Global Political Economy
Theory and Practice

Global Political Economy
Theory and Practice

Theodore H. Cohn
Simon Fraser University

 LONGMAN

An imprint of Addison Wesley Longman, Inc.

New York • Reading, Massachusetts • Menlo Park, California • Harlow, England
Don Mills, Ontario • Sydney • Mexico City • Madrid • Amsterdam

Editor-in-Chief: Priscilla McGeehon
Acquisitions Editor: Eric Stano
Associate Editor: Jennie Errickson
Supplements Editor: Mark Toews
Marketing Manager: Megan Galvin
Project Manager: Ellen MacElree
Design Manager: John Callahan
Cover Design: Maria Ilardi
Cover Photo: PhotoDisk
Graphic Art: Joanne Del Ben
Electronic Production Specialist: Joanne Del Ben
Print Buyer: Hugh Crawford
Electronic Page Makeup: Joanne Del Ben
Printer and Binder: Maple-Vail Book Manufacturing Group
Cover Printer: Coral Graphic Services, Inc.

Library of Congress Cataloging-in-Publication Data

Cohn, Theodore H., 1940–

    Global political economy: theory and practice / Theodore H. Cohn.
       p.   cm
    Includes bibliographical references and index.
    ISBN 0-321-01165-1
    1. International economic relations.   2. International trade.
   3. International finance.   I. Title.
    HF1359.C654   2000
    337—dc21

                                                  99-29540
                                                      CIP

Please visit our website at http://longman.awl.com

0-321-01165-1

12345678910—MA—02010099

To Shirley

BRIEF CONTENTS

Chapter 9 Regionalism and the Global Trade Regime 238

Chapter 10 Multinational Corporations and Global Production 274

Chapter 11 International Development 317

PART IV CONCLUDING COMMENTS 353

Chapter 12 Current Trends in the Global Political Economy 355

PREFACE

In the Cold War period of the 1950s and 1960s, the academic study of international relations focused primarily on strategic-security issues. However, events such as the global food and oil crises in the early 1970s demonstrated the importance of understanding the relationship between the political, economic, and social aspects of international relations, and international political economy (IPE) emerged as a major area of study. With the breakup of the Soviet bloc and Soviet Union and the end of the Cold War in the late 1980s and the 1990s, IPE matters such as trade, foreign investment, international development, and monetary and financial relations have become even more central. This book introduces undergraduate students and beginning graduate students to the complex but vital issues surrounding the global political economy. I wrote the text because of a long-held conviction that it is possible for students to understand the broader implications of IPE issues only by examining them in a theoretical context. Without the organizing framework of theory, it is difficult to make sense of the growing body of IPE facts and statistics and to interpret events in the global political economy. Thus, the text takes a comprehensive approach to the study of IPE, focusing on both theory and practice.

To help in drawing connections between the theory and the substantive issues, I focus on three major themes or challenges throughout the text: globalization, North-North relations (among the advanced industrial states), and North-South relations (among the industrial states of the North and the less developed countries of the South). Considerable space is also devoted to the emerging centrally planned economies of Eastern Europe and the former Soviet Union. Nevertheless, East-West relations is not a major theme of the book; the Cold War has virtually ended, and the former Second World is becoming increasingly integrated in the capitalist global political economy.

Although a major focus of the book is globalization, I do *not* claim that globalization is leading to some sort of world society or world government. Indeed, considerable space is devoted to the increasing importance of regional blocs and organizations such as the European Union and the North American Free Trade Agreement, and Chapter 9 is devoted specifically to the subject of regionalism. Furthermore, there is discussion throughout the book of the interconnections between domestic and international issues both globally and regionally. These domestic-international interactions are generally more important in the study of international political economy than in the study of strategic-security issues.

I am grateful for the comments, advice, and support of a number of individuals in writing this book. First, I would like to thank Mark Zacher of the University of British Columbia and Michael Webb of the University of Victoria for providing helpful advice with regard to the organization and content of the book. I would also like to thank the following reviewers for providing criticisms and suggestions that were extremely useful in making revisions: Sherry L. Bennett, Rice University; Kurt Burch, University of Delaware; Vincent Ferraro, Mount Holyoke College; Vicki L. Golich, California State University, San Marcos; Beverly G. Hawk, University of Alabama at Birmingham; Michael J. Hiscox, University of California, San Diego; Matthias Kaelberer, University of Northern Iowa; Quan Li, Florida State University; David E. Spiro, University of Arizona; and Kenneth P. Thomas, University of Missouri—St. Louis. In addition, I have appreciated the suggestions of several colleagues at Simon Fraser University, including Stephen McBride, Michael Howlett, Yoshi Kawasaki, and James Busumtwi-Sam.

The competent editorial staff at Addison Wesley Longman has given active support to this book, and I especially want to thank Jennie Errickson for the time, effort, and abilities she has focused on the project. Thanks are also due to Ellen MacElree, Peter Glovin, Rich Wohl, Pam Gordon, and Leo Wiegman.

My acknowledgements would not be complete without mentioning the role my students have played over the years in asking insightful questions, raising important issues, and giving me feedback as to what aspects of IPE they found clear or confusing. My sons Daniel and Frank also gave me assistance in a variety of areas, ranging from computer advice to the typing of some tables and figures. Finally I am dedicating this book to my wife Shirley for her caring advice, support, and encouragement.

THEODORE H. COHN

PART I

Introduction and Overview

The field of international relations traditionally focused primarily on the study of strategic-security issues and largely ignored economic issues, but it has become increasingly evident that the political, economic, and social aspects of international relations are closely intertwined. As a result, *international political economy* (IPE) has emerged as an important area of study in international relations. Chapter 1 provides answers to some basic questions such as "What is international political economy?" and "Why is international political economy a relatively new area of study?" It then discusses the basic themes of this book, and introduces the main theoretical perspectives in the field. Chapter 2 provides a general overview of the world economy since World War II, with particular emphasis on the institutions developed to manage international economic relations.

Introduction

In July 1944, while World War II was still raging in Europe and the Pacific, delegates from 44 countries held a conference in the small resort town of Bretton Woods, New Hampshire, to reach a broad-ranging agreement for economic cooperation. The **Bretton Woods system** that emerged from the conference helped to shape international economic relations in the postwar era. After World War II, however, the emergence of the Cold War between the United States and the Soviet Union became the central concern of Western policymakers, and international economic issues often seemed to be of lesser priority. Thus, postwar international relations scholars placed primary emphasis in their research on strategic-security issues related to the Cold War, or "high politics." International economic issues, by contrast, were considered to be relatively nonpolitical and were relegated to the area of "low politics." As this book will discuss, by the late 1960s and early 1970s it became increasingly evident to both policymakers and academics that they had underestimated the political importance of international economic issues. Indeed, some of the most contentious international issues in the 1970s were both economic and political by nature. It was at about this time that international political economy, which examines the interaction between the political, economic, and social aspects of international relations, emerged as an important field of study. A few examples of major issues and events clearly demonstrate how international politics and economics are often closely intertwined.

The Persian Gulf War   In August 1990, Iraq invaded its much smaller neighbor Kuwait and was in a position to control about one-fifth of the oil production of the Organization of Petroleum Exporting Countries (OPEC). The Western industrial states and Japan were concerned not only about the strategic implications of the Iraqi invasion, but also about the possible economic effects in view of their high degree of dependence on Middle East oil imports. When Iraq failed to withdraw from Kuwait by a specified date, the United Nations Security Council endorsed the use of force by a United States–led military coalition against Iraq. Because one Communist regime after another in Eastern Europe had disintegrated in 1989 and the Soviet Union itself was on the verge of dissolution, the United States was able to engage in military actions against Iraq without concerns about any counteraction from the

Soviets. Nevertheless, the American *economic* position was no longer as predominant as it had been in the 1950s and 1960s. The United States therefore insisted that Japan, Germany, Saudi Arabia, and Kuwait provide a substantial amount of funding to help finance the Gulf War effort (Japan and Germany did not participate in the military operations). A close relationship exists between economic "wealth" and political "power" internationally, and the cost-sharing plan agreed to in the Gulf War could serve as a model for some future U.S.-led military operations.

European Integration   In 1951, six Western European countries (France, West Germany, Italy, Belgium, the Netherlands, and Luxembourg) joined together to form the European Coal and Steel Community (ECSC), which was designed to coordinate the policies of member states and reduce their trade barriers in coal and steel. Although the ECSC was designed to promote *economic* integration of the member countries' coal and steel resources, the reasons for its formation in 1951 were primarily *political.* The French foreign minister, Robert Schuman, had two major purposes in developing the plan for the ECSC: first, to meet U.S. demands that West Germany be rebuilt to help deter any aggression by the Soviet Union, and second, to allay French domestic fears of renewed aggression by a rearmed Germany. Over the centuries, Germany and France had repeatedly fought over access to coal and steel resources in border areas such as Alsace-Lorraine. It was therefore felt that a sharing of coal and steel resources in the ECSC would help rebuild Germany and also make future wars between France and Germany virtually impossible. Thus, the preamble to the ECSC treaty states that the member countries wish "to create, by establishing an economic community, the basis for a broader and deeper community among peoples long divided by bloody conflicts."[1]

The ECSC was successful in integrating the coal and steel resources of the six member states, which agreed to extend it to a full-scale regional integration agreement with the formation of the European Economic Community in 1957. Today, this community—which is now called the **European Union (EU)**—has 15 full members and a large number of associate member states. One of the original purposes of economic integration in Europe—to end armed hostilities and war between France and Germany—has certainly been achieved.

World Bank Loans to Third World Countries   This book will show that politics and economics often are inextricably linked in the decision making of the major international economic organizations. Such linkages are evident in the lending activities of the *World Bank,* which is the largest source of **multilateral** development finance for Third World countries (also called less developed countries or LDCs). The *Articles of Agreement* of the World Bank state that the bank "shall not interfere in the political affairs of any member" and that "only economic considerations shall be relevant" to its lending decisions.[2] Many analysts argue, however, that the bank's loans are inevitably based on political as well as economic considerations. For example, the World Bank has had a clear preference for lending to countries that emphasize private enterprise, and this preference became far more pronounced after the Third World foreign debt crisis in the 1980s (the debt crisis is discussed in Chapter 8). Although bank officials argue that those countries with a private market orientation are more likely to be economically efficient, the bank's preference for private enterprise is also based on the political and ideological leanings of its most powerful members—the advanced industrial states. In the 1950s to 1970s, the bank gave some support to a Third World development strategy that combined state action with private entrepreneurship, and it provided finance for some infrastructure projects such as roads, railways, airports, water systems, and public utilities which involved state-owned corporations. Even in these early years, however, the bank showed a definite preference for private enterprise, and one noted observer of the global political economy has written that Eugene Black who was World Bank president from 1949 to 1962 was "inclined to talk as if there were some kind of exclusive relationship between political freedom and private enterprise, and as if he believed that his main task is therefore to defend the only true economic faith throughout the world."[3]

In the 1980s the bank followed such national leaders as British Prime Minister Margaret Thatcher and U.S. President Ronald Reagan in a shift to the Right, and was far more inclined to view governments and public enterprise as hindrances to growth. Thus, World Bank structural adjustment loans (SALs) to indebted Third World countries in the 1980s and 1990s have been linked with the agreement of these countries to institute policies promoting privatization, deregulation, and trade liberalization. In sum, international politics and international economics have been so intertwined in the area of Third World development policy that the World Bank has been both unwilling and unable to fully follow the directive of it Articles of Agreements that its loans should be based solely on economic considerations.

The Boeing Company's Merger with McDonnell Douglas Corporation   This book demonstrates that the economic activities of private actors such as international banks and multinational corporations often have major political implications. A prime example of such political-economic linkages is evident in the decision of two American aircraft companies—Boeing and McDonnell Douglas—to merge their operations in early 1997. When the merger proposal was first announced, the European Union swiftly raised objections and threatened to retaliate against Boeing, which is based in Seattle, Washington. The EU's concerns stemmed largely from the fact that Boeing has the largest market share for large commercial aircraft (about 70 percent), while Europe's Airbus Consortium's market share is only 30 percent. The Europeans feared that spillovers as a result of the McDonnell Douglas Corporation's experience with defense production would enable Boeing to increase its domination of the civil aircraft business. Furthermore, the Europeans objected to the 20-year contracts with exclusive-supplier provisions that Boeing signed with three U.S. airlines—Delta, American, and Continental. Although the merger was approved by the U.S. Federal Trade Commission and supported by the White House, Boeing had to be concerned about European retaliation. The Europeans could not block a merger between two U.S. companies, but they could impose fines making it difficult for Boeing to operate in Europe. Thus, Boeing eventually agreed not to enforce the exclusive-supplier provisions of its agreements with the three U.S. airlines.

The United States has initiated similar clashes with Europe over civil airlines issues. Indeed, after years of bitter disputes over European government subsidies to Airbus, which contributed to its growing sales vis-à-vis Boeing, the United States pressured the Europeans to sign an agreement in 1992 limiting the Airbus subsidies. The civil airline industry has been described as being "the most politicized in the world—apart from the defense industry," with which it is closely tied.[4] However, as global competition increases in a wide range of economic areas, disputes such as those involving Boeing and Airbus will become more frequent. Because governments often feel a stake in the welfare of their domestically based multinational corporations, disputes over economic market share often become highly politicized.

The foregoing examples demonstrate that politics and economics are often inextricably linked in the real world of international relations. Before discussing the purposes and themes of this book, we need to address two important questions: What is international political economy? And why is international political economy a relatively new area of study?

WHAT IS INTERNATIONAL POLITICAL ECONOMY?

As a field of study that bridges the disciplines of politics and economics, IPE is concerned with the interaction between "the state" and "the market." The state and the market, in turn, are associated with the (political) pursuit of power and the (economic) pursuit of wealth. As the political component of IPE, a *state* is a sovereign territorial unit with a government and a population. As the economic component, the **market** is "the co-ordinating mechanism where the forces of supply and demand in an economy determine prices, output and methods of production via the automatic adjustment of price movements."[5]

An inherent tension often exists between the state and the market. The state is concerned with preserving national sovereignty and unity while the market is associated with economic openness and the breaking down of state barriers.[6] For example, the 1988 Canada-U.S. Free Trade Agreement (CUSTA) extended the "geographic space" to include an open market between the two countries, but many Canadians feared that this expanded market posed a threat to Canadian sovereignty in some areas such as energy, foreign investment, and cultural industries. When CUSTA was extended to form the **North American Free Trade Agreement (NAFTA)** in 1994, many Mexicans were concerned that NAFTA might encroach on their sovereignty in areas such as energy and agriculture. Although the United States is a much larger economy than its two North American neighbors, many Americans feared that NAFTA would lead to a loss of national control over such issues as employment and the environment.

Despite the inherent tensions between states and markets, they also often have a complementary and even symbiotic relationship. Domestically, states establish rules to protect private property rights and to provide infrastructure such as transportation and communications facilities required for market transactions. Internationally, states join in agreements and form organizations to promote economic openness and stability. Furthermore, there is often a close relationship between a state's wealth and market size on the one hand and its military and political power on the other. As interdependence has increased, states have been drawn more closely into the competitive forces of the world economy. Thus, states today are sometimes called *competition states* because they are closely involved in supporting research and development in high-technology sectors, in the restructuring of industry, and in the deregulation of financial markets.[7] The impressive economic growth rates of some states seem to be closely related to their success in fostering a symbiotic relationship with the competitive marketplace. As we will discuss, Japan and the newly industrializing countries (NICs) of East Asia (Hong Kong, Singapore, South Korea, and Taiwan) were especially successful in fostering such state-market relationships from the 1960s to the 1980s.

While state-market interactions continue to be the core issue in the study of IPE, we are also concerned with other types of organizational relationships. Primary among these is the interaction between states and multinational corporations (MNCs)—also referred to as transnational corporations. The MNC is the main nonstate actor with which the state must contend today. Indeed, the 600 largest MNCs now each benefit from worldwide sales of over $1 billion, and together they produce more than 25 percent of world gross domestic product; the 350 largest corporations account for about 40 percent of world trade. As is the case with states and markets, there is an inherent tension between the state and the MNC, but they can also have a complementary and cooperative relationship.

The traditional view of the MNC is that it is closely linked with the "home" state where its headquarters are located. Although the MNC opens foreign branch plants in "host" countries, its main financial, and research and development activities remain firmly planted in the home country. The directors and shareholders in the home county also retain primary responsibility for management of the MNC's foreign operations. From this perspective, the home state is in a more powerful position than its MNCs, because it provides the basic environment and legal structure within which its MNCs must function. However, this traditional model has been supplemented by other models in which the host country gains more control over its MNC branch plant operations, and in which the MNC extricates itself from control by any single state. This latter type is sometimes referred to as a "geocentric" or "stateless" corporation, since its ownership and board of directors become internationalized. Some MNCs follow a deliberate strategy of internationalizing their operations to increase their freedom of operation. Although "stateless" corporations have to take different national markets into account in their production and marketing strategies, they are no longer beholden to any single country. As discussed in Chapter 10, IPE scholars differ over the importance they attach to these various models of MNC-state relationship.[8]

Whether one focuses on state-market, state–multinational corporation, or power-wealth interactions, there is general agreement that the field of IPE is interdisciplinary in nature. It draws on contributions from political scientists, economists, sociologists, anthropologists, historians, and geographers. IPE theorists also seek to overcome the limitations imposed by the current disciplinary boundaries. On the one hand, they criticize some economists for **economism**—that is, for overestimating the importance of the economic sphere and for underestimating the importance and autonomy of the political sphere.[9] On the other hand, IPE theorists accuse some political scientists of devoting too much attention to politics and the exercise of power and too little attention to the impact of economic structures and processes on political relationships.

The challenge of engaging in interdisciplinary study is obviously magnified when we examine political economy at the international level. How does one develop an IPE theory that examines international influences and also accounts for the multitude of social, cultural, economic, political, and developmental variations across nation-states? Furthermore, IPE scholars find it more essential than strategic-security specialists to focus on the linkages between international and domestic politics. Foreign policy and defense officials normally have considerable leeway in dealing with strategic-security matters because domestic groups and individuals are generally willing to leave decision making on these issues to the government experts. By contrast, domestic groups often see a close relationship between their own economic welfare and international economic issues such as trade and foreign investment, and they therefore demand a greater role in government decision making on these issues. Thus, "scholars and practitioners alike have begun to understand that effective international economic cooperation depends not only on the external interests and actions of states, but on their ability to manage, channel, or circumvent domestic political pressures as well."[10] IPE scholars thus have the daunting tasks of focusing on domestic as well as international interactions and of crossing the boundaries between a number of social science disciplines.

WHY IS INTERNATIONAL POLITICAL ECONOMY A RELATIVELY NEW AREA OF STUDY?

The relative newness of international political economy as an academic area of study is ironic, not only because of the close interaction between politics and economics, but also because awareness of these linkages extends back to ancient times. Indeed, Thucydides (471–400 B.C.), who has often been described as the founder of international relations, demonstrated an acute awareness of the linkages between power and wealth. In his *History of the Peloponnesian War* dealing with conflict among the Greek city-states, Thucydides wrote that "war is a matter not so much of arms as of money, which makes arms of use."[11] Our earlier discussion of the cost-sharing arrangements in the 1990s Persian Gulf War demonstrates that Thucydides' work continues to be relevant. Aristotle (384–322 B.C.) also demonstrated a sensitivity to political-economic interconnections, and he in fact subsumed economics under the study of politics.[12]

Despite this early awareness of the linkages between politics and economics, several factors led to the tendency in modern times to view them as distinct areas of study: the influence of the liberal school of thought, the "hierarchy" of international concerns after World War II, and the organization of disciplines in universities. As discussed in Chapter 4, liberal-economic theorists such as Adam Smith (1723–90) considered economic and political matters to be largely separable. In Smith's view, economic activity operates under a naturally harmonious system of laws, whereas politics does not obey either natural laws or harmony. As a result, Adam Smith is often associated with calls for "laissez-faire" capitalism, in which the economic system functions best with minimal interference from the government. The liberal tendency to view politics as separable from economics, and to believe that the state should have a minimal role in operation of the market, contributed to a turning away from the study of political economy.

In the post–World War II period, the most pressing international concerns were in the strategic-security area. The rapid emergence of the Cold War led scholars to view the questions of war and peace as the truly important ones, or "high politics." Postwar international economic relations, by contrast, were marked by a large degree of stability and cooperation under U.S. leadership, and scholars therefore viewed international economic matters as being outside the realm of high diplomacy, or as "low politics."[13] International relations specialists in the postwar period therefore accepted the liberal dictum that politics was separable from economics; but one could say that they "turned Adam Smith on his head," because they gave clear priority to political security over economic issues. A perusal of many international politics texts dating from the 1950s to the 1970s and even later clearly demonstrates the lack of attention given to political-economic interactions.[14]

Beginning in the late 1960s and early 1970s, several factors contributed to a reversal of these trends and to a new interest in IPE among both policymakers and academics. On the one hand, détente between the United States and the Soviet Union ushered in a period of decreased tension and concern about global strategic-security matters. On the other hand, the relative decline of U.S. economic power, combined with economic threats resulting from such events as the oil price increases in the 1970s and the Third World foreign debt crisis in the 1980s, heightened concerns about international economic stability. Thus, it was evident that international economic issues had become "high politics" and required urgent attention.

Since the mid-1970s, the North American academic community has made great strides in developing the field of IPE. Nevertheless, the social sciences in most universities continue to be organized in separate disciplines, with political science and economics in different departments. These disciplinary divisions in universities have considerable influence over "rewards, interactions, and the flow of thought itself."[15] It is evident that despite the obstacles posed by the inflexibility of academia, world events will make the study of IPE increasingly relevant. In recent years, armed strife has led to horrific human suffering in conflicts around the world, in places such as the former Yugoslavia, Somalia, and Rwanda. Nevertheless, with the end of the Cold War, the advanced industrial states in the North, the Third World countries in the South, and the emerging economies in Eastern Europe and the former Soviet Union (FSU) are all directing much of their attention to economic problems.

THE PURPOSE AND THEMES OF THIS BOOK

This book provides a comprehensive approach to the study of international political economy. Part II introduces the student to the main theoretical perspectives in the field, and Part III examines current issues in IPE in historical perspective relating to monetary and financial relations, foreign debt, foreign trade, foreign investment, and international development. It is possible to understand the broader implications of current IPE issues only by examining them in a theoretical context. The substantive chapters in Part III, on trade, monetary relations, and so forth, therefore direct the reader to the interaction between theory and practice. To help draw connections between the theory and the substantive issues, this book focuses on three major themes or challenges: globalization, North-North relations, and North-South relations.

Globalization

Globalization is a process that has two major aspects: the broadening and the deepening of interactions and interdependence among societies and states throughout the world. In regard to broadening, globalization extends linkages geographically to encompass virtually all major societies and states. Thus, events and policies adopted in one part of the world are likely to have a major impact on distant locations. In regard to deepening, globalization involves a marked increase in the frequency and intensity of interactions and interdependence among societies and states. Globalization is contributing to fundamental changes in the relationship between markets and states—the subject of international political economy. Although states have often adopted policies that promote it, globalization is basically an economic process with political consequences.[16] The chapters in Part III point to indications of globalization in various aspects of the political economy. For example, the *daily* volume of foreign exchange trading in currencies rose from about $1 billion in the mid-1970s to $1.2 trillion in the mid-1990s; foreign direct investment (FDI) flows reached $315 billion in 1995, nearly a sixfold increase over the 1981–85 level; and global trade grew twelvefold in the postwar period, amounting to over $4 trillion a year by 1995.[17]

This book is concerned with both the causes and the effects of globalization. In terms of effects, we are particularly interested in the impact of globalization on interactions among states, between the state and the market, and between the state and multinational corporations. For example, state policies that were traditionally considered to be domestic now often have a significant impact on other states and on international business. Pressures have therefore increased to subject "domestic" factors such as competition policies, trade-distorting subsidies, and financial market activity to international regulation. MNCs are also demanding nondiscriminatory trade and investment rules so that they can operate without restrictions internationally, and these new rules could impose additional restrictions on the policymaking autonomy of nation-states.

Globalization is a controversial term, especially because some extreme globalizers claim that we are entering a "borderless world" in which MNCs are losing their national identities and distinct national economies are being subsumed under the global marketplace.[18] This book adopts a less extreme version of globalization in four respects. First, globalization is not a uniform process throughout the world. The effects of globalization are far more evident, for example, in major urban centers than they are in rural areas, on remote islands, and in extremely underdeveloped areas of the Third World. Second, globalization is *not* causing the state to wither away. Although autonomy in regard to implementing economic policies is eroding in some important respects, the state is also adopting some new and more complex functions to deal with a highly interdependent world. Furthermore, governments continue to have choices in how they respond to the forces of globalization. When domestic groups have appealed for assistance in dealing with global competitive pressures, some states have resorted to trade protectionism, other states have adopted industrial policies to promote competitiveness, and still others have permitted the market to function without interference.[19]

Third, globalization is *not* leading to some sort of world society or world government. Indeed, the forces of globalization can lead to fragmentation and conflict as well as to unity and cooperation. For example, some writers argue that the increase in global **competitiveness** is contributing to the formation of three economic blocs in the world, centered in Europe, North America, and Japan/East Asia. Opinions differ widely as to whether the relationship among these three blocs will become more cooperative or conflictual in nature. And fourth, interdependence and globalization are not unique to the present-day period. A survey of history shows that the internationalization of finance, trade, and production has fluctuated over time, and it is possible that international events could eventually reverse the current moves toward globalization. For example, before World War I there was a high degree of interdependence in trade, foreign investment, and other areas. In 17 industrial countries for which there are comparative data, exports as a share of gross domestic product or total output averaged 12.9 percent in 1913, which is comparable with the 1993 level of 14.5 percent; and the migration of people around the world was more extensive in some earlier periods than it is today. The interdependent linkages of the nineteenth and early twentieth centuries were subsequently eroded during World War I, and in the interwar period these linkages virtually collapsed as a result of increased nationalism and the Great Depression. Only after World War II did global economic ties begin to increase again.[20]

Despite the historical changes in interdependence over time, globalization is more encompassing today than it was at any time in the past. With advances in technology, communications, and transportation, the activities of states are being internationalized to a degree not previously experienced. In communications, for example, the cost of an international telephone call fell by more than 90 percent from 1970 to 1990; telecommunications traffic increased by about 20 percent a year in the 1980s; and over 50 million people were using the Internet by the late 1990s. Indeed, the spread of ideas through the media, television, videos, and the Internet seems to be contributing to the emergence of a global culture. In transportation, shipping costs fell by more than two-thirds between 1920 and 1990, and the operating costs per mile for the world's airlines fell by 60 percent from 1960 to 1990.[21] Global interdependence today is also qualitatively different than it was in the past. Although a number of corporations globalized their activities in the nineteenth century, the role of the MNC in generating foreign direct investment, trade, and technology is a modern-day phenomenon. By 1988, there were about 19,000 MNCs, which accounted for 25 to 30 percent of the gross domestic product of all market economies and for 80 percent of the trade in managerial and technology skills.[22]

The geographic reach of the capitalist economic system is for the first time also encompassing virtually the entire globe, with LDCs becoming more actively involved in the global economy and the "emerging" centrally planned economies (CPEs) of

Eastern Europe and the former Soviet Union liberalizing their economies since the demise of communism. Thus, for the first time, membership in the major international economic organizations such as the International Monetary Fund, the World Bank, and the World Trade Organization is becoming truly global in scope.[23] This book examines the implications of these changes as well as the differing attitudes of IPE theorists as to whether globalization is a positive or negative phenomenon.

North-North Relations

The second theme of this book concerns the relationship among the advanced industrial states in the North. As globalization has increased, countries have found it more difficult to manage their economic affairs individually, and they have been inclined to seek regional and global solutions. The Northern states in Western Europe, North America, and Japan are the only countries with the wealth and power to look after international management of the global economy. Thus, the international management issue is primarily a North-North issue involving the advanced industrial states. This book discusses two factors that IPE scholars have focused on as contributing to international economic management: hegemony and international institutions.

Because of its combined economic and military power, the United States was the undisputed leader or *hegemon* in the early postwar period. One important measure of a country's economic power is its **gross domestic product (GDP),** the total value of the goods and services produced by the country over a specified time period—usually a year. Alternatively, some economists measure a country's total output in terms of its **gross national product (GNP).** The GNP is similar to the GDP except that the GNP also includes a country's net amount of earnings from foreign investment. Because it provides a better measure of economic activity within a country's borders, the GDP is more widely used than the GNP. In keeping with this custom, this book generally uses the term *GDP*. However, movements in the GDP and GNP normally do not differ greatly, and sometimes data are given in terms of a country's GNP.[24]

Regardless of whether GDP or GNP is used as a measure, the United States was clearly the economic hegemon after World War II. Indeed, during the war the GDP of the United States increased by about 50 percent, while Western European countries lost one-quarter of their GDPs on the average and the economies of the Soviet Union and Japan were severely damaged. Thus, in 1950 the U.S. economy was 3 times the size of the Soviet Union's, 5 times the size of Britain's, and 20 times the size of Japan's. The Western European countries and Japan at this time were also highly dependent on U.S. aid and foreign investment for postwar reconstruction.[25]

In the 1950s and 1960s, the *relative* economic position of the United States vis-à-vis other advanced industrial states inevitably began to decline as Western Europe and Japan gradually recovered from the war. The extent of the U.S. decline and the possibilities for a renewal of U.S. predominance are matters of intense debate among IPE theorists. However, almost all would agree that U.S. power resources relative to those of other advanced industrial states have fallen since the end of World War II. For example, the U.S. dollar continued to be the top currency for international economic transactions, but the Japanese yen and German mark gained in importance; in 1971 the United States shifted from having balance-of-trade surpluses every year to having balance-of-trade deficits (i.e., imports greater than exports); the United States increasingly became a recipient as well as a source of foreign direct investment; and in 1989 Japan surpassed the United States for the first time as the largest single donor of development assistance to the Third World. This book examines the effects of the relative decline of U.S. economic hegemony on the management of the global economy. We are particularly interested in whether or not economic management has become more difficult and in how the nature of management has changed over time.

The second factor in global management of interest to us is the role of international institutions. Under U.S. and British leadership, three international economic organizations were established to help manage the global economy at the end of World War II: the International Monetary Fund (IMF), the International Bank for Reconstruction and Development (IBRD or the World Bank), and the General Agreement on Tariffs and Trade (GATT). Because the advanced industrial states have been the dominant powers affecting the policies of these organizations, the institutional management of the global economy has been largely a North-North issue. This book examines the role of these institutions in the management (or mismanagement) of the international political economy.

Although the rich Northern states have often acted in concert to look after global economic management, there are also significant differences and divisions among these states. For example, with the demise of the Cold War between the United States and the Soviet Union and the relative decline of U.S. economic hegemony, three major economic blocs have emerged: in Europe, North America (led by the United States), and East Asia (led by Japan). Because much of the world's economic, technological, scientific, and military power is encompassed in these three major blocs, the competitiveness between them has major consequences for the future of the global economy.[26] Thus, the second theme of this text relates to both the linkages and the divisions among the advanced industrial states of the North.

North-South Relations

Some analysts question whether it is meaningful today to speak of "the South" as a group of countries with common characteristics when there are major differences in the level of income and economic development among Southern countries. On the one hand, the East Asian NICs—South Korea, Taiwan, Singapore, and Hong Kong—have relatively high per capita incomes and literacy rates, and they are quite competitive in some areas with the industrial states of the North. On the other hand, the UN's list of 48 least developed countries—mostly in sub-Saharan Africa and South Asia—have extremely low per capita incomes and literacy rates, and there are formidable problems to overcome before their populations can be elevated above the subsistence level.[27] Despite the disparities in wealth and economic development among Southern countries, it is meaningful to generalize about the problems of the South because countries such as the East Asian NICs tend to be the exception rather than the rule. Indeed, two of the four East Asian NICs—Singapore and Hong Kong—have a unique status in the Third World. Both are so small geographically that they are more akin to city-states, and Hong Kong was a British crown colony before it was incorporated into mainland China. Furthermore, even some East Asian NICs such as South Korea have been vulnerable to financial and currency crises in recent years (see Chapter 11). Thus, a major characteristic of the global economy today is the marked inequality in wealth and power between the advanced industrial states of the North on the one hand and the *great majority* of LDCs in the South on the other.

This book uses the terms *less developed countries* or *LDCs* and *Third World* to refer to the countries in the South. These countries often have colonial histories and low levels of social and political as well as economic development. Economically, LDCs generally have low per capita incomes, inadequate infrastructure facilities (such as poor transportation and communications), and limited availability of modern technology. The poorer LDCs, which include many countries in sub-Saharan Africa and in Asia, have widespread poverty and malnutrition. The lack of economic resources in LDCs also limits their abilities to foster social development. Thus, many Third World countries have limited educational facilities, low literacy rates, and inadequate health and sanitary facilities. Assessing political development in a country is a more difficult and contentious issue. However, Third World countries are more likely than advanced industrial states to have unstable and authoritarian governments.[28]

The Third World includes almost all the countries of Latin America and the Caribbean, Asia and Oceania, and Africa and the Middle East. In 1950, the Third World accounted for almost 65 percent of the total world population, and by 1996, the Third World population had climbed to almost 80 percent of the world total. A number of countries in the former Soviet Union and Eastern Europe that were previously part of the Communist Second World are now receiving foreign debt and development financing from the advanced industrial states and are in effect also a part of the Third World. When we speak of the world, we therefore must give a great deal of attention to the LDCs or the Third World.[29] Although our main concern when discussing international inequality is with the differences between the industrial states of the North and the less developed countries of the South, it is important to note that the global economy is also marked by differences in the wealth and power of individuals *within* states. As noted in Chapter 11, some groups within Third World states, such as women and children, are often in especially disadvantageous positions. (Disparities in wealth of course are also prevalent within many Northern industrial states.) This book discusses the effects of changes in the global economy, such as globalization and the liberalization of trade and financial flows, on the inequalities between rich and poor both within states and among states.

Third World countries have relatively little influence in setting the agenda and making decisions regarding the international political economy. This is evident, for example, in important international economic organizations such as the World Trade Organization, the International Monetary Fund, and the World Bank. Over the years, a variety of strategies have been followed to promote Third World economic development, and the LDCs have also sought to increase their power and influence over international economic issues. Although a relatively small number of LDCs—particularly in East and Southeast Asia and in Latin America—have improved their economic positions, the great majority of Third World countries have been frustrated in their efforts to promote development and exert more influence. Even among the more successful Third World countries in East Asia and Latin America, recent events indicate that their economic progress may be precarious.[30] Thus, the United Nations Development

Program reported in 1996 that "the world has become more polarized, and the gulf between the poor and rich of the world has widened even further."[31] This book examines competing views as to why most Third World countries continue to be poor and why they continue to have little influence in IPE issues, and it also explores the strategies Third World countries have employed to promote economic development and increase their influence.

Finally, considerable space is devoted to the former Second World, that is, the former centrally planned economies that are liberalizing as a result of the breakup of the Soviet bloc and the Soviet Union itself. (Chapter 7, for example, discusses the fact that the foreign debt crisis has had a major impact on debtor countries in the former Eastern bloc as well as in the Third World.) Nevertheless, East-West relations is not a major theme of this book because the Cold War has virtually ended, and the former CPEs are becoming increasingly involved in the capitalist global political economy. The more developed emerging countries, such as the Czech Republic and Hungary, are approaching the level of development of some of the advanced industrial states in the North, while the poorer countries of the former Second World are essentially becoming members of the South.

THE IPE THEORETICAL PERSPECTIVES

Many students have a natural tendency to avoid studying "theory," and this seems to be particularly true in the case of international political economy. Without theory, however, we are basically studying a series of facts, and we are unable to assess the broader implications of these facts for international political and economic relations in general. One might argue that the facts speak for themselves, but in reality a person will interpret "the facts" quite differently depending on whether he or she is viewing them "from a bank office in Zurich, a *maquiladora* [border factory] in Mexico, a shantytown in Peru, a rice paddy in Sri Lanka ... [or] a trade office in Washington, D.C."[32] We all interpret "the facts" on the basis of our theoretical views of the world, and the only choice is whether our views remain implicit or whether we explicitly examine the theories we use to interpret issues and events.

A scholar's choice of theoretical perspective will also determine what "facts" he or she chooses to focus on or ignore. For example, theorists writing from the realist perspective place considerable emphasis on the struggle for power in international relations, and some realists claim that "power is the essence of politics."[33] While realists provide us with many useful insights regarding relations among the most powerful industrial states, they normally have little interest in examining the conditions of the poorest and weakest Third World countries. Only when Third World entities such as OPEC or the newly industrializing countries challenge the predominant position of the North do realists usually take notice. Dependency theorists writing from the historical structuralist perspective, by contrast, devote most of their attention to examining the conditions of Third World countries in the periphery of the global economy. However, they are so concerned with examining external exploitation of the Third World by the advanced industrial states that they often fail to look at purely *domestic* factors in Third World countries that interfere with their development.

International political economy is a field of study in which scholars apply a wide range of theories and analytical methods. Three theoretical perspectives have been most prominent in the study of IPE: the realist, liberal, and historical structuralist perspectives. Realism is the oldest theoretical perspective in both international relations and IPE. According to realists, the state is the principal or dominant actor in international politics. Realists also view the international system as a "self-help" system without a centralized authority, in which each state must build up its own power to prevent being dominated by other states. International relations is often characterized by realists as a zero-sum game, in which one state's gain is another state's loss. "Relative gains," or the gains a state achieves in relation to the gains achieved by other states, are therefore extremely important to realists. Each state can be expected to manipulate the market in order to capture relative gains vis-à-vis other states.

While realism is the most important perspective in international relations in general, liberalism is the most important school of thought in IPE. To avoid confusion, it is important to note that the use of the term *liberal* is different in international political economy and American domestic politics. In the United States, "liberals" are viewed as supporting greater government involvement in the market to prevent inequalities and stimulate growth. "Conservatives" in the United States, by contrast, are committed to free markets and minimal intervention by the government. Orthodox liberals in IPE are more akin to U.S. conservatives; they emphasize the importance of free markets and private property rights and prescribe only a limited government role in economic activities. However, Chapter 4 discusses the fact that some nonorthodox liberals are more accepting of government intervention. Liberals are more optimistic than realists about the prospects for cooperation among states, and they believe that international organizations and other institutions can help promote such cooperation. Thus, in the view of liberals, economic relationships are a positive-sum game in which all states benefit, even if they do not benefit equally.

This book uses the term *historical structuralism* for the third perspective because scholars in this group argue that history has been marked by structural means of exploitation, in which one class dominates over another.[34] The main characteristic of the current system is the dominance of capitalist relations of production, with the capitalist class (the bourgeoisie) exploiting the workers (the proletariat). Some historical structuralists, such as dependency and world-system theorists, focus on the exploitation of Third World states in the periphery by the advanced capitalist states in the core of the global economy. Unlike liberals and realists, who are generally supportive of the capitalist system, historical structuralists typically advocate a transformation to socialism as the key to an end to exploitation.

Becoming familiar with realism, liberalism, and historical structuralism is an important starting point in developing alternative "lenses" for viewing the various substantive issue areas (such as trade and monetary relations) in IPE. However, the field of IPE is not neatly divided into these three perspectives. First, the margins separating these perspectives have often become blurred as these views have evolved and influenced each other over time. Second, some of the most important theoretical approaches in IPE, such as regime theory and hegemonic stability theory, are "hybrid" theories that draw on more than one of the three perspectives. Third, much of the recent literature examining the relationship between domestic institutions and IPE does not fit easily into any one of the three traditional perspectives. In addition to the three main theoretical perspectives, this book looks at the hybrid theories and at domestic-international interactions. For example, the chapters in Part III discuss the fact that major decisions and events in such areas as monetary relations, trade, foreign investment, and international development are affected by domestic as well as international interests and developments.

Three major perspectives and a growing range of theoretical approaches are used in the study of IPE. Some social scientists view this diversity as an indication of our failure to develop an all-embracing theory. However, the existence of different perspectives and theories should not be viewed as a weakness. Social science theory "is always *for* someone and *for* some purpose,"[35] and because the three IPE perspectives are based on differing sets of values, it is unlikely that they will ever be entirely compatible. The three IPE perspectives have differing interpretations of the three main themes in this book relating to globalization, North-North relations, and North-South relations. In regard to the first theme, for example, realists, with their emphasis on the importance of the nation-state, question whether significant globalization is in fact occurring; liberals believe that there is a significant level of globalization, and they view it in very positive terms; and historical structuralists also believe that globalization is significant, but they feel that it is having extremely negative consequences for lower classes and poorer nations in the periphery of the global economy. In regard to the second theme, liberals are far more inclined than realists or historical structuralists to argue that international institutions can play an important role in promoting international economic cooperation. In regard to the third, historical structuralists place far more emphasis than liberals or realists on the inequalities between the North and the South and on the North's exploitation of the South.

FOCUS OF THIS BOOK

This book introduces undergraduate students and beginning graduate students to the study of international political economy. Several distinguishing features of the book have already been discussed. First, it provides an in-depth background to IPE theory, a discussion of current IPE issues in historical perspective, and an examination of the interplay of theory and practice. Without the organizing framework of theory, discussions about trade, foreign investment, development, and other substantive IPE issues simply become a series of disparate facts. Second, Part III of the book focuses on three major themes relating to globalization, North-North relations, and North-South relations.

Third, this book emphasizes the role of international economic organizations such as the World Trade Organization, the International Monetary Fund, and the World Bank in the management of the global political economy. It also devotes considerable attention to important regional organizations such as the European Union, the North American Free Trade Agreement, and the Asia-Pacific Economic Cooperation forum. Most IPE textbooks devote some space to international organizations, but the coverage is very limited and unsystematic. This is a reflection of the relative lack of emphasis on international organizations in the field of international relations in general. Early scholarship on international organizations had a strong idealistic and legal focus on the bodies, rules, and procedures in the League of Nations and then the United Nations. Post–World War II realists understandably felt that these legalistic studies provided us with little information about the real world of power politics, and they turned away from the study of international organizations. In recent years, however, a number of scholars have recognized the importance of studying international organizations as part of, rather than divorced from, the realities of international politics. It is especially important that we devote more attention to international organizations in the case of IPE, where the World Trade Organization, the European Union, the North American Free Trade Agreement, and other organizations have very significant roles.[36]

The book does *not* attempt to glorify international organizations, and it discusses their limitations and problems as well as their possibilities. For example, international organizations always remain to a considerable degree "creatures" of the nation-states that created them, even though the leaders of these bodies have some leeway in formulating objectives and conducting their operations. Furthermore, international institutions are having great difficulty managing the international economy in an age of globalization. Indeed, the total resources of the United Nations, the World Bank, and the International Monetary Fund are far smaller than the daily flows of foreign exchange on global markets. Developing mechanisms for global management is nevertheless a major challenge today. International organizations often serve as important forums for negotiation of management issues, and they also assist in upholding critical principles, norms, and rules of the global political economy.

A fourth emphasis of this book is on regional as well as global relations in the international political economy. Most IPE texts focus almost exclusively on the global political economy and contain no systematic discussion of trends toward regionalism. Yet these trends are inevitably affecting the management of the global political economy, and this book therefore devotes a full chapter to regionalism and globalism in trade. With the formation of NAFTA, "the trade and economic relations of the two largest markets in world trade—the European Community and the United States—are increasingly conditioned by regional agreements."[37] Two other major economies, Japan and China, are not yet members of regional integration agreements. However, the Asia-Pacific Economic Cooperation forum (which includes Japan and China as well as the United States) has a goal of establishing a free and open trade and investment area for developed country members by the year 2010 and for less developed members by 2020. Regionalism of course affects other areas in addition to trade, and Part III devotes some attention to regional trends in the chapters on monetary relations, foreign investment, and development. It is impossible to devote a great deal of space to regionalism in an IPE text, and we are therefore mainly concerned with the *relationship between* regionalism and globalism in the international economy.

A fifth focus of this book relates to its coverage of North-South issues. Instead of discussing North-South issues in a separate section, the book integrates the North-North and North-South discussions as much as possible for several reasons. The three main IPE perspectives should be assessed in terms of their approach to global political economy issues, which relate to *all* countries both rich and poor. Indeed, the historical structuralist perspective (discussed in Chapter 5) focuses almost exclusively on the weaker and exploited classes and countries, and an adequate examination of it necessarily includes a discussion of the Third World. Chapters 3 through 5 therefore discuss each perspective's approach to North-South as well as North-North issues. Part III also integrates the discussion of North-North and North-South relations because the process of globalization in trade, foreign investment, and monetary relations is by definition affecting all areas of the globe. Two chapters are largely devoted to the Third World. Chapter 7 on the foreign debt crisis deals with an issue that specifically has affected LDCs. Even this chapter, however, includes a discussion of Eastern Europe and the former Soviet Union. Chapter 11 is devoted to a detailed discussion of alternative strategies to promote Third World development.

Finally, this book provides substantial coverage of the issues surrounding the emerging states of Eastern Europe, the FSU, and China. These countries are undergoing a gradual (and often extremely difficult) transition from centrally planned economies to more market-oriented economies. As part of this change, they are seeking to establish closer economic ties with the advanced industrial states and to become active members of the major international economic organizations. The emerging CPEs are discussed along with other countries in Part III.

Political leaders and international relations scholars have devoted much more attention to international economic issues in recent years, particularly since the decline of the Cold War. This book focuses on the major theoretical perspectives and substantive issues in IPE and on the interaction between theory and practice. To assess some of the changes occurring in the international political economy, we focus on three major themes: globalization, North-North relations, and North-South relations. Chapter 2 provides an overview of the development of the international political economy in the post–World War II period, with an emphasis on the development of postwar institutions. Chapters 3 through 5 discuss the basic assumptions and historical evolution of the three main IPE theoretical perspectives and also examine how each perspective approaches North-South relations. Chapters 6 to 11 cover monetary relations, foreign debt, global trade, trade regionalism, multinational corporations, and international development.

NOTES

1. Preamble to *Treaty Establishing the European Coal and Steel Community*, Paris, April 18, 1951 (London: Her Majesty's Stationery Office, 1972).
2. International Bank for Reconstruction and Development, *Articles of Agreement* as amended effective February 16, 1989 (Washington, DC: World Bank, August 1991), Article 4, section 10.
3. Andrew Shonfield, *The Attack on World Poverty* (New York: Random House, 1960), p. 147. On the World Bank's changing political and ideological leanings see David A. Baldwin, "The International Bank in Political Perspective," *World Politics* 18 (October 1965), pp. 68–81; Theodore H. Cohn, "Politics in the World Bank: The Question of Loans to the Asian Giants," *International Organization* 28-3 (Summer 1974), pp. 561–571; and Luiz Carlos Bresser Pereira, "Development Economics and the World Bank's Identity Crisis," *Review of International Political Economy* 2-2 (Spring 1995), pp. 211–247.

4. "Boeing v. Airbus," *The Economist*, July 26, 1997, pp. 59–61; Edmund L. Andrews, "Europeans Take Boeing to Brink," *New York Times*, July 24, 1997, pp. A1, C5.

5. Robert Boyer and Daniel Drache, "Introduction," in Robert Boyer and Daniel Drache, eds., *States Against Markets: The Limits of Globalization* (London: Routledge, 1996), p. 3.

6. Robert Gilpin, with Jean M. Gilpin, *The Political Economy of International Relations* (Princeton, NJ: Princeton University Press, 1987), pp. 8–11. The tensions between the state and the market are reflected in the titles of some books on IPE, such as Boyer and Drache, eds., *States Against Markets*, and Herman M. Schwartz, *States Versus Markets: History, Geography, and the Development of the International Political Economy* (New York: St. Martin's Press, 1994).

7. Philip G. Cerny, *The Changing Architecture of Politics: Structure, Agency and the Future of the State* (London: Sage, 1990), pp. 228–229.

8. Lorraine Eden, "Bringing the Firm Back In: Multinationals in International Political Economy," in Lorraine Eden and Evan H. Potter, eds., *Multinationals in the Global Political Economy* (New York: St. Martin's Press, 1993), pp. 25–26; United Nations Development Programme, Human Development Report—1997 (New York: Oxford University Press, 1997), p. 92; Stephen D. Krasner, "Power Politics, Institutions, and Transnational Relations," in Thomas Risse-Kappen, ed., *Bringing Transnational Relations Back In: Non-State Actors, Domestic Structures and International Institutions* (Cambridge: Cambridge University Press, 1995), pp. 277–279; Wyn Grant, "Perspectives on Globalization and Economic Coordination," in J. Rogers Hollingsworth, ed., *Contemporary Capitalism: The Embeddedness of Institutions* (Cambridge: Cambridge University Press, 1997), pp. 322–325.

9. Richard K. Ashley, "Three Modes of Economism," *International Studies Quarterly* 27-4 (December 1983), p. 463.

10. Michael Mastanduno, David A. Lake, and G. John Idenberry, "Toward a Realist Theory of State Action," *International Studies Quarterly* 33-4 (December 1989), p. 458.

11. Thucydides, *The History of the Peloponnesian War*, translated by Richard Crawley (London: Dent & Sons, Everyman's Library), p. 41.

12. Martin Staniland, *What Is Political Economy? A Study of Social Theory and Underdevelopment* (New Haven, CT: Yale University Press, 1985), p. 11; Aristotle, *Politics*, translated by Benjamin Jowett (New York: Modern Library, 1943).

13. Postwar international relations scholars were more inclined than government officials to differentiate between high and low politics. See Richard N. Cooper, "Trade Policy Is Foreign Policy," *Foreign Policy* 9 (Winter 1972–73), p. 18.

14. Some scholars called for greater emphasis on the study of IPE from an early period. See, for example, Klaus Knorr, "Economics and International Relations: A Problem in Teaching," *Political Science Quarterly* 62-4 (December 1947), p. 560; Susan Strange, "International Economics and International Relations: A Case of Mutual Neglect," *International Affairs* 46 (April 1970), p. 307; and Christopher Brown, "International Political Economy: Some Problems of an Interdisciplinary Enterprise," *International Affairs* 49-1 (January 1973), p. 52.

15. James Caporoso, "International Political Economy: Fad or Field?" *International Studies Notes* 13 (Winter 1987), p. 2.

16. Anthony G. McGrew, Paul G. Lewis, et al., *Global Politics: Globalization and the Nation-State* (Cambridge: Polity Press, 1992), p. 23; Claire Turenne Sjolander, "The Rhetoric of Globalization: What's in a Wor(l)d?" *International Journal* 51-4 (Autumn 1996), p. 605.

17. United Nations Development Programme, *Human Development Report 1997*, p. 83.

18. See Paul Hirst and Grahame Thompson, *Globalization in Question: The International Economy and the Possibilities of Governance* (Cambridge: Polity Press, 1996), ch. 1. The

term *borderless world* is taken from Kenichi Ohmae, *The Borderless World: Power and Strategy in the Interlinked Economy* (New York: Harper Perennial, 1990).

19. Philip G. Cerny, "Globalization and Other Stories: The Search for a New Paradigm for International Relations," *International Journal* 51-4 (Autumn 1996), pp. 617–637; Ethan B. Kapstein, *Governing the Global Market: International Finance and the State* (Cambridge, MA: Harvard University Press, 1994), p. 7.

20. United Nations Development Programme, *Human Development Report 1997*, p. 83. For a historical discussion of globalization, see Paul Bairoch, "Globalization Myths and Realities: One Century of External Trade and Foreign Investment," in Boyer and Drache, eds., *States Against Markets,* pp. 173–192. For a study that questions how extensive globalization is today, see Hirst and Thompson, *Globalization in Question.*

21. United Nations Development Programme, *Human Development Report 1997*, p. 83.

22. John H. Dunning, *Multinational Enterprises and the Global Economy* (Wokingham, UK: Addison-Wesley, 1993), pp. 14–15.

23. China and Russia are not yet members of the World Trade Organization, but both countries are observers in the WTO and are actively seeking to join.

24. See Paul R. Krugman and Maurice Obstfeld, *International Economics: Theory and Policy* (New York: HarperCollins, 3rd edition, 1994), pp. 305–306.

25. Joseph S. Nye, Jr., *Bound to Lead: The Changing Nature of American Power* (New York: Basic Books, 1990), p. 70.

26. For a dramatic portrayal of this competitiveness, see Lester Thurow, *Head to Head: The Coming Economic Battle Among Japan, Europe, and America* (New York: Morrow, 1992).

27. For information on the least developed countries, see United Nations Conference on Trade and Development, *The Least Developed Countries, Annual Reports* (New York: United Nations).

28. Howard Handelman, *The Challenge of Third World Development* (Upper Saddle River, NJ: Prentice Hall, 1996), pp. 3–10.

29. Mike Mason, *Development and Disorder: A History of the Third World Since 1945* (Toronto: Between the Lines, 1997), p. 1.

30. For example, see "South-East Asia Loses Its Grip," *The Economist,* July 19, 1997, p. 15; and Edward A. Gargan, "Currency Assault Unnerves Asians," *New York Times,* July 29, 1997, pp. A1, C15.

31. United Nations Development Programme, *Human Development Report 1996* (New York: Oxford University Press, 1996), p. 2.

32. James A. Caporaso, "Global Political Economy," in Ada Finifter, ed., *Political Science: The State of the Discipline II* (Washington, DC: American Political Science Association, 1993), p. 451.

33. Hans J. Morgenthau, revised by Kenneth W. Thompson, *Politics Among Nations: The Struggle for Power and Peace* (New York: Knopf, 6th edition, 1985), p. 10.

34. The term *historical structuralism* emerged in discussions with a colleague, Professor James Busumtwi-Sam, for which I am grateful.

35. Robert W. Cox, "Social Forces, States and World Orders: Beyond International Theory," *Millennium* 10-2 (1981), p. 128. See also Roger Tooze, "Perspectives and Theory: A Consumer's Guide," in Susan Strange, ed., *Paths to International Political Economy* (London: Allen & Unwin, 1984), pp. 3–4.

36. For a detailed discussion of the inadequate attention given to the study of international organizations, see J. Martin Rochester, "The Rise and Fall of International Organization as a

Field of Study," *International Organization* 40-4 (Autumn 1986), pp. 777–813; Pierre de Senarclens, "Regime Theory and the Study of International Organizations," *International Social Science Journal* 45–138 (November 1993), pp. 453–462; and J. Martin Rochester, "The United Nations in a New World Order: Reviving the Theory and Practice of International Organization," in Charles W. Kegley, Jr., ed., *Controversies in International Relations Theory: Realism and the Neoliberal Challenge* (New York: St. Martin's Press, 1995), pp. 199–221.

37. World Trade Organization, *Regionalism and the World Trading System* (Geneva: World Trade Organization, April 1995), p. 27.

Managing the Global Economy Since World War II: The Institutional Framework

After three years of preliminary negotiations, delegates from 44 countries met in July 1944 in Bretton Woods, New Hampshire, to convene the United Nations Monetary and Financial Conference, known as the Bretton Woods conference. Within 22 days, the delegates endorsed agreements to institute a framework for international economic cooperation after World War II. These Bretton Woods agreements were of historic significance because they marked "the first successful attempt consciously undertaken by a large group of nations to shape and control their economic relations."[1] The Bretton Woods conference led directly to the establishment of two new international economic organizations—the International Monetary Fund (IMF) and the International Bank for Reconstruction and Development (IBRD) or World Bank. Several years later, the General Agreement on Tariffs and Trade (GATT) was to become the main global trade organization. These three organizations became part of a complex institutional framework that developed to help manage the global economy in the postwar period.

    The critical negotiations preceding the Bretton Woods conference, and the conference itself, were in fact "very much an Anglo-American affair, with Canada playing a useful mediating role."[2] Some other major countries had less important roles in the conference or did not even attend the meetings: Although a French delegation under Pierre Mendés France participated in the conference, France was still occupied by Germany at the time of Bretton Woods; Germany, Italy, and Japan, as enemy countries, were not represented; and the Soviet Union had only a limited role in the conference and did not sign the final agreements. Twenty-seven less developed countries were present (19 of them Latin American), but their role was rather marginal. The chief planners for the conference were Harry Dexter White of the U.S. Treasury and John Maynard Keynes of Britain. Although the delegates had some fundamental differences of outlook, there was a large degree of consensus on the type of institutional order required for the postwar period. They were particularly concerned with avoiding a repetition of the disastrous events of the interwar period, when increased exchange controls and trade protectionism had contributed to the Great Depression of the 1930s and to World War II itself.

GLOBAL ECONOMIC RELATIONS BEFORE WORLD WAR II

Britain was the first country to industrialize, and by the 1820s it was the dominant or *hegemonic state* in the global political economy. (The concept of hegemony is discussed in Chapter 3.) In 1846, Britain abolished its *Corn Laws*, which had restricted agricultural imports, and this decision contributed to an extended period of free trade in the nineteenth century. Both domestic and external factors accounted for the liberalization of Britain's trade policies at this time. Domestically, legislative and demographic changes caused industrial groups to gain in representation vis-à-vis landed agricultural groups in the British Parliament. Because the agricultural elite's ability to promote agricultural protectionism in the Parliament declined, this group was unable to prevent the repeal of the Corn Laws. Externally, Britain opened its markets to imports of agricultural goods and raw materials so that foreign countries would accept its manufactured goods in return. As the leading industrial power, Britain clearly found such a division of labor in its interest. In addition to the repeal of the Corn Laws, another free trade landmark was the 1860 *Cobden-Chevalier Treaty* between Britain and France, which resulted in a network of commercial treaties lowering **tariff** barriers throughout Europe.[3] By the late nineteenth century, however, industrial protectionism on the European continent, depressed economic conditions, and a decline of British hegemony slowed the growth of trade liberalization. With the outbreak of World War I, the network of trade and commercial treaties was almost completely disrupted.

The United States emerged from World War I as a net creditor nation and the world's largest industrial power. Some of its policies, however, did not facilitate a return to an open, liberal economy. As the largest creditor nation in the interwar period, the United States initially insisted that European nations repay all their war debts, even though this policy contributed to serious financial problems for the country's World War I allies. Indeed, Britain and France had the largest war debts to the United States, amounting to almost $5 billion and more than $4 billion, respectively (before interest multiplied the totals).[4] The United States also imposed trade barriers during this period, which made it extremely difficult for the Europeans to gain needed revenues from exports. The U.S. Congress responded to a recession with the Fordney-McCumber Act of 1922, raising customs duties on agricultural and other products. When the U.S. economy moved into depression after the 1929 stock market crash, Congress passed the 1930 Smoot-Hawley Act, which increased American tariffs to their highest level in the twentieth century.[5] European countries rushed to retaliate against the Smoot-Hawley tariff with their own restrictions on imports, and from 1929 to 1933, world trade declined from $35 billion to $12 billion.[6]

The disastrous experience of the interwar period resulted in part from a lack of economic leadership. Hegemonic stability theorists argue that a global hegemon or predominant power increases the likelihood that there will be a more stable, open international economy. (Debates over the validity of hegemonic stability theory are discussed in Chapter 3.) According to these theorists, Britain served as the global hegemon in the nineteenth century. However, in the interwar period Britain was no longer able, and the United States was not yet willing, to assume the hegemonic duties of promoting freer trade and an open, stable economic system.[7] Other theorists argue that domestic politics was a major factor explaining the economic disarray and conflict. For example, the domestic policymaking system in the United States during the interwar period contributed to the rise in U.S. tariffs despite the country's growing economic power. The U.S. Constitution gives Congress the authority to regulate commerce with foreign nations, and during most of the interwar period, Congress was responsible for setting tariffs. However, the U.S. Congress is a large, unwieldy body subject to special interests, and it was unable to resist the demands of its constituents for higher protection. In efforts to reverse the damage caused by the increase in trade restrictions, Congress passed the *Reciprocal Trade Agreements Act (RTAA)* in 1934. Most importantly, the RTAA delegated tariff-setting policy to the President, who was better able than Congress to resist the pressures of special interests. Although the RTAA resulted in a number of bilateral trade agreements, tariff rates were so high in the early 1930s that these agreements were not sufficient to stem the forces of trade protectionism.[8]

Another major problem in the interwar period was the lack of international organizations to promote economic openness and stability. Although economic conferences were held in the 1920s and 1930s, they failed to deal with the problems of war reparations and debts, disorderly exchange conditions among currencies, and a decline in world trade. In 1933, during the Great Depression, a World Economic and Monetary Conference held in London could not even agree on establishing an **exchange rate** for the U.S. dollar.[9] This experience demonstrated that permanent international economic organizations were needed to support open and stable economic relations after World War II.

THE FUNCTIONS OF THE IMF, THE WORLD BANK, AND GATT

In contrast to the interwar period, the United States emerged as a more mature power at the end of World War II, both willing and able to assume a leadership position. In addition, the major powers established an institutional framework to help prevent a recurrence of the interwar problems. Although some writers refer to the IMF, the

World Bank, and GATT as the Bretton Woods institutions, GATT was in fact established several years after the Bretton Woods conference. In this book the three organizations are referred to as *keystone international economic organizations (KIEOs)* to indicate the central role they have played in international finance, trade, and monetary relations.[10]

The **International Monetary Fund (IMF)** was created to support international monetary stability and the elimination of currency exchange restrictions. To promote monetary stability, the IMF monitored a system of fixed or pegged exchange rates, in which currencies were given official exchange rates in relation to gold and the U.S. dollar. The pegged exchange rate system was designed in part to avoid the competitive devaluation of currencies, which had led to trade wars during the interwar period. **Devaluation** refers to a reduction in the official rate at which one currency is exchanged for another. When a country devalues its currency, the prices of its imported goods and services increase, while its exports become less expensive to foreigners. Countries with deficits in their **balance of payments** (that is, with more money leaving than entering the country) are inclined to devalue their currencies to increase their revenue from exports. The IMF was authorized to provide short-term loans to help countries deal with temporary balance-of-payments problems and maintain the **fixed exchange rates** of their currencies.

The *International Bank for Reconstruction and Development (IBRD)* or *World Bank* was created to provide long-term loans (unlike the IMF's short-term loans) for postwar reconstruction in Europe and for economic development in the Third World. As with the IMF, the World Bank's role was designed to prevent problems that had occurred in the interwar period. After World War I, numerous problems stemming from the cost of servicing war debts and bringing about economic recovery had contributed to economic tensions and conflicts. To prevent a recurrence of these problems after World War II, the World Bank had the role of providing long-term loans for postwar reconstruction and for development. The **General Agreement on Tariffs and Trade (GATT)** was designed to lower countries' tariff rates in multilateral negotiations so that they would not resort to protectionist trade barriers as they had during the interwar period. In addition to providing a forum for trade negotiations, GATT also established rules for the conduct of international trade relations and developed procedures for settling disputes among member states over trade issues.

Because the IMF, the World Bank, and GATT were established partly to avoid problems that had developed during an earlier period (the interwar years), the functions of these institutions inevitably had to evolve along with changes after World War II. For example, the task of European reconstruction proved to be larger than originally anticipated, and the United States therefore established the European Recovery Program (the Marshall Plan) in 1948 to give **bilateral aid** to the Western European countries. As a result, the World Bank played only a minor role in European reconstruction and shifted its attention almost completely to providing loans for economic development. As for the IMF, it lost one of its main functions when the fixed exchange rate system for currencies collapsed in the early 1970s and was replaced by a system of **floating exchange rates.** However, the IMF's profile increased again in the early 1980s when it became the lead international agency dealing with the foreign debt crisis, which began when Mexico threatened to default on its loans in 1982 (see Chapter

7). The World Bank also has provided financing to the foreign debtor countries, and recipients of IMF and World Bank loans now include countries in Eastern Europe and the former Soviet Union as well as the Third World.

GATT was created under special circumstances, and to understand its evolution as an organization, it is necessary to be aware of its origins. Negotiations were held for several years after the Bretton Woods conference to create an international trade organization (ITO) comparable in strength with the IMF and the World Bank. However, trade is one of the most sensitive economic issues to countries, and the U.S. Congress was unwilling to support the formation of a strong trade organization such as the ITO. As a result, the "temporary" General Agreement on Tariffs and Trade, which was signed by 23 governments in 1947 to initiate postwar trade negotiations, became the main global trade organization by default. Because GATT was designed to be only a provisional treaty, it never became a fully developed international organization. Indeed, countries that joined GATT became "contracting parties" rather than formal "members" of the agreement (this book uses the term *GATT membership* for the sake of brevity). Despite its humble origins, GATT proved quite effective for a number of years in liberalizing trade. However, GATT was not well equipped to deal with many new areas of trade, and in January 1995 it was superseded by a new **World Trade Organization (WTO),** which is a full-fledged international organization. Unlike GATT, the WTO deals not only with trade in goods but also with trade in services, intellectual property rights, and trade-related investment measures.

THE INTERNATIONAL ECONOMIC ORGANIZATIONS AND THE UNITED NATIONS

Figure 2.1 shows that the IMF, the World Bank, and the WTO are specialized agencies theoretically under the auspices of the *Economic and Social Council,* which is one of the six principal organs of the United Nations. Under the current structure of the UN system, the World Bank has now become a **World Bank group** of four institutions (see Chapter 11). Unlike the IMF and the World Bank group, GATT never became a full specialized agency of the United Nations, but its successor, the World Trade Organization, is a UN specialized agency.

Although the IMF, the World Bank, and the WTO are part of the United Nations system, the UN in fact has little authority or influence over these organizations. Indeed, the UN signed an agreement with the World Bank when it was formed (and a similar agreement with the IMF), acknowledging that "it would be sound policy to refrain from making recommendations to the Bank with respect to particular loans or with respect to terms or conditions of financing."[11] A major reason for the lack of UN leverage is that the IMF and the World Bank are far more financially sound as institutions than the UN. Indeed, the United States and some other member countries have withheld part of their dues from the UN, and in September 1995 the UN even indicated that it might try to borrow money from the World Bank to deal with its deficit problem. (This action was vetoed by some major UN member states.) Chapters 6 and

Principal Organs of the United Nations

| INTERNATIONAL COURT OF JUSTICE | GENERAL ASSEMBLY | ECONOMIC AND SOCIAL COUNCIL | SECURITY COUNCIL | TRUSTEESHIP COUNCIL | SECRETARIAT |

- Main and other sessional committees
- Standing committees and ad hoc bodies
- Other subsidiary organs and related bodies

➤ **UNRWA**
UN Relief and Works Agency

■ **IAEA**
International Atomic Energy Agency

➤ **INSTRAW**
International Research and Training Institute for the Advancement of Women

➤ **ODCCP**
UN Office for Drug Control and Crime Prevention

➤ **OHCHR**
Office of the UN High Commissioner for Human Rights

➤ **UNCHS**
UN Centre for Human Settlements (Habitat)

†➤ **UNCTAD**
UN Conference on Trade and Development

†➤ **UNDP**
UN Development Programme

　➤ **UNIFEM**
　UN Development Fund for Women

　➤ **UNV**
　UN Volunteers

➤ **UNEP**
UN Environment Programme

➤ **UNFPA**
UN Population Fund

➤ **UNHCR**
Office of the UN High Commissioner for Refugees

➤ **UNICEF**
UN Children's Fund

➤ **UNICRI**
UN Interregional Crime and Justice Research Institute

➤ **UNIDIR**
UN Institute for Disarmament Research

➤ **UNITAR**
UN Institute for Training and Research

➤ **UNOPS**
UN Office for Project Services

➤ **UNU**
UN University

PEACEKEEPING OPERATIONS

- Military Staff Committee
- Standing committees and ad hoc bodies
- International Tribunal For the former Yugoslavia
- International Criminal Tribunal for Rwanda
- **UNSCOM**
UN Special Commission (Iraq)

➤**WFP (UN/FAO)**
World Food Programme

➤**ITC**
International Trade Centre UNCTAD/WTO

- **FUNCTIONAL COMMISSIONS**
Commission for Social Development

　➤UN Research Institute for Social Development (UNRISD)

Commission on Human Rights

Commission on Narcotic Drugs

Commission on Science and Technology for Development

Commission on Sustainable Development

Commission on the Status of Women

Commission on Population and Development

Statistical Commission

- **REGIONAL COMMISSIONS**
Economic Commission for Africa (ECA)

Economic Commission for Europe (ECE)

† Economic Commission for Latin America and the Caribbean (ECLAC)

Economic and Social Commission for Asia and the Pacific (ESCAP)

Economic and Social Commission for Western Asia (ESCWA)

- **SESSIONAL AND STANDING COMMITTEES**

- **EXPERT, AD HOC AND RELATED BODIES**

■ **ILO**
International Labor Organization

■ **FAO**
Food and Agriculture Organization of the UN

■ **UNESCO**
UN Educational, Scientific and Cultural Organization

■ **WHO**
World Health Organization

† **WORLD BANK GROUP**

† ■ **IBRD**
International Bank for Reconstruction and Development

† ■ **IDA**
International Development Association

† ■ **IFC**
International Finance Corporation

† ■ **MIGA**
Multilateral Investment Guarantee Agency

†■ **IMF**
International Monetary Fund

■ **ICAO**
International Civil Aviation Organization

■ **UPU**
Universal Postal Union

■ **ITU**
International Telecommunication Union

■ **WMO**
World Meterological Organization

■ **IMO**
International Maritime Organization

■ **WIPO**
World Intellectual Property Organization

■ **IFAD**
International Fund for Agricultural Development

■ **UNIDO**
UN Industrial Development Organization

†■ **WTO**
World Trade Organization

➤ UN programmes and organs.

■ Specialized agencies and other autonomous organizations within the system.

• Other commissions, committees and ad hoc and related bodies.

† Organizations discussed in this book.

Published by the United Nations Department of Public Information, DPI/1857/Rev. 1—June 1998.

Figure 2.1

Source: The United Nations System, United Nations Department of Public Information, June 1998.

11 discuss the fact that the IMF and the World Bank have weighted voting systems in which the rich northern states have the most votes. This contrasts with the one nation, one vote system of many UN bodies. Because the Northern states prefer weighted voting, they have directed most of their funding for multilateral economic management away from the UN and toward the KIEOs.[12]

Although the KIEOs generally act independently of the United Nations, UN bodies have sometimes induced them to revise their policies and adopt new programs. Examples include the UN's role in the World Bank's creation of a soft-loan agency (see Chapter 11), the IMF's establishment of a compensatory financing facility (see Chapter 6), and the decision of the IMF and the World Bank to introduce human and social dimensions in their lending programs. The World Bank has also cooperated with a number of UN bodies in providing development assistance to the Third World.[13]

POSTWAR ECONOMIC INSTITUTIONS AND THE ADVANCED INDUSTRIAL STATES

The role of the advanced industrial states in the international political economy is marked by three major characteristics, which are also evident in the management of the postwar economic institutions. First, the United States has been and continues to be the most powerful single state, but its hegemony is gradually giving way to a three-way predominance shared by a *triad* composed of the North America, Western Europe, and Japan–East Asia. (The chapters in Part III demonstrate how influential the triad has become in each of the issue areas we examine.) Second, the triad led by the advanced industrial states is responsible for the largest share of international economic transactions today, such as foreign investment, trade in manufactures and services, and **capital** flows. For example, in 1995 the advanced industrial states were the largest source *and* the largest recipients of foreign direct investment (FDI), accounting for 92.1 percent of the outward stocks and 71.9 percent of the inward stocks of FDI. In 1995, North America, Western Europe, and Asia also accounted for almost 93 percent of the world exports of manufactures and for 89.3 percent of world exports of commercial services.[14]

The third characteristic is that countries within the triad conduct most of their international economic transactions with each other, and their trade and investment flows with other parts of the world are relatively small. U.S. multinational corporations have shown a strong preference for investing in Europe, intra-European investment has accelerated, and Japan and Western European countries have invested heavily in the United States. The advanced industrial states still occupy the dominant position in the global political economy. Although Third World countries and the emerging countries of Eastern Europe and the former Soviet Union are increasing their linkages with the industrial states, they continue to occupy peripheral economic positions.

The IMF, the World Bank, and the WTO

In view of their role in global economic transactions, the advanced industrial states have the most influence in determining the agenda and operations of the keystone international economic organizations. For example, the rich Northern states provide most of the funding for IMF and World Bank loans and have the most votes in these weighted-voting institutions. The five countries with the largest number of votes in the IMF and World Bank are the United States, Japan, Germany, France, and Britain. Although the WTO has a one nation, one vote system, the major trading nations, which are mainly Northern countries, have the largest role in setting the agenda in multilateral trade negotiations. Northern dominance in these institutions is also evident from the nationalities of their chief executive officers. By tacit agreement, the World Bank president has always been an American, and the managing director of the IMF has always been a European; all the directors-general of GATT and the WTO as of early 1999 have also been European. Third World countries have been underrepresented on the professional staffs of these organizations, and most Communist countries were not members of the KIEOs from the 1940s to the 1970s.[15]

The Bretton Woods system and its institutions are often credited with contributing "to almost unprecedented global economic growth and change over the past five decades."[16] However, the type of growth these institutions foster has closely followed the prescriptions of the United States and other advanced capitalist countries. The KIEOs therefore support a liberal approach to economic growth, which holds that international prosperity and peace are most likely when there is a free flow of goods and capital around the world. As discussed in Chapter 5, historical structuralists argue that this liberal approach to growth benefits the wealthy capitalist countries in the core of the global economy but disadvantages the lower classes and peripheral Third World countries.

Judged by liberal criteria, the KIEOs were quite effective in the 1950s and 1960s in promoting economic liberalization, growth, and stability. A number of factors help to account for their effectiveness. First, the Cold War increased the incentive of the United States to cooperate economically with Western Europe and Japan; vigorous economic recovery was viewed as a prerequisite for a strong anti-Soviet alliance system. Second, the United States as the global hegemon was able and willing to provide leadership in establishing principles and rules for the conduct of postwar trade, finance, and monetary relations. Third, a relatively small number of politically and economically like-minded countries that accepted U.S. leadership were involved in developing the postwar economic system. Finally, the postwar international institutions were designed so that governments could pursue domestic policy objectives such as full employment and also abide by international rules and obligations.[17]

Despite the early effectiveness of the KIEOs, they encountered increasing problems in managing the global economy beginning in the late 1960s. With Europe and Japan growing much faster than the United States in the 1960s, the United States became less confident about its economic dominance and less inclined to support economic liberalism. For example, pressures for trade protectionism increased in the United States when its balance of trade shifted to a deficit position in 1971. Europe and Japan also began to question U.S. leadership, and the decline of the Cold War permitted the frictions among the advanced capitalist states to increase. A second factor posing a challenge to the KIEOs was the increased influence of the Third World. Less developed countries had long been dissatisfied with the policies of the KIEOs, and in the 1970s the LDCs became able to put some force behind their protests. A critical turning point was the first oil shock following the October 1973 Middle East

War. At this time, the members of OPEC were able to limit the supply of Persian Gulf oil and increase its price by more than 400 percent. The subsequent disruption in the global economy challenged the management capabilities of advanced industrial states and the KIEOs.

A third challenge to the KIEOs resulted from the forces of globalization, such as increased capital flows. As discussed in Part III, increased capital mobility has made it difficult for the KIEOs to manage, and even to monitor, many activities in the global economy. The total economic resources of the KIEOs "pale in comparison to daily market-driven foreign exchange cash flows,"[18] and no international organization effectively oversees the activities of multinational corporations and international banks, which are major contributors to these massive capital flows. As a result, a number of analysts today are skeptical about the ability of the KIEOs to oversee the effective management of the global economy.[19] Finally, the growing membership of the KIEOs with the influx of Third World and former Soviet bloc countries has also interfered with their management capabilities. By 1996, there were 181 members of the IMF, 180 members of the World Bank, and 128 members of the WTO. While some argue that the KIEOs must become more broadly representative, others point to the problems of decision making in such large, unwieldy institutions. The large, diverse memberships of these organizations can contribute to serious difficulties and frustrations in consultation, coordination, and the supervision of policies.

While the IMF, the World Bank, and the WTO continue to have important functions in the global economy, their large memberships have led some liberal analysts to argue that "they must be led by a much smaller core group whose weight confers on them the responsibility of leadership."[20] Since the 1960s, the advanced industrial states have in fact often conferred among themselves in smaller groups before seeking endorsement of their policies by the larger KIEOs. As Figure 2.2 shows, these groups include the Organization for Economic Cooperation and Development, the Group of Ten, the Group of Five, and the Group of Seven. These smaller groups are often more manageable for dealing with coordination of policies among the advanced industrial states in an age of globalization and power sharing among the United States, Europe, and Japan. Furthermore, the industrial states can meet in these groups without sharing information and decision-making power with the LDCs. Unlike liberal economists, who view these smaller groups as essential for promoting economic leadership and stability, historical structuralists argue that the groups permit the most powerful capitalist countries to exclude peripheral states from the decision-making process. Although the IMF and the World Bank have weighted voting, they are nevertheless preferable to the smaller groups from this perspective because the LDCs are at least present at the bargaining table.

The Organization for Economic Cooperation and Development

The Organization for Economic Cooperation and Development (OECD) is a group of mainly advanced industrial states that is based in Paris, France. As Figure 2.2 shows, the OECD had 29 members as of mid-1997. From the time of its creation in 1961, the OECD has been committed to liberalizing international transactions such as trade and

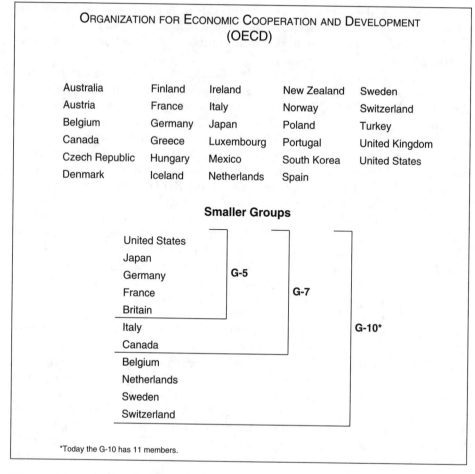

Figure 2.2   Groups of Advanced Industrial States

capital flows. The OECD is well known for its policy studies of economic and social is-sues, but it also serves as a forum for the industrial states to discuss members' eco-nomic policies, review common problems, and promote cooperation and policy coor-dination. In an age of globalization, a country's domestic policies can often have international consequences, and OECD members seek to achieve a consensus on im-plementing domestic policies that will minimize conflict. Although the OECD has the authority to adopt binding as well as nonbinding agreements, it usually operates through a system of mutual persuasion, in which governments exert peer pressure on each other to meet their commitments.[21]

The advanced capitalist states use the OECD not only to promote cooperation but also to develop a more unified developed country position in setting the agenda and conducting negotiations in the IMF, the World Bank, and the WTO. For example, as early as 1963, an OECD report recommended that the World Bank establish an inter-national agency to guarantee funds that private investors direct to LDCs. This report eventually served as the basis for the World Bank's decision to establish the Multilateral Investment Guarantee Agency (MIGA) in 1988. The OECD's work on liberalization of trade in services also led to the decision that the new World Trade Organization should be responsible for liberalizing trade in services as well as goods, and the OECD has been working for several years on a draft multilateral agreement on investment (MAI) that might eventually be monitored by the WTO. (Currently the negotiations for an MAI have been suspended.) In addition to coordinating industrial state policies, the OECD serves as a forum in which the industrial states can respond as a group to the demands of the LDCs.[22]

Although OECD membership was for years limited to the advanced capitalist states, a debate in the early 1990s resulted in a decision that the organization should be open to some enlargement. Thus, Figure 2.2 shows that five countries outside the industrial core group have become OECD members since 1994: Mexico, Hungary, Poland, the Czech Republic, and South Korea. Other countries are also seeking membership in the organization. Some countries are open to this enlargement, but others warn that "transforming the OECD into a mini–United Nations could well jeopardize its ability to achieve high quality agreements among like-minded countries."[23]

Three smaller groupings that are limited to the most important countries in the OECD—the Groups of Ten, Five, and Seven—have taken on significant functions in recent years. The **Group of Ten (G-10)** was the first of these small groups to be formed, in 1962. As Figure 2.2 shows, the G-10 now actually includes 11 countries: the United States, Japan, Germany, France, Britain, Italy, Canada, Belgium, the Netherlands, Sweden, and Switzerland. As mentioned in Chapter 6, the IMF lacked sufficient funding in the early 1960s to meet the borrowing requirements of its member countries. The G-10 countries therefore established the General Arrangements to Borrow (GAB) in 1962, under which they agreed to provide loans to the IMF in their own currencies when it needed supplementary resources. When the G-10 countries meet, they also discuss important issues that affect international monetary relations in general.

While the OECD and G-10 coordinated the economic policies of the advanced industrial countries throughout the 1960s, the main focus of policy coordination shifted to two smaller groupings in the 1970s: the Group of Five and the Group of Seven. With the increase in globalization, it was felt that these groups would have special advantages in policy coordination: their numbers are very small, they include the most powerful industrial states in the global economy, they are flexible groupings without formal constitutions, and top political leaders with the authority to implement agreements often attend their meetings.[24]

The Group of Five and Group of Seven

The **Group of Five (G-5)** includes the finance ministers and governors of the **central banks** of the five largest industrial economies: the United States, Japan, Germany, France, and Britain (see Figure 2.2). These five countries also have the most votes in the IMF and World Bank policymaking bodies. The G-5 first met in 1967 to informally discuss international monetary issues, and it was felt that such meetings were useful and should be continued.[25] In 1975, the G-5 agreed to hold more formal summit meetings at which their heads of government or state could discuss international economic issues. The interest in more formal meetings followed major changes in the global economy, including the need for more collective leadership with the decline of U.S. hegemony, the growing interdependence among the advanced industrial states, the oil crisis, and the world economic recession. Italy was invited along with the G-5 countries to attend the first summit in 1975, and Canada was invited to the second summit in 1976. Once invited, they continued attending the summits, and the **Group of Seven (G-7)** was created. Russia now participates in G-7 summit discussions on political and security matters and in some of the economic discussions, but it is not a full economic participant.[26]

From 1975 to 1986, the G-5 and G-7 met as two largely separate entities. While the G-5 finance ministers and central bank governors held informal and confidential meetings on monetary and financial issues, the G-7 heads of state and government held highly publicized meetings on political as well as economic matters. In 1986, the G-7 largely displaced the G-5, and today there are two different layers of the G-7: at the top are the heads of state or government, who meet in annual summits, and at the second level are the ministers of finance and central bank governors.

The G-5 and G-7 meetings performed some critical functions in the 1970s and 1980s, coordinating **macroeconomic,** currency, and monetary policies among the advanced industrial states. (Macroeconomic policies deal with problems such as employment income, and prices in the economy as a whole, while microeconomic policies refer to the decisions of individual households and firms.) The meetings were also important in arranging financing and other measures to deal with the 1980s Third World debt crisis and the 1991 Gulf War. In recent years, however, the G-7 meetings of finance ministers and central bank governors have become far less effective, and serious concerns have been raised about "the apparent inability of G-7 macroeconomic cooperation to ensure stability in the markets, or to sustain global economic growth."[27] Two major factors account for the decline of the G-7's effectiveness. First, with the demise of the Cold War, economic policy coordination among the capitalist states seems to have less urgency, and conflicts among the G-7 countries have increased. The lack of a common purpose has been exacerbated by the decline of the United States' ability and willingness to exert economic leadership. The second reason for the G-7 decline relates to its difficulties in coping with the increase in globalization. For example, the massive international flows of private capital today interfere with the ability of G-7 monetary authorities to influence currency markets.

The G-7's decline has received considerable attention lately, and some scholars and policymakers warn that continued G-7 leadership is essential for international economic stability and prosperity.[28] In attempting to regain its influence, the G-7 must make the necessary transition from unilateral U.S. leadership to effective collective leadership. This involves both U.S. willingness to share decision making and the willingness of countries such as Japan and Germany to assume more global responsibilities. The G-7 must also address the question of its legitimacy among countries outside its select group, especially because some of these countries are becoming important global economic actors. Indeed, it is striking that the G-7 has no LDC members, considering the size and economic importance of such countries as China, India, Brazil, and Indonesia. The G-7 also has no oil-exporting country among its members (e.g., Saudi Arabia), despite the effect of petroleum on economic developments since the 1970s. Although the G-7 is not likely to expand its membership in the near future, countries such as China, India, and Brazil cannot be ignored, and the G-7 must be willing to consult with nonmembers more seriously if it is to regain its influence.[29]

Divisions Among the Advanced Industrial States

To this point, we have focused mainly on groupings in which the advanced capitalist states cooperate and coordinate their policies on a global basis. However, divisions have developed among the industrial states as U.S. economic hegemony has declined and as the end of the Cold War has permitted differences among these countries to emerge. Globalization has also had the dual effect of creating pressures for cooperation and coordination of policymaking on the one hand and adding to sources of conflict on the other hand as states seek to preserve their autonomy. This book discusses numerous instances of divisions among the advanced industrial states. The following examples relate to the postwar economic institutions.

In recent years, some industrial states have expressed dissatisfaction with their level of representation in the KIEOs. A number of critics in Germany and Japan in particular have argued that their countries' influence in these organizations has not kept pace with their growing economic importance. Thus, a German representative at the 1988 annual meetings of the IMF–World Bank boards of governors asserted that "the Americans have the power, the French get the top jobs, and the Germans and the Japanese come up with the money."[30] Thus, none of the chief executive officers of the three KIEOs has been from Germany or Japan.[31] Even the United States has expressed dissatisfaction in recent years with the fact that all directors-general of GATT have been European. When it came time to select the first WTO director-general in 1995, the United States therefore supported a Mexican for the post. However, as discussed in Chapter 8, this was a battle that the United States lost.

The most important institutional sign of divisions among the advanced industrial states in recent years has been the development and growth of regional integration agreements (RIAs). Although some analysts view these regional groups as stepping-stones to global cooperation, others warn that they may promote divisiveness and interfere with globalism. Many factors account for this turn to regionalism, including impatience of countries with decision making in the large, heterogeneous global organizations; the growing interest of the United States in regionalism as its global hegemonic position has declined; and increased competitiveness among three major regional blocs in the world centered in the European Union, the United States, and Japan. (Chapter 9 provides a detailed discussion of regionalism.) The European Union has advanced to a further stage of integration than most other regional agreements, such as NAFTA, and to understand the phenomenon of regionalism it is necessary to briefly discuss the stages of regional economic integration.

The Stages of Regional Economic Integration   As Figure 2.3 shows, there are five levels of regional economic integration.

1. **Free trade area (FTA).** In an FTA, member countries progressively eliminate tariffs on substantially all their trade with each other. Every country in the FTA retains the right, however, to follow its own trade policies toward

nonmember states. As a result, an FTA poses a lower threat to national sovereignty and tends to be more acceptable to countries with politically sensitive relationships. One of the most important FTAs established in recent years is NAFTA. Most economic integration agreements are free trade agreements.

2. **Customs union (CU).** A CU has the same characteristics as an FTA *plus* a common external tariff toward outside countries. Because a CU involves common trade barriers, member countries must surrender more of their ability to make independent decisions. Thus, Britain was originally unwilling to join the European Community (a customs union) because it wanted to retain its Commonwealth preference system with countries such as India, Canada, and Australia. Britain's trade became increasingly Europe-oriented, and it eventually joined the EC in 1973 and agreed to phase out its Commonwealth preferences. Compared to the number of FTAs, the number of customs unions is relatively small.

3. **Common market.** A common market has the same characteristics as a customs union *plus* the free mobility of factors of production (labor and capital) among the member countries. Because a common market leads to increased labor mobility, there is a tendency to establish similar health, safety, educational, and social security standards so that no country's workers have a competitive advantage. The European Union has generally progressed to the common market stage.

4. **Economic union.** An economic union has the characteristics of a common market, but it also involves the harmonization of industrial, regional, transport, fiscal, monetary, and other economic and social policies. A full economic union also includes a monetary union, with the adoption of a common currency by the members. In January 1999, 11 members of the European Union

	Free trade area (FTA)	Customs union (CU)	Common market	Economic union	Political union
Removal of all tariffs among members	X	X	X	X	X
Common external tariff		X	X	X	X
Free movement of factors (labor and capital)			X	X	X
Harmonization of economic policies				X	X
Political unification					X

Figure 2.3 Stages of Regional Economic Integration

Year of membership	Members	
1957	*France Germany (Federal Republic) *Italy *Belgium *Netherlands *Luxembourg	
1973	Britain Denmark *Ireland	} First enlargement
1979	Greece	} Second enlargement
1986	*Spain *Portugal	
1989	*Germany unified	
1995	*Austria *Finland Sweden	} Third enlargement

*Founding members of the European Economic and Monetary Union (January 1, 1999).

Figure 2.4   Expanding the Membership of the European Union

joined in an economic and monetary union, and moved to adopt a new currency—"the Euro"—in place of their national currencies. (The 11 founding members of the EMU have an * in Figure 2.4.)

5. **Political union.** A political union has all the characteristics of an economic union but extends from the economic area to such political areas as foreign and defense policy. A fully developed political union is more akin to a federal political system than to an agreement among sovereign states.

It is important to note that these stages of regional integration are pure models; they do not fully describe reality. NAFTA, for example, is primarily at stage 1 (an FTA). However, NAFTA contains some provisions requiring more openness toward foreign investment, normally identified with stage 3 (a common market).

The Growing Impact of Regionalism   In the postwar period, it is possible to identify two major phases in the growth of regionalism. The first phase began in 1957, when six countries joined to form the European Economic Community, now called the European Union (see Figure 2.4). Following the example of the European Community, a number of Third World countries sought to establish their own regional agreements in the 1960s. However, this first phase of regionalism "had virtually died by the end of the [1960s] decade, except for the original European Community."[32] In the 1980s there was a revival of regionalism, and many analysts believe that this second phase of regionalism is likely to be far more successful. The United States had refused to join RIAs in the first phase but became more supportive of regionalism in the second phase. Thus, in the 1980s the United States concluded free trade agreements with Israel and Canada, and in the early 1990s it formed NAFTA with Canada and Mexico.

Several possible reasons can be given for the willingness of the United States to participate in RIAs in the 1980s. First, the United States was reacting to the broadening and deepening of integration in the European Union, an expanding trade bloc from which it was excluded. As Figure 2.4 shows, membership in the EU grew from 6 states in 1958 to 15 in 1995, and a number of Eastern European countries would like to join in the future. A second factor in the U.S. conversion was dissatisfaction with the slow progress of multilateral trade negotiations. Indeed, it was during the protracted eighth round of GATT negotiations (the Uruguay round) that the United States established its free trade agreements with Israel, Canada, and Mexico. A third factor relates to the relative decline in U.S. economic hegemony. During the first phase of regionalism, the United States as global hegemon took the main responsibility for upholding the GATT trade regime as the best path to trade liberalization. However, frustration over its chronic trade deficits has pushed the United States to seek regionalism as another possible route to expanding its export markets.

As discussed in Chapter 9, some U.S. domestic groups strongly oppose NAFTA and any attempts to extend it to other countries such as Chile. Nevertheless, since the U.S. conversion to regionalism in the 1980s, all major advanced industrial states except Japan are now members of RIAs. Japan and the United States are both members of the *Asia-Pacific Economic Cooperation (APEC)* forum, which was formed in 1989. APEC has a goal of establishing a free and open trade and investment area for its developed country members by the year 2010, and if this goal is achieved, Japan will also be a member of an RIA.

What is the significance of the growth of regionalism for relations between the advanced industrial states? Some observers think this is a period of "open regionalism" that will serve as a stepping-stone to global cooperation, and they point out that APEC has a broad range of members from Asia, Australasia, and North and South America. Others argue, however, that regionalism is a divisive force that could eventually result in the splitting of the world into three major economic blocs based in Europe, the Western Hemisphere, and East Asia.

Despite the divisions among the advanced industrial states, they are normally able to cooperate when necessary to preserve their predominant influence vis-à-vis the Third World in the IMF, the World Bank, and the WTO. It is therefore important to examine why Third World countries have had so little influence in these institutions and what actions they have attempted to take to remedy this situation.

POSTWAR ECONOMIC INSTITUTIONS AND THE THIRD WORLD

The Bretton Woods system and its institutions are often credited with contributing "to almost unprecedented global economic growth and change over the past five decades."[33] This economic growth, however, has not been shared by all. Poverty and its attendant problems, such as disease and hunger, are prevalent in much of the

world, and there is a major gulf between the rich nations of the North and the poor nations of the South. Third World countries are characterized not only by low levels of
economic development but also by low levels of social development. Economic development indicators include such factors as per capita income, infrastructure facilities
(for example, transportation, communications, and electrical power and water facilities), and the availability of modern technology. Social development indicators include
literacy rates, health and sanitary facilities, and infant mortality and life expectancy
rates.

Table 2.1 includes figures on one of the main indicators of economic development, per capita income. The first column shows that Northern states have much
higher per capita incomes than most Southern states. Thus, the average per capita income in the United States in 1993 ($24,240) was almost 8 times greater than the per
capita income in Indonesia ($3,150), almost 20 times greater than the per capita in-
come in India ($1,220), and more than 40 times greater than the per capita income in
Tanzania ($580). The second column shows that there is also a major gap between the
rich and the poor within countries of the north as well as the south. Thus, the per
capita income of the poorest 20 percent of people in Japan ($9,070) is less than one-
half of the average per capita income in Japan ($20,850); the per capita income of the
poorest 20 percent in the United States ($5,814) is less than one-fourth of the U.S. av-
erage ($24,240); and the per capita income of the poorest 20 percent in Guatemala
($352) is barely one-tenth of the Guatemalan average ($3,350).

The following examples show that the economic gap between the rich states in the
North and the poor states in the South is not only great but is widening.

TABLE 2.1
AVERAGE PER CAPITA INCOME AND PER CAPITA INCOME
OF THE POOREST 20%, 1993 (U.S. DOLLARS)

Country	Average Per Capita Income	Per Capita Income of the Poorest 20%
United States	$24,240	$5,814
Japan	20,850	9,070
Netherlands	17,330	7,105
United Kingdom	17,210	3,958
Korea, Republic of	9,630	3,563
Chile	8,400	1,386
Hungary	6,050	2,297
Brazil	5,370	564
Guatemala	3,350	352
Indonesia	3,150	1,370
Nigeria	1,400	357
India	1,220	537
Bangladesh	1,290	613
Nepal	1,020	464
Guinea-Bissau	840	88
Tanzania	580	70

Source: Human Development Report 1996, p. 13, table 1.1. Copyright © 1996 by the
United Nations Development Programme. By permission of Oxford University Press.

- In 1993, the global GDP amounted to about $23 trillion. (The global GDP refers to the total value of production of goods and services in the world.[34]) Of this $23 trillion, the LDCs, with almost 80 percent of the world's population, accounted for only $5 trillion, while the industrial countries accounted for $18 trillion.
- The share of global income of the poorest 20 percent of the world's people fell from 2.3 to 1.4 percent in the last 30 years, while the share of the richest 20 percent rose from 70 to 85 percent.
- The gap in per capita income between the industrial countries and the LDCs almost tripled from $5,700 in 1960 to $15,400 in 1993.[35]

Although the economic gap between the Northern and Southern states has generally increased in recent years, there are also growing divisions *within the South.* Thus, Table 2.2 shows that the East Asian and Latin American countries generally score higher in terms of both economic and social indicators than the South Asian and sub-Saharan African countries. The sub-Saharan Africans and East Asians demonstrate some of the most striking differences in development levels. The per capita GDP in sub-Saharan Africa in 1960 ($990) was slightly higher than the per capita GDP in East Asia excluding China ($869). By 1994, however, the per capita GDP in East Asia excluding China ($11,088) was almost 8 times higher than the per capita GDP in sub-Saharan Africa ($1,460). Sub-Saharan Africa also registered lower levels of development than most other regions on such social measures as infant mortality, adult literacy rate, and access to safe water, while East Asia's development level was well above the average in these areas.

TABLE 2.2
HUMAN DEVELOPMENT INDICATORS

Region	Real GDP Per Capita (U.S. dollars)		Infant Mortality Rate (per 1,000 live births)		Adult Literacy Rate (%)		Safe Water Access (percentage of the population)	
	1960	1994	1960	1994	1970	1994	1975–80	1990–96
Sub-Saharan Africa	$990	$1,460	166	97	27	56	24	42
South Asia	698	1,687	163	73	32	49	30[b]	76[b]
East Asia	729	2,983	146	41	88	98[a]	—	—
East Asia excluding China	869	11,088[a]	84	17	88	98[a]	70	94
Southeast Asia and Pacific	732	4,149	127	50	65	87	15	67
Latin America and Caribbean	2,137	5,933	107	38	72	86	60	75
Arab states	931	4,263[a]	166	67	30	57	71	83
All LDCs	915	2,923	149	64	43	64	41	69

[a]1993 figures.
[b]Excluding India.

Source: Human Development Report 1996, p. 209. Copyright © 1996 by the United Nations Development Programme. By permission of Oxford University Press.

Recognizing the major divisions among LDCs, the United Nations in 1971 compiled a list of 24 of the poorest countries which it identified as "least-developed countries" (LLDCs), and the UN list of LLDCs has grown to 31 countries in 1980 and to 48 countries today. The UN has singled out the LLDCs for special attention, because they generally have extremely low per capita GDPs, literacy rates, and shares of manufacturing. Table 2.3 shows that almost three-quarters of the 48 LLDCs are in Africa, and that there are also a substantial number in the Asia/Pacific. The third column in the table shows that a large percent of those LLDCs for which statistics are available had *negative* GNP per capita growth rates from 1970 to 1995.

Although a relatively small number of LDCs—particularly in East and Southeast Asia—have improved their economic positions, the great majority of Third World countries have been frustrated in their efforts to promote development and exert more influence. As discussed in Chapter 11, even some East and Southeast Asian countries, such as South Korea, Indonesia, Malaysia, and Thailand, which had been viewed as exemplars of economic development, confronted serious financial crises in the late 1990s. The most significant gap in economic and social development therefore continues to be the division between the advanced industrial states of the North on the one hand and the large majority of less developed countries in the South on the other. Because most LDCs are in a very weak position individually, only collective action has provided some opportunity for extracting costly concessions from the North. Thus, the Third World has often attempted to present a unified front vis-à-vis the Northern industrial states in the United Nations and other institutional forums.

LDC Efforts to Alter the Institutional Framework

Many LDCs have been dissatisfied with the KIEOs because of their lack of influence in these organizations. From the perspective of many LDCs, the KIEOs also promote policies that either do not contribute to, or pose major obstacles to, LDC economic development.[36] This chapter briefly discusses LDC efforts to bring about changes in the postwar international institutions and also to create new institutions that would increase their influence and development prospects. Subsequent chapters examine the position of LDCs on issues such as foreign debt and foreign investment, and Chapter 11 outlines alternative strategies the LDCs have followed for promoting development.

The 1950s   An early target of LDC dissatisfaction was the International Bank for Reconstruction and Development or World Bank, which was designed to provide long-term loans for economic development. As discussed in Chapter 11, the IBRD provides *hard loans,* with relatively high interest rates and shorter repayment periods; for example, the interest rate on IBRD loans in 1995 was about 7.1 percent. Because the poorest LDCs require **concessional** or **soft loans,** the IBRD funding is available mainly to middle-income LDCs. Third World countries were also dissatisfied with the weighted voting system of the IBRD, which favored—and continues to favor—the rich northern states. In 1997, for example, the 26 developed countries had 61.6 percent of the votes in the World Bank board of governors, and the G-7 countries alone had 47.8 percent of the governors' votes. The 163 LDC members of the World Bank, by contrast, had only 38.4 percent of the votes.[37]

TABLE 2.3
DEVELOPMENT INDICATORS OF THE LEAST
DEVELOPED COUNTRIES (LLDCs)

	1995 GNP per capita (U.S. dollars)	1995 Population (millions)	1970–1995 Real growth rate percent (GNP per capita)
LLDCs			
Afghanistan	—	23.48	—
Angola	410	10.77	—
Bangladesh	240	119.77	1.5
Benin	360	5.48	0.1
Bhutan	380	0.70	5.4
Burkina Faso	210	10.38	1.5
Burundi	160	6.26	0.6
Cambodia	280	10.02	—
Cape Verde	1030	0.38	5.5
Central African Republic	350	3.27	−1.5
Chad	160	6.45	−0.1
Comoros	480	0.49	−0.7
Congo, Dem. Rep.	110	43.85	−4.0
Djibouti	—	0.63	—
Equatorial Guinea	380	0.40	—
Eritrea	—	3.57	—
Ethiopia	110	56.40	—
Gambia	320	1.11	0.2
Guinea	540	6.59	0.1
Guinea-Bissau	240	1.07	—
Haiti	250	7.17	−1.3
Kiribati	780	0.08	—
Laos	350	4.88	—
Lesotho	650	1.98	2.3
Liberia	—	2.73	−3.0
Madagascar	230	13.65	−2.5
Malawi	170	9.76	−0.2
Maldives	990	0.25	—
Mali	250	9.79	0.2
Mauritania	460	2.27	−0.7
Mozambique	80	16.17	−0.2
Myanmar	—	45.11	—
Nepal	210	20.80	1.3
Niger	200	9.03	−2.6
Rwanda	180	6.40	−0.2
Sao Tome and Principe	420	0.13	−1.0
Sierra Leone	170	4.51	−1.0
Solomon Islands	910	0.38	2.8
Somalia	—	9.49	−0.6
Sudan	—	26.71	−0.6
Tanzania	130	29.65	—
Togo	300	4.11	−1.1
Tuvalu	—	0.01	—

TABLE 2.3 CONTINUED

	1995 GNP per capita (U.S. dollars)	1995 Population (millions)	1970–1995 Real growth rate percent (GNP per capita)
Uganda	240	19.17	—
Vanuatu	1 220	0.17	—
Western Samoa	1 140	0.16	—
Yemen	280	15.27	—
Zambia	400	8.98	–2.4
LLDCs, TOTAL	—	579.88	—

Source: Organisation for Economic Co-operation and Development, *Development Co-operation—1997 Report* (PARIS: OECD, 1998), pp. A87-A88.

Throughout the 1950s, the LDCs repeatedly pressured the United Nations to establish a new agency that would have a more equitable voting system than the World Bank, and would provide grants or soft loans (with low or no interest and long repayment periods) to Third World countries. These proposals repeatedly failed, however, because of opposition from the advanced industrial states. With decolonization increasing and LDC needs for capital becoming more evident, in 1960 the developed states finally agreed to establish a soft-loan aid agency, the *International Development Association (IDA)*. As is often the case, however, the Northern states were *not* willing to accede to LDC demands for greater power over decision making, and they insisted that the IDA become a part of the World Bank group with its weighted voting system (see Figure 2.1). Furthermore, the largest share of World Bank group loans continues to be hard loans provided by the IBRD. The soft IDA loans are limited in amount and are generally available to only the poorest of the LDCs.

The 1960s   In the 1960s decolonization transformed North-South relations as many new African and Asian LDCs gained their independence and joined the United Nations. (Most Latin American LDCs had gained their political independence in the nineteenth century.) Thus, the number of new African and Asian states in the UN increased from 10 in 1955 to 55 in 1966, and by 1966 they accounted for about 45 percent of the countries in the United Nations.[38] In 1964, the 77 Third World countries in the UN from Africa, Asia, and Latin America met to express their dissatisfaction with the KIEOs and to prepare for a major conference on trade and development.[39] This caucus of LDCs now has well over 100 members, but it is still referred to as the **Group of 77 (G-77).**

The conference organized by the G-77 in Geneva in March 1964 was the first **United Nations Conference on Trade and Development (UNCTAD).** In view of the growing numbers of LDCs in the United Nations, the G-77 was able to convene UNCTAD I despite the initial opposition—and then the grudging acceptance—of the advanced industrial states. UNCTAD I was "the first institutional response in the economic sphere to the entry of the Third World on the international scene," and UNCTAD subsequently became a permanent organ of the UN General Assembly (see Figure 2.1).[40] Although all members of the UN are members of UNCTAD, the LDCs with their greater numbers have had the predominant role in setting UNCTAD's agenda and work program. In marked contrast to the KIEOs, the secretariat of the UNCTAD has openly supported LDC interests, and the UNCTAD secretary-general has always been from a Third World country.

UNCTAD experienced some success in espousing an alternative approach to trade and economic development, in inducing GATT to give more priority to Third World trade interests, and in overseeing certain areas of trade negotiation such as the establishment of international commodity agreements. However, GATT/WTO continues to be the unrivaled international organization monitoring the principles, norms, and rules of the global trade regime. Because UNCTAD's orientation posed a direct challenge to the liberal-economic order and to the power position of the North, the advanced industrial states simply refused to accept it as a major forum for negotiations on international economic relations. Thus, UNCTAD's main role has not been in international management but in serving as a pressure group for Third World interests.

The 1970s   Although Third World countries attempted to improve their position vis-à-vis the North in the 1960s, their stance became far more militant in the 1970s when OPEC drastically increased oil prices. A number of factors contributed to OPEC's success in raising prices, including the increased dependence of the advanced industrial states on Middle Eastern oil and the unifying effect on Arab OPEC members of the October 1973 Middle East War. Although LDC oil importers as well as industrial states were hurt by the OPEC price increases, most LDCs nevertheless viewed OPEC as an example of what they might also do to increase their power and wealth vis-à-vis the North. Thus, the OPEC example, along with increases in the prices of a number of commodities that LDCs exported, led to LDC calls for a **New International Economic Order (NIEO)** in the 1970s. The NIEO was a multilateral strategy designed to gain major economic concessions from the North and to increase the economic and political power of the South.

The advanced industrial states were willing to join in NIEO negotiations with the Third World in the 1970s because of their concerns about the increased leverage of OPEC. Indeed, implicit linkages were drawn between guaranteed supplies of OPEC oil at lower prices on the one hand and Northern willingness to discuss the NIEO demands on the other. Third World demands in the NIEO negotiations were numerous, including an increase in **foreign aid,** LDC sovereignty over their economies and natural resources, increased LDC control over foreign direct investment, more access to Northern technology on easier terms, preferential treatment for LDC exports to Northern states, international commodity agreements, and increased LDC decision-making power in the IMF and the World Bank group.[41]

The Third World countries did register some gains in the NIEO negotiations. For example, the voting shares of OPEC countries increased somewhat in both the IMF and the World Bank, and the industrial states eventually agreed to a generalized system of preferences (GSP) for LDC exports (see Chapter 8). These gains, however, were clearly limited, and industrial states became less willing to make concessions to the Third World as bargaining power gradually shifted back in favor of the North. Indeed, oil proved to be a unique commodity; LDC producers of other commodities could not acquire similar marketing power. The industrial states also gradually gained access to other sources of oil and became less dependent on the OPEC producers. The most significant factor shifting the balance of power back toward the North, however, was the Third World foreign debt crisis that began in the 1980s.

The 1980s and 1990s   Chapter 7 focuses on the Third World foreign debt crisis, which began in 1982 when Mexico threatened to default on its loans. As discussed in Chapter 7, the debt crisis was closely related to the OPEC oil price increases of the 1970s. OPEC countries deposited a large share of their oil revenues in international banks, which recycled these "petrodollars" by extending massive loans to LDC oil importers. A combination of imprudent lending, imprudent borrowing, and unexpected international events contributed to overborrowing by many LDCs in the 1970s and to the LDCs' dependence on debt relief assistance in the 1980s and the 1990s. In return for extending structural adjustment loans to the debtor LDCs, the IMF and the World Bank, backed by the advanced industrial states, imposed conditions requiring that LDCs open their economies to trade, foreign investment, and other economic linkages with the North. Thus, Third World countries have generally taken a more conciliatory approach toward the North since the 1980s, and they have been more willing to accept Northern demands for such policies as liberalization, privatization, and deregulation.

This shift in the balance of power toward the North is evident in changes occurring in UNCTAD, which has been "the principal locus of Third World efforts to obtain changes in the trade and other economic relationships between developed and developing countries."[42] UNCTAD's pressures on behalf of the Third World had increased during the 1970s when the Third World was demanding a New International Economic Order. By the late 1980s, however, UNCTAD began to shift its policy toward a more conciliatory approach because of threats that it could become totally irrelevant. This change was evident in UNCTAD's relationship with GATT, which shifted from an emphasis on conflicting to complementary interests between the two organizations. The change was also evident in the tone of discussion in UNCTAD conferences, which are normally held once every four years. The sixth UNCTAD conference (UNCTAD VI) in 1983 was marked by confrontation, but UNCTAD VII and VIII in 1987 and 1992 were notable for efforts to identify common North-South interests. Because it was the first UNCTAD conference since the breakup of the Soviet bloc, UNCTAD VIII "brought together a virtually universal view that economic policies based on market forces were the best basis for achieving development."[43] UNCTAD's reversal of policy was only one indication that most Third World countries in the 1990s saw little alternative to operating within the framework of the KIEOs and the liberal-economic system of the advanced industrial states.

POSTWAR ECONOMIC INSTITUTIONS AND THE CENTRALLY PLANNED ECONOMIES

International organization scholars generally consider the IMF, the World Bank, and GATT/WTO to be universal membership organizations, in which all states can become members.[44] For much of the history of these organizations, however, the centrally planned economies (CPEs) of Eastern Europe, the Soviet Union, and China either were nonmembers or played a very limited role. At the end of World War II there was an institutional division of labor, with the UN concentrating primarily on political and military security matters and the Bretton Woods institutions taking responsibility for economic cooperation. Nevertheless, political security issues were inevitably a factor in the deliberations of the KIEOs.[45] The Western allies generally felt that universalism was the best approach to creating a more secure environment, and Harry Dexter White of the U.S. Treasury Department wrote in his April 1942 draft Bretton Woods plan that "to exclude a country such as Russia would be an egregious error. Russia, despite her socialist economy could both contribute and profit by participation."[46] The allied governments also expected that the Eastern European states, which previously had close economic ties with the West, would become full members of the Bretton Woods organizations.[47]

Although the Soviet Union was fearful of capitalist encirclement, it wanted to gain access to economic and financial aid to reconstruct its war-damaged economy. The USSR therefore was actively involved in the deliberations leading up to and including the Bretton Woods conference. As the only Communist state at Bretton Woods (Poland and Czechoslovakia were not yet Communist), the Soviet Union expressed a number of concerns regarding such issues as special consideration for state-trading countries, the paid-in subscriptions and voting procedures of the IMF and World Bank, and the amount of information the IMF and World Bank would require of member states. The major Western countries made limited concessions to the USSR in the *IMF Articles of Agreement* concerning the payment of subscriptions and the provision of information to the IMF, and the Soviet Union signed the Bretton Woods agreements. However, it continued to oppose the method of allocating votes in the IMF and the World Bank, the transfer of gold to U.S. territory, and the conditions that the IMF would place on its loans. After the first IMF/World Bank board of governors meeting in March 1946, the Soviet Union stopped participating, and it did not become a member of these organizations. By this time, Cold War issues were intruding (e.g., disputes over the administration of Berlin and the Soviet occupation of Eastern Europe), and both the USSR and the West backed away from the goal of universality. Thus, the Soviet Union did not even attend the conferences designed to develop a global trade organization.[48]

In 1947, the United States responded to the continuing economic problems in Western Europe—the near exhaustion of foreign exchange reserves for purchasing needed food, energy, and raw materials—with the European Recovery Program, or Marshall Plan. When U.S. Secretary of State George C. Marshall introduced the plan, he invited the Soviet Union and Eastern Europe to participate. However, the Soviets refused to join in and also vetoed the idea of participation by the East Europeans. Particularly objectionable to the Soviets were U.S. requirements that the United States have some advisory authority over the internal budgets of Marshall Plan aid recipients, that the European countries cooperate with each other in the use of Marshall Plan aid, and that most of the aid be used to purchase U.S. exports. Only Western European states therefore joined with the United States in the Marshall Plan, and the Soviet Union established the *Council for Mutual Economic Assistance (CMEA)* in January 1949 as a counterweight. Composed of the Soviet Union and Eastern European states other than Yugoslavia, the CMEA solidified the economic and political divisions between Eastern and Western Europe.[49]

The Soviet-led CMEA was involved with a number of economic activities such as technical cooperation and joint planning, and its strategies for promoting cooperation among the CPEs sharply differentiated it from the market-oriented Bretton Woods system. For example, the CMEA emphasized central planning for almost all economic decisions, such as resource allocation; the nationalization of the factors of production, including capital, natural resources, and in most cases land; the collectivization of agriculture; and a rather rigid separation of the domestic economy from external economic influences. The main purpose of CMEA was to reorient Eastern European trade away from the West and to solidify the economic linkages between the Soviet Union and Eastern Europe. Thus, the CMEA established two institutions, the International Bank for Economic Cooperation (in 1964) and the International Investment Bank (in 1971), which were designed to assume functions similar to those of the IMF and the World Bank. These two CMEA banks were very inadequate substitutes, however, because they were associated with increased bilateralism, a currency (the ruble) with unrealistic conversion rates that limited trade, and inward-looking policies vis-à-vis the world economy.[50]

The growing economic rift between East and West resulted not only from actions of the Soviet Union but also from policies of the Western industrial states. For example, the United States restricted trade with Communist countries from 1948, and the 1949 U.S. Export Control Act authorized the President to establish a licensing system that would regulate exports to the Communist states. The United States also pressured its allies to join in the *Coordinating Committee (COCOM)*, which was established to coordinate Western embargoes of strategic goods to the Soviet bloc. COCOM was an effort to limit the Soviet Union's military advances, and it was also designed to hurt the USSR economically and isolate it politically. Furthermore, the U.S. Congress passed the Trade Agreements Extension Act in 1951, which withdrew trade concessions previously granted to all Communist countries other than Yugoslavia.

The liberal-economic orientation of the KIEOs was yet another factor contributing to the East-West split. Theoretically, the lending decisions of the IMF and World Bank are to be nonpolitical in nature, and the IBRD Articles of Agreement explicitly state that "only economic considerations shall be relevant" to the bank's decisions.[51] A number of analysts argue, however, that these institutions are committed to a capitalist world economy and that they make decisions on the basis of political and ideological as well as economic considerations.[52] Even when these organizations are not consciously promoting Western-style capitalism, the values of their professional staff members, who have received their education and training mainly in Western capitalist countries, affect the decision-making process.[53]

In view of the major East-West divisions, it is not surprising that most linkages between the Communist states and the KIEOs were severed during the 1950s. Although

Czechoslovakia, Poland, Yugoslavia, China, and Cuba had been founding members of the IMF and the World Bank, their membership ended or their status changed after they became centrally planned socialist economies (the sole exception was Yugoslavia). As Table 2.4 shows, Poland withdrew from the IMF and the World Bank in 1950, charging that these institutions were largely controlled by the U.S. government, and Czechoslovakia was expelled from the World Bank and the IMF in 1954. The ostensi-

TABLE 2.4

MEMBERSHIP OF THE EMERGING ECONOMIES IN THE KEYSTONE INTERNATIONAL ECONOMIC ORGANIZATIONS

	IMF	World Bank	GATT/WTO
1946	Poland, Czechoslovakia, Yugoslavia, and China (founding members of IMF and World Bank)		
1948			Czechoslovakia and China (founding members)
1950	Poland withdraws from IMF and World Bank		Republic of China (Taiwan) withdraws from GATT
1954	Czechoslovakia ousted from IMF and World Bank		
1966			Yugoslavia
1967			Poland
1971			Romania
1972	Romania	Romania	
1973			Hungary
1980	People's Republic of China (PRC) replaces Taiwan in IMF and World Bank		
1982	Hungary	Hungary	
1984			Special observer status: People's Republic of China (PRC)
1986	Poland	Poland	
1990	Czech and Slovak Federal Republic, Bulgaria		East Germany accedes to GATT by virtue of reunification
1991	Albania	Albania, Bulgaria, Czech and Slovak Federal Republic	
1992	Russian Federation, other FSU[a] republics	Russian Federation, other FSU republics	Special observer status: Russian Federation and other FSU[a] republics
1993	Croatia, Slovenia, Macedonia, Czech Republic, Slovak Republic	Croatia, Slovenia, Czek Republic, Slovak Republic	Czech Republic, Slovak Republic
1994		Macedonia	Slovenia
1996	Bosnia and Herzegovina	Bosnia and Herzegovina	Bulgaria

[a]FSU = former Soviet Union.

Sources: International Monetary Fund, Annual Report of Executive Board (Washington, DC: IMF, various years); World Bank Annual Report (Washington, D.C.: World Bank, various years); General Agreement on Tariffs and Trade, GATT Activities (Geneva, Switzerland: GATT, various years).

ble reasons for expulsion related to Czechoslovakia's failure to pay part of its capital subscription to the IBRD and its refusal to consult with the IMF and provide it with information.[54] Yugoslavia was the only Eastern European country to remain in the IMF and the World Bank in the 1950s, but it was a special case because of its independence from the Soviet Union. The Republic of China (Taiwan) occupied the China seat in these institutions after the People's Republic of China took over the mainland in October 1949, and Cuba under Fidel Castro withdrew from the World Bank in 1960 and from the IMF in 1964.

Table 2.4 shows that China and Czechoslovakia were founding members of GATT in 1948, but the Chiang Kai-shek government (which had fled from the mainland to Taiwan) withdrew from the organization in 1950, purportedly on behalf of China. Czechoslovakia remained a member of GATT (but not of the IMF and the World Bank), even though its membership was basically inactive for a number of years. Czechoslovakia was able to retain membership because of GATT's status as a highly informal organization.

As nonmembers of the KIEOs, the Soviet bloc countries joined the Third World in supporting the formation of alternative organizations in which the advanced capitalist states would have less control. For example, the Soviet Union strongly endorsed the formation of the United Nations Conference on Trade and Development. By the late 1960s, however, the Soviet bloc countries became less interested in UNCTAD and other alternative organizations for a number of reasons. These included the growth of East-West détente, the increase of tensions and economic problems within the Eastern bloc's CMEA, the growing dependence of Eastern European countries on Western markets for their exports, and the political desire of Eastern Europeans to gain more independence from the Soviet Union. Thus, Table 2.4 shows that some Eastern European countries (Poland, Romania, and Hungary) joined the KIEOs beginning in the late 1960s. The People's Republic of China also replaced Taiwan in the IMF and the World Bank in 1980, and Russia and other FSU republics joined the two Bretton Woods institutions in the early 1990s after the breakup of the Soviet Union. Russia and China are currently seeking to join the WTO, but they have not yet been accepted as members. The emerging economies have had to accept more market reforms when joining the KIEOs, and the KIEOs in turn have had to become more open to some degree of central planning. Later chapters discuss in greater detail the gradual moves toward integration of the emerging economies with the IMF, the World Bank group, and GATT/WTO.

POSTWAR ECONOMIC INSTITUTIONS AND THE GENDER ISSUE

Although Third World countries have been the main disadvantaged group, other groups have also been largely excluded from positions of power in the KIEOs. For example, no head of the IMF, the World Bank, or GATT/WTO has been a woman. Women have been appointed to head some UN agencies, including the UN Children's Fund (UNICEF), the UN Development Fund for Women, the office of the UN High Commissioner for Refugees, and the Population Fund; but these agencies deal primarily with social areas, which are considered to be within the woman's domain.

Although 35 percent of the 2500 professional posts at United Nations headquarters were held by women in late 1996, women occupied only 18 percent of the policy- and decision-making posts. Some feminist theorists argue that the small number of women in high foreign policy and international organization positions is "symptomatic of a much deeper issue . . . the extent to which international politics is such a thoroughly masculinized sphere of activity that women's voices are considered inauthentic."[55]

In December 1995, the assistant secretary general for political affairs (a Mexican woman) became the first coordinator for all women's issues in the UN system, and in January 1998 a French Canadian woman became the first person to occupy the post of deputy secretary-general. (The deputy secretary-general can temporarily assume responsibility for the UN at the discretion of the secretary-general.) The extent to which these moves will affect the role of women in the KIEOs remains to be seen.[56]

CONCLUSION

This chapter has examined the changing institutional framework for managing the global economy in the postwar era. The member states at the 1944 Bretton Woods conference had great faith in the establishment of international institutions to prevent a recurrence of the problems of the interwar years, and the three keystone international economic organizations have been important contributors to prosperity in the postwar period. Nevertheless, there is a hierarchy of states within the IMF, the World Bank, and GATT/WTO, and postwar prosperity has not been equally distributed among states and peoples. The United States and other advanced industrial countries have been at the top of the hierarchy, in a position to establish and uphold the principles and rules for the functioning of the global economic order. The Third World countries have sought to alter the KIEOs and to establish alternative organizations such as the UN Conference on Trade and Development. However, their gains have been limited, and events such as the foreign debt crisis of the 1980s have greatly weakened their position.

Unlike the Third World countries, the centrally planned economies for many years were nonparticipants in the KIEOs, and the Soviet Union established the Council for Mutual Economic Assistance as an alternative organization for the Eastern bloc. However, economic problems, political tensions, and growing economic dependence on advanced capitalist states gradually pushed the Eastern bloc countries to join the Western-dominated KIEOs. The breakup of the Soviet bloc and the Soviet Union has sped up this integration process. The Third World debt crisis has similarly forced many LDCs to become more dependent on the IMF and the World Bank for structural adjustment loans and to become more closely integrated with the capitalist economic order. Thus, one student of globalization argues that "we can no longer identify three worlds or two superpowers but rather a singular system in which the critical basis for international relations is no longer the ownership of military hardware but both economic muscle and the ability to influence ideas and commitments."[57]

The globalization process has therefore contributed to the increase in membership of the IMF, the World Bank, and the World Trade Organization, and for the first time they are in fact becoming universal membership organizations. Although globalization has contributed to the increased size of the KIEOs, it has also made it more difficult for these international institutions to manage global economic relations. The rapid movement of capital around the world is simply one indication of the pervasive influence of private actors such as multinational corporations and international banks in an age of "cascading interdependence."[58] These changes are posing an increasing challenge not only to the management capabilities of the large international organizations but also to the nation-states that undergird these organizations. In efforts to coordinate their activities, the advanced capitalist states have therefore often turned to smaller, more informal groupings such as the Group of Seven.

Although globalization is challenging the management capabilities of states and international organizations, it is *not* leading to a "borderless world." In fact, states are seeking to survive and prosper in the new age of global competitiveness. With the demise of the Cold War, new economic power centers have been able to emerge in Europe and East Asia, posing a challenge to U.S. economic hegemony. These three regional blocs have extended competitiveness among the advanced industrial states to the global level. Despite these regional divisions, however, one can argue that the advanced capitalist states "are still committed through the G7, the IMF, the World Bank, and the World Trade Organisation to continue to manage the international system."[59]

Divisions have become more evident not only among the advanced industrial states but also among the LDCs. Indeed, some analysts argue that the so-called Third World has fragmented into a number of groups, with the largest gap developing between the least-developed countries (LLDCs) on the one hand and the East Asian NICs on the other. The Third World has also been fragmenting on a regional basis, with some LDCs joining in regional groupings along with advanced industrial states. Notable examples include the associate membership of the African, Caribbean, and Pacific countries in the European Union; Mexico's membership in NAFTA; and the joining of industrial and Third World countries in the APEC.

NOTES

1. Armand Van Dormael, *Bretton Woods: Birth of a Monetary System* (London: Macmillan, 1978), p. ix.

2. Richard N. Gardner, "The Political Setting," in A. L. K. Acheson, J. F. Chant, and M. F. J. Prochowny, eds., *Bretton Woods Revisited* (Toronto: University of Toronto Press, 1972), p. 20; Margaret Garritsen de Vries, "The Bretton Woods Conferences and the Birth of the International Monetary Fund," in Orin Kirshner, ed., *The Bretton Woods-GATT System: Retrospect and Prospect After Fifty Years* (Armonk, N.Y.: M.E. Sharpe, 1996), pp. 3–18.

3. See Edward John Ray, "Changing Patterns of Protectionism: The Fall in Tariffs and the Rise in Non-Tariff Barriers," *Northwestern Journal of International Law and Business* 8 (1987), pp. 294–295; and Stephen D. Krasner, "State Power and the Structure of International Trade," *World Politics*, 28-3 (April 1976), pp. 330–335.

4. Sally Marks, *The Illusion of Peace: International Relations in Europe 1918–1933* (New York: St. Martin's Press, 1976), p. 47; Charles P. Kindleberger, *The World in Depression: 1929–1939* (Berkeley: University of California Press, revised and enlarged edition, 1986), pp. 23–26.

5. Robert A. Pastor, *Congress and the Politics of U.S. Foreign Economic Policy, 1929–1976* (Berkeley: University of California Press, 1980), p. 78; John M. Dobson, *Two Centuries of Tariffs: The Background and Emergence of the U.S. International Trade Commission* (Washington, DC: U.S. International Trade Commission, December 1976), p. 32.

6. For a discussion of the effects of the 1930 U.S. tariff, see Joseph M. Jones, Jr., *Tariff Retaliation: Repercussions of the Hawley-Smoot Bill* (Philadelphia: University of Pennsylvania Press, 1934).

7. See Kindleberger, *The World in Depression.*

8. The classic study on domestic pressures on the U.S. Congress during the interwar period is E. E. Schattschneider, *Politics, Pressures and the Tariff: A Study of Free Private Enterprise in Pressure Politics, as Shown in the 1929–1930 Revision of the Tariff* (Hamden, CT: Archon Books, 1963, unaltered from the 1935 edition). On the role of domestic forces in protectionism, see Helen V. Milner, *Resisting Protectionism: Global Industries and the Politics of International Trade* (Princeton, NJ: Princeton University Press, 1988).

9. It was not until 1936 that the United States, Britain, and France finally reached a tripartite agreement to stabilize exchange rates among currencies. See Edward M. Bernstein, "The Making and Remaking of the Bretton Woods Institutions," in Orin Kirshner, ed., *The Bretton Woods–GATT System: Retrospect and Prospect After Fifty Years* (Armonk, NY: Sharpe, 1996), p. 89.

10. The term *KIEOs* is used in Harold Jacobson and Michel Oksenberg, *China's Participation in the IMF, the World Bank, and GATT: Toward a Global Economic Order* (Ann Arbor: University of Michigan Press, 1990).

11. Quoted in Sidney Dell, "Relations Between the United Nations and the Bretton Woods Institutions," *Development* 4 (1989), p. 28. The UN General Assembly has tried to influence the World Bank's loan-giving activities at various times, but these efforts have been largely unsuccessful. See Samuel A. Bleicher, "UN v. IBRD: A Dilemma of Functionalism," *International Organization* 24-1 (Winter 1970), pp. 31–47.

12. "United Nations–Bretton Woods Collaboration: How Much Is Enough?" *Report of the Twenty-sixth United Nations Issues Conference* (Muscatine, IA: Stanley Foundation, February 24–26, 1995), p. 18.

13. For a detailed discussion of the range of UN interactions with the Bretton Woods institutions, see Dell, "Relations Between the United Nations and the Bretton Woods Institutions," pp. 27–38; and Edward S. Mason and Robert E. Asher, *The World Bank Since Bretton Woods* (Washington, DC: Brookings Institution), pp. 566–576.

14. United Nations Conference on Trade and Development, *World Investment Report 1996* (New York: United Nations, 1996), pp. 239–247; World Trade Organization, *WTO Annual Report 1996,* Vol. 2 (Geneva: WTO, 1996), pp. 24, 67.

15. There are a number of reasons for the underrepresentation of LDCs. See Theodore Cohn, "Developing Countries in the International Civil Service: The Case of the World Bank Group," *International Review of Administrative Sciences* 41-1 (1975), pp. 47–56.

16. Bretton Woods Commission, *Bretton Woods: Looking to the Future;* Commission Report, Staff Review, Background Papers (Washington, DC: Bretton Woods Committee, July 1994), p. B-3.

17. Robert O. Keohane, "Comment," in Peter B. Kenen, ed., *Managing the World Economy: Fifty Years After Bretton Woods* (Washington, D.C.: Institute for International Economics, 1944), p. 59; Eichengreen and Kenen, "Managing the World Economy," pp. 5–6; John Ger-

ard Ruggie, "International Regimes, Transactions, and Change: Embedded Liberalism in the Postwar Economic Order," in Stephen D. Krasner, ed., *International Regimes* (Ithaca, NY: Cornell University Press), pp. 195–231.

18. "United Nations–Bretton Woods Collaboration: How Much Is Enough?" p. 2.

19. Aaron Segal, "Managing the World Economy," *International Political Science Review* 11-3 (1990), p. 367.

20. C. Fred Bergsten and C. Randall Henning, *Global Economic Leadership and the Group of Seven* (Washington, DC: June, 1996), p. 15.

21. Organisation for Economic Co-operation and Development, *The OECD in the 1990s* (Paris, OECD, 1994), p. 9; David Henderson, "The Role of the OECD in Liberalising International Trade and Capital Flows," in Sven Arndt and Chris Miller, eds., Special issue of *The World Economy* on "Global Trade Policy" (1996), pp. 11–28.

22. Bernard Colas, "The OECD's Legal Influence in a Global Economy," *World Economic Affairs* 1-3 (Spring/Summer 1997), pp. 66–67.

23. Colas, "The OECD's Legal Influence in a Global Economy," p. 67; Henderson, "The Role of the OECD," pp. 21–22.

24. Michael C. Webb, *The Political Economy of Policy Coordination: International Adjustment Since 1945* (Ithaca, NY: Cornell University Press, 1995), pp. 176–177.

25. Michael P. Blackwell, "From G-5 to G-77: International Forums for Discussion of Economic Issues," *Finance & Development* 23-4 (December 1986), p. 40.

26. Segal, "Managing the World Economy," p. 362; Robert D. Putnam and Nicholas Bayne, *Hanging Together: Cooperation and Conflict in the Seven-Power Summits* (London: Sage, revised edition, 1987), pp. 150–154.

27. Stephen Gill, "Global Finance, Monetary Policy and Cooperation Among the Group of Seven, 1944–92," in Philip G. Cerny, ed., *Finance and World Politics: Markets, Regimes and States in the Post-Hegemonic Era* (London: Elgar, 1993), p. 104; Paul Lewis, "An Eclipse for the Group of Seven," *New York Times*, May 1, 1995, p. C2; C. Fred Bergsten, "A Clinton Round or a Pacific Free Trade Area?" *New Perspectives Quarterly* 10-2 (Spring 1993), pp. 19–22.

28. Bergsten and Henning, *Global Economic Leadership and the Group of Seven*, pp. 6–7.

29. Bergsten and Henning, *Global Economic Leadership and the Group of Seven*, pp. 43–49.

30. Quoted in Klaus Engelen, "Comment," in Kenen, ed., *Managing the World Economy*, p. 79. See also Klaus C. Engelen, "Anger and Angst: Why the Germans Hate the World Bank and the IMF," *The International Economy* 2-5 (Sept./Oct. 1988), pp. 74–78.

31. Of the seven IMF managing directors, 3 have been French, 2 Swedish, 1 Belgian, and 1 Dutch. Of the five directors-general of GATT/WTO, 2 have been Swiss, 1 British, 1 Irish, and 1 Italian.

32. Jagdish Bhagwati, "Regionalism and Multilateralism: An Overview," in Jaime de Melo and Arvind Panagariya, eds., *New Dimensions in Regional Integration* (Cambridge: Cambridge University Press, 1993), p. 29.

33. Bretton Woods Commission, *Bretton Woods,* p. B-3.

34. See the glossary for a more precise definition of the GDP.

35. United Nations Development Programme, *Human Development Report 1996* (New York: Oxford University Press, 1996), p. 2.

36. There are numerous studies of Third World dissatisfaction with the KIEOs, mainly from a historical structuralist perspective but also from a realist perspective. See, for example,

Kevin Danaher, ed., *Fifty Years Is Enough: The Case Against the World Bank and the International Monetary Fund* (Boston: South End Press, 1994); John Cavanagh, Daphne Wysham, and Marcos Arruda, eds., *Beyond Bretton Woods: Alternatives to the Global Economic Order* (London: Pluto Press, 1994); and Stephen D. Krasner, *Structural Conflict: The Third World Against Global Liberalism* (Berkeley: University of California Press, 1985).

37. *The World Bank Annual Report 1997* (Washington, DC: World Bank, 1997), pp. 227–230.

38. David A. Kay, *The New Nations in the United Nations, 1960–1967* (New York: Columbia University Press, 1970), pp. 2–3.

39. The term *Third World* was apparently first used by a French demographer, Alfred Sauvy, in 1952.

40. Michael Zammit Cutajar, ed., *UNCTAD and the North-South Dialogue: The First Twenty Years* (Oxford: Permagon Press, 1985), p. vii.

41. There are many books on the LDCs' call for a new international economic order. See, for example, Jeffrey A. Hart, *The New International Economic Order: Conflict and Cooperation in North-South Economic Relations, 1974–77* (London: Macmillan, 1983); and Ervin Laszlo, et al., *The Obstacles to the New International Economic Order* (New York: Pergamon Press, 1980).

42. Tyrone Ferguson, *The Third World and Decision Making in the International Monetary Fund: The Quest for Full and Effective Participation* (London: Pinter Publishers, 1988), p. 33.

43. Grant B. Taplin, "Revitalizing UNCTAD," *Finance & Development* 29-2 (June 1992), pp. 36–37; Marc Williams, *International Economic Organisations and the Third World* (New York: Harvester Wheatsheet. 1994), p. 192; Carlston B. Boucher and Wolfgang E. Siebeck, "UNCTAD VII: New Spirit in North-South Relations?" *Finance & Development* 24-4 (December 1987), p. 14.

44. Harold K. Jacobson, *Networks of Interdependence: International Organizations and the Global Political System* (New York: Knopf, 1979), p. 13.

45. Henry Morgenthau, Jr., "Bretton Woods and International Cooperation," *Foreign Affairs* 23-2 (January 1945), p. 186.

46. Quoted in Joseph Gold, *Membership and Nonmembership in the International Monetary Fund: A Study in International Law and Organization* (Washington, DC: IMF, 1974), p. 129.

47. Jozef M. van Brabant, *The Planned Economies and International Economic Organizations* (Cambridge: Cambridge University Press, 1991).

48. Valerie J. Assetto, *The Soviet Bloc in the IMF and the IBRD* (Boulder, CO: Westview Press, 1988), pp. 56–66, 185; Brabant, *The Planned Economies and International Economic Organizations*, pp. 45–48; Laszlo Lang, "International Regimes and the Political Economy of East-West Relations," *Occasional Paper Series* no. 13 (New York: Institute for East-West Security Studies, 1989), pp. 19–22.

49. For a discussion of the relationship between the Marshall Plan and the formation of the CMEA (also called COMECON), see William R. Keylor, *The Twentieth Century World— An International History* (New York: Oxford University Press, 1984), pp. 274–275, 359; and Michael Kaser, *Comecon: Integration Problems of the Planned Economies* (London: Oxford University Press, 1965), pp. 9–12.

50. Klaus Schröder, "The IMF and the Countries of the Council for Mutual Economic Assistance," *Intereconomics* 2 (March/April 1982), p. 87; Brabant, *The Planned Economies and International Economic Organizations*, p. 70.

51. *IBRD—Articles of Agreement,* as amended effective February 16, 1989 (Washington, DC: IBRD, August 1991), Article 4, section 10.

52. For a discussion of the involvement of politics in World Bank decision making, see David A. Baldwin, "The International Bank in Political Perspective," *World Politics* 18-1 (October 1965), pp. 68–81; and Theodore H. Cohn, "Politics in the World Bank Group: The Question of Loans to the Asian Giants," *International Organization* 28-3 (Summer 1974), pp. 561–571. For critiques of the IMF and World Bank's political/ideological orientation from a historical structuralist perspective, see Cheryl Payer, *The Debt Trap: The IMF and the Third World* (Middlesex, UK: Penguin, 1974); and Teresa Hayter, *Aid as Imperialism* (Middlesex, UK: Penguin, 1971).

53. Valerie J. Assetto, *The Soviet Bloc in the IMF and the IBRD* (Boulder, CO: Westview Press, 1988), pp. 53–54.

54. Gold, *Membership and Nonmembership in the International Monetary Fund,* pp. 342–379; Marie Lavigne, "Eastern European Countries and the IMF," in Béla Csikós-Nagy and David G. Young, eds., *East-West Economic Relations in the Changing Global Environment* (London: Macmillan, 1986), p. 298; and Assetto, *The Soviet Bloc in the IMF and the IBRD,* pp. 69–93.

55. J. Ann Tickner, *Gender in International Relations: Feminist Perspectives on Achieving Global Security* (New York: Columbia University Press, 1992), p. 4.

56. Barbara Crossette, "Mexican Diplomat at U.N. New Advocate for Women," *New York Times,* February 16, 1996, p. A6; "UN Retreats from Goal to Hire Women for Half of Professional Jobs," *Vancouver Sun,* October 26, 1996, p. A9; Barbara Crossette, "French Canadian Is a U.N. Chief's First Right-Hand Woman," *New York Times,* January 13, 1998, p. A7.

57. Malcolm Waters, *Globalization* (London: Routledge, 1995), p. 116.

58. See James N. Rosenau, "The State in an Era of Cascading Politics: Wavering Concept, Widening Competence, Withering Colossus, or Weathering Change?" *Comparative Political Studies* 21-1 (April 1988), pp. 13–44.

59. Andrew Gamble and Anthony Payne, "Conclusion: The New Regionalism," in Andrew Gamble and Anthony Payne, eds., *Regionalism and World Order* (London: Macmillan, 1996), p. 253.

PART II

The Theoretical Perspectives

Part II of this book focuses on the three main theoretical perspectives in the study of international political economy: realism, liberalism, and historical structuralism. Before discussing these perspectives, it is necessary to make some general points about them. First, the three main perspectives are not mutually exclusive ideologies. Although the perspectives remain distinctive, they have interacted and influenced one another over time, and the margins between them are sometimes blurred. Many IPE theories such as regime theory, hegemonic stability theory, and the business conflict model also are "hybrids" that draw on more than one of the three major perspectives. In addition, the research of an increasing number of scholars on the intersection of domestic and foreign policy variables in IPE cannot be neatly classified under one of the three traditional perspectives. Chapters 3 through 5 discuss some of these hybrid theories under the perspective with which they are *most* closely identified.

Second, it is somewhat simplistic to state that there are three main IPE perspectives; in fact, each perspective contains a wide diversity of writings. Liberalism is perhaps the most broad-ranging of the perspectives, and historical structuralism encompasses writings ranging from classical Marxism to dependency theory and world-system theory. Nevertheless, a diversity of writings can be grouped within each school of thought because the authors generally agree on a core set of assumptions about IPE.[*]

And third, the three perspectives do not adequately address some of the "newer" issues in IPE relating to the environment, gender, technology, and migration. Nevertheless, no new theoretical approaches to this point have posed a major challenge to

---

[*]See Thomas J. Biersteker, "Evolving Perspectives on International Political Economy: Twentieth-Century Contexts and Discontinuities," *International Political Science Review* 14-1 (January 1993), pp. 7–33.

the three traditional IPE perspectives in terms of the scope and importance of their explanations.† Becoming familiar with these perspectives is an important starting point in the study of IPE.

It is useful to provide a brief preview here of how Chapters 3 through 5 are organized. To compare the main IPE perspectives, each chapter begins with a discussion of how the perspective deals with three key questions: (1) What is the role of domestic actors, particularly the individual, the state, and societal groups? (2) What are the nature and purpose of international economic relations? and (3) What is the relationship between politics and economics? While these three questions provide a basis for comparing the IPE perspectives, they gloss over the differences among writers *within* each perspective. The second part of each chapter therefore examines the historical development of the perspective, with particular emphasis on the diversity of views contained within the perspective. Each chapter concludes with a discussion of the perspective's approach to North-South relations.

---

†See Stephen D. Krasner, "International Political Economy: Abiding Discord," *Review of International Political Economy* 1-1 (Spring 1994), pp. 13–14.

CHAPTER 3

The Realist
Perspective

Part II begins in this chapter with a discussion of the realist perspective, the oldest school of thought in international relations. Indeed, Thucydides (ca. 471–400 B.C.) is often credited with writing the first important work on international relations—*The History of the Peloponnesian War* on war between the Greek city-states—and also with being the first writer in the realist tradition.[1] In addition to being the oldest school of thought, realism was also the most influential school affecting the views and policies of American foreign policy leaders after World War II. Despite realism's prominence in international relations in general, it has been far less important than the liberal perspective in the subfield of IPE, for several reasons. First, realists have developed their theories by drawing mainly on politics and history rather than economics; and second, the realists' emphasis on power has most often directed their attention to strategic-security issues rather than to economic issues.

There are variations among writers in all three main IPE perspectives. Thus, we can in fact identify two major strains of realism, one that has largely neglected economic matters and a second that has been far more attuned to economic-political interactions. The first strain stems from the views of Niccolò Machiavelli, an Italian philosopher and diplomat who lived from 1469 to 1527. Machiavelli is best known for his classic work *The Prince*, in which he provided advice to leaders on how to gain and maintain power. Machiavelli saw little connection between economics and politics, and he wrote, "Fortune has decreed that, as I do not know how to reason either about the art of silk or about the art of wool, either about profits or about losses, it befits me to reason about the state."[2] Machiavelli also considered military strength to be far more important than wealth in making war because "gold alone will not procure good soldiers, but good soldiers will always procure gold."[3] As discussed in this chapter, postwar American realists, like Machiavelli, relegated economics to a relatively low level of importance.

59

The other strain of realism, stemming from Thucydides and the mercantilists, has been associated with a distinctive realist approach to IPE. Theorists in this strain draw close linkages between traditional realist concerns with power and security on the one hand and economic relations on the other hand. In *The History of the Peloponnesian War*, for example, Thucydides attributed war among the Greek city-states to a number of economic changes, including the growth of trade, the emergence of new commercial powers such as Athens and Corinth, and the use of money in traditional agrarian economies. Thucydides (unlike Machiavelli) also considered wealth to be a vitally important source of military strength, and he wrote that "war is a matter not so much of arms as of money, which makes arms of use."[4] Thucydides often referred to economic issues, but it was the classical mercantilists of the sixteenth to nineteenth centuries who first engaged in *systematic* theorizing on IPE from a realist perspective.[5] The explicit emphasis of the mercantilists on the linkages between wealth and power was a major factor in the establishment of a realist perspective on IPE.

BASIC TENETS OF THE REALIST PERSPECTIVE

The Role of the Individual, the State, and Societal Groups

Realists emphasize the fact that there is no central authority above nation-states in the international system. Unlike most domestic societies, international relations is a "self-help" system in which each state must look after its own interests.[6] Thus, realists consider the state to be the principal or dominant actor in international politics, and they place considerable emphasis on the preservation of national sovereignty and the pursuit of the national interest. A state has internal sovereignty when it has a monopoly on the legitimate use of force within its territory, and it has external sovereignty when it is free of control by any outside authority. To retain its sovereignty, a state must have sufficient power to defend its interests against outside forces. Realists therefore consider the pursuit of power to be a primary objective in furthering the national interest. Indeed, Hans Morgenthau, the foremost realist writer in the post–World War II period, wrote in *Politics Among Nations* that "international politics, like all politics, is a struggle for power."[7] Power is an essential requirement for the pursuit of state goals, whether they be security, wealth, or power itself; but in a ranking of objectives, realists give top priority to the survival and security of the state.

The state, according to realists, is not only the most important international actor but also a rational, unitary actor that seeks to maximize the benefits and minimize the costs involved in achieving national objectives. Realists studying foreign economic policymaking have recognized the need to focus on domestic as well as international variables in explaining a state's actions.[8] Nevertheless, most modern-day realists continue to emphasize the unitary nature of the state in foreign policy and to downgrade the political importance of subnational and nonstate actors such as interest groups and multinational corporations (MNCs). In the realist view, nonstate actors generally operate within the rubric of state policies. Realists therefore argue that liberals overestimate the role of interest groups, international institutions, and MNCs in state policymaking and that historical structuralists overestimate the degree to which the state is beholden to major industrial and financial interests.[9]

The Nature and Purpose of International Economic Relations

According to realists, because international relations is a self-help system, each state must above all look after its own survival and security. Nevertheless, a "security dilemma" results when each state takes actions to bolster its own security because such actions increase the fear and insecurity of other states. For example, a state may build up its armaments solely for defensive purposes, but this action may raise the fears of other states and contribute to an arms race. In view of the security dilemma, realists argue that states are most concerned about *relative gains,* and each state tries to improve its position vis-à-vis other states. Thus, a number of realist writers contend that "even though two states may be gaining absolutely in wealth, in political terms it is the effect of these gains on relative power positions which is of primary importance."[10] Unlike realists, liberals concentrate more on *absolute gains,* in which each state seeks to maximize its own gains and is less concerned with the gains or losses of others.

The emphasis of realists on relative gains stems from their view that economic relations in an anarchical international system is often a zero-sum game in which one group's gain equals another group's loss. This contrasts with the liberal view of economic relations as a positive-sum game in which different groups may gain together. The liberal versus realist view of international institutions provides a prime example of this difference in outlook. Liberals assume that the major international economic organizations—the International Monetary Fund, the World Bank, and the World Trade Organization—are politically neutral and benefit all states that adhere to their liberal-economic guidelines. Realists, by contrast, believe that the most powerful states shape the rules of these organizations to fit with their own particular national interests and that international organizations serve primarily as "arenas for acting out power relationships."[11]

Although in the realist view, all states are concerned with relative gains, the objectives of states may be either offensive or defensive in nature. Aggressive states may use the international economy to promote imperialist expansion or to extend their national power over others, while defensive states may simply seek to maintain their economic positions in the system. Whether a state is more aggressive or defensive in nature, its interests and policies are determined by its power position in the international system. Thus, realists believe that a hegemonic state with dominant power is likely to have very different interests and policies than less powerful states.

Despite the realist attention to changes in the relative power among states, historical structuralists argue that realists are mainly concerned with redistribution of power *within* the capitalist system and that they share the commitment of the liberals to capitalism. Historical structuralists, by contrast, believe that a more equitable distribution of wealth and power is not possible under capitalism, and they therefore question the capitalist system itself. In the view of historical structuralists, there are only "two main modes of development in contemporary history: capitalist and redistributive," and they group realism along with liberalism in the capitalist mode.[12]

The Relationship Between Politics and Economics

Realists give priority to politics over economics, and they assume that the state has considerable capacity to structure economic relations at the international level. Thus, they are highly critical of liberal theorists who argue that increasing interdependence and globalization are eroding state control. Some realists question the very premise that interdependence and globalization are increasing.[13] Others acknowledge that globalization may be occurring, but they disagree with liberals about both the causes and the consequences of this phenomenon. While liberal theorists attach considerable importance to technological change and advances in communications and transportation as factors behind globalization, realists believe that globalization (to the extent that it is occurring) increases only because states permit it to increase. Thus, the largest states have the capability of either opening or closing world markets, and they can also use the globalization process to improve their power positions vis-à-vis smaller and weaker states.[14] Realists also place considerable emphasis on the ability of a hegemonic state to create an open and stable economic order that can further the globalization process. (The different versions of hegemonic stability theory are discussed later in this chapter.)

THE MERCANTILISTS

The term **mercantilism** was first used by Adam Smith, an eighteenth-century economist and philosopher, in reference to much of the economic thought and practice in Europe from about 1500 to 1750.[15] As discussed in Chapter 4, Smith, as a liberal economist, was highly critical of the mercantilists. After the demise of feudalism, mercantilism played an important role in state building and territorial unification through its emphasis on national power. Mercantilists believed that a state's power depended above all on the amount of gold and silver it could accumulate in the public treasury. With these precious metals, the state could build up its armed forces, hire mercenaries, and influence its allies as well as its enemies. Mercantilist states therefore took all necessary measures to increase their exports and decrease their imports as a means of accumulating gold. It is impossible for all states to have a balance-of-trade surplus (i.e., more exports than imports), so mercantilists believed that conflict was central to international economic relations and that relative gains were more important than absolute gains. Thus, the mercantilists stood firmly within the realist school of thought.

A number of writers from different countries contributed to classical mercantilist thought over several centuries; thus, it is not surprising that there are disputes over the interpretation of their ideas. For example, some analysts argue that classical mercantilists considered national power to be the most important goal and that they viewed the acquisition of wealth as simply a means of gaining power—the ultimate objective. Others, by contrast, maintain that the mercantilists placed power and wealth on an equal footing, viewing them both as "proper ultimate ends of national policy."[16] Despite these differences of view, analysts generally agree that mercantilism focused on the national interest and on the pursuit of wealth as well as power by the state.

In the late eighteenth century, important thinkers began to develop comprehensive critiques of mercantilism on political and ethical as well as economic grounds. The mercantilists were criticized, for example, for not guaranteeing the freedom of the individual from intrusive regulation by the state and for contributing to the continuous cycle of wars and preparation for wars in Europe. Adam Smith also launched a vigorous economic attack on mercantilism, arguing that it encouraged states to engage in "beggaring all their neighbours" and caused trade and commerce to become a "fertile source of discord and animosity."[17] The liberal criticisms of mercantilism were highly effective, and liberal views of free trade became dominant in England—the major power of the time—for much of the nineteenth century.

It is important to note that some authors use the term *mercantilism* in a more general sense in reference to realist thought and/or practice in IPE. Thus, they refer not only to the mercantilist period in the sixteenth to eighteenth centuries but also to "neomercantilist" states today, which rely on government involvement and various forms of protectionism to promote self-sufficiency and increase their power and wealth. To avoid confusion, this book uses the term *realism* in reference to the general school of thought in IPE; it uses the term *mercantilism* to refer only to the specific period when states sought to accumulate precious metals and increase their national power in the sixteenth to eighteenth centuries.

REALISM AND THE INDUSTRIAL REVOLUTION

Although the liberal critics of mercantilism were highly successful, some thinkers and policymakers continued to emphasize realist practices. Mercantilism was basically a preindustrial doctrine, and the advent of the Industrial Revolution gave a new impetus to realist thought. Industrialization in the realist view had become a central requirement for countries seeking to gain national security, military power, and economic self-sufficiency. Foremost among the realist thinkers at this time were the first U.S. Secretary of the Treasury, Alexander Hamilton (1755–1804); and a German civil servant, professor, and politician who was imprisoned and exiled because of his dissident political views, Friedrich List (1789–1846).

The classical mercantilists were the first to engage in systematic realist theorizing on IPE, but Alexander Hamilton's 1791 *Report on the Subject of Manufactures* "contains the intellectual origins of modern economic nationalism and the classic defense of economic protectionism."[18] Hamilton considered the strengthening of the American economy and the promotion of economic development to be essential for the preservation of national independence and security. His preferred policies to achieve economic growth were largely realist, including an emphasis on industry over agriculture, economic self-sufficiency, government intervention, and trade protectionism. Although Hamilton realized that agriculture was important, he believed that the growth of manufacturing was more essential for diversifying the U.S. economy and decreasing its vulnerability to external forces. In his *Report on Manufactures,* Hamilton therefore wrote:

> Not only the wealth; but the independence and security of a Country, appear to be materially connected with the prosperity of manufactures. . . . The extreme embarrassments of the United States during the late War, from an incapacity of supplying themselves, are still matter of keen recollection.[19]

Because the British government had discouraged manufacturing in the American colonies, Hamilton felt that U.S. government intervention was necessary to help establish an industrial base. To counter the advantages of British over American industries, Hamilton argued that the U.S. government should encourage the introduction of foreign technology, capital, and skilled labor. The government should also adopt protectionist trade policies, including tariffs, quotas, and bounties, to bolster its fledgling industries. Hamilton's advocacy of protectionism differed from classical mercantilism, however; he did not consider the accumulation of gold and a positive balance of trade to be the primary objectives. Instead, he emphasized the development of a strong manufacturing economy.

Friedrich List was strongly influenced by Hamilton's ideas, and like Hamilton, he placed considerable emphasis on the development of manufacturing industries for a country's economic development. Indeed, in his seminal work, *The National System of Political Economy* (1841), List wrote that "a nation which exchanges agricultural products for foreign manufactured goods is an individual with *one* arm, which is supported by a foreign arm."[20] List had lived in the United States as well as in Germany, and he argued that these two countries would never equal Britain's wealth and power if they did not develop their manufacturing industries. In regard to promoting the development of manufacturing, List placed particular emphasis on the imposition of trade barriers, the importance of national unity, and the development of "human capital."

If Germany and the United States were to catch up with the British, List argued, they would have to provide some degree of trade protection for their infant industries. Indeed, Britain itself had adopted a protective commercial policy that had enabled it to attain manufacturing supremacy, and only after it became the economic leader did it support free trade. By turning to a free trade policy in the nineteenth century, Britain was able to promote a division of labor that enabled it to retain its supremacy in industry and technology. Thus, in the first half of the nineteenth century, trade between Britain and the United States consisted mainly of the export of British manufactured products in exchange for U.S. wool and cotton. Although states can benefit from free trade in the long term, List argued, the economic development of Germany and the United States would be constrained in an open competitive economy as long as they lagged behind Britain. It was therefore necessary for the state to impose some protective trade policies in the United States and Germany so that these nations could build up their productive potential.

List also emphasized the importance of national unity, which would enable the state to implement policies promoting economic development. List's preoccupation with national unification was understandable because of the prevalence of internal duties on trade within Germany at the time. A strong, unified state was necessary, List believed, not only to impose external trade barriers and engage in national projects such as the building of railroads but also to promote the development of human capital. List attributed British leadership in manufacturing and trade to the superiority of the British educational system, and he thought that governments had special responsibilities for the education of their citizens.[21]

As a realist, List strongly criticized the views of the liberal economist Adam Smith, who favored a division of labor in production and free trade. In List's view, liberals like Smith placed too much emphasis on the existence of natural harmony and peace and underestimated the extent to which the world is divided by national rivalries and conflict. It is important to note, however, that List recognized the importance of a division of labor and free trade *in the long term.* In the short term, he believed, government involvement in developing human capital and protecting infant industries was necessary in countries such as Germany and the United States, which were lagging behind. Only when the less advanced nations could be "raised by artificial measure," as the British had been, wrote List, could "freedom of trade . . . operate naturally."[22]

REALISM IN THE INTERWAR PERIOD

As discussed in Chapter 2, Britain repealed its Corn Laws in 1846, opening its markets to agricultural imports and ushering in a period of free trade that continued until the latter part of the nineteenth century. However, changes occurring in the late nineteenth century caused liberal free trade ideas to lose some of their appeal. Under the pressures of World War I and the economic crises and conflicts of the interwar years, there was a virtual breakdown of cooperative relations based on liberalism. Realist ideas gained more influence as each country sought to protect its own national interest, and countries turned to policies of protectionism, competitive currency devaluations, and foreign exchange controls. The dire economic circumstances also encouraged extremists, especially on the right, who "took advantage of the economic dislocation to attack the entire liberal-capitalist system and to call for assertive 'national' policies, backed if necessary by the sword."[23]

The experience of extreme nationalism and trade protectionism in the interwar years, and its linkage with the Great Depression and the outbreak of World War II, provided an impetus for leaders at the Bretton Woods conference to establish a more liberal economic system. Thus, liberalism became the dominant school of thought in the postwar international economic system. In the postwar international *political* system, however, realist thought was to reign supreme. Unlike the earlier mercantilists, the postwar realists were to be largely unconcerned with economic matters.

REALISM IN THE POST–WORLD WAR II PERIOD

Although realists such as Thucydides, the mercantilists, Alexander Hamilton, and Friedrich List had been highly attuned to economic issues, U.S. realists after World War II focused almost exclusively on strategic-security issues. With the rapid emergence of the Cold War between East and West, strategic-security matters were a major preoccupation, and international economic issues by contrast seemed to be relatively unimportant. Under U.S. leadership, a consensus developed at Bretton Woods that seemed to usher in a period of economic stability and prosperity. Third World countries felt that their interests received too little attention at Bretton Woods, but they had little ability to influence the postwar economic policies. The Cold War was also largely excluded from the postwar economic system because most Soviet bloc countries were not members of the IMF, the World Bank, and GATT. Their nonparticipation did not interfere with the functioning of these organizations because the Eastern bloc accounted for only a small share of global economic interactions. These organizations were largely dominated by the Western industrial states and espoused liberal principles; realists therefore tended to view them as involved with "low politics" and therefore not worthy of much attention.

Postwar realists were also influenced by liberal views on the separability of economics and politics. However, unlike liberals such as Adam Smith, who supported the idea of a laissez-faire economy free of political constraints, the realists emphasized political forces and largely ignored economics. Traditional U.S. views that there *should be* a clear separation between the state and the economy were yet another source of influence on postwar realists. Government involvement in military and defense matters was fully accepted in the United States, but state involvement in the economy was viewed as somehow less legitimate. Finally, the superpower status of the United States led U.S. realists to fix their attention so firmly on the power struggle with the Soviet Union that they "overlooked the economic relations beneath the flux of political relations."[24] As a result, liberalism and Marxism clearly overshadowed realism as schools of thought on IPE in the 1950s and 1960s.

THE REVIVAL OF REALIST INTERNATIONAL POLITICAL ECONOMY

In the 1970s and 1980s, some realist writers began to return "to a realist conception of the relationship of economics and politics that had disappeared from postwar American writings."[25] For example, one of the leading scholars in the realist rediscovery of IPE was Robert Gilpin, who devoted an entire book to the study of U.S. power and the multinational corporation in 1975.[26] Several major factors contributed to the reemergence of realism as a major perspective on IPE. First, the decline of the Cold War and the increasing disarray in the global economy forced many realists to broaden their focus beyond strategic-security issues; and second, realists were highly critical of the liberal and Marxist economic analyses of IPE.

While Western monetary, trade, and aid relations had prospered under U.S. leadership in the 1950s and 1960s, major changes occurred in the 1970s and 1980s with destabilizing consequences for the global economy. These changes included the emergence of OPEC as a powerful new world actor; the relative decline of U.S. economic hegemony; the increase in economic frictions and competitiveness among the United States, the European Community, and Japan; and the emergence of a foreign debt crisis in many LDCs. The new sources of instability in the postwar economic system forced realists to confront the fact that economic issues were of central importance and could no longer be relegated to the category of "low politics."

Realists also criticized liberals and Marxist students of IPE for being "economistic," that is, for exaggerating the importance of economics and underestimating the importance of politics.[27] A number of developments in the postwar period demonstrated the necessity for realist studies of IPE, with their emphasis on political issues and the role of the state. For example, the "Keynesian revolution" from the 1930s to the 1950s caused industrial states to become heavily involved in macroeconomic management and public social expenditures; the breakdown of colonialism led to the establishment of many newly independent states that developed forms of government quite different from the Western liberal democratic model; and the growing international competition facing the United States in the 1970s and 1980s led to protestations that the state should be doing more to promote U.S. industry. An updated realist perspective was therefore needed to "bring the state back in" to the study of IPE.[28]

In their approach to IPE, the newer realists posed a direct challenge to liberal interpretations of economic change. According to liberals, international economic relations had flourished after World War II because of the growth of interdependence. This interdependence in turn was closely linked with advances in communications, transportation, and technology and with the increased role of nongovernmental actors such as MNCs. Realists, by contrast, with their emphasis on the state and power, argued that *the distribution of power among states* (not advances in technology and communications) is the most important factor determining whether or not international economic relations will flourish. A major factor to consider in power distribution is whether or not there is a global hegemonic state with predominant power, willing and able to provide leadership. Thus, the newer realists have been strong advocates of hegemonic stability theory, which draws linkages between the existence of a hegemonic state and the nature of global economic relationships.[29]

Again, although hegemonic stability theory is closely tied with the realist school of thought, it is a "hybrid" theory that also draws on the liberal and historical structuralist perspectives. The discussion that follows therefore demonstrates that hegemonic stability theory cannot be neatly categorized. Nevertheless, the main aspects of hegemonic stability theory are discussed in this chapter because it forms such a central part of the realist approach to IPE.

HEGEMONIC STABILITY THEORY

Hegemonic stability theory asserts that a relatively open and stable international economic system is most likely when there is a single dominant or hegemonic state with two characteristics: it has a sufficiently large share of resources that it is *able* to provide leadership, and it is *willing* to pursue policies necessary to create and maintain a liberal economic order. In addition to being willing and able to lead, the hegemon must follow policies that other major actors believe are relatively beneficial. When a global hegemon is lacking or declining in power, economic openness and stability are more difficult—but not impossible—to maintain. It is generally agreed that hegemonic conditions have occurred at least twice—under Britain in the nineteenth century, and under the United States after World War II. Some writers maintain that the United Provinces (the present-day Netherlands) was a hegemonic power in the mid-seventeenth century,[30] but most do not believe that Dutch international influence was comparable to British and American influence during their hegemonic periods.

Hegemonic stability theory has spawned a vast array of literature as well as lively discussion and debate in the field of IPE. Scholars have critiqued virtually all aspects of the theory, some simply calling for revisions, others questioning its basic assumptions. In response, hegemonic stability theorists have defended the theory and revised certain aspects of it. Many of the criticisms are based on empirical grounds. For example, critics question whether theorists can draw meaningful generalizations about hegemonic behavior based on the experiences of only two or three global hegemons during limited historical periods. There is also considerable disagreement as to the definition and measurement of hegemony, with different authors focusing variously on the military, political, economic, and cultural aspects. In view of the differences over measurement, it is not surprising that analysts differ over whether or not U.S. hegemony is declining. Even those theorists who agree that the United States is a declining hegemon have different views about timing. Furthermore, some theorists question one of the basic premises of the theory: that a global hegemon in fact contributes to economic openness and stability. Rather than examining the numerous studies critiquing and defending hegemonic stability theory, we focus here on four questions that have been a major source of division among theorists:

1. What is hegemony?
2. What are the strategies and motives of hegemonic states?
3. Is hegemony necessary and/or sufficient for producing an open economic system?
4. Is U.S. hegemony declining?

What Is Hegemony?

The distribution of power among major states is rarely equal. Indeed, realists and some historical structuralists (such as world-system theorists, discussed in Chapter 5) believe that the international system is marked by unequal growth, with some states increasing and others declining in power. The term **hegemony** is used when the distribution of power is *extremely* unequal, and realists view hegemony in state-centric terms. For example, one important realist writer describes the international system as "imperial" or "hegemonic" when "a single powerful state controls or dominates the lesser states in the system."[31] A definition of this sort, however, does not provide us with answers as to how much control, and what types of control, are necessary for a state to be hegemonic. Can a state attain a hegemonic position based on military or economic power alone, or must it achieve a leadership position in both areas? Most theorists have rather stringent conditions for hegemonic status, and they therefore believe that hegemonic conditions have been fulfilled on only two or three occasions. Thus, one prominent definition limits hegemony to a relationship among states that is so unbalanced that "one power can largely impose its rules and wishes (at the very least by effective veto power) in the economic, political, military, diplomatic and even cultural arenas."[32]

Although most theorists define hegemony in state-centric terms, *Gramscian* theorists use the term *hegemony* in a cultural sense to connote the complex of *ideas* that social groups use to assert their legitimacy and authority. (Gramscian analysis, which stems from the writings of Antonio Gramsci, an Italian Marxist, is discussed in Chapter 5.[33]) Thus, Gramscians refer to the hegemony of ideas such as capitalism and to the global predominance of American culture. According to Gramscians, the capitalist class agreed to provide a wide range of concessions—such as welfare, unemployment insurance, and workers' rights to organize—to subordinate social classes. In return for these concessions, subordinate social classes viewed the hegemony of the capitalist class as being perfectly acceptable and legitimate. As globalization has proceeded in such areas as trade, foreign investment, and finance, some Gramscians refer to the emergence of a "transnational capitalist class" that is establishing its hegemony at the global level. The transnational capitalist class is ensuring that all impediments to the free flow of capital around the world are being removed.[34]

The Gramscian views clearly enrich our understanding by focusing on aspects of hegemony that are not adequately covered in the state-centric definitions. Nevertheless, the state-centric definition is used by most writers involved in debates over hegemonic stability theory.

What Are the Strategies and Motives of Hegemonic States?

Although hegemonic stability theorists agree that a hegemon must be willing and able to lead, they have differing views regarding the hegemon's leadership methods and goals. Thus, authors refer to three different models of hegemony, ranging from "benevolent" at one end of the spectrum to "coercive" at the other end.[35] In the first model, the hegemon is benevolent in methods as well as goals. It is more concerned about promoting generalized benefits than its self-interest, and it relies on rewards rather than threats to ensure compliance by other states. In the second, "mixed" model, the hegemon has an interest in general as well as personal benefits, but it relies on coercive methods when necessary to achieve its objectives. In the third model, the hegemon is exploitative because it exerts leadership out of self-interest, and it is more inclined than hegemons in the first two models to use coercion to enforce compliance. Benvolent hegemons are more concerned with the absolute gains of states, coercive hegemons are more concerned with relative gains, and hegemons with "mixed" motives and methods are interested in both absolute and relative gains.

Liberals view hegemony in the most benevolent terms, emphasizing the degree to which the hegemon is willing to "take on an undue share of the burdens of the system."[36] According to the liberal view, the hegemon is willing to provide public goods in order to create and maintain open, stable economic regimes. **Public goods** have two main characteristics: they are nonexcludable and nonrival. Nonexcludability means that others can benefit from the good, even if they do not contribute to its provision. A sidewalk can be considered a public good, for example, because even those individuals who have not helped pay for it through taxes are free to use it. Nonrivalness means that one state's (or individual's) use of the good does not seriously decrease the amount available to others. Again, a sidewalk is nonrival because many individuals can simultaneously benefit from using it.

In the liberal view, a benevolent hegemon is willing to provide a wide range of public goods to ensure that there is economic openness and stability. For example, the United States as global hegemon permits its currency to be used as the principal reserve asset, supplies adequate U.S. dollars to permit the growth of international trade, provides financing for economic growth of Third World countries, and maintains a relatively open market for other countries' exports. There are very few pure public goods because a hegemon may be able to enforce at least partial exclusion of countries. In contrast to public goods, private goods are both excludable and rival.[37] States receive a public good even if they do not help to provide it, so they tend to become noncontributors or *free riders,* and public goods are underproduced in relation to private goods.

Realists are more inclined than liberals to portray the hegemon as assuming leadership to further its national self-interest rather than the general good. In the realist view, a rising hegemonic state prefers an open international system because such openness can contribute to the hegemon's rate of economic growth, national income, and political power.[38] Realists are also more likely than liberals to portray the hegemon as coercive, threatening to cut off trade, investment, and aid in efforts to force other states to share the costs of public goods. Nevertheless, many realists indicate that hegemonic states can have mixed motives and that the overall effects of hegemony can be beneficial. One important realist writer therefore argues that

> there is no question that the creation of a system of multilateral trade relations was in the interests of the United States. . . . It does not follow from this fact, however, that American efforts to achieve such a system were solely self-serving. . . . Nor does it follow that what is good for the United States is contrary to the general welfare of other nations.[39]

Among proponents of the three main IPE perspectives, historical structuralists are the least likely to view the hegemon as benevolent. Some historical structuralists argue that the hegemon coordinates the responses of the developed states in the core of the global economy, enabling them to solidify their dominance over the LDCs in the periphery. Only when the hegemonic power declines is there disarray among the leading capitalist states, which undermines their ability to continue extracting surplus from the periphery. Thus, Gramscian theorists advocate the development of a "counterhegemony" among disadvantaged groups in the periphery as a means of freeing themselves from their disadvantageous position vis-à-vis the hegemonic forces in the core.[40]

Is Hegemony Necessary and/or Sufficient for Producing an Open Economic System?

Hegemonic stability theorists believe that the existence of a hegemonic state increases the likelihood that there will be an open and stable international economy. One of the ways in which a hegemon promotes openness and stability is by helping to create and maintain liberal international regimes (discussed in detail in Chapter 4). International **regimes** can be defined as "sets of implicit or explicit principles, norms, rules, and decision-making procedures around which actors' expectations converge in a given area of international relations."[41] In other words, the regime concept addresses the fact that a degree of governance above the nation-state level exists in specific areas of international relations, even without a centralized world government. Member states of the World Trade Organization, for example, abide by certain trade regime principles such as nondiscrimination, reciprocity, and trade liberalization; and they follow trade regime rules that (with certain exceptions) ban the use of import quotas and export subsidies.

According to hegemonic stability theorists, the United States as global hegemon has played a major role in creating and maintaining open and stable monetary, trade, and aid regimes since the end of World War II. Through the provision of public goods and rewards and the use of coercion, the United States as global leader gives other states the incentive to abide by the regime principles, norms, and rules. Thus, hegemonic stability theorists assume that open, stable economic regimes are more difficult to maintain if a hegemonic state is declining or there is no hegemon. On the basis of these assumptions, hegemonic stability theorists have made a number of assertions about the liberalizing effects of British and American hegemony:

- British hegemony in the nineteenth century was a major factor contributing to trade liberalization.
- The decline of British hegemony after 1875 led to a decline in free trade.
- The lack of a hegemon willing and able to lead between World Wars I and II resulted in increased protectionism culminating in the Great Depression.
- The emergence of the United States as a global hegemon after World War II resulted in the reemergence of open and stable international economic regimes.

A number of empirical studies, however, have questioned the assumption that hegemony is necessary and/or sufficient for producing economic openness. For example, some empirical findings reveal that there was no widespread return to protectionism when British hegemony declined after 1875 and that it was World War I, *not* Britain's relative decline as a hegemon, "that sounded the death knell for liberalized international trade."[42] Some critics concede that a hegemonic state may play an important role in creating open international economic regimes but argue that these open regimes will not necessarily collapse after the hegemon declines. Open economic regimes can have beneficial effects on the major states, which may thus have sufficient incentive to maintain these open regimes through cooperative efforts even after the hegemon declines.[43]

Others point out that hegemonic powers were not uniformly committed to free trade and that domestic interest groups in a hegemonic state can cause it to be protectionist in some sectors. For example, as noted in Chapter 6, the United States generally supported an open international trade regime in the 1940s but did *not* endorse an open, liberal international financial order. Instead, the United States joined European countries in supporting the use of national controls on capital flows. Even in the trade area, the United States was not uniformly liberal in the postwar era (for example, responding to domestic interests after World War II by insisting that GATT provide several major exceptions for agriculture and by supporting the creation of a restrictive Multi-Fiber Agreement to limit textile imports).[44]

Some writers also maintain that factors other than hegemony can account for economic openness and stability. For example, general world prosperity can result in open economic regimes, while economic downturns can cause countries to adopt more closed, protectionist policies. Furthermore, industries are more inclined to pressure for trade protectionism when they produce surpluses and are more likely to support trade openness during periods of shortages.[45] Most critics therefore seem to agree that there may be *some* connection between hegemony and economic openness. However, they question whether hegemony is necessary and/or sufficient for creating and maintaining open, liberal economic regimes.

Is U.S. Hegemony Declining?

One of the most vigorous debates in the hegemony literature focuses on whether or not U.S. hegemony has declined. A number of theorists are "declinists" who argue that hegemony is inherently unstable and that "one of the most important features of American hegemony was its brevity."[46] Declinists cite a variety of reasons for U.S. hegemonic decline, including the hegemon's tendency to overextend itself in both military and economic terms, the tendency of free riders to gain more from economic openness than the hegemon does, and the emergence of more dynamic and competitive economies that challenge the hegemon's predominant position.

Pitted against the declinists are a number of "renewalists" who challenge the assumption that the United States is a declining hegemon. Although most renewalists acknowledge that U.S. economic power has declined in a relative sense since 1945, they argue that this fact has not had a significant effect on U.S. hegemony. U.S. predominance at the end of the war was so great that the country's relative position was bound to decline as a result of economic reconstruction in Europe and Japan. Nevertheless, U.S. economic power today, even with some decline, is "quite enormous when compared to that of any other country, and has an international aspect which gives the US government a unique prerogative *vis-à-vis* the rest of the world."[47] Some renewalists also argue that most of the U.S. economic decline occurred before the mid-1970s and that the U.S. share of global economic output has been fairly constant since that time.

As evidence of its continued hegemony, renewalists maintain that the United States has a considerable amount of co-optive power (also referred to as "structural" or "soft" power): it is often successful in getting "other countries to *want* what it wants."[48] Thus, the United States continues to have a large degree of control over setting the global agenda and determining how issues are dealt with in international politics. In explaining the continued U.S. influence, renewalists criticize declinists for failing to consider noneconomic factors. Thus, U.S. television, movies, and magazines have an enormous effect on cultural tastes and habits around the world, despite the efforts of some countries to limit such influences; and U.S. supremacy in the military-security area also permits it to exercise power in the economic sphere. Although the decline of the Cold War has decreased the scope of security threats to Western Europe and Japan, new global security threats are likely to emerge; and the breakup of the Soviet bloc has solidified American military/security predominance.[49]

The financial crisis in East and Southeast Asia in the late 1990s, and Japan's inability to assume a leadership role and revive its own lackluster economy, also has led renewalists to argue that the United States is regaining its economic predominance. Compared with East Asia and Japan, the United States was experiencing high economic growth and low unemployment and inflation rates. Thus, articles have appeared in such journals as *Foreign Affairs* projecting that the United States will continue to be the global hegemon in the twenty-first century as it has been in the twentieth. However, while renewalists consider the American economic revival in the 1990s to be a long-term structural phenomenon, declinists describe it as a sign of short-term cyclical fluctuations. In the declinist view, the mid- to long-term trend is clearly operating against U.S. hegemony.[50]

Hegemonic stability theory has contributed to a wide range of literature and discussion among scholars of IPE. Indeed, some international relations theorists have described hegemonic stability theory as "the most prominent approach among American political scientists for explaining patterns of economic relations among the advanced capitalist countries since 1945."[51] However, this discussion has shown that the tenets of hegemonic stability theory are controversial and have contributed to vigorous debates among theorists. Although realists at first turned to hegemonic stability theory partly as a response to liberal interpretations of IPE, liberal versions of the theory have also been prominent, and historical structuralists (e.g., world-system and Gramscian theorists) have also focused on hegemony. It is not surprising that realists have been particularly interested in hegemonic stability because of their preoccupation with interactions among the most powerful states. In IPE, the most powerful countries are the advanced capitalist states of the North.

REALISM AND NORTH-SOUTH RELATIONS

Although realists are very concerned about relative gains, their preoccupation with power and influence usually leads them to examine distributional issues only among the most powerful states, that is, among the advanced industrial states of the North. As a result, realist international relations scholars have until recently only rarely focused on issues involving North-South relations.[52] A prime example of the realist tendency to ignore the interests of the poorer countries of the South is found in the nineteenth century writings of Friedrich List. As discussed earlier in this chapter, List believed that Northern countries such as Germany and the United States should develop their manufacturing industries so that they could compete more effectively with Britain. However, List did not consider industrialization to be a legitimate objective for the colonial territories of the South, which served as a source of raw materials and agricultural goods for the North. In *The National System of Political Economy,* List therefore wrote that the Northern countries were "specially fitted by nature for manufacturing" and that the Southern countries should therefore provide the North with "colonial produce in exchange for their manufactured goods."[53]

Realists have written more studies on North-South relations in recent years, but this is only because some Southern countries have posed a challenge to the power position of the North. In the 1970s, for example, realists became interested in OPEC when it wrested control over oil prices and production levels from the international oil companies and launched "the most effective exercise of power by the South against the North since the conclusion of the Second World War."[54] (Membership in the OPEC cartel is limited to LDCs.) When OPEC supported the Group of 77's demands in the United Nations for a New International Economic Order (NIEO) which was designed to alter the imbalance of power between the North and the South, realists also wrote a number of studies on the NIEO's possible impact. In the 1980s and 1990s, realists became less interested in OPEC as its ability to control oil supplies and prices declined. They turned their attention instead to the newly industrializing countries in East Asia, which seemed to pose a new challenge to the power position of the North. Thus, realists became involved in a vigorous debate with liberals: were the economic successes of the East Asian NICs (South Korea, Taiwan, Singapore, and Hong Kong) due more to their market orientation (the liberal view) or to government-business cooperation and government involvement in the market (the realist view)? Even when realists study North-South relations, however, they generally do not have a sustained interest in Third World development as a legitimate area of inquiry. Thus, an author of one of the major realist studies on North-South relations written in the 1970s warned the reader that his book dealt with issues that do not normally fall within the domain of international relations.[55]

The realist and liberal perspectives on North-South relations differ in some important respects. While the liberals assert that LDCs are primarily interested in achieving economic growth and prosperity, realists argue that the LDCs are seeking increased power as well as wealth so that they can become less vulnerable to the North. In the realist view, most of the problems of the LDCs can be traced not only to their poverty but also to their position of weakness in the international system. Even when LDCs experience absolute economic gains, they continue to feel vulnerable because of their relatively weak position vis-à-vis the North.[56] The section that follows briefly discusses three strategies realists claim LDCs employ to decrease their vulnerability. (These strategies are discussed in more detail in Part III.)

The first strategy realists note is that LDCs often depend on their greater numbers by employing collective action vis-à-vis the North because they have little power individually. The Group of 77, for example, was formed in the early 1960s (see Chapter 2). This caucus of LDCs, which now has well over 100 member states, has served as a major vehicle for the expression of Third World interests. Other joint actions by LDCs to strengthen their position have included producer associations such as OPEC and regional integration movements (discussed in Chapter 9). Second, realists argue, LDCs emphasize government involvement in the promotion of development. As discussed in later chapters, LDCs have often opted for economic development policies (both import substitution and export-led growth) in which the government has played a major role in supplementing the market. The premise of these policies draws on the assumptions of Alexander Hamilton and Friedrich List, that is, that free trade is in the interest of early industrializers but that late industrializers will never be able to catch up if there is open competition. Thus, for late industrializers, the state often takes responsibility for actively promoting development and industrialization.[57]

A third strategy realists identify is the effort of Third World countries to alter international regimes and organizations governing economic relations. At the end of World War II, the United States used its hegemonic position to establish international regimes that upheld liberal principles, norms, rules, and decision-making procedures.

LDCs, which are at a disadvantage in purely market-oriented transactions, often seek to alter the principles and rules of these liberal regimes. Third World countries would prefer more authoritative, less market-oriented regimes in which international organizations would make decisions redirecting both power and wealth from the advanced industrial states to the LDCs. The LDCs would also prefer to have international economic organizations (such as UNCTAD) based on the one nation, one vote principle rather than weighted-voting organizations such as the IMF and the World Bank. As discussed in Chapter 11, Third World efforts to alter market-oriented regimes was most evident in the demands for a New International Economic Order in the 1970s.[58]

Although realists, unlike liberals, focus on the struggle for a redistribution of power and wealth between North and South, they do not question whether such a redistribution is possible within the capitalist system. In other words, both realists and liberals generally accept capitalism as the most desirable system for the conduct of economic relations. As discussed in Chapter 5, however, many historical structuralists believe that a redistribution of power and wealth between the North and the South is impossible under capitalism and that such a redistribution can occur only under socialism.

CRITIQUE OF THE REALIST PERSPECTIVE

This discussion focuses on some of the more important general criticisms of the realist perspective. Realists often correctly criticize both the liberals and historical structuralists for "economism," that is, for exaggerating the importance of economics and underestimating the importance of politics. In seeking to remedy this deficiency, however, realists sometimes go to the other extreme and overemphasize the centrality of politics and the state in relation to economics. The preoccupation of U.S. realists in the early postwar period with international strategic-security issues, and their almost total neglect of economic issues, was a prime example of this mistake.

Since the 1970s and 1980s, some writers have revitalized the realist study of IPE and have contributed to important theorizing in this area, for example, with the realist approach to hegemonic stability theory. Nevertheless, these theorists often continue to downgrade the importance of economic issues that are not closely related to the realists' central concerns with power and security and relative gains. This chapter noted, for example, that realists have not had a sustained interest in North-South relations and that liberal and historical structuralist analyses have therefore been far more important in this area.

Realists often pride themselves on being the most parsimonious of international relations theorists. Their simplifying assumptions regarding the rational, unitary state and other issues have enabled them to develop some elegant theories; nevertheless, the "state as unitary actor" view is probably the most controversial of the realist assumptions.[59] As interdependence and globalization increase, domestic processes and nongovernmental actors have a greater role in foreign policy, but the realist perspective is less attuned to this vision of the state. Transnational actors such as MNCs and international banks are particularly important in the economic arena; therefore, the parsimonious habits of realists sometimes limit their analyses of important economic issues. In recent years, some students of foreign economic policymaking have tried to develop a realist theory of state action that takes account of domestic as well as international factors.[60] However, liberal IPE theorists continue to be far more attuned to domestic-level variables than realists.[61]

Realists also place more emphasis on relative than absolute gains, an attitude that is a direct result of their concern with state survival and security in an anarchic self-help system. Relative gains are clearly of primary concern in some interstate relationships, such as U.S.-Soviet relations during the Cold War and relations between India and Pakistan during periods of hostility. However, absolute gains are often of greater concern in interdependent relationships in which states cooperate and do not threaten each other with force.[62] Even when realists study international economic organizations, they are more attuned to concerns about relative than absolute gains in these institutions. For example, one realist study of the European Union concludes that "the weaker but still influential partners will seek to ensure that the rules" established give them the opportunity "to voice their concerns and interests and thereby prevent their domination by stronger partners."[63] The preoccupation of realists with relative gains causes them to be highly skeptical about the possible influence of international institutions. If member states are always concerned that they may gain less than others, realists argue, they will be very reluctant to transfer significant authority to these international bodies. Nevertheless, international economic organizations at the global and regional levels—such as the IMF, the World Bank, the World Trade Organization, the European Union, and the North American Free Trade Agreement—have had a significant effect on some areas of the international economy. To better understand the functioning of the global economy, theorists must study such institutions further.

Although the realist perspective has had remarkable longevity and success in international relations in general, its preoccupation with strategic-security issues has limited its influence in the study of international economic matters. We now turn to a discussion of liberalism, which has been the most important theoretical perspective in IPE.

NOTES

1. For a discussion of Thucydides and realism, see Michael W. Doyle, "Thucydidean Realism," *Review of International Studies* 16-3 (1990), pp. 223–237; and Laurie M. Johnson Bagby, "The Use and Abuse of Thucydides in International Relations," *International Organization* 48-1 (Winter 1994), pp. 131–153.

2. Quoted in Albert O. Hirschman, *National Power and the Structure of Foreign Trade* (Berkeley: University of California Press, expanded edition, 1980), p. xv.

3. Niccolò Machiavelli, *The Prince and the Discourses* (New York: Modern Library, 1940), pp. 308–310.

4. Thucydides, *The History of the Peloponnesian War*, translated by Richard Crawley (London: Dent, Everyman's Library, 1910), p. 41; Robert G. Gilpin, "The Richness of the Tradition of Political Realism," *International Organization* 38-2 (Spring 1984), p. 293.

5. Thomas J. Biersteker, "Evolving Perspectives on International Political Economy: Twentieth-Century Contexts and Discontinuities," *International Political Science Review* 14-1 (1993), p. 25.

6. On a "self-help" system, see Kenneth N. Waltz, *Theory of International Politics* (Reading, MA: Addison Wesley, 1979), pp. 105–107.

7. Hans J. Morgenthau, revised by Kenneth W. Thompson, *Politics Among Nations: The Struggle for Power and Peace* (New York: Knopf, 6th edition, 1985), p. 31.

8. See, for example, Stephen D. Krasner, *Defending the National Interest: Raw Materials Investments and U.S. Foreign Policy* (Princeton, NJ: Princeton University Press, 1978); and Michael Mastanduno, David A. Lake, and G. John Ikenberry, "Toward a Realist Theory of State Action," *International Studies Quarterly* 33-4 (December 1989), pp. 457–474.

9. Robert O. Keohane, "Theory of World Politics: Structural Realism and Beyond," in Robert O. Keohane, ed., *Neorealism and Its Critics* (New York: Columbia University Press, 1986), pp. 164–65.

10. Robert Gilpin, *U.S. Power and the Multinational Corporation: The Political Economy of Foreign Direct Investment* (New York: Basic Books, 1975), p. 34. See also Waltz, *Theory of International Politics,* p. 126; and Joseph M. Grieco, "Anarchy and the Limits of Cooperation: A Realist Critique of the Newest Liberal Institutionalism," *International Organization* 42-3 (Summer 1988), p. 498.

11. Tony Evans and Peter Wilson, "Regime Theory and the English School of International Relations: A Comparison," *Millennium* 21-3 (Winter 1992), p. 330.

12. Robert W. Cox, *Production, Power, and World Order: Social Forces in the Making of History* (New York: Columbia University Press, 1987), p. 6.

13. See, for example, Kenneth N. Waltz, "The Myth of National Interdependence," in Charles P. Kindleberger, ed., *The International Corporation* (Cambridge, MA: MIT Press, 1970), pp. 222–223; Janice E. Thomson and Stephen D. Krasner, "Global Transactions and the Consolidation of Sovereignty," in Ernst-Otto Czempiel and James N. Rosenau, eds., *Global Changes and Theoretical Challenges: Approaches to World Politics for the 1990s* (Lexington, MA: Heath, 1989), p. 197.

14. Andrew Hurrell and Ngaire Woods, "Globalisation and Inequality," *Millennium* 24-3 (1995), p. 458.

15. Adam Smith used the term *mercantile system,* and German writers in the 1860s used the term *Merkantilismus* to describe this doctrine. Only afterward did the term *mercantilism* become standard in the English language. See Jacob Viner, "Mercantilist Thought," in David L. Sills, ed., *International Encyclopedia of the Social Sciences* (New York: Free Press, 1968), vol. 4, p. 436; and David A. Baldwin, *Economic Statecraft* (Princeton, NJ: Princeton University Press, 1985), p. 72.

16. Jacob Viner, "Power Versus Plenty as Objectives of Foreign Policy in the Seventeenth and Eighteenth Centuries," *World Politics* 1 (October 1948), pp. 10, 17; Eli F. Heckscher, *Mercantilism* (London: Allen and Unwin, 1934), vol. 2, p. 17.

17. Adam Smith, *The Wealth of Nations* (London: Dent & Sons, Everyman's Library no. 412, 1910), vol. 1, bk. 4, p. 436.

18. Robert Gilpin with Jean M. Gilpin, *The Political Economy of International Relations* (Princeton, NJ: Princeton University Press, 1987), p. 180.

19. Alexander Hamilton, *The Report on the Subject of Manufactures,* December 5, 1791, in Harold C. Syrett, ed., *The Papers of Alexander Hamilton,* Vol. 10 (New York: Columbia University Press, 1966), p. 291.

20. Friedrich List, *The National System of Political Economy,* translated by Sampson S. Lloyd (London: Longmans, Green 1916), p. 130.

21. List's emphasis on the importance of human capital is discussed in David Levi-Faur, "Friedrich List and the Political Economy of the Nation-State," *Review of International Political Economy* 4-1 (Spring 1997), pp. 154–178.

22. List, *The National System of Political Economy,* p. 107.

23. Paul Kennedy, *The Rise and Fall of the Great Powers: Economic Change and Military Conflict from 1500 to 2000* (New York: Random House, 1987), p. 283.

24. Gilpin, "The Richness of the Tradition of Political Realism," p. 294.

25. Gilpin, *The Political Economy of International Relations,* p. xii.

26. See Gilpin, *U. S. Power and the Multinational Corporation.*

27. Richard K. Ashley, "Three Modes of Economism," *International Studies Quarterly* 27-4 (December 1983), p. 463.

28. Theda Skocpol, "Bringing the State Back In: Strategies of Analysis in Current Research," in Peter B. Evans, Dietrich Rueschemeyer, and Theda Skocpol, eds., *Bringing the State Back In* (Cambridge: Cambridge University Press, 1985), pp. 6–7.

29. The first realists writing about hegemonic stability theory were Robert Gilpin and Stephen Krasner.

30. See Immanuel Wallerstein, "The Three Instances of Hegemony in the History of the Capitalist World-Economy," in *The Politics of the World-Economy: The States, the Movements and the Civilizations* (London: Cambridge University Press, 1984), pp. 37–46.

31. Robert Gilpin, *War and Change in World Politics* (Cambridge: Cambridge University Press, 1981), p. 29; Joseph S. Nye, Jr., *Bound to Lead: The Changing Nature of American Power* (New York: Basic Books, 1990), pp. 37–40.

32. Wallerstein, "The Three Instances of Hegemony in the History of the Capitalist World-Economy," p. 38.

33. See Antonio Gramsci, *Selections from the Prison Notebooks of Antonio Gramsci,* edited and translated by Quintin Hoare and Geoffrey Nowell Smith (New York: International Publishers, 1971).

34. See Stephen Gill, ed., *Gramsci, Historical Materialism and International Relations* (Cambridge: Cambridge University Press, 1993).

35. See Duncan Snidal, "The Limits of Hegemonic Stability Theory," *International Organization* 39-4 (Autumn 1985), pp. 585–586.

36. Charles P. Kindleberger, *The World in Depression 1929–1939* (Berkeley: University of California Press, 1973), p. 28.

37. James A. Caporaso, "Global Political Economy," in Ada Finifer, ed., *Political Science: The State of the Discipline* II (Washington: American Political Science Association, 1993), p. 453; Snidal, "The Limits of Hegemonic Stability Theory," pp. 590–592; Charles P. Kindleberger, "Dominance and Leadership in the International Economy," *International Studies Quarterly* 25-2 (June 1981), p. 244. See also the definition of public goods in Mancur Olson's classic study *The Logic of Collective Action: Public Goods and the Theory of Groups* (Cambridge, MA: Harvard University Press, 1965), pp. 14–15.

38. Stephen D. Krasner, "State Power and the Structure of International Trade," *World Politics* 28 (April 1976), p. 322.

39. Robert Gilpin, "The Politics of Transnational Economic Relations," in Robert O. Keohane and Joseph S. Nye, Jr., eds., *Transnational Relations and World Politics* (Cambridge, MA: Harvard University Press, 1972), p. 58.

40. Wallerstein, "The Three Instances of Hegemony in the History of the Capitalist World-Economy," pp. 44–46; Robert W. Cox, "Gramsci, Hegemony and International Relations:

An Essay in Method," in Stephen Gill, ed. *Gramsci, Historical Materialism and International Relations* (Cambridge: Cambridge University Press, 1993), pp. 64–65.

41. Stephen D. Krasner, "Structural Causes and Regime Consequences: Regimes as Intervening Variables," in Stephen D. Krasner, ed., *International Regimes* (Ithaca, NY: Cornell University Press, 1983), p. 2.

42. Arthur A. Stein, "The Hegemon's Dilemma: Great Britain, the United States and the International Economic Order," *International Organization* 38-2 (Spring 1984), p. 373.

43. See Robert O. Keohane, *After Hegemony: Cooperation and Discord in the World Political Economy* (Princeton, NJ: Princeton University Press, 1984); and Robert O. Keohane, "The Demand for International Regimes," in Stephen D. Krasner, ed., *International Regimes* (Ithaca, NY: Cornell University Press, 1983), pp. 141–171.

44. Eric Helleiner, *States and the Reemergence of Global Finance: From Bretton Woods to the 1990s* (Ithaca, NY: Cornell University Press), p. 4; Theodore H. Cohn, "The Changing Role of the United States in the Global Agricultural Trade Regime," in William P. Avery, ed., *World Agriculture and the GATT, International Political Economy Yearbook* (Boulder, CO: Rienner, 1993) vol. 7, pp. 20–24; Vinod K. Aggarwal, *Liberal Protectionism: The International Politics of Organized Textile Trade* (Berkeley: University of California Press, 1985), pp. 77–81.

45. Timothy J. McKeown, "Hegemonic Stability Theory and Nineteenth Century Tariff Levels in Europe," *International Organization* 37-1 (Winter 1983), p. 89; Peter F. Cowhey and Edward Long, "Testing Theories of Regime Change: Hegemonic Decline or Surplus Capacity?" *International Organization* 37-2 (Spring 1983), pp. 157–188.

46. Robert O. Keohane, *After Hegemony: Cooperation and Discord in the World Political Economy* (Princeton, NJ: Princeton University Press, 1984), p. 139. The IPE literature is replete with statements about the decline of U.S. hegemony. See, for example, Michael C. Webb and Stephen D. Krasner, "Hegemonic Stability Theory: An Empirical Assessment," *Review of International Studies* 15 (Spring 1989), p. 185; and Wallerstein, "The Three Instances of Hegemony in the History of the Capitalist World-Economy," p. 46.

Other declinist literature includes Kennedy, *The Rise and Fall of the Great Powers;* David P. Calleo, *Beyond American Hegemony: The Future of the Western Alliance* (New York: Basic Books, 1987), and Walter Russel Mead, *Mortal Splendor: The American Empire in Transition* (Boston: Houghton Mifflin, 1987).

47. Stephen Gill, "American Hegemony: Its Limits and Prospects in the Reagan Era," *Millennium* 15-3 (Winter 1986), p. 331. See also Samuel Huntington, "The U.S.—Decline or Renewal?" *Foreign Affairs* 67-2 (Winter 1988–89), pp. 76–96.

48. Joseph S. Nye, Jr., "Soft Power," *Foreign Policy* 80 (Fall 1990), p. 166. See also Nye, *Bound to Lead;* and Susan Strange, "The Persistent Myth of Lost Hegemony," *International Organization* 41-4 (Autumn 1987), pp. 551–574.

49. Bruce Russett, "The Mysterious Case of Vanishing Hegemony; or, Is Mark Twain Really Dead?" *International Organization* 39-2 (Spring 1985), p. 230; Susan Strange, "The Future of the American Empire," *Journal of International Affairs* 42 (Fall 1988), pp. 1–17.

50. For differing views of the 1990s U.S. economic revival, see Mortimer B. Zuckerman, "A Second American Century," *Foreign Affairs* 77-3 (May/June 1998), pp. 18–31; Paul Krugman, "America the Boastful," *Foreign Affairs* 77-3 (May/June 1998), pp. 32–45; and "United States: Too Triumphalist by Half," *The Economist,* April 25, 1998, pp. 29–30.

51. Webb and Krasner, "Hegemonic Stability Theory," p. 183.

52. David A. Lake, "Power and the Third World: Toward a Realist Political Economy of North-South Relations," *International Studies Quarterly* 31-2 (June 1987), p. 217.

53. List, *The National System of Political Economy*, p. 154.

54. Stephen D. Krasner, *Structural Conflict: The Third World Against Global Liberalism* (Berkeley: University of California Press, 1985), pp. 108–109.

55. Robert L. Rothstein, *The Weak in the World of the Strong: The Developing Countries in the International System* (New York: Columbia University Press, 1977), p. ix.

56. Krasner, *Structural Conflict*, p. 3; Rothstein, *The Weak in the World of the Strong*, p. 8.

57. Chalmers Johnson, *MITI and the Japanese Miracle: The Growth of Industrial Policy, 1925–1975* (Stanford, CA: Stanford University Press, 1982), p. 19.

58. Krasner, *Structural Conflict*, p. 7.

59. Joseph M. Grieco, "Realist International Theory and the Study of World Politics," in Michael W. Doyle and G. John Ikenberry, eds., *New Thinking in International Relations Theory* (Boulder, CO: Westview Press, 1997), p. 168.

60. See Mastanduno, Lake, and Ikenberry, "Toward a Realist Theory of State Action," pp. 457–474.

61. For an alternative view, see Jennifer Sterling-Folker, "Realist Environment, Liberal Process, and Domestic-Level Variables," *International Studies* Quarterly 41-1 (March 1997), pp. 1–25.

62. Robert O. Keohane, "Neoliberal Institutionalism: A Perspective on World Politics," in Robert O. Keohane, *International Institutions and State Power: Essays in International Relations Theory* (Boulder, CO: Westview Press, 1989), pp. 10–11.

63. Joseph M. Grieco, "The Maastricht Treaty, Economic and Monetary Union and the Neo-realist Research Programme," *Review of International Studies* 21 (January 1995), p. 34.

The Liberal
Perspective

Liberalism is the most influential perspective in IPE. Most important international economic organizations, and the economic policies of most states today, are strongly influenced by liberal principles. The term *liberal,* however, is used differently in IPE and U.S. domestic politics. Liberalism in the United States is often contrasted with conservatism. While U.S. conservatives are committed to free markets and minimal intervention by the government, U.S. liberals are inclined to support greater government involvement in the market to prevent inequalities and stimulate growth. Liberal economists, by contrast, have many similarities with U.S. conservatives; they emphasize the importance of the free market and private property rights and call for only a limited government role in economic activities. However, there are also variations among economic liberals. While some liberal economists believe that there should be as little government involvement in the economy as possible, others consider a degree of government intervention to be necessary for the effective functioning of markets.

BASIC TENETS OF THE LIBERAL PERSPECTIVE

Liberal international theory is exceedingly diverse in nature, and it is extremely difficult to provide a single "core statement of the liberal credo."[1] Compared with the liberal perspective, the core statements in realism and Marxism are easier to identify. A major reason for this difference is that realists and Marxists place more emphasis than liberals on developing "parsimonious" theories, that is, on economy and simplicity in the assumptions they make. While realists oversimplify by focusing on the rational, unitary state as their guiding principle, Marxists view the world in terms of class relations. Liberals are pluralist by nature, so they focus on a wider range of actors and levels of analysis. Although this broader outlook enables liberals to capture many of the complexities of international relations that realists and Marxists overlook, it also interferes with their development of a coherent and encompassing liberal international theory.

This chapter focuses primarily on three variants of liberalism that are directly relevant to the study of IPE: orthodox, interventionist, and institutional liberalism.[2] *Orthodox liberals* are mainly concerned with promoting "negative freedom," or the freedom of the private sector and the market to function with minimal interference from the state. The earliest economic liberals, such as Adam Smith and David Ricardo, adhered to liberal orthodoxy. *Interventionist liberals* believe that an exclusive focus on negative freedom is too narrow because we cannot always be certain that the private sector and the market will be progressive and produce widespread benefits. Interventionist liberals therefore see benefits from some government involvement to promote more equality, fairness, and justice in a free **market economy.** *Institutional liberals* also believe that some outside involvement is necessary to supplement the functioning of the market, and they favor the development of strong international institutions such as the World Trade Organization, the International Monetary Fund, and the World Bank.

The Role of the Individual, the State, and Societal Groups

The liberal perspective takes a "bottom-up" approach to politics and gives primacy of place in society to the individual consumer, firm, or entrepreneur.[3] In the liberal view, individuals have inalienable natural rights that must be protected from both private and public collectivities such as labor unions, churches, and the state. If individuals are free to pursue their own political and economic interests, the welfare of society and its inhabitants is most likely to be achieved. Thus, Adam Smith, an orthodox liberal writing in the eighteenth century, discussed the "invisible hand," which converts the individual's selfish interest into advantage for society as a whole:

> Every individual is continually exerting himself to find out the most advantageous employment for whatever capital he can command. It is his own advantage, indeed, and not that of the society, which he has in view. But the study of his own advantage naturally, or rather necessarily, leads him to prefer that employment which is most advantageous to the society.[4]

Because the hidden hand of the market performs so efficiently, society can regulate itself best with minimal interference from the state. Some liberals even reject the idea that the state can be an important autonomous actor, with motivations and resources different from those of other societal institutions. Instead, they view the state as simply an aggregation of private interests, with public policy resulting from a struggle among interest groups.[5] The interventionist strain of liberalism, however, points to the limitations of markets in dealing with some economic problems, such as unemployment, and foresees some role for the government in these situations.

The Nature and Purpose of International Economic Relations

After World War II, three major international economic organizations were established: the International Monetary Fund (IMF), the International Bank for Reconstruction and Development (IBRD or the World Bank), and the General Agreement on Tariffs and Trade (GATT). These organizations are all based on liberal-economic principles, and it is therefore not surprising that liberals have a rather positive view of international economic relations as currently structured. They maintain that the formal rules of behavior of the keystone international economic organizations are politically neutral and that all states' growth and economic efficiency benefit when their economic interactions conform to the liberal principles of the KIEOs. If existing international relationships do not bring about growth and efficient allocation of resources, liberals often argue that the problem is not with the international economic system but with the unwillingness of governments to pursue rational liberal-economic policies.

Liberalism assumes that international economic interactions can be mutually beneficial, or a positive-sum game, if they are permitted to operate freely. All states and individuals are likely to gain from open economic relationships, even if they do not gain equally. In view of the overall positive effect of economic relations, liberals are often less concerned with *distributional* issues and are less likely to differentiate between rich versus poor or large versus small states. Certainly liberalism encompasses a range of views on distributional issues, with interventionist liberals emphasizing equality and social democracy as well as liberty and efficiency. All liberals, however, believe that the international economic system will function most efficiently if it ultimately depends on the price mechanism and the market. This emphasis on the market generally causes liberals to be more preoccupied with such values as liberty and efficiency.

Many liberals believe that less developed countries today face basically the same challenges that countries in Europe and North America did during the nineteenth century. Unlike the case in the earlier period, however, LDCs today can benefit from a diffusion of advanced technology and modern forms of organization from the advanced industrial states. Greater integration with the centers of modern economic and political activity therefore spurs modernization and rapid economic growth in Third World countries, while relative isolation from these centers of activity results in LDC backwardness. In sum, liberals believe that all states, including the LDCs, can benefit from the growth of interdependence and globalization if they follow open, liberal policies.

According to the liberals, the purpose of international economic activity is to achieve the optimum or most efficient use of the world's scarce resources and the maximization of economic growth and efficiency. Liberals are therefore primarily concerned with *aggregate* measures of economic performance such as the growth of GDP, trade, foreign investment, and per capita income. If the global level of foreign trade and investment are increasing, this is more important to liberals than any relative gains and losses in trade and foreign investment among states.

The Relationship Between Politics and Economics

Liberals tend to view politics and economics as basically separable and autonomous areas of activity. Many liberals also assume that international economic interests are in basic harmony with a state's national interest, and they therefore believe that governments should not interfere with international economic transactions. To the extent that the government has a substantive role, it should be to create an open environment within which individuals and private firms can freely express their economic preferences. Thus, the state has a role in preventing restraints on competition and free trade and in providing public goods such as national defense and infrastructure, including roads and railways to facilitate production and the transport of goods and people. Everyone will benefit from the more efficient use of the world's scarce resources if government restrictions do not impede the free exchange of commodities and investment flows. If governments permit the market to operate freely, a natural division of labor develops in which each country specializes in producing those goods for which it has a comparative advantage.

ORTHODOX LIBERALISM

The liberal tradition dates back to at least the seventeenth century with the writings of John Locke (1632–1704). Locke believed that government should be able to take limited enforcement actions to extract taxes and require military service, but he argued that the primary role of the state was to ensure the *"Preservation of . . . [peoples']* Lives, Liberties and Estates, which I call by the general Name, *Property."*[6] Although Locke predated Adam Smith (1723–1790) by almost a century, Smith is considered to be the central figure adopting the orthodox liberal approach to political economy. Unlike Locke, who based his support for the minimal state largely on political doctrines, Adam Smith emphasized laissez-faire economics and led the way in opposing mercantilist economic thought (discussed in Chapter 3). Smith argued that freely operating markets based on a division of labor serve to maximize efficiency and prosperity and that such productive gains are likely to be positive-sum in nature. (In a positive-sum game, all states can gain together, unlike a zero-sum game, in which one state's gain is equal to another state's loss.) The mercantilists believed that a country could gain wealth and power only at the expense of other countries, but Smith cautioned against such views:

> By such maxims as these . . . nations have been taught that their interest consisted in beggaring all their neighbours. Each nation has been made to look with an invidious eye upon the prosperity of all the nations with which it trades, and to consider their gain as its own loss. Commerce, which ought naturally to be, among nations, as among individuals, a bond of union and friendship, has become the most fertile source of discord and animosity.[7]

As a strong advocate of free trade, Smith opposed the barriers that mercantilist states erected against the free exchange of goods and the enlargement of markets. While Smith realized that merchants who benefited from protectionism would try to retain their advantages, he differentiated such specific groups from the populace in general, who would benefit from prosperity as a result of free trade. Smith's arguments for free trade were based on the principles of division of labor and economic interdependence. Each state in an unregulated international economy would find a productive niche based on **absolute advantage;** it could produce particular goods more efficiently than other states. David Ricardo (1772–1823) subsequently strengthened the free trade defense by explicitly arguing that two countries could benefit from trade because of **comparative advantage.** Even if one of the countries had no absolute advantage in the production of any good, it should specialize in and export those products for which it had a *relative* advantage (i.e., the least cost disadvantage). The concepts of absolute and comparative advantage are explained in detail in Chapter 8.

Although Smith was a strong supporter of free trade, he did not believe that it should be a unilateral or unconditional policy. For example, he thought that a country should be able to impose limits on free trade to meet national security requirements and to retaliate against unfair trade restrictions imposed by foreign countries. Smith also believed that by implementing free trade gradually, a government could ensure that domestic industry and labor groups would have time to adjust to international competition. Furthermore, Smith tempered his arguments for limited government intervention with an awareness of political realities. Thus, he indicated that the state should perform three important but circumscribed functions: to provide for national defense, to protect members of society from injustice or oppression, and to provide public works and institutions (i.e., public goods), which private individuals and groups would not provide on their own.[8]

It is important to note that despite their openness to some government involvement, Smith and other orthodox liberals believed this involvement should be extremely circumscribed and limited to actions that would promote the functioning of the market.

THE INFLUENCE OF JOHN MAYNARD KEYNES

John Maynard Keynes (1883–1946) was a liberal economist who called for a much greater degree of government interventionism than the orthodox liberals. Keynes strongly opposed the extreme level of nationalism and beggar-thy-neighbor policies of the interwar years associated with realism. However, he also viewed the Great Depression as an indication that the orthodox liberal belief in the convergence between self-interest and the public interest was overdrawn. Orthodox liberal theory provided virtually no guidance or remedies for dealing with the high levels of unemployment in the 1930s, which had devastating economic and social consequences.

In contrast to the orthodox liberal view that markets tend inherently toward a socially beneficial equilibrium, Keynes argued that production and consumption often balance at a point where the unemployment level is relatively high. In other words, market-generated equilibrium might occur at a point where labor and capital are underutilized. Keynes noted that economic adjustment tended to result in unemployment rather than wage cuts because labor unions often resisted the downward movement of wages. This rise of unemployment in turn led to decreased demand and to a reduction in production and the level of investment. Governments could remedy this situation, in Keynes's view, by becoming involved in the management of aggregate demand. Thus, Keynes called on governments to implement fiscal and monetary policies designed to increase demand, and he supported government investment when necessary in public projects. In his major work *The General Theory of Employment, Interest, and Money,* Keynes wrote that "the central controls necessary to ensure full employment will, of course, involve a large extension of the traditional functions of government."[9]

Keynes's emphasis on full employment caused him to place less priority than the orthodox liberals on specialization and international trade. Indeed, he argued that it was sometimes justifiable to limit imports in order to bolster domestic employment, even if the goods could be produced more cheaply abroad. When unemployment levels reached record highs in the 1930s, Keynes in fact wrote that goods should "be homespun whenever it is reasonably and conveniently possible."[10] After World War II, Keynes moved toward supporting more multilateral, internationalist solutions in the Bretton Woods negotiations, but this was largely because he foresaw the possibility of planning on a global scale (the United States basically overruled this objective). Keynes's concessions to multilateralism were also contingent on solutions to Britain's financial problems. As Britain's chief postwar negotiator, he pressured the Labour government to pursue open liberal policies, and in return the United States provided the British with $3.75 million in loans.[11]

Keynes's support of a greater role for economic management at both the national and international levels had a major impact on liberal-economic thought. Because markets often behave differently than the orthodox liberals predicted, Keynes explicitly called for the state to play a role in combating the problem of unemployment. However, he remained firmly within the liberal-economic tradition, believing in the importance of individual initiative and in the inherent efficiency of the market. Greater management, in Keynes's view, would facilitate rather than impede the efficient functioning of world market forces. Thus, Keynes favored intervention by the government, not for the purpose of replacing capitalism but to rescue and revitalize it. Keynes's views, calling for greater government intervention in the economy, gave rise to the interventionist strand of liberalism.[12]

LIBERALISM IN THE POSTWAR PERIOD

Post-1945 liberal-economic theories developed in efforts to avoid the economic problems of the interwar years, including trade wars, financial crises, and the depression. The postwar economic planners were influenced not only by the ideas of John Maynard Keynes, but also by those of Karl Polanyi. In his classic 1944 work *The Great Transformation,* Polanyi warned of the dangers of the orthodox liberals' commitment to the "self-regulating market," with little concern about the effects on society. In Polanyi's view, society would move to protect itself from unregulated market activities, because disasters such as the depression of the interwar years would result if society was unprotected.[13] Influenced by Keynes's and Polanyi's ideas, the postwar planners designed the international economic order on the basis of an interventionist or embedded liberal compromise. The "embedded" term refers to the fact that postwar efforts to maintain an open liberal international economy were "embedded" in societal efforts to provide domestic security and stability for the populace.[14] Thus, movement toward greater openness in the international economy included measures to cushion domestic economies from external disruptions, and policies to provide domestic stability in turn were designed to minimize interference with the expansion of global economic relations. In trade policy, for example, Western leaders called for tariff reductions on a multilateral basis, but they also permitted countries to include safeguards and exemptions from the trading regulations to protect their balance of payments and promote full employment.

Underlying the postwar interventionist liberal compromise was a domestic class compromise between business and labor. Thus, labor unions largely abandoned their demands that the economy be socialized, and in return they benefited from collective bargaining, the welfare state, and political acceptance. Business for its part accepted a greater role for the government, welfare, and collective bargaining, and in return it won broad societal acceptance of freer international trade, private ownership, private profit, and the market.[15]

The predominant strand of liberalism in the postwar period was interventionist in nature; it viewed government intervention as necessary to counteract the socially unacceptable aspects of the market. These interventionist liberals, however, opted for government measures that would reinforce rather than replace the market, and they looked to the market as the preferred means of determining production and distribution.

A RETURN TO ORTHODOX LIBERALISM

Although the liberalism of Western policymakers in the postwar period was highly accepting of government interventionism, orthodox liberal theorists retained considerable influence in some circles. In 1947 Friedrich Hayek organized the first meeting of what became known as the Mont Pelerin Society, a transnational private forum of scholars and political figures committed to orthodox liberal ideas. Proponents of a return to orthodox liberalism, such as Hayek, Ludwig von Mises, and Milton Friedman, placed the highest priority on competitive markets and the efficient allocation of resources, and they often viewed economics and politics as being even more separable than did Adam Smith and David Ricardo. Thus, Friedman (b. 1912) wrote in 1962 that "the kind of economic organization that provides economic freedom directly, namely, competitive capitalism, also promotes political freedom because it separates economic power from political power."[16] Hayek and Friedman also expressed extremely negative views of state interference with the market. For example, Milton Friedman and Rose Friedman argued:

> Wherever we find any large element of individual freedom, some measure of progress in the material comforts at the disposal of ordinary citizens, and widespread hope of further progress in the future, there we also find that economic activity is organized mainly through the free market. Wherever the state undertakes to control in detail the economic activities of its citizens . . . there ordinary citizens are in political fetters, have a low standard of living, and have little power to control their own destiny.[17]

Proponents of orthodox liberalism also rejected the notion that free market policies contribute to inequality, and they were extremely critical of Keynes's emphasis on government involvement to combat unemployment. Private initiative and free enterprise rather than government intervention, in their view, were most likely to result in full employment, rising wages, and a high standard of living for the average person.[18]

Despite the ongoing influence of orthodox views, the policies of interventionist liberalism maintained their centrality during the expansive years of the 1950s and 1960s. However, the OPEC oil price shock in 1973 and the prolonged global recession after 1974 made it more costly for governments to continue with welfare and full-employment policies, and the contradictions between capital accumulation and the redistribution of wealth became more evident. Orthodox writings of economists such as Hayek and Friedman therefore experienced a revival in the late 1970s and 1980s and began to exert more influence over government policies. Foremost among political leaders pushing for this revival were Prime Minister Margaret Thatcher in Britain and President Ronald Reagan in the United States.

In the view of many critics, the Thatcher-Reagan policies concentrated on revitalizing the confidence of business in government, largely rejecting the attempt to ease the effects of liberalism on vulnerable groups. These policies therefore resulted in open conflict with government employees, trade unions, and welfare recipients. As the changes initiated under Reagan and Thatcher spread to other countries, there were growing pressures on governments to adopt orthodox liberal policies in the 1980s and 1990s, with an emphasis on privatization, deregulation, and the promotion of free trade and foreign investment. To legitimize their confrontational approach toward excluded groups, the newer orthodox leaders sometimes appealed to traditional values such as "the work ethic, family, neighborhood, and patriotism."[19]

This return to orthodox liberalism is very different from the liberalism of Adam Smith in some important respects. Most importantly, the pressures for liberal orthodoxy are now global in extent, for several reasons. First, advances in technology, communications, and transportation have enabled multinational corporations and international banks to shift their funds and their activities around the world. Second, the IMF, the World Bank, and the industrial countries have provided Third World debtors with financing since the foreign debt crisis erupted in 1982, but the conditions on this financing have included pressures for Third World countries to privatize, deregulate, and liberalize their economies. Third, with the breakup of the Soviet bloc and the Soviet Union, orthodox liberal pressures have also spread to the former centrally planned economies. To differentiate this new liberal orthodoxy from the liberalism of Adam Smith and David Ricardo, some scholars use the term "neoliberalism."

LIBERALISM AND INSTITUTIONS

As discussed in Chapter 1, theorists point to "hegemony" and "institutions" as two of the mechanisms for management of the international political economy. Although hegemonic stability theory draws on more than one IPE perspective, it was covered in Chapter 3 because of its close links with realism. This chapter examines the role of international institutions because liberals believe that these institutions have a significant role in promoting economic cooperation. Two types of institutions are important here: international regimes and international organizations.[20] Regime theory is the main theoretical approach of international relations scholars to the study of institutions. International regimes help to promote cooperation in issue areas (such as international trade and monetary relations) in which there is high degree of interdependence among states.[21]

Interdependence Theory

Interdependence can be defined as "mutual dependence," in which "there are reciprocal (although not necessarily symmetrical) costly effects of transactions."[22] Interdependence is not a new phenomenon in international relations; a number of theorists wrote thoughtful studies on the subject in the early 1900s.[23] By the 1940s, scholars were publishing works on interdependence in international trade and monetary relations.[24] Despite these early studies, Richard Cooper's book *The Economics of Interdependence* (1968) is credited with being the first systematic study of the growing economic interdependence among states.[25] Cooper suggests that advances in transportation, communications, and technology have basically altered the conditions of international economics and that new policies are needed to address the unprecedented conditions of interdependence. He questions the decentralization of policymaking among states and argues that international policy coordination is the best means of achieving national economic goals in an interdependent world:

> The growing interdependence of the world economy creates pressures for common policies, and hence for procedures whereby countries discuss and coordinate actions that hitherto were regarded as being of domestic concern exclusively. These pressures arise because market forces increasingly circumscribe the ability of nation-states to achieve their desired aims, regardless of their formal retention of sovereignty.[26]

Although Cooper considers cooperation to be the best response to the challenge of interdependence, he does not consider how *political* conditions can promote or undermine international cooperation. In their seminal work *Power and Interdependence*, published almost a decade after Cooper's study, Robert Keohane and Joseph Nye go a step further and analyze how international politics is transformed by interdependence. Although Keohane and Nye agree with Cooper that interdependence offers new opportunities for cooperation, they argue against an overly optimistic view of global harmony. Thus, they maintain that economic changes do not negate politics but simply create a new type of politics:

> Asymmetrical interdependence [i.e., mutual dependence that is not evenly balanced] can be a source of power. . . . A less dependent actor in a relationship often has a significant political resource, because changes in the relationship . . . will be less costly to that actor than to its partners.[27]

Nevertheless, Keohane and Nye as well as Cooper have a rather benign view of the effects of asymmetrical interdependence on smaller states. Indeed, they argue that interdependent relationships increase the opportunities for bargaining and permit smaller states to achieve their objectives in disputes with larger states more often than one might anticipate. In a study of asymmetrical interdependence between the

United States and Canada, Keohane and Nye conclude that Canada's ability to successfully confront the United States in conflicts results largely from the highly interdependent relationship among the two countries.[28] However, some Canadian foreign policy analysts strongly disagree with these conclusions; they are more inclined to characterize Canada's relationship with the United States in terms of dependence rather than interdependence.[29]

Interdependence theorists explicitly question the realist assumptions that states are unitary rational actors, that states are the only important actors in international relations, and that military force is always useful for promoting a state's national interest. In Keohane and Nye's complex interdependence model, by contrast, multiple channels (nongovernmental as well as governmental) connect societies, military-security issues do not necessarily dominate the agenda, and states do not use military force against each other.[30] Interdependence theorists also maintain that the scope of international relations has expanded dramatically, encompassing "new" areas such as environmental pollution, human rights, immigration, monetary and trade instabilities, and **sustainable development.** These new areas are more *intermestic* in nature (domestic as well as international) than traditional strategic-security issues.[31] Thus, interdependence theorists question the tendency of realists to view international politics as being distinct and separable from domestic politics.

Although interdependence theorists are critical of many realist assumptions, they view their model as supplementing rather than replacing realism. Thus, they acknowledge that realism is still the best model for understanding many strategic-security situations, in which power and force are of prime importance. They maintain, however, that interdependence theory is often more applicable than realism in explaining international socioeconomic relations.

The Liberal Approach to Cooperation

Achieving cooperation in a world of nation-states is problematic because there is no centralized international authority to establish and enforce rules for state behavior. Game theory is useful for assessing the prospects for cooperation among states, and the **prisoners' dilemma** is the game most often used by international relations theorists. The prisoners' dilemma game examines situations in which cooperation provides mutual benefits to states if they can rely on each other to honor agreements, but each state has an incentive to cheat regardless of the actions taken by others.

The term *prisoners' dilemma* derives from the story used to describe the game: The police arrest two individuals, actor A and actor B, for committing fraud. The police suspect that A and B have also committed robbery, but they cannot prove it without a confession. The police put A and B in different cells so they cannot communicate with each other, then question each prisoner separately. In Figure 4.1, prisoners A and B "cooperate" with each other if they do not confess to committing robbery, and they "defect" (or cheat on each other) if they confess to the crime. The prisoners receive "payoffs" (i.e., benefits or losses) depending on the decisions they make. The numbers at the top right-hand corner of the squares in Figure 4.1 are the payoff figures for A, and the numbers at the bottom left-hand corners are the payoffs for B. The police

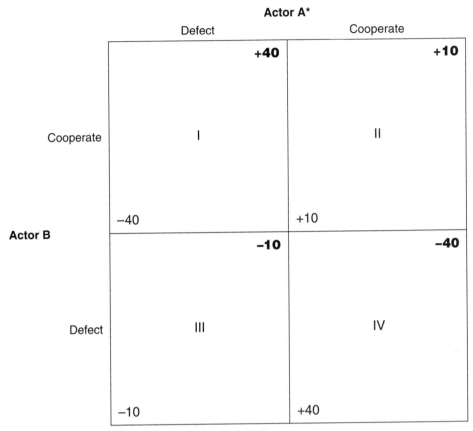

Figure 4.1   Prisoners' Dilemma

make a tempting offer to induce A to confess (i.e., to defect). First, the police tell A that conviction for fraud is certain and will result in a sentence of 1 year for both prisoners if they do not confess (square II in Figure 4.1). However, if A confesses to robbery (i.e., defects) and B does not (i.e., cooperates), A will go free and B will get 10-years' imprisonment (square I). If both A and B defect and confess to robbery, they will get a reduced sentence of 5 years (square III). Finally, if A does not confess to robbery (i.e., cooperates) but B confesses (i.e., defects), A will get 10-years' imprisonment and B will go free (square IV). The police offer the same set of conditions to B.

The question is, what will the prisoners do? According to individual rationality, if B defects, A is better off defecting (a payoff of –10) rather than cooperating (–40). If B cooperates, A is also better off defecting (+40) than cooperating (+10). Regardless of what B does, therefore, it would seem rational for A to defect! The same reasoning would apply to B's decisions. A fears that B will defect, and A wants to avoid ending up with the worst possible penalty by cooperating (–40 in square IV); thus, A is almost certain to defect; and B, too, who similarly mistrusts A, is likely to defect. A and B are therefore both likely to defect and end up with the third-best outcome (square III), even though both would have been better off cooperating and ending up with the second-best outcome (square II). Square III is referred to as a *Pareto-suboptimal* or *Pareto-deficient* outcome because *all* actors (A and B) would prefer another outcome (II). Square II, by contrast, is the **Pareto-optimal** outcome or the best collective outcome for A and B; no one actor can be made better off without making someone else worse off (that is, if A's payoff increases to +40 in square I, B's payoff decreases to −40).[32]

The dilemma in this game results from the fact that individual rationality leads to an outcome (square III) that is Pareto-suboptimal for both prisoners.[33] In international relations, we ask how (and whether) states can move from a Pareto-suboptimal outcome (mutual defection or DD) to the Pareto-optimal outcome (mutual cooperation or CC). In the view of liberals, "cheating" by states can inhibit cooperation, but the move to CC is often possible if cheating can be controlled. The existence of a global hegemon, and the existence of international institutions, can limit cheating and facilitate movement toward mutual cooperation. A global hegemon prevents cheating by providing public goods and coercing other states to abide by agreed rules and principles. Institutions such as international organizations prevent cheating simply by bringing states together on a regular basis. A state that interacts regularly with other states in international organizations is less likely to cheat because the other states will have many opportunities to retaliate. International institutions also enforce principles and rules to ensure that cheaters will be punished, and they collect information on each member state's policies, increasing "transparency" or confidence that cheaters will be discovered. Finally, international organizations contribute to a mutual learning process in which states become aware of the mutual gains that result from cooperation.[34]

Realists are far more skeptical than liberals that international institutions can play a major role in promoting cooperation. In the realist view, institutions often cater to the interests of the great powers instead of affecting their behavior. Realists also place more emphasis than liberals on the concern of states with *relative gains* as a major obstacle to cooperation. Realists are highly skeptical of the liberal view that international institutions can refocus a state's interests toward absolute, mutual gains. States will continue to be concerned about their capabilities *relative to* those of other states because of their basic interest in survival and independence. Even when two states have common interests, they may be unwilling to cooperate because of each state's concern that the other will receive greater gains. Institutions can play a significant role in promoting cooperation, according to realists, only if the institutions can ensure member states that their gains will be balanced and equitable. However, gains are rarely equal, so this will be a very difficult objective for international institutions to achieve.[35]

Regime Theory

While realists simply assume that the international system is anarchic because a central authority above nation-states is lacking, regime theory first developed in efforts to explain why international interactions seem to be more orderly in some issue areas than in others.[36] With the growth of interdependence, states have established some principles, norms, and rules to regulate each others' behavior in such areas as trade, aid, and monetary relations. Thus, *regimes* can be defined as "sets of implicit or explicit principles, norms, rules, and decision-making procedures around which actors' expectations converge in a given area of international relations."[37] International regimes are normally associated with international organizations. For example, the World Trade Organization is embedded in the global trade regime, and the International Monetary Fund is embedded in the global monetary regime. Regime *principles* and *norms* refer to general beliefs and standards of behavior that determine how relations are conducted in a specific issue area. Important principles of the global trade regime, for example, include trade liberalization, reciprocity, and nondiscrimination. Regime *rules* are more specific than norms and principles; rules refer to the types of behavior that are considered to be permissible and impermissible. According to the rules of the global trade regime, for example, countries should normally refrain from using import quotas and export subsidies in efforts to improve their trade balances. The sections that follow briefly examine some of the research done on the formation and consequences of regimes.

The Formation of Regimes   Some theorists argue that the existence of a hegemonic state or group of states is necessary for both the formation and persistence of regimes. Others draw a distinction between the creation and maintenance of a regime. A hegemonic power plays a major role in the creation of regimes through providing public goods and coercing other states; but it is easier to maintain regimes than it is to establish them. Thus, countries that have benefited from a regime may be willing to cooperate with each other to maintain it, even after a hegemonic state has declined.[38] Some theorists go even further and argue that hegemony is not necessary for either the creation or the maintenance of regimes. For example, some regimes may arise through negotiations among willing states that are relatively equal in stature. In such cases, the common interests of these states is sufficient to form the regime even in the absence of a dominant hegemon.[39]

Are Regimes Important?   Research on the formation of regimes is of interest, but a more central question to ask is whether regimes "make a difference" in international relations. In assessing the importance of regimes, some researchers examine whether member states regularly abide by regime principles, norms, and rules; whether regimes cause states to alter their perceptions of self-interest; whether regimes persist even when there is a deterioration in overall relations; and whether regimes adequately manage the international problems they were formed to deal with. Some scholars claim that regimes are often quite effective. For example, studies have shown that a Baltic environmental protection regime established in 1974 continued to be reasonably effective even when East-West relations deteriorated and that countries were often willing to abide by GATT's dispute settlement decisions even when they were required to alter their policies. The number of empirical studies on regime effectiveness are still limited, however, and there is considerable need for more sustained, in-depth research on the significance of regimes in affecting international behavior.[40]

In this book we assume that regimes do affect the international behavior of at least some states in certain issue areas. Regime principles, norms, and rules can help to establish standards in specific areas by which member states can assess their own and others' actions. In setting standards, regimes can provide countries with reliable information, decrease the likelihood of misunderstandings, and increase the possibilities for cooperation. Regimes can also induce national governments to follow consistent policies, limit actions that adversely affect other states, and become less responsive to special interest groups. To say that regimes and their international organizations can influence international behavior does not indicate that their effect is always as positive as liberals imply. As both realists and historical structuralists point out, the principles, norms, and rules of a regime may simply reflect or further the interests of the most powerful states, and it is the least powerful states that are expected to abide by them. The chapters in Part III examine the role of regimes and international organizations in greater detail.

LIBERALISM AND DOMESTIC-INTERNATIONAL INTERACTIONS

Scholars of international political economy are more likely than strategic-security specialists to focus on the linkages between international and domestic politics. A major reason relates to the fact that domestic groups and individuals often see a close relationship between international economic interactions (such as trade and foreign investment) and their own welfare. Much of the literature on domestic structure and IPE cannot be neatly categorized under any one of the three IPE perspectives; however, the liberals most closely adhere to the view that domestic societal pressures affect state policy (as discussed in Chapter 5, one strand of Marxism also considers the state to be an "instrument" of the dominant capitalist class).

One IPE area in which international relations specialists have examined domestic-international interactions extensively is foreign economic policymaking. Foreign policy specialists are more inclined than other international relations theorists to recognize the need to examine domestic politics. A state's foreign economic policy results at least as much from domestic factors as it does from international factors.[41] For example, some analysts have argued that more centralized states such as Japan and France can often respond more decisively to external events than more decentralized states such as the United States. It is argued that the separation of powers in the United States between the President and the Congress, and the division of powers between the federal government and the states, make the U.S. government more vulnerable to interest group pressures and less able to respond promptly to international crises. Thus, France promptly took actions to increase its autonomy and security of energy supplies after the 1973 OPEC oil price increases by supporting French oil companies, promoting special relations with former French colonies that had oil, and developing nuclear energy as an alternative source of supply. The decentralized U.S. government, by contrast, acted far more indecisively because it was subject to a variety of competing societal pressures from oil companies, environmentalists, and other groups.[42]

While the strong state/weak state distinction may be helpful in comparing industrial state policies in a general sense, more recent studies have argued that states are not uniformly strong or uniformly weak across different issue areas and time periods.[43] Thus, the U.S. executive has been able to implement monetary policy far more easily than trade policy because societal groups see their economic fortunes as being far more affected by trade. While societal groups exert pressures on Congress to express their interests on controversial trade issues such as NAFTA, they give government leaders considerable latitude in the formulation and implementation of monetary policy. States such as Japan, which are considered to be highly centralized, also do not necessarily act decisively in regard to every issue. Thus, when a financial crisis affected East and Southeast Asia in the late 1990s, Japan had great difficulty in adopting some of the bold policy measures required to alleviate the crisis (see Chapter 11).

As long as one takes account of variations over issue areas and time periods, domestic structure can be an important factor in explaining a country's foreign economic policies. For example, hegemonic stability theorists look at U.S. economic and political resources, but they largely ignore the *domestic* constraints confronting U.S. policymakers. The domestic divisions within both the U.S. polity (for example, between the President and Congress) and the U.S. society can make it difficult for the United States to provide international leadership *even if* the United States has the external strength one associates with a hegemon. Japan, by contrast, with fewer external power resources, may benefit from a greater unity of purpose in its polity and society under certain circumstances.

International relations specialists have also focused on domestic-international interactions when examining international economic negotiations. For example, theorists often view international negotiations as a "two-level game" involving a relationship between a state's international interests and obligations (level 1) on the one hand and its domestic interactions (level 2) on the other.[44] At the international level of the two-level game, state representatives bargain with each other to reach an agreement. At the domestic level, these representatives must bargain with their own domestic constituencies, whose concurrence is often needed to arrive at legitimate and effective agreements. A certain degree of consistency must develop between the international and domestic interests if agreements are to be signed and implemented. The two-level game framework is especially useful in examining issues such as agricultural trade, in which a wide range of domestic interests come into conflict with the international interests of the state.[45]

In addition to examining foreign economic policymaking and international negotiations, IPE specialists have sought to explain international economic cooperation and conflict in terms of domestic variables.[46] Chapters 6 and 8, for example, refer to some writers who argue that domestic factors have been more important than the existence of a hegemon in explaining cooperation and conflict in the global monetary and trade regimes. There is a wealth of literature on domestic interactions in the field of international political economy; this book can only begin to discuss the subject.

LIBERALISM AND NORTH-SOUTH RELATIONS

Liberals generally agree that the key factors in development are the efficient use of scarce resources and economic growth, which is often defined as an increase in the total per capita income of a country. Beyond these broad areas of agreement, however, the liberal development school "lacks a central unifying, theoretical argument."[47] When discussing liberal theory in general, we referred to orthodox liberals such as Adam Smith and Milton Friedman and to interventionist liberals such as John Maynard Keynes. The same division is evident among liberal development theorists.

Orthodox Liberals and North-South Relations

North-South distributional issues are not a major concern of the orthodox liberals. Because orthodox liberals consider international economic relations to be a positive-sum game, they believe that the growth of interdependence will have a mutually beneficial effect on states. Indeed, orthodox liberals often argue that North-South linkages provide even more benefits to the LDCs than to the advanced industrial states. The economic problems of LDCs, in the orthodox liberal view, stem from irrational or inefficient domestic policies and not from their unfavorable position in the global economy. The sections that follow outline the views of orthodox liberals regarding domestic and external determinants of development.

Domestic Development Factors   Orthodox liberals assume that development problems in the Third World stem largely from irrational or inefficient policies of LDCs. In the 1950s and 1960s, liberal *modernization theorists* compared traditional and modern societies and traced the development process from traditionalism to modernity. Although modernization theory was considered to be largely passé by the 1970s, its precepts continue to influence orthodox liberal thought. Modernization theory asserts that the Northern industrial states achieved economic development by abandoning traditional methods of organizing society and that the North's development experience serves as an indispensable guide to development for the South. From the modernization perspective, LDCs must replace their traditional values, institutions, and patterns of activity if they are to overcome the obstacles to development. The individual and societal changes required may produce considerable dislocation and hardship, but the rewards and opportunities in societies that successfully modernize are also great. To bring about modernization, society must develop a system of rewards for innovation. Innovation and other internal mechanisms for generating surpluses contribute to increased investment, which in turn leads to self-sustaining growth.[48]

It is generally conceded today that modernization theorists' concepts of "traditional" and "modern" were imprecise, that the two concepts are not mutually exclusive, and that modern values and practices are not always superior to traditional ones. Nevertheless, orthodox liberals continue to believe that the main factors hindering Third World development are domestic. For example, they argue that the countries of Western Europe that protected private property rights experienced early success in industrialization and development and that Third World governments that do not enforce these rights hinder foreign investment and the adoption of new technologies. In the orthodox liberal view, LDC governments should permit private producers to operate freely through the price mechanism and should limit their own involvement to providing public goods such as national security, education, and services designed to improve the functioning of markets.[49]

Paths to Development   A number of modernization theorists were quite deterministic, arguing that LDCs must follow the same path to development that was previously taken by Northern states. For example, one theorist wrote in the 1960s that the Western development model "reappears in virtually all modernizing societies of all continents of the world, regardless of variations of race, color or creed."[50] The best-known study prescribing a single development path is Walt Rostow's *The Stages of Economic Growth*, which received widespread attention from the time of its publication. Rostow takes a highly deterministic position, claiming that societies move through five specific stages on their way to modernity: traditional society, the preconditions for takeoff, the takeoff, the drive to maturity, and the age of high mass consumption.[51]

Although Rostow's model initially had considerable influence, his stages were extremely difficult to apply to specific Third World countries, and his predictions regarding LDC growth were unduly optimistic. Thus, Rostow argued that an LDC reaching the takeoff stage would be transformed in such a way that its growth would be self-sustaining thereafter. Such predictions raised false hopes that Third World economic development was a readily achievable and irreversible process. While some modernization theorists were more open to the idea that LDCs could follow different routes to development, much modernization theory was—like Rostow's—marked by determinism.[52]

Critics of modernization theory have strongly challenged the view that all countries can or should follow similar paths to development, pointing out that the challenges facing LDCs today are very different from those that confronted early developers. The forces of globalization, the need to compete with advanced industrial states, and the proliferation of multinational corporations all indicate that development today cannot simply be a repetition of the earlier Western model.[53] Nevertheless, even after modernization theory was considered to be passé, orthodox liberals continued to view the Western model as the only legitimate path to development. In the 1970s, for example, orthodox liberals strongly opposed the OPEC cartel's strategy to raise oil prices because it interfered with market-oriented pricing; and they also opposed the Third World prescription for a New International Economic Order, objecting that it would redistribute wealth and power on the basis of political pressure rather than efficient economic performance.[54] With the breakup of the Soviet bloc, orthodox liberals became even more assertive. Thus, by the late 1980s and early 1990s, some theorists were writing that "third-world countries are much like those of the first world and will, with a modicum of external aid and internal stability, follow in the path of their predecessors" and that "what we may be witnessing is not just the end of the Cold War" but "the universalization of Western liberal democracy as the final form of human government."[55]

External Development Factors   Internationally, orthodox liberals view North-South relations as a positive-sum game that benefits the South, and they strongly reject the idea that the advanced industrial states are responsible for poverty in the Third World. On the contrary, orthodox liberals often argue that "the late-comers to modern economic growth tend to catch up with the early-comers."[56] In the liberal orthodox view, Third World countries are more likely to achieve development if they are closely integrated in the global economy through freer trade and capital flows. Those LDCs that have few trade and foreign investment linkages with the North are the poorest and least developed countries. Because LDCs have shortages of capital and technology, foreign investment and the diffusion of advanced technologies are of particular importance to them. Exports are also of critical importance to LDCs because of their small domestic markets, and international trade permits LDCs to specialize in the goods they can produce most efficiently. Thus, two well-known orthodox liberal economists have written in regard to the African country of Tanzania that "such economic development as has taken place is in large measure due to access to Western markets and to Western enterprise, capital, and ideas."[57]

Because orthodox liberals advocate free trade, they were extremely critical of the **import-substituting industrialization (ISI)** policies followed by a number of LDCs in the 1950s and 1960s. (Some Latin American LDCs continued to follow ISI policies in the 1970s and early 1980s.) These policies involved protection of local industry through a wide array of tariffs and **nontariff barriers (NTBs),** with an emphasis on production for the domestic market over production for export. In the orthodox liberal view, ISI causes economic distortions in LDC economies and fosters uncompetitive industries with high prices and low-quality products.[58]

Orthodox liberals, by contrast, attributed the economic success of the East Asian newly industrialized countries (NICs) to their "export-led development" model, which these theorists viewed as clearly preferable to the import substitution model. As its name implies, **export-led growth** relies on deep involvement in international trade as a "motor" to development. Thus, the orthodox liberals Milton Friedman and Rose Friedman argued that "Malaysia, Singapore, Korea, Taiwan, Hong Kong and Japan— all relying extensively on private markets, are thriving" while "India, Indonesia, and Communist China, all relying heavily on central planning, have experienced economic stagnation and political repression."[59] As discussed in Chapter 3, realists disputed the liberal view that the East Asian NICs' success in exporting depended mainly on market-oriented policies. Instead, the realists argue that government-business cooperation and selective government involvement was key to East Asian economic development. Chapter 11, on international development, examines this debate in greater detail.

Interventionist Liberals and North-South Relations

Interventionist liberals begin with the same basic assumptions as orthodox liberals that LDCs with efficient, market-oriented policies are most likely to achieve economic growth. In contrast to orthodox liberals, however, interventionists point to the pronounced inequalities between North and South, and they call on the advanced industrial states to give more consideration to the special needs of LDCs. The interventionists believe that "economic forces left entirely to themselves tend to produce growing inequality," especially when income distribution is highly distorted (as is the case between North and South).[60] They therefore recommend a variety of changes that involve some degree of intervention in the market, including the removal of Northern trade barriers to Southern states while permitting some degree of protectionism for LDC industries, the provision of increased financial resources to indebted LDCs through the IMF and the World Bank, and the assurance that multinational corporations will not take undue advantage of LDC needs for foreign investment and technology. Interventionists also argue that Northern assistance to the South is a matter of enlightened self-interest because "the countries of the North, given their increasing interdependence with the South, themselves need international economic reform to ensure their own future prosperity."[61]

Although interventionists argue that corrective devices are needed to provide for the special needs of the South, they believe that the necessary changes can occur within the international liberal order and that a radical redistribution of wealth and power between North and South is not necessary. They also share the faith of other liberals in private enterprise, believing that private sector interactions between North and South should be encouraged. Finally, interventionist and orthodox liberals agree that many Southern development problems are rooted in domestic inefficiencies and that LDCs therefore have the primary responsibility for confronting their development problems.[62]

CRITIQUE OF THE LIBERAL PERSPECTIVE

It is impossible to provide a detailed critique of the liberal perspective here. This section focuses only on some of the more important general criticisms that theorists from the two competing perspectives (realists and historical structuralists) level against the liberals. As this chapter notes, liberals tend to view international economic relations as occurring in a competitive market among equals, in which all countries benefit from trade, foreign investment, and other economic linkages. Because these exchange relations produce mutual benefits, orthodox liberals are not particularly concerned about the fact that all countries do not benefit equally. Although interventionist liberals point out that unemployment can occur under pure market conditions and that LDCs may require special and differential treatment, they feel that these problems can be resolved by supplementing the liberal-economic system rather than replacing it.

Both realists and historical structuralists criticize liberals for their inattention to power and distributional issues. In contrast to liberals, who emphasize the mutual gains from exchange, realists emphasize the relative distribution of gains across states, with the more powerful states capturing a larger share of the benefits. Realists argue that economic exchanges are in fact rarely free and equal and that bargaining power based on monopoly and coercion can have important political effects. Thus, the more powerful states can injure the weaker states simply by reducing or terminating their linkages in such areas as trade, aid, and foreign investment.[63] Historical structuralists often accuse liberals of seeking to legitimize inequalities and exploitation. Domestically, liberals mislead the working class into believing that it will reap the benefits of economic prosperity along with the capitalist class; and internationally, liberals disguise exploitation and imperialism under the cloak of "interdependence." Critics also question the liberal view that technology, rather than global redistribution, can solve many of the world's most urgent economic and environmental problems. Even with technological advances, the liberal international order that seemed so positive-sum in the immediate postwar years is becoming more intensely competitive as we move away from a world of abundant resources. A world where resources are becoming scarce will inevitably become more zero-sum in nature.

In regard to North-South relations, orthodox liberals simply assume that open economic policies will improve LDC opportunities, without considering the political and power relationships between North and South. Aside from some aberrant cases such as OPEC and the East Asian NICs, critics argue, North-South relationships are highly asymmetrical, with LDCs far more dependent on the advanced industrial states than vice versa. Thus, President Julius Nyerere of Tanzania remarked to the ministerial meeting of the Group of 77 Third World states in February 1979 that

> what we have in common is that we are all, in relation to the developed world, dependent—not interdependent—nations. Each of our economies has developed as a by-product and a subsidiary of development in the industrialized North, and is externally oriented.[64]

It is evident that this dependent relationship provides the North with a potent source of power over the South. The liberal perspective, however, tends to avoid the subject of power, discounting the effects of North-South asymmetries by arguing that North-South relations are a positive-sum game in which everyone benefits. One liberal assessment of NAFTA, for example, indicates that the United States, Canada, and Mexico agreed to "a partial surrender of autonomy in order to achieve the benefits that are available from mutual relaxation of protectionism."[65] However, orthodox liberals avoid asking whether the Southern states (i.e., Mexico in NAFTA) must surrender more autonomy than the Northern states (the United States and Canada).

Liberals are also criticized for putting too much faith in the market and for disregarding the role of the state. Although liberals such as Adam Smith recognized that the state had to perform certain essential functions, orthodox liberalism generally provides for a minimal role for the state. Interventionist liberals such as John Maynard Keynes have viewed states as performing various corrective functions, but even interventionists can be criticized for undertheorizing the role of the state. Liberal theory portrays the state as simply performing functions that the market does not perform, and it does not sufficiently explore either the capacities or constraints of the state. Thus, realists argue that we should "bring the state back in" to our research because of its central role in policymaking.[66]

Chapters 3 and 4 have demonstrated that realists and liberals have differing perceptions regarding a wide range of issues in IPE. However, these two schools of thought are much closer together than the third school—the historical structuralists—in one important respect. While liberals and realists accept and basically approve of the capitalist system as a given, historical structuralists generally view capitalism as an exploitative system that should—and will—eventually be replaced by socialism. It is to the historical structuralists that we now turn.

NOTES

1. R. D. McKinlay and R. Little, *Global Problems and World Order* (London: Pinter, 1986), p. 41. Andrew Moravcsik attempts to identify the core analytical propositions of liberalism in "Taking Preferences Seriously: A Liberal Theory of International Politics," *International Organization* 51-4 (Autumn 1997), pp. 513–553.

2. For a discussion of the various strands of liberalism, see Mark W. Zacher and Richard A. Matthew, "Liberal International Theory: Common Threads, Divergent Strands," in Charles W. Kegley, Jr., ed., *Controversies in International Relations Theory: Realism and the Neoliberal Challenge* (New York: St. Martin's Press, 1995), pp. 107–150.

3. Moravcsik, "Taking Preferences Seriously," p. 517.

4. Adam Smith, *The Wealth of Nations* (London: Dent, Everyman's Library no. 412, 1910), vol. 1, bk. 4, p. 398.

5. See, for example, E. E. Schattschneider, *Politics, Pressures and the Tariff: A Study of Free Enterprise in Pressure Politics, as Shown in the 1929–1930 Revision of the Tariff* (Hamden, CT: Archon Books, 1963, reprint of the 1935 edition).

6. John Locke, *Two Treatises of Government* (Cambridge: Cambridge University Press, 1964), ch. 9 of the Second Treatise, p. 368.

7. Adam Smith, *The Wealth of Nations,* vol. 1, bk. 4, p. 436.

8. Smith, *The Wealth of Nations,* vol. 2, bk. 4, pp. 180–181; George T. Crane and Abla Amawi, *The Theoretical Evolution of International Political Economy: A Reader* (New York: Oxford University Press, 1991), p. 56.

9. John Maynard Keynes, *The General Theory of Employment, Interest, and Money* (New York: Harcourt, Brace & World, 1935), pp. 378–379.

10. John Maynard Keynes, "National Self-Sufficiency," *The Yale Review* 22 (1933), p. 758.

11. Fred L. Block, *The Origins of International Economic Disorder: A Study of United States International Monetary Policy from World War II to the Present* (Berkeley: University of California Press, 1977), pp. 62–69; D. E. Moggridge, *Keynes* (London: Macmillan, 1976), p. 147.

12. Anthony Arblaster, *The Rise and Decline of Western Liberalism* (New York: Basil Blackwell, 1984), p. 292; B. Greenwald and J. E. Stiglits, "Keynesian, New Keynesian and New Classical Economics," *Oxford Economic Papers* 39-1 (1987), p. 119.

13. Karl Polanyi, *The Great Transformation* (Boston: Beacon Press, sixth printing, 1965).

14. The term "embedded liberalism compromise" was coined by John Gerard Ruggie in his article "International Regimes, Transactions, and Change: Embedded Liberalism in the Postwar Economic Order," in Stephen D. Krasner, ed., *International Regimes* (Ithaca, NY: Cornell University Press, 1983), pp. 204–214.

15. Peter Gourevitch, *Politics in Hard Times: Comparative Responses to International Economic Crises* (Ithaca, NY: Cornell University Press, 1986), pp. 166–169; Adam Przeworski, *Capitalism and Social Democracy* (Cambridge: Cambridge University Press, 1985), pp. 205–211.

16. Milton Friedman, *Capitalism and Freedom* (Chicago: University of Chicago Press, 1962), p. 9.

17. Milton Friedman and Rose Friedman, *Free to Choose: A Personal Statement* (New York: Harcourt Brace Jovanovich, 1980), pp. 54–55.

18. See Friedman, *Capitalism and Freedom,* pp. 171–172; F.A. Hayek, *New Studies in Philosophy, Politics, Economics and the History of Ideas* (Chicago: University of Chicago Press, 1978), p. 209; and Ludwig von Mises, *Planning for Freedom* (South Holland, IL: Libertarian Press, 1974), p. 17.

19. Robert Cox, *Production, Power, and World Order: Social Forces in the Making of History* (New York: Columbia University Press, 1987), pp. 286–288. See also Alain Lipietz, *Towards a New Economic Order: Postfordism, Ecology and Democracy,* translated by Malcolm Slater (New York: Oxford University Press, 1992), pp. 30–31.

20. Robert O. Keohane, "Neoliberal Institutionalism: A Perspective on World Politics," in Robert O. Keohane, *International Institutions and State Power: Essays in International Relations Theory* (Boulder, CO: Westview Press, 1989), pp. 3–4.

21. Ernst B. Haas, "Words Can Hurt You; or, Who Said What to Whom About Regimes," in Krasner, ed., *International Regimes*, p. 27.

22. Robert O. Keohane and Joseph S. Nye, *Power and Interdependence*, 2nd ed. (Glenview, IL: Scott, Foresman, 1989), pp. 8–9.

23. See Sir Norman Angell, *The Foundations of International Polity* (London: Heinemann, 1914); Francis Delaisi, *Political Myths and Economic Realities* (London: Douglas, 1925); Ramsay Muir, *The Interdependent World and Its Problems* (Boston: Houghton Mifflin, 1933); and David A. Baldwin, "Interdependence and Power: A Conceptual Analysis," *International Organization* 34-4 (Autumn 1980), pp. 481–482.

24. See W. A. Brown, Jr., *The International Gold Standard Reinterpreted, 1914–1934,* 2 vols. (New York: National Bureau of Economic Research, 1940); and Albert O. Hirschman, *National Power and the Structure of Foreign Trade* (Berkeley: University of California Press, 1945).

25. Richard N. Cooper, *The Economics of Interdependence: Economic Policy in the Atlantic Community* (New York: McGraw-Hill, 1968).

26. Richard N. Cooper, "Economic Interdependence and Foreign Policy in the Seventies," *World Politics* 24 (January 1972), p. 179.

27. Keohane and Nye, *Power and Interdependence*, p. 11. See also Crane and Amawi, *The Theoretical Evolution of International Political Economy*, pp. 14, 107–109.

28. See Keohane and Nye, *Power and Interdependence*, ch. 7.

29. See, for example, Wallace Clement, *Continental Corporate Power: Economic Linkage Between Canada and the United States* (Toronto: McClelland and Stewart, 1976); Glen Williams, "On Determining Canada's Location Within the International Political Economy," *Studies in Political Economy* 25 (Spring 1988), pp. 107–140; and Duncan Cameron and Mel Watkins, eds., *Canada Under Free Trade* (Toronto: Lorimer, 1993).

30. Keohane and Nye, *Power and Interdependence*, pp. 24–25.

31. Bayless Manning coined the term *intermestic* in "The Congress, The Executive and Intermestic Affairs: Three Proposals," *Foreign Affairs* 55 (June 1977), pp. 306–324.

32. The term *Pareto-optimal* is named after an Italian sociologist, Vilfredo Pareto (1848–1923).

33. Robert Axelrod, *The Evolution of Cooperation* (np: Basic Books, 1984), p. 9.

34. See Keohane, "Neoliberal Institutionalism," pp. 1–20; and Robert Axelrod and Robert O. Keohane, "Achieving Cooperation Under Anarchy: Strategies and Institutions," in Kenneth A. Oye, ed., *Cooperation Under Anarchy* (Princeton, NJ: Princeton University Press, 1986), pp. 226–254.

35. For the realist view of institutions, see John J. Mearsheimer, "The False Promise of International Institutions," *International Security* 19-3 (Winter 1994–95), pp. 5–49; and Joseph Grieco, *Cooperation Among Nations: Europe, America, and Non-Tariff Barriers to Trade* (Ithaca, NY: Cornell University Press, 1990).

36. Mark W. Zacher with Brent A. Sutton, *Governing Global Networks: International Regimes for Transportation and Communications* (Cambridge: Cambridge University Press, 1996), p. 1.

37. Krasner, "Structural Causes and Regime Consequences: Regimes as Intervening Variables," in Krasner, ed., *International Regimes*, p. 2.

38. Robert O. Keohane, *After Hegemony: Cooperation and Discord in the World Political Economy* (Princeton, NJ: Princeton University Press, 1984), pp. 49, 244–245.

39. Oran R. Young, "Regime Dynamics: The Rise and Fall of International Regimes," in Krasner, ed., *International Regimes,* pp. 98–101; and Mark A. Levy, Oran R. Young, and Michael Zürn, "The Study of International Regimes," *European Journal of International Relations* 1-3 (1995), p. 286.

40. Robert O. Keohane, "The Analysis of International Regimes: Towards a European-American Research Programme," in Volker Rittberger, ed., with the assistance of Peter Mayer, *Regime Theory and International Relations* (Oxford: Clarendon Press, 1993), pp. 32–34; Volker Rittberger and Michael Zürn, "Towards Regulated Anarchy in East West Relations: Causes and Consequences of East-West Regimes," in Volker Rittberger, ed., *International Regimes in East-West Politics* (London: Pinter, 1990), pp. 20–22.

41. Even realists who examine foreign economic policy must be more attuned to domestic issues. See Stephen D. Krasner, *Defending the National Interest: Raw Materials Investments and U. S. Foreign Policy* (Princeton, NJ: Princeton University Press, 1978), pp. 12–13; and Michael Mastanduno, David A. Lake, and G. John Ikenberry, "Toward a Realist Theory of State Action," *International Studies Quarterly* 33-4 (December 1989), pp. 457–474.

42. See Peter J. Katzenstein, "International Relations and Domestic Structures: Foreign Economic Policies of the Advanced Industrial States," *International Organization* 30-1 (Winter 1976), pp. 41–42; Peter J. Katzenstein, ed., *Between Power and Plenty: Foreign Economic Policies of Advanced Industrial States,* special issue of *International Organization* 31-4 (Autumn 1977); Matthew Evangelista, "Domestic Structure and International Change," in Michael W. Doyle and G. John Ikenberry, eds., *New Thinking in International Relations Theory* (Boulder, CO: Westview Press, 1997), pp. 206–208.

43. See G. John Ikenberry, David A. Lake, and Michael Mastanduno, ed., *The State and American Foreign Economic Policy,* special issue of *International Organization* 42-1 (Winter 1988); and William D. Coleman and Grace Skogstad, *Policy Communities and Public Policy in Canada: A Structural Approach* (Mississauga, ONT: Copp Clark Pitman, 1990), p. ix.

44. The two-level game approach was developed by Robert Putnam. See Robert D. Putnam, "Diplomacy and Domestic Politics: The Logic of Two-Level Games," *International Organization* 42-3 (Summer 1988), pp. 427–460; and Peter B. Evans, Harold K. Jacobson, and Robert D. Putnam, eds., *Double-Edged Diplomacy: International Bargaining and Domestic Politics* (Berkeley: University of California Press, 1993).

45. See William P. Avery, ed., *World Agriculture and the GATT* (Boulder, CO: Rienner, 1993); Theodore H. Cohn, "The Intersection of Domestic and Foreign Policy in the NAFTA Agricultural Negotiations," *Canadian-American Public Policy,* no. 14 (Orono: University of Maine, September 1993); and William P. Avery, "American Agricultural and Trade Policymaking: Two-Level Bargaining in the North American Free Trade Agreement," *Policy Sciences* 29 (1996), pp. 113–136.

46. See, for example, Peter Alexis Gourevitch, "Squaring the Circle: The Domestic Sources of International Cooperation," *International Organization* 50-2 (Spring 1996), pp. 349–373.

47. David A. Lake, "Power and the Third World: Toward a Realist Political Economy of North-South Relations," *International Studies Ouarterly* 31-2 (June 1987), p. 218.

48. C. E. Black, *The Dynamics of Modernization: A Study in Comparative History* (New York: Harper & Row, 1966), p. 27; Daniel Lerner, "Modernization: Social Aspects," in David Sills,

ed., *International Encyclopedia of the Social Sciences* (New York: Macmillan, 1968) vol. 10, pp. 386–388.

49. Robert Wade, *Governing the Market: Economic Theory and the Role of Government in East Asian Industrialization* (Princeton, NJ: Princeton University Press, 1990), pp. 11–14.

50. Daniel Lerner, *The Passing of Traditional Society: Modernizing the Middle East* (New York: Free Press, 1964), pp. viii–ix. (This quotation appears in the preface to the paperback edition.)

51. See W. W. Rostow, *The Stages of Economic Growth: A Non-Communist Manifesto* (Cambridge: Cambridge University Press, 1960), pp. 4–92.

52. Studies that were less deterministic include Gabriel A. Almond and James S. Coleman, eds., *The Politics of the Developing Areas* (Princeton, NJ: Princeton University Press, 1960); Samuel P. Huntington, *Political Order in Changing Societies* (New Haven, CT: Yale University Press, 1968); and Alexander Gerschenkron, *Economic Backwardness in Historical Perspective: A Book of Essays* (Cambridge, MA: Belknap Press of Harvard University Press, 1962).

53. Alejandro Portes, "On the Sociology of National Development: Theories and Issues," *American Journal of Sociology* 82-1 (July 1976), p. 60.

54. McKinlay and Little, *Global Problems and World Order*, p. 96; Peter T. Bauer and Basil S. Yamey, "World Wealth Redistribution: Anatomy of the New Order," in Karl Brunner, ed., *The First World and the Third World: Essays on the New International Economic Order* (Rochester, NY: University of Rochester Policy Center Publications, 1978), p. 193.

55. Lloyd G. Reynolds, *Economic Growth in the Third World, 1850–1980* (New Haven, CT: Yale University Press, 1985), p. 6; Francis Fukuyama, "The End of History?" *The National Interest 16* (Summer 1989), p. 4.

56. W. W. Rostow, *Why the Poor Get Richer and the Rich Slow Down* (Austin: University of Texas Press, 1980), p. 259.

57. P.T. Bauer and B.S. Yamey, "Against the New Economic Order," *Commentary* 63-4 (April 1977), p. 27.

58. For a useful survey of literature criticizing LDC import substitution policies, see Carlos F. Díaz-Alejandro, "Trade Policies and Economic Development," in Peter B. Kenen, ed., *International Trade and Finance: Frontiers for Research* (London: Cambridge University Press, 1975), pp. 112–116.

59. Milton Friedman and Rose Friedman, *Free to Choose: A Personal Statement* (New York: Harcourt Brace Jovanovich, 1980), p. 57. See also Bela Balassa, "The Process of Industrial Development and Alternative Development Strategies," in Bela Balassa, ed., *The Newly Industrializing Countries in the World Economy* (New York: Pergamon Press), pp. 16–17.

60. Independent Commission on International Development Issues (henceforth, Brandt Commission I), North-South: *A Program for Survival* (Cambridge, MA: MIT Press, 1980), pp. 103–104.

61. Brandt Commission I, *North-South,* p. 33. See also Albert Fishlow, "A New International Economic Order: What Kind?" in Albert Fishlow, Carlos F. Díaz-Alejandro, Richard R. Fagen, and Roger D. Hansen, *Rich and Poor Nations in the World Economy* (New York: McGraw-Hill, 1978), pp. 51–76.

62. Stephen D. Krasner, *Structural Conflict: The Third World Against Global Liberalism* (Berkeley: University of California Press, 1985), pp. 22–25.

63. Charles E. Lindblom, *Politics and Markets: The World's Political-Economic Systems* (New York: Basic Books, 1977), p. 48.

64. "Address by His Excellency Mwalima Julius K Nyerere, President of the United Republic of Tanzania, to the Fourth Ministerial Meeting of the Group of 77," Arusha, 12–16 February 1979, in Karl P. Sauvant, *The Group of 77: Evolution, Structure, Organization* (New York: Oceana Publications, 1981), p. 133.

65. Steven Globerman and Michael Walker, "Overview," in Steven Globerman and Michael Walker, eds., *Assessing NAFTA: A Trinational Analysis* (Vancouver, B.C.: The Fraser Institute, 1993), p. ix.

66. Theda Skocpol, "Bringing the State Back In: Strategies of Analysis in Current Research," in Peter B. Evans, Dietrich Rueschemeyer, and Theda Skocpol, eds., *Bringing the State Back In* (Cambridge: Cambridge University Press, 1985), p. 6.

CHAPTER 5

The Historical Structuralist Perspective

The term *historical structuralism* encompasses a wide range of theoretical approaches, including Marxism, dependency theory, world-system theory, and Gramscian analysis. All the theoretical approaches in this perspective have some roots in Marxism, but some have diverged quite substantially from mainstream Marxist ideas. As we will discuss, Marxists sometimes accuse dependency and world-system theorists of not being sufficiently Marxist and of being mistaken in their interpretation of Third World development.

There are several reasons why this book refers to the third IPE perspective as historical structuralism. The term *structuralist* reflects this perspective's focus on structural means of exploitation, in which one class dominates another or rich Northern states in the core of the global economy dominate poorer Southern states in the periphery. However, some realists are also structuralists; they explain state behavior on the basis of the structure of the international system. To these realists, a state's power and position in the system are the critical factors affecting its behavior.[1] To differentiate this third perspective from structural realism, we add the word *historical* because theorists in the third perspective take a historical approach to the study of IPE.[2] According to this group of theorists, history has been marked by exploitation, and the main characteristic of the current system is the dominance of capitalism, with the capitalist class (the *bourgeoisie*) exploiting the workers (the *proletariat*). Thus, the term *historical structuralism* best describes this school of thought.

It is especially difficult to generalize about the basic tenets of the third IPE perspective because of the wide diversity of historical structuralist approaches. The discussion of theoretical developments is therefore particularly important in this chapter; it provides some indication of the wide differences among writers in this school of thought. There is no separate section on North-South relations in this chapter because some historical structuralist approaches—especially the dependency approach—focus almost exclusively on North-South issues.

BASIC TENETS OF THE HISTORICAL STRUCTURALIST PERSPECTIVE

The Role of the Individual, the State, and Societal Groups

Marxists identify the relationship among classes as the main factor affecting the economic and political order. Each mode of production (e.g., feudalism and capitalism) is associated with two opposing classes, an exploiting nonproducing class and an exploited class of producers. Classes are absent only in the simplest mode of production, the primitive-communal, and in the future Communist mode. Thus, Karl Marx and Friedrich Engels write in *The Communist Manifesto:*

> The history of all hitherto existing society is the history of class struggles. . . . The modern bourgeois society that has sprouted from the ruins of feudal society, has not done away with class antagonisms. It has but established new classes, new conditions of oppression, new forms of struggle in place of the old ones.[3]

In most of Marx and Engels' writings, they depict the state as being nothing more than an agent acting at the behest of the dominant class—in capitalism, the bourgeoisie. Indeed, the bourgeoisie uses the state as an instrument for the exploitation of wage labor. Marx and Engels suggest that under certain conditions, the state may have some autonomy from a dominant class. For example, the state's autonomy may increase temporarily during transition periods, when the power of warring classes is more equally balanced.[4] But in the long run, Marx and Engels argue, the state cannot escape from its dependence on the owners and controllers of capital. Only when the proletarian revolution eliminates private ownership and class distinctions will the state no longer be needed as an instrument of class oppression. A number of later writers—both within and outside the Marxist tradition—have been highly critical of the Marx and Engels position that state actions simply reflect the views of the dominant class.

The Nature and Purpose of International Economic Relations

While liberals consider economic relations to be a positive-sum game, historical structuralists as well as realists view economic relations as being basically conflictual and zero-sum in nature. Thus, Marx and Engels argue that "one fact is common to all past ages, *viz.,* the exploitation of one part of society by the other."[5] This exploitation takes the form of a class struggle, with capitalism being the most advanced stage. Under capitalism, a class of private owners of the means of production extracts surplus value from a class of free but propertyless wage laborers. The private owners then convert this surplus value into capital, which is invested in new means of production.

It is well known that the views of historical structuralists evolved along with changes in the international system. Thus, Marx and Engels initially predicted that the contradictions within the capitalist world would contribute to the absolute poverty of the working class, surplus production, economic downturns, and the eventual collapse of the capitalist system. When this dire prediction was not realized, Lenin and others maintained that *imperialism* explained the continued survival of capitalism.[6] Imperialism delayed the downfall of capitalism because colonies supplied the "metropole" states with a cheap source of agricultural and raw materials and provided an outlet and market for the metropoles' surplus of capital and manufactured goods.

When the process of decolonization marked an end to the age of imperialism, capitalism continued to demonstrate resilience, and some historical structuralists turned their attention from colonialism to *neocolonialism* as the explanation. Although the imperial powers had ceded direct political control over their former colonies, they continued to control the newly independent Third World states economically.[7] Others who have sought to explain the persistence of capitalism and Third World underdevelopment include dependency theorists and world-system theorists. *Dependency theorists* argue that the world is hierarchically organized, with the leading capitalist states in the *core* of the global economy dominating and exploiting poor states in the *periphery*. Only the core states can make autonomous choices about domestic and foreign economic policies, and market mechanisms simply reinforce socioeconomic and political inequalities. Some early dependency theorists asserted that the core states *underdeveloped* the peripheral states, but LDC success stories such as the emergence of the newly industrialized countries caused later theorists to acknowledge that development is possible in some Third World states. Nevertheless, these theorists argue that LDC economic growth takes the form of *dependent development,* which involves a close association between elites in the core and the periphery.

Historical structuralists focus on the exploitative nature of capitalism and are thus similar to realists in considering the purpose of economic and political activity to be the redistribution of wealth and power. Unlike realists, however, historical structuralists reject the idea that a meaningful redistribution of wealth and power can occur within the capitalist system. Actively taking the side of the poor and less powerful, historical structuralists argue that the inequalities under capitalism will disappear only after there is a transformation to socialism. The ultimate goal of exploited states and classes, according to historical structuralists, should be to break linkages with the capitalist states and/or to overthrow the capitalist system.

The Relationship Between Politics and Economics

History, according to Marx, is a dialectical process in which there is a contradiction between evolving economic modes of production (e.g., feudalism, capitalism, and socialism) on the one hand and the political system on the other. This contradiction is resolved when changes in the mode and relations of production eventually cause the political "superstructure" to undergo similar changes. Marx viewed politics as being subordinate to economics, and his writings provided the foundation for the instrumentalist tradition in Marxist thought.[8] **Instrumental Marxism,** like liberalism, perceives formal government institutions as responding in a rather passive manner to socioeco-nomic pressures. Liberals, however, believe that any societal interest group may have political influence, while instrumental Marxists believe that the state's policies reflect the interests of the capitalist class. To support their position, instrumental Marxists point to the personal ties between leading capitalists and public officials and to the movement of individuals back and forth between business and government. One in-strumental Marxist, for example, argues that the individuals in "*all* command positions in the state system have largely, and in many cases overwhelmingly, been drawn from the world of business and property, or from the professional middle classes."[9]

After World War II, many Marxist as well as non-Marxist scholars strongly criti-cized the instrumental Marxist views because industrial states were adopting a number of social policies such as welfare and unemployment insurance *despite* the opposition of important business groups. As a result, a second tradition of **structural Marxism** emerged. In contrast to the instrumentalists, structural Marxists argue that the state is relatively autonomous from direct political pressure by the capitalist class. Thus, the state may adopt some policies that provide benefits to all major groups in society, in-cluding the working class. Although in the short term, some capitalists oppose these state policies, they in fact serve the longer-term interests of the bourgeoisie. The bour-geoisie, which has internal divisions, may be less well placed than the state to recog-nize what policies best serve its own long-term interests. Thus, by providing welfare and other benefits, the state often placates the workers and gains their support for the continuance of capitalism.[10]

Although they consider the state to be relatively autonomous, structural Marxists differ from realists in some important respects. The state is not under the direct con-trol of the bourgeoisie in the structural Marxist view, but it shares with that class a commitment to the long-term maintenance of the capitalist system. Realists, by con-trast, believe that the state has genuine independence from the economic interests of any societal group. Thus, the state in the realist view is free to take those actions it deems necessary to further the "national interest."

KARL MARX AND INTERNATIONAL POLITICAL ECONOMY

Karl Marx (1818–1883) did not write systematically on international relations, but his theory of capitalism and class struggle provided the basic framework for historical structuralist approaches to IPE. Although Marx wrote a number of articles about the effect of Western capitalism on non-European areas, his specific references to the pre-sent-day Third World focused primarily on India and China.[11] It was no accident, in Marx's view, that capitalism first emerged in Europe, where the feudal mode of pro-duction was prevalent. Feudal landholdings were private, so these landholdings could be converted into private bourgeois property when the feudal mode of production was replaced by capitalism.

Marx argued that in contrast to the situation in Europe, an "Asiatic" mode of pro-duction that was outside the mainstream of Western development was prevalent in such countries as India and China. The state's presence was much greater in the

Asiatic mode, because climate and geography made centralized irrigation important in agriculture. Thus, strong central governments in China and India developed large public work projects to provide water over extensive land areas. At the local level, Marx portrayed oriental society as characterized by small, self-sufficient village communities in which there was communal rather than individual ownership. Because communal property (locally) and public property (centrally) overshadowed private property in the Asiatic mode, Marx saw no basis for a transformation—as there was in feudalism—from private feudal landholdings to private capitalist holdings. As a result, Marx believed that "oriental societies" such as China and India had no internal mechanisms for change and that external pressure from Western imperialism was necessary if these countries were to progress to capitalism—and then to socialism. (It is important to note that there were some major defects in Marx's analysis of Asiatic societies, which are attributed to his lack of first-hand knowledge and his Eurocentric prejudices.)[12]

Marx certainly does not glorify British imperialism in India in his writings. Indeed, he harshly criticizes England's role in destroying the Indian handicraft textile industry, first by preventing India from exporting cotton to the European market and then by inundating India with British textiles. Nevertheless, Marx views the stagnant Asiatic society as being even worse than capitalism because it lacked capitalism's capacity for development. He therefore warns us that India's village communities "restrained the human mind within the smallest possible compass, making it the unresisting tool of superstition, enslaving it beneath traditional rule, depriving it of all grandeur and historical energies."[13]

In contrast to his view of stagnating Asiatic societies, Marx considered capitalism to be a dynamic, expansive system with a historical mission to move the development process forward throughout the world. Thus, Marx viewed England as performing a dual function in India—first, in destroying the old Asiatic society, and second, in providing the foundation for Western society in Asia. Without this introduction of Western capitalism, Marx reasoned, the conditions for a Communist revolution in Asia would not be met:

> Can mankind fulfill its destiny without a fundamental revolution in the social state of Asia? If not, whatever may have been the crimes of England, she was the unconscious tool of history in bringing about that revolution.[14]

Although Marx strongly criticized the exploitative nature of British imperialism, he nevertheless viewed it as enabling India to move from the stagnant Asiatic mode of production to the dynamic exploitative mode. The move to the capitalist mode, according to Marx, was a necessary evil because it was a prerequisite for subsequent moves to socialism and communism.

MARXIST STUDIES OF IMPERIALISM

Although Marx raised some important—and contentious—questions about the impact of Western capitalism on non-European societies, systematic studies of imperialism depended on later writers. In contrast to most liberal theories, which emphasize the mutual benefits of international interactions, theories of imperialism portray the world as hierarchically organized, with some societies engaging in conquest and control over others. Most non-Marxists have used the term *imperialism* in reference to a political rather than an economic relationship between advanced metropolitan countries and their colonies or dependencies. It is therefore ironic that a non-Marxist English economist, John A. Hobson (1858–1940), developed one of the most influential economic theories of imperialism. Hobson argued that three major problems plague capitalist societies: low wages and underconsumption by workers, oversaving by capitalists, and overproduction. Although capitalism is highly efficient and contributes to the production of growing surpluses, private owners increase their profits by paying extremely low wages to their workers. As a result, workers in the capitalist countries have very limited purchasing power, and the capitalists must look to countries abroad as an outlet for their excess goods and profits. Their forays into what is now termed the Third World give rise to imperialism.[15]

Despite the influence of Hobson's writings, the most important group of theories of imperialism are Marxist. Indeed, *Imperialism: The Highest Stage of Capitalism* by Vladimir Lenin (1870–1924) became the most widely cited work in this area, even though Lenin borrowed many of his ideas from earlier Marxist and non-Marxist writers.[16] Lenin was interested in the new, expanded form of imperialism of the late nineteenth century, "in which the dominance of monopolies and finance capital [had] established itself" and "the division of all territories of the globe among the great capitalist powers [had] been completed."[17] Lenin, writing in the Marxist tradition, took a far more doctrinaire approach than Hobson. Thus, he maintained that imperialism was the *inevitable* outcome of the highest stage of capitalism and that imperialism could disappear only with the advent of universal socialism.

Like Marx, Lenin argued that capitalism contributes to overproduction and underconsumption, to lower wages and lower employment for the working class, and to falling rates of profit for the capitalists. However, Marx had predicted that the growing misery of the proletariat would lead to revolution in the advanced capitalist countries, and Lenin turned to imperialism to explain why such a revolution had not occurred. Under imperialism, the export of capital and goods to colonial areas provided new "superprofits" for capitalist firms, which helped them avert economic crises. By using a portion of these superprofits to bribe the working class (or "labor aristocracy") in their home countries with higher wages, the capitalists were able to delay the revolution. However, Lenin argued that imperialism did not mark an end to capitalism's underlying contradictions and that the revolution was still inevitable. Once the capitalist states had divided up the globe into colonial areas, competition among them would lead to interimperialist wars and the downfall of capitalism.

Lenin's position on the effects of colonialism on capitalist development in Third World countries was somewhat ambivalent. On the one hand, Lenin predicted that capitalist monopolies would oppose industrialization in the colonial territories and would use the colonies as sources of raw materials and markets for their manufactures. On the other hand, Lenin agreed with Marx that colonialism was also a progressive force that was essential for Third World modernization. Indeed, Lenin maintained that capitalism has an inherent contradiction: it develops rather than underdevelops the Third World. As the Western capitalist states export capital and technology to their colonies, they help create foreign competitors with lower wages, which can outcompete them in world markets. The increase of economic competition between rising and declining capitalist powers eventually leads to economic conflict and imperial rivalries.

Although Marx and Lenin viewed colonialism as a necessary evil that would bring capitalist development to the colonial territories, industrialization and development did not occur as anticipated. For example, even after most Latin American colonies gained their independence from Spain and Portugal in the early nineteenth century, their production continued to be concentrated on primary products, their industrialization was limited, and they were highly dependent on capital and technology from the advanced industrial states. The failure to bring about capitalist development in the colonies and former colonies led to major rifts among the Marxists. Most notably, Otto Kuusinen, a Finnish member at the Sixth Congress of the Communist International (Comintern) in 1928, argued that imperialism was economically regressive rather than progressive as Lenin had maintained. The views of Marxists such as Kuusinen were particularly important: they provided a basis for the arguments of the Latin American dependency movement that emerged after World War II.[18] As the following discussion demonstrates, dependency theorists "turned classical Marxism on its head" and focused on capitalism's role in hindering rather than facilitating Third World development.

DEPENDENCY THEORY

Writers on dependency (or *dependencistas*) were originally Latin American and/or focused on Latin America, and **dependency theory** became the dominant approach to development among Latin American intellectuals in the 1960s. Many of the early studies were published only in Spanish; it was not until a number of years later that most English-speaking scholars became aware of dependency theory.[19] Dependency theorists reject the optimism of liberal modernization theorists (discussed in Chapter 4) and maintain that the advanced capitalist countries either underdevelop the Third World or prevent Third World countries from achieving genuine autonomous development. The discussion here examines the origins, basic tenets, and critiques of dependency theory.

The Origins of Dependency Theory

Dependency theory is based on two major theoretical traditions: Marxism and Latin American structuralism. Some of the most prominent writers on dependency explicitly express their allegiance to Marxism.[20] Dependency theorists, like Marxists, limit their studies almost exclusively to capitalist development, and they adopt much of the language of Marxists, using terms such as *class, mode of production,* and *imperialism.* Dependency theorists and Marxists also have a common commitment to taking political action as well as conveying ideas, and both groups advocate the replacement of capitalism with socialism. However, Marxists take a more doctrinaire approach than many dependency theorists regarding the inevitability of socialism.[21]

A fundamental difference between Marxism and dependency theory is the fact that dependency theorists focus almost exclusively on North-South relations and on development problems in the Third World. As we discussed, dependency theorists also strongly reject Marxist views that Northern industrial countries are performing a service to Third World countries in the long term by contributing to the spread of capitalism. A key figure in the transition from classical Marxism to dependency theory was Paul Baran, whom some refer to as the father of the dependency approach. Baran was the first important Marxist theorist to view the Third World as a major area of study, and he also differed from his predecessors in arguing that capitalist development was a fundamentally different process in advanced and underdeveloped countries. Unlike Marx, who viewed colonialism as enabling countries such as India to advance from the Asiatic to the capitalist mode of production, Baran emphasized the contradictions between the objectives of the advanced capitalist states on the one hand and the development of "backward" nations on the other. Thus, Baran wrote that

> economic development in underdeveloped countries is profoundly inimical to the dominant interests in the advanced capitalist countries. Supplying many important raw materials to the industrialized countries, providing their corporations with vast profits and investment outlets, the backward world has always represented the indispensable hinterland of the highly developed capitalist West. Thus the ruling class in the United States (and elsewhere) is bitterly opposed to the industrialization of the so-called "source countries."[22]

Baran further argued that foreign capitalists prevent Third World industrialization by forming alliances with elites in LDCs who also oppose it. These elites include feudal landed interests and a *comprador class* composed of merchants who import manufactured goods from the industrial states. Baran moved away from the Marxist position to the view that capitalist development in the industrial states occurs *at the expense of* autonomous development in the Third World. His view was to become a fundamental tenet of the dependency approach.

In addition to its beginnings in Marxism, dependency theory also has origins from Latin American structuralism, particularly the ideas of the Argentinian economist Raúl Prebisch, who became director of the United Nations Economic Commission for Latin America (ECLA) in the late 1940s. Prebisch and his followers were called structuralists because they focused on the structural obstacles to Third World development. Prebisch particularly questioned the assumptions of liberal trade theory that everyone benefits from trade, and he argued instead that Third World countries in the periphery of the global economy suffer from declining **terms of trade** with advanced industrial states in the core. Third World countries, according to Prebisch, are at a marked disadvantage because they export mainly primary commodities and import finished goods from the core. While demand for finished goods increases with rising incomes, demand for primary products remains relatively constant (for example, wealthy individuals drink only so much coffee or tea, regardless of their incomes). Furthermore, the industrial states can often develop substitute or synthetic products if Third World countries attempt to charge higher prices for their raw materials.

According to Prebisch and his followers, Third World countries could develop only through government involvement to promote industrialization and decrease dependence on trade with the advanced industrial states. Thus, they advised Third World states to follow import-substituting industrialization policies to protect their industries, imposing tariff and nontariff barriers and emphasizing domestic production rather than exports.[23] A number of LDCs, especially in Latin America, were influenced by Prebisch's structuralist views, and they adopted ISI policies in the 1950s and 1960s. By the 1960s, however, there was growing disillusionment with ISI policies, which contributed to a wide range of problems for LDCs, including uncompetitive industries and growing balance-of-payments deficits. Scholars challenged the Prebisch approach from both the right and the left, and many left-leaning scholars turned to dependency theory. Dependency theorists adopted many of Prebisch's ideas, but their views of both the problems and solutions for the Third World were generally more extreme than those of Prebisch. Unlike Prebisch, for example, most dependency theorists did not believe that the core would ever willingly transfer resources to the periphery, and many dependency theorists called for a domestic social revolution in Third World countries and a severing of contacts with the advanced industrial states.[24]

The Basic Tenets of Dependency Theory

A discussion of the basic tenets of dependency theory is complicated by the fact that there is considerable variation among writers in this tradition. In efforts to organize the discussion and draw comparisons among dependency theorists, the next sections examine the source of Third World problems, possibilities for development in the periphery, and prescriptions for change.

The Source of Third World Problems   Dependency theorists reject the views of liberal theorists that Third World economic problems result primarily from inefficient domestic policies and that greater North-South interdependence promotes Third World development. In contrast, dependency theorists argue that structural factors related to the global capitalist economy are primarily responsible for constraining development possibilities in the Third World. While the core countries benefit from their capitalist global linkages and experience dynamic development based on internal needs, development in the peripheral countries is severely constrained as a result of their interaction with the core.

Although dependency theorists attach primary importance to external constraints on development, they are also interested in the class linkages between individuals within the peripheral and core states. Thus, they describe the development of a class alignment in the South, where elites in Third World countries (*compradores*) act as intermediaries between the capitalist international order on the one hand and the subjected local peoples on the other. While this collaborating *comprador* class may have local concerns, it ultimately depends on the international economic order to ensure its survival as a class. Thus, the main political alliances of the *compradores* are with foreign capitalists, and the elites in the South often take actions that reinforce the pattern of Third World dependency.[25]

LDC Possibilities for Development   Dependency theorists have had differing views regarding LDC possibilities for development. Some early theorists argued that the development of the capitalist economies in the core *requires* the underdevelopment of the periphery. These theorists were highly deterministic: they believed that LDCs cannot escape from underdevelopment as long as they maintain linkages with the wealthy capitalist states. Although today's developed countries may have been *un*developed in the past, they were never *under*developed because they were not part of the periphery in the global capitalist economy. The peripheral countries of today, by contrast, became underdeveloped *as a result of* their involvement with the countries in the capitalist core.[26]

However, theorists who argued that underdevelopment was the only possible fate for peripheral countries found it increasingly difficult to explain why industrialization *was* occurring in some LDCs. Liberals, realists, and some Marxists all pointed to the fact that newly industrialized countries such as South Korea, Taiwan, Brazil, and Mexico were experiencing impressive economic growth rates. Dependency theorists responded to this dilemma by introducing the concept of *dependent development.*[27] Certain LDCs can undergo development, according to this view, when a particularly favorable alliance forms between foreign capital, domestic capital, and the Third World state. This alliance enables the Third World country to benefit from capital accumulation and from some degree of industrialization.

Those who write about dependent development are more attuned than earlier dependency theorists to the wide variety of local conditions and dependency relations in the Third World. Despite recognizing the diversity of LDC situations, however, these authors maintain that even the more favored LDCs remain fundamentally dependent and cannot attain genuine autonomous development. In the final analysis, those LDCs experiencing dependent development cannot escape from their dependent linkages with the core countries, and their development is therefore conditioned by the requirements of the core. Dependency theorists argue that although the NICs seem to be examples of success in the Third World, workers in these countries often receive low wages and produce less technologically sophisticated goods than those of the industrial states in the core.[28]

Prescriptions for Change   Dependency theorists believe that LDCs cannot escape from their dependent position in the capitalist system; thus, they often prescribe a breaking of linkages with the core countries and/or a socialist revolution to bring about more social justice and equality. The goals of autonomy and socialism are not necessarily compatible, however, and theorists do not explicitly state which of these two goals is more important for decreasing dependency. Those who emphasize autonomy tend to call for highly nationalistic and antiforeign actions such as the cutting of linkages with the developed core states. Such actions do not ensure that the other goal of dependency theorists will be achieved; policies that increase a state's autonomy do not ensure that there will be more social justice or equality for the bulk of the population.

Nevertheless, dependency theorists at least hope that an end to dependent linkages will lead a country to "emphasize distribution and participation rather than accumulation and exclusion."[29]

Although dependency theorists call for socialism as one of their two main goals, they do not clearly indicate what they mean by the term, they do not explain how a socialist revolution will enable countries to escape dependency, and they do not describe how the revolution will occur. Dependency theorists also do not explain how peripheral countries can become more autonomous and "de-link" themselves from the core countries. The vagueness of prescriptions in dependency theory relates partly to the tension between the goals of autonomy and socialism and partly to the fact that Marxist-Leninist predictions regarding a socialist revolution in the advanced industrial states often proved to be inaccurate.

Critiques of Dependency Theory

Dependency theory became a favorite target of criticism in the 1970s and 1980s, and other theories have subsequently become more important in the historical structuralist school. One major criticism is that dependency theorists do not adequately define their basic concepts. For example, theorists tend to view countries in dichotomous terms as either dependent or not dependent, and it is unclear how one can measure lesser or greater *degrees* of dependence. There are also different *forms* of dependence, such as military, economic, and cultural dependence, but these different forms are not usually identified. Furthermore, "developed versus underdeveloped" or "core versus periphery" are extremely broad categories that include a wide range of countries. What does the term *underdeveloped* signify when it includes countries as diverse as Brazil, India, and Haiti? How does one justify including Portugal along with the United States, Japan, and Germany as a developed country in the core? Critics argue that these concepts are too vague to make the types of distinctions required for good theorizing.[30]

A second criticism relates to the preoccupation of dependency theorists with capitalism and their failure to consider other forms of exploitation. Some critics argue that the most important factor in dependency is not capitalism (as dependency theorists maintain) but unequal power among states. As long as power is unequal, larger and more powerful states are able to impose dependence on smaller states.[31] Thus, some scholars have done studies of the former Soviet bloc to demonstrate that dependency relations can also exist in noncapitalist systems. These studies show some marked differences between the Soviet and Western systems. For example, postwar Soviet dominance contributed to rapid industrialization with an emphasis on heavy industry in Eastern Europe, which was quite different from the Western model in the Third World; and political linkages were more important in the Soviet bloc, while economic linkages were central to the West's relations with the South. Despite the differences, however, both the Soviet and the capitalist systems were marked by "asymmetric and unequal linkages between a dominant center and its weaker dependencies."[32]

A third criticism is that dependency theory attaches too much importance to the international system and too little to domestic policies and behavior as a source of LDC development problems. Although some of the more astute dependency theorists do focus on domestic structures in Third World states, they continue to give primacy to the importance of external factors. Dependency theorists therefore have a tendency to portray LDCs as being virtually helpless vis-à-vis outside forces, and they cannot adequately explain why Third World countries sometimes respond in very different ways to similar external constraints. To explain such differences, critics charge, it is necessary to consider the importance of domestic economic and political factors.[33]

A fourth criticism is that dependency theory's predictions regarding Third World development prospects are often incorrect. For example, China was often held up as a model of agrarian self-reliance, but in 1976 it turned to a policy of openness rather than closure to promote national development. This change in policy contributed to rapid economic growth in China, and LDCs that are the most integrated in the world economy are sometimes the fastest-growing countries. Finally, we should note that even Marxists criticize dependency theorists for being overly nationalistic and not sufficiently Marxist. These scholars insist that the most fundamental problem is not *foreign* control or domination, as some dependency theorists maintain, but *private* control and domination of the means of production. Thus, they criticize dependency theorists for putting more emphasis on "relations of exchange" (i.e., between core and peripheral states) than on "relations of production" (i.e., between the proletariat and the bourgeoisie).[34]

The numerous criticisms of dependency theory from both the right and the left have had a telling effect. Thus, one noted dependency theorist predicted in 1985 that the dependency label would disappear because the term was "too closely associated with simplistic hypotheses of external determination" and "the impossibility of either capitalism or democracy on the periphery."[35] Some writers have tried to bring back dependency theory or examine its relevance today, but historical structuralists have in general turned their attention to other theoretical approaches. Despite the demise of dependency theory, many of the concerns of these theorists still have relevance today and serve an important role in counterbalancing the biases of the liberal and realist perspectives. In an age of global competition, there is a persistence of hierarchy among states, and a further marginalization of some countries and regions, particularly in the Third World. It is therefore important to heed the message of dependency theorists that genuine economic development can only occur in "a world respecting equality and difference."[36] The next section raises questions about the future of the historical structuralist perspective in view of the breakup of the Soviet bloc and the Soviet Union, and the final sections of the chapter discuss some historical structuralist approaches that seem to be particularly promising.

WHITHER THE HISTORICAL STRUCTURALIST SCHOOL OF IPE?

With the failed predictions of the Marxist-Leninists regarding the downfall of capitalism and the problems with some historical structuralist approaches such as dependency theory, numerous questions were raised about the vitality of the historical structuralist perspective in general. Since the breakup of the Soviet bloc and the end of the

Cold War in the late 1980s and early 1990s, some theorists have launched the harshest criticism of all: that the historical structuralist perspective has become irrelevant. For example, one liberal theorist argues that "the implosion of the Soviet Union, and domestic changes in Eastern Europe, have eliminated the significance of the socialist economic model"; and another claims that the discrediting of Marxism-Leninism is leading to "an unabashed victory of economic and political liberalism."[37] Many observers are also referring to the "triumph" of liberalism in the Third World. LDCs in the 1960s and 1970s turned to economic nationalism, state socialism, and trade protectionism, but there has been a marked turnaround in their policies today. For a number of reasons discussed in this book, LDCs since the 1980s have been moving en masse toward liberal policies of reduced state intervention in the economy, increased reliance on the market, and liberalized trade and foreign investment policies.[38]

Despite these negative prognostications about the historical structuralist perspective, it continues to have major relevance today. Most importantly, historical structuralists devote considerable attention to the poorest and weakest individuals and states and to distributive justice issues, which are not dealt with adequately by either liberals or realists. While liberals and realists accept the capitalist system largely as a given, the historical structuralists raise serious questions about inequality and exploitation under capitalism, and they discuss the possibilities of alternative systems. Historical structuralism continues to be an important perspective in IPE, and the following sections discuss three theoretical approaches with linkages to this school of thought that are currently of considerable interest: world-system theory, Gramscian theory, and the business conflict model.

World-System Theory

World-system theory has many similarities with dependency theory, and some former dependency theorists now identify themselves as world-system theorists. Like dependency theorists, world-system theorists view capitalism as basically exploitative, and they openly advocate major changes in global economic relations. Nevertheless, world-system theory is accepted as more relevant than dependency theory today because the world-system approach is more broad-ranging and flexible. Instead of limiting their inquiry to the peripheral states as dependency theorists do, world-system theorists (as their name indicates) focus on the entire world system. They are concerned not only with the exploitation of states in the periphery but also with relationships among states in the core and with the rise and decline of hegemonic states. World-system theorists also delve more deeply than dependency theorists into the historical development of capitalism in their attempts to explain the core's exploitation of the periphery. Indeed, much world-system analysis extends back to at least the sixteenth century. Finally, as we will discuss, world-system analysts introduce the concept of the semiperiphery, and they question the dependency theorists' view that all Third World states must be permanently relegated to the periphery.[39]

Only a brief discussion of world-system theory is provided here; the student should refer to more detailed sources.[40] Although the fundamentals of the world-system approach derive largely from the voluminous works of Immanuel Wallerstein, there are of course other important world-system theorists, such as Christopher

Chase-Dunn. There are some major differences in view among world-system theorists; the discussion that follows refers primarily to the writings of Wallerstein.

The main unit of analysis in world-system theory is the world-system, which can be defined as "a unit with a single division of labor and multiple cultural systems."[41] World-systems can be of two major types: *world-empires*, which have a common political system, and *world-economies*, which do not have a common political system. Today there is only one world-system, a world-economy that is capitalist in form. This capitalist system became predominant with the emergence of the modern world-economy in Europe during the "long" sixteenth century (1450–1640). The essential feature of a capitalist world-economy is production for sale in a market with the goal of realizing the maximum profit. Capitalism is also characterized by unequal exchange relationships, which strong core states enforce on weak peripheral areas. Thus, Wallerstein argues that "capitalism involves not only appropriation of the surplus value by an owner from a laborer, but an appropriation of surplus of the whole world-economy by core areas."[42]

World-system theorists take the capitalist world-economy as their main unit of analysis; they do not consider states to be meaningful actors in their own right, apart from their position in the world-economy.[43] Thus, long before the breakup of the Soviet Union, Wallerstein always rejected the idea that truly socialist states could exist in a capitalist world-economy:

> There are today no socialist systems in the world-economy any more than there are feudal systems because there is *one* world-system. It is a world-economy and it is by definition capitalist in form.[44]

World-system theorists also believe that neither the internal nor the external strength of a state can be viewed separately from its position in the world-economy. Core states are therefore relatively strong states by definition, and peripheral states are relatively weak.

In response to the fact that some Third World states, such as the East Asian and Latin American NICs, are industrializing, world-system theorists modify the classical dependency argument by asserting that a limited number of countries can ascend to a *semiperiphery*, which is situated somewhere between the periphery and the core. Semiperipheral states have more capital-intensive industry than peripheral states but less than core states, and they also are stronger and more autonomous from the core than peripheral states.[45] Although some states in the semiperiphery seem to be models of economic success, they are in fact simply "the more advanced exemplars of dependent development" because they are still dependent on the core.[46] It is possible, according to world-system theorists, for states to ascend from the periphery to the semiperiphery and then from the semiperiphery to the core. It is also possible for some states to descend from the core to the semiperiphery. Nevertheless, world-system theorists are far more pessimistic than liberal theorists about the future prospects for today's Third World countries, and they believe that a country's ascent from the periphery is a relatively rare occurrence. Thus, world-system theorists consider the division of the world-economy into the core, periphery, and semiperiphery to be an enduring feature of the capitalist world-economy.[47]

In the world-system view, the existence of the semiperiphery contributes to the stability of the capitalist world-economy and to the continued predominance of the industrial states in the core. The distribution of wealth and power in the capitalist world-economy is highly unequal, and it would be natural for the peripheral countries to directly confront the core countries that acquire most of the benefits. The periphery includes the overwhelming majority of states, and a rebellion against the minority of states within the core would have a good chance of success if the periphery remained united. However, the semiperipheral states divide the majority in the periphery so that the core states are not faced with a unified opposition. Even though the semiperipheral states are disadvantaged by capitalism, they "tend to think of themselves primarily as better off than the lower sector rather than as worse off than the upper sector."[48] They therefore have a dual role as both exploiter and exploited, effectively dividing the periphery and stabilizing the capitalist world-economy.

The continued expansion of the core combined with some growth of the semiperiphery has contributed to a less polarized and more politically stable capitalist world-economy and to a further weakening of the periphery. Despite this apparent political stability, however, the capitalist world-economy continues to have contradictions that could threaten its long-term survival. World-system theorists therefore raise the prospect of the decline of the capitalist world-economy and its replacement by socialism, but their predictions regarding the timing of these changes are surprisingly vague and long-term. For example, Wallerstein asserts that the internal contradictions in the capitalist world-economy should "bring it to an end in the twenty-first or twenty-second century."[49] Wallerstein believes that socialism could become a new type of world-system, but he is vague about when such a new world-system will develop.

Liberal, realist, and Marxist scholars express numerous criticisms of world-system theory, which in many cases are similar to the critiques of dependency theory. For example, both liberals and Marxists claim that world-system theorists place too much emphasis on external factors and too little emphasis on internal factors in explaining conditions in the periphery; they also criticize world-system analysis for disregarding the positive effects that the core capitalist states may have on the peripheral states. Furthermore, some classical Marxists charge that world-system theorists (like dependency theorists) place more emphasis on "relations of exchange" between core, semiperipheral, and peripheral states than on the far more important "relations of production" between capitalists and workers.

Realists are especially critical of world-system theorists for overemphasizing economic relationships and underemphasizing the role of the state. Thus, they accuse Wallerstein of rather simplistically assuming that "strong states" naturally exist in the core and that "weak states" are found in the periphery. Many authors have provided counterexamples that challenge such statements. First, they argue that some of the strongest states in the sixteenth century (e.g., Spain and Sweden) were in the periphery, while the core states of this period, Holland and England, had relatively weak state structures. Second, they note that "late industrializers" have often demonstrated successful development because of strong state leadership. This was true of Russia and Germany in the past, and it is true of the East Asian NICs (the semiperiphery) today. Finally, some writers argue that the United States, which remains the leading economic and military power today, is a relatively weak state because of its separation of powers and its federal division of powers.[50]

Despite the numerous criticisms of world-system theory, it provides us with an important alternative approach to the study of IPE. As historical structuralists, world-system theorists offer a long-term historical view of social, economic, and political change going back to at least the sixteenth century. This contrasts with theorists in the other two IPE perspectives, who either have been ahistorical in their approach or have devoted too little attention to historical change. For example, the views of liberal modernization theorists that Third World countries could and should follow the development path of Western industrial states proved to be misguided, but many liberals still adhere to a (more sophisticated) variation on these views today. Critics understandably argue that liberals underestimate the importance of historical differences between the industrializing countries in the past and the Third World countries today. In view of historical and other changes, Third World countries today neither may be able nor may choose to follow the development path Western developed countries have taken in the past.

World-system theory also avoids some of the pitfalls of dependency theory by asserting that countries can sometimes ascend from the periphery to the semiperiphery and the core. However, world-system theorists avoid the overoptimism of liberal theorists regarding the prospects for ascent from the periphery. Unlike realists and liberals, world-system theorists focus on the poorest and weakest in the periphery of society and on the exploitation of the periphery by the core. While world-system theorists may be accused of overestimating the degree to which external exploitation causes Third World problems, realists and liberals err in the opposite direction by largely ignoring the role of external exploitation of the poor and weak in the capitalist world-economy. Even those realists and liberals who are critical of some aspects of capitalism, accept it largely as a given.

World-system theorists have proved to be flexible and dynamic as a group, able to adjust their theoretical views in response to criticism. This brief description of the world-system approach does not convey the degree to which there is a wide variation of views among world-system theorists or the degree to which world-system theory is evolving.

Gramscian Analysis

Antonio Gramsci, a former leader of the Italian Communist party, drew many of his ideas from Marxism. Gramsci argued, however, that Marxism was overly economistic; that is, it exaggerated the importance of economics relative to political, social, and cultural factors. Thus, classical Marxists were unable to explain crucial aspects of political and social reality during Gramsci's time, such as the role of Catholicism and the rise of Mussolini in Italy. The domination of capitalism, Gramsci asserted, depends only partly on economic factors such as the private ownership of the means of production. To understand capitalist domination, the student must also be familiar with the political, ideological, and cultural aspects of class struggle. Similarly, we must consider politics and culture as well as economics when discussing the reorganization of society under socialism. Thus, Gramsci placed much more emphasis than classical Marxists on the role of culture and ideas in explaining societal organization and change.[51]

As noted in Chapter 3, the Gramscian view of hegemony is quite different from that of the realists. Unlike the realists, who identify hegemony solely with the predominant power of a nation-state (or a group of core states), Gramscians also view hegemony in terms of class relationships. The hegemonic rule of a particular class, according to Gramsci, is based not only on coercion but even more importantly on social-moral leadership. In other words, the ruling class gains the active consent of the subordinate class on the basis of shared values, ideas, and material interests. The bourgeoisie often achieve such a consensus by providing the subordinate classes with a range of concessions, such as social and economic benefits and support for workers' efforts to organize labor unions. In return, the subordinate classes are accepting or even supportive of continued leadership by the bourgeoisie. When a hegemonic structure of thought and action develops, subordinate groups therefore find it very difficult to even conceive of developing an alternative structure based on different ideas and values.

Gramscian theorists use the term *historic bloc* to refer to the congruence between state power on the one hand and the prevailing ideas guiding the society and the economy on the other. The historic bloc established under bourgeois hegemony is difficult for subordinate groups to replace because it is supported not only by physical power but also by the power of ideas. Like the classical Marxists, Gramsci was committed to political action as well as theory, and he wrote about the importance of building a *counterhegemony* among subordinate groups. A counterhegemony is an alternative ethical view of society that poses a challenge to the dominant bourgeois-led view. If subordinate groups become sufficiently dissatisfied, a proletarian-led counterhegemony organized around socialist ideas could pose a challenge to the bourgeois-led hegemony organized around capitalism. For example, the propensity of governments today to decrease socioeconomic benefits to subordinate classes in an age of global competitiveness might eventually cause disadvantaged groups to pose such a counterhegemonic challenge. If the proletariat succeeded in supplanting bourgeois hegemony with their own counterhegemony, they would create a new historic bloc based on socialism.[52]

Gramsci's analysis was limited primarily to the national level. Writers such as Robert Cox and Stephen Gill have extended his ideas and applied them to international relations. They argue that in this age of globalized production and exchange, a *transnational historic bloc* may be developing. The main institutions in this bloc are the largest multinational corporations, international banks, international organizations such as the IMF and the World Bank, and international business groups in the most powerful capitalist states. With the development of a transnational bloc, class relations can now be viewed on a global scale. As discussed in Chapter 4, the predominant strand of liberalism in the post–World War II period was interventionist in nature; it drew on Keynesianism and viewed government intervention as necessary to counteract the socially unacceptable aspects of the market. Thus, countries balanced movement toward greater openness in the international economy with measures to cushion the effects on vulnerable groups in society through such measures as welfare and unemployment insurance. According to Gramscian theorists, the developing transnational historic bloc is threatening the interventionist liberal compromise of the postwar period.

A crucial element of this transnational historic bloc is the power and mobility of transnational capital, which is putting both national labor unions and national business groups on the defensive. As discussed in Chapter 6 on monetary relations, the advanced industrial states imposed controls on capital flows in the 1950s and 1960s, but these controls were gradually removed beginning in the 1970s. The increased ability of transnational capital and MNCs to shift location from one country to another enables them to play off national labor groups—which are relatively immobile—against one another. Those workers who are employed by MNCs in both the core and the periphery also tend to identify their own interests with those of transnational capital, and this attitude divides the working class and further limits its ability to build a counterhegemony. The transnational historic bloc is also posing a threat to the ability of elected governments to make autonomous policy decisions. The recessionary conditions in the 1980s, for example, induced states to engage in "competitive deregulation" of their national **capital markets** in efforts to attract more capital and foreign investment, accelerating the reduction of barriers to capital mobility. Further solidifying this transnational historic bloc is a hegemonic ideology, which portrays capital mobility as contributing to economic efficiency, consumer welfare, and economic growth.[53]

Despite the emergence of a bourgeois transnational historic bloc, there are indications that dissatisfaction with the transnational liberal forces could eventually stimulate a counterhegemonic response. For example, IMF and World Bank structural adjustment loans or SALs (discussed in Chapter 7), which are linked to pressures for privatization, deregulation, and trade liberalization, are creating resentment in some Third World recipient countries; and there is disillusionment with moves toward a market economy in Eastern European and former Soviet Union countries. Gramscian theorists therefore argue that although the forces of transnational capital are currently in the ascendancy, this situation may not continue indefinitely.

Gramscian analysis, like world-system theory, has been criticized on a number of grounds. For example, critics charge that Gramscians (like Marxists, dependency theorists, and world-system theorists) are so preoccupied with examining the problems of capitalism and the hegemony of transnational capital that they do not explore the potential problems of dominance and subordination in other possible global systems (e.g., socialism). Gramscians may have avoided some of the pitfalls of classical Marxists, who often made unrealized predictions regarding the downfall of capitalism; in efforts to avoid being proved wrong, however, Gramscians provide little guidance as to when a counterhegemony to the emerging transnational historic bloc might develop and what form this counterhegemony might take. As a result, Gramscians, like world-system theorists, are better at pointing to the problems with the capitalist system than they are at offering solutions.

Despite these criticisms, Gramscian analysis, like world-system theory, has many important strengths. For example, the Gramscian view of hegemony has many advantages over the realist and liberal views. As we discussed, realists and liberals define hegemony in state-centric terms, and they can identify only two or three times when there was a hegemonic state (Britain, the United States, and perhaps the Netherlands). Their ability to examine the effects of hegemony on IPE is therefore limited to only two or three relatively brief historical periods. *Gramscian* theorists, by contrast, use the term *hegemony* in a cultural sense to connote the complex of *ideas* that social groups use to assert their legitimacy and authority, and they also extend the concept of hegemony to include nonstate actors such as multinational corporations and international banks as well as nation-states. Thus, the Gramscian concept of hegemony is far less restrictive, and we can use it to examine a far wider range of events in the international economy.

The Business Conflict Model

The business conflict model, like hegemonic stability theory and regime theory, is a hybrid approach that draws on more than one theoretical perspective (in this case, historical structuralism and liberalism).[54] According to business conflict theorists, business groups—especially large corporations—are the most important societal groups affecting government policymaking, but there are major cleavages within the business community over policy issues. The cleavages include "divisions among corporations of different nationalities, among corporations of the same nationality, and among internationally owned corporations."[55] These divisions lead to conflicts within and among states with regard to policy, and they have a major impact on government policy processes and output. Business conflict theorists examine conflicts that occur within as well as across state borders, providing another example of the growing trend in IPE toward studying domestic-international interactions.

The business conflict model is discussed with historical structuralism because it emphasizes class (that is, business) as a major factor in foreign policymaking and views business firms as being motivated primarily by profit. Nevertheless, there are significant differences between business conflict theorists and instrumental Marxists, who argue that "the state serves the interests of the capitalist class because it is controlled by this class."[56] Instrumental Marxists simply assume that the capitalist class is united in furthering its interests, while business conflict theorists maintain that divisions among capitalists are pervasive. Business conflict theorists are also highly critical of structural Marxists, who believe that the state (while committed to ensuring the long-term survival of capitalism) is relatively autonomous from direct political pressure of the capitalist class. In the view of business conflict theorists, the state does not have relative autonomy from the pressure of business groups, even in the short term.[57] The business conflict model has some similarity with liberal pluralism. Both are society-centered theories that emphasize the role of interest groups in government policymaking. In the view of pluralists, however, no single interest group or class dominates society and the state. Business conflict theorists, by contrast, believe that "business groups have often been able to shape and direct . . . foreign investment and trade strategy independent of other pressure groups."[58]

In the view of business conflict theorists, the most significant division in the business community is between internationalist and nationalist business groups.[59] Nationalist firms are smaller and oriented primarily to the domestic market; internationalist firms are larger, more competitive, and heavily involved with foreign trade and investment. The diverse positions of the nationalist and internationalist firms give them different vested interests in policymaking. For example, nationalist firms often feel threatened by imports and favor trade protectionism, while internationalist firms with integrated multinational operations and substantial dependence on exports resist protectionism and favor open international markets.[60]

In pressuring for more open foreign trade and investment policies, internationalist business firms usually benefit from a close working relationship with the executive branch in the United States. Business internationalists also form organizations to influence and work with U.S. foreign policy officials, who are more likely to listen to the internationalists than to other groups. Smaller domestic business groups, which are more inclined to favor economic closure and protectionism, do not benefit from such connections with the U.S. foreign policy establishment. As a result, business nationalists often concentrate their efforts on influencing congressional committees that affect foreign policy outcomes. Although domestic businesses lack the wealth, connections, and expertise of the business internationalists, the diverse membership of Congress permits domestic business to gain influence by targeting individual representatives. Thus, protectionist pressures from domestic business in Congress often collide with business internationalist pressures for liberalization in the executive branch of government.

Even internationalist business groups are sometimes divided among themselves over foreign economic strategies, and this situation can have an impact on their ability to influence policymaking. For example, internationalist firms that depend extensively on labor-intensive production in Third World countries often favor military force to quell leftist insurgencies, and they support military governments that discipline the domestic labor force and ensure that wages are low. Internationalist firms that are less labor-intensive, by contrast, are less likely to support military action.[61] The business conflict model postulates that divisions between business nationalists and internationalists and divisions among internationalists are reflected in foreign policy outcomes. The model is a promising new approach to foreign economic policymaking that draws on both historical structuralism and liberal pluralism.

CONCLUSION

The relative influence of the three major perspectives on IPE as a discipline varies over time. The historical structuralist perspective may have faltered in recent years, but there are a number of promising new theoretical approaches in this school of thought. It is also certainly possible that the historical structuralist perspective could gain more influence in the future. Current pressures to replace postwar interventionist liberalism with a return to liberal orthodoxy is causing considerable dissatisfaction among many "have-nots" in society, providing a stimulus to a possible revival of historical structuralism. Furthermore, although some historical structuralist approaches, such as dependency theory, have been discredited in recent years, many of the concerns of dependency theorists continue to be relevant. Recent advances in world-system, Gramscian, business conflict, and other theories in this school clearly indicate that historical structuralism provides an important alternative perspective to the liberal and realist views.

NOTES

1. The seminal structural realist (or neorealist) study is Kenneth N. Waltz, *Theory of International Politics* (Reading, MA: Addison-Wesley, 1979). See also Robert O. Keohane, "Theory

of World Politics: Structural Realism and Beyond," in Robert O. Keohane, ed., *Neorealism and Its Critics* (New York: Columbia University Press, 1986), pp. 158–203.

2. The term *historical structuralism* emerged in discussions with a colleague, Professor James Busumtwi-Sam, for which I am grateful.

3. Karl Marx and Friedrich Engels, *The Communist Manifesto* (New York: International Publishers, 1948), p. 9.

4. For a discussion of the two strands of Marxist writing on the state, see Bob Jessop, *The Capitalist State: Marxist Theories and Methods* (Oxford, UK: Martin Robertson, 1982), pp. 1–31; and David Held, *Models of Democracy* (Cambridge, UK: Polity Press, 1987), pp. 113–121.

5. Marx and Engels, *The Communist Manifesto*, p. 29.

6. See V. I. Lenin, *Imperialism: The Highest Stage of Capitalism* (New York: International Publishers, revised translation, 1939).

7. See, for example, Jack Woddis, *An Introduction to Neo-Colonialism* (London: Lawrence & Wishart, 1967); and Harry Magdoff, "Imperialism Without Colonies," in Roger Owen and Bob Sutcliffe, eds., *Studies in the Theory of Imperialism* (London: Longman, 1981), pp. 144–169.

8. Some authors argue that Marx was not a strict economic determinist. See, for example, David McLellan, *Marx* (London: Fontana/Collins, 7th ed., 1980), p. 41; and Gabriel Palma, "Dependency: A Formal Theory of Underdevelopment or a Methodology for the Analysis of Concrete Situations of Underdevelopment?" *World Development* 6-7/8 (July/August 1978), pp. 883–884.

9. Ralph Miliband, *The State in Capitalist Society* (New York: Basic Books, 1969), p. 66. On instrumental Marxism, see David A. Gold, Clarence Y. H. Lo, and Erik Olin Wright, "Recent Developments in Marxist Theories of the Capitalist State," *Monthly Review* 27-5 (October 1975), pp. 32–35.

10. For a discussion of structural Marxism, see Gold, Lo, and Wright, "Recent Developments in Marxist Theories of the Capitalist State," pp. 35–40; and Pat McGowan and Stephen G. Walker, "Radical and Conventional Models of U.S. Foreign Economic Policy Making," *World Politics* 33-3 (April 1981), pp. 357–360.

11. Marx's writings on the non-European world are contained in Shlomo Avineri, ed., *Karl Marx on Colonialism and Modernization: His Despatches and Other Writings on China, India, Mexico, the Middle East and North Africa* (Garden City, NY: Doubleday, 1968). For conflicting interpretations of Marx's views of the Third World, see Carlos Johnson, "Ideologies in Theories of Imperialism and Dependency," in Ronald H. Chilcote and Dale L. Johnson, eds., *Theories of Development: Mode of Production or Dependency?* (Beverly Hills, CA: Sage, 1983), pp. 75–104.

12. Brendan O'Leary, *The Asiatic Mode of Production: Oriental Despotism, Historical Materialism and Indian History* (Oxford, UK: Basil Blackwell, 1989), p. 263. See also see Anthony Giddens, *Capitalism and Modern Social Theory: An Analysis of the Writings of Marx, Durkheim and Max Weber* (Cambridge: Cambridge University Press, 1971), pp. 24–27; Lawrence Krader, *The Asiatic Mode of Production: Sources, Development and Critique in the Writings of Karl Marx* (Assen, The Netherlands: Van Grocum & Comp., 1975); and Timothy Brook, ed., *The Asiatic Mode of Production in China* (Armonk, NY: M.E. Sharpe, 1989).

13. Karl Marx, "The British Rule in India," in Avineri, ed., *Karl Marx on Colonialism and Modernization*, pp. 86–88.

14. Marx, "The British Rule in India," p. 481.

15. J. A. Hobson, *Imperialism: A Study* (Ann Arbor: University of Michigan Press, 1965), p. 81.

16. For differing views of Lenin's contribution to the study of imperialism, see Anthony Brewer, *Marxist Theories of Imperialism: A Critical Survey* (London: Routledge, 2nd ed., 1990), p. 116; and Tom Kemp, "The Marxist Theory of Imperialism," in Roger Owen and Bob Sutcliffe, eds., *Studies in the Theory of Imperialism* (London: Longman, 1972), pp. 26–30.

17. Lenin, *Imperialism: The Highest Stage of Capitalism,* p. 89.

18. Thomas Biersteker, "Evolving Perspectives on International Political Economy: Twentieth-Century Discontinuities," *International Political Science Review* 14-1 (January 1993), p. 12; Palma, "Dependency," pp. 896–897.

19. For example, a seminal study on dependency theory is *Dependencia y desarrollo en América Latina* by Cardoso and Faletto, but it was not available in an English edition until eight years after it was published. See Fernando Henrique Cardoso and Enzo Faletto, *Dependency and Development in Latin America,* translated by Marjory Mattingly Urquidi (Berkeley: University of California Press, 1979).

20. See, for example, Peter Evans, "After Dependency: Recent Studies of Class, State, and Industrialization," *Latin American Research Review* 20-2 (1985), p. 159; and Cardoso and Faletto, *Dependency and Development in Latin America,* p. ix.

21. Aidan Foster-Carter, "From Rostow to Gunder Frank: Conflicting Paradigms in the Analysis of Underdevelopment," *World Development* 4-3 (March 1976), p. 175.

22. Paul A. Baran, *The Political Economy of Growth* (New York: Monthly Review Press, 1962), pp. 11–12.

23. See Raúl Prebisch, "The Economic Development of Latin America and Its Principal Problems," *Economic Bulletin for Latin America* 7-1 (February 1962), pp. 1–22 (First published in Spanish in May 1950).

24. Joseph L. Love, "The Origins of Dependency Analysis," *Journal of Latin American Studies* 22 (February 1990), pp. 143–60.

25. Tony Smith, "Requiem or New Agenda for Third World Studies?" *World Politics* 37-4 (July 1985), pp. 546–547.

26. The most important early dependency theorist taking such a deterministic approach was André Gunder Frank. See, for example, Frank's "The Development of Underdevelopment," *Monthly Review* 18-4 (September 1966), pp. 17–31. Not all early dependency theorists were as deterministic as Frank. For example, see Cardoso and Faletto, *Dependency and Development in Latin America.*

27. See, for example, Peter Evans, *Dependent Development: The Alliance of Multinational, State, and Local Capital in Brazil* (Princeton, NJ: Princeton University Press, 1979); and Gary Gereffi, *The Pharmaceutical Industry and Dependency in the Third World* (Princeton, NJ: Princeton University Press, 1983).

28. André Gunder Frank, "Asia's Exclusive Models," *Far Eastern Economic Review* 116-26 (June 25, 1982), p. 23.

29. Evans, *Dependent Development,* p. 329. See also Gereffi, *The Pharmaceutical Industry and Dependency in the Third World,* p. 24.

30. See Colin Leys, "Underdevelopment and Dependency: Critical Notes," *Journal of Contemporary Asia* 7-1 (1977), pp. 92–107.

31. David Ray, "The Dependency Model of Latin American Underdevelopment: Three Basic Fallacies," *Journal of Interamerican Studies and World Affairs* 15-1 (February 1973), pp. 7–8.

Although some dependency theorists acknowledge that dependent relationships can exist between socialist countries, they generally limit their analyses to the capitalist system.

32. Cal Clark and Donna Bahry, "Dependent Development: A Socialist Variant," *International Studies Quarterly* 27-3 (September 1983), p. 286.

33. Tony Smith, "The Underdevelopment of Development Literature: The Case of Dependency Theory," *World Politics* 31-2 (January 1979), pp. 257–258; Stephan Haggard, "The Newly Industrializing Countries in the International System," *World Politics* 38-2 (January 1986), p. 346.

34. Ernesto Laclau, "Feudalism and Capitalism in Latin America," *New Left Review* 67 (May–June, 1971), p. 25. See also Bill Warren, "Imperialism and Capitalist Industrialization," *New Left Review* 81 (September–October 1973), pp. 3–45.

35. Evans, "After Dependency," p. 158.

36. David L. Blaney, "Reconceptualizing Autonomy: The Difference Dependency Theory Makes," *Review of International Political Economy* 3-3 (Autumn 1996), p. 485. See also Geisa Maria Rochal, "Redefining the Role of the Bourgeoisie in Dependent Capitalist Development: Privatization and Liberalization in Brazil," *Latin American Perspectives* 21-1 (Winter, 1994), pp. 72–98; and Jill Hills, "Dependency Theory and Its Relevance Today: International Institutions in Telecommunications and Structural Power," *Review of International Studies* 20-2 (April, 1994), pp. 169–186.

37. John Gerard Ruggie, "Multilateralism: The Anatomy of an Institution," in John Gerard Ruggie, ed., *Multilateralism Matters: The Theory and Praxis of an Institutional Form* (New York: Columbia University Press, 1993), p. 33; Francis Fukuyama, "The End of History?" *The National Interest* 16 (Summer 1989), pp. 3, 11.

38. Thomas J. Biersteker, "The 'Triumph' of Neoclassical Economics in the Developing World: Policy Convergence and Bases of Governance in the International Economic Order," in James N. Rosenau and Ernst-Otto Czempiel, eds., *Governance Without Government: Order and Change in World Politics* (Cambridge: Cambridge University Press, 1992), pp. 102–131.

39. For a discussion of the differences between dependency and world-system theory, see Peter Evans, "Beyond Center and Periphery: A Comment on the Contribution of the World System Approach to the Study of Development," *Sociological Inquiry* 49-4 (1979), pp. 15–20.

40. A very useful beginning source on world-system theory is Thomas R. Shannon, *An Introduction to the World-System Perspective* (Boulder, CO: Westview Press, 2nd edition, 1996).

41. Immanuel Wallerstein, "The Rise and Future Demise of the World Capitalist System: Concepts for Comparative Analysis," in Immanuel Wallerstein, *The Capitalist World-Economy* (New York: Cambridge University Press, 1979), p. 5.

42. Wallerstein, "The Rise and Future Demise of the World Capitalist System," pp. 18–19.

43. Immanuel Wallerstein, "Class Formation in the Capitalist World-Economy," in Wallerstein, *The Capitalist World-Economy*, p. 230.

44. Wallerstein, "The Rise and Future Demise of the World Capitalist System," p. 35.

45. Wallerstein was not the first to refer to a middle "class" between the center and the periphery. Ruy Mauro Marini referred to "subimperial states," and Johan Galtung described "go-between" nations. See Ruy Mauro Marini *Subdesarollo y Revolución* (Mexico: Siglo Veintiuno, 9th edition, 1978); and Johan Galtung, "A Structural Theory of Imperialism," *Journal of Peace Research* 8-2 (1971), p. 104.

46. Evans, *Dependent Development,* p. 33.

47. Shannon, *An Introduction to the World-System Perspective,* pp. 146–149.

48. Immanuel Wallerstein, "Dependence in an Interdependent World: The Limited Possibilities of Transformation Within the Capitalist World-Economy," in Wallerstein, *The Capitalist World-Economy,* p. 69.

49. Wallerstein, "Dependence in an Interdependent World," p. 67; Wallerstein, "The Rise and Future Demise of the World Capitalist System," p. 35.

50. Theda Skocpol, "Wallerstein's World Capitalist System: A Theoretical and Historical Critique," *American Journal of Sociology* 82-5 (March 1977), pp. 1084–1088; Alexander Gerschenkron, "Economic Backwardness in Historical Perspective," in Alexander Gerschenkron, *Economic Backwardness in Historical Perspective: A Book of Essays* (Cambridge, MA: Belknap Press of Harvard University Press, 1962), pp. 16–21; Peter J. Katzenstein, ed., "Between Power and Plenty: Foreign Economic Policies of Advanced Industrial States," special issue of *International Organization* 31-4 (Autumn 1977).

51. For an exposition of Gramsci's ideas, see Antonio Gramsci, *Selections from the Prison Notebooks of Antonio Gramsci,* edited and translated by Quintin Hoare and Geoffrey Nowell Smith (New York: International Publishers, 1971). See also John Merrington, "Theory and Practice in Gramsci's Marxism," in New Left Review, ed., *Western Marxism: A Critical Reader* (London: New Left Review, 1977), pp. 142–150.

52. See Robert W. Cox, "Gramsci, Hegemony and International Relations: An Essay in Method," *Millennium* 12-2 (1983), pp. 162–175; and Mark Rupert, *Producing Hegemony: The Politics of Mass Production and American Global Power* (Cambridge: Cambridge University Press, 1995), p. 29.

53. See Stephen Gill and David Law, "Global Hegemony and the Structural Power of Capital," in Stephen Gill, ed., *Gramsci, Historical Materialism and International Relations* (Cambridge: Cambridge University Press, 1993), pp. 93–124.

54. This discussion of the business conflict school relies on David N. Gibbs, *The Political Economy of Third World Intervention: Mines, Money, and U.S. Policy in the Congo Crisis* (Chicago: University of Chicago Press, 1991); Ronald W. Cox, *Power and Profits: U.S. Policy in Central America* (Lexington: University Press of Kentucky, 1994); and David Skidmore, "The Business of International Politics," *Mershon International Studies Review* 39, suppl. 2 (October 1995), pp. 246–254. See also Gregory P. Nowell, *Mercantile States and the World Oil Cartel, 1900–1939* (Ithaca, NY: Cornell University Press, 1994); and Robert Vitalis, *When Capitalists Collide: Business Conflict and the End of Empire in Egypt* (Berkeley: University of California Press, 1995).

55. Gibbs, *The Political Economy of Third World Intervention,* p. 30.

56. McGowan and Walker, "Radical and Conventional Models of U.S. Foreign Economic Policy Making," p. 352.

57. Gibbs, *The Political Economy of Third World Intervention,* pp. 13–19.

58. Cox, *Power and Profits,* p. 4.

59. Skidmore, "The Business of International Politics," p. 246.

60. Helen Milner, *Resisting Protectionism: Global Industries and the Politics of International Trade* (Princeton, NJ: Princeton University Press, 1988), pp. 24–25.

61. Cox, *Power and Profits,* p. 15.

PART III

The Issue Areas

Part III focuses on the main substantive issue areas in IPE. Chapter 6 begins by examining international monetary relations because the most significant types of transactions in the international economy—including trade, investment, and finance—all depend on the availability of money and credit. The chapter is devoted mainly to monetary relations but also discusses some of the crucial connections between monetary and financial issues. Next, Chapter 7 covers the issue of foreign debt, which is closely linked with international monetary and financial relations. Thus, the International Monetary Fund has been the lead international organization dealing with both monetary and foreign debt issues.

Chapters 8 and 9 deal with trade relations at both the global and regional levels. Regionalism is a major issue affecting all the substantive issue areas we examine. For example, Chapter 6 on monetary relations devotes some attention to the establishment of an economic and monetary union in Europe. Chapter 9 is devoted to regionalism and globalism in trade because trade liberalization has been so central to regional integration agreements such as the European Union and the North American Free Trade Agreement. Chapter 10 deals with the most important private actor in the international economy, the multinational corporation. With the increase of globalization and international competitiveness, the relationship between the MNC and the state is a matter of great concern to policymakers. Chapter 11 deals with the issue of international development. Most of the chapters in Part III devote some attention to Third World issues; Chapter 11 focuses specifically on alternative strategies and approaches to promoting economic development. The final section of each chapter in Part III draws linkages between the issue area on the one hand and the main themes and theoretical perspectives in IPE on the other.

International Monetary Relations

International monetary relations, the first substantive area addressed in this book, is the most central issue area in IPE. The most important types of transactions in the international economy—including trade, investment, and finance—all depend on the availability of money and credit. Thus, one long-term analyst of global monetary issues states that the most critical issue to hegemonic stability theorists should "not [be] what the hegemon does or does not do in trade . . . but what it does or fails to do to maintain peace and what it does or fails to do to keep the monetary system stable and credit flowing in a steady fashion."[1] Although international monetary relations is one of the most difficult issues for students to master, some background in this area can provide a sound basis for understanding other major issues in IPE.

The sheer volume of monetary and financial transactions is playing a major role in reshaping the global political economy. Indeed, the amount of money handled *daily* by foreign exchange markets increased from negligible amounts in the late 1950s, to $10 to $15 billion in 1975, and to about $1 trillion in the early 1990s. This latter figure is almost 40 times greater than the daily value of international trade.[2] Liberal interdependence theorists assert that this marked increase in financial transactions has resulted largely from advances in communications, technology, and transportation and that nation-states are therefore finding it increasingly difficult to regulate economic activities. Realist scholars, by contrast, argue that financial transactions have increased with the permission (and sometimes the encouragement) of the most powerful states and that these states continue to dictate the terms for such transactions.[3]

Realists can also point to the fact that international monetary transactions still rely primarily on the existence of separate national currencies. As discussed later in this chapter, some assets, such as special drawing rights, are more international in scope, and the establishment of a new "euro" currency for a number of countries in the European Union may pose a major challenge to the predominance of the nationally based U.S. dollar in the future. Nevertheless, the global monetary regime continues to function primarily in a world of separate national currencies, where states must inevitably be concerned about their balance of payments—the total flows of money into and out of the state.[4] A country's balance of payments tells us not only about its overall financial position but also about its position in other areas such as trade and foreign investment. It is therefore necessary to provide some background on the balance-of-payments issue.

THE BALANCE OF PAYMENTS

The **balance of payments,** which records the debit and credit transactions of a country with foreign countries and international institutions, is composed of two broad categories: the **current account,** which includes all transactions related to a country's current expenditures and national income, and the **capital account,** which includes all transactions related to movements of financial capital into and out of a country. As Table 6.1 shows, the current account comprises four different types of transactions:

1. *Merchandise trade,* or the export and import of tangible goods that can be seen and touched. The difference between the value of merchandise exports and imports is the *merchandise trade balance.*
2. *Services trade,* or intangible items such as insurance, information, transportation, and banking, provided to or by foreigners. A country's merchandise and services exports minus its merchandise and services imports (items 1 and 2 in the table) are equal to its *balance of trade.*[5]
3. *Investment income and payments,* which measure interest and dividend payments on investments by citizens of the home country to foreigners and by foreigners to citizens of the home country.
4. *Remittances and official transactions,* which include income that migrant workers or foreign companies send out of a country, military and foreign aid, and salaries and pensions paid to government employees abroad.

Table 6.1 shows that Japan had a current account *surplus* of $117.64 billion (U.S.) in 1992, while the United States had a current account *deficit* of $66.30 billion. The critical item for both countries was the merchandise trade balance, with Japan having a merchandise trade *surplus* of $132.40 billion and the United States having a merchandise trade *deficit* of $96.14 billion. As noted in Chapter 8, the United States has had merchandise trade deficits almost every year since 1971, while Japan has had substantial trade surpluses. The largest U.S. trade deficits are often with Japan; this fact has been a constant source of friction between the two countries. Table 6.1 shows that in contrast to its merchandise trade deficit, the United States had a positive balance in its *services* trade in 1992 (+$42.32 billion). This helps to explain why the United States exerted strong pressure to include services trade in the Canada-U.S. Free Trade Agreement and in the last round of GATT negotiations (the Uruguay round in 1986–93). The United States also had a positive balance in the investment income and payments item of the current account in 1992 (+$20.40 billion) because of interest and dividend payments received on past investments, but the positive balances on services and investment income were not sufficient to overcome the large U.S. negative bal-

TABLE 6.1

Balance-of-Payments Data, 1992 (billions of dollars)

	United States	Japan
Current account		
1. Merchandise trade		
Exports	+440.14	+330.81
Imports	−536.28	−198.47
Merchandise trade balance	−96.14	+132.40
2. Services trade		
Credit	+159.40	+48.31
Debit	−117.08	−89.73
Services trade balance	+42.32	−41.42
Balance of trade (1 + 2)	−53.82	+90.98
3. Investment income and payments		
Credit	+130.95	+145.75
Debit	−110.55	−114.47
Balance	+20.40	+31.28
4. Remittances and official transactions	−32.88	−4.62
Current account balance	**−66.30**	**+117.64**
Capital account		
5. Direct investment and other long-term capital	−17.61	−30.78
6. Short-term capital	+54.19	−75.77
Capital account balance	**+36.58**	**−106.55**
Statistical discrepancy	**−12.34**	**−10.46**
Total	**−42.06**	**+0.63**
Change in reserves	**+42.06**	**−0.63**

Increase in reserves: −; decrease in reserves: +.

Source: International Monetary Fund, *Balance of Payments Statistics Yearbook,* vol. 44, part 1, 1993 (Washington, DC: IMF, 1993), pp. 366, 742.

ance on merchandise trade. Thus, the overall U.S. current account balance in 1992 was negative (−$66.30 billion).

The second major item in the balance of payments is the *capital account,* which measures long-term and short-term flows of investment (items 5 and 6 in Table 6.1). A country's capital exports are *debit* items because they involve payments to foreigners and use foreign exchange; its capital imports are *credit* items because they involve payments from foreigners and earn foreign exchange. (This is the opposite of merchandise trade, in which exports are credits and imports are debits.) Short-term investments normally have a maturity of less than one year, while long-term investments extend beyond this period. Long-term capital flows are further subdivided into foreign direct investment (FDI) and portfolio investment. Direct investment is capital investment in a branch plant or subsidiary of a multinational corporation in which the investor has voting control. **Portfolio investment,** by contrast, is investment in bonds or a minority holding of shares that does not involve legal control.

Governments tend to offset imbalances in their current accounts with changes in their capital accounts. Thus, a country with a current account deficit often seeks to offset this deficit by seeking foreign investment or an inflow of funds into its capital account. A current account surplus, on the other hand, permits a country to have a capital account deficit through investment abroad or the accumulation of foreign assets. Accordingly, Table 6.1 reveals that Japan (which had a current account *surplus*) had a capital account *deficit* of $106.55 billion in 1992 and that the United States (which had a current account *deficit*) had a capital account *surplus* of $36.58 billion.

In addition to the current and capital accounts, the balance of payments also includes two items of lesser importance. The first is referred to as the *statistical discrepancy*. This item results partly from errors in collecting and computing data; but, more importantly, it stems from a government's failure to include all the goods, services, and capital flows that cross its borders. The final item in the balance of payments is the *change in official reserves*. Each country has a **central bank** (for example, the U.S. Federal Reserve or the Bank of Canada) that holds reserves of foreign exchange and gold. When a country has a deficit in its current *and* capital accounts (the total in Table 6.1), this amount must be matched by an equivalent reduction in reserves. When a state has a surplus in its current and capital accounts, it accumulates the surplus money in its reserves. The total of a country's current account, capital account, statistical discrepancy, and change in reserves always equals zero; hence the term *balance of payments*. Note in Table 6.1 that, by standard balance-of-payments accounting, a *minus* figure equals an *increase* in reserves, and a *plus* figure equals a *decrease* in reserves. (This is merely a bookkeeping exercise so that the balance of payments will equal zero, and it should not be of concern to the student.) Thus, in 1992 U.S. reserves *decreased* by $42.06 billion, and Japanese reserves *increased* by $0.63 billion.

Although all international payments in the balance-of-payments account always balance (i.e., equal zero) in a bookkeeping sense, this fact does not indicate that a country never has payments difficulties. On the contrary, analysts commonly speak of a country as having a *balance-of-payments surplus* or a *balance-of-payments deficit*. These terms refer only to the current and capital account parts of the balance of payments; they exclude any changes in official financing. A government with a balance-of-payments surplus reduces its liabilities to foreign governments and/or adds to its holdings of official reserves, and a government with a balance-of-payments deficit increases its liabilities and/or reduces its official reserves. The main body of the balance of payments therefore informs us about a state's overall position in terms of financial assets and liabilities.[6]

GOVERNMENT RESPONSE TO A BALANCE-OF-PAYMENTS DEFICIT

Countries with balance-of-payments deficits normally feel far more pressure to correct the imbalances than countries with balance-of-payments surpluses. A deficit country's reserves can eventually be depleted, but a surplus country can continue to increase its reserves indefinitely. Furthermore, realists believe that a balance-of-payments surplus, even if it is maintained with the help of government policy, is an indication of "superior competitive performance."[7] Surplus countries can in fact feel both economic and political pressures to correct their surpluses in the longer term. For example, excessive official reserves can lead to rising prices and inflationary pressures at home, and large balance-of-payments surpluses can force up the value of a country's currency, in turn making the country's exports more expensive for foreigners. Nevertheless, surplus countries normally view their payments disequilibrium as an economic asset rather than a liability, and we therefore focus here on a country's response to a payments deficit. When governments have a balance-of-payments deficit, they have two basic policy choices: they can either *finance* the disequilibrium or *adjust* to it. Governments often prefer financing measures because they can defer the costs to the future, when foreign debts must be repaid. Adjustment measures, by contrast, can have major political risks because some societal groups must bear the costs of adjustment in the present.[8]

Adjustment Measures

Governments opting for adjustment measures rely on three types of policy instruments to affect the balance of payments: monetary policy, fiscal policy, and commercial policy. While monetary and fiscal policy affect the level of economic activity, commercial policy directly influences a country's trade flows. **Monetary policy** influences the economy through changes in the money supply. When a government uses monetary policy to deal with a balance-of-payments deficit, its central bank limits public access to funds for spending purposes and makes such funds more expensive. For example, the central bank raises interest rates to make borrowing more costly; it decreases the amount of money available for loans by requiring commercial banks to hold larger reserves; and it sells government bonds so that money is withdrawn from the economy. These policies are designed to produce a contraction of the economy, less spending on goods and services, and hence a lowering of the payments deficit. **Fiscal policy** affects the economy through changes in government spending and/or taxes. When a government uses fiscal policy to deal with a balance-of-payments deficit, it lowers government expenditures and/or raises taxes to withdraw purchasing power from the public. Economies with balance-of-payments surpluses often follow the opposite policies; for example, they may adopt measures to expand the money supply, increase the budget deficit, and inflate the economy.

Governments using various combinations of monetary, fiscal, and commercial policy may opt for adjustment measures that are *external* or *internal* in nature. *External adjustment methods,* which cause foreigners to pay more of the adjustment costs, include such measures as tariffs, import quotas, export subsidies, tax incentives, and currency devaluation. External measures are designed to reduce payments to foreigners (by decreasing imports and outflows of foreign investment) and to increase payments from foreigners (by increasing exports and foreign investment inflows). Because external adjustment measures are aimed at foreign countries, a major pitfall of this approach is that others often retaliate and everyone loses in the long run. The competitive devaluation of currencies, with each country attempting to lower the value of its currency—and thus the relative price of its exports—is a prime example of the results of such retaliation. Although a government may adopt external measures to avoid making politically unpopular decisions at home, even external measures impose costs on some domestic groups. For example, a reduction in imports may promote domestic production and employment, but it also has adverse effects on importing businesses and on the choice of products available to consumers.

Internal adjustment methods cause individuals and groups at home to pay more of the adjustment costs. These are usually deflationary monetary and fiscal measures designed to slow down business activity in efforts to decrease the deficit. Examples of such measures include higher taxes and higher interest rates to reduce spending levels by individuals, businesses, and the government. The costs of internal adjustment methods are most evident domestically; they can contribute to unemployment, a reduction in living standards, business bankruptcies, and a phasing out of publicly financed programs. However, internal adjustment measures can also affect foreigners by deflating the economy and lowering the demand for foreign imports.

Financing

Instead of using adjustment methods, a country may seek *financing* to deal with its balance-of-payments deficit. Governments that choose financing must borrow from external credit sources and/or decrease their foreign exchange reserves. Governments often prefer to postpone difficult political decisions and to opt for future over current costs, so they tend to shift from adjustment to financing when reserves and access to credit are available. However, financing is difficult to arrange over a lengthy period; a country's reserves can be depleted, and foreigners are reluctant to invest in a country with chronic foreign debt problems.

In recent years the United States has often depended on inflows in its capital account (+$36.58 billion in 1992, as shown in Table 6.1) to counter the deficit in its current account (−$66.30 billion in 1992). The United States has been able to rely on financing because its large economy and its political stability attract foreign investors. Nevertheless, if the United States continues to rely on large capital inflows, it could eventually be paying out more in interest and dividends to foreigners than it receives (the investment income and payments item under the current account). Canada is a prime example of a country that has a long history as a net international borrower, and its investment income and payments has therefore been a high-debit item. Although Canada had a *positive* merchandise trade balance of $8.18 U.S. billion in 1992, it had a *negative* balance on investment income and payments of −$27.42 billion, contributing to a *negative* current account balance of −$23.02 billion. Like the United States, Canada had to turn to the capital account to help counter its current account deficit (the Canadian capital account balance in 1992 was +$13.79 billion).[9]

In reality, states usually employ a combination of external adjustment, internal adjustment, and financing measures to deal with their payments deficits. Although economic factors may have some effect on the country's choice of methods, its decision on this issue is basically political.[10] Liberals, realists, and historical structuralists have differing preferences regarding these policy instruments. Orthodox liberals generally believe that payments deficits result from domestic inefficiencies and that governments should adopt internal adjustment measures as a necessary form of discipline. Liberals oppose external adjustment measures, which contribute to trade barriers and the distortion of economic exchange, and they also oppose external financing because it permits countries to delay instituting necessary internal reforms.

Realists and historical structuralists, by contrast, often oppose internal adjustment methods that interfere with domestic autonomy in policymaking. Dependency theorists believe that the international system serves the interests of the rich Northern states, so they view the situation as doubly unjust if LDCs must bear the costs of adjustment internally. External adjustment measures are far more acceptable to both realists and historical structuralists. Realists view such external measures as "fair game" in a state's efforts to improve its competitive position vis-à-vis other states, and historical structuralists believe that Third World countries may have to impose import controls because of their unfavorable terms of trade with industrial states. Some historical structuralists also argue that the North, which benefits most from the international system, should provide Southern states with liberal financing to help alleviate their balance-of-payments problems.

INTERNATIONAL MONETARY RELATIONS BEFORE BRETTON WOODS

The literature on the modern period of international monetary relations commonly refers to the existence of four successive monetary regimes.[11] The first regime, which lasted from the 1870s to the outbreak of World War I in 1914, marked the period of the international gold standard; the second regime, identified with a gold exchange standard, was in effect during the first part of the interwar period; the third regime under the Bretton Woods system extended from 1944 to 1973; and the fourth regime from 1973 to the present is identified with a system of floating exchange rates. This chapter focuses primarily on the third and fourth regimes, which developed after World War II. However, to understand the Bretton Woods regime it is necessary to provide some background discussion of the first two regimes.

The International Gold Standard (1870s to 1914)

The international **gold standard** was a *fixed exchange rate* regime in which each country's currency was given an official exchange rate in relation to gold. By making the real values of national currencies more stable, the gold standard was designed to facilitate transactions between economies. For example, if the U.S. dollar was pegged at $35 per ounce of gold and the British pound was pegged at £14.5 per ounce of gold, the exchange rate between the dollar and the pound would remain constant at $2.41 per £1 (35 divided by 14.5). Although all countries had to undergo adjustments to maintain their exchange rates, the gold standard functioned reasonably well because it was backed by British hegemony and by cooperation among the core countries at the time (especially Britain, France, and Germany).[12] By providing public goods to other countries, such as investment capital, loans, and an open market for imports, Britain assumed a leadership role in stabilizing the gold standard. Thus, Western Europe and the United States generally maintained their official gold parities for about 35 years.[13]

The gold standard regime was based on orthodox liberal ideas in some important respects. The primary objective was to promote monetary openness and stability through the maintenance of stable exchange rates. This was a period before John Maynard Keynes introduced his interventionist liberal ideas to combat unemployment, and countries were expected to sacrifice domestic social objectives for the sake of monetary stability. Orthodox liberals have sometimes referred to the gold standard in highly idealized terms, and in 1981 President Ronald Reagan even created a special commission to determine whether the United States should return to the gold standard (the commission's recommendation was negative).[14] However, critics maintain that the poorest countries, and the poorest classes within countries, often assumed the largest burden of adjustment under the gold standard through sacrifices in both welfare and employment.

The Interwar Period (1914 to 1944)

World War I completely disrupted international monetary relations, but after the war Great Britain attempted to establish a *gold exchange standard* regime. A gold exchange standard, like a gold standard, is based on fixed exchange rates among currencies. The international reserves of a country under the nineteenth-century gold standard, however, were officially held in gold, while official reserves under a gold exchange standard consist of both gold and reserve currencies (such as the British pound or U.S. dollar). Although many central banks had in fact held reserve currencies as well as gold in earlier years, the gold exchange standard institutionalized this practice.[15] Because gold itself is in scarce supply and depends on new discoveries, a gold *exchange* standard permits more flexibility in increasing international reserves. (Furthermore, the largest gold producers are South Africa and Russia, which were not always the most favored countries.)

British efforts to reestablish monetary stability with the gold exchange standard continued for several years, but these efforts eventually failed. As a result, monetary relations for much of the interwar period were marked by competitive devaluations, a shift to floating rather than fixed exchange rates, destabilizing speculative capital movements, and increased trade protectionism, which culminated in the Great Depression. Some theorists maintain that the failure to reestablish monetary stability in the interwar period resulted from the decline of British hegemony and Britain's inability to pursue effective stabilizing policies as it had before World War I. Others, however, argue that the main factor in the breakdown of monetary stability was the growing reluctance of countries to sacrifice domestic goals such as full employment for the sake of currency stability.

Those who argue that domestic factors were mainly responsible for the breakdown of monetary stability point to major differences in domestic politics before World War I and in the interwar period. In most countries before World War I, voting was limited, labor unions were weak, farmers were not organized, and left-leaning parties were restricted. Thus, governments generally felt free to raise interest rates, decrease government expenditures, and raise taxes if necessary to bolster the value of their currencies in relation to gold, even if these policies contributed to unemployment and other domestic hardships. By the end of World War I, however, domestic groups had gained more influence through the extension of suffrage, the legalization of labor unions, the organization of farmers, and the development of mass political parties. It was no accident that John Maynard Keynes introduced his interventionist liberal ideas at this time, positing that some government intervention is necessary to deal with domestic economic problems such as unemployment. Thus, governments could no longer easily sacrifice the domestic welfare of their citizens to maintain external balance in support of the gold exchange standard, and one government after another responded to economic difficulties in the interwar period by turning away from international openness.[16]

THE FORMATION OF THE BRETTON WOODS MONETARY REGIME

World War II was marked by a breakdown of monetary cooperation and a period of exchange controls, and planning for a postwar monetary regime culminated in the 1944 Bretton Woods conference. The Bretton Woods monetary regime was a gold exchange system in which the value of each country's currency was pegged to gold or the U.S. dollar. Unlike the previous two regimes, however, the Bretton Woods system was based on the postwar interventionist liberal compromise (see Chapter 4).[17] On the one hand, postwar planners assumed that the pegged exchange rates would provide sufficient monetary stability to permit a resumption of normal international trade. On the other hand, the planners ensured that there was some flexibility and assistance so that countries could pursue domestic objectives related to employment and inflation. This marked a contrast with the classical gold standard, in which long-term exchange rate stability took precedence over domestic socioeconomic requirements.[18]

The interventionist liberal compromise had three major elements. First, a country was to maintain the par value of its currency in the short term, but it could devalue its currency (with the approval of the IMF) in the longer term if it had a "fundamental disequilibrium" in its balance of payments. (The classical gold standard, by contrast, had been committed to long-term exchange rate stability.)[19] The second element of the interventionist liberal compromise was the creation of the International Monetary Fund, which would provide short-term loans to countries with temporary balance-of-payments problems. The third element of the compromise was the support for national controls over capital flows. Speculative capital flows had contributed to great instability during the interwar period, and the postwar negotiators feared that such speculation could similarly undermine efforts to maintain fixed exchange rates and promote freer trade under the Bretton Woods regime. The chief negotiators also believed that unrestricted capital flows would interfere with the functioning of the welfare state. If corporations and citizens could freely move their funds abroad to evade taxes, funding that the state required for welfare expenditures would be jeopardized.[20]

THE INTERNATIONAL MONETARY FUND

The most important international organization embedded in the Bretton Woods monetary regime was the International Monetary Fund (IMF). The IMF, which is located in Washington, D.C., was created to promote stable and orderly exchange rates and to provide member states with short-term loans for temporary balance-of-payments problems. Under the IMF Articles of Agreement, members had to peg their currencies to gold or the U.S. dollar, which was valued at $35 per ounce of gold. Member countries were also to contribute to a "pool" of national currencies; those funds would be available for the IMF loans to deficit countries.[21] Each IMF member was given a *quota* based on its relative economic importance, and this quota determined the size of its *subscription,* or contribution to the IMF resource pool. The IMF has a weighted voting system in which the most economically powerful countries have the largest quotas and subscriptions and also have the most votes.

The IMF approves loans to members in a series of stages, or *tranches.* In the 1980s, the IMF developed a number of new programs to deal with the foreign debt crisis, and member countries can now borrow amounts far above the level of their IMF quotas. IMF **conditionality** has become a major factor in its loan giving: members agree to adopt specific economic policies in return for IMF funding.[22] The more a member country borrows from the IMF (in relation to its quota), the more stringent are the IMF's conditionality requirements. Third World countries feel strong pressures to abide by IMF conditionality, not only because of the loans the IMF can provide but because the advanced industrial countries and private international banks often make the acceptance of IMF conditions a requirement for their own granting of loans and development assistance. The IMF usually requires the borrowing country to adopt contractionary monetary and fiscal policies that are liberal-economic in nature. In the view of IMF officials, these requirements are designed to ensure that the borrower addresses its balance-of-payments problems so that it can repay the IMF loan. From the perspective of many LDC loan recipients, however, the IMF's conditionality requirements often infringe on their sovereignty and do not address the basic structural problems hindering their economic development (see Chapter 7 for further discussion of this issue).

The two main policymaking bodies of the IMF are the *board of governors* and the *board of executive directors.* As is the case for the UN General Assembly, each IMF member appoints one representative (usually the finance minister or central bank governor) to the board of governors; but in the IMF, the voting power of each governor depends on the weighted voting system. The IMF board of governors meets only once a year in conjunction with the board of governors of the World Bank, and most of its powers are delegated to the board of executive directors (or executive board), which is in continuous session. The executive board, which also has weighted voting, is responsible for the IMF's daily business, including requests for financial assistance, economic consultations with member countries, and the development of policies. It consists of the IMF managing director as chair and 24 executive directors.

The countries with the largest subscriptions and the most votes in the IMF governing bodies are the Group of Five—the United States, Japan, Germany, France, and Britain. As of 1997, the U.S. executive director had 17.78 percent of the votes on the IMF executive board, followed by Japan and Germany with 5.54 percent each and

France and Britain with 4.98 percent each. The G-5 countries all have a sufficient number of votes to appoint their own executive directors. Coalitions of member countries elect the other executive directors every two years.[23] The advanced industrial states not only have the most voting power in the IMF governing bodies; they also have considerable influence in the operating staff. Thus, by tacit agreement, the top executive officer of the IMF, the managing director, has to this point always been European, and the World Bank president has always been American.[24]

In practice, the board of governors and the executive board arrive at most decisions through consensus rather than formal votes, but the weighted voting procedure gives the advanced industrial states the most influence in both bodies. The Third World countries nevertheless are able to influence IMF decision making through bloc voting under certain circumstances. Most IMF decisions are made with a simple majority vote, but majorities of 70 and 85 percent are required for some important decisions. The provision for these special majorities gives an effective veto to the United States, the European Union, and the Third World countries *if* they act as a group. Although the Third World has on rare occasions blocked some initiatives requiring special majorities, it is not able to alter the existing structure of the IMF, which clearly favors the advanced industrial states. Because it includes such a large, amorphous group of countries, the Third World also has difficulty acting as a monolithic group to block IMF decisions.[25]

Not surprisingly, the LDCs have expressed dissatisfaction with the industrial states' dominance in the IMF, and the non-oil LDCs joined with OPEC after the 1973–74 oil price increases to demand greater voting power.[26] As a result of these demands, the OPEC countries benefited from the readjustment of IMF quotas and voting allocations, and Third World countries were included in more of the IMF's deliberations. Nevertheless, the IMF's weighted voting system continues to favor the interests and objectives of the advanced industrial states.

Chapter 2 noted that all the centrally planned economies except Yugoslavia withdrew or were ousted from the IMF and the World Bank in the 1950s and 1960s. Membership issues in the two institutions are closely related; a country cannot join the World Bank without also becoming a member of the IMF. This requirement deterred most Communist countries from joining the World Bank for a number of years, even though they were interested in receiving World Bank financing, because they would have been subject to IMF conditionality. Although Romania joined the IMF and the World Bank in 1972, most former Soviet bloc countries did not join these institutions until the 1980s and 1990s. A number of the emerging economies of Eastern Europe and the former Soviet Union have experienced foreign debt problems; Chapter 7 discusses their membership in the Bretton Woods institutions.

THE FUNCTIONING OF THE BRETTON WOODS MONETARY REGIME

The Bretton Woods monetary regime was a gold exchange regime in which the main reserves were gold and the U.S. dollar. Economists generally ask three questions about the adequacy of reserve assets in upholding a monetary regime. First, is there a sufficient amount of reserves (that is, gold and the U.S. dollar) for **liquidity,** or financing purposes? As interdependence increases, more liquidity is necessary to cover the growing number of economic transactions among states, but if there is a surplus of liquidity, inflation and other problems can result. Second, is there a *confidence* problem with the existing reserve currencies? When countries lack confidence that a currency's value will remain stable, they are reluctant to hold that currency in its reserves. Confidence problems have led to periodic efforts to sell off British pounds and U.S. dollars. And third, what *adjustment* options do reserve-currency countries have in dealing with their balance-of-payments deficits? An effective regime should provide all deficit countries (including the top-currency country, the United States) with a sufficient range of adjustment options. The discussion that follows examines the problems with liquidity, confidence, and adjustment that developed in the Bretton Woods monetary regime.[27]

The Central Role of the U.S. Dollar

Events in the early postwar years dictated that the United States rather than the IMF would take initial responsibility for managing the international monetary regime. Monetary relations immediately after the war were more unstable than expected, with balance-of-payments deficits and lack of foreign exchange seriously hindering recovery in Europe. Because the IMF's available funds were inadequate to meet the needs, the United States as global hegemon assumed much of the responsibility for providing finance. Thus, the United States opened its market for the export of foreign goods, provided long-term loans and grants to Europe through the European Recovery Program or Marshall Plan, and supplied the U.S. dollar as the main source of international liquidity. In opting for the Marshall Plan and other bilateral aid for postwar reconstruction, the United States effectively sidelined the IMF as a financing institution for Europe, and the IMF's main clients soon became the less developed countries. However, LDCs were often deterred by the conditionality requirements that the IMF imposed on its loans; total drawings from the IMF fell to zero in 1950 and did not exceed 1947 levels again until 1956.[28]

Because the Bretton Woods monetary regime was based on a gold exchange standard, central banks could hold their international reserves in two forms—gold and foreign exchange—in any proportion they chose.[29] It is ironic, however, that the original attraction of gold as a reserve asset—its scarcity—became a liability as increased trade and foreign investment led to growing demand for international reserves. Gold-mining sources were limited, so only the U.S. dollar could meet this need for increased liquidity. Although it was vital that there be a sufficient number of dollars available for global liquidity purposes, large U.S. balance-of-trade surpluses in the late 1940s contributed to a dollar shortage. To remedy this problem, the United States distributed dollars around the world through economic aid and military expenditures from 1947 to 1958, providing liquidity for the international economy.

Other countries at times changed the par value of their currencies relative to gold and the U.S. dollar, but the dollar's value was to remain fixed at the 1934 rate of $35 per ounce of gold, and the United States agreed to exchange all dollars held by foreign central banks and treasuries for gold at the official rate. This commitment seemed to be perfectly reasonable because the United States held a much larger share of the world's gold reserves than any other country after the war. The fixed rate of the dollar was designed to ensure that it would be "as good as gold." However, most other countries actually preferred U.S. dollars to gold for their reserves and international transactions; dollars (unlike gold) earned interest, and they did not have to be shipped and stored. Although the IMF Articles of Agreement stated that "the par value of the currency of each member shall be expressed in terms of gold . . . or in terms of the United States dollar," IMF members in fact related their par values to the dollar.[30]

While the United States as global hegemon was providing its currency as a public good to meet international liquidity needs, it was also receiving the private benefit of seignorage. **Seignorage** is "the profit that comes to the seigneur, or sovereign power, from the issuance of money."[31] As the supplier of the key world currency, the United States gained financial power and influence, and it was largely exempt from the discipline that the international financial system imposed on other states. The United States was also able to trade and borrow in domestic currency and thus avoid exchange rate risks and transaction costs, and the dollar's leading role enabled New York City to retain its position as the world's financial capital. U.S. policy from 1947 to the late 1950s was therefore based on a mixture of altruism and self-interest, and other major countries acquiesced in U.S. monetary leadership because of the benefits they received.[32]

Despite the early emergence of the United States as hegemon in the global monetary regime, several changes in the late 1950s led to concerns about its continued leadership. The United States regularly had a substantial balance-of-trade surplus in the postwar period, but it had even larger debits due to the economic and military financing it was providing through the Marshall Plan and other assistance programs. As a result, the U.S. had an overall balance-of-payments deficit beginning in 1950. U.S. payments deficits averaged about $1.5 billion per year for most of the decade, but they increased rapidly in the late 1950s, and observers began to speak of a dollar "glut" rather than a dollar shortage. In 1960, the U.S. payments deficit was $3.7 billion, and foreign dollar holdings exceeded U.S. gold reserves for the first time.[33] Thus, European governments, which had eagerly sought to obtain dollars, were now reluctant to accumulate excessive dollar reserves.

To some economists, the dollar's declining fortunes demonstrated that there were fundamental problems with a monetary regime that relied on a single key currency. On the one hand, the need for sufficient liquidity caused the United States to spread dollars around the world by running balance-of-payments deficits. On the other hand, these payments deficits would eventually make it impossible for the United States to continue exchanging dollars for gold at $35 per ounce, and this would lead to the collapse of confidence in the dollar as the top currency. Any U.S. actions to drastically reduce its balance-of-payments deficit in order to restore confidence in the dollar would contribute to a shortage of global liquidity. The **Triffin dilemma** (named after economist Robert Triffin) refers to the problem confronting a monetary regime that depends on a single key currency: the liquidity and confidence functions of the currency eventually come into conflict.[34]

A second major change that raised questions about U.S. control over monetary relations was the growth of the *Eurocurrency market* (or *Euromarket*). **Eurocurrencies** are national currencies traded and deposited in banks outside the home country, mainly (but not necessarily) in Europe. The most common form of Eurocurrencies are *Eurodollars* held in banks outside the United States. The origins of the Eurocurrency market extend back to 1917, when the Communist government in Russia deposited its U.S. dollars in European banks to prevent the United States from seizing them. After World War II, the Communist governments in the Soviet Union and China deposited their dollars from export earnings in offshore banks to avoid U.S. banking regulations.

The Eurocurrency market as we know it developed in the 1960s when President Lyndon Johnson responded to the U.S. balance-of-payments deficits by imposing restrictions on foreign lending by American banks. To avoid these restrictions, U.S. companies began to finance their foreign operations from offshore banks, which were not subject to U.S. banking legislation. The Eurodollar market also grew because European banks involved with foreign transactions found it easier to use U.S. dollars than to constantly exchange their currencies. The main appeal of Eurodollars to depositors is that they are not subject to domestic government regulations. For example, the U.S. Federal Reserve requires banks to hold a certain percentage of their deposits as reserves, but the United States does not have this control over Eurodollar deposits. U.S. banks are not permitted to pay interest on deposits held less than 30 days, but European banks can pay interest on very short-term deposits.[35]

Although liberal interdependence theorists point to the role that private actors such as international bankers played in the expansion of the Euromarket, the leading states also contributed to the growth of the Euromarket because of the advantages it offered to them.[36] For example, the British government allowed the Euromarket to operate without regulation in efforts to promote the City of London as a leading financial center, and the American government permitted U.S. bankers to retain their dominant position in international finance by avoiding the U.S. capital control program and moving their international dollar business to London. In view of the declining confidence in its currency, the U.S. government also felt that the Euromarket would enhance the appeal of U.S. dollars to foreigners.[37] The central role that the British and American governments played in supporting the expansion of the Eurodollar business is ironic: "it may prove to have been the most important single development of the century undermining national monetary sovereignty."[38] Persistent U.S. balance-of-payments deficits, combined with the growth of the Eurodollar market in the 1960s, posed questions about the United States' ability to manage international monetary relations, and this in turn contributed to a shift toward multilateralism.

A Shift Toward Multilateralism

As U.S. balance-of-payments deficits continued to increase, the dollar slipped from top currency to negotiated-currency status in the 1960s. A *top currency* is favored for international monetary transactions because others have confidence in the strong economic position of the issuing state. A *negotiated currency* does not benefit from this high degree of confidence, and the issuing state must offer inducements so that others will continue to accept its leadership.[39] A negotiated-currency state must also be open to multilateral management, and this was in fact the response to the U.S. problems. In 1962, 10 advanced industrial countries (the Group of Ten or G-10) agreed to establish the General Arrangements to Borrow (GAB), in which they would lend the IMF up to $6 billion in their own currencies when there was a need for supplementary resources to cope with international monetary problems. As discussed in Chapter 2, the G-10 actually consists of 11 countries today: the G-7 countries (the United States, Japan, Germany, France, Britain, Italy, and Canada) plus Belgium, the Netherlands, Sweden, and Switzerland. The G-10 had to approve each request for supplementary support; this represented a shift from unilateral U.S. management to more collective management of international monetary issues.[40]

Another indication of the shift from unilateral to multilateral management was the increased role accorded to the **Bank for International Settlements (BIS)** in the 1960s. Located in Basel, Switzerland, the BIS is in fact the oldest of the international financial institutions. It was formed in 1930 to oversee the settlement of German reparations after World War I (thus the term *settlements* in the name). Since World War II, the BIS has become the main forum for cooperation and consultation among central bankers of countries in the Organization for Economic Cooperation and Development (OECD). Central banks deposit part of their official currency reserves with the BIS, which can use them to deal with exchange rate problems and to provide credit to central banks that lack liquidity. When the U.S. dollar came under downward pressure in the 1960s, the BIS organized mutual lines of credit among the central banks to help stabilize exchange rates and the price of gold. The United States had refused to attend the monthly meetings of the BIS in the 1940s and 1950s, but it began to accept the need for multilateral management of international financial issues in the 1960s and has attended the BIS meetings since that time.[41]

While Western European countries viewed the establishment of the G-10 and the upgraded role of the BIS as something of a victory, Third World countries were highly dissatisfied with the propensity of the G-10 and BIS to hold discussions about monetary issues outside the framework of the IMF, where the LDCs were represented.[42] The LDCs were not content with pressing their demands for greater participation only within the confines of the IMF, and they responded to the G-10 by setting up their own group in 1972. The **Group of 24 (G-24),** which is composed of eight finance ministers or central bank governors from each of the three main LDC regions (Africa, Asia, and Latin America), regularly reviews international monetary relations and tries to coordinate LDC monetary policies. It also has responded to G-10 reports on international monetary reform by presenting its own "counterreports." Although the G-24's ideas on monetary issues have received some recognition, its influence (like the influence of UNCTAD and the G-77) is clearly circumscribed because it consists of the borrowers rather than the lenders in the IMF.[43]

Although the G-10 could jointly supply a substantial amount of financial resources, there were concerns that G-10 resources were not sufficient to defend the dollar if it came under attack. A rush to change dollars into gold became more likely as the U.S. balance-of-payments deficit continued to increase. A series of measures were therefore adopted to bolster the dollar, and the United States also sought to improve its balance of payments by reducing capital outflows. In 1963, for example, the United States imposed an interest equalization tax on U.S. purchases of foreign securities; and in 1965, it imposed limits on foreign investments and loans by U.S. firms and banks. Despite these efforts, U.S. gold stocks fell from about $22.7 billion in 1950 to $10.7

billion in 1970 while dollar claims against the U.S. gold supply rose from about $5 billion to $70 billion. Thus, the dollar had in effect become inconvertible into gold by 1968.[44]

Disagreement continues today about the basic causes of the U.S. balance-of-payments deficit. Some observers attribute the U.S. payments deficit to the public goods the United States as the hegemonic state provided to others, such as the Marshall Plan, the U.S. dollar as the key currency, and an open market for other countries' exports. However, critics argue that Americans and their governments have been unwilling to achieve a balance between revenues and expenditures. During the Vietnam War, for example, the U.S. Congress refused to raise taxes to pay for the war effort, and President Lyndon Johnson refused to cut domestic social programs. The United States also has a lower personal savings rate than the other G-5 countries. In 1980, for example, the personal savings ratio as a percentage of disposable income was 19.2 percent for Japan, 12.3 percent for Britain, 11.0 percent for France, 10.9 percent for West Germany, and only 6.0 percent for the United States. The difference in personal savings habits of Japan and the United States results both from cultural factors and from Japanese monetary and fiscal policies such as increasing interest rates on bank deposits. Thus, high-saving Japan has been the source of large-scale capital flows to the low-saving United States in recent years.[45]

Yet another possible reason for the U.S. balance-of-payments problem relates to the decline of U.S. competitiveness after the postwar recovery in Western Europe and Japan. Unlike other countries, the United States could not devalue its dollar to become more competitive under the gold exchange standard. Thus, the Bretton Woods regime did not provide the United States with sufficient adjustment options, in view of the country's decreased competitiveness. To confront the problem of declining confidence in the U.S. dollar, proposals were developed in the 1960s to create a new artificial reserve asset. The United States initially opposed this idea because it wanted to maintain the dollar's reserve role, but it eventually changed its position to take pressure off the dollar in international money markets.[46] France, however, resented U.S. privileges as the top-currency state, and it wanted the United States to deal with its balance-of-payments problems before a new reserve was created. After several years of negotiation, IMF members finally agreed in 1969 to create a new international reserve termed special drawing rights.[47]

Special drawing rights (SDRs) are artificial international reserves, created and managed by the G-10 and used among central banks outside U.S. control. The Europeans have a veto over the creation of new SDRs, which thus represent a marked decrease in U.S. financial power.[48] All IMF members are allocated SDRs in proportion to their quotas, so that those with the highest quotas (the G-5 countries) receive the most SDRs. The first distribution of SDRs was an allocation of $9.5 billion over three years beginning in 1970, and a second allocation of $12 billion occurred in the 1977–81 period. In September 1997, the IMF approved a third allocation of SDRs, which enabled countries that had joined the IMF after the second allocation (mainly emerging countries of Eastern Europe and the former Soviet Union) to receive an SDR allocation for the first time.[49] At first, 35 SDRs were equal to $35 or to an ounce of gold; but from 1974 to 1980, after the move to floating currencies, the SDR value was determined by a *basket,* weighted average of 16 currencies. In 1981, the basket was changed to a weighted average of the G-5 currencies.

Because movements in the exchange rates of the G-5 countries' currencies tend to offset one another (that is, some currencies rise while others drop in value), the value of the SDR is more stable than that of any single currency in the basket. This stability makes the SDR attractive as a unit of account to the IMF and other international and regional organizations. Nevertheless, the SDR has been far less successful as a reserve asset, and as of April 1997, IMF member countries' holdings of SDRs amounted to only 1.7 percent of their total nongold reserves.[50] This is still a world of nation-states, so a truly international reserve unconnected with an economically powerful state(s) may simply be ahead of its time. Major conflict between industrial states and Third World countries over the issuance of additional SDRs has also limited their role (this issue is discussed below).

The U.S. balance-of-payments deficit was not the only problem confronting the Bretton Woods system in the 1960s and 1970s. Despite the continuance of national controls on capital flows, investors lacked confidence in the existing exchange rates of currencies, and speculative capital flows increased significantly.[51] Speculative activity in the Euromarket was especially difficult to regulate, and multinational corporations were able to evade controls through transactions among their affiliates in different countries. Thus, MNCs became adept at moving their capital from one country to another to take advantage of interest rate spreads and expected exchange rate adjustments, and this increased capital mobility put growing pressures on states to realign their exchange rates. In efforts to prevent a run on their currencies, leaders often committed themselves to the established parities, severely limiting their policy options. Powerful domestic interest groups also often prevented governments from instituting needed realignment of their currencies. As a result, modest changes in parities were difficult to institute, and the monetary regime became overly rigid despite the need for flexibility.[52]

The Demise of the Bretton Woods Monetary Regime

By the late 1960s, the Bretton Woods monetary regime had become untenable. France's Charles de Gaulle was deliberately converting dollars into gold to bring about an end to the United States' hegemonic privilege as the key currency state; and the United States was increasingly making it awkward for foreign central banks to change their dollars into gold. Although U.S. balance-of-payments deficits extended back to 1950, these deficits had resulted from the huge amount of foreign investment and loans the United States was extending around the world. In 1971, however, the United States had its first balance-of-*trade* deficit since 1893, indicating that its trade competitiveness was seriously declining. President Richard M. Nixon therefore decided to suspend the official convertibility of the dollar into gold on August 15, 1971. This action sent shock waves throughout the world. The Nixon administration also imposed a 10 percent tariff surcharge on all dutiable imports, promising to remove it when other countries such as West Germany and Japan altered their "unfair" exchange rates. At the time of the Nixon shocks, the U.S. share of international reserves had fallen from a postwar level of 50 percent to 16 percent, while the European Community's share had risen from 6.1 to 32.5 percent. In December 1971, the G-10 countries therefore agreed to lower the dollar's value by 10 to 20 percent vis-à-vis other major currencies in the first Smithsonian Agreement (negotiated at the Smithsonian Institute in Washington, D.C.). The U.S. balance-of-payments problem continued, and a second Smithsonian Agreement devaluing the dollar further was negotiated in February 1973.[53]

After announcing the first Smithsonian Agreement, the industrial states decided that monetary reform was urgently needed and that a **Committee of Twenty (C-20)** should be established to decide on the reforms. The industrial states occupied 11 seats in the C-20, and the LDCs (which had been angered by their exclusion from the G-10's Smithsonian Agreement) occupied the other 9 seats. Following two years of discussion, the C-20 reached an agreement for international monetary reform in June 1974. The agreement recommended that the system of stable but adjustable exchange rates be continued and that the SDR become the principal reserve asset, with a reduced role for gold and the U.S. dollar. The C-20 proposals ultimately failed, however, because of differences between the Europeans, the Americans, and the LDCs and because of destabilizing global changes such as the 1973–74 increases in OPEC oil prices. With the failure of the C-20 efforts, it was evident that the Bretton Woods regime of fixed exchange rates would collapse and would be replaced by a regime based on floating rates.[54]

It is impossible to detail all the differences among C-20 members; we refer here to only one conflict over the creation of SDRs to illustrate the difficulties the committee had in reaching a consensus on monetary issues. In the C-20 meetings, the Third World countries proposed that a "link" be established between the creation of new SDRs and the transfer of resources to LDCs for development purposes. If LDCs received most of the new SDRs, they reasoned, this would benefit the Third World while also providing an increase in liquidity.[55] When the industrial states had first decided to create SDRs in 1969, they had initially not even planned to include the LDCs in the allocation, and the decision to distribute SDRs in accordance with IMF quotas was a compromise agreement. Thus, the 11 industrial states on the C-20 argued that the LDCs' link proposal would undermine the monetary integrity of the SDR and that issues regarding monetary relations and development assistance should be kept strictly separate. The industrial countries were particularly concerned that the LDCs' needs for development assistance were almost limitless and might lead to the creation of an excessive amount of SDRs from a monetary standpoint. The LDCs tried to allay this fear by agreeing that new SDRs should be created only to satisfy international liquidity requirements and *not* on the basis of LDC needs. Furthermore, the G-10 and not the LDCs would retain decision-making power over when to create new SDRs. The developed states, however, were unmoved; they decided that any new SDRs should be allocated (as in the past) only according to a country's quota in the IMF.[56] In view of such major differences as the North-South split over SDR allocations, it is not surprising that the C-20 reached no agreement on altering the global monetary regime.

A multitude of problems confronted the Bretton Woods monetary regime by the early 1970s. First, while the U.S. role as the top-currency state was premised on the idea that it was an unrivaled hegemon, this no longer seemed to be the case; second, as capital flows around the world increased, the Bretton Woods system of pegged exchange rates became increasingly untenable; and third, the three characteristics of reserves—liquidity, confidence, and adjustment—all presented serious problems. Thus, countries were reluctant to hold large supplies of U.S. dollars for liquidity purposes; the persistent U.S. balance-of-payments deficit contributed to a crisis of confidence in the dollar; and the dollar could not be adjusted through devaluation, even when the United States became less competitive. The Bretton Woods regime collapsed when the C-20 could not agree on a viable plan for saving it.

THE REGIME OF FLOATING (OR FLEXIBLE) EXCHANGE RATES

The Bretton Woods agreement had outlawed freely floating exchange rates, so all the major trading nations were "living in sin" by 1973.[57] The IMF meeting in Jamaica in January 1976 finally legalized the existing situation by permitting each government to decide whether to establish a par value for its currency or to shift to floating rates. In a *free-floating* regime, member countries do not intervene in currency markets, and the market alone determines currency valuations. IMF members have in fact relied extensively on *managed floating* in recent years, in which central banks intervene to deal with disruptive conditions such as excessive fluctuations in exchange rates. Although managed floating is considered to be legitimate, the IMF calls on central banks to avoid *dirty floating,* or "manipulating exchange rates . . . in order to prevent effective balance of payments adjustment or to gain an unfair competitive advantage."[58] Today the monetary regime is "mixed" in nature: major industrial countries such as the United States, Japan, and Canada (and a number of LDCs) independently float their currencies; the European Union countries seek increased regional coordination of their policies; and many Third World countries peg the value of their currencies to a key currency or basket of currencies. Not surprisingly, some observers refer to the current system of monetary relations as a "non-system."[59]

Liberal economists were generally supportive of the move to floating rates, for a variety of reasons. First, a system of flexible rates had intellectual appeal for many liberals because adjustment of international exchange rates would depend on market pressures rather than government involvement. Thus, as early as 1953 the orthodox liberal economist Milton Friedman wrote a classic article strongly favoring the establishment of "a system of exchange rates freely determined in open markets, primarily by private transactions, and the simultaneous abandonment of direct controls over exchange transactions."[60] While some liberals feared that floating rates could lead to instability because of speculative capital flows, as had occurred in the 1930s, Friedman argued that the instability in the 1930s had resulted more from fundamental economic and financial problems than from the floating of currencies. By the 1970s, there were additional reasons for liberal economists to favor a shift to floating rates. Liberals argued that with the marked increase in capital flows and speculative pressures, governments could no longer defend fixed exchange rates for currencies and that floating rates would contribute to rapid adjustments of international payments imbalances in response to market pressures.[61]

The results of the change to floating exchange rates, however, have not been as positive as expected. Most economists in the early 1970s underestimated the extent to which capital mobility would increase and thus disrupt exchange rates. Partly as a response to the return of orthodox liberalism, the United States and Britain rejected the postwar imposition of national controls on capital flows under Bretton Woods, shifting to policies of allowing capital to move more freely. Countries were competing for the inflow of foreign investment in the 1980s, and others followed the U.S. and British example. Thus, the United States and Britain removed their capital controls in the 1970s; Australia, New Zealand, Japan, and members of the European Community removed most of their capital controls in the 1980s. The removal of capital controls, combined with technological advances in such areas as telecommunications, contributed to a massive growth in speculative capital flows, which had far-reaching effects on the world's financial markets.[62] In the face of these changes, two problems developed with the floating exchange rate regime: volatility and misalignment of exchange rates. *Volatility* refers to short-term instability in the exchange rate, and *misalignment* refers to the long-term departure of an exchange rate from its competitive level.[63]

The Bretton Woods pegged rate regime had limited the variability in exchange rates, but exchange rates are much more volatile under the floating system. Highly volatile exchange rates can create uncertainty, inhibit productive investments, and possibly interfere with international trade. Misalignment, however, is a more serious problem than volatility: misalignment can lead to prolonged changes in international competitiveness. Although some economists believed that misalignments would be eliminated with floating currencies, this has not been the case. Indeed, exchange rate misalignment under the floating regime has been as high as 20 to 30 percent for both the U.S. dollar and the Japanese yen.[64] Depending on whether a currency is under- or overvalued, misalignment can give a country substantial price advantages or disadvantages vis-à-vis its competitors.

When the industrial states abandoned the Bretton Woods regime, the IMF's original role in stabilizing the pegged exchange rates largely disappeared, and the IMF faced a crisis of purpose. The industrial states often held policy discussions regarding problems with the floating regime in the Groups of Five and Seven, outside IMF auspices. At the G-7 summits, member governments engaged in a limited degree of policy coordination to stabilize monetary relations. For example, at the 1978 Bonn Summit, the United States agreed to adopt policies to deal with its balance-of-payments deficits, while Germany and Japan agreed to adopt expansionary economic policies that would increase their demand for American goods.[65] This limited degree of policy coordination ended, however, with the Reagan administration in January 1981. When Ronald Reagan became President, he lowered taxes and raised spending for military-defense purposes. These policies contributed to a huge U.S. government deficit, which exceeded $200 billion annually by the mid-1980s. The United States required foreign investment to service its debt, so it raised interest rates to attract foreign capital. However, the increase in capital imports simply strengthened the U.S. dollar, and the American balance-of-trade and payments deficits began to spiral out of control.

The Plaza-Louvre Accords

With the U.S. dollar continuing to appreciate in value and U.S. deficits climbing, the United States became far more concerned with foreign exchange rates. In efforts to bring down the dollar, Secretary of the Treasury James Baker III assembled the finance ministers and central bank heads of the G-5 in New York City's Plaza Hotel in September 1985. Here the G-5 agreed on joint intervention to raise the value of the major nondollar currencies through coordinated market intervention (that is, the buying and selling of currencies), and the United States in return promised to reduce government spending. The dollar depreciated significantly after the Plaza Agreement, so the G-5 met at the Louvre in Paris in February 1987 to prevent the dollar's value from slipping even further. The major countries involved at this point were the *Group of Three*—the United States, Japan, and Germany.[66]

The Plaza and Louvre accords marked a shift to managed floating, in which the major governments intervened to correct serious volatility and misalignment of currency rates. However, the major economies have not coordinated their interventions on a consistent basis since the Louvre accord. Although policy coordination is important for the maintenance of international currency stability today, it is difficult to achieve because of the high degree of mobility of international capital flows.[67] The unwillingness of governments to accept constraints on adopting fiscal and monetary policies as they see fit also limits the degree to which policy coordination is likely to occur. Thus, the floating monetary regime is far more unstable today than liberal economists had predicted, and it is uncertain that the major industrial states will coordinate their policies sufficiently to prevent future misalignment of currency rates.

ONE MONETARY REGIME, TWO, OR THREE?

With unstable monetary relations under the flexible exchange rate regime and a continuance of large U.S. balance-of-trade deficits, questions have arisen as to whether the U.S. dollar will eventually lose its role as the top reserve currency. Considerable attention has been given to the emergence of three major economic regions or blocs in Western Europe, North America, and East Asia. In monetary terms, this situation translates into three currency areas centered on the euro, the U.S. dollar, and the yen. Although the German deutschmark has been the anchor for other currencies in the European Union, the EU is in the process of developing an Economic and Monetary Union with a new European currency—the euro—at its center. The Western Hemisphere has no formal monetary arrangements comparable with those in Europe, but the supremacy of the U.S. dollar in the hemisphere is not in doubt. When a Latin American country decides to peg its currency, it normally pegs it to the U.S. dollar.

The yen's position in the Asia-Pacific region is somewhat less certain. Japan's economic strength and its role as an exporter of goods and capital have contributed to the importance of the yen as an international currency. Unlike the case in Europe and

North America, however, economic integration is not a clearly defined regional objective in East Asia. The Asia-Pacific Economic Cooperation forum includes a goal of free trade and an open investment area by the year 2010 for industrial country members, but APEC is not limited to Asia. It includes such countries as the United States, Canada, and Mexico. Although the Japanese yen may not serve as the anchor for an integrated-currency area, it is certainly a key international currency.[68]

EUROPEAN MONETARY RELATIONS

With the future of global monetary relations uncertain, "the only initiative that might be held out as a serious experiment" in international monetary reform today is taking place in Europe.[69] It is therefore important to examine the European approach to monetary relations. The Treaty of Rome creating the European Community in 1957 provided specific details on eliminating trade barriers, but monetary integration was *not* one of the treaty's goals. Nevertheless, a number of European leaders have long viewed monetary union as a central objective, and as early as 1959 the European Parliament proposed that an institution similar to the U.S. Federal Reserve System be formed. Since the 1960s, a series of events have given concrete form to the idea of European monetary integration, and in early May 1998, 11 members of the European Union formally committed to replacing their national currencies with the euro as a single European currency.[70] The discussion that follows examines the reasons why the EU is establishing an economic and monetary union (EMU), the implications of the EMU for European countries, and the problems and tensions surrounding the formation of the EMU.

From 1958 to 1973, the Bretton Woods monetary regime provided the European Community with a framework for coordinating monetary policies, and with some degree of stability under the system of fixed exchange rates. Several major changes as early as the 1960s, however, caused the EC countries to consider proposals for regional monetary integration more seriously. First, U.S. balance-of-payments deficits and decreased confidence in the dollar began to pose a threat to exchange rate stability. This threat rose dramatically in the 1960s when President Lyndon Johnson continued to pursue the Vietnam War at great expense to the United States and also launched ambitious domestic social programs. Second, rapid European progress in establishing a customs union and the development of the EC's Common Agricultural Policy (CAP) increased the need for exchange rate stability among EC members.[71]

In response to these changes, Pierre Werner, the prime minister and minister of finance of Luxembourg, proposed in 1968 that the six EC member states lock the exchange rates among their currencies at fixed levels. At their December 1969 summit meeting in The Hague, the national leaders of the six EC states also endorsed the concept of eventually establishing an economic and monetary union (EMU).[72] One practical result of these proposals was the establishment in 1972 of the "snake," which was the first European exchange rate arrangement. In the snake, EC members agreed to hold their currencies within a 2.25 percent band against each other. However, the 1973–74 oil price hike and the 1975 global recession, combined with different inflation rates among EC countries, made it impossible for countries with weaker currencies to adhere to the narrow fluctuation band, and France, Ireland, Italy, and Britain soon left the snake agreement.[73]

Despite the failure of the snake, it had an important role in creating habits of co-operation among European central banks, facilitating later integration efforts. When variability in the exchange rates of EC currencies began to interfere with the integration process, renewed calls for monetary integration resulted in the establishment of the *European Monetary System* (EMS) in 1979. The EMS had two main features, an *exchange rate mechanism (ERM)* and a *European currency unit (ECU)*. The ERM was a form of adjustable peg system, similar to the original Bretton Woods system. Participating countries decided on exchange rates for their currencies, setting bands beyond which the rates could not fluctuate (+2.25 and −2.25 percent for most EC countries). When the limits of a band were reached, central banks intervened to keep the exchange rates within the required levels. After consultation with other EMS members, countries could decide to realign their currencies. The second feature, the ECU, was a monetary unit based on a weighted basket of the EMS countries' currencies. Although the ECU served as a unit of account, it did not have a major role in the monetary system.[74]

The EMS experienced a reasonable degree of success for more than a decade, contributing to further habits of cooperation on monetary issues. In 1986, EC members signed the *Single European Act* calling for the removal of all barriers on the movement of goods, people, and capital within the EC by January 1, 1993; and in December 1991, a European conference produced the *Treaty on European Union* or *Maastricht Treaty*. One of the central objectives of the Maastricht Treaty was to establish an EMU in 1999. The EMU was to include the creation of a central bank and a single currency, central control over the money supply, and wide-ranging influence over national tax and financial policies.[75]

In addition to the historical reasons outlined for the moves toward European monetary integration, other factors have contributed to pressures for monetary union. First, European Union states now conduct more than 60 percent of their trade with each other. European business groups in particular believe that a common currency—the euro—will end uncertainties over exchange rate fluctuations and facilitate this growing European trade. Second, in an age of globalization there are feelings that greater European unity is necessary so that Europe can compete more effectively with the United States and Japan. Third, there are strong domestic pressures in some European countries such as France, Italy, and even Germany for a continuance of costly social programs, and political leaders with liberal leanings feel that a European monetary union will force these countries to decrease their government spending.

When EU member states signed the Maastricht Treaty in 1991, many economists predicted that monetary integration would progress smoothly.[76] However, the steps toward monetary union have been difficult for a number of reasons. The most important obstacle stemmed from the fact that the Maastricht agreement had rather rigid requirements for developing a single currency. These requirements were included mainly at the insistence of Germany. To join the EMU, countries were to have (or be showing substantial progress toward) budget deficits that did not exceed 3 percent of their gross domestic products, public debt that was no greater than 60 percent of their GDPs, and relatively low inflation rates. Only some of the EU countries were likely to meet these targets, and the required cuts in domestic welfare and social expenditures caused considerable discontent. For example, in December 1995 French workers staged massive strikes in Paris to protest planned cutbacks in social security programs.

Another related problem was that many Germans were fearful of sacrificing the deutschmark, which reflects the country's economic strength, for what could be a much weaker euro. Germany accounts for about 25 percent of the European Union's total economic output today, and the deutschmark is the second largest currency (after the U.S. dollar) held in official reserves of countries throughout the world. As a result, there was considerable concern among Germans that weaker countries such as Italy could detract from the strength of the euro. Despite the economic requirements for joining the EMU, many Germans believed that monetary integration would not be good for their country. Nevertheless, Chancellor Helmut Kohl of Germany strongly supported the EMU and staked his reputation on monetary integration. While many Germans were fearful of the euro, other countries had different concerns. Thus, Britain, Denmark, and Sweden did not seek membership in the EMU in the "first wave" for political as well as economic reasons. In Britain in particular, the issue of preserving national sovereignty is extremely sensitive, and the fact that the new European central bank (ECB) is to be located in Frankfurt, Germany, delighted neither the British nor the French.

Despite the obstacles to implementing the goals of the Maastricht Treaty, the European commitment to monetary union remained very much alive. Thus, in early May 1998, the European Union's heads of government agreed that 11 EU members (the Euro-11) would replace their national currencies with the euro: Austria, Belgium, Finland, France, Germany, Ireland, Italy, Luxembourg, the Netherlands, Portugal, and Spain. Only 4 EU members did not participate in the agreement: Britain, Sweden, and Denmark chose not to join initially; and Greece was too weak economically. In view of the combined strength of the 11 countries' economies, the euro will be the world's second currency, and it could eventually supplant the dollar as the key currency in the global monetary regime: the 11 EU countries account for 19.4 percent of the world's GDP, compared with 19.6 percent for the United States and 7.7 percent for Japan. These EU countries also account for 18.6 percent of global trade (not counting internal trade), compared with 16.6 percent for the United States and 8.2 percent for Japan.[77]

Nevertheless, an important question remains regarding the degree to which the euro will be a strong currency that attracts confidence. One possible source of contention is the extent to which the EU interpreted its own requirements for membership in the EMU in a flexible manner so that 11 countries could join. For example, 8 of the 11 countries had debts exceeding 60 percent of their total output, and France also had a budget deficit above the 3 percent of GDP required for admission. Many analysts argue that the policies of the new European central bank will be more important than the flexibility in admitting members in determining whether or not the euro will be a strong currency, and the ECB is required by its founding statute to promote price stability as its main objective. The question arises, however, as to whether or not the EMU countries will subsume their national priorities to the development of a common monetary policy and permit the European central bank to act independently.

A bitter debate over the nationality of the president of the ECB (French President Jacques Chirac insisted that the Dutch nominee for the ECB position serve only 4 years of an 8-year term so that a French candidate could then take over) does not bode well for an effective and independent bank. The Social Democratic party's victory in Germany in September 1998 also signaled a further shift to the left in Europe, with center-left groups forming the main governing party in 13 of the 15 EU countries. It is uncertain as to whether these governments will permit the ECB to follow orthodox liberal policies designed to promote price stability and curb inflation, or whether the governments will try to exert more political control over the ECB to ensure that it gives greater priority to interventionist liberal policies such as combatting unemployment.[78] Divisions over these competing objectives could interfere with the effective functioning of the EMU. It is interesting to note, however, that some skeptics questioned whether the euro would ever be created. Now that Europe has moved to establish a common currency, it could serve more as a partner with the United States in managing international monetary relations, and in the future the euro could vie with the U.S. dollar for key currency status.

THE ROLE OF THE JAPANESE YEN

Unlike the case in Europe, formal currency links are lacking in East Asia. The role of the Japanese yen, however, has increased dramatically in the last decade, and some analysts believe that a "yen bloc" with financial, monetary, and trade implications is likely to emerge in East Asia. There are a number of indications of the yen's increased influence. For example, the yen's share of the Eurobond market grew from about 5 percent in 1980 to 13 percent in 1993. Although the yen's global share of foreign exchange reserves is still only about 9 percent, its share is significantly higher in East Asia; in Indonesia, the Philippines, Singapore, and Taiwan, the yen's share of foreign exchange reserves is at least 30 percent. Nevertheless, no country has yet pegged its exchange rate specifically to the yen, and in East Asia most countries have maintained currency links with the U.S. dollar or a basket of currencies. Japan's traditional lack of openness in trade and finance has also produced obstacles to the development of the yen as a major reserve for international trade and financial transactions.[79]

Despite the continued dominance of the U.S. dollar and the agreement to establish a common European currency, some writers believe that the yen's importance as an international currency could increase in the future for several reasons: Japan's large capital exports will give it influence in determining the currency in which debts are denominated; the yen's global position should be strengthened if the impressive growth of the East Asian economies from the 1960s to the 1980s resumes; and a shift by Japan to more open, liberal policies could make the yen more acceptable in international trade and financial transactions. The U.S. dollar is likely to retain its role as the top (albeit negotiated) currency in the medium term because of the size and diversity of the U.S. economy and the efficient nature of the dollar payment system. Nevertheless, the new European currency (and to a much lesser extent the Japanese yen) could pose a growing threat to the central position of the dollar in the future.[80]

CONCLUSION

At the end of World War II, the Bretton Woods negotiators opted for a monetary regime based on Keynes's ideas of interventionist liberalism, in which exchange rates were pegged to the U.S. dollar and gold and the IMF provided short-term loans for balance-of-payments problems. To maintain exchange rate stability, the negotiators agreed that IMF member states should be able to impose controls on capital flows. Pressures of globalization, combined with pressures for a return to orthodox liberalism, contributed to a shift from pegged to floating exchange rates in 1973 and to a gradual freeing of capital controls throughout the 1970s and 1980s.

Liberal interdependence theorists believe that advances in technology and communications have made these changes irrevocable and that to return to the pegged rates of Bretton Woods in "today's world of globalizing capital markets, capital controls would have to be fierce."[81] In 1973, only $10 to $20 billion of currency was traded on world markets each day, and in 1983, the figure was still a modest $60 billion per day. Since 1983, however, trading of currencies has increased 20-fold, aided by new financial instruments and advanced-technology computers and telecommunications. Central bank reserves, by contrast, have grown far more slowly. Thus, the ability of central banks to cope with currency traders has greatly decreased.[82] In the view of many liberals, the shift to floating currencies and to a freeing of capital flows is a positive development enabling markets to function more freely, with little interference from the state.

Historical structuralists, by contrast, view the increased mobility of capital as a highly negative development because the fear of capital outflows can force governments to adopt policies that adversely affect the poorest and weakest in society. If governments do not adopt "capital-friendly" policies, multinational corporations and international banks today can readily shift their funds to more welcoming locations. Thus, governments are inclined to lower their tax rates on corporate income even if this means a sacrifice in social programs.[83] The mobility of capital flows, according to historical structuralists, also increases the vulnerability of the working class. Unlike capital, labor is still largely immobile between countries, and countries with weaker labor unions will often draw investment away from countries where labor unions are stronger and more independent.[84]

Many realists, by contrast, argue that the degree to which globalization has occurred in monetary and financial relations is greatly exaggerated. Indeed, they often present evidence to show that there was more openness to capital flows before World War I than there is today.[85] To the extent that global financial flows have increased in recent years, realists believe that this has occurred with the permission (and sometimes the encouragement) of the most powerful states and that these states continue to dictate the terms for such transactions. Some writers take a position that combines realism with liberalism, arguing that powerful states initially adopted policies that contributed to the globalization of finance but that this globalization "has had unintended consequences for those who promoted it."[86] Thus, it may no longer be possible for states to regain control over the global market forces that they unleashed. Realists also argue that states have a more important role in the current regime of floating exchange rates than many liberals would lead us to believe. Indeed, the Plaza and Louvre accords show that the industrial states can manage exchange rates by intervening collectively in the market when they so choose. When this does not occur, it is because the most powerful states cannot agree on the need for, or type of, intervention, not because exchange rates are uncontrollable.

Realists also remind us that this is primarily a world of *national* currencies, in which the U.S. dollar still is the top currency. In some respects, U.S. hegemony has declined in global monetary relations. For example, the United States' percentage of votes in the IMF decision-making bodies has steadily fallen from about 40 percent to slightly below 18 percent, and collective leadership has replaced unilateral U.S. leadership in this area. Nevertheless, the dollar continues to serve as the top—albeit negotiated—currency. Efforts to increase the role of special drawing rights as an alternative to the dollar have been largely unsuccessful, and in 1997 SDRs amounted to only 1.7 percent of IMF members' total nongold reserves. Although its importance has declined, the dollar still accounts for more than 60 percent of reserves and more than half of global private financial wealth, and about 67 percent of world trade and 75 percent of international bank lending is invoiced in U.S. dollars.

Despite the dollar's continued importance, confidence in the U.S. currency continues to be problematic because of U.S. economic decline in other areas. For example, the United States now accounts for only 20 percent of global output and 14 percent of global exports; furthermore, countries with the world's key currencies have traditionally been international creditors, but the United States is now the world's largest debtor.[87] Major international creditor countries such as Japan and Germany, however, do not have economies as large as that of the United States, and they do not have financial markets with the same degree of depth and liquidity. Both Japan and Germany have also been reluctant to permit greater international use of their currencies because of their fears of losing control over monetary policy. Although the euro could challenge the position of the U.S. dollar in the future, continuing political divisions in Europe could preclude this possibility. One possibility is that the top currencies—the dollar, the euro, and perhaps the yen—might share power more evenly in the future.

While realists and liberals are concerned with the status of U.S. hegemony in the international monetary regime, many historical structuralists believe that this question will have little significance for less developed countries in the periphery of the global economy. The rich Northern states have dominated the South in global monetary relations, from this perspective, and they will continue to do so even if U.S. hegemony declines.

NOTES

1. Susan Strange, "Protectionism and World Politics," *International Organization* 39-2 (Spring 1985), p. 257.
2. Eric Helleiner, *States and the Reemergence of Global Finance: From Bretton Woods to the 1990s* (Ithaca, NY: Cornell University Press, 1994), p. 1; Joseph S. Nye, Jr., "Soft Power," *Foreign Policy* 80 (Fall 1990), pp. 153–171.
3. Susan Strange, *Casino Capitalism* (Oxford: Basil Blackwell, 1986), p. 29.
4. Benjamin J. Cohen, "Introduction," in Benjamin J. Cohen, ed., *The International Political Economy of Monetary Relations* (Aldershot, UK: Elgar, 1993), pp. xi–xiv.

5. The term *balance of trade* is sometimes used to refer to the merchandise trade balance alone. However, this book also includes services because of their growing importance in overall trade flows.

6. Richard G. Lipsey, Douglas D. Purvis, and Peter O. Steiner, *Economics* (New York: Harper & Row, 5th edition, 1985), pp. 765–772; Benjamin J. Cohen, *Organizing the World's Money: The Political Economy of International Monetary Relations* (New York: Basic Books, 1977), pp. 20–24.

7. David Calleo and Susan Strange, "Money and World Politics," in Susan Strange, ed., *Paths to International Political Economy* (London: Allen & Unwin, 1984), p. 97.

8. This section on adjustment and financing relies partly on Mordechai E. Kreinin, *International Economics: A Policy Approach,* 6th edition (San Diego, CA: Harcourt Brace Jovanovich, 1991), pp. 123–124; and Richard N. Cooper, *The Economics of Interdependence: Economic Policy in the Atlantic Community* (New York: McGraw-Hill, 1968), pp. 13–23, chs. 7–9.

9. International Monetary Fund, *Balance of Payments Statistics Yearbook* (Washington, DC: IMF, 1993), vol. 44, pt. 1, p. 118.

10. Cooper, *The Economics of Interdependence,* p. 22.

11. See Kenneth W. Dam, *The Rules of the Game: Reform and Evolution in the International Monetary System* (Chicago: University of Chicago Press, 1982), p. 6; and Benjamin J. Cohen, *Organizing the World's Money; The Political Economy of International Monetary Relations* (New York: Basic Books, 1977), ch. 3.

12. Barry Eichengreen argues that cooperation among the major powers, and the willingness of these powers to undergo domestic adjustments when necessary, were more important than British hegemony in maintaining the pre–World War I gold standard. See Barry Eichengreen, *Golden Fetters: The Gold Standard and the Great Depression, 1919–1939* (New York: Oxford University Press, 1992), ch. 2.

13. John Gerard Ruggie, "International Regimes, Transactions, and Change: Embedded Liberalism in the Postwar Economic Order," in Stephen D. Krasner, ed., *International Regimes* (Ithaca, NY: Cornell University Press, 1983), pp. 204–207; Ronald I. McKinnon, "The Rules of the Game: International Money in Historical Perspective," *Journal of Economic Literature* 31-1 (March 1993), pp. 3–11.

14. Paul R. Krugman and Maurice Obstfeld, *International Economics: Theory and Policy* (New York: HarperCollins, 3rd edition, 1994), p. 507.

15. Charles P. Kindleberger, *The World in Depression 1929–1939* (Berkeley: University of California Press, revised and enlarged edition, 1986), pp. 46–49.

16. Peter Alexis Gourevitch, "Squaring the Circle: The Domestic Sources of International Cooperation," *International Organization* 50-2 (Spring 1996), pp. 349–373. Two books which argue convincingly that domestic factors played a major role in the breakdown of monetary stability in the interwar period are Eichengreen, *Golden Fetters;* and Beth A. Simmons, *Who Adjusts? Domestic Sources of Foreign Economic Policy During the Interwar Years* (Princeton, NJ: Princeton University Press, 1994).

17. John Gerard Ruggie calls this the "embedded liberal compromise." See Ruggie, "International Regimes, Transactions, and Change," pp. 209–214.

18. Dam, *The Rules of the Game,* p. 38; Edward M. Bernstein, "The Search for Exchange Stability: Before and After Bretton Woods," in Omar F. Hamouda, Robin Rowley, and Bernard M. Wolf, eds., *The Future of the International Monetary System: Change, Coordination or Instability?* (Aldershot, UK: Elgar, 1989), p. 29.

19. As we will discuss, the United States was the only country that could not devalue its currency under the Bretton Woods regime.

20. Eric Helleiner, "From Bretton Woods to Global Finance: A World Turned Upside Down," in Richard Stubbs and Geoffrey R. D. Underhill, eds., *Political Economy and the Changing Global Order* (Toronto: McClelland & Stewart, 1994), p. 164; J. Keith Horsefield, ed., *The International Monetary Fund 1945–1965: Twenty Years of International Monetary Cooperation, Vol. 3: Documents* (Washington, DC: IMF, 1969), p. 67.

21. *Articles of Agreement of the International Monetary Fund,* adopted July 22, 1944 (Washington, DC: IMF, April 1993).

22. See Sidney Dell, "On Being Grandmotherly: The Evolution of IMF Conditionality," *Essays in International Finance,* no. 144 (Princeton, NJ: Princeton University, October 1981); and "Conditionality: Ensuring Effective Use of Revolving Resources," *IMF Survey—Supplement on the IMF,* vol. 24 (September 1995), p. 9.

23. For a list of the executive directors and their voting power, see *Annual Report of the International Monetary Fund—1997* (Washington, DC: IMF, 1997) pp. 215–218; *Articles of Agreement of the IMF,* Article 12, section 3.

24. In addition to the board of governors and executive board, an interim committee was established in October 1974, which meets at the ministerial level and has become increasingly important. *Annual Report of the IMF—1996.*

25. Marc Williams, *International Economic Organisations and the Third World* (New York: Harvester Wheatsheaf, 1994), pp. 67–68; Stephen D. Krasner, *Structural Conflict: The Third World Against Global Liberalism* (Berkeley: University of California Press, 1985), pp. 138–140.

26. See Tyrone Ferguson, *The Third World and Decision Making in the International Monetary Fund: The Quest for Full and Effective Participation* (London: Pinter Publishers, 1988), pp. 90–91.

27. The three problems of liquidity, confidence, and adjustment were first identified by a group of 32 economists. See Fritz Machlup and Burton G. Malkiel, eds., *International Monetary Arrangements: The Problem of Choice: Report on the Deliberations of an International Study Group of 32 Economists* (Princeton, NJ: Princeton University, International Finance Section, 1964), p. 24.

28. Ruggie, "International Regimes," p. 223; Cohen, *Organizing the World's Money,* pp. 94–97.

29. See Dam, *The Rules of the Game,* pp. 64–69.

30. *Articles of Agreement of the IMF,* Article 4, section 1; John Charles Pool, Stephen C. Stamos, and Patrice Franko Jones, *The ABCs of International Finance* (Lexington, MA: Heath, 2nd edition, 1991), pp. 67–68.

31. Charles P. Kindleberger, "Dominance and Leadership in the International Economy: Exploitation, Public Goods and Free Rides," *International Studies Quarterly* 25-2 (June 1981), p. 248.

32. Marina V. N. Whitman, "Leadership Without Hegemony," *Foreign Policy,* no. 20 (Fall 1975), p. 140; "Will the Buck Stop Here?" *The Economist,* November 12–18, 1994, p. 88.

33. Robert A. Isaak, *Managing World Economic Change: International Political Economy* (Englewood Cliffs, NJ: Prentice-Hall, 2nd edition, 1995), pp. 84–85.

34. See Robert Triffin, *Gold and the Dollar Crisis: The Future of Convertibility* (New Haven: Yale University Press, revised edition, 1961).

35. Harold James, *International Monetary Cooperation Since Bretton Woods* (Washington, DC, and New York: IMF and Oxford University Press, 1996), pp. 179–181; Stuart Corbridge, *Debt and Development* (Oxford: Blackwell, 1993), pp. 30–31.

36. Michael C. Webb, *The Political Economy of Policy Coordination: International Adjustment Since 1945* (Ithaca, NY: Cornell University Press, 1995), p. 16.

37. For a detailed discussion of U.S. and British support for the Euromarket in the 1960s, see Helleiner, *States and the Reemergence of Global Finance,* pp. 81–100.

38. Susan Strange, *Sterling and British Policy: A Political Study of an International Currency in Decline* (London: Oxford University Press, 1971), p. 209.

39. Strange, *Sterling and British Policy,* pp. 5, 17.

40. C. Fred Bergsten and C. Randall Henning, *Global Economic Leadership and the Group of Seven* (Washington, DC: Institute for International Economic, June 1996), pp. 22–23.

41. Although the United States attended meetings, it was not until September 1994 that Alan Greenspan, governor of the U.S. Federal Reserve System, occupied the seat that had been reserved for him in the BIS. For a detailed discussion of the BIS, see Age F. P. Bakker, *International Financial Institutions* (New York: Longman, 1996), ch. 6.

42. Keith J. Horsefield, *The International Monetary Fund, 1945–65: Twenty Years of Monetary Cooperation,* Vol. 1 (Washington, DC: 1969), p. 514.

43. Ngaire Woods, "A Third World Voice within the IMF?" *The Round Table,* no. 314 (April 1990), p. 196. See also C. Randall Henning, "The Group of Twenty-four: Two Decades of Monetary and Financial Co-operation Among Developing Countries," in United Nations Conference on Trade and Development, *International Monetary and Financial Issues for the 1990s—Vol. 1* (New York: United Nations, 1992), pp. 137–154.

44. Barry Eichengreen and Peter B. Kenen, "Managing the World Economy Under the Bretton Woods System: An Overview," in Peter B. Kenen, ed., *Managing the World Economy: Fifty Years After Bretton Woods* (Washington, DC: Institute for International Economics, September 1994), pp. 26–34.

45. Krugman and Obstfeld, *International Economics,* pp. 311–313; Marin Bronfenbrenner and Yasukichi Yasuba, "Economic Welfare," in Kozo Yamamura and Yasukichi Yasuba, eds., *The Political Economy of Japan: The Domestic Transformation,* Vol. 1 (Stanford, CA: Stanford University Press, 1987), p. 100.

46. For a discussion of the reasons for the shift in U.S. Policy, see John S. Odell, *U.S. International Monetary Policy: Markets, Power, and Ideas as Sources of Change* (Princeton, NJ: Princeton University Press, 1982), pp. 79–164.

47. For a discussion of the lengthy negotiations leading to the decision to create SDRs, see Susan Strange, *International Monetary Relations* (London: Oxford University Press, 1976), pp. 229–262.

48. Pierre-Paul Schweitzer, "Political Aspects of Managing the International Monetary System," *International Affairs* 52-2 (April 1976), p. 214.

49. "IMF Given Role in Fostering Freer Capital Flows; Quota Increase, SDR Allocation Agreed," *IMF Survey,* vol. 26, no. 18, October 6, 1997, p. 292.

50. "SDR: An International Reserve Asset," *IMF Survey—Supplement on the IMF,* vol. 26 (September 1997), pp. 20–21.

51. Helleiner, *States and the Reemergence of Global Finance,* p. 102.

52. John Williamson and C. Randall Henning, "Managing the Monetary System," in Kenen, ed., *Managing the World Economy,* p. 89.

53. For a discussion of President Nixon's August 1971 decision and the Smithsonian agreements, see Robert Solomon, *The International Monetary System, 1945–1981* (New York: Harper & Row, 2nd edition, 1982), pp. 176–234.

54. When the C-20's efforts failed, the Interim Committee of the IMF board of governors was established to carry on its work of monetary reform. For a discussion of the C-20's failed negotiations, see John Williamson, *The Failure of World Monetary Reform, 1971–74* (Sunbury-on-Thames, UK: Nelson, 1977).

55. The idea of linking development assistance with international liquidity creation was not new. Maxwell Stamp is credited with making the first linkage proposal in 1958. See Hon. Maxwell Stamp, "The Fund and the Future," *Lloyds Bank Review* (October 1958), pp. 14–20.

56. Graham Bird, *The International Monetary System and the Less Developed Countries*, 2nd edition (London: Macmillan, 1982), p. 254. For a discussion of the link debate in the Committee of 20, see Williamson, *The Failure of World Monetary Reform*, pp. 143–147.

57. Cohen, *Organizing the World's Money*, p. 115. Canada was an exception in the Bretton Woods regime, since it had floated its currency from 1950 to 1962. The United States (and the IMF) had agreed to this exception partly because of its "special relationship" with Canada. See A. F. W. Plumptre, *Three Decades of Decision: Canada and the World Monetary System, 1944–75* (Toronto: McClelland and Stewart, 1977).

58. *Articles of Agreement of the IMF*, Article 4, section 1-iii.

59. Yusuke Kashiwagi, "Future of the International Monetary System and the Role of the IMF," in Bretton Woods Commission, *Bretton Woods: Looking to the Future, Background Papers* (Washington, DC: Bretton Woods Committee, July, 1994), p. C-1.

60. See Milton Friedman, "The Case for Flexible Exchange Rates," *Essays in Positive Economics* (Chicago: University of Chicago Press, 1953), p. 203.

61. John Williamson, *The Exchange Rate System* (Washington, DC: Institute for International Economics, revised edition, June, 1985), p. 9; Michael Devereux and Thomas A. Wilson, "International Co-ordination of Macroeconomic Policies: A Review," *Canadian Public Policy* 15, special issue (February 1989), pp. S22–S23; Kashiwagi, "Future of the International Monetary System and the Role of the IMF," p. C-1.

62. Helleiner, *States and the Reemergence of Global Finance*, pp. 115–116; Gordon G. Thiessen, "Foreign Exchange Markets Viewed from a Macro-Policy Perspective," *Canadian Public Policy* 15, special issue (February 1989), p. S68.

63. Williamson, *The Exchange Rate System*, pp. 9–10.

64. Williamson, *The Exchange Rate System*, p. 39.

65. Devereux and Wilson, "International Co-ordination of Macroeconomic Policies," pp. S23–S24.

66. Williamson and Henning, "Managing the Monetary System," p. 100.

67. For a discussion of the difficulties in bringing about policy coordination, see Webb, *The Political Economy of Policy Coordination*.

68. Yusuke Kashiwagi, "Future of the International Monetary System and the Role of the IMF," p. C-3.

69. Barry Eichengreen, "Prerequisites for International Monetary Stability," in *Bretton Woods: Looking to the Future*, p. C-50.

70. See "Fanfare for the Euro," *The Economist*, May 2, 1998, pp. 45–46.

71. Michele Fratianni and Jürgen von Hagen, *The European Monetary System and European Monetary Union* (Boulder, CO: Westview Press, 1992), pp. 11–12.

72. See David R. Cameron, "Transnational Relations and the Development of European Economic and Monetary Union," in Thomas Risse-Kappen, ed., *Bringing Transnational Relations Back In: Non-State Actors, Domestic Structures and International Institutions* (Cam-

bridge: Cambridge University Press, 1995), pp. 39–41; Andrew Britton and David Mayes, *Achieving Monetary Union in Europe* (London: Sage Publications, 1992), pp. 6–9.

73. A. J. Kondonassis and A. G. Malliaris, "Toward Monetary Union of the European Community: History and Experiences of the European Monetary System," *American Journal of Economics and Sociology* 53-3 (July 1994), pp. 292–294; Helmut Schlesinger, "On the Way to a New Monetary Union: The European Monetary Union," *Federal Reserve Bank of St. Louis Review* 76-3 (May/June 1994), p. 4.

74. Paul De Grauwe, *The Economics of Monetary Union* (Oxford: Oxford University Press, 2nd revised edition, 1994), pp. 98–102.

75. See Michael H. Abbey and Nicholas Bromfield, "A Practitioner's Guide to the Maastricht Treaty," *Michigan Journal of International Law* 15-4 (Summer 1994), pp. 1329–1357.

76. Brian K. Kruzmann, "Challenges to Monetary Unification in the European Union: Sovereignty Reigning Supreme?" *Denver Journal of International Law and Policy* 23-1 (Fall 1994), p. 158.

77. "Fanfare for the Euro," p. 45.

78. Edmund L. Andrews, "Politicians Seek Wider Role in European Central Bank," *New York Times,* October 9, 1998, p. C2; "A Continental Drift—To The Left," *The Economist,* October 3, 1998, pp. 59–60; "Euro Brief: Eleven into One May Go," *The Economist,* October 17, 1998, pp. 81–82. The 13 EU countries with center-left governments in October, 1998 were Austria, Belgium, Britain, Denmark, Finland, France, Germany, Greece, Italy, Luxembourg, Netherlands, Portugal, and Sweden.

79. This section on Japan relies extensively on David D. Hale, "Is It a Yen or a Dollar Crisis in the Currency Market?" in Brad Roberts, ed., *New Forces in the World Economy* (Cambridge, MA: MIT Press, 1996), pp. 304–320; and Jeffrey A. Frankel and Shang-Jun Wei, "Is a Yen Bloc Emerging?" in symposium on "Economic Cooperation and Challenges in the Pacific," *Joint U.S.-Korea Academic Studies,* vol. 5 (1995), pp. 145–175.

80. Hale, "Is It a Yen or a Dollar Crisis in the Currency Market?" pp. 308–310.

81. Richard G. Lipsey, "Agendas for the 1988 and Future Summits," *Canadian Public Policy* 15, special issue (February 1989), p. S90.

82. "Big: The Foreign-exchange Market," *The Economist,* September 23, 1995, pp. 63–64.

83. The standard rate of corporate income tax in OECD countries did in fact fall from 43 percent in 1986 to 33 percent in 1995, while the average tax rate for workers increased. See "Survey: World Economy," *The Economist,* September 20, 1997, p. 33.

84. Stephen Gill and David Law, "Global Hegemony and the Structural Power of Capital," in Stephen Gill, ed., *Gramsci, Historical Materialism and International Relations* (Cambridge: Cambridge University Press, 1993), p. 108.

85. Paul Hirst and Grahame Thompson, *Globalization in Question: The International Economy and the Possibilities of Governance* (Cambridge, UK: Polity Press, 1996), p. 27.

86. Ethan B. Kapstein, *Governing the Global Economy: International Finance and the State* (Cambridge, MA: Harvard University Press, 1994), p. 6. This is also one of the themes in Helleiner, *States and the Reemergence of Global Finance.*

87. "Will the Buck Stop Here," *The Economist,* November 12, 1994, p. 88.

CHAPTER 7

Foreign Debt

The international debt crisis that erupted in the early 1980s was "one of the most traumatic international financial disturbances" of the twentieth century.[1] Debt crises had occurred frequently in the nineteenth century, and widespread defaults on loans in the 1930s had severely disrupted capital flows to Latin America and to Southern and Eastern Europe. Nevertheless, the world seemed unprepared for the 1980s debt crisis, which threatened the international banking system as well as some of the largest Third World countries. A number of authors have examined the similarities and differences between the 1980s debt crisis and earlier crises.[2] One significant difference relates to changes in lending mechanisms. In the 1920s, most lending to Latin America occurred through the bond markets, so country debt was held by numerous individual bondholders located in many different countries. When LDCs defaulted on their debts in the 1930s, these bondholders suffered the loss, and the debt crisis was fragmented.

In the 1970s, by contrast, private bank lending to middle-income LDCs greatly increased. When the debtor countries threatened to default on their loans in the 1980s, the possible losses were therefore much more concentrated in the largest commercial banks, which occupied a central position in international finance. Indeed, the 9 largest U.S. banks had loans outstanding to 17 highly indebted countries, amounting to 194 percent of the banks' capital and reserves in 1982; a major debt default could have affected the core of the banking system. Because the 1980s debt crisis posed a major threat to international financial stability, creditor governments felt more pressure to intervene in the debt settlement process during this period.[3] Thus, another historical difference relates to the role of international organizations and the advanced industrial states.

In earlier periods of default, international institutions to deal with debt problems did not exist, and governments generally were less willing to intervene. In the 1980s, by contrast, the International Monetary Fund cajoled private banks to continue lending to LDC debtors on the one hand and pressured debtor countries to alter their economic policies on the other. There was also no hegemonic power to deal with the debt crisis in the 1930s, but in the 1980s the United States filled this position. Together the United States and the IMF orchestrated the response to the 1980s debt crisis, with other actors such as the World Bank, the Paris and London Clubs, and the Bank for International Settlements (discussed below) playing supporting positions.[4]

WHAT IS A DEBT CRISIS?

As discussed in Chapter 6, a country has a current account deficit when its payments abroad are greater than those it receives. Countries must either finance their deficits or adjust to them, and those governments that choose financing must borrow from external credit sources and/or decrease their foreign exchange reserves. As governments continue to borrow to finance their budget deficits, they are burdened with growing foreign debt problems. However, the level of a borrower's outstanding debt is *not* the main factor determining whether or not it is facing a debt crisis. The United States today is the world's largest debtor country, and in 1991 the U.S. debt amounted to about $370 billion. The total foreign debt owed by all the LDCs in the Western Hemisphere in 1991, by comparison, was about $434 billion. Nevertheless, the U.S. GNP is also the world's largest, and there is no danger that the United States will be unable to service the repayments on its outstanding debt. While the U.S. net foreign debt amounted to only about 6.4 percent of its GNP in 1991, the net foreign debt of the LDCs in the Western Hemisphere amounted to over 40 percent of their collective GNP.[5]

In determining the severity of a country's debt problem, therefore, we need to know not only the size of the debt, but also whether or not the country has the ability and commitment to service its debt repayments. A "debt crisis" results when countries lack sufficient foreign exchange to make the principal and/or interest payments on their debt obligations. Debt crises vary both in terms of severity and in terms of the length of time and types of measures required to bring about a resolution.[6] This chapter focuses primarily on the debt crisis of the 1980s, particularly on the origins of the debt crisis, the strategies adopted to deal with it, and the effects of the crisis on the debtor countries and the international banks.

THE ORIGINS OF THE 1980S DEBT CRISIS

According to most observers, the debt crisis began in August 1982, when Mexico announced that it could no longer service its public sector debt obligations. The announcement produced shock waves because of the magnitude of the Mexican external debt, which was estimated at $78 billion by the end of 1981.[7] However, earlier warning signs of a possible crisis had been largely ignored. From 1976 to 1980, a number of LDCs, including Zaire, Argentina, Peru, Sierra Leone, Sudan, and Togo, had been involved in debt rescheduling negotiations; and the external debt of LDCs in general had increased six-fold to $500 billion between 1972 and 1981. Foreign debt was also a growing problem in Eastern Europe, and Poland's indebtedness had reached serious proportions by 1981.[8] After Mexico's 1982 announcement, the debt crisis therefore quickly spread as private creditor banks moved to decrease their loan exposure to other LDC borrowers. Thus, 25 LDCs requested debt restructuring on their commercial bank debt by the end of 1982, and in 1983 the World Bank reported that "almost as many developing countries have had to reschedule loans in the last two years as in the previous twenty-five years."[9]

Analysts have differing views regarding the causes of the 1980s debt crisis, stemming partly from their divergent ideological perspectives. Most commonly, the crisis is explained in terms of unexpected changes in the global economy, irresponsible behavior of the lenders, irresponsible behavior of the debtor countries, and dependence of the Third World countries on the advanced capitalist states.

Unexpected Changes in the Global Economy

Some observers attribute the debt crisis primarily to external shocks, as a result of unexpected global economic changes.[10] The first external shocks occurred in the early 1970s, when there was a sharp rise in the prices of foodgrains and oil. In the late 1960s, major surpluses of wheat and grain had accumulated, leading to a decline in international food prices and production cutback programs in the United States, Canada, and some other grain-exporting countries. As a result of these cutback programs, the world was especially vulnerable to unanticipated events such as inclement weather and crop shortfalls in the Soviet Union, which resulted in massive Soviet grain purchases and serious foodgrain shortages. In 1972–73, global food stocks fell to their lowest level in twenty years, the volume of food aid was drastically reduced, and there were substantial increases in foodgrain prices.[11] After the October 1973 Middle East war, the Arab countries in OPEC also managed to limit the supply of oil and drastically raise its price. Thus, those LDCs that imported oil as well as food were doubly hit by the food and oil crises.

While many importing states were severely hurt by the increased oil prices, the OPEC countries accumulated unprecedented amounts of excess reserves—or "petrodollars"—which they deposited in the largest commercial banks. These banks played a major role in recycling the petrodollars through loans to middle-income developing countries, which were considered to be creditworthy for receiving commercial bank loans. Thus, about 60 percent of external financing for non-OPEC LDCs came from commercial bank credits between 1974 and 1979.[12] A second oil shock occurred in 1979, when OPEC more than doubled its prices. The private banks provided additional loans to help the LDCs pay for the new round of oil price increases, and they also offered loans to oil-exporting LDCs to help develop their industries and diversify their economies.

The second oil shock contributed to a severe contraction in the industrial economies and thus to the worst global recession since the 1930s. As a result, LDCs faced a sharp decline in demand for their commodity exports, and they found it increasingly difficult to earn foreign exchange to service their debts. The 1979 oil price increases also produced inflationary pressures, which the industrial states sought to control by raising interest rates. In the United States, the Reagan administration's need to borrow abroad to cover its huge federal budget deficits was yet another source of upward pressure on interest rates. The creditor banks were providing short-term loans at variable interest rates, and the impact of the higher rates on LDC debt levels was rapid and severe.[13] It may seem ironic that the debt crisis began with Mexico—an oil exporter. Oil-exporting LDCs, however, had also borrowed private funds to launch ambitious development projects and other programs, without anticipating that oil prices—and thus their oil revenues—would fall sharply after 1979. Thus, the unexpected global economic changes in the 1970s and 1980s contributed to the external debt problems of Third World oil exporters as well as importers.

Unanticipated global changes certainly were a factor in the debt crisis, but critics point out that these changes were not the only cause. While the external shocks affected a large number of LDCs, the East Asian newly industrializing countries fared far better than the Latin American LDCs. Both commercial banks and debtor countries often favor the "external shocks" explanation for the debt crisis because it awards "primary responsibility to economic policy shifts beyond their control."[14] Nevertheless, the policies of both the lenders and the borrowers must also be considered as explanations for the crisis.

Irresponsible Behavior of the Lenders

Historical structuralists and some interventionist liberals often consider irresponsible behavior by the creditor banks to be a major cause of the debt crisis. The commercial banks, according to this perspective, engaged in overlending, without being sufficiently concerned about the creditworthiness of borrowers or the nature of the activities they were financing. When the OPEC countries deposited a large amount of petrodollars in private commercial banks (mainly in New York and London), the banks aggressively sought to increase their loan activity in the Third World. The competition to lend funds, combined with inflationary conditions, meant that the large commercial banks charged extremely low interest rates, which did not give LDCs adequate signals as to when to stop borrowing. By the time the interest rates rose sharply in the early 1980s, LDC debtors had become overly dependent on commercial bank loans, and this factor heightened the severity of the crisis.[15] Thus, the commercial banks were often accused of "loan pushing" and of "urging the debtor countries to increase their liabilities."[16]

Some critics of the lender's policies argue that the banks could not have engaged in overlending completely on their own, and that governments of the industrial countries shared responsibility for this development. After the first oil shock in 1973, the industrial states collectively and individually adopted a number of policies that encouraged the flow of private bank funds to the Third World. For example, in 1974 the central bankers in the Group of 10 countries provided assurances that they would assist banks recycling petrodollars if they encountered financial difficulties. The IMF also introduced new lending programs for LDC oil importers such as the 1974 oil facility and the 1974 Extended Fund Facility, that in turn encouraged private banks to upgrade their own lending activities. Furthermore, the gradual lifting of capital controls in the industrial states (discussed in Chapter 6) eased the process by which banks in the United States and Western Europe could recycle surplus petrodollars to the Third World. From this perspective, both the creditor international banks, and the advanced industrial states in which they were located, shared responsibility for overlending which was a major cause of the debt crisis.[17]

Irresponsible Behavior of the Borrowing States

Many liberal theorists, especially orthodox liberals, attribute primary responsibility for the debt crisis to the imprudent behavior of the borrowing states. These critics often argue that the LDCs sought the easy route to borrowing from private banks in the 1970s in efforts to avoid the conditionality requirements of IMF loans. Unlike the IMF, private banking institutions were not inclined (and did not have the legal authority) to make loans to sovereign governments subject to policy conditions. Basic principles of the IMF financing regime—that governments should not have unlimited access to balance-of-payments financing and that countries with financing problems should undergo adjustment measures—were jeopardized due to the accessibility of private funds. As a liberal-economic institution, the IMF itself seemed to endorse this view in its 1977 *Annual Report:*

> Access to private sources of balance of payments finance may . . . in some cases permit countries to postpone the adoption of adequate domestic stabilization measures. This can exacerbate the problem of correcting payments imbalances, and can lead to adjustments that are politically and socially disruptive when the introduction of stabilization measures becomes unavoidable.[18]

In addition to citing imprudent borrowing behavior, liberals attribute the debt crisis at least in part to the domestic policies of borrowing states. While some LDCs used the commercial bank loans wisely to finance productive investments and economic growth, a goodly number, according to this view, used the funds to make poor investments, increase public expenditures, import consumer goods, and pay off corrupt officials. Some LDCs reacted to the debt crisis in a timely manner with readjustment policies, but many others demonstrated unwillingness—or inability—to change. Liberal economists often contrast the strong economic performance of the East Asian debtor countries such as South Korea and Indonesia in the 1980s with the generally weak performance of the Latin American debtors. (The most notable exception to this comparison was the weak performance of the Philippines.)

The differential economic performance of the East Asians and Latin Americans, from this perspective, cannot be explained by differences in external shocks or even by the amount of external borrowing. Instead, the most important differences relate to these countries' policies on foreign trade and exchange rates. While Latin American LDCs employed import substitution policies, the East and Southeast Asian LDCs placed far more emphasis on export-led growth. Exports are a critical source of foreign exchange for servicing a country's debts, so the East and Southeast Asians' outward-oriented policies placed them in a much stronger position to deal with their debt problems. Overvalued exchange rates also encouraged capital flight in Latin American countries such as Mexico and Argentina because residents feared precipitous declines in the value of their countries' currencies. The East and Southeast Asian LDCs, by contrast, had realistic exchange rates and generally avoided the Latin American problem of capital flight.[19]

Table 7.1 illustrates the more favorable position of the East and Southeast Asians vis-à-vis the Latin Americans in 1982. The largest debtors in Table 7.1 are Latin American (the debts of Brazil, Mexico, and Argentina exceeded $92, $86, and $43 billion, respectively); some East and Southeast Asian countries such as South Korea, Indonesia, and the Philippines also had substantial debt levels (exceeding $37, $24, and $24 billion, respectively). However, the stronger export position of the East and Southeast Asians (except the Philippines) demonstrates that they were in a much better position

TABLE 7.1

TOTAL DEBT AND DEBT INDICATORS, 1982 (MILLIONS OF DOLLARS)

	Total Debt	**Debt/Exports** (%)	**Debt Service** Ratio[a](%)
Latin America			
Argentina	43,634	447.3	50.0
Brazil	92,990	396.1	81.3
Chile	17,315	335.9	71.3
Colombia	10,306	204.3	29.5
Mexico	86,019	311.5	56.8
Peru	10,712	255.9	48.7
Venezuela	32,153	159.8	29.5
East and Southeast Asia			
Indonesia	24,734	116.3	18.1
Republic of Korea	37,330	131.6	22.4
Malaysia	13,354	93.4	10.7
Philippines	24,551	297.8	42.6
Thailand	12,238	130.0	20.6

[a]Debt service ratio: the ratio of a country's interest and principal payments to its export income.

Source: World Bank, *World Debt Tables 1992–93, Vol. 2: Country Tables* (Washington, DC: IBRD, 1992).

than the Latin Americans to service their debts. Economists often use the **debt service ratio,** which measures the ratio of a country's interest and principal payments on its debt to its export income, as a measure to assess the ability of a country to service its debt. The lower the debt service ratio (and also the debt-to-export ratio), the more favorable are the prospects that a country will meet its debt obligations. Thus, Table 7.1 shows that the debt service ratios of Malaysia and Indonesia were as low as 10.7 and 18.1 percent in 1982, while the debt service ratios of Brazil and Chile had reached the very unfavorable levels of 81.3 and 71.3 percent.

The view that irresponsible LDC behavior was the major factor explaining the debt crisis, like the other perspectives, has been subjected to some severe criticism. While the differing reactions of LDCs to the debt crisis indicates that some LDCs followed more prudent policies than others, critics charge that the attribution of LDC responsibility ignores the fact that the debt crisis was *systemic* in nature. Indeed, "the simultaneous onset of the crisis in more than forty developing countries" indicates that some of the major contributing factors were external to the LDCs and largely beyond their control.[20] Furthermore, East and Southeast Asian LDCs such as Thailand, Malaysia, Indonesia, and South Korea, which liberals identified as following responsible policies during the 1980s debt crisis, were the first to be hit by a severe financial crisis in the late 1990s (this issue is discussed in Chapter 11).

LDC Dependence on the Advanced Capitalist States

Some historical structuralists argue that the 1980s debt crisis cannot be traced simply to proximate actors and events but that it resulted from the long-term structural nature of the capitalist system. Thus, dependency and world-system theorists view LDC debt crises as simply extreme instances of a "debt trap," which exploits LDCs in the periphery and binds them to rich Northern states in the core.[21] Some writers draw linkages between Third World debt crises and the legacy of colonialism. The colonial powers established a division of labor in which the colonies provided agricultural products and raw materials to the metropole and served in turn as markets for the metropole's manufactures. This pattern still characterizes the export and import structures of many LDCs today, preventing them from earning the foreign exchange necessary for development. Although some LDCs are industrializing, they remain dependent on multinational corporations and other institutions in the core for technology and finance, and they therefore find it impossible to escape from their indebtedness.[22]

Other historical structuralists point to foreign aid as a source of LDC debt crises because more than half of all official development assistance is disbursed as loans. A substantial share of World Bank financing is also disbursed to the Third World as *hard loans* with high interest rates and relatively short repayment periods (see Chapter 11). A large percentage of multilateral and bilateral foreign aid today is required simply to cover the LDCs' repayments of past aid disbursements. Thus, development assistance loans become simply another mechanism by which surpluses are transferred from the peripheral to the core states. Many historical structuralists also view IMF and World Bank conditionality requirements as infringing on LDC sovereignty and as incorrect prescriptions for reducing LDC debt problems. Thus, official IMF and World Bank loans, like commercial bank loans, serve to perpetuate rather than alleviate LDC dependency:

> If they seek official help on softer than commercial terms, they have to accept outside scrutiny . . . and accept conditions which doom their efforts at industrial, diversified development. If they accept suppliers' credits on commercial terms in order to go through with their cherished projects, they are caught anyway when the payments come due before they are able to meet them.[23]

Like the other interpretations of the debt crisis, the dependency interpretation has been subject to considerable criticism. Liberals in particular argue that dependency theorists attribute the LDCs' debt problems solely to external causes beyond their control and thereby avoid looking at the *domestic* sources of LDC problems— traditional attitudes, domestic inefficiencies, and a reluctance to follow policies of economic openness.

We can safely conclude that all the above views regarding the origins of the foreign debt crisis have some validity. The unexpected food and oil price increases in the 1970s encouraged countries to increase their borrowing, and the monetary policy changes and world recession after the 1979 price increases added to the debt load of many LDC borrowers. While these unexpected global changes made a debt crisis more likely, the behavior of the commercial banks, some industrial states, and some debtor governments certainly exacerbated the debt situation. Furthermore, the long-term structural dependency of Third World countries on the industrial states increased the vulnerability of LDCs to protracted debt problems. Mexico's minister of finance and public credit from 1982 to 1986 clearly identified the multiple causes of the debt crisis, and the failure of the world community to foresee it, when he stated that

> the origin of the debt itself is clearly traceable to a decision by both develop-ing and developed countries that . . . resulted in the channeling of tens of bil-lions of dollars to the debtor community of today. . . . The whole world con-gratulated itself on the success, smoothness, and efficiency with which the recycling process was achieved. *We all were responsible.*[24]

THE FOREIGN DEBT REGIME

Before discussing the world's reaction to the 1980s debt crisis, it is important to de-scribe the elements of a foreign debt regime that developed to monitor and manage the crisis. A debt regime was more evident in the 1980s than it had been in the 1930s because a global hegemon (the United States) and a more developed institutional framework (including the IMF and the World Bank) existed to deal with the 1980s cri-sis. Before World War II, the mechanisms for coping with a debt crisis were largely limited either to unilateral actions by the creditors or debtors or to two-party solutions in which the debtors and creditors reached a compromise at the bargaining table. In-ternational debt settlements in the postwar period, by contrast, have often been three-party affairs involving international organizations such as the IMF and the World Bank and less formal groupings such as the Paris and London Clubs (discussed below). The United States has also acted as a third party in the postwar period, using its hegemonic position to pressure for debt settlements and to coordinate settlement efforts.[25]

Some regimes encompass only one sector or issue while others are broader in scope, and specific regimes may be nested within more diffuse regimes. For example, some authors have described textile and agricultural trade regimes as being nested within the more diffuse global trade regime.[26] While the global trade regime princi-ples, norms, and rules provide a general framework for the textile and agricultural trade regimes, textile and agricultural trade relations have their own unique character-istics and have often been treated as "exceptions" by the GATT/WTO. This chapter views the 1980s foreign debt regime as a specific regime nested within a more diffuse balance-of-payments financing regime, because foreign debt crises are a specific, more extreme type of balance-of-payments problem. While there have been continuous ef-forts to negotiate agreements with individual debtor countries throughout the postwar period, the pressures resulting from the 1980s debt crisis produced more coordinated, longer-term efforts to establish rules and decision-making procedures that we nor-mally associate with an international regime.

A basic principle underlying the balance-of-payments financing regime is that an adequate but not unlimited amount of supplementary financing should be available to states for dealing with their balance-of-payments deficits. A second principle is that those providing this financing may attach conditions to the funding that they believe will correct the recipient states' balance-of-payments problems. The rules of the balance-of-payments financing regime include the explicit conditions that the IMF places on its borrowers.[27] In the 1970s, the balance-of-payments regime's basic principle of conditional lending was threatened because private banks provided debtor countries loans with extremely low interest rates and minimal conditions. While these private bank loans were readily available to many middle-income and newly industrializing countries in the 1970s, low-income LDCs generally lacked creditworthiness to receive private bank loans, so they remained highly dependent on lending from the IMF and donor governments. Thus, Table 7.2 shows that in 1980 private bank loans accounted for only 6 percent of the debt of low-income LDCs (LICs) but for 38 percent of middle-income country (MIC) debt and for 65 percent of the debt of the NICs. **Official development assistance (ODA),** by contrast, accounted for 67 percent of LIC debt in 1980, but for only 25 percent of MIC debt and 4 percent of the debt of the NICs. The willingness of the private banks to provide for much of the financing needs of the more creditworthy LDCs greatly limited the IMF's ability to set conditions for these borrowers.

With the emergence of the debt crisis in 1982, however, private banks moved quickly to limit their loan exposure to LDCs, and the MICs and NICs therefore had to look to the IMF, the World Bank, and official government aid agencies for assistance with their growing debt problems. This dependence on official financing provided the international organizations and the U.S. government with considerable leverage in establishing what we call the foreign debt regime. As with the pre-1970s balance-of-payments regime, the basic principle of the debt regime revolved around conditionality—that the provision of new loans and debt rescheduling were contingent on the debtor countries' commitment to market-oriented reforms. However, the 1980s debt regime was also different from the pre-1970s regime in some important respects.

First, the IMF (with U.S. backing) adopted a new role when it imposed pressures on the private commercial banks in the 1980s to continue providing loans to the debtor LDCs. Second, creditor clubs such as the Paris and London Clubs were used much more frequently during the 1980s and 1990s than in earlier periods. Third, both the IMF and the World Bank became involved in providing structural adjustment loans to indebted LDCs and to the emerging countries of Eastern Europe and the former Soviet Union. These SALs were conditioned on far more demanding requirements than previously that the recipient LDCs adopt orthodox liberal reforms such as deregulation, privatization, and greater openness to trade and foreign investment. The changing roles of the IMF and the World Bank in the foreign debt regime are examined later in this chapter. We discuss here two sets of actors whose roles were also important: the emerging economies of Eastern Europe and the FSU, which became major debtor countries along with the LDCs; and the Paris Club and private creditor committees, which had a significant role in rescheduling loans.

The IMF, the World Bank, and the Emerging Economies

Chapter 2 noted that the Soviet bloc countries were nonmembers of the IMF and the World Bank for most of the early postwar period. Before examining the role of these countries in the foreign debt regime, we need to understand how they came to join the IMF and the World Bank. Membership issues in the two institutions are closely

TABLE 7.2

TOTAL DEBT, AND SHARE OF DEBT BASED ON ODA AND PRIVATE BANK LOANS FOR NONOIL LDCs

Income Group	1971			1975			1980			1982		
	Total Debt[a]	Percentage ODA	Percentage Private Banks	Total Debt	Percentage ODA	Percentage Private Banks	Total Debt	Percentage ODA	Percentage Private Banks	Total Debt	Percentage ODA	Percentage Private Banks
LICs	$18	74	2	$40	73	7	$86	67	6	$110	69	6
MICs	$25	45	14	$40	33	29	$107	25	38	$144	24	39
NICs	$32	16	38	$72	9	60	$192	4	65	$266	3	67

[a]Total debt figures in billions.

Abbreviations: ODA = official development assistance
LICs = low-income countries
MICs = middle-income countries
NICs = newly industrializing countries

Source: External Debt of Developing Countries—1982 Survey, p. 34. Copyright © OECD, 1982. By permission of the Organisation for Economic Co-operation and Development.

related: a country cannot join the World Bank without also becoming a member of the IMF. As Table 7.3 shows, Yugoslavia remained a member of the IMF and the World Bank from the time they were established. This was not surprising in view of Yugoslavia's defection from the Soviet Bloc in 1948 and its moves to develop an independent, nonaligned foreign policy. The Yugloslavs were also adopting policies such as workers' self-management and market socialism, which were more compatible with the liberal-economic orientation of the Bretton Woods institutions.

Table 7.3 shows that Romania was the first centrally planned economy (CPE) to join these institutions after the withdrawals or expulsions of the 1950s. Romania, like Yugoslavia, was atypical. It had distanced itself politically from the Soviet Union (but unlike Yugoslavia, Romania was still a member of the Soviet bloc). From Romania's perspective, the integration policies of the Council for Mutual Economic Assistance (CMEA) were hindering its industrialization, and membership in the IMF and the World Bank would enable Romania to benefit from their loans, upgrade its economic relations with the West, and further its political objectives. Remarkably, Romania became an IMF and World Bank member in 1972 without having to pass through a transition phase, even though its moves toward economic reform and decentralization were halting and it was building up a sizable foreign debt. Western countries downgraded the importance of these economic issues, largely because Romania's membership

TABLE 7.3
MEMBERSHIP OF THE EMERGING ECONOMIES IN THE IMF AND WORLD BANK

	IMF	World Bank
1946	Poland, Czechoslovakia, Yugoslavia, and China (founding members of IMF and World Bank)	
1950	Poland withdraws from IMF and World Bank	
1954	Czechoslovakia ousted from IMF and World Bank	
1972	Romania	Romania
1980	People's Republic of China (PRC) replaces Taiwan in IMF and World Bank	
1982	Hungary	Hungary
1986	Poland	Poland
1990	Czech and Slovak Federal Republic, Bulgaria	
1991	Albania	Albania, Bulgaria, Czech and Slovak Federal Republic
1992	Russian Federation, other FSU[a] republics	Russian Federation, other FSU[a] republics
1993	Croatia, Slovenia, Macedonia, Czech Republic, Slovak Republic	Croatia, Slovenia, Czech Republic, Slovak Republic
1994		Macedonia
1996	Bosnia and Herzegovina	Bosnia and Herzegovina

[a]FSU = former Soviet Union

Sources: International Monetary Fund, *Annual Report of the Executive Board* (Washington, DC: IMF, various years); World Bank, *Annual Report* (Washington, DC: World Bank, various years).

contributed to significant divisions within the Soviet bloc. Although Romania provided sensitive economic information to the IMF and the World Bank, the two institutions abided by a special agreement not to disclose this information in their statistical reports.[28]

The People's Republic of China was the next CPE to participate in IMF and World Bank meetings, and its case, too, was atypical. The IMF and the World Bank both permitted the PRC to take over the China seat from Taiwan and thus treated the issue as one of representation rather than new membership. The PRC's decision to "return" to the Bretton Woods institutions in 1980 followed a radical change in its policies. The Sino-Soviet dispute of the late 1950s and early 1960s had caused Mao Zedong's PRC to turn inward with a policy of "self-reliance," and this inward-looking policy became far more extreme and autarkic from 1966 to 1969 during the PRC's Cultural Revolution. The political and economic problems wrought by the Cultural Revolution, however, caused China to become somewhat more open to the outside world. In response, the UN General Assembly voted to seat the PRC delegation in October 1971, and China's commercial contacts with the advanced industrial states increased.[29]

Although China's foreign policy was changing, there was little change in its domestic economic policy. It was not until Mao's death in 1976 and the subsequent arrest of cultural revolutionaries that the PRC launched the Four Modernizations program to increase economic productivity and efficiency and to develop a more active role for China in the global economy. Thus, China wanted to renew its membership in the IMF and the World Bank as a means of gaining access to capital finance for infrastructure projects that were essential for its economic modernization. In the negotiations that followed, several factors facilitated China's reentry application, including the active support of the United States and a compromise worked out regarding Taiwan's subscription.[30]

After the PRC's takeover of the China seat in 1980, both Hungary and Poland requested accession in late 1981. Unlike Romania, Hungary came much closer to meeting the IMF's normal economic requirements. In 1968, Hungary had introduced its New Economic Mechanism (NEM), designed to increase the country's economic decentralization, outward economic orientation, and competitiveness in international markets; and in the 1970s and 1980s, Hungary introduced other economic reforms. Hungary sought IMF membership in order to safeguard these reforms and also to obtain assistance with its foreign debt, which was partly an outgrowth of its development plans. The debt situation was far more urgent for Poland, which had borrowed in international financial markets in the early 1970s as a substitute for introducing meaningful economic reform. Poland needed to reassure the financial community that it was committed to servicing its debt in the early 1980s, and IMF membership would be a part of this reassurance process. While Hungary was admitted to the IMF and the World Bank in 1982, Poland's application was stalled by its imposition of martial law in December 1981. Thus, it was not until 1986 that Poland was admitted to the Bretton Woods institutions (see Table 7.3).[31]

Poland was the last Eastern European country to become a member of the IMF and World Bank before the cataclysmic changes in the Soviet bloc transformed East-West relations. After Mikhail Gorbachev took office, he attempted to revive the Soviet economy through a combination of economic restructuring (*perestroika*) and a turn to political openness (*glasnost*). Although Gorbachev's economic efforts failed, his policies contributed to a series of revolutionary changes. Thus, the disintegration of one Communist regime after another in Eastern Europe in 1989 and the unification of Germany in June 1990 led to the decision to dissolve the CMEA in June 1991. This was followed by the Moscow coup in August 1991, which led to the independence of the Baltic states, and the formal dissolution of the Soviet Union itself in December 1991. Czechoslovakia and Bulgaria joined the Bretton Woods institutions in 1990 and 1991, but the most significant change was the accession of Russia and other former Soviet Union (FSU) republics in 1992–1993. Because Russia was facing an economic crisis, the IMF and Western donors offered it a $24 billion assistance package in return for Russia's commitment to decrease its budget deficit and inflation rate.[32]

The Bretton Woods institutions have worked closely together to assist the emerging economies of Eastern Europe and the FSU to make the transition to market orientation. The IMF has taken the lead in this process, estimating financing needs, providing policy advice, and setting conditions for economic reform. The World Bank has provided its usual financing for infrastructure and has also offered technical assistance and funding to promote the development of market incentives, privatization of state monopolies, and a legal framework for the emerging private sector.[33] Tensions have of course existed between the emerging economies and the Bretton Woods institutions in view of their different economic outlooks. Nevertheless, the addition of so many new countries has put new pressures on IMF and World Bank resources, and Third World countries sometimes charge that the emerging economies are receiving favored treatment.

There does in fact seem to be some truth to these LDC charges. For example, the findings of one study revealed that Romania, Poland, and Hungary have received more IMF loans than one would expect on the basis of economic criteria.[34] Charges have also been made that Russia received a "sweetheart deal" when it joined the IMF in 1992: it was permitted to borrow more funds in relation to its IMF quota than other countries. These charges of favored treatment, however, do not seem to apply to all emerging economies. For example, a study in 1990 concluded that China has not received any special treatment in funding from the Bretton Woods institutions.[35] There may be disagreements over the extent to which the emerging economies have received favorable treatment, but there is no doubt that their membership has enhanced the universality of the Bretton Woods organizations. As noted later in this chapter, the foreign debt crisis in the 1980s affected the emerging as well as the Third World economies. The globalization of membership in the IMF and World Bank has inevitably meant that more debtor countries are competing for the limited funds of these two institutions.

The Paris Club and the Private Creditor Committees

Three major types of negotiations have occurred between creditors and debtors to deal with the 1980s debt crisis. In the first type of negotiation, the IMF and the World Bank agree to provide structural adjustment loans to Third World debtor governments in exchange for the debtors' commitment to follow prescribed economic policies to eliminate their balance-of-payments problems. The other two types of negotiations involve meetings between the debtors and less formal creditor groupings than the IMF and World

Bank: the Paris and London Clubs. The **Paris Club** is a quasi-institutional grouping of creditor governments, which in most cases are members of the OECD. The **London Club** is the term informally used for private creditor committees, which are composed of the largest commercial banks. The Paris and London Clubs have no charters or formal institutional structures, and their memberships vary with each rescheduling negotiation. The ad hoc nature of these clubs stems partly from the creditors' view that debt reschedulings should be unusual rather than common occurrences, and partly from the desire to avoid high-profile negotiations. Thus, the Paris Club has no legal status or written rules, no voting procedure (decision making occurs on the basis of consensus), and no regular office (meetings are usually held in the French Ministry of Finance).[36]

The Paris Club's first meeting was held in 1956 to negotiate a rescheduling of Argentina's foreign debt. Argentina was in arrears to several European governments, and this meeting was designed to provide a multilateral rescheduling forum as an alternative to a series of uncoordinated bilateral reschedulings. Paris Club meetings were originally limited in number, but they became much more frequent as debt problems increased. Indeed, the Paris Club concluded over twice as many agreements in the seven-year period from 1978 to 1984 as it did in the previous 22 years; these agreements from 1978 to 1984 resulted in the deferment of about $27 billion of debt service obligations. Participants in Paris Club debt reschedulings usually include the debtor country government, the governments of the main official creditors, and representatives of the IMF, the World Bank, the United Nations Conference on Trade and Development (UNCTAD), and sometimes the regional development banks. In its deliberations, the Paris Club emphasizes three basic principles: imminent default, conditionality, and burden sharing.[37]

The first principle of imminent default is designed to limit requests for relief to those with a serious, justifiable need. To avoid unnecessary negotiations, the Paris Club will not even consider a debtor's request for relief unless the debtor has substantial external payments arrears and is likely to default on its payments. The second principle of conditionality stems from the creditor governments' concerns that the debtor will be able to service its external debts on schedule. Thus, the debtor country must first conclude a standby arrangement with the IMF, based on the IMF's conditionality requirements, before the Paris Club will agree to hold its own negotiations with the debtor.[38] In the small number of cases in which the debtor country was not an IMF member at the time of rescheduling (e.g., Poland, Cuba, and Mozambique), the Paris Club established its own conditionality program of stabilization measures. As for the third principle of burden sharing, all creditors must provide relief in proportion to their loan exposure to the debtor country. The burden-sharing principle is designed to avoid the problem of free riding among creditors, and it also extends to the private creditor banks; thus, the Paris and London Clubs cooperate and communicate with each other regularly.

Private debt reschedulings have a number of similarities with Paris Club agreements. In both cases, rescheduling is done on a case-by-case basis by mutual agreement between a single debtor and its creditors, and the debtor must normally commit to adjustment policies as agreed with the IMF. A fundamental difference, however, is that commercial banks are of course far more numerous than nation-states. A relatively small number of states can agree on rescheduling loans at Paris Club meetings, but the coordination problems for private creditors are more complicated. The most common method private creditors use to coordinate their activities is to establish "creditor committees" for the various debtor countries, with the largest international banks (those holding the most loans outstanding) representing the smaller creditor banks. The international banks on a creditor committee bargain with each other and with the debtor country to establish the terms for debt rescheduling, then present the agreement to the smaller creditor banks for ratification. Although the largest creditors would like to limit their loan exposure to a troubled debtor, they realize that the debtor country could default if all individual creditors withheld loans. Because the major international banks have high loan exposure and a long-term interest in the stability of international capital markets, they have a common interest in successful debt restructuring.

Smaller creditor banks, by contrast, have fewer loans at risk and less of a vested interest in maintaining the international credit system. Thus, they are reluctant to ratify restructuring agreements that require them to provide additional loans. Because smaller creditor banks are more inclined to think on the basis of individual rationality, in line with prisoners' dilemma (discussed in Chapter 4), there is a danger that all banks could defect and that massive debtor default could disrupt the international banking system. To prevent a Pareto-suboptimal outcome of this nature, the large international banks put considerable pressure on the smaller banks to avoid free riding and to participate in the debt restructuring agreements.[39] As discussed in the next section, this system of private creditor committees worked quite effectively in earlier years but was insufficient to deal with the 1980s debt crisis.

Historical structuralists, and many Third World debtors, have been highly critical of the Paris and London Club meetings. When a single debtor meets with all its major creditors at the bargaining table, the creditors are in a position to exert unusually strong pressures on the debtor government. The case-by-case approach of the Paris and London Clubs also prevents the debtors from developing a united front, and it ignores the systemic nature of the 1980s debt crisis by operating on the assumption that each debtor's situation can be treated individually. Finally, historical structuralists criticize the two clubs for the strong emphasis they place on IMF conditionality as a prerequisite for their negotiations.[40] At the UNCTAD V conference in 1979, the Third World's Group of 77 sought to replace the Paris and London Clubs with an international debt commission that would be more favorable to LDC interests. Although the creditor governments agreed to invite an observer from the UNCTAD secretariat to future Paris Club negotiations, it did not accede to LDC demands for an international debt commission. Thus, the creditors continue to set the rules and procedures for Paris and London Club negotiations.

STRATEGIES TO DEAL WITH THE 1980s DEBT CRISIS

The debt crisis was more prolonged than many observers had anticipated, and the major creditor states and international institutions gradually adopted more activist policies as it became evident that milder measures were insufficient. Two of the main actors involved in devising and implementing strategies were the United States and the

International Monetary Fund. Although the IMF had lost some importance with the collapse of the pegged exchange rate system and the increase in private bank lending in the 1970s, the debt crisis of the 1980s placed it "back at the center of the international financial system, first as a coordinator in a crisis, and then . . . as a source of information, advice, and warning on the mutual consistency of national policies."[41] The IMF owed its more central role largely to the support of U.S. administration officials, who believed that U.S. (and Western) policies on debt issues could best be implemented through the multilateral institutions. The IMF could exert pressure on both the private banks and the Third World debtors, avoiding major protests over U.S. government interference with private sector lending and LDC sovereignty.[42]

The international debt strategies had three major objectives: to prevent the collapse of the international banking and financial systems, to restore capital market access for the debtor countries, and to minimize economic dislocation and restore economic growth in the debtor countries. The strategies employed to achieve these objectives can be divided into three successive phases: (1) from 1982 to 1985, the provision of emergency loans and private "involuntary" loans to debtor countries; (2) from 1986 to 1988, the introduction of the Baker Plan, which continued with private involuntary lending and placed new emphasis on official lending; and (3) from 1989 to 1994, the implementation of the Brady Plan, which emphasized debt reduction agreements.

Emergency Measures and Involuntary Lending: 1982 to 1985

The first phase in dealing with the debt crisis was a "firefighting" strategy in which the United States, the IMF, and other creditors provided short-term emergency financing to Mexico, Brazil, Venezuela, and other LDCs to avert a 1930s-style financial collapse. As part of this firefighting strategy, the Bank for International Settlements (see Chapter 6) provided some "bridging" finance to Third World debtor countries until IMF loans were approved.[43] This emergency lending was followed by a medium-term strategy in which the private banks engaged in "involuntary" lending. Involuntary lending, which is referred to more politely in official circles as *concerted lending*, can be defined as "the increase in a bank's exposure to a borrowing nation that is in debt-servicing difficulty and that, because of a loss of creditworthiness, would be unable to attract new lending from banks not already exposed in the country."[44]

In the late 1970s and early 1980s, the private creditor committees were quite successful in managing the debt situation; the largest international creditor banks induced the smaller banks to engage in involuntary lending when necessary in debt restructuring agreements. Only nine countries had to restructure their commercial debts from the mid-1970s to 1982, so interbank coordination was sufficient to manage the debt situation. Although the IMF had a role in supervising the debtors' economic policies, its involvement during this period was quite limited. The Mexican debt crisis in August, 1982, however, drastically altered the system of debt management. The large international banks in this case were simply unable to cope with the debt crisis because of its massive scope, and many small banks in the U.S. Southwest with loans outstanding to Mexico were unwilling to increase their loan exposure. It was therefore necessary for the IMF to intervene with an activist policy:

In November 1982, the Fund's Managing Director . . . took the unprecedented step of establishing mandatory levels of forced private lending before the I.M.F. would sign a stabilization agreement with Mexico. This bold action, repeated in the Brazilian case, was a turning point in the treatment of sovereign debt. It staked out a new leadership role for the Fund, and a new relationship between the Fund and private banks.[45]

In addition to pressuring the creditor banks, the IMF insisted that the debtor nations develop adjustment programs as the price for debt rescheduling and the provision of new lending. Thus, realists point out that it was creditor *states* operating through the IMF that managed the debt crisis, and not private banks and the market. The debt crisis posed such a major threat to the international financial system that only states were able to mobilize sufficient resources to deal with the crisis. Furthermore, only official pressures were sufficient to induce banks to continue lending to the debtors on the one hand and to force debtor governments to meet conditionality requirements on the other.[46] Liberals, by contrast, emphasize the role that the IMF played as an institution in managing the debt crisis, and they disagree with the realist view that the IMF was simply doing the bidding of the major creditor states.

The general assumption of the IMF and creditor states in these early years was that the debt crisis was only a short-term problem stemming from the temporary inability of LDCs to service their debts. However, it soon became evident that the debt crisis posed an insolvency problem for many Third World states, which were unable to stem their growing debt problems even after significantly adjusting their policies.[47] Although the early firefighting tactics dealt with the immediate crisis, it was evident by 1985 that many LDC debtors had longer-term economic and financial problems. Economic activity and investment in most debtor countries were declining, and international pressures for continued adjustment programs in the LDCs were interfering with their economic growth objectives. Furthermore, the private commercial banks were resisting IMF pressures and reducing their loan exposure in the debtor countries. Thus, official creditors such as the IMF rather than the private banks were assuming an increasing share of the lending risk. When James A. Baker III became secretary of the U.S. Treasury in 1985, he therefore moved to adopt a more structured approach to the debt crisis.

The Baker Plan: 1986 to 1988

In late 1985, Secretary Baker introduced a plan that provided a more concrete formula for dealing with the debt crisis but did not change the basic assumptions about the best strategy to follow. As was the case in the 1982–85 period, those who devised the **Baker Plan** underestimated the insolvency problem confronting many LDCs, and they therefore rejected the idea that major portions of the Third World debt should be forgiven. Thus, the Baker Plan emphasized the postponement of some debt payments, the provision of new loans, and changes in the debtor countries' policies. This strategy rested on the assumption "that principal debtor countries could grow their way out of debt and could expand their exports enough to reduce their relative debt burdens to levels compatible with a return to normal credit market access."[48]

TABLE 7.4

GROSS EXTERNAL DEBT AND EXTERNAL DEBT AS A PERCENTAGE
OF GNP FOR THE BAKER-17 COUNTRIES, 1985 AND 1992
(MILLIONS OF DOLLARS)

	1985		1992	
	Debt	**EDT/GNP%**	**Debt**	**EDT/GNP%**
°Brazil	106,148	50.3	121,110	30.1
°Mexico	96,867	55.2	113,378	35.2
°Argentina	50,946	84.2	67,569	83.6
°Venezuela	35,334	°	37,193	62.5
Philippines	26,622	89.1	32,589	60.7
Yugoslavia	22,251	48.2	16,294	°
°Chile	20,384	143.3	19,360	49.3
Nigeria	19,550	25.1	30,998	110.7
Morocco	16,529	136.6	21,418	77.8
°Peru	12,884	85.3	20,297	95.4
°Colombia	14,245	42.6	17,204	36.7
Cote d'Ivoire	9,745	154.2	17,997	207.1
°Ecuador	8,703	77.4	12,280	102.1
°Bolivia	4,805	176.6	4,243	83.6
°Costa Rica	4,401	120.8	3,965	63.2
°Jamaica	4,068	234.9	4,304	153.6
°Uruguay	3,919	89.7	5,253	46.8

EDT/GNP % = ratio of total external debt to gross national product. °indicates Latin American and Caribbean countries.

Source: World Bank, *World Debt Tables, 1992–93 and 1993–94, Vol. 2: Country Tables* (Washington, DC: IBRD, 1992 and 1993).

The Baker Plan also focused primarily on Latin American debtors. When Secretary Baker referred to the heavily indebted countries, he identified 15 middle-income LDCs (later increased to 17) as the main target group for his international debt measures. As the asterisks in Table 7.4 show, 12 of the 17 countries targeted were Latin American and Caribbean, and the "Baker-17" list did not include the low-income LDCs that were heavily indebted to official (rather than private) creditors.[49] Table 7.4 lists these 17 highly indebted countries in order of their total gross external debt in 1985, from highest to lowest (the order of countries changed somewhat in 1992). As the table shows, the 4 countries with the highest debts among the 17 in 1985 (Brazil, Mexico, Argentina, and Venezuela) were all Latin American. However, we require more than figures on gross external debt level to assess a country's debt servicing abilities. We must also examine *debt indicators* such as a country's debt-to-export ratio and debt service ratio (shown in Table 7.1) and its debt as a percentage of total output or GNP. Table 7.4 shows that the countries with the highest gross external debts ranked well below some of the smaller, poorer LDCs in terms of debt as a percentage of

GNP. Thus, Brazil's and Mexico's external debts as a percentage of GNP were 50.3 and 55.2 percent in 1985, compared with Jamaica's 234.9 percent, Bolivia's 176.6 percent, and the Cote d'Ivoire's 154.2 percent.

Although the Baker Plan focused only on a select group of indebted LDCs and did not recognize the severity of the debt problem, it did mark a turning point in one important respect. Recognizing that the debt crisis was becoming a longer-term problem, the Baker Plan shifted emphasis from short-term balance-of-payments adjustment to long-term structural change and the resumption of economic growth in the LDC debtor states. In view of the new emphasis on long-term change, the World Bank and the Inter-American Development Bank (IDB)—with their longer-term loans—assumed a more central role in the debt strategy. Thus, the Baker Plan proposed that the multilateral development banks increase their total lending by $10 billion to a gross level of $20 billion over three years and that the private banks also lend $20 billion to the major debtors. In return, the debtor countries were to institute significant liberal-economic reforms, including the liberalization of their trade and foreign investment policies and the privatization of state firms. These reforms had particular significance for many Latin American LDCs, which had previously followed protectionist import substitution policies.

Any possibilities that the Baker Plan could succeed were upset by unexpected changes in the global economy. For example, international oil prices collapsed shortly after the Baker Plan was announced, upsetting the recovery plans of oil-exporting debtor countries such as Mexico. The decline of oil prices also gave some oil-importing LDCs less incentive to adopt economic policy reforms that were necessary for their recovery. Thus, the Baker initiative lost much of its momentum by mid-1986. The Baker Plan also did not achieve adequate results in terms of economic growth in the debtor countries, and many LDC debtors refused to comply with IMF conditionality requirements (for example, Brazil declared a moratorium on paying its debts in 1987). Furthermore, commercial banks sought to reduce their loan exposure in the LDCs, and the lending risks continued to shift from the private banks to governments and multilateral agencies. The multilateral development banks also disbursed less funding than the Baker Plan had anticipated. As a result, the debt repayments of LDCs began to exceed the funding they were receiving in new loans. The net transfer of financial resources to LDCs shifted from a *positive* $29 billion in 1982 to a *negative* $34 billion by 1987, and the net resource transfer to the Baker-17 list of highly indebted countries shifted from +$11 billion to −$17 billion during the same period.[50]

Because the debtor countries' repayment requirements greatly exceeded their access to new financing, they experienced their deepest economic problems during the Baker Plan period. From 1981 to 1988, real per capita income in almost every South American country declined in absolute terms, and living standards in many LDCs fell to levels comparable with the 1950s and 1960s. Indeed, many analysts referred to the 1980s as a "lost development decade." Although the Baker Plan's failure resulted partly from unforeseen external events such as the collapse of international oil prices, historical structuralists viewed the plan as an "attempt to maintain the fiction that the debt crisis was only temporary and could be surmounted if all parties cooperated."[51]

The Brady Plan: 1989 to 1994

The failure of the Baker Plan to promote economic recovery and growth in the Latin American LDCs posed a serious threat to U.S. exports in Latin American markets. Concerns were also voiced in the U.S. Congress about the possible negative effects of the continued debt problems on the revival of democratic governments in Latin America. Serious riots in Caracas, Venezuela, in February 1989 were associated with government austerity measures, providing further evidence that the Baker measures were insufficient, and the new U.S. Secretary of the Treasury, Nicholas J. Brady, announced what is known as the **Brady Plan** in March 1989.

The Brady Plan was similar to the Baker Plan in several respects. For example, the Brady Plan opted for handling the debt problem on a case-by-case basis, in which each debtor LDC negotiated separately with its creditors, and it linked the easing of credit terms with the debtors' acceptance of IMF and World Bank requirements for liberal economic reform. However, the Brady Plan differed from the Baker Plan with its new emphasis on *debt reduction,* or partial forgiveness of existing debt. The Baker Plan had rejected the idea of debt reduction on the grounds that banks would not lend to countries that had failed to repay their debts and that LDCs would be able to repay their debts and return to prosperity if the debt repayment period was simply extended. The Brady Plan, by contrast, recognized that LDCs could not regain their creditworthiness if their debt burden was too onerous and that extending the debt repayment period without debt reduction had not led to a return of LDC prosperity and economic growth.[52]

The Brady Plan therefore encouraged U.S. private banks to accept a certain amount of debt reduction, and the IMF and World Bank to support some debt reduction through their lending policies.[53] Those creditor banks that agreed voluntarily to reduce the value of the principle or interest on the debt owed to them would receive guarantees of repayment on the remaining portion of the debt. The IMF and World Bank would help finance these guarantees, and Japan also committed funds for this purpose.

The World Bank, the IMF, and a number of academics had supported the need for debt reduction long before the U.S. policy change under the Brady Plan. Indeed, a World Bank vice president later referred to this time lag, stating that "so long as the United States was not willing to move, the IFIs [international financial institutions] were not free to speak—though to be sure the repeated emphasis on debt reduction . . . by the heads of the World Bank and IMF, was signaling their conclusion that it was time to move on."[54]

By May 1994, Brady Plan deals for debt reductions were completed or announced for 18 major debtor countries, accounting for $191 billion in original bank claims. The Brady Plan has contributed to improvement of the debt profile in some LDCs, but Table 7.4 shows that the 17 countries on the Baker Plan's list still had substantial debts in 1992.[55] While many of the countries on the Baker Plan's list are middle-income LDCs, the situation has been far worse for the poorest LDCs. This was evident at a meeting of the Group of Seven countries in Washington, D.C., in September 1996, when it was estimated that 20 low-income LDCs—most of them in sub-Saharan Africa—had debt burdens considered to be "possibly unsustainable." The G-7 countries and the World Bank and IMF therefore approved yet another debt relief plan for the poorest LDCs in fall 1996. All these countries' debts owed to the IMF and World Bank would also be eligible for relief under the plan.[56] In view of the continuance of debt problems, it is necessary to examine the overall effectiveness of debt strategies employed since the 1980s.

Assessing the Effectiveness of Debt Strategies

The international debt strategies had three main objectives: to prevent the collapse of the international banking and financial systems, to restore capital market access for the debtors, and to minimize economic dislocation and restore economic growth in the debtor countries. The debt strategies were most successful in achieving the first two objectives. In regard to the first objective, by the late 1980s "the banks were no longer in the serious jeopardy that they faced at the outset of the debt crisis."[57] From 1982 to 1992, the loan exposure of all U.S. banks to the Baker list of 17 highly indebted countries fell from 130 percent of the banks' capital and reserves to only 27 percent; the loan exposure of British banks to these 17 countries fell from 85 percent of capital to 12 percent; and the loan exposure of German and French banks fell from 31 to 19 percent and from 135 to 23 percent, respectively. In 1988, the Bank for International Settlements also oversaw an agreement that commercial banks in the OECD countries must have equity and reserves amounting to at least 8 percent of their outstanding loans, and this measure helped to restore some confidence in the international banking system.[58] In regard to the second objective, many of the LDC debtor countries were able to return to the international financial markets far more rapidly after the 1980s debt crisis than they had after the 1930s crisis. Academics and policymakers with a liberal-economic orientation view these first two criteria as the most important for assessing the effectiveness of international debt strategies, and they therefore have generally considered the debt strategies to be successful.[59]

In marked contrast, historical structuralists (and some interventionist liberals) believe that the third objective of debt strategies—restoring economic growth in the Third World debtor countries—should be the most important, and they have considered the debt strategies to be largely ineffective. For example, one critic argues that the major creditor states and the IMF have been primarily concerned with increasing "the immediate payment capacity of the debtor nations and not their development."[60] Historical structuralists also believe that the strategies for dealing with the debt crisis have required much sacrifice from the Third World, and especially from the poorest peoples within Third World countries. The international bankers and the industrial states, by contrast, have sustained few losses and in fact have often registered gains as a result of the debt strategies employed. These critics therefore conclude that "the debt crisis is by no means over yet; a banking crisis may have been tidied up, but a development crisis is in full swing."[61]

The IMF and the World Bank have been special targets of criticism for historical structuralists, who argue that the Bretton Woods institutions have given greatest priority to ensuring that LDC debtors adopt liberal-economic policies and repay their loans. According to these critics, a radical restructuring of LDC debtor economies is required to promote their economic development, but IMF conditionality precludes such possibilities. While some liberal economists concede that IMF and World Bank conditionality has contributed to economic dislocation in LDC debtor countries, they nevertheless argue that, in liberalizing their policies, the debtor countries have "laid the foundations for subsequent sustainable growth." However, critics of the debt strategies believe that

> there is some reason to be sceptical about the view that the Third World economies are now "leaner and fitter" to face the world ahead beyond the debt crisis. They are certainly leaner but whether they are fitter remains to be seen.[62]

To this point in the chapter, we have discussed only the effects of the debt crisis on the Third World countries. However, many emerging states in Eastern Europe and the former Soviet Union were also major foreign debtors in the 1980s and 1990s.

THE EMERGING ECONOMIES AND FOREIGN DEBT

The Soviet bloc countries contended with many of the same economic problems as the Third World during the 1980s debt crisis, including growing balance-of-payments deficits, declining terms of trade, and stagnant economic growth. The increased need for financing was also causing Soviet bloc countries to look toward the IMF and the World Bank. Thus, Hungary and Poland joined these institutions in the 1980s, partly in efforts to deal with their growing debt problems.[63]

Eastern Europe

During the 1970s, the Eastern Europeans borrowed heavily on international financial markets to finance industrial investment. However, poor investment decisions, economic inefficiency, lack of export competitiveness, and high interest rates on their foreign debt created severe economic problems. Indeed, as early as 1981 an acute foreign exchange shortage forced Poland to negotiate a rescheduling of its debt with official and private creditors. Poland had financed an ambitious program of industrial investment with external funding, but its economic performance and export levels were insufficient to service its debt. Like the Third World, the Eastern European countries have followed alternative development strategies with major implications for their foreign debt. The two basic strategies for dealing with debt are often referred to as the Polish and Czech-Hungarian models.[64]

The Polish model has involved large debt buildup followed by repeated debt reschedulings and eventually official debt relief, partly based on political considerations. After a number of debt reschedulings in the 1980s, the Polish government sought major debt reduction from Western governments, which held two-thirds of its debt. In Paris Club negotiations, the industrial countries offered Poland a 50 percent forgiveness of its bilateral official debt in 1991. Although Poland had requested 80 percent forgiveness, the Paris Club's 50 percent offer was exceptionally high; the club had previously offered a maximum forgiveness of 33 percent to low-income countries. Under pressure from the Group of Seven governments, the commercial banks also reached an agreement with Poland in March 1994 to reduce its private debt by 45 percent. Bulgaria in many respects followed the Polish model, and the private banks agreed in principle to a substantial reduction of Bulgaria's debt in late 1993 (most of Bulgaria's debt was private). In contrast to the Polish-Bulgarian model, the former Czechoslovakia and Hungary followed more restrained and prudent economic policies in efforts to achieve a favorable creditworthiness record. These countries never accumulated large amounts of debt and did not find it necessary to seek debt relief.

As with the Third World countries, the differences in debt strategies of the emerging countries stemmed partly from domestic economic and political factors. For example, the Polish model of large debt buildup resulted partly from political events in the 1970s, which prevented the Polish government from taking decisive action to deal with its looming debt problems. After Wladyslaw Gomulka was removed as first secretary of the Communist party in Poland in 1970, policies were adopted that eventually led to decentralization of the party and divisions within the top political leadership. When high oil prices and difficulty in exporting goods contributed to serious economic problems in the late 1970s, the fractured political leadership in Poland enabled societal groups such as workers to resist austerity moves (which would have been made at the workers' expense). For example, when the leaders attempted to raise prices and hold down wages as part of an economic austerity program, several hundred strikes by workers forced them to reverse these moves. It was not until December 1981, when the military took control in Poland and dominated strong societal groups such as Solidarity, that an austerity program was introduced (which contributed to domestic hardship and eventually to further protests).[65]

In contrast to the case in Poland, in Hungary domestic political developments contributed to the implementation of more prudent economic policies. While Hungary instituted some austerity measures, it also adopted a series of reforms to make the economy more efficient and to give profits and prices a larger role in resource allocation. The national trauma resulting from the suppression of the 1956 revolt in Hungary had led to a number of developments that contributed to these economic reforms. For example, Hungary turned to collective instead of one-person leadership, and these leaders supported the introduction of a limited market mechanism and a more balanced development strategy based on specific Hungarian conditions. Unlike reformers elsewhere, Hungarian supporters of economic reform also "sought not to weaken the [Communist] party but to use it to pursue their particular economic goals."[66] When Hungary was confronted with debt problems, its earlier reforms and its political ability to institute changes enabled it to meet its debt service obligations far more effectively than Poland.

Despite the different development strategies followed by Eastern European countries, their debt problems (as was the case for LDC debtors) also resulted from external events that were largely beyond their control. All Eastern European countries, for example, suffered economically from their increased dependence on imports from nonsocialist countries to promote economic growth and investment after 1985, from the collapse of the Soviet bloc's CMEA in 1991, and from deterioration in their terms of trade as the Soviet Union ended subsidized oil exports. External disruptions had a particularly severe effect on some Eastern European countries such as Bulgaria. Thus, the Gulf War adversely affected Bulgaria's exports to Iraq; the breakup of the CMEA had major consequences for Bulgaria because of its high share of exports to the Soviet Union; and the war in Yugoslavia seriously disrupted Bulgarian export routes to Western Europe. The structural transition to market-oriented economies produced further instability, and domestic output in Eastern Europe fell by almost 25 percent in 1990–91. This combination of internal and external factors contributed to the foreign debt problems of the Eastern European states.

The Former Soviet Union Countries

The Soviet Union also had an external debt problem, which was greatly exacerbated by the breakup of the country. In mid-1992, Russia began negotiations with the other states of the FSU on "zero-option" agreements, in which Russia assumed responsibility for the entire debt of the FSU while also taking control of all the FSU's foreign assets. The external debt of the FSU was about $60 billion in 1990 and almost $80 billion by 1992, while the assets included gold and foreign exchange, embassies abroad, and a portfolio of loans to countries such as India, Cuba, Libya, and Vietnam. Russia was willing to assume the entire FSU debt because it had the strongest resource base with which to service the debt, because the division of assets such as embassies seemed to make little sense, and because the assumption of the debt could help preserve Russia's hegemonic role in the region.

However, the collapse of the Russian economy severely undercut the country's debt-servicing capacity, and Russia had to seek IMF loans and negotiate Paris Club reschedulings. It is unlikely that there will be a meaningful resolution of Russia's external debt problem until its domestic economy is stabilized, and stabilization will involve reducing the huge fiscal deficit. As in the Third World and some Eastern European countries, the two alternatives to consider are debt rescheduling (the Baker Plan model) and debt forgiveness (the Brady Plan model). Those opposed to debt forgiveness argue that Russia is not a low-income LDC, its severe economic problems are only temporary, debt forgiveness would jeopardize Russia's chances to obtain better lending terms in the future, and debt forgiveness would be politically unacceptable for a former superpower. Nevertheless, if Russia's debt problems prove to be serious and prolonged, forgiveness may have to be considered.[67]

THE DEBT CRISIS AND THE CHANGING ROLES OF THE IMF AND THE WORLD BANK

A major new element in the 1980s debt crisis was the central role played by the international financial institutions—the IMF and the World Bank. The debt crisis also had a major effect on the relationship between the IMF and the World Bank as the two institutions adopted new functions that overlap in some significant respects. The problem of overlap was recognized when these two institutions were created, and the Bretton Woods negotiators deliberately excluded references to Third World development in the IMF Articles of Agreement. The "development" function was assigned to the World Bank.[68] Thus, the IMF was to provide short-term loans to *any* country with balance-of-payments problems, while the World Bank was to provide long-term loans specifically for reconstruction and development (see Chapter 11). The only direct linkage between the two organizations was that membership in the IMF was made a prerequisite for membership in the World Bank.[69]

Despite the initial separation of these two institutions, in the 1960s the World Bank began to infringe directly on the IMF's territory. Diverging from its practice of providing loans for specific development projects, the World Bank provided large-scale *program lending* to India for general balance-of-payments support. The bank also attempted to link this support with general conditions for policy reform by the Indian government.[70] The World Bank justified its actions by arguing that India's balance-of-payments deficit resulted from development problems that were long-term rather than transitory in nature. However, IMF officials argued that the World Bank's balance-of-payments funding with conditionality attached was a direct infringement on the IMF's functions. In 1966 the two organizations signed an agreement in efforts to avoid further overlap problems, but the agreement did not fully clarify the differences in their responsibilities.[71]

Several changes in the 1970s contributed to a marked increase in overlap between IMF and World Bank functions. First, the IMF became less involved with promoting exchange rate stabilization when the Bretton Woods system of pegged exchange rates collapsed. The IMF's other major function of providing loans to countries, in which there are possibilities of overlap with the World Bank, therefore became more prominent. Second, the IMF initially provided loans to all countries, but by the late 1970s it was lending almost exclusively to LDCs—the same group of countries receiving World Bank loans. Third, although the World Bank Articles of Agreement (Article 3, Section 4) state that the bank should provide loans for specific projects "except in special circumstances," bank officials became increasingly aware of situations in which LDCs could not obtain needed funding for their development programs by borrowing only for specific projects. In 1971, the bank's executive directors therefore decided that program lending of the type they had provided to India in the mid-1960s was appropriate under certain circumstances. World Bank program lending to finance commodity imports has distinct similarities with IMF lending for balance-of-payments purposes.[72]

The most important reason for increased overlap related to the oil shocks in the 1970s and the foreign debt crisis in the 1980s. In reacting to the debt crisis, the IMF and the World Bank developed some remarkably similar new lending programs for indebted LDCs. The IMF found that its traditional short-term loans for balance-of-payments problems with three- to five-year repayment periods were not adequate for a number of LDCs that had protracted payments problems. To deal with the debt crisis, the IMF therefore also provided *medium-term* structural adjustment loans with repayment periods ranging from 5.5 to 10 years. As for the World Bank, it found that its long-term loans for development projects with repayment periods of 15 to 20 years (and in some cases 40 years) were also not the type of funding Third World debtors required to deal with their more immediate balance-of-payments problems. Like the IMF, the World Bank therefore developed medium-term SALs for Third World debtors. While the IMF still provided short-term balance-of-payments loans and the World Bank still provided long-term development loans, they *both* were now providing medium-term SALs to deal with the debt crisis.[73]

The greater overlap of functions between the IMF and the World Bank has increased both the potential for conflict and the need for collaboration between the two organizations. The overlapping of functions also raises questions as to whether both should continue to exist as separate institutions. Indeed, *The Economist* predicted in 1991 that a merger between the two Bretton Woods institutions "makes sense, and in time it will happen."[74] Despite this prediction, several reasons are given for maintaining the two as distinctive bodies. First, the World Bank group is composed of four financial institutions, and it is already too large by itself for efficient management (see Chapter 11). Joining the World Bank and the IMF would simply compound the problems related to size. Second, development issues are exceedingly complex, and it is important that a range of institutions provide advice and establish conditions for loans. Although historical structuralists argue that IMF and World Bank policies are virtually identical, liberal economists can point to IMF–World Bank disputes as an indication of competing perspectives. Third, the IMF's responsibilities extend well beyond providing loans to LDCs. Although the IMF's monetary role declined when the pegged exchange rate regime collapsed in the early 1970s, the IMF continues to provide advice to states on monetary issues, and it could play a more important role in global monetary and financial issues in the future.[75]

A final reason for maintaining a separate IMF and World Bank is that the disintegration of the Soviet bloc and the dire economic circumstances in much of sub-Saharan Africa provide sufficient economic challenges for both institutions, helping to restore a differentiation of their functions.[76] While the IMF has been given the lead role in dealing with debt problems of the emerging states in Eastern Europe and the FSU, the World Bank as the main multilateral development institution has been coordinating aid efforts in sub-Saharan Africa.

THE IMF, THE WORLD BANK, AND THE DEBTOR COUNTRIES

Although new efforts at IMF–World Bank collaboration are partly designed to avert institutional conflict, Third World countries are highly suspicious of these moves. Historical structuralists and LDC debtors often criticize IMF conditionality as an unwarranted infringement on LDC sovereignty, and they argue that the liberal-economic conditions placed on IMF and World Bank loans hinder rather than facilitate development.[77] With moves toward IMF–World Bank collaboration, LDCs are concerned about the increased likelihood of *cross-conditionality*, in which the IMF's determination that a loan applicant is uncreditworthy prevents the applicant from receiving World Bank as well as IMF funding. Thus, Third World countries fear that the conditions placed on official loans will become even more onerous. Although the IMF and World Bank have ruled out cross-conditionality in a formal, legal sense, there is no doubt that they sometimes engage in this practice on an informal basis.[78]

Critics also charge that the IMF and World Bank's structural adjustment loans put the onus of adjustment on the LDC debtor countries—and on the most vulnerable groups within LDCs—even though responsibility for the debt crisis was shared between North and South. SALs pressure LDC debtors to reduce the role of the state and increase the role of the market, with little concern for the distributional and social welfare effects of these policies. Because SALs are intended to improve LDCs' balance of payments by reducing spending for social services, lowering wages, emphasizing production for export over local consumption, and ending subsidies for local industries, it is the poorer, more vulnerable individuals in LDCs who are often the most severely affected. Thus, a large body of literature exists on the effects of IMF and World Bank SALs on poorer women and children in LDCs.

Historical structuralists argue that it is necessary to be aware of the negative distributional effects of IMF and World Bank SALs. Poorer women in LDCs, who have the responsibility for the unpaid work of managing the household, are the most severely affected by IMF and World Bank pressures for a reduction in LDC funding for public services. Women have primary responsibility in the household for cooking, cleaning, and health care, so public sector services such as clean water supplies, waste disposal, public transport, and health facilities lighten women's household work and enable them to gain education and skills so they can enter the paid work force. Thus, the burdens on poorer women increase as IMF and World Bank structural adjustment programs require cutbacks in social expenditures on health and nutrition. As the government provides less of these services, women must make up the difference by providing them through the home. The school dropout rate of young girls is also likely to increase as a result of SALs because girls must help with the household labor and also often work in sweatshops to supplement the family's income. Children, and pregnant and lactating mothers, are also the groups most seriously affected by IMF and World Bank pressures to remove food subsidies and increase food prices for consumers in LDCs. In other words, the informal sector in LDCs grows because of structural adjustment programs, and poorer women often pay the price through increased unpaid work and a deterioration of health and nutrition.[79]

In response to these criticisms, the World Bank has taken some measures to ameliorate the effects of LDC structural adjustment programs on the poor while retaining its concerns for promoting efficiency and liberal-economic growth. For example, the Bank continues to view cuts in food subsidies as desirable in terms of efficiency, but it has attempted to ameliorate the negative effects on the poor through school lunches, food stamps, and the provision of food aid.[80] Nevertheless, while IMF and World Bank officials would argue that structural adjustment programs aimed at market efficiency and decreased public sector involvement can be compatible with distributional and social welfare goals, they have not convinced many of their critics.

CONCLUSION

What is the relevance of the three IPE theoretical perspectives and the three major themes of the text—globalization, North-North relations, and North-South relations—

for the issue of foreign debt? The 1980s foreign debt crisis provides a prime example of the effects of growing interdependence and globalization on the policies of indebted Third World and emerging states. The origins of the debt crisis stemmed back to the 1970s, when commercial banks extended a large volume of loans to Third World countries after the OPEC price increases. These private loans were particularly attractive to the borrowing LDCs because of their low interest rates and lack of conditionality. While orthodox liberals emphasize the imprudent borrowing behavior and inefficient domestic policies of LDCs as major causes of the debt crisis, historical structuralists focus instead on the long-term dependency of LDCs and the irresponsible behavior of the commercial banks and creditor governments. Despite these differences of view regarding the culpability of debtors versus creditors, most would agree that unexpected changes resulting from global interdependence, such as the oil and food crises of the 1970s, should be included among the major factors causing the debt crisis.

There is also broad agreement that the IMF and the World Bank have used structural adjustment loans to induce debtor countries to adopt liberal-economic policies, thus opening their economies to the forces of globalization. For example, ever since Mexico declared in 1982 that it could no longer service its foreign debt, Mexican governments have steadily moved toward policies of economic liberalization. These moves include Mexico's shift from import-substituting industrialization to export-led growth policies, the massive withdrawal of public subsidies in most economic sectors, domestic economic changes to attract foreign investment, and the opening of the economy to international trade. In the trade area, Mexico joined GATT in 1986 and engaged in further liberalization of its trade and foreign investment policies before joining NAFTA in 1993. Mexico is of course not alone in making such changes, and one can see them throughout the Third World. Thus, the average import tariffs in Latin America as a whole declined from 56 percent in 1985 to 16 percent in mid-1992, largely as a result of unilateral trade liberalization, and Latin American states signed at least 31 agreements to liberalize trade from 1990 to 1996.[81]

Although these Third World policy changes resulted partly from evidence that some previous policies such as import substitution had been unsuccessful, there is no doubt that pressure from the major industrial states and the IMF and World Bank were also critical factors in the decision of indebted countries to open their economies. Sharp differences of view exist, however, regarding the effects of these liberal-economic policies on the indebted states. Liberal economists often argue that the strategies to deal with debt have been quite successful, preventing the collapse of the international banking system and restoring access to the capital market for many of the indebted states. Liberals assume that though the changes in policy required of debtor states have caused hardship for some groups and individuals, the long-term effects of the shift to economic openness will be beneficial for Third World and emerging countries.

Realists and historical structuralists, by contrast, argue that liberals largely ignore the effect of political and economic inequality among states on the debt issue. While globalization has facilitated the *transmission* of liberal values and policies to the advanced industrial states, these values and policies have been *imposed on* the Third World debtor states. Liberals also consider the IMF and the World Bank to be politically neutral institutions, while realists and historical structuralists view them as conduits for the imposition of policies favored by the most powerful industrial states and private actors on the least powerful. Although IMF and World Bank SALs require borrowing countries to adopt prescribed liberal-economic policies, these conditions are ultimately set not by the international organizations but by their most powerful member states.[82] Historical structuralists also argue that the debt strategies required far more sacrifice from the Third World debtors than from the international banks and that IMF and World Bank conditionality requirements have been designed to meet the needs of international capital rather than those of the indebted states. Indeed, IMF requirements that debtor countries reduce their social service expenditures, increase their exports, remove their restrictions on capital flows, and devalue their currencies have often had the most negative impact on the poorest and weakest groups in society.

This chapter on the debt crisis tells us a good deal not only about the themes of globalization and North-South inequality but also about the theme of North-North relations. Although the United States has declined as a hegemon in some economic areas, it clearly took a leadership position in helping to manage the debt crisis. Thus, the central actors in managing the crisis were the United States and the IMF, with the Paris and London Clubs (composed mainly of the Group of Ten industrial states) and the World Bank playing supporting roles. As a result, realists point out that it was the most powerful industrial states, and the international institutions such as the IMF and the World Bank which they supported, that managed the debt crisis, not the private banks and the market. Only states were able to mobilize sufficient resources to deal with the crisis, and only official pressures were sufficient to induce banks to continue lending to the debtors on the one hand and to force debtor governments to meet conditionality requirements on the other.

Despite the relative decline in U.S. hegemony in some economic areas, the United States continued to maintain its dominant position with regard to financial, monetary, and debt issues "well into the 1980s because of the relative attractiveness of U.S. financial markets, the preeminence of U.S. financial institutions and the dollar in global markets, and the relative size of the U.S. economy."[83] The United States continues to have a major role in the international monetary and debt regimes.

NOTES

1. William R. Cline, *International Debt Reexamined* (Washington, DC: Institute for International Economics, 1995), p. 1.
2. See Albert Fishlow, "Lessons from the Past: Capital Markets During the 19th Century and the Interwar Period," *International Organization* 39-3 (Summer 1985), pp. 383–439; Barbara Stallings, *Banker to the Third World: U.S. Portfolio Investment in Latin America, 1900–1986* (Berkeley: University of California Press, 1987); Barry Eichengreen and Richard Portes, "Dealing with Debt: The 1930s and the 1980s," in Ishrat Husain and Ishac Diwan, eds., *Dealing with the Debt Crisis: A World Bank Symposium* (Washington, DC: World Bank, 1989), pp. 69–86; and Barry Eichengreen and Peter H. Lindert, eds., *The International Debt Crisis in Historical Perspective* (Cambridge, MA: MIT Press, 1989).

3. Stuart Corbridge, *Debt and Development* (Oxford: Blackwell Publishers, 1993), p. 25; Cline, *International Debt Reexamined*, p. 6.

4. Stallings, *Banker to the Third World*, pp. 313–314.

5. Paul R. Krugman and Maurice Obstfeld, *International Economics: Theory and Policy* (New York: HarperCollins, 3rd edition, 1994), p. 327.

6. Rudiger Dornbusch and Stanley Fischer, "Third World Debt," *Science* 234, November 14, 1986, p. 836; Corbridge, *Debt and Development*, p. 15.

7. John T. Cuddington, "The Extent and Causes of the Debt Crisis of the 1980s," in Husain and Diwan, eds., *Dealing with the Debt Crisis*, p. 15.

8. World Bank, *World Debt Tables 1992–93*, Vol. 1 (Washington, DC: IBRD, 1992), pp. 41–45. For a historical structuralist perspective on early warning signs of a debt crisis, see Cheryl Payer, *Lent and Lost: Foreign Credit and Third World Development* (London: Zed Books, 1991), pp. 83–89.

9. The World Bank, *Annual Report—1983* (Washington, DC: IBRD, 1983), p. 34.

10. William R. Cline, "International Debt: Analysis, Experience and Prospects," *Journal of Development Planning* 16 (1985), p. 26.

11. Theodore H. Cohn, *Canadian Food Aid: Domestic and Foreign Policy Implications*, Monograph Series in World Affairs (Denver, CO: University of Denver, Graduate School of International Studies, 1979), pp. 25–26.

12. Charles Lipson, "The International Organization of Third World Debt," *International Organization* 35-4 (Autumn 1981), p. 611; Benjamin J. Cohen, "Balance-of-Payments Financing: Evolution of a Regime," in Stephen D. Krasner, ed., *International Regimes* (Ithaca, NY: Cornell University Press, 1983), p. 329.

13. Albert Fishlow, "Lessons from the Past," p. 433.

14. Miles Kahler, "Politics and International Debt: Explaining the Crisis," *International Organization* 39-3 (Summer 1985), pp. 358–359.

15. John Loxley, "International Capital Markets, the Debt Crisis and Development," in Roy Culpeper, Albert Berry, and Frances Stewart, eds., *Global Development Fifty Years After Bretton Woods: Essays in Honour of Gerald K. Helleiner* (New York: St. Martin's Press, 1997), pp. 138–142.

Some analysts argue that the share of the OPEC surplus that was recycled through the banking system was actually quite small and that the low interest rates were the main reason for the increase in commercial bank loans to LDCs. See Edwin M. Truman, "U.S. Policy on the Problems of International Debt," *Federal Reserve Bulletin* 75-11 (November 1989), p. 728.

16. Stallings, *Banker to the Third World*, pp. 184–186; Ricardo Ffrench-Davis, "External Debt, Adjustment, and Development in Latin America," in Richard E. Feinberg and Ricardo Ffrench-Davis, eds., *Development and External Debt in Latin America: Bases for a New Consensus* (Notre Dame, IN: University of Notre Dame Press, 1988), p. 40.

17. Ethan B. Kapstein, *Governing the Global Economy: International Finance and the State* (Cambridge, MA: Harvard University Press, 1994), pp. 60–69.

18. International Monetary Fund, Annual Report of the Executive Directors for the Fiscal Year ended April 30, 1977 (Washington, DC: IMF, 1977), pp. 40–41.

19. Cline, *International Debt Reexamined*, pp. 2–3; Jeffrey Sachs, "External Debt and Macroeconomic Performance in Latin America and East Asia," in William C. Brainard and George L. Perry, eds., *Brookings Papers on Economic Activity* 2 (Washington, DC: Brookings Institution, 1985), pp. 523–535.

20. Sachs, "External Debt and Macroeconomic Performance in Latin America and East Asia," p. 526.

21. Cheryl Payer, *The Debt Trap: The IMF and the Third World* (Middlesex, UK: Penguin, 1974), pp. 45–49.

22. Peter Körner, Gero Maass, Thomas Siebold, and Ranier Tetzlaff, *The IMF and the Debt Crisis: A Guide to the Third World's Dilemma*, translated by Paul Knight (London: Zed Books, 1986), pp. 30–31; Peter Evans, *Dependent Development: The Alliance of Multinational, State, and Local Capital in Brazil* (Princeton, NJ: Princeton University Press, 1979).

23. Payer, *The Debt Trap*, p. 48. See also Robert E. Wood, *From Marshall Plan to Debt Crisis: Foreign Aid and Development Choices in the World Economy* (Berkeley: University of California Press, 1986), pp. 233–241.

24. Jesús Silva-Herzog, "The Costs for Latin America's Development," in Robert A. Pastor, ed., *Latin America's Debt Crisis: Adjusting to the Past or Planning for the Future?* (Boulder, CO: Rienner, 1987), p. 33.

25. Peter H. Lindert and Peter J. Morton, "How Sovereign Debt Has Worked," in Jeffrey D. Sachs, ed., *Developing Country Debt and Economic Performance, Vol. 1: The International Financial System* (Chicago: University of Chicago Press, 1989), pp. 66–77. The concept of an international debt regime is discussed in Thomas J. Biersteker, "International Financial Negotiations and Adjustment Bargaining: An Overview," in Thomas J. Biersteker, ed., *Dealing with Debt: International Financial Negotiations and Adjustment Bargaining* (Boulder, CO: Westview Press, 1993), pp. 1–15.

26. The "nesting" terminology was first used by Vinod Aggarwal. For a discussion of the textile and agricultural trade regimes, see V. K. Aggarwal, *Liberal Protectionism: The International Politics of Organized Textile Trade* (Berkeley: University of California Press, 1985); and Theodore H. Cohn, "The Changing Role of the United States in the Global Agricultural Trade Regime," in William P. Avery, ed., *World Agriculture and the GATT*, International Political Economy Yearbook, Vol. 7 (Boulder, CO: Rienner, 1993), pp. 17–38.

27. Cohen, "Balance-of-Payments Financing: Evolution of a Regime," pp. 319–323.

28. Valerie J. Assetto, *The Soviet Bloc in the IMF and the IBRD* (Boulder, CO: Westview Press, 1988), pp. 186–187; Jozef M. van Brabant, *The Planned Economies and International Economic Organizations* (Cambridge: Cambridge University Press, 1991), p. 126.

29. Harold K. Jacobson and Michel Oksenberg, *China's Participation in the IMF, the World Bank, and GATT: Toward a Global Economic Order* (Ann Arbor: University of Michigan Press, 1990), pp. 46–52.

30. William Feeney, "Chinese Policy in Multilateral Financial Institutions," in Samuel S. Kim, ed., *China and the World: Chinese Foreign Policy in the Post-Mao Era* (Boulder, CO: Westview Press, 1984), pp. 266–271; Samuel S. Kim, "Whither Post-Mao Chinese Global Policy?" *International Organization* 35-3 (Summer 1981), pp. 455–457.

31. Klaus Schröder, "The IMF and the Countries of the Council for Mutual Economic Assistance," *Intereconomics* 2 (March/April 1982), pp. 88–90; Marie Lavigne, "Eastern European Countries and the IMF," in Béla Csikós-Nagy and David G. Young, eds., *East-West Economic Relations in the Changing Global Environment* (London: Macmillan, 1986), pp. 300–304.

32. Leah A. Haus, *Globalizing the GATT: The Soviet Union's Successor States, Eastern Europe, and the International Trading System* (Washington, DC: Brookings Institution, 1992), p. 104; "Sorting Out Russia," *The Economist*, September 26, 1992, pp. 97–98.

33. Aziz Ali Mohammed, "The Role of International Financial Institutions," in John P. Hardt and Richard F. Kaufman, eds., *East-Central European Economies in Transition* (Armonk, NY: Sharpe, for the Joint Economic Committee, U.S. Congress, 1995), pp. 192–195.

34. Assetto, *The Soviet Bloc in the IMF and the IBRD*, p. 50.

35. Jacobson and Oksenberg, *China's Participation in the IMF, the World Bank, and GATT*, p. 128; Feeney, "Chinese Policy in Multilateral Financial Institutions," p. 274; Richard W. Stevenson, "In Borrowing from the I.M.F., Did Yeltsin Get a Sweetheart Deal?" *New York Times*, March 3, 1996, p. A5.

36. Sources on the Paris and London Clubs include Alexis Rieffel, *The Role of the Paris Club in Managing Debt Problems* (Princeton, NJ: Princeton University, Essays in International Finance, no. 161, December 1985); Alexis Rieffel, "The Paris Club, 1978–1983," *Columbia Journal of Transnational Law* 23-1 (1984), pp. 83–110; and Christine A. Kearney, "The Creditor Clubs: Paris and London," in Biersteker, ed., *Dealing with Debt*, pp. 61–76.

37. Rieffel, *The Role of the Paris Club in Managing Debt Problems*, pp. 4–14.

38. Michael G. Kuhn with Jorge P. Guzman, *Multilateral Official Debt Rescheduling: Recent Experience, World Economic and Financial Surveys* (Washington, DC: November 1990), p. 7.

39. Charles Lipson, "International Debt and International Institutions," in Miles Kahler, ed., *The Politics of International Debt* (Ithaca, NY: Cornell University Press, 1986), pp. 222–226; and Charles Lipson, "Bankers' Dilemmas: Private Cooperation in Rescheduling Sovereign Debts," in Kenneth A. Oye, ed., *Cooperation Under Anarchy* (Princeton, NJ: Princeton University Press, 1986), pp. 200–225.

40. See Payer, *Lent and Lost*, pp. 52–56.

41. James, *International Monetary Cooperation Since Bretton Woods*, p. 347.

42. Benjamin J. Cohen, "International Debt and Linkage Strategies: Some Foreign-policy Implications for the United States," *International Organization* 39-4 (Autumn 1985), p. 722.

43. Paul Krugman, "LDC Debt Policy," in Martin Feldstein, ed., *American Economic Policy in the 1980s* (Chicago: University of Chicago Press, 1994), pp. 692–694; Age F. P. Bakker, *International Financial Institutions* (New York: Longman, 1996), pp. 95–96.

44. William R. Cline, *International Debt and the Stability of the World Economy*, Policy Analyses in International Economics 4 (Washington, DC: Institute for International Economics, September 1983), p. 74.

45. Lipson, "Bankers' Dilemmas: Private Cooperation in Rescheduling Sovereign Debts," p. 223; Lipson, "International Debt and International Institutions," pp. 220–227.

46. Kapstein, *Governing the Global Economy*, p. 82.

47. Dornbusch and Fischer, "Third World Debt," p. 838.

48. William R. Cline, "The Baker Plan and Brady Reformulation: An Evaluation," in Husain and Diwan, eds., *Dealing with the Debt Crisis: A World Bank Symposium*, p. 177.

49. Corbridge, *Debt and Development*, p. 65.

50. Edwin M. Truman, "U.S. Policy on the Problems of International Debt," *Federal Reserve Bulletin* 75-11 (November 1989), p. 730; Richard E. Feinberg and Delia M. Boylan, "Modular Multilateralism: North-South Economic Relations in the 1990s," in Brad Roberts, ed., *New Forces in the World Economy* (Cambridge, MA: MIT Press, 1996), p. 45.

51. Payer, *Lent and Lost*, p. 97.

52. Jeffrey Sachs, "Making the Brady Plan Work," *Foreign Affairs* 68-3 (Summer 1989), p. 92.

53. Sachs, "Making the Brady Plan Work," p. 87.

54. Stanley Fischer, "Foreword," in Husain and Diwan, *Dealing with the Debt Crisis,* p. v.

55. For a detailed discussion of the results of the Brady Plan, see Cline, *International Debt Reexamined,* pp. 231–273.

56. Paul Lewis, "I.M.F. and World Bank Clear Debt Relief," *New York Times,* September 30, 1996, p. C2.

57. Cline, *International Debt Reexamined,* p. 70.

58. Cline, *International Debt Reexamined,* pp. 70–76; Bakker, *International Financial Institutions,* p. 94.

59. For example, see "Summary of Discussion on LDC Debt Policy," in Feldstein, ed., *American Economic Policy in the 1980s,* p. 737; Stallings, *Banker to the Third World,* pp. 313–315. See also Theodore H. Cohn, "The United States and Latin America: Ambivalent Ties," *The Canadian Review of American Studies* 20-2 (Fall 1989), pp. 255–263.

60. Ffrench-Davis, "External Debt, Adjustment, and Development in Latin America," p. 31.

61. Richard E. Feinberg, "Latin American Debt: Renegotiating the Adjustment Burden," in Feinberg and Ffrench-Davis, eds., *Development and External Debt in Latin America,* pp. 57–58; Corbridge, *Debt and Development,* p. 85.

   William Cline provides some strong arguments from a liberal-economic perspective against the view that the debt strategies favored the banks over the debtor countries. See Cline, *International Debt Reexamined,* pp. 255–262.

62. H. W. Singer, "Beyond the Debt Crisis," *Development* 1 (1992), p. 36.

63. Valerie J. Assetto, *The Soviet Bloc in the IMF and the IBRD* (Boulder, CO: Westview Press, 1988), pp. 189–190.

64. The discussion of East European and former Soviet Union debt that follows relies extensively on Cline, *International Debt Reexamined,* pp. 345–367.

65. Matthew Evangelista, "Domestic Structure and International Change," in Michael W. Doyle and G. John Ikenberry, eds., *New Thinking in International Relations Theory* (Boulder, CO: Westview Press, 1997), pp. 212–214; Kazimierz Poznanski, "Economic Adjustment and Political Forces: Poland Since 1970," *International Organization* 40-2 (Spring 1986), pp. 455–488.

66. Ellen Comisso and Paul Marer, "The Economics and Politics of Reform in Hungary," *International Organization* 40-2 (Spring 1986), p. 422. See also Laura D'Andrea Tyson, "The Debt Crisis and Adjustment Responses in Eastern Europe: A Comparative Perspective," *International Organization* 40-2 (Spring 1986), pp. 239–285.

67. Cline, *International Debt Reexamined,* pp. 346–360.

68. References to developing countries were later included in the second amendment to the IMF Articles of Agreement, when LDC members were more numerous. See Joseph Gold, "The Relationship Between the International Monetary Fund and the World Bank," *Creighton Law Review* 15 (1982), pp. 509–510.

69. Richard E. Feinberg, "The Changing Relationship Between the World Bank and the International Monetary Fund," *International Organization* 42-3 (Summer 1988), p. 547.

70. For a discussion of the bank's 1960s program lending to India, see Michael Lipton and John Toye, *Does Aid Work in India? A Country Study of the Impact of Official Development Assistance* (London: Routledge, 1990), ch. 3.

71. Jacques Polak, "The World Bank and the IMF: The Future of their Coexistence," in *Bretton Woods: Looking to the Future* (Washington, DC: Bretton Woods Commission, July 1994), p. C-149; Edward S. Mason and Robert E. Asher, *The World Bank Since Bretton Woods* (Washington, DC: Brookings Institution, 1973), pp. 551–554.

72. Hiroyuki Hino, "IMF–World Bank Collaboration," *Finance & Development* 23-3 (September 1986), p. 11.

73. There is a wide range of literature on IMF and World Bank structural adjustment loans. See, for example, Jacques J. Polak, *The World Bank and the International Monetary Fund: A Changing Relationship,* Brookings Occasional Papers (Washington, DC: Brookings Institution, 1994); Paul Mosley, Jane Harrigan, and John Toye, *Aid and Power: The World Bank and Policy-based Lending,* vol. 1 (London: Routledge, 1991); and Stanley Please, "The World Bank: Lending for Structural Adjustment," in Richard E. Feinberg and Valeriana Kallab, eds., *Adjustment Crisis in the Third World* (New Brunswick, NJ: Transaction Books, 1984), pp. 83–98.

74. "Survey: The IMF and the World Bank," *The Economist,* October 12, 1991, p. 48.

75. James, *International Monetary Cooperation,* p. 326; Polak, *The World Bank and the IMF: A Changing Relationship,* pp. 44–45.

76. Jeffrey Sachs, "Beyond Bretton Woods: A New Blueprint," *The Economist,* October 1, 1994, p. 23.

77. There are numerous critiques of IMF conditionality and the debt crisis. For example, see Kevin Danaher, ed., *Fifty Years Is Enough: The Case Against the World Bank and the International Monetary Fund* (Boston: South End Press, 1994); Payer, *Lent and Lost;* Martin Honeywell, ed., *The Poverty Brokers: The IMF and Latin America* (London: Latin America Bureau, 1983); and Körner, et al., *The IMF and the Debt Crisis.*

78. Feinberg, "The Changing Relationship Between the World Bank and the International Monetary Fund," pp. 552–556; Polak, *The World Bank and the IMF: A Changing Relationship,* pp. 16–17.

79. Diane Elson, "From Survival Strategies to Transformation Strategies: Women's Needs and Structural Adjustment," in Lourdes Benería and Shelley Feldman, eds., *Unequal Burden: Economic Crises, Persistent Poverty, and Women's Work* (Boulder, CO: Westview Press, 1992), pp. 26–48; Gita Sen and Caren Grown, *Development, Crises, and Alternative Visions: Third World Women's Perspectives* (New York: Monthly Review, 1987), pp. 62–63.

80. Marc Williams, *International Economic Organisations and the Third World* (New York: Harvester Wheatsheaf, 1994), p. 127.

81. Gerardo Otero, "Neoliberal Reform and Politics in Mexico: An Overview," in Gerardo Otero, ed., *Neoliberalism Revisited: Economic Restructuring and Mexico's Political Future* (Boulder, CO: Westview Press, 1996), pp. 6–7; Sebastian Edwards, "Latin American Economic Integration: A New Perspective on an Old Dream," *The World Economy* 16-3 (May 1993), p. 325; "Mercosur: The End of the Beginning," *The Economist,* October 12, 1996, pp. 3–4.

82. See Anthony Hurrell and Ngaire Woods, "Globalisation and Inequality," *Millennium* 24-3 (1995), pp. 447–470.

83. Eric Helleiner, *States and the Reemergence of Global Finance: From Bretton Woods to the 1990s* (Ithaca, NY: Cornell University Press, 1994), p. 13.

CHAPTER 8

Global Trade
Relations

From the earliest times, trade relations have aroused strong positive and negative emotions among societies and peoples. On the one hand, some early Christian philosophers argued that trade was divinely ordained and a part of the natural order; and proposals for world peace stemming from at least the seventeenth century drew strong linkages between free trade and the achievement of peaceful conditions.[1] On the other hand, trade conflicts have been common since the latter part of the Middle Ages, when the number of sovereign entities was increasing. Although these conflicts are often limited in scope, they sometimes escalate to the point of becoming major trade wars.[2] The high degree of controversy surrounding trade issues stems largely from the fact that interest groups and the broader public within states view their own welfare as being more affected by trade policy than by monetary, investment, or financial policy. Thus, business, labor, agricultural, consumer, environmental, and cultural groups have strongly vested interests in policies promoting trade liberalization or protectionism, and they regularly attempt to influence government trade policies.

Trading relations, like monetary and financial relations, have been strongly affected by the forces of globalization. Thus, trade as a share of global output rose from 7 percent in 1950 to more than 22 percent in 1997, and trade grew 2.8 times faster than global output from 1984 to 1994. While foreign investment flows are increasing even faster than trade flows, the two are closely related. A growing share of trade is taking place within multinational corporations and their affiliates. Indeed, *intrafirm trade* within MNCs or related partners now accounts for about one-third of total world trade. As the director-general of the WTO has stated, "businesses now trade to invest and invest to trade—to the point where both activities are increasingly part of a single strategy to deliver products across borders."[3]

As global interdependence has increased and has had growing domestic effects, major societal groups have expressed strongly held views on trade liberalization agreements. On the one hand, internationalist firms and industries, which have become dependent on exports, imports, and multinational production, strongly favor global and regional trade liberalization agreements because protectionism is very costly to them. On the other hand, domestically oriented firms, threatened by surging import competition, may strongly oppose freer trade agreements.[4] A number of labor, environmental, and cultural groups in the United States and Canada have also opposed regional agreements such as the Canada-U.S. Free Trade Agreement (CUSTA) and the North American Free Trade Agreement (NAFTA), fearing that they will infringe on the state's ability to impose its own labor, environmental, and (in the case of Canada) cultural standards.

This chapter discusses the characteristics of the postwar global trade regime and the changing role of the advanced industrial states, the less developed countries, and the emerging economies in this regime. A major theme relates to the competing pressures for the liberalization of trade on the one hand and for various forms of protectionism on the other.

TRADE THEORY

The promotion of free trade is a central tenet of liberal theorists, who argue that trade is a positive-sum game that provides mutual benefits to states. Realists, by contrast, tend to view trade as a zero-sum game in which each state strives to increase its exports (especially of high-value-added goods) and decrease its imports. Historical structuralists view trade as a form of unequal exchange in which the advanced capitalist states in the core export manufactured and high-technology goods and import raw materials and lower-technology goods from the periphery. Of the three main IPE perspectives, liberal theories of trade have clearly been the most influential among economists in the industrial states.

While liberal trade theory has evolved considerably over time, the views of Adam Smith and David Ricardo still form a central part of the justification for freer trade. Adam Smith argued that the gains from free trade result from *absolute advantage,* in which each state benefits if it specializes in the goods it produces best, and trades with others. For example, if France can produce wine more cheaply than England and England can produce cloth more cheaply than France, both countries can benefit from specialization and trade. David Ricardo's theory of *comparative advantage* is less intuitive—and also a more powerful theory—because it indicates that trade is beneficial even if absolute advantage does not exist. In his 1817 study *Principles of Political Economy and Taxation,* Ricardo argued that England and Portugal could gain from trading wine for cloth even if Portugal produced *both* goods more cheaply than England.[5] The tables below use arbitrary figures to demonstrate Ricardo's theory of comparative advantage. Table 8.1 gives the amount of labor required (for example, workerdays) in Portugal and England to produce one bottle of wine and one bolt of cloth.

As Table 8.1 shows, Portugal can produce *both* wine and cloth with fewer labor inputs than England. Nevertheless, the two countries can gain from specialization and trade because England has less of a cost disadvantage in cloth than in wine production. In other words, England has a *comparative* advantage in cloth, and Portugal has a *comparative* advantage in wine. To demonstrate these gains, we assume that England

TABLE 8.1
LABOR REQUIRED TO PRODUCE
ONE BOTTLE OF WINE AND
ONE BOLT OF CLOTH

	Wine	Cloth
England	6	5
Portugal	2	4

shifts 30 units of labor from wine to cloth production and that Portugal shifts 12 units of labor from cloth to wine production. The total amount of labor used in the two countries remains constant, but this reallocation of labor causes the production changes given in Table 8.2.

As Table 8.2 shows, the shift of 30 units of labor from the wine to the cloth industry in England raises cloth production by 6 bolts (30 divided by 5) and reduces wine production by 5 bottles (–30 divided by 6). The shift of 12 units of labor from the cloth to the wine industry in Portugal raises wine production by 6 bottles (12 divided by 2) and reduces cloth production by 3 bolts (–12 divided by 4). Table 8.2 shows that with England specializing more in cloth and Portugal specializing in wine, the two countries together produce one more bottle of wine and three more bolts of cloth. Liberals therefore argue that two countries can enjoy mutual (but not necessarily equal) benefits from specialization and trade *even if* one of the two countries has an absolute advantage in producing all of the products traded.

Although Ricardo's theory provided a powerful liberal argument in favor of free trade, his assumption that comparative advantage results only from differences in labor productivity is far too limiting. In reality, comparative advantage also results from other factors of production such as capital and natural resources. In the 1920s and 1930s, liberal economists therefore turned to a more elaborate theory to explain a country's comparative advantage: the **Heckscher-Ohlin theorem.** According to this theory, developed by two Swedish economists, a country's comparative advantage is determined by its relative abundance and scarcity of various factors of production, such as capital, labor, and resources. Thus, the more advanced economies, which are capital-rich states, will specialize in the production and export of capital-intensive

TABLE 8.2
CHANGES IN PRODUCTION OF
WINE AND CLOTH

	Bottles of Wine	Bolts of Cloth
England	–5	+6
Portugal	+6	–3
Total	+1	+3

goods, while the LDCs, which have an abundant supply of cheap labor, will specialize in labor-intensive goods.

Building on the Heckscher-Ohlin theorem, in the 1940s two economists in the United States developed the *Stolper-Samuelson theory,* which helps to explain why some domestic groups in a state are free-trade-oriented and other groups are protectionist. According to the Stolper-Samuelson theory, trade liberalization benefits abundantly endowed factors of production and hurts poorly endowed factors of production in a state. Thus, if a state is rich in labor and productive land but poor in capital, freer trade would be beneficial to workers and farmers but detrimental to the owners of capital. The Stolper-Samuelson theory has been used to explain why blue-collar labor in the United States and Canada has opposed NAFTA (Mexico is more abundantly endowed with less skilled workers) and why wheat farmers in France have opposed moves to liberalize agricultural trade in GATT/WTO (the United States, Canada, Australia, and Argentina are more abundantly endowed with land for wheat production).[6]

The Heckscher-Ohlin and Stolper-Samuelson models are controversial. Some empirical studies contradict their assumption that countries are always more successful in exporting goods produced with their abundantly endowed factors.[7] Nevertheless, these models continue to occupy a central place in international trade theory. The Stolper-Samuelson theory is also of considerable interest to us here because it points to the fact that there are inevitably both winners and losers as a result of freer trade. While liberals concede that freer trade may produce job losses in some sectors, they argue that trade liberalization is nevertheless desirable because the gains in overall efficiency are greater than any losses and because even the losers can be compensated and will benefit in the long term. Realists and historical structuralists, by contrast, believe that the losers will not be adequately compensated and will suffer as a result of their disadvantageous position.

Although liberal theories extending from Ricardo's comparative advantage to the Heckscher-Ohlin theorem are still considered important for explaining interindustry trade, they do not adequately explain the rapid increase in intraindustry and intrafirm trade. In *intraindustry trade,* differentiated products are traded within the same industry group; for example, the United States and Japan may export electrical products to each other. The Heckscher-Ohlin assumption that trade is most beneficial between countries with different factor endowments does not provide an adequate explanation for intraindustry trade, which often occurs among advanced industrial states with similar factor endowments. Thus, liberals have developed new theories which postulate that intraindustry trade provides benefits such as economies of scale, the satisfaction of consumer tastes for variety, and the production of more specialized and sophisticated manufactured products.[8] Much trade today is also *intrafirm* trade between parent companies of multinational corporations and their subsidiaries. Chapter 10 discusses the fact that theories of the firm best explain why trade occurs between an MNC's affiliates in different countries.

Realists have often argued that liberal assumptions about comparative advantage are overly static, underestimating the ability of a state to upgrade its advantages in trade. The growing amount of intraindustry and intrafirm trade among countries with similar factor endowments has added force to the realist arguments. Thus, realists question whether David Ricardo's advice to Portugal in fact served its long-range interests. By following Ricardo's prescriptions and specializing in wine, Portugal might have gained some short-term advantages. However, it would have been less competitive than England over the long term because cloth production was a high-growth, high-technology industry at the time. According to realists, Portugal would have been better off *creating* a comparative advantage for itself in cloth through government assistance to the cloth industry, even if it had a "natural" comparative advantage in wine.[9]

Strategic trade theory emphasizes the creation of comparative advantage through industrial targeting. Strategic trade theorists justify and even promote the idea of government intervention in the economy, and they often prefer the terms *arbitrary comparative advantage* or *competitive advantage* to comparative advantage. Although efforts to gain competitive advantage in trade are not really new, the growing emphasis on high-technology industries provides "a fertile breeding ground for interventionist policies."[10] Strategic trade theorists have produced a wide range of studies to demonstrate that interventionist policies can improve a country's position in manufacturing and technology, and they often point to Japan and the East Asian NICs as examples of states that have mobilized a limited amount of resources to create competitive advantage. However, liberal theorists argue that the benefits of strategic trade policy are likely to be small while the risks are great. Although individual rationality might lead a country to attempt to increase its competitive advantage at the expense of others, other countries are likely to retaliate, and everyone will be worse off as a result (see the discussion of the prisoners' dilemma in Chapter 4).[11] Despite these liberal warnings, the temptations remain strong in an age of global competition for countries to gain a competitive advantage by targeting particular industrial and high-technology sectors.

GLOBAL TRADE RELATIONS BEFORE WORLD WAR II

Throughout modern history, countries have alternated between periods of trade liberalization and protectionism. Thus, mercantilist trade restrictions gave way to a period of freer trade in 1815, when Britain first lowered its import duties and then repealed its Corn Laws and opened its borders to food imports in 1846. Following the British lead, Latin America's newly independent republics adopted liberal trade policies; Prussia moved Germany to lower its trade barriers; and France joined with Britain in the Cobden-Chevalier Treaty of 1860, which resulted in a network of commercial treaties lowering tariff barriers between Britain and France and throughout Europe. After 1875, however, the enthusiasm for free trade waned somewhat because of the decline of British hegemony, the defeat of France in the 1870 Franco-Prussian War, and the depression of 1873–96. With the outbreak of World War I the network of European trade and commercial treaties was completely disrupted.[12]

After World War I, renewed efforts to remove trade restrictions were largely unsuccessful as countries reacted to harsh economic conditions by increasing their tariffs. Tariffs were rising not only in European nations recovering from the war but also in the United States, which had emerged from the war as a net creditor nation and the world's largest industrial power. Thus, the U.S. Congress enacted the Fordney-McCumber Tariff in 1922, which increased import duties to an average of 38 percent, well above the duty levels in the 1913 Underwood Tariff. After the 1929 stock market crash, Congress passed the 1930 Smoot-Hawley Tariff Act, which increased average U.S. ad valorem rates on dutiable imports to 52.8 percent, "the highest American tariffs in the twentieth century."[13]

The question arises as to why the United States as the top economic power in the interwar period did not act more forthrightly to limit the rise of trade protectionism. Hegemonic stability theorists often argue that the United States was able but unwilling to become the hegemonic leader until its position became more firmly established after World War II.[14] However, some analysts question whether the United States in fact had the ability to establish an open economic system during the interwar period. Although the United States was the top economic state at the time, its share of world trade and investment was well below that of Britain during the latter part of the nineteenth century.[15]

Others look to domestic politics rather than to the U.S. global position in explaining American protectionism. Although the United States emerged as the largest industrial power in the interwar period, a number of U.S. industries were fearful of renewed European competition, and U.S. agricultural groups were dismayed by a rapid decrease in agricultural prices. In their efforts to pressure for trade protectionism, these domestic groups benefited from the fact that the U.S. Constitution gives Congress the sole power to regulate commerce and impose tariffs. The members of Congress do not have national constituencies, so they are far more susceptible than the President to protectionist pressures. Producers and workers who wanted to limit imports were also politically organized and concentrated in specific industries, and by joining together they were able to convince Congress to enact the Smoot-Hawley tariff. Those groups benefiting from freer trade, such as consumers, by contrast, were far more diffuse in nature and had little influence. Party politics also played a role in the Smoot-Hawley tariff; the Republicans—who were more protectionist than the Democrats—held a majority in the Senate at the time.[16]

Regardless of the reasons for the U.S. Smoot-Hawley tariff, it had disastrous consequences as other countries rushed to retaliate with their own import restrictions.[17] Between 1929 and 1933, world trade therefore declined from $35 billion to $12 billion, and U.S. exports fell from $488 million to $120 million. In efforts to reverse this damage, the U.S. Congress passed the Reciprocal Trade Agreements Act (RTAA) in 1934. The RTAA in effect transferred tariff-setting authority from Congress to the President, who could lower tariffs by up to 50 percent from Smoot-Hawley levels in trade negotiations with other countries.[18] Although Congress authorized the President to conduct only bilateral (not multilateral) tariff negotiations, the RTAA marked a significant turning point because it directly linked the setting of tariffs to international negotiations. Instead of having Congress set tariffs on a unilateral, statutory basis, the President was now authorized to establish "bargaining tariffs" as a result of bilateral agreements.

The introduction of bargaining tariffs indicated a recognition that the United States would gain greater access to foreign markets only by opening its own market to imports.[19] From 1934, when the RTAA was approved, until 1945, the United States concluded bilateral trade agreements with 27 countries and lowered its tariff rates by an average of 44 percent. Tariff rates were so high in the early 1930s, however, that these agreements mainly served to correct earlier excesses. The decision of the Roosevelt administration to lower tariffs only in exchange for similar concessions by other countries (hence the name *Reciprocal* Trade Agreements Act) also limited the scope of the agreements. Furthermore, many countries were unwilling to lower their tariffs, and the RTAA agreements did not stimulate a worldwide movement toward trade liberalization. Thus, protectionism continued to affect trade relations during the rest of the interwar period.[20]

GATT AND THE POSTWAR GLOBAL TRADE REGIME

The United States and Britain wanted to ensure that the devastating effects of protectionism in the interwar period were not repeated, and they began to hold bilateral discussions in 1943 to lay the groundwork for postwar trade negotiations. In fall 1945 the U.S. State Department issued a document on trade and employment, which formed the basis for multilateral negotiations resulting in the Havana Charter or Charter for an international trade organization (ITO) in March 1948. The charter was unusually broad in scope, dealing not only with commercial policy but also with economic development, full employment, international investment, international commodity arrangements, restrictive business practices, and the administration and functions of an international trade organization.[21] In view of the protracted nature of the Havana Charter negotiations, the participating governments decided to begin negotiating a lowering of tariffs before the charter was actually approved and ratified. These negotiations were concluded in October 1947 when 23 governments signed the final act of the General Agreement on Tariffs and Trade (GATT).

It was assumed that GATT would simply be folded into a new ITO; but the U.S. Congress never ratified the Havana Charter, and GATT therefore became permanent by default. The reasons for the U.S. failure to ratify the charter are complex and ironic, especially because the United States had originally proposed the creation of an international trade organization.[22] In drafting the ITO charter, the trade negotiators were sensitive to the problems of different countries, such as the Europeans recovering from the war. However, in trying to meet everyone's demands, the negotiators satisfied neither the protectionists nor the free traders. While U.S. protectionists argued that the ITO would lead to the import of low-cost goods and threaten the U.S. ability to form its own trade policy, free traders felt that the numerous escape clauses and exceptions in the charter would interfere with trade liberalization. Because the charter had little support within the United States, President Harry Truman agreed not to submit it to Congress for ratification, and the ITO was never formed.[23]

With the failure to establish the ITO, GATT became a permanent global trade organization. GATT did not even require ratification by the U.S. Congress because it was simply a trade agreement. Thus, countries that signed GATT were referred to as contracting parties rather than members as was the case for other international organizations. (This chapter uses the less accurate term *GATT members* for the sake of brevity.) Unlike the ITO, which would have become a United Nations specialized agency on a par with the IMF and the World Bank, GATT never attained specialized agency status. GATT continued to be primarily a written code of behavior on international trade, and it had more limited legal obligations and more primitive dispute settlement procedures than the planned ITO. GATT also lacked the Havana Charter's provisions relating to investment, employment, commodity agreements, and restrictive business practices.

Despite its informal origins, GATT gradually developed some of the characteristics of an international organization; for example, it had a small secretariat and a number of committees and working parties, and it made decisions that were binding on its member states.[24] Some analysts even argue that GATT's informality enabled it to become a more effective organization than the IMF and the World Bank:

> Many observers would now conclude that the GATT was the more effective arrangement. The strength of a formal arrangement such as the IMF is its rigidity; that of an informal, ideas-based institution such as the GATT is its adaptability. The greater success of the GATT thus illustrates the importance for postwar economic performance of an adaptable institutional framework.[25]

Indications of GATT's strengths included its success in reducing tariffs, its negotiation of disciplines for nontariff barriers, and its steadily increasing membership. However, GATT's informality and flexibility also proved to be a source of weakness in several respects. First, some trade sectors such as agriculture and textiles were largely exempted from GATT regulations. From the time GATT was formed, agriculture was treated as an exception to the trade organization's restrictions on import quotas and export subsidies; and industrial states imposed textile import quotas that contravened the spirit and rules of GATT, first through bilateral export restraints beginning in the 1950s and then through the multilateral Multi-Fiber Arrangement.

Second, GATT was more of a club than a formal organization, and its members could easily waive its regulations and avoid noticing violations. For example, some countries circumvented the GATT ban on import quotas by imposing **voluntary export restraints,** in which they pressured others to "voluntarily" decrease their exports. Third, when conflicts developed between countries over trade-distorting practices, GATT's rather weak dispute settlement procedures were often inadequate to deal with them. Fourth, burgeoning U.S. balance-of-trade deficits in the 1980s caused the United States to charge others with being unfair traders and to turn more often to trade unilateralism. Only by enhancing the trade regime's authority could the United States be assured that unilateral measures to ensure fair trade were unnecessary. And fifth, GATT's inadequacies became more evident as globalization increased, and the United States in particular demanded that the scope of GATT's activities be extended beyond trade in goods to such areas as trade in services, intellectual property, and investment.

By the mid-1980s, a number of trade experts therefore warned that GATT would become irrelevant if it did not tighten its regulations, improve its dispute settlement procedures, and extend its discipline to "older" areas such as agriculture and textiles and to "newer" areas such as services, intellectual property, and investment.[26] Although the GATT Uruguay round began with plans to upgrade the agreement, the decision was made during the round to replace GATT with a new World Trade Organization. (GATT continues to exist as the largest trade agreement under the WTO.)

PRINCIPLES OF THE GLOBAL TRADE REGIME

In some respects the GATT trade regime was not really new; its principles and rules codified past commercial practices, and its basic approach—that trade policy should be made through international negotiation—was established earlier by the 1934 U.S. RTAA. The GATT regime marked a turning point in one critical respect, however: it relied on *multilateral* negotiation. The postwar trading arrangements also reflected the interventionist liberal compromise. While the major trading nations approved of measures to liberalize trade, they also agreed to accept safeguards and exemptions to protect countries' balance of payments and domestic social policies.[27] Despite GATT's informal origins, the global trade regime became one of the most established regimes in terms of principles, norms, rules, and decision-making procedures. The sections that follow discuss the main trade regime principles and some of the threats posed to them.

Trade Liberalization

Liberalization is a central trade regime principle that GATT tried to enforce, first by lowering tariffs and then by regulating **nontariff barriers (NTBs).** Tariffs, or taxes levied on products that pass through a customs border, are usually imposed on imports but may also be applied to exports. GATT has always preferred tariffs to import quotas because tariffs (at reasonable levels) permit efficient producers to continue increasing their sales, whereas quotas set an arbitrary limit on the amount imported and provide no reward for efficiency. Thus, GATT Article 11 called for the "general elimination of quantitative restrictions" or import quotas. A number of exceptions were permitted to Article 11, however, relating to balance-of-payments problems, infant industry protection for LDCs, enforcement of health standards, and national security. Countries could also impose import quotas on agricultural products when such regulations were needed to enforce domestic supply management measures.[28]

GATT explicitly permitted tariffs, not import quotas, but it sought to lower tariffs through successive rounds of multilateral trade negotiations (MTNs). As Table 8.3 shows, eight rounds of MTNs were held under GATT auspices. In the first five rounds, countries negotiated tariff reductions on a product-by-product basis. However, product-by-product negotiations became more complex and time-consuming as GATT membership increased, and the sixth round (the Kennedy round) therefore shifted to "linear cuts" or across-the-board tariff reductions on industrial products. These linear tariff cuts resulted in an average tariff reduction of 35 percent in the Kennedy round for the OECD countries.[29]

TABLE 8.3
THE ROUNDS OF GATT NEGOTIATIONS

Name	Years	Subjects Covered	Countries Participating
Geneva	1947	Tariffs	23
Annecy	1949	Tariffs	13
Torquay	1951	Tariffs	38
Geneva	1956	Tariffs	26
Dillon	1960–61	Tariffs	26
Kennedy	1964–67	Tariffs and antidumping measures	62
Tokyo	1973–79	Tariffs, nontariff measures, plurilateral agreements	102
Uruguay	1986–93	Tariffs, nontariff measures, rules, services, intellectual property, dispute settlement, trade-related investment, textiles, agriculture, creation of World Trade Organization	123

Source: WTO Focus Newsletter, No. 30, May 1998, p. 2. By permission of the World Trade Organization.

The first five rounds of trade negotiations dealt only with the reduction of tariffs. However, GATT soon became a victim of its own success in reducing tariffs as member countries turned increasingly to nontariff barriers as an alternative means of protecting their producers. NTBs include an incredibly large array of measures that restrict imports, assist domestic production, and promote exports, and they are often more restrictive, ill-defined, and inequitable than tariffs. Negotiations to reduce NTBs are also more problematic than those for tariffs because it is difficult to quantify and measure the impact of NTBs, and countries tend to view NTBs as adjuncts of their domestic policies (and therefore as not subject to international regulation).[30]

The Kennedy round was the first round to go beyond tariff negotiations and begin the process of negotiating NTBs. The Tokyo round of negotiations on NTBs was far more extensive and resulted in a number of NTB codes dealing with technical barriers to trade, government procurement, subsidies and countervailing duties, customs valuation, and import licensing procedures. The use of codes resulted partly from the fact that LDCs opposed the extension of GATT discipline to nontariff barriers. Thus, the NTB codes were *plurilateral trade agreements* that were not multilateralized in the GATT. They bound only the signatories, and many LDCs did not participate in them. The Uruguay round was the most complicated set of GATT negotiations because it widened the agenda to include not only trade in goods but also trade in services, intellectual property, and trade-related investment measures; and it also began the process of applying global trade rules to sensitive areas such as agriculture and textiles.

Both the broadening of issues covered and the increased number of participants in the Uruguay round reflected the degree to which trade was increasingly affected by the forces of globalization. Thus, Table 8.3 shows that the number of participating countries rose from 23 in the first round (Geneva) to 123 in the eighth (Uruguay). Table 8.3 also shows that beginning with the Dillon round, each successive GATT negotiating round was more lengthy and complicated than the previous one. The Uruguay round involved seven years of difficult negotiations, and there were often concerns that the negotiators would never reach a final agreement. Nevertheless, the Uruguay round *was* completed, and it resulted in the establishment of a new World Trade Organization with jurisdiction over a much wider array of trade and related areas (such as investment and intellectual property) than the GATT.

One question asked by IPE scholars is *why* the trade liberalization principle has not only endured but been expanded, despite periodic threats to it and despite the decline in U.S. trade hegemony. In 1953, for example, the United States was clearly the trade hegemon, accounting for almost 30 percent of all manufactured exports. By the late 1970s, however, the United States had fallen to second place as an exporter of manufactures, accounting for only 13 percent of the world total. West Germany had moved into first place with 16 percent, and Japan was close behind the United States with 11 percent. Although there was an increase in the "new protectionism" of NTBs in the late 1970s, the trade liberalization principle was *not* as seriously threatened in the late 1970s as it had been in the 1920s when Britain's trade hegemony was declining. Indeed, the GATT Tokyo round (1973–79) reduced weighted-average industrial tariffs to extremely low levels (5 percent in the European Community, 4 percent in the United States, and 3 percent in Japan) and also resulted in the regulation of NTBs through a series of codes.[31]

Some scholars believe that the difference between the 1920s and 1970s demonstrates the importance of regimes in upholding principles and norms that are eventually internalized by states. In contrast to the 1920s, a major global trade organization—GATT—existed in the 1970s, and the GATT-centered global trade regime maintained the trade liberalization principle even as U.S. trade hegemony was declining. Other scholars point to domestic politics to explain the different outcomes in the 1920s and the 1970s. As noted previously, the U.S. Congress alone has the power to regulate commerce and impose tariffs under the Constitution, and in the 1920s Congress responded to domestic interest group pressures and dramatically increased tariffs. By the 1970s, however, Congress was regularly transferring its tariff-making authority to the President, who was more insulated from interest group pressures (this transfer to the President had begun with the RTAA in 1934). Thus, a major change in the domestic structure of trade policymaking in the United States helps to account for the post-war vitality of the trade liberalization principle.

Another domestic factor of importance stems from the forces of globalization. Many industries in the United States and other countries in the 1920s had few international ties, and they were therefore domestically oriented and supported trade protectionism to limit external competition. By the 1970s, however, "the increased economic integration of advanced industrial states into the world economy . . . altered the domestic politics of trade."[32] Now there were many more internationalist firms than there had been in the 1920s, and these firms were highly dependent on multinational production, exports, imports, and intrafirm trade. Thus, despite the decline in the U.S. trade position, the resistance of industries and firms to the forces of protectionism was much greater in the 1970s than it had been in the 1920s. Domestic as well as international factors account for the resilience of the trade liberalization principle in the post–World War II era.

Nondiscrimination

Nondiscrimination is another basic principle of the global trade regime. Indeed, the first GATT director-general referred to nondiscrimination as "the fundamental cornerstone" of the global trade organization.[33] The nondiscrimination principle has two dimensions, one external (most-favored-nation treatment) and the other internal (national treatment). The unconditional **most-favored-nation (MFN)** principle in Article 1 of the General Agreement stipulates that every trade advantage or privilege that a GATT member gives to any country must be extended, immediately and unconditionally, to all other GATT members. By requiring equal treatment of imports from different origins, the MFN principle helps to ensure that imports come from the lowest-cost foreign suppliers and that comparative advantage determines trading patterns. Unconditional MFN treatment can be traced back to fifteenth-century Europe and to the Cobden-Chevalier Treaty of 1860. However, unlike these earlier models, the GATT-centered MFN principle was based on *multilateral* commitments and regular multilateral consultations and negotiations.[34]

Despite the importance the GATT negotiators gave to MFN treatment, the GATT permitted exceptions to MFN on the basis of colonial preferences, regional integration agreements, balance of payments, and national security and allowed exceptions as a response to "unfair" trade actions. Of these exceptions, the proliferation of free trade agreements and customs unions such as the NAFTA and the European Union has posed the greatest threat to the MFN principle in recent years. The member states of these RIAs abolish tariff barriers among themselves, giving each other more favorable treatment than they give to other members of GATT/WTO. (Chapter 9 discusses the relationship between RIAs and GATT/WTO in more detail.)

While MFN treatment is designed to prevent discrimination at a country's border, **national treatment** seeks to prevent internal discrimination. The national treatment provisions in GATT Article 3 require member countries to treat foreign products— once they have been imported—at least as favorably as domestic products with regard to internal taxes and regulations. This provision is designed to prevent countries from using domestic measures to limit foreign competition as their tariffs and other external trade barriers decline. The importance of the national treatment provision is seen by the frequency with which it has been tested in GATT dispute settlement cases. In a 1988 case, for example, a GATT panel found that pricing and listing practices of Canadian provincial liquor boards, which discriminated against foreign wines, were inconsistent with Canada's national treatment obligations.[35]

Reciprocity

Reciprocity, the concept that a country benefiting from another country's trade concessions should provide roughly equal benefits in return, is a fundamental principle in MTNs and in the admission of new members to GATT/WTO. By ensuring that agreements are reached through a balanced exchange of concessions, the reciprocity principle limits free riding under the unconditional MFN principle. Liberal economists often argue that a country gains by liberalizing its trade unilaterally as well as through negotiation. However, unilateral trade liberalization is often not politically acceptable because protectionist forces in specific industries are usually well organized and able to mobilize domestic opposition to such policies. In reaching agreement on *reciprocal* trade concessions, by contrast, governments can depend on support from export-oriented domestic industries that will clearly gain from the agreement. New members in the WTO obtain all the benefits of market access resulting from earlier negotiating rounds, and they are also expected to provide reciprocal benefits. Thus, joining the WTO involves negotiations in which an applicant must agree to liberalize access to its market.

In practice, the reciprocity principle ensures that tariff negotiations reflect the interests of the major trading nations. States benefiting from other countries' tariff reductions must be able to offer reciprocal concessions, and those states with large domestic markets and high trade volumes have the greatest concessions to offer and thus the most leverage.[36] As a result, there is a pecking order in the global trade regime as there is in the global monetary regime. Although the Group of Seven has played an important role in coordinating monetary and macroeconomic policies, it has not taken the lead responsibility for trade policy. A parallel grouping known as the **Quadrilateral Group of Trade Ministers** or **Quad** acts as an informal committee guiding the global trade regime. The European Commission which is responsible for the EU's commercial policy—the United States, Japan, and Canada—regularized their long-term cooperation in the GATT by forming the Quad in 1981. The trade ministers of the Quad meet periodically to help set the agenda for trade negotiations, and they played an important role in all stages of the Uruguay round. For example, when the Uruguay round negotiations were stalled, the Quad announced a market-access agreement at the Group of Seven Economic Summit meeting in Tokyo in July, 1993 which resulted in a relaunching of the negotiations.[37]

The states with the largest reciprocal concessions to offer are the Big Three in the GATT: the United States, the European Union, and Japan. Of these three, the United States and the EU have been the most important. Thus, the four years of negotiations in the Kennedy round culminated in marathon talks to resolve differences between the United States and the European Community. When the Americans and Europeans reached a compromise on various sectoral issues, the Kennedy round was successfully completed.[38] The Tokyo round negotiations were also a pyramidal process, in which the principal actors—the United States and European Community—usually initiated agreements and other states were then involved in discussions to reach a consensus. Even among the LDCs there was a pecking order, with more important states such as Brazil, Mexico, and India taking priority. Although pyramidal negotiations realistically give priority to those with the power to veto an agreement, such negotiations limit the ability of smaller states to affect the outcome or protect their interests.[39] The LDCs had more influence in the Uruguay round than in previous rounds, but even in this case U.S. agreements with the European Community and Japan on agriculture were critical to ultimate success.[40]

Reciprocity may be either specific or diffuse in nature. *Specific reciprocity* refers to "situations in which specified partners exchange items of equivalent value in a strictly delimited sequence"; *diffuse reciprocity* has a less precise definition of equivalence because "one's partners may be viewed as a group rather than as particular actors, and the sequence of events is less narrowly bound."[41] While diffuse reciprocity can coexist with *unconditional* MFN treatment, specific (or aggressive) reciprocity is more akin to *conditional* MFN treatment. In conditional MFN, two countries granting concessions to each other extend these concessions to a third country *only if* it offers equivalent concessions.

Liberal economists argue that diffuse reciprocity is more conducive to interstate cooperation than specific reciprocity because of the difficulty of determining whether concessions are exactly equivalent. If countries always demanded specific reciprocity from each other, it would also be impossible to conduct negotiations. Nevertheless, the United States responded to its declining trade hegemony and its balance-of-trade deficits since 1971 with claims that specific reciprocity is sometimes necessary to prevent other countries from acting as free riders. The United States has been particularly inclined to demand specific reciprocity from countries such as Japan with which it has large trade deficits. While Japan argues that its trade surpluses are due to its competitive advantages, the United States maintains that Japan has numerous hidden trade barriers and does not provide reciprocal access to its market.[42]

Safeguards

Safeguards refer to government actions to limit imports that may cause harm to the importing country's industry or economy. The safeguard principle is an essential part of most trade liberalization agreements; countries would not agree to commitments if rigid adherence was necessary in all situations. Safeguard actions are usually temporary, but Table 8.4 shows that a government may also impose permanent trade barriers under certain circumstances. The most prominent temporary safeguard mechanism is the *general escape clause* (GATT Article 19), which permits a country to counter unforeseen "import surges" that cause, or are likely to cause, *serious* injury to a domestic

TABLE 8.4
SAFEGUARDS AND CONTINGENT TRADE MEASURES

Safeguards	
Temporary	**Permanent**
Import surges	General exceptions
Balance-of-payments problems	National security
Infant industries	Tariff renegotiations
General waivers	

Contingent Trade Measures
Antidumping duties (ADDs)
Countervailing duties (CVDs)

Sources: Bernard M. Hoekman and Michel Kostecki, *The Political Economy of the World Trading System: From GATT to WTO* (Oxford: Oxford University Press, 1995), pp. 161–195; John H. Jackson, *The World Trading System: Law and Policy of International Economic Relations* (Cambridge, MA: MIT Press, 1989), pp. 149–187.

industry. Such safeguard actions must be applied to all WTO members, and affected countries can request compensation. In view of these stringent requirements, countries do not often utilize the escape clause.[43] Table 8.4 shows that in addition to escape clause actions, a country may impose temporary import restrictions to safeguard its balance of payments and infant industries, and it may also seek a general waiver from a specific obligation. Furthermore, a country may apply permanent safeguard measures under GATT clauses relating to general exceptions (e.g., to safeguard public morals, health, and natural resources), national security, and tariff renegotiations.

Safeguard provisions, permissible even when other countries engage in "fair" trade, are usually distinguished from *contingent trade measures* taken to counter unfair trade activities. The two main types of contingent trade measures are antidumping and countervailing duties (see Table 8.4). **Dumping** occurs when a firm sells a product in an export market at a lower price than it charges in the home market or below the cost of production. The WTO permits a country to impose **antidumping duties (ADDs)** if foreign goods are being dumped and the dumping is causing or threatening material injury to its domestic producers. A country may also impose **countervailing duties (CVDs)** against imports benefiting from *trade-distorting subsidies* in an exporting country that produce or threaten material injury to domestic producers.[44] Unlike safeguard actions, contingent trade measures may be imposed in response to *material* injury (which is less than *serious* injury), and the measures are targeted at specific countries charged with engaging in unfair trade.

Contingent trade measures may be legitimate responses to unfair trade, but they can also be used as a justification for trade protectionism. Thus, ADD and CVD actions are highly controversial, and dispute settlement panels in GATT/WTO and NAFTA have often examined complaints about such actions. The United States was the first country to use CVDs, and it has been the largest user of CVDs in the post–World War II period. With the U.S. balance-of-trade deficits since 1971 and the decline of tariffs resulting from GATT negotiations, the U.S. Congress responded to domestic pressures by changing the rules and procedures so that CVDs could be imposed more easily. Thus, the United States was responsible for about 58 percent of all the countervail investigations launched from 1980 to 1992; and the United States also initiated the largest number of antidumping investigations during this period. Other frequent initiators of antidumping investigations include Australia, the European Union, Canada, and Mexico.[45]

Development

The failed Havana Charter contained a number of provisions on economic development that did not become part of the 1947 General Agreement, and development issues played only a minor role in the global trade regime in the 1940s and 1950s.[46] As the number of Third World GATT members increased, however, a "development principle" began to emerge. Several GATT provisions were added that gave LDCs special treatment and thus diverged from the nondiscrimination and reciprocity principles. However, development remains a less central trade regime principle because the major trading nations have agreed to only limited concessions to promote the interests of LDCs.[47] Later in this chapter we examine the changing role of development issues in the global trade regime.

FORMATION OF THE WORLD TRADE ORGANIZATION

By the early 1980s, the trade regime principles discussed above were all in a state of flux, and many of the earlier GATT achievements in promoting freer trade seemed to be in jeopardy. In terms of the liberalization principle, previous GATT rounds had lowered tariffs, but countries were resorting to NTBs such as voluntary export restraints that were not even covered by GATT rules. Furthermore, liberalization did not extend to major areas such as textiles and agriculture, and the GATT procedures for dealing with trade disputes were inadequate. The nondiscrimination principle was also increasingly threatened by RIAs that did not adhere to MFN treatment. As for the reciprocity and safeguard principles, the United States was demanding specific rather than diffuse reciprocity from some of its trading partners, and countries dissatisfied with the GATT safeguards were sometimes resorting to unilateral protectionist actions. Finally, in regard to the development principle, Third World countries were only marginally involved in the GATT; most of them refused to sign the Tokyo round NTB codes.

In view of GATT's evident shortcomings, the United States in particular pressured for a new round of trade negotiations. With its balance-of-trade deficits increasing rapidly in the 1980s, the United States was especially interested in extending the trade regime rules to areas such as services and agriculture, where it continued to have a comparative advantage.[48] The trade regime inadequacies were also evident to other GATT members, and agreement was reached to begin the Uruguay round negotiations in 1986. The negotiators at first focused on extending GATT's jurisdiction, but Canada proposed in 1990 that a more formal trade organization replace GATT, and others eventually supported this proposal. Thus, a new World Trade Organization replaced GATT in January 1995 as the main global trading organization.[49] In contrast to GATT, the WTO is a formal, legally constituted organization like the IMF and the World Bank. GATT has not disappeared but has reverted to its original status as an agreement for trade in goods. The trade rules that the WTO oversees are contained in various treaties, including GATT and several new treaties negotiated in the Uruguay round: the *General Agreement on Trade in Services (GATS)*, the *Agreement on Trade-Related Intellectual Property Rights (TRIPs)*, and the *Agreement on Trade-Related Investment Measures (TRIMs)*. Trade in goods is the largest aspect of international trade; thus, GATT is the most important trade agreement under WTO auspices.[50]

The *Ministerial Conference*, which includes all member countries and meets every two years, is the highest authority in the WTO; it can take decisions on all matters under the multilateral trade agreements (see Figure 8.1). However, a number of subsidiary bodies are responsible for the day-to-day work of the WTO. The most important of these bodies is the *General Council* which is also composed of all WTO members. In addition to performing functions on behalf of the Ministerial Conference, the General Council oversees the activities of three major bodies: the *Councils for Trade in Goods, Trade-Related Aspects of Intellectual Property Rights,* and *Trade in Services* (relating to the GATT, TRIPs, and GATS agreements). A number of committees also reporting to the General Council (listed on the left of Figure 8.1) deal

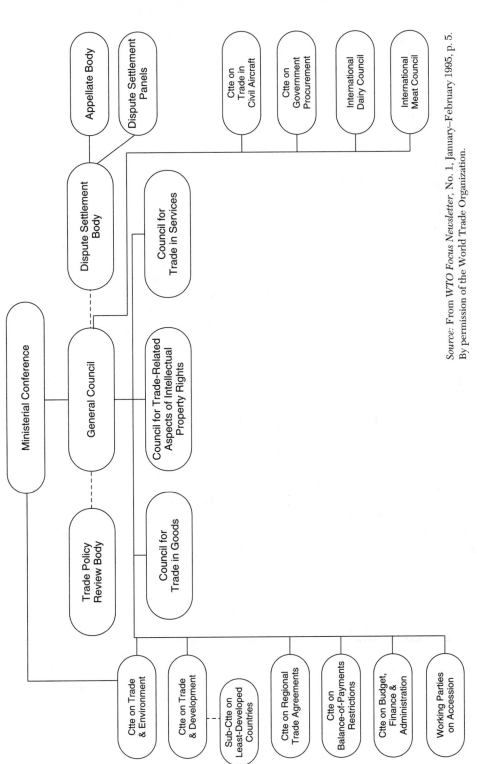

Figure 8.1 The Structure of the World Trade Organization

Source: From *WTO Focus Newsletter*, No. 1, January–February 1995, p. 5. By permission of the World Trade Organization.

with such subjects as trade and environment, trade and development, regional trade agreements, balance-of-payments restrictions, and accession to the WTO.

The General Council also convenes in two particular forms when necessary—as the *Trade Policy Review Body* and the *Dispute Settlement Body*. The trade policy review body conducts regular reviews of the trade policies of individual WTO members and ensures that others are promptly notified of policies that may interfere with trade. By increasing the transparency of members' policies, the WTO helps to promote trust that agreements are being enforced. The dispute settlement body establishes panels to investigate complaints and adjudicate trade disputes. A member country may invoke the WTO's dispute settlement procedures if another member has broken a WTO regulation or has reneged on previously negotiated concessions. A WTO member may appeal a decision against it to the *Appellate Body* (see Figure 8.1), but if the appellate body agrees with the panel report, the member must implement the panel's recommendations or pay compensation. Dispute settlement procedures are designed to be more binding and timely under the WTO than they were under the GATT. One of the parties to a dispute could block the adoption of a GATT panel report, but WTO reports can be blocked only by the consensus of member states, a highly unlikely possibility. If a country refuses to implement a panel report or provide adequate compensation, the dispute settlement body can authorize the complainant to take retaliatory action. Although the WTO dispute settlement procedures are a definite improvement over those of the GATT, they could prove to be problematic. A larger country may refuse to implement a panel report that it considers threatening to its interests, and a smaller country may be reluctant to "retaliate" against the larger country even if it could legally do so.[51]

The chief administrative officer of the WTO (and also of the GATT in earlier years) is the director-general. Tacit agreement in the 1940s provided that the World Bank president would always be an American and the IMF managing director a European, but there was no similar agreement for GATT. As a result, appointment of the director-general has recently been a contentious process. As Table 8.5 shows, all directors-general of GATT were Europeans. When it came time to select the first WTO director-general, the United States supported a non-European for the post, the former Mexican President Carlos Salinas de Gortari. Japan and most Asian countries supported a South Korean candidate (the trade minister, Kim Chul-su), and the Euro-

TABLE 8.5
DIRECTORS-GENERAL OF GATT[a] AND WTO

	Years in Office	Nationality
Sir Eric Wyndham-White	1948–68	British
Olivier Long	1969–80	Swiss
Arthur Dunkel	1980–93	Swiss
Peter Sutherland	1993–95	Irish
Renato Ruggiero	1995–present	Italian

[a]The title of GATT's chief administrative officer was changed from *secretary-general* to *director-general* in 1965.

pean Union supported an Italian (the former minister of foreign trade, Renato Ruggiero). Although Ruggiero of Italy was the clear favorite in the one nation, one vote GATT, the major trading nations sought a consensus to avoid a divisive vote on the issue. The United States finally agreed to the selection of Ruggiero as director-general, partly because it had chosen the wrong candidate (Salinas was indirectly linked to several political scandals). In return for its support, the United States insisted that Ruggiero should serve only one four-year term and that the next WTO head should be non-European.[52] This dispute reflects the growing trade rivalry between Europe, the United States, and Japan and the greater assertiveness of the United States in response to its declining hegemony in trade.

In contrast to the voting systems in the IMF and the World Bank, the WTO's voting system (like GATT's before it) is based on the one nation, one vote principle. Depending on the issue, WTO votes require a simple majority, a special majority of two-thirds or three-fourths, or unanimity. The one nation, one vote system has given Third World countries less influence than one might expect, however, because consensus decision making is far more common than formal vote taking. The LDCs also do not normally pressure for more formal voting in the WTO against the will of the major trading nations.[53] Furthermore, in trade negotiations, the Quad (the United States, the EU, Japan, and Canada) acts as an important informal group in setting the agenda.

THE THIRD WORLD AND GLOBAL TRADE ISSUES

The main participants in the GATT negotiations after World War II were advanced industrial states; the LDCs were largely uninvolved. This lack of involvement related partly to the nature of GATT and partly to LDC policies. The Havana Charter gave some attention to Third World issues in areas such as finance for economic development, preferential agreements among LDCs, and commodity agreements. When the charter was not approved, very few of these provisions were incorporated into GATT. Third World countries were also wary of participating in GATT because they felt that it did not take account of LDC needs for special and differential treatment.[54] For many years the LDCs therefore sought exemptions from some of the trade regime's principles and rules, and they wanted special access to developed country markets. In the 1980s, however, the LDCs became more accepting of the regime's liberal-economic values and more interested in participating as full partners in the global trade regime. Liberals and historical structuralists have very different views regarding the needs of LDCs for special treatment, the reasons why LDC policies changed in the 1980s, and the effects of the trade regime on LDC interests. The discussion that follows identifies four general stages of LDC participation in the postwar trade regime:

1. *The 1940s to early 1960s.* LDCs had only limited involvement in the GATT.
2. *The early 1960s to early 1970s.* LDCs increased their GATT membership and sought special and differential treatment.

3. *The early 1970s to 1980.* North-South confrontation increased, along with LDC demands for a New International Economic Order (NIEO).
4. *1980 to the present.* LDCs became more willing to accept the liberal-economic principles of the GATT/WTO centered global trade regime.

The 1940s to Early 1960s: A Period of Limited LDC Involvement

Third World countries had only limited involvement in the global trade regime in the early postwar years because of their relatively small numbers (many were still colonial territories), their protectionist trade policies, and GATT's inattention to their development problems. Most LDCs in the 1950s adopted protectionist import-substituting industrialization (ISI) policies, which were designed to replace industrial imports with domestic production. Raúl Prebisch, an Argentinian economist, was the most influential figure supporting ISI policies in the postwar period. Prebisch argued that structural inequality between the industrial states in the core and the LDCs in the periphery was a major characteristic of the capitalist world economy. As long as LDCs were dependent on exports of primary products, they could not achieve high economic growth rates. Prebisch therefore advised LDCs to pursue ISI policies to increase their production of manufactures.[55]

Latin American LDCs in particular, influenced by Prebisch's arguments, adopted policies that emphasized industrial over agricultural development, production for the domestic market over production for export, and protection of local industry through trade barriers. With this focus on inward-looking policies, most LDCs did not seek to actively participate in GATT. Thus, only 10 of the original 23 GATT members were LDCs. While 20 LDCs had joined GATT by 1960, only 7 participated in the fifth (Dillon) round of GATT negotiations.[56] The only major provision in the General Agreement dealing directly with the trade problems of LDCs was GATT Article 28, which gave Third World countries some flexibility in imposing import quotas to protect their infant industries and alleviate their balance-of-payments problems. Although the LDCs insisted that GATT should be doing more to give them special and differential treatment, their influence in the 1950s was extremely limited.[57]

The Early 1960s to Early 1970s: Growing Pressures for Special Treatment

Two major changes occurred in the 1960s and 1970s, contributing to growing LDC pressures for special treatment. First, many LDCs began to modify their import-substituting industrialization strategies or shift to export-oriented growth strategies; and second, the bargaining power of LDCs increased. By the 1960s, many LDCs following ISI policies were experiencing serious economic problems, including a slowdown in the growth of exports, dependence on intermediate imports for the production of industrial goods, and growing balance-of-payments problems. (See Chapter 11 for further discussion of LDC development strategies.) As Third World countries turned from inward- to outward-looking policies, they demanded special treatment to promote their exports. The LDCs also became better able to press their demands as the North-South balance shifted because of decolonization. Thus, in 1961 the United Nations General Assembly declared the 1960s to be the UN Development Decade, and the United Nations Conference on Trade and Development (UNCTAD I), the first major North-South conference on development issues, convened in 1964. Third World countries also established the Group of 77 at this time, which became the main vehicle for expressing their economic interests vis-à-vis the advanced industrial states.[58]

Although UNCTAD never posed a serious challenge to GATT as the main global trading organization, it did have some influence in directing attention to Third World issues. Thus, GATT members added a new Part IV to the General Agreement in February 1965, calling for special treatment for LDCs. Although Part IV called on the developed countries to reduce their import barriers to LDC goods, this was not a legally binding obligation, and Part IV was in fact largely symbolic in nature. Indeed, the industrial states were actually raising their trade barriers in the 1960s for some products in which LDCs had a comparative advantage. A prime example of developed country protectionism vis-à-vis LDCs was the case of textiles and clothing. To protect their domestic producers in the 1950s, some industrial states (for example, the United States and Britain) violated GATT Article 11, which outlaws import quotas, and imposed "voluntary" restraints on textile/clothing exports from Japan, Hong Kong, India, and Pakistan. The industrial states then sought to legalize these restrictions through multilateral agreements. In 1961, a Short-Term Arrangement on Cotton Textiles was negotiated, and this was succeeded by several Long-Term Arrangements and four successive Multi-Fiber Arrangements (MFAs). In marked contrast to GATT, these multilateral textile agreements endorsed industrial state protectionism and restricted the exports of LDCs.[59]

GATT Part IV was largely a symbolic gesture. The LDCs received a more concrete concession in 1971 when GATT permitted industrial states to establish a *generalized system of preferences* for LDCs through a 10-year renewable waiver from the most-favored-nation clause.[60] The United States and some other industrial states had at first strongly opposed the GSP idea, but their position on the issue gradually softened. The GSP lowers tariff rates in industrial states for certain imports from LDCs. Although some LDCs have benefited from these special preferences, the benefits have been limited. Thus, the industrial states refused to accept any legal obligation to provide preferences or to bind themselves to an internationally agreed GSP scheme. Instead, each state established its own GSP scheme, often limited the amount of imports that could enter at lower duties, and excluded sensitive products such as textiles and apparel from preferential status. In view of the complexities of the different GSP schemes, the more competitive LDCs such as the East Asian NICs have benefited most from the GSP, and it has offered very few benefits to poorer LDCs. One study, for example, found that only three countries—Hong Kong, South Korea, and Taiwan—accounted for 44 percent of the total gains from GSP tariff reductions. Finally, industrial states often reduced or eliminated their GSP for those LDCs that were especially successful in increasing their exports.[61]

The Early 1970s to 1980: Increased North-South Confrontation

The success of OPEC in increasing oil prices in 1973–74 was a major factor encouraging the LDCs to issue calls for a New International Economic Order in the UN General Assembly.[62] To bring about the NIEO, the LDCs sought a wide range of concessions from the North relating to LDC sovereignty over their natural resources, increased control over foreign investment, greater assistance for LDC debt and development problems, greater LDC influence in the international economic organizations, improved LDC access to industrial state markets, and increased prices for LDC commodity exports.[63] We focus here on a central trade-related demand of the LDCs—the negotiation of an *Integrated Program for Commodities (IPC)*.

For a number of years, the first secretary-general of UNCTAD, Raúl Prebisch, had insisted that commodity agreements were necessary to redress the problems of unstable earnings and declining terms of trade for LDC commodity exports. A resolution to establish the IPC was finally approved in 1976 at the UNCTAD IV conference, with the goal of establishing agreements for 18 commodities that accounted for a substantial share of LDC primary product exports. The two most important elements of the IPC were to be the creation of international buffer stocks and the creation of a common fund that would be used to acquire the stocks. By enlarging the stockpiles of those commodities with declining prices and selling stockpiles of those commodities with increasing prices, the IPC was designed to avoid excessive price fluctuations and to ensure producers of remunerative returns.

Despite UNCTAD's passage of the IPC resolution, implementation of the program proved to be difficult for several reasons. First, some major developed countries opposed the IPC proposal on liberal-economic grounds because of its strong emphasis on market intervention to stabilize prices. Industrial states were to be the largest contributors to the common fund, so their opposition did not bode well for implementation. Second, the LDCs' ability to influence the industrial states declined abruptly in the 1980s with the emergence of the foreign debt crisis. Third, some of the assumptions of the IPC were defective, and doubts were raised about the actual effect of raising commodity export prices. Less developed and developed countries are not neatly divided into commodity exporters and importers, and the raising of commodity prices would benefit some industrial state exporters and hurt some LDC importers.

In view of the opposition of the industrial states, the agreement to establish a common fund was not ratified until 1989; and since 1989, the industrial states have contributed only limited amounts to the common fund. Furthermore, only one new international agreement, the International Natural Rubber Agreement, was instituted under the IPC, and the International Tin Agreement collapsed in 1985. The IPC gave UNCTAD an opportunity to raise its profile as a negotiating forum, and the willingness of industrial states to negotiate (albeit reluctantly) represented something of a success for the LDCs. Nevertheless, the failure of the IPC to meet LDCs' expectations demonstrates the aversion most industrial states have to nonmarket solutions and points out their ability to prevent successful implementation of such North-South agreements.[64]

While the LDCs were confronting the industrial states in the UN in the 1970s, they were also participating in the Tokyo round GATT negotiations from 1973 to 1979.

One result of the Tokyo round was the approval of the *enabling clause*, which "established for the first time in trade relations . . . a permanent legal basis for preferences in favour of developing countries."[65] The clause gave permanent legal authorization for the GSP preferences and for preferential trading agreements among LDCs. To gain approval of the enabling clause, LDCs had to support the principle of "graduation" for those countries that demonstrated notable progress in development. Because some exports from more advanced LDCs were threatening American producers, the U.S. government demanded that these LDCs (e.g., South Korea, Taiwan, and Brazil) give up special treatment and accept greater GATT discipline.[66]

Another significant development in the GATT Tokyo round was the creation of codes to decrease NTBs in areas such as government procurement, subsidies, technical barriers to trade, import licensing, and antidumping duties. Most LDCs were unwilling to limit their use of NTBs, so the industrial states negotiated the codes among themselves. Only a small number of LDCs signed the codes, and some of the major industrial states threatened to deny the benefits of the codes to GATT members that were nonsignatories. However, the attitude of LDCs toward participation in the global trade regime was to change markedly in the 1980s and 1990s.

1980s to the Present: More Active and Cooperative LDC Participation in GATT/WTO

Initially, Third World countries opposed the idea of a new round of trade negotiations in the 1980s. They pointed to continued inequities in the international trade regime, and they were suspicious of efforts to include new areas in GATT, such as services, intellectual property, and investment, in which the developed countries had a competitive advantage. The opposition of LDCs gradually softened, however, and they actively participated in negotiations with the advanced industrial states in the GATT Uruguay round. This contrasted sharply with previous rounds, when many LDCs had sought special and differential treatment and had not participated actively in the exchange of concessions. The agenda of the Uruguay round included issues of interest to LDCs, such as trade in textiles and tropical agriculture, and issues of interest to industrial states, such as trade in services, intellectual property, and investment measures. Most significantly, the LDCs agreed to treat the many different Uruguay round agreements as a *single undertaking*: acceptance of the Uruguay round accord meant acceptance of *all* its agreements. The single undertaking was a marked contrast with the Tokyo round's NTB codes, in which most LDCs did not participate.[67]

The more active LDC role in the Uruguay round was directly related to the decision of many of these countries to liberalize their trade policies in the 1980s. Liberal economists and historical structuralists cite different reasons for this dramatic shift in Third World policies. According to liberals, LDCs became increasingly aware of the advantages of adopting liberal-economic policies, for several reasons. First, the tariff preferences LDCs received through the GSP were eroding as tariffs on trade among the industrial states were falling with each round of trade negotiations. Thus, LDCs were gaining fewer advantages from special and differential treatment. Second, the industrial states viewed LDCs as free riders receiving special treatment, and the LDCs were therefore marginalized in trade negotiations. Many products of interest to the LDCs, such as textiles and tropical agriculture, were either excluded from the GATT negotiations or subjected to special protectionist rules. And third, liberals attributed the shift in LDC policies to the failure of inward-looking ISI policies and to the notable success of the East Asians' export-led growth strategies.[68]

Historical structuralists strongly disagree with liberals as to the reasons why LDCs shifted their trade policies in the 1980s. According to historical structuralists, LDCs were *forced* to alter their policies. In response to the foreign debt crisis in the 1980s, the IMF and the World Bank provided structural adjustment loans to LDCs only on the condition that they decrease government spending, privatize, and liberalize their trade. Because industrial states and private lenders are unlikely to extend loans to LDC debtors that do not first receive the IMF's stamp of approval, the debtor countries had no choice but to liberalize their trade policies. Thus, one writer argues that "the current rush toward free trade follows on the heels of 10 years of structural adjustment, a logical 'next step' in the overhaul of the global economy."[69]

Liberals and historical structuralists also disagree in their assessment of the effects of the GATT Uruguay round on Third World countries. Liberals concede that the LDCs had to make concessions to the industrial states in such areas as intellectual property, services trade, and investment. However, they argue that these were short-term concessions and that LDCs will benefit in the long term from liberalizing their policies. Liberals also point to the advantages LDCs gained from participating in the Uruguay round in such areas as textiles and tropical agriculture. Finally, liberals note that LDCs still benefit from special and differential treatment in some areas; for example, LDCs have a lower level of obligations and more flexible implementation timetables, and they will benefit from special provisions for the least developed countries (LLDCs) and from technical assistance and training.[70]

Historical structuralists, by contrast, argue that LDCs gave up far more than they received in the Uruguay round. The inclusion of trade in services and intellectual property ensures that income will be transferred from the poor to the rich countries because the LDCs cannot yet compete effectively in these areas. As for the "concessions" to LDCs, the agreement to phase out the protectionist Multi-Fiber Arrangement on textiles was "backloaded" so that almost one-half of the industrial states' import quotas are to be removed only at the end of a 10-year transition period. Historical structuralists are highly skeptical that the industrial states will comply with an agreement that is extended so far into the future.[71] Liberals and historical structuralists agree that LDCs are becoming more closely involved in the global trade regime but have very different views of the possible consequences for these countries.

THE EMERGING ECONOMIES AND GLOBAL TRADE RELATIONS

The Third World countries only gradually increased their involvement in the GATT trade regime, but most centrally planned economies were not even members of GATT for many years after World War II. As was the case for LDCs, the General Agreement also largely ignored the issues of concern to CPEs.[72] The lack of attention to state trading and central planning was not surprising; the Soviet Union had turned down an invitation to attend the Havana Charter negotiations (see Chapter 2), and it was simply assumed that GATT members would be free market economies. Indeed, one of the major functions of GATT was to limit government actions that interfered with market forces.

As Table 8.6 shows, Czechoslovakia was a founding member of GATT and remained a member even after it became Communist (for many years its membership was largely inactive). Other Eastern European countries (Yugoslavia, Poland, Romania, and Hungary) joined GATT in the 1960s and 1970s. CPEs exclude foreign products through administrative control over pricing and purchasing; thus, a lowering of tariffs does not necessarily increase access to CPE markets. GATT therefore admitted these Eastern European countries under special provisions (see the discussion below). In the late 1980s and 1990s, however, the requirements for membership became more rigorous, and nonmarket economies were expected to institute specific reforms as a condition for admission. The more stringent requirements resulted from concerns about the possible admission of China and the Soviet Union (later Russia), the revival of orthodox liberalism in the 1980s, and the more formal characteristics of the WTO compared with its predecessor, GATT.

Although relations between GATT and its Eastern European members were often difficult, the problems were limited because these countries had a relatively small impact on global trade relations. This would not necessarily be the case if China or Russia joined the WTO, where their membership could have significant economic and political consequences. China and Russia were readily admitted to the IMF and the World Bank because they are loan recipients and have little influence in these weighted-voting institutions.[73] The WTO, by contrast, does not have weighted voting, and the major trading nations are concerned that these two countries could shift the balance of power. Furthermore, if economies as large as China and Russia are admitted to the WTO before they evolve sufficiently toward developing market economies,

TABLE 8.6
MEMBERSHIP OF THE EMERGING ECONOMIES IN GATT/WTO

	GATT/WTO
1948	Czechoslovakia and China (founding members)
1950	Republic of China (Taiwan) withdraws from GATT
1966	Yugoslavia
1967	Poland
1971	Romania
1973	Hungary
1984	Special observer status: People's Republic of China (GATT Council)
1990	East Germany accedes to GATT by virtue of German reunification
1992	Special observer status: Russian Federation and other FSU[a] republics (GATT Council)
1993	Czech Republic, Slovak Republic
1994	Slovenia
1996	Bulgaria

[a]FSU = former Soviet Union.

Sources: General Agreement on Tariffs and Trade, GATT Activities (Geneva, Switz.: GATT, various years).

there are fears that trade protectionism in the WTO could increase.[74] The sections that follow examine GATT/WTO relations with Eastern Europe, China, and the former Soviet Union countries.

The Eastern European Countries and GATT/WTO

Czechoslovakia was a founding member of GATT as well as the IMF and the World Bank. Although Czechoslovakia was ousted from the IMF and the World Bank shortly after it became a nonmarket economy, it was able to remain as a largely inactive member of the GATT for many years because of the informality of the General Agreement. Table 8.6 shows that four other Eastern European countries (Yugoslavia, Poland, Romania, and Hungary) joined GATT in the 1960s and early 1970s. While some of these countries were becoming more market oriented, the decision to admit them also resulted from the Western policy of *differentiation*. Designed to contain the Soviet Union, the differentiation strategy rewarded Eastern European countries for adopting more independent foreign or domestic policies. The strong U.S. support for Romanian accession to GATT, for example, stemmed mainly from that country's collision with the Soviet Union on foreign policy issues. The GATT secretariat also exerted pressure for the admission of Eastern European states because it aspired to the goal of universal membership.[75]

In accordance with the West's differentiation policy, GATT imposed a diverse range of conditions for admission of the Eastern European states. After its break with the Soviet bloc in 1948, Yugoslavia sought to redirect its trade to the West. When Yugoslavia first explored GATT affiliation in 1950, it was a full CPE; but it began efforts to engage in economic decentralization in 1952. Yugoslavia did not become a full member of GATT until 1966 because major reforms were required to move it from CPE protection toward the GATT model. This experience showed that a CPE could decentralize enough to permit participation in the GATT under conditions very similar to those for a market economy.

Unlike the case of Yugoslavia, Poland and Romania applied for accession to GATT when they were not yet moving toward market reform. Tariffs have little influence over the import decisions of CPEs, so Poland and Romania had to commit to increasing their imports from GATT members in return for the benefits of GATT membership. When Poland became a GATT member in 1967, it agreed to increase its total value of imports from GATT members by 7 percent per year, and in return Poland received limited MFN treatment. The agreement with Poland had some major shortcomings. First, Poland's 7 percent import commitment was based on an estimate that its exports to GATT members would increase by the same amount. Because Poland did not meet the 7 percent import requirement, as a quid pro quo it had to decrease its exports to other GATT countries. Some analysts therefore argue that the 7 percent requirement served as a *disincentive* to Polish trade in GATT.[76]

When Romania applied for membership, GATT agreed to classify it as an LDC, and it was therefore subject to less rigid requirements than Poland. Instead of providing a specific commitment, Romania expressed a "firm intention" to increase its imports from GATT members by at least as much as its total imports from all countries were increasing. Although this approach avoided the problems of specific commitments encountered with Poland, the Romanian undertakings were so vague that they were unenforceable.[77] The conditions for Hungary's admission to GATT (in 1973) were somewhere in between those for Yugoslavia on the one hand and Poland and Romania on the other. Because Hungary had been instituting some liberal economic reforms under its New Economic Mechanism, GATT members permitted it to provide tariff concessions as an alternative to firm commitments to increase its imports. In contrast to other Eastern European countries, Bulgaria was rebuffed for many years in its attempts to join GATT. Bulgaria's efforts failed because it was a close Soviet ally during the Cold War and because of fears that its admission would create a precedent for the Soviet Union. With the decline of the Cold War, the strategic rationale for denying Bulgaria WTO membership became less important, but the Bulgarian case continued to be enmeshed with the issue of WTO membership for Russia and China. It was not until 1996 that the WTO finally approved the entry of Bulgaria.[78]

Despite the openness of GATT to the admission of Eastern European countries, the acceptance of these countries was clearly conditional. For example, the accession agreements for Poland, Romania, and Hungary permitted the European Community to continue imposing discriminatory quantitative restrictions. Trade between the CPEs and the United States was also subject to special restrictions under U.S. law. Thus, in some respects the Eastern Europeans were second-class citizens in GATT. With the breakup of the Soviet bloc, there were growing pressures to normalize the terms of participation for Eastern European countries. The European Union agreed to dispense with its quantitative restrictions on Eastern European exports, and the WTO extended virtually the same treatment to Poland and Hungary as it does to market economies. However, normalization of membership for Eastern European countries is still not complete.[79]

China

China's decision to seek membership in GATT/WTO marked a significant departure from its policies in earlier years. In the early 1960s, China had followed a policy of "self-reliance," which emphasized import substitution, and the PRC's policies became even more autarkic in 1966 to 1969 during the Cultural Revolution. In the early 1970s, however, the PRC occupied the China seat in the UN General Assembly and moved to expand its commercial contacts with the West. After Mao Zedong's death in 1976 and the imprisonment of Cultural Revolution leaders, the PRC began to move toward more market orientation in agriculture and industry and also sought to establish contacts with the global trade organization. In 1982, China was given observer status in GATT, permitting it to attend the annual meetings of the Contracting Parties, and in 1984 China was given special observer status allowing it to attend meetings of the GATT Council. In 1986 the PRC indicated that it wanted to "rejoin" GATT as a full member.[80]

Compared to the relative ease with which it took over the China seat in the IMF and the World Bank (in 1980), China's accession to GATT/WTO has been a protracted affair. The delay in reconciliation stems from the policies of both the PRC and the global trade organization. Although the PRC wanted to increase its linkages with all the major international economic organizations in the late 1970s, it had a more restrained attitude toward GATT than toward the IMF and the World Bank. To participate in the IMF and the World Bank, China would have to provide economic data on itself and pay its subscription, but the benefits of receiving external financing and economic advice from these organizations greatly outweighed the drawbacks. As a full participant of GATT, by contrast, the requirements of China would be greater (e.g., submitting to the GATT rules and opening its market) and the benefits more uncertain. Thus, the PRC did not formally seek full participation in GATT until 1986.[81] China also insisted on three conditions for its membership, which have been highly contentious in the negotiations: its accession should be considered a resumption of membership rather than a new membership; it should be able to provide tariff concessions in return for membership privileges; and it should be classified as a less developed country.

Resumption of Membership Versus New Membership   The issue regarding the status of China's membership is quite complex. China was a founding member of GATT when it came into force in 1948. However, it was in the midst of a civil war during the early years of GATT, and in 1950 the government of Chiang Kai-shek (which had fled to Taiwan) sent a cable withdrawing China from GATT membership. The PRC maintains that the 1950 cable has no legal effect because Chiang Kai-shek was no longer leading the legally constituted government of China. The PRC also argues that it had reoccupied the China seat without having to apply as a new member in the United Nations, the Food and Agriculture Organization, and the IMF and World Bank. Thus, the PRC's desire to join GATT/WTO should be regarded as a resumption of membership rather than a new membership issue. A number of WTO members point out, however, that China did not participate in GATT negotiations or abide by GATT obligations for 35 years. Because China still has many characteristics of a CPE, WTO members should place conditions on its membership. Despite continuing conflict over the legal status of China's membership, it is generally accepted today that a negotiation must precede China's accession and that procedures to be followed will be similar to those for new WTO members.[82]

Tariff Concessions in Return for Full Participation   China objects to the fact that Poland and Romania had to commit to increasing their imports when they joined the GATT and that the contracting parties were able to maintain discriminatory quantitative restrictions against the Eastern European countries. In China's view, it has moved a considerable distance toward becoming a market economy, and the imposition of special conditions for its accession to the WTO are unnecessary. Thus, a Chinese member of the UNCTAD secretariat has stated that "China expects unconditional most favoured-nation treatment equivalent to that accorded to all other Contracting Parties."[83]

Major trading countries in the WTO, by contrast, argue that the Chinese government continues to have considerable control over trade and depends on strategic trade rather than comparative advantage as a basis for its policies. Although some Eastern European countries joined GATT as CPEs, China's sheer size and huge trading capacity make the imbalance in market access a much greater concern. The terms for admitting China to the WTO are therefore of considerable importance and might involve significant departures from the conditions applying to market economies. While WTO members might permit some special safeguards for Chinese products, they will want assurances that China limits those measures which distort trade. The United States also charges that China consistently violates trade regime principles in areas such as intellectual property rights.[84]

The Question of Developing Country Status   As a Chinese official in the UNC-TAD secretariat has stated, the PRC expects "the same differential and more favourable treatment" in the WTO that is "accorded to developing countries at similar stages of economic development."[85] Romania was given developing country status when it was admitted to the GATT, so there is a precedent for conceding to China's request in this area. With developing country status, China would be eligible for the special treatment granted to other LDCs, such as protection for infant industries and the generalized system of preferences. Many industrial countries and LDCs in the WTO, however, are apprehensive about growing competition from China, and they are therefore likely to demand that China meet the reciprocity conditions expected of more developed states. To the extent that the WTO considers granting China some degree of developing country status, it would probably impose severe limitations and expect major concessions from China in return.

Russia and Other FSU Countries

After avoiding participation in GATT for more than three decades, the Soviet Union sought observer status in GATT and quietly explored the possibility of membership in the early 1980s. However, some important GATT members strongly opposed these efforts. Undeterred, the Soviets in August 1986 asked for observer status at the Punta del Este meetings to launch the GATT Uruguay round negotiations. This request came along with the announcement of Soviet plans to introduce extensive domestic economic and trade reforms.

The Soviet Union's change in policy should not have been surprising; a sharp drop in oil prices was posing a serious threat to Mikhail Gorbachev's five-year plan to restructure and modernize the economy. However, the major trading countries limited invitations to the GATT Uruguay round to contracting parties or to countries that had given formal notification of their intention to join GATT. This decision was designed to permit China's participation in the round, but to exclude the Soviet Union and Bulgaria. American officials in particular expressed strong opposition to Soviet participation, arguing that the Soviet economic system was incompatible with the trade regime's principles, norms, and rules. The major trading nations were also concerned that the Soviet Union would benefit more than the West from accession to the GATT and that the Soviets would politicize GATT activity, making it difficult to conduct trade negotiations.[86]

The breakup of the Soviet Union in December 1991 drastically changed the attitudes of the United States and other Western countries, and negotiations with regard to WTO membership are ongoing with states of the former Soviet Union. Serious economic problems in the FSU countries and their halting steps toward establishing market economies pose obstacles to their accession to the WTO. However, in 1998 negotiations were concluded successfully with the Kyrgyz Republic and Latvia, paving the way for them to become the first two FSU countries in the WTO; and others were certain to follow.[87] Although China and Russia have not yet joined the WTO, a number of factors favor their eventual inclusion. As long as countries the size of China and Russia are not included, the WTO cannot claim to be a truly global trade organization. Furthermore, China and Russia are more likely to liberalize their economies from within than outside the WTO, and they are more likely to follow disruptive economic policies as long as they remain outsiders.[88]

CONCLUSION

This chapter demonstrates that international trade has been strongly affected by the forces of globalization. The changes are evident in the growing importance of international trade to national economies and to domestic groups within those economies, in the closer linkages between trade and other international issues, and in the increased membership of countries in GATT/WTO. Trade as a share of global output increased from 7 percent in 1950 to over 22 percent in 1997, and trade grew 2.8 times faster than global output from 1984 to 1994. Internationalist firms have a major stake in an open trading system today because of their reliance on multinational operations, exports, imports, and intrafirm trade. GATT was designed to deal almost exclusively with trade in tangible goods, but this coverage proved to be too narrow as trade in services increased. Furthermore, the WTO today is addressing a wide range of nontrade issues such as foreign investment, intellectual property, labor standards, and the environment, which have become closely intertwined with trade issues.[89] Foreign direct investment and trade, for example, are highly complementary because about one-third of trade today is conducted among affiliates of international firms. (While some accords such as TRIPS extend well beyond the trade area, internationalist firms are pleased to have them included in the WTO.)

Finally, membership and participation in GATT/WTO is for the first time becoming truly global in scope. For many years Third World countries in GATT did not fully participate in the negotiations, and a number of LDCs did not even join the organization. The foreign debt crisis that began in 1982 marked a turning point in LDC participation in the global economy in general and in the global trade regime in particular. Indeed, Table 8.7 shows that 33 LDCs joined GATT from 1981 to 1994 (the year before the WTO was formed). Another major turning point was the breakup of the Soviet Union in the early 1990s, which led to a new wave of emerging countries seeking membership in GATT/WTO. As of May 1998 there were 132 member states in the WTO and 34 observer governments waiting to join the WTO. The majority of the 34 observer governments were emerging economies, including most notably China and Russia.[90]

Liberals, realists, and historical structuralists have very different reactions to these changes in the global trade regime. Liberal economists believe that industrial, Third World, and emerging countries are all benefiting from trade liberalization and the expanding membership in the WTO. Thus, one liberal researcher argues that "in one country after another, farsighted leaders have recognized that they themselves have the means to invigorating their economies by opening their borders."[91] Orthodox liberals also applaud the moves by many LDCs in recent years to liberalize their trade barriers unilaterally, arguing that the primary benefits go to those who liberalize. As for the service, investment, and intellectual property agreements that resulted from the GATT Uruguay round, liberals feel that they should and do "mark only the beginning, not the completion, of new liberalization."[92]

Many realists question whether there is a genuine globalization of trading activity, and they also point to the fact that countries today are not uniformly moving in the direction of trade liberalization. Today's "globalization," from this perspective, is actually a form of "triadization," in which the three most powerful and developed regions of

TABLE 8.7
NEW LDC ACCESSIONS TO GATT, 1982–94
(DATES OF ACCESSION)

Angola	1994	Hong Kong	1986
Antigua and Barbuda	1987	Lesotho	1988
Bahrain	1993	Macao	1991
Belize	1983	Maldives	1983
Bolivia	1990	Mali	1993
Botswana	1987	Mexico	1986
Brunei	1993	Morocco	1987
Colombia	1981	Mozambique	1992
Djibouti	1994	Namibia	1992
Dominica	1993	Paraguay	1993
El Salvador	1991	Qatar	1994
Fiji	1993	Solomon Islands	1994
Grenada	1994	Swaziland	1993
Guatemala	1991	Thailand	1982
Guinea, Republic of	1994	Venezuela	1990
Guinea-Bissau	1994	Zambia	1982
Honduras	1994		

Source: Bernard Hoekman and Michel Kostecki, *The Political Economy of the World Trading System: From GATT to WTO* (Oxford: Oxford University Press, 1995), pp. 275–276.

the world—Western Europe, North America, and East Asia—have the most interactions. By far the largest amount of trade occurs between and within these three major regions, and trade flows involving other regions are relatively small. The Quad group composed of the United States, the European Union, Japan, and Canada also plays an important role in setting the agenda for global trade negotiations. Triadization is evident not only from facts and figures but also from general attitudes. Thus, Western Europeans, Japanese, and North Americans tend to believe that the "world that counts is their world in which is located the scientific power, technological potentials and supremacy, military hegemony, economic wealth, cultural power and, therefore, mastery of conditions and ability to govern the world economy."[93]

Realists point out that within the industrial world, the decline of U.S. trade hegemony has led to growing competition among the three major trading blocs. In this increasingly competitive world, strategic trade policies that involve selective intervention by governments can greatly improve a country's trade position. Strategic trade theorists often point to Japan and the East Asian NICs as examples of states that have mobilized a limited amount of resources to create competitive advantage. Thus, realists have often suggested that other countries should follow the example of the East Asians rather than relying on static views of comparative advantage.

Historical structuralists, like realists, point to a hierarchy among states, in which the industrial states clearly dominate the global trade regime. However, historical structuralists are more concerned than realists with the consequences for Third World states. In the view of historical structuralists, LDCs have become more active participants in the global trade regime not by choice but by necessity. IMF and World Bank structural adjustment loans since the 1980s have been linked with LDC commitments to engage in trade liberalization, privatization, and deregulation, and Third World debtors have had to comply with these conditions to receive international financing. The GATT Uruguay round agreement, from this perspective, was an unequal agreement in which industrial states received concrete gains in areas such as intellectual property and services trade while LDCs had to settle for the promise of possible future gains in areas such as textile trade.

The TRIPs agreement on intellectual property is a prime example of the differing views of liberals and historical structuralists regarding the Uruguay round. The Uruguay round agreement requires all signatories to provide intellectual property rights protection in a number of areas. For example, WTO members must develop legislation that provides at least 20 years of protection for patents. Liberals argue that most innovation occurs privately, and groups and individuals will have little incentive to engage in research and development if they are not rewarded with sufficient patent protection. Thus, intellectual property rights are essential for the development of new inventions and innovations. Historical structuralists, by contrast, can point to the fact that many of the TRIPs measures "are not explicitly related to trade—except in the name of the agreement."[94] While Third World countries in the GATT Uruguay round had wanted the TRIPs discussions to be limited to trade-related measures, the industrial states used these discussions to develop measures they wanted that were outside the competence of GATT.[95] Thus the TRIPs agreement, according to historical structuralists, will limit and distort trade, hinder the transfer of technology to the Third World, and lead to a net transfer of resources in rents from the LDCs to the advanced industrial states. Indeed, more than 80 percent of the patents in the Third World are owned by foreigners, mainly multinational corporations with headquarters in the North.[96]

In reality, both liberals and realists point to important trends in the global trade regime. On the one hand, trade interdependence has been increasing, and there are strong pressures for further trade liberalization. On the other hand, this growing interdependence and the decline of U.S. trade hegemony have led to increased competitiveness and greater temptations to resort to strategic trade policy. Nevertheless, if one considers the role of domestic and transnational (i.e., nongovernment) actors today, it would seem that the forces for trade liberalization are inexorable. As globalization as increased, a growing proportion of domestic firms in the advanced industrial states have become reliant on multinational operations, imports, exports, and intrafirm trade. These internationalist firms have played a major role in pressuring for trade liberalization at both the global and regional levels.[97]

NOTES

1. Jacob Viner, *Studies in the Theory of International Trade* (New York: Augustus M. Kelly, Reprint of Economic Classics, 1965), p. 100; David A. Baldwin, *Economic Statecraft* (Princeton, NJ: Princeton University Press, 1985), pp. 75–76.
2. A trade war is "a category of intense international conflict where states interact, bargain, and retaliate primarily over economic objectives directly related to the traded goods or service

sectors of their economies, and where the means used are restrictions on the free flow of goods or services"; see John A. C. Conybeare, *Trade Wars: The Theory and Practice of International Commercial Rivalry* (New York: Columbia University Press, 1987), p. 3.

3. Renato Ruggiero (director-general of the World Trade Organization), "Charting the Trade Routes of the Future: Towards a Borderless Economy," address delivered to the International Industrial Conference, San Francisco, September 29, 1997, *World Trade Organization Press Release*, Geneva, Press/77, p. 4.

4. Helen V. Milner, *Resisting Protectionism: Global Industries and the Politics of International Trade* (Princeton, NJ: Princeton University Press, 1988), pp. 290–291.

   Business conflict theory is directly relevant to disputes between internationalist and nationalist business groups over international trade. See the discussion of business conflict theory in Chapter 5 of this book.

5. David Ricardo, *The Principles of Political Economy and Taxation* (Homewood, IL: Irwin, 1963). See also Cletus C. Coughlin, K. Alec Chrystal, and Geoffrey E. Wood, "Protectionist Trade Policies: A Survey of Theory, Evidence, and Rationale," *Federal Reserve Bank of St. Louis Review* 70-1 (January–February, 1988), pp. 12–13.

6. Wolfgang F. Stolper and Paul A. Samuelson, "Protection and Real Wages," *Review of Economic Studies* 9-1 (November 1941), pp. 58–73; Ronald Rogowski, *Commerce and Coalitions: How Trade Affects Domestic Political Alignments* (Princeton, NJ: Princeton University Press, 1989).

7. For example, one researcher found that the United States was highly successful in exporting labor-intensive goods in the 1950s, a period in which it was the most capital-rich country. See Wassily Leontief, "Domestic Production and Foreign Trade: The American Capital Position Re-examined," *Proceedings of the American Philosophical Society* 97-4 (September 1953), pp. 332–349. See also Harry P. Bowen, Edward E. Leamer, and Leo Sveikauskas, "Multicountry, Multifactor Tests of the Factor Abundance Theory," *American Economic Review* 77-5 (December 1987), pp. 791–809.

8. Elhanan Helpman and Paul R. Krugman, *Market Structure and Foreign Trade: Increasing Returns, Imperfect Competition, and the International Economy* (Cambridge, MA: MIT Press, 1985), p. 3; Robert Gilpin, with Jean M. Gilpin, *The Political Economy of International Relations* (Princeton, NJ: Princeton University Press, 1987), pp. 175–178.

9. Bruce R. Scott, "National Strategies: Key to International Competition," in Bruce R. Scott and George C. Lodge, eds., *U.S. Competitiveness in the World Economy* (Boston: Harvard Business School Press, 1985), pp. 93–95.

10. Laura D'Andrea Tyson, *Who's Bashing Whom? Trade Conflict in High-Technology Industries* (Washington, DC: Institute for International Economics, November 1992), p. 4; F. M. Scherer and Richard S. Belous, *Unfinished Tasks: The New International Trade Theory and the Post–Uruguay Round Challenges*, Issues Paper no. 3 (Washington, DC: British–North American Committee, May 1994), p. 42.

11. Klaus Stegemann, "Policy Rivalry Among Industrial States: What Can We Learn from Models of Strategic Trade Policy?" *International Organization* 43-1 (Winter 1989), p. 99.

12. See Edward John Ray, "Changing Patterns of Protectionism: The Fall in Tariffs and the Rise in Non-Tariff Barriers," *Northwestern Journal of International Law & Business,* 8 (1987), pp. 294–295; and Rogowski, Commerce and Coalitions, pp. 168–169.

13. Robert A. Pastor, *Congress and the Politics of U.S. Foreign Economic Policy, 1929–1976* (Berkeley: University of California Press, 1980), p. 78.

14. The classic statement of this position is found in Charles P. Kindleberger, *The World in Depression 1929–1939* (Berkeley: University of California Press, 1973), pp. 291–307.

15. Stephen D. Krasner, "State Power and the Structure of International Trade," *World Politics* 28-3 (April 1976), p. 338.

16. See E. E. Schattschneider, *Politics, Pressures and the Tariff: A Study of Free Private Enterprise in Pressure Politics, as Shown in the 1929–1930 Revision of the Tariff* (Hamden, CT: Archon Books, 1963, unaltered from the 1935 edition); and Pastor, *Congress and the Politics of U.S. Foreign Economic Policy*, pp. 80–84.

17. For a discussion of the effects of the U.S. 1930 tariff, see Joseph M. Jones, Jr., *Tariff Retaliation: Repercussions of the Hawley-Smoot Bill* (Philadelphia: University of Pennsylvania Press, 1934).

18. For a discussion of the reasons for Congressional passage of the RTAA, see I. M. Destler, *American Trade Politics* (Washington, DC: Institute for International Economics and The Twentieth Century Fund, 2nd edition, June 1992), pp. 14–15.

19. Jones, *Tariff Retaliation,* pp. 303–305; Gilbert R. Winham, *The Evolution of International Trade Agreements* (Toronto: University of Toronto Press, 1992), p. 19; Henry J. Tasca, *The Reciprocal Trade Policy of the United States: A Study in Trade Philosophy* (New York: Russell & Russell, 1938), chs. 2–4.

20. John W. Evans, *The Kennedy Round in American Trade Policy: The Twilight of the GATT?* (Cambridge, MA: Harvard University Press, 1971), pp. 5–7.

21. Robert E. Hudec, *The GATT Legal System and World Trade Diplomacy* (New York: Praeger, 1975), pp. 7–18; Simon Reisman, "The Birth of a World Trading System: ITO and GATT," in Orin Kirshner, ed., *The Bretton Woods–GATT System: Retrospect and Prospect After Fifty Years.* (Armonk, NY: Sharpe, 1996), pp. 83–85. For detail on the early U.S.-U.K. bilateral discussions on trade, see E. F. Penrose, *Economic Planning for Peace* (Princeton, NJ: Princeton University Press, 1953), pp. 87–115.

22. William Diebold, Jr., *The End of the I.T.O.,* Essays in International Finance no. 16 (Princeton, NJ: International Finance Section, Department of Economics and Social Institutions, Princeton University, October, 1952), p. 2. See also Richard N. Gardner, *Sterling-Dollar Diplomacy in Current Perspective: The Origins and Prospects of Our International Economic Order* (New York: Columbia University Press, new expanded edition, 1980), pp. 348–380.

23. For studies favoring the ITO charter at the time, see Clair Wilcox, *A Charter for World Trade* (New York: Macmillan, 1949); and William Adams Brown, Jr., *The United States and the Restoration of World Trade: An Analysis and Appraisal of the ITO Charter and the General Agreement on Tariffs and Trade* (Washington, DC: Brookings Institution, 1950). For a study highly critical of the charter, see Philip Cortney, *The Economic Munich: The I.T.O. Charter, Inflation or Liberty, The 1929 Lesson* (New York: Philosophical Library, 1949).

24. John H. Jackson, *World Trade and the Law of GATT* (Indianapolis, IN: Bobbs-Merrill, 1969), pp. 120–121.

25. Barry Eichengreen and Peter B. Kenen, "Managing the World Economy Under the Bretton Woods System: An Overview," in Peter B. Kenen, ed., *Managing the World Economy: Fifty Years After Bretton Woods* (Washington, DC: Institute for International Economics, September 1994), p. 7.

26. Bernard M Hoekman and Michel M. Kostecki, *The Political Economy of the World Trading System: From GATT to WTO* (Oxford: Oxford University Press, 1995), pp. 1–3; Richard N.

Gardner, "The Bretton Woods–GATT System After Fifty Years: A Balance Sheet of Success and Failure," in Orin Kirshner, ed., *The Bretton Woods–GATT System: Retrospect and Prospect After Fifty Years* (Armonk, NY: Sharpe, 1996), p. 199.

27. John Gerard Ruggie, "International Regimes, Transactions, and Change: Embedded Liberalism in the Postwar Economic Order," in Stephen D. Krasner, ed., *International Regimes* (Ithaca, NY: Cornell University Press, 1983), p. 212.

28. Jock A. Finlayson and Mark W. Zacher, "The GATT and the Regulation of Trade Barriers: Regime Dynamics and Functions," in Stephen D. Krasner, ed., *International Regimes* (Ithaca, NY: Cornell University Press, 1983), pp. 282–286; Hoekman and Kostecki, *The Political Economy of the World Trading System*, pp. 27–30.

29. Item-by-item negotiations continued in the Kennedy round for agricultural goods and some other sensitive products. See Hoekman and Kostecki, *The Political Economy of the World Trading System*, pp. 72–74; Robert E. Hudec, *Enforcing International Trade Law: The Evolution of the Modern GATT Legal System* (Salem, NH: Butterworth Legal Publishers, 1993), pp. 12–13.

30. Theodore H. Cohn, *The International Politics of Agricultural Trade: Canadian-American Relations in a Global Agricultural Context* (Vancouver: University of British Columbia Press, 1990), pp. 141–42.

31. Milner, *Resisting Protectionism*, p. 8; Marc L. Busch and Helen V. Milner, "The Future of the International Trading System: International Firms, Regionalism, and Domestic Politics," in Richard Stubbs and Geoffrey R. D. Underhill, eds., *Political Economy and the Changing Global Order* (Toronto: McClelland & Stewart, 1994), p. 264.

32. Milner, *Resisting Protectionism*, p. 290. The Milner volume focuses on a number of case studies to demonstrate the difference in domestic firms' trade preferences in the 1920s and the 1970s.

33. Eric Wyndham-White, "Negotiations in Prospect," in C. Fred Bersten, ed., *Toward a New World Trade Policy: The Maidenhead Papers* (Lexington, MA: Heath, 1975), p. 322.

34. Charles Lipson, "The Transformation of Trade: The Sources and Effects of Regime Change," in Stephen D. Krasner, ed., *International Regimes* (Ithaca, NY: Cornell University Press, 1983), p. 242.

35. Winham, *The Evolution of International Trade Agreements*, pp. 46–48; Hoekman and Kostecki, *The Political Economy of the World Trading System*, pp. 26–27.

36. Finlayson and Zacher, "The GATT and the Regulation of Trade Barriers," pp. 286–290.

37. Robert Wolfe, *Farm Wars: The Political Economy of Agriculture and the International Trade Regime* (London: Macmillan, 1998), p. 89; General Agreement on Tariffs and Trade, "The QUAD's Initial Market-Access Package," *GATT Focus Newsletter* no. 101, August-September 1993, p. 3; Fred Bergsten and Randall Henning, *Global Economic Leadership and the Group of Seven* (Washington, D.C.: Institute for International Economics, 1996), pp. 17–18.

38. Ernest Preeg, *Traders and Diplomats: An Analysis of the Kennedy Round of Negotiations Under the General Agreement on Tariffs and Trade* (Washington, DC: Brookings Institution, 1970), p. 195.

39. Gilbert Winham, *International Trade and the Tokyo Round Negotiations* (Princeton, NJ: Princeton University Press, 1986), pp. 172–175.

40. Theodore H. Cohn, "NAFTA, GATT and Canadian-U.S. Agricultural Trade Relations," *The North-South Agenda Papers*, no. 10 (Coral Gables, FL: North-South Center, University of Miami, November 1994), pp. 5–8.

41. Robert O. Keohane, "Reciprocity in International Relations," *International Organization* 40-1 (Winter 1986), p. 4.
42. Carolyn Rhodes, "Reciprocity in Trade: The Utility of a Bargaining Strategy," *International Organization* 43-2 (Spring 1989), p. 276; Keohane, "Reciprocity in International Relations," p. 24.
43. John Whalley and Colleen Hamilton, *The Trading System After the Uruguay Round* (Washington, DC: Institute for International Economics, July 1996), pp. 49–50; John H. Jackson, *The World Trading System: Law and Policy of International Economic Relations* (Cambridge, MA: MIT Press, 1989), p. 149.
44. Hoekman and Kostecki, *The Political Economy of the World Trading System*, pp. 161–162; Winham, *The Evolution of International Trade Agreements*, pp. 50–51; Finlayson and Zacher, "The GATT and the Regulation of Trade Barriers," pp. 290–293.
45. J. Michael Finger and Julio Nogues, "International Control of Subsidies and Countervailing Duties," *The World Bank Economic Review* 1 (1987), pp. 713–714; Hoekman and Kostecki, *The Political Economy of the World Trading System*, p. 164. For a comparison of American and Canadian contingent trade measures, see Theodore H. Cohn, "Emerging Issues in Canada-U.S. Agricultural Trade Under the GATT and FTA," *Canadian-American Public Policy*, no. 10 (Orono: University of Maine, June 1992), pp. 18–22.
46. For a discussion of economic development issues addressed in the Havana Charter and ITO, see Wilcox, *A Charter for World Trade*, pp. 140–152.
47. Finlayson and Zacher, "The GATT and the Regulation of Trade Barriers," pp. 293–296.
48. Jeffrey J. Schott, assisted by Johanna W. Buurman, *The Uruguay Round: An Assessment* (Washington, DC: Institute for International Economics, November 1994), pp. 4–5.
49. See Minister for International Trade, "Canada Proposes Strategy for Creation of a World Trade Organization," *News Release* no. 077, External Affairs and International Trade Canada, April 11, 1990.
50. Hoekman and Kostecki, *The Political Economy of the World Trading System*, p. 1.
51. Hoekman and Kostecki, *The Political Economy of the World Trading System*, pp. 44–50; Ernest H. Preeg, *Traders in a Brave New World: The Uruguay Round and the Future of the International Trading System* (Chicago: University of Chicago Press, 1995), p. 42.
52. Nathaniel C. Nash, "U.S. Backed Candidate for Trade Post Is Trailing," *New York Times*, December 3, 1994, p. 3; Madelaine Drohan, "Americans, Europeans at Odds Over Who Should Lead WTO," *Globe and Mail*, March 15, 1995, p. B6; David E. Sanger, "Yielding, U.S. Bows to Europe on Trade Chief," *New York Times*, March 21, 1995, p. C1.
53. Gardner Patterson and Eliza Patterson, "The Road from GATT to MTO," *Minnesota Journal of Global Trade* 3-1 (Spring 1994), p. 37.
54. Martin Wolf, "Two-Edged Sword: Demands of Developing Countries and the Trading System," in Jagdish N. Bhagwati and John Gerard Ruggie, *Power, Passions, and Purpose: Prospects for North-South Negotiations* (Cambridge, MA: MIT Press, 1984), p. 202.
55. See Raúl Prebisch, *The Economic Development of Latin America and Its Principal Problems* (New York: United Nations Economic Commission for Latin America) 7-1, pp. 1–59; Albert O. Hirschman, "The Political Economy of Import-Substituting Industrialization in Latin America," *Quarterly Journal of Economics* 82-1 (February 1968), pp. 1–32; Hollis Chenery, "The Structuralist Approach to Development Policy," *American Economic Review* 65-2 (May 1975), pp. 310–316.
56. Marc Williams, *Third World Cooperation: The Group of 77 in UNCTAD* (London: Pinter Publishers, 1991), p. 23.

57. Kenneth W. Dam, *The GATT: Law and International Economic Organization* (Chicago: University of Chicago Press, 1970), pp. 227–228; Robert E. Hudec, *Developing Countries in the GATT Legal System* (Aldershot, UK: Gower, for the Trade Policy Research Centre, 1987), pp. 23–24.

58. Karl P. Sauvant, *The Group of 77: Evolution, Structure, Organization* (New York: Oceana Publications, 1981), p. 3; Williams, *Third World Cooperation,* pp. 89–90.

59. Vinod K. Aggarwal, *Liberal Protectionism: The International Politics of Organized Textile Trade* (Berkeley: University of California Press, 1985), p. 8.

60. For a discussion of UNCTAD's role in pressuring GATT to develop the GSP, see Anindya K. Bhattacharya, "The Influence of the International Secretariat: UNCTAD and Generalized Tariff Preferences," *International Organization* 30-1 (Winter 1976), pp. 75–90.

61. Anne O. Krueger, *Trade Policies and Developing Nations* (Washington, DC: Brookings Institution, 1995), pp. 40–42. See also Rolf J. Langhammer and André Sapir, *Economic Impact of Generalized Tariff Preferences,* Thames Essay no. 49 (Aldershot, UK: Gower, for the Trade Policy Research Centre, 1987).

62. The LDCs' demands were contained in several documents submitted to the General Assembly in 1974: the *Declaration on the Establishment of a New International Economic Order (NIEO),* the *Program of Action on the Establishment of a NIEO,* and the *Charter of Economic Rights and Duties of States.*

63. Jeffrey A. Hart, *The New International Economic Order: Conflict and Cooperation in North-South Economic Relations, 1974–77* (New York: St. Martin's Press, 1983), ch. 2.

64. Hart, *The New International Economic Order,* pp. 36–40; Williams, *Third World Cooperation,* pp. 133–159; Alfred Maizels, "Reforming the World Commodity Economy," in Michael Zammit Cutajar, ed., *UNCTAD and the South-North Dialogue: The First Twenty Years* (Oxford: Pergamon Press, 1985), pp. 101–121.

65. Olivier Long, *Law and Its Limitations in the GATT Multilateral Trade System* (Dordrecht, Neths: Nijhoff, 1985), p. 101.

66. Hudec, *Developing Countries in the GATT Legal System,* pp. 70–91.

67. See Robert Wolfe, "Global Trade as a Single Undertaking: The Role of Ministers in the WTO," *International Journal* 51-4 (Autumn 1996), pp. 690–709; and Wolfe, *Farm Wars,* pp. 91–97.

68. John Whalley, "Recent Trade Liberalisation in the Developing World: What Is Behind it and Where Is it Headed?" in David Greenaway, Robert C. Hine, Anthony P. O'Brien, and Robert J. Thornton, eds., *Global Protectionism* (London: Macmillan, 1991), pp. 225–253; Krueger, *Trade Policies and Developing Nations,* pp. 48–50.

69. John Gershman, "The Free Trade Connection," in Kevin Danaher, ed., *Fifty Years Is Enough: The Case Against the World Bank and the International Monetary Fund* (Boston: South End Press, 1994), p. 24.

70. See Bernard R. Hoekman, "Developing Countries and the Multilateral Trading System After the Uruguay Round," in Roy Culpeper, Albert Berry, and Frances Stewart, eds., *Global Development Fifty Years After Bretton Woods: Essays in Honour of Gerald K. Helleiner* (New York: St. Martin's Press, 1997), pp. 252–279.

71. For more detail on historical structuralist arguments, see Chakravarthi Raghavan, *Recolonization: GATT, the Uruguay Round and The Third World* (London: Zed Books, 1990); and Chakravarthi Raghavan, "A New Trade Order in a World of Disorder?" in Jo Marie Griesgraber and Bernhard G. Gunter, eds., *World Trade: Toward Fair and Free Trade in the Twenty-first Century* (London: Pluto Press, 1997), pp. 1–31.

72. See M. M. Kostecki, *East-West Trade and the GATT System* (London: Macmillan, for the Trade Policy Research Centre, 1979), p. 2; Zdenek Augenthaler, "The Socialist Countries and GATT," in Frans A. M. Alting von Geusau, ed., *Economic Relations After the Kennedy Round* (Leyden, Neths: Sijthoff-Leyden, 1969), p. 81.

73. In 1995, China and Russia together accounted for only 5.2 percent of the votes in the IMF and only 6.04 percent of the votes in the World Bank.

74. Jackson, *The World Trading System,* pp. 283–286; *International Monetary Fund—Annual Report, 1995* (Washington, DC: IMF, 1995), pp. 218–219; *The World Bank—Annual Report, 1995* (Washington, DC: World Bank, 1995), p. 196.

75. Leah A. Haus, *Globalizing the GATT: The Soviet Union's Successor States, Eastern Europe, and the International Trading System* (Washington, DC: Brookings Institution, 1992), pp. 15, 28; Bohdan Laczkowski, "Poland's Participation in the Kennedy Round," in Geusau, ed., *Economic Relations After the Kennedy Round,* pp. 83–93.

76. Eliza R. Patterson, "Improving GATT Rules for Nonmarket Economies," *Journal of World Trade Law* 20-2 (March/April 1986), p. 188; Jozef M. van Brabant, *The Planned Economies and International Economic Organizations* (Cambridge: Cambridge University Press, 1991), pp. 199–201.

77. Patterson, "Improving GATT Rules for Nonmarket Economies," p. 189; Paul D. McKenzie, "China's Application to the GATT: State Trading and the Problem of Market Access," *Journal of World Trade* 24-5 (October 1990), pp. 141–143.

78. "Preparations Intensify for Singapore; Membership of Bulgaria and Panama Approved," World Trade Organization, *WTO Focus Newsletter* no. 12, August-September, 1996, pp. 1–2.

79. Laszlo Lang, "International Regimes and the Political Economy of East-West Relations," *Occasional Paper Series 13* (New York: Institute for East-West Security Studies, 1989), pp. 35–36; Haus, *Globalizing the GATT,* ch. 3.

80. McKenzie, "China's Application to the GATT," pp. 144–145; Robert E. Herzstein, "China and the GATT: Legal and Policy Issues Raised by China's Participation in the General Agreement on Tariffs and Trade," *Law and Policy in International Business* 18-2 (1986), pp. 373–374.

81. Harold K. Jacobson and Michel Oksenberg, *China's Participation in the IMF, the World Bank, and GATT: Toward a Global Economic Order* (Ann Arbor: University of Michigan Press, 1990), pp. 83–92.

82. Chung-chou Li, "Resumption of China's GATT Membership," *Journal of World Trade Law* 21-4 (1987), p. 26; Herzstein, "China and the GATT," pp. 404–405; Jackson, *The World Trading System,* pp. 287–288.

83. Li, "Resumption of China's GATT Membership," p. 30.

84. McKenzie, "China's Application to the GATT," pp. 144–145; Herzstein, "China and the GATT," pp. 375–377.

85. Li, "Resumption of China's GATT Membership," p. 30.

86. Jacobson and Oksenberg, *China's Participation in the IMF, the World Bank, and GATT,* p. 94; Brabant, *The Planned Economies and International Economic Organizations,* pp. 1–6; Lang, "International Regimes and the Political Economy of East-West Relations," pp. 53–60.

87. World Trade Organization, "Way Cleared for Kyrgyz Republic to Become 133rd Member of the WTO," *WTO Press Release* 109, July 17, 1998; World Trade Organization, "Latvia to Become WTO Member," *WTO Press Release* 115, October 14, 1998.

88. McKenzie, "China's Application to the GATT," p. 150.
89. John Whalley and Colleen Hamilton, *The Trading System After the Uruguay Round* (Washington, DC: Institute for International Economics, July 1996), pp. 2–3.
90. World Trade Organization, *WTO Focus Newsletter*, no. 30, May 1998, p. 5.
91. Jim Powell, "Self-Determination Through Unilateral Free Trade," in Doug Bandow and Ian Vásquez, eds., *Perpetuating Poverty: The World Bank, the IMF, and the Developing World* (Washington, DC: CATO Institute, 1994), p. 345.
92. Whalley and Hamilton, *The Trading System After the Uruguay Round*, p. 2; Hoekman and Kostecki, *The Political Economy of the World Trading System*, pp. 268–271.
93. Riccardo Petrella, "Globalization and Internationalization: The Dynamics of the Emerging World Order," in Robert Boyer and Daniel Drache, eds., *States Against Markets: The Limits of Globalization* (London: Routledge, 1996), p. 77; Hoekman and Kostecki, *The Political Economy of the World Trading System*, pp. 9–10.
94. Whalley and Hamilton, *The Trading System After the Uruguay Round*, p. 52.
95. For the North-South divisions on this issue, see John Croome, *Reshaping the World Trading System: A History of the Uruguay Round* (Geneva: World Trade Organization, 1995), pp. 130–138.
96. For contending views on this issue, see Krueger, *Trade Policies and Developing Countries*, pp. 52–54; and Raghavan, *Recolonization: GATT, the Uruguay Round and the Third World*, pp. 114–141.
97. See Milner, *Resisting Protectionism*.

Regionalism and the Global Trade Regime

The major trading nations gave strong support to multilateral trade liberalization with the formation of the General Agreement on Tariffs and Trade after World War II. However, regionalism also began to emerge as a significant force in international trade with the formation of a number of regional integration agreements (RIAs). As noted in Chapter 2, a regional agreement may exist at various stages of economic integration, ranging from a free trade area to a customs union, a common market, or an economic union (see Figure 2.3). There have been two major waves of regionalism in the postwar period, the first in the 1950s and 1960s and the second since the mid-1980s. The second wave has been especially significant, with the European Union increasing its membership and deepening the integration process and the United States reversing its long-standing policy of refusing to join RIAs. Thus, of the 109 regional agreements reported to the GATT from 1947 to 1994, 33 were concluded from 1990–1994. Most of the major trading nations in the World Trade Organization today also belong to at least one RIA (Japan is an important exception).[1] Table 9.1 shows that a wide range of reciprocal and nonreciprocal RIAs were in force as of January 1995 (the nonreciprocal RIAs are between developed and less developed countries).

From one perspective, regionalism and multilateralism are competing approaches to trade and foreign investment policy. While multilateralism contributes to worldwide liberalization of foreign trade and investment flows, regionalism may act as a balkanizing force that divides the world into competing trade blocs. From a second perspective, however, "open" regionalism can be an important force in breaking down national trade barriers and thus in serving as a stepping-stone rather than an obstacle to global free trade. States and multinational corporations today often consider regionalism and multilateralism to be complementary strategies, which they can use simultaneously to promote market forces and increase their competitiveness in the global economy.

Theorists from the three IPE perspectives have very different views of RIAs. Liberal economists consider GATT/WTO multilateralism to be the best possible route to

TABLE 9.1

REGIONAL INTEGRATION AGREEMENTS (RIAs) NOTIFIED TO GATT AND IN FORCE AS OF JANUARY 1995

Reciprocal RIAs

Europe

European Community (EC)

Austria	Germany	Netherlands
Belgium	Greece	Portugal
Denmark	Ireland	Spain
Finland	Italy	Sweden
France	Luxembourg	United Kingdom

EC Free Trade Agreements with

Estonia	Latvia	Norway
Iceland	Liechtenstein	Switzerland
Israel	Lithuania	

EC Association Agreements with

Bulgaria	Hungary	Romania
Cyprus	Malta	Slovak Rep.
Czech Rep.	Poland	Turkey

European Free Trade Association (EFTA)

Iceland	Norway	Switzerland
Liechtenstein		

EFTA Free Trade Agreements with

Bulgaria	Israel	Slovak Rep.
Czech Rep.	Poland	Turkey
Hungary	Romania	

Norway Free Trade Agreements with

Estonia	Latvia	Lithuania

Switzerland Free Trade Agreements with

Estonia	Latvia	Lithuania

Czech Republic and Slovak Republic Customs Union

Central European Free Trade Area

Czech Rep.	Poland	Slovak Rep.
Hungary		

Czech Republic and Slovenia Free Trade Agreement

Slovak Republic and Slovenia Free Trade Agreement

North America

Canada-United States Free Trade Agreement (CUSTA)

North American Free Trade Agreement (NAFTA)

Latin America and the Caribbean

Caribbean Community and Common Market (CARICOM)

Central American Common Market (CACM)

Latin American Integration Association (LAIA)

Andean Pact

Southern Common Market (Mercosur)

Middle East

Economic Cooperation Organization (ECO)

Gulf Cooperation Council (GCC)

Asia

Australia–New Zealand Closer Economic Relations Trade Agreement (CER)

Bangkok Agreement

ASEAN Preferential Trade Arrangement

Lao People's Dem. Rep. and Thailand Trade Agreement

Other

Israel–United States Free Trade Agreement

Nonreciprocal RIAs

Europe

EEC-Association of certain non-European countries and territories (EEC-PTOM II)

EEC Cooperation Agreements with

Algeria	Lebanon	Syria
Egypt	Morocco	Tunisia
Jordan		

ACP-EEC Fourth Lomé Convention

Asia

Australia–Papua New Guinea Agreement

South Pacific Regional Trade Cooperation Agreement (SPARTECA)

Source: Regionalism and the World Trading System, April 1995, p. 26, Table 1. By permission of the World Trade Organization.

trade liberalization because it breaks down regional as well as national barriers to trade. Negotiating difficulties in the large multilateral arena often pose obstacles to free trade, however, so liberals generally support open RIAs as a second-best route to trade liberalization. (Open RIAs do not raise trade barriers to the outside world.) Most liberals acknowledge that some groups such as displaced workers may lose as a result of RIAs, but they nevertheless argue that the gains in efficiency from open regionalism outweigh any costs incurred. Liberals also generally assume that all member states will benefit in the long run from open regional agreements, even if they do not benefit equally. Power disparities are not a major problem for smaller states in regional agreements, according to liberals. Indeed, they argue that RIAs provide more benefits to a small country than to a large country in terms of economies of scale and increased market demand for its exports.[2]

In contrast to liberals, realists and historical structuralists believe that RIAs have important distributional effects and that some member states and groups within states will benefit *at the expense of* others. Of particular concern to these theorists are RIAs with major asymmetries of power and/or levels of economic development among the member states. Realists, for example, argue that the larger partner in an RIA either will not permit the smaller partner to receive disproportionate benefits or will expect some "side payments" in return. These side payments will be greater than any economic benefits the smaller partner receives from gains in market access and economies of scale. As noted in this chapter, Canada and Mexico sought free trade with the United States partly to gain more assured access to the large U.S. market. The United States, however, expected side payments in such areas as foreign investment, trade in services, and access to natural resources (especially energy).[3] In the long term, realists expect the distribution of benefits in regional agreements to reflect the asymmetries of power, wealth, and technology among the member states.

In the view of historical structuralists, MNCs and other sources of transnational capital are the main beneficiaries of some regional agreements such as NAFTA. The main losers are the working class and the poorest people within both industrial and Third World states. Regional agreements, from this perspective, permit MNCs to locate their production facilities in those member states that have the lowest wages, environmental standards, and taxes, then export freely to other states within the region. Historical structuralists also view some regional arrangements as means by which states in the core (often in association with transnational capital) exploit states in the periphery. For example, they argue that the institutional linkages of the European Union with 70 African, Caribbean, and Pacific (ACP) "associate members" simply consolidates "the vertical economic relationship of the colonial period."[4] (See the discussion of associate membership in the European Union later in this chapter.)

This chapter begins with a discussion of regionalism and how it relates to the process of globalization. It provides a brief historical background of the development of RIAs and presents competing views as to why states form such agreements, examines the institutional relationship between GATT/WTO and regional agreements, and examines regionalism in the three major trading blocs—Europe, North America, and East Asia.

REGIONALISM AND GLOBALIZATION

Regionalism is a difficult term to define because it usually involves not only geographic proximity but also a sense of cultural, economic, political, and/or organizational cohesiveness. Efforts by international relations specialists to precisely define and identify regions have therefore usually met with frustration.[5] In this chapter the term *regionalism* is used primarily in reference to interactions among states in a particular geographic area, where there is certain degree of economic and often organizational cohesiveness. A large portion of the chapter is devoted to a discussion of RIAs, which usually limit their membership to countries within a particular region.[6] However, Japan and the East Asian countries have close regional economic ties even though they are not joined together in an RIA. This discussion of trade regionalism is therefore not limited to RIAs.

Globalization and regionalism are both increasing today, and the relationship between these two processes is quite complex. In some respects, globalization limits the growth of regionalism. As global interdependence increases, many problems, such as financial crises, trade wars, and environmental degradation, take on worldwide dimensions and require multilateral management techniques at the global level. Thus, multilateral institutions such as GATT/WTO, the IMF, and the World Bank are better equipped than regional organizations to deal with many of the problems resulting from globalization. Globalization also promotes growing linkages among regions as well as states, and in this sense it can undermine national and regional cohesiveness.

Despite some inherent contradictions between the global and regional processes, globalization may also act to stimulate the rise of regionalism. States must often rely on institutions above the national level to deal with problems arising from the increase in global interdependence. However, it is often easier to utilize institutions composed of like-minded states at the regional level than the far more diverse universal membership institutions at the multilateral level. Globalization also contributes to an increase in the intensity and scope of competition, and states and MNCs often find that they can improve their global competitiveness by organizing regionally. Finally, globalization has been closely associated with the revival of classical liberalism, which favors a shift in authority from the state to the market. The heightened market pressures weaken state barriers and contribute to the growth of institutions at both the regional and global levels.

Globalization pressures may both conflict with and contribute to the growth of regionalism. The revival of regionalism since the 1980s, however, has generally complemented rather than conflicted with the globalization process.[7]

A HISTORICAL OVERVIEW OF REGIONAL INTEGRATION AGREEMENTS

Regional integration is not a new phenomenon. From the seventeenth century to World War II there were many integration proposals involving colonies, provinces, and states, and some of the more successful agreements resulted in political as well as commercial union. Examples of early integration efforts in Europe and North America include a proposal for commercial union among Austria, Bavaria, Spain, and some German principalities in 1665; a customs union between England and Ireland in 1826; a customs treaty establishing a single German *Zollverein* among German splinter states in 1833; and a Reciprocity Treaty removing all import tariffs on natural products between the United States and Canada in 1854. In the Southern Hemisphere, early agreements included a South African Customs Union among the Union of South Africa, Bechuanaland, Basutoland, and Swaziland in 1910; and a customs union between the British colonies of Kenya and Uganda in 1917, which was extended to include Tanganyika in 1927.[8]

Despite these early attempts to establish RIAs, regional integration in its modern form did not develop until after World War II, with the creation of the European Economic Community. This chapter is primarily concerned with the two major waves of regionalism in the postwar period, the first wave in the 1950s and early 1960s and the second since the mid-1980s.

The First Wave of Regionalism

In 1949, the Soviet Union signed a treaty with Bulgaria, Czechoslovakia, Hungary, Poland, and Romania, establishing the Council for Mutual Economic Assistance. Although CMEA members engaged in technical cooperation and joint planning, the state-centered orientation of these centrally planned economies precluded any genuine moves toward regional economic integration.[9] As a result, most writers view the first wave of regionalism as beginning with the formation of the European Community in 1957 and the European Free Trade Association (EFTA) in 1960.[10] These European agreements provided a stimulus for the spread of regionalism throughout Latin America and Africa in the early 1960s. However, the RIAs in the Third World were formed for very different reasons than those in Western Europe. Because the small domestic markets of less developed countries interfered with their efforts to pursue import substitution industrialization policies, LDCs looked to preferential trade agreements as a means of providing larger markets—and economies of scale—for their production of industrial goods. Thus, Third World regional agreements in the 1950s to 1960s were quite inward-looking and were designed to pursue import substitution at the regional level.

By the early 1970s the first wave of regionalism had proved to be largely unsuccessful outside Europe, for several reasons. First, numerous problems arose with the Third World RIAs. Only a limited number of industries were willing to locate in Third World regions, so competition among LDC members of regional agreements for these industries was fierce; and most of these industries located in the larger and more advanced LDCs. In the East African Common Services Union, for example, Tanzania and Uganda resented the fact that the major industries were concentrated in Kenya. Thus, the benefits of regional integration in LDC areas were often distributed very unequally, leading to numerous disputes among member states. To counter such inequities, some Third World RIAs tried to allocate industries among the member countries by bureaucratic means rather than relying on the market, but this practice led to economic inefficiencies and political conflicts. A second reason for the failure of the first wave of integration outside Europe was that the United States as the global hegemon was a firm supporter of multilateralism and generally did not endorse regional agreements. Although the United States made an exception in supporting the European Community largely for political-security reasons, it tried to open up the European integration process in the GATT Dillon and Kennedy rounds. In the second wave of regionalism, by contrast, the United States was to become an active participant in regional agreements.[11]

The Second Wave of Regionalism

The second wave of regionalism started in the mid-1980s, and this time regionalism seems to be more durable, in non-European as well as European areas. The European Community moved to widen and deepen its integration in the second wave. Widening occurred with the accession of Spain and Portugal in 1986 and Austria, Finland, and Sweden in 1995; and deepening occurred with the adoption of a single market in "Europe 1992" and the signing of the Maastricht Treaty (see the discussion below). The most significant change in the second wave was the dramatic turnaround in the United States. Shifting from its position as the key defender of the multilateral trade order in the postwar years, the United States has been willing to participate in RIAs since the mid-1980s. Finally, there has been a revival of regional agreements among LDCs, and unlike the case in the 1960s, these agreements are associated with the opening of the Third World to liberalism and global market forces.[12]

WHAT ARE THE REASONS FOR THE RISE OF REGIONALISM?

Although there is widespread agreement on some of the reasons for the rise of regionalism, realists, liberals, and historical structuralists emphasize different factors in their theoretical explanations. While realists usually look to strategic-security factors and changing power relationships as explanations, liberals focus on the growth of interdependence, and historical structuralists emphasize the influence and demands of transnational capital.

Realist Explanations

Realists explain the development of Western European regional integration in the first wave (the 1950s to 1960s) as a response to changing power and strategic-security relationships. The United States as global hegemon viewed a speedy economic recovery in Western Europe as essential to meet the strategic threat of the Soviet Union, and it therefore was generally supportive of Western European integration. Indeed, the United States' insistence that the Europeans develop a common recovery program in which they would jointly administer U.S. Marshall Plan aid resulted in the formation of the *Organization for European Economic Cooperation (OEEC)* in 1948. In addition to developing a program for economic reconstruction and organizing a fair distribution of Marshall Plan funds, the OEEC oversaw the moves toward convertibility of European currencies and the liberalization of trade in Western Europe. Furthermore, the OEEC contributed to the rapid integration of West Germany in Europe, laying the foundations for the eventual formation of the European Economic Community.[13] Realists point out that another forerunner of the EC, the *European Coal and Steel Community (ECSC)*, was also created for strategic-security reasons. In 1951, six countries (Belgium, France, West Germany, Italy, Luxembourg, and the Netherlands) formed the ECSC primarily to prevent France and Germany from renewing their age-old rivalries and conflict. Seven years later, the six member countries in the ECSC expanded the integration process by forming the EC. Finally realists note that Western European concerns about changing global power relationships contributed to the formation of the EC. With the European countries facing the eventual loss of their colonies and the United States and the Soviet Union emerging as the world's two superpowers, the Europeans realized that integration was necessary if they were to have continuing influence on the global scene.

Realists also attribute the second wave of integration in the 1980s to shifting balances in strategic and economic power. For example, they view the change from a bipolar to a multipolar international system as highly significant. In the postwar bipolar system, the Western Europeans and Japanese were willing to accept American leadership because of their dependence on U.S. nuclear deterrence and economic assistance. With the demise of the Soviet Union and the breakdown of bipolarity, U.S. allies have been more inclined to act independently of the United States, and a multilateral system has emerged centered in three major regional economic blocs in Europe, North America, and Japan/East Asia.[14] Another important factor in the second wave, according to realists, has been the relative decline of American economic hegemony. After World War II, the United States as global hegemon used its power and resources to help develop an open and integrated world economy. As its economic hegemony declined, however, the United States was less willing to provide the public goods to maintain an open multilateral trade regime, and it sought to regain some of its economic leverage and power by joining RIAs.[15]

Liberal Explanations

Liberals focus on the growth of interdependence as a major factor in the revival of regionalism in the 1980s. As economic interdependence increased, states turned to economic liberalization to promote their exports, attract foreign investment, and upgrade their technological capabilities. However, numerous problems were confronting the multilateral GATT trade regime in the 1980s (see Chapter 8), and regionalism therefore served as a second-best route for establishing trade linkages.[16] Regional trade negotiations, which involved small groups of like-minded states in geographically focused areas, were easier to conduct than multilateral negotiations. RIA members also had a number of objective similarities, such as comparable levels of income and development, which often made negotiations easier. (Mexico's membership as an LDC in NAFTA was a notable exception.) Trade negotiations in the larger, more diverse GATT were by contrast more complicated and difficult. Thus, liberals note approvingly that Canada and the United States negotiated issues in their 1988 free trade agreement (such as trade in services and agriculture) that had not yet been dealt with globally.[17]

The growth of interdependence, according to liberals, also led to increased demands by societal groups such as industries and firms for regional agreements, and states in the 1980s were willing to supply these domestic groups with agreements. Along with the trend toward globalization, a growing number of firms became highly dependent on exports and imports, and they shifted their operations from the national to the multinational level. These internationalist firms pressured for a freeing of economic relationships at *both* the global and the regional levels. Regionalism in particular often improves the competitiveness of international firms, which can benefit from "the larger regional markets as their base rather than just the home market."[18]

Historical Structuralist Explanations

Historical structuralists, like liberals, believe that MNCs and other sources of transnational capital played a central role in the revival of regionalism in the 1980s. Unlike liberals, however, historical structuralists view this as a highly negative development. Regional integration agreements such as NAFTA, from this perspective, have permitted MNCs to become more competitive by locating their production facilities in states and regions with the lowest taxes, wages, and environmental standards. While the capitalist class has benefited from this growth of regionalism, the greater mobility of capital often drives down the price for domestic labor. Historical structuralists also explain the revival of regionalism in terms of the desire of the most powerful states to seek regional hegemony over others. As its economic hegemony declined globally, the United States sought to recoup its losses by establishing its hegemony more firmly on a regional basis. Thus, some critics charge that NAFTA was "designed to fit Canada and Mexico into the American model of development, on terms amenable to American corporations."[19]

GATT/WTO AND REGIONAL INTEGRATION AGREEMENTS

The United States as global hegemon at the end of World War II strongly opposed preferential agreements and any other type of discrimination in international trade that would interfere with an open multilateral trade regime. The British, however, wanted to preserve their discriminatory imperial preference tariffs, and a number of countries wanted to have the prerogative to conclude RIAs. Thus, John Maynard Keynes expressed strong opposition to U.S. pressures for an end to imperial preferences, referring to "all the old lumber, most-favored-nation clause and the rest which was a notorious failure and made such a hash of the old world."[20] U.S. views on this issue prevailed to a large extent, and Article 1 of GATT was devoted to unconditional MFN treatment. Nevertheless, GATT also permitted regional exceptions to the unconditional MFN clause: GATT Article 24 permits member countries to form customs unions (CUs) and free trade areas (FTAs) that discriminate against other members, as long as these regional agreements meet specific conditions.[21] An examination of the reasoning behind the Article 24 provisions is crucial to an understanding of the relationship between the WTO and regional agreements.

Liberal economists consider global free trade to be the best possible route to maximizing welfare, and this was also the approach taken by GATT as a liberal-economic institution. RIAs, which discriminate against outsiders, are clearly inferior to multilateral agreements, which liberalize trade without discrimination. Nevertheless, liberals generally believe that regional agreements may offer a second-best route to trade liberalization when there are obstacles to freeing trade at the global level.[22] GATT Article 24 therefore sanctions the formation of regional CUs and FTAs, but it seeks to ensure they are more trade-creating than trade-diverting.[23] Before discussing the GATT Article 24 provisions, it is necessary to describe the different ways in which RIAs may be trade-creating and trade-diverting.

Trade Diversion

RIAs inevitably result in some trade diversion because the reduction or elimination of trade barriers on intraregional trade produces some shifting of imports from more efficient outside suppliers to less efficient regional suppliers. As trade within an RIA is liberalized, competition also increases within member countries' markets. This competition can lead to greater adjustment pressures for inefficient industries, which try to shift some of the adjustment burden onto third countries by pressuring for increased external barriers. Thus, trade diversion can result when RIAs raise protectionist barriers against outsiders. Outside countries may also be harmed by investment diversion when a multinational firm decides to invest inside an RIA and produce locally instead of producing in the least-cost location and shipping goods to the region.

A customs union may be more trade diverting in some respects than a free trade area. (As Figure 2.3 shows, a CU, unlike an FTA, has a common external tariff.) Even if there is no increase in average external tariffs when the CU is formed, other types of protectionism can increase. For example, import-competing industries often petition successfully for an increase in the CU's contingent trade actions, such antidumping and countervailing duties. The European Union's experience shows that the threat or imposition of such duties can pose a formidable trade barrier to outsiders. Contingent trade actions pose less of a problem for outsiders in an FTA because FTAs have no common external tariff and industries cannot pressure for area-wide protection. Although import-competing firms in member states have an incentive to obtain contingent protection in an FTA, each industry must depend on only its own government for support.[24]

While contingent protection actions can have trade-diverting effects in a CU, **rules of origin** often have serious trade-diverting effects in an FTA. Because each FTA member retains its own external tariffs, FTAs must have rules of origin to prevent importers from bringing goods in through the lowest-duty member and shipping them to partner countries whose duties are higher. The rules of origin are designed to determine whether goods crossing borders within the FTA should qualify for duty-free treatment. These rules are extremely difficult to develop and implement, however, because so many goods today are manufactured with numerous components originating in a number of countries. Domestic firms in an FTA often pressure successfully for stiffer rules of origin, which become a form of trade protectionism against outside countries. Unlike the case with FTAs, rules of origin are not a major issue in CUs because of the common external tariff.[25]

The impact of RIAs depends not only on internal political dynamics but also on how nonmember countries react to them. When one regional agreement is formed, nonmembers may have the incentive to establish their own RIAs in response, and regionalism proliferates. Thus, some countries establish RIAs in efforts to "better defend themselves against the discriminatory effects of *other* regional groups."[26] This proliferation of regionalism can increase trade conflicts and lead to fragmentation of the global trade regime. From this perspective, regionalism by its very nature causes trade diversion.

Trade Creation

The main source of trade creation in RIAs is the increased trade among member countries, which shifts demand from less efficient domestic country production to more efficient partner country production. RIAs also can often achieve a deeper level of integration than multilateral agreements because negotiations are occurring among a smaller number of like-minded partners. As a result, regional agreements may provide a positive demonstration effect and contribute to more effective multilateral trade negotiations. For example, the deepening of European Community integration to include services trade was followed by the decision to also include services trade in the GATT Uruguay round; and the inclusion of agriculture, services, intellectual property, and investment provisions in the CUSTA and NAFTA agreements also provided a stimulus for negotiating these issues in the Uruguay round.

GATT Article 24 and Regional Agreements

GATT Article 24 could not deal with all types of trade diversion, but it was designed to ensure that RIAs result in as much trade creation and as little trade diversion as possible. To ensure that regional agreements are trade-creating, Article 24 stipulates that free trade agreements and CUs are to eliminate tariffs and other trade restrictions on "substantially all" trade among the member states within a "reasonable" time period.[27] This condition may seem ironic because maximum preferential liberalization diverges more from MFN treatment and therefore can be more injurious to nonmembers than partial liberalization, but it is included for several reasons. First, the GATT founders felt that a rigorous requirement to remove all tariff barriers in RIAs would prevent the proliferation of preferential agreements, which involve only partial trade liberalization among members. Preferential arrangements of this nature had contributed to the trade discrimination and protectionism of the 1930s. Second, in the GATT/WTO view, genuine FTAs or CUs are more likely to facilitate trade liberalization at the global level. When regional agreements involve deeper integration than has occurred multilaterally (i.e., the removal of all tariffs), they can serve as stepping-stones to multilateral free trade. Preferential agreements with only partial trade liberalization, by contrast, would not have this positive demonstration effect.[28]

To ensure that a regional agreement minimizes the amount of trade diversion, Article 24 stipulates that trade barriers should not rise on the average to countries outside the agreement when the RIA is formed. While the individual member states in an FTA are not to raise their average level of duties, the common external tariff of a CU may not "on the whole" be higher or more restrictive than the member countries' duties were before the CU was established. These trade diversion provisions are designed to limit reductions in imports from nonmembers as a result of the regional agreement.[29]

Although GATT Article 24 seems to provide a mechanism for regulating RIAs, in reality GATT/WTO has often had very little influence in this area. It is therefore necessary to examine how effective GATT/WTO has been in monitoring and regulating regionalism.

The Effectiveness of GATT Article 24

When countries form an RIA, GATT/WTO establishes a working party to assess whether or not the RIA meets the requisite conditions. While Article 24 has permitted GATT to exert some influence over regional agreements, its influence in practice has been quite limited. GATT's regulations on regional arrangements were drafted with smaller agreements in mind, such as the Benelux customs union negotiated by Belgium, the Netherlands, and Luxembourg in 1944, and the regulations were rarely used during the first decade of GATT's existence. This situation changed dramatically in 1957, when the Treaty of Rome establishing the European Community was notified to the GATT. In view of its size and importance, the EC was simply not willing to wait for GATT's approval under Article 24 before proceeding with economic integration. Indeed, negotiating the Treaty of Rome had been a difficult and sensitive process, and EC members indicated that they would not readjust the treaty to satisfy GATT.[30]

In the end, GATT acceded to the EC's demands and never completed its examination of the Treaty of Rome, even though GATT members had reached no consensus regarding the treaty's consistency with Article 24. GATT's acquiescence in this case had a detrimental effect on its ability to exert authority over subsequent regional agreements. Thus, GATT working parties have had little success in bringing about changes in the terms of regional agreements after the member states in the region have negotiated them. Early agreements such as the European Community and the Latin American Free Trade Association (LAFTA) were notified to the GATT *before* they entered into force, but more recent regional arrangements have sometimes been notified to the GATT/WTO belatedly. For example, two agreements that entered into force *before* GATT working parties were established to examine them were NAFTA in January 1994 and the agreement in which Austria, Finland, and Sweden acceded to the European Union in January 1995.[31]

It is not surprising that GATT working parties have had little influence over RIAs after they are established; governments that have already engaged in extensive bargaining are reluctant to reopen their negotiations in response to outside criticism. The most GATT/WTO working parties can accomplish is to embarrass RIA members over allegations of noncompliance and thus encourage countries to comply with GATT/WTO guidelines in the future. Nevertheless, the GATT/WTO rules *can* influence national decision making at earlier stages in the process. One authority on international trade issues points out that GATT Article 24 in fact influenced the European Community and CUSTA at an early stage by setting broad parameters for the conduct of the regional negotiations:

> The diplomats negotiating each of these agreements were operating under instructions to make maximum efforts to comply with GATT rules, and the actual results of these negotiations testify that a quite important degree of GATT compliance was achieved. Except for agriculture . . . and except for the EC's relationship with former colonies, the . . . developed-country agreements . . . were essentially GATT-conforming. To be sure, GATT was unable to do anything further once the agreements were signed and deposited in Geneva for review.[32]

Some analysts point out that GATT/WTO is less effective because the conditions it requires of regional agreements are not clearly specified. Legitimate differences exist over the interpretation of Article 24 requirements that RIAs cover "substantially all" trade, do not become more restrictive "on average," and be fully implemented in a "reasonable length of time." The GATT Uruguay round negotiators tried to clarify the criteria and procedures for assessing regional agreements, but their success in removing the ambiguities in Article 24 was limited. In addition to its imprecise wording, Article 24 does not adequately address such issues as contingent protection measures (antidumping and countervailing duties) and rules of origin, which may significantly increase the protectionism of regional agreements vis-à-vis outside countries.[33]

In view of the ambiguous GATT/WTO requirements, Article 24 working parties are reluctant to give RIAs their unqualified approval. By the end of 1994, only 6 of 69 working parties had reached a consensus that particular regional agreements conformed with the Article 24 conditions, and only 2 of the 6 "approved" regional agreements are still operative.[34] In the great majority of cases, working parties have simply noted that members had divergent views regarding the conformity of the regional agreement with GATT/WTO. However, GATT/WTO has never explicitly concluded that a regional agreement has *not* met the legal requirements![35]

Special Treatment for Less Developed Countries

While the GATT Article 24 provisions were designed to apply to all RIAs, less developed countries over time were given special and differential treatment. Two types of regional arrangements involving LDCs have been especially prominent: the European Union's association agreements and RIAs among developing countries.

The European Union's Association Agreements with LDCs   When the European Community was formed in 1957, France insisted that the trade preferences it had given to its African Overseas Territories be continued. The French wanted to ensure that exports from its former colonies would have free access to the EC and that other EC members would eventually share the costs of providing economic assistance to its former colonies. Despite the opposition of some EC members, the French were adamant, and Part 4 of the Treaty of Rome provided for an extension of France's preferential arrangements under EC auspices. Initially, there were 18 LDCs with "associate" status, known as the Associated African States and Madagascar (AASM). Although Part 4 called for the gradual removal of tariffs between EC members and the associates, the associates could protect their infant industries and retain some tariffs for revenue purposes, and the EC was to provide financial aid to the associates through a European Development Fund.[36]

A number of countries in GATT argued that the EC was providing discriminatory trade preferences to the African associates because the associate system did not constitute a genuine FTA (that is, the African associates did not provide fully reciprocal free trade to the EC members). As a result, the association agreements were in direct conflict with GATT's nondiscrimination principle.[37] The EC insisted, however, that the association agreements were fully coordinate with United Nations proposals that the North should promote economic and social development in the South. At a 1966 GATT working party examining the association agreements, for example, EC members

> expressed the view that in a free-trade area consisting of industrialized and less-developed countries the industrialized countries should not require reciprocal advantages from their less-developed partners. . . . In their view, Article XXIV had never been meant to apply to free-trade areas between developed and less-developed countries.[38]

Despite the controversy over the association agreements, the EC solidified them in the *Yaoundé Conventions,* signed at Yaoundé, Cameroon, in 1963 and 1969. After Britain joined the EC in 1973, the Yaoundé convention was replaced by the first *Lomé Convention* at Lomé, Togo, in 1975, and the former British colonies gained associate status. The fourth Lomé Convention (Lomé IV) covers a 10-year period from 1990 to 2000 and includes agreements with 70 African, Caribbean, and Pacific (ACP) countries. GATT/WTO has never resolved the dispute over the European Union's trade preferences granted to associate countries, and problems continue to recur. For example, some Latin American countries with the backing of the United States have repeatedly registered complaints in the WTO over EU preferences given to banana imports from the ACP associate countries. (U.S. interest in the issue stems largely from the fact that the EU has refused to open its market to bananas shipped by two U.S. firms, Dole Food Company and Chiquita Brands International.) In a dispute settlement case regarding the issue, the WTO ruled in September 1997 that the EU's policies violated international trade rules by discriminating in favor of banana imports from the ACP states and four Latin American countries which had special arrangements with the EU (Costa Rica, Colombia, Venezuela, and Nicaragua). The WTO gave the EU until January 1, 1999 to develop a revised banana import regime. Although the EU agreed on a revised quota structure for banana imports, the United States and several Latin American countries (Ecuador, Guatemala, Honduras, and Mexico) complained in late 1998 that the EU's proposed changes were "primarily cosmetic," and still discriminatory. Despite these ongoing tensions, in the Lomé Conventions the European Union has agreed to eliminate the trade preferences the EU members receive from the ACP associates, and the United States in turn has toned down its opposition to the association agreements.[39]

The European Union has also established association agreements with a number of other countries inside and outside Europe. As Table 9.1 shows, most of these EU associate and free trade agreements are *reciprocal* RIAs and therefore can be viewed more legitimately as FTAs under GATT Article 24. Unlike the case of the ACP countries, which have nonreciprocal associate agreements, the reciprocal agreements are with countries that were not former colonies of EU members.

Regional Arrangements Among LDCs   Historically, GATT's examination of RIAs among LDCs was even less stringent than its examination of RIAs among developed countries. This partly reflected a recognition that LDCs were forming RIAs for different reasons than developed countries. Thus, GATT did not openly object to the formation of the Latin American Free Trade Association in 1960, even though LAFTA was quite protectionist and "did not even approach the requirements of total integration."[40] In the 1960s and 1970s, GATT agreements granting special and differential treatment to LDCs further strengthened the LDCs' case for forming preferential regional agreements. After Part IV on trade and development was added to GATT in 1965, the LDCs sometimes invoked it to justify forming preferential trade arrangements that did not meet the "substantially all trade" requirement of GATT Article 24. When the 1979 decision on differential treatment for developing countries (the enabling clause) was approved during the GATT Tokyo round, it became the main legal cover for LDCs forming questionable regional agreements. Because the enabling clause does not explicitly refer to Article 24, there is some controversy over the extent to which it provides LDCs with special treatment in forming regional agreements. Nevertheless, many LDCs claim that the enabling clause permits them to form agreements that reduce rather than eliminate tariffs and that apply to only a limited range of products (that is, not to "substantially all trade"). *Mercosur,* the Southern Common Market Treaty signed by Argentina, Brazil, Paraguay, and Uruguay in 1991, is a recent example of an agreement notified to GATT under the enabling clause rather than Article 24.[41]

GATT was historically rather accepting of RIAs among LDCs with protectionist characteristics, and this acceptance increased over the years. Despite this permissiveness, however, recent LDC moves toward trade liberalization have inevitably affected their regional arrangements. The positive experience of Japan and the East Asian NICs with export-led growth has contributed to the abandonment of ISI policies, decreasing the likelihood that LDCs will seek inward-looking regional agreements. Furthermore, IMF and World Bank structural adjustment loans have forced LDCs to liberalize their trade policies, and this is reflected in more open regional agreements. The fact that Mexico is not given special and differential treatment in NAFTA may be the strongest indication of the influence of liberalism on LDC participation in RIAs today.[42]

EUROPE

Postwar regional integration has been centered mainly in Western Europe, where the European Union has emerged as the largest and most successful RIA in the world. Indeed, European countries were parties in 76 of the 109 agreements notified to GATT from 1948 to 1994. The breakup of the Soviet bloc has given new impetus to the European integration process, and trade agreements involving Central and Eastern

European countries accounted for 24 of the 33 agreements notified to GATT from 1990 to 1994.[43] Proposals for commercial union in Europe in fact extend back to the seventeenth century. A more immediate precursor of postwar integration was a French proposal in the interwar period that a European customs union be formed to resolve the continent's political and economic problems. After World War II, these plans for European integration were realized with U.S. support and encouragement, but the union was limited to Western European countries because of the ensuing Cold War.

In 1951, six countries (Belgium, France, West Germany, Italy, Luxembourg, and the Netherlands) formed the European Coal and Steel Community (ECSC), and these countries extended their integration under the Treaty of Rome to establish the European Economic Community and the European Atomic Energy Community (Euratom) in 1957. In 1960, seven European countries (Austria, Britain, Denmark, Norway, Portugal, Sweden, and Switzerland) responded to the EC by forming the European Free Trade Association (EFTA). While these "outer seven" countries wanted to be included in an FTA, they were not prepared to join the "inner six" countries in the EC for several reasons. Most importantly, the EC customs union required a common external tariff and a degree of policy coordination that threatened both Britain's Commonwealth preference system and the nonaligned policies of countries such as Sweden and Switzerland. The EFTA did not pose the same threat to these countries' autonomy because it did not require a common external tariff (see Figure 2.3). Since the formation of the EC and the EFTA, there has been a gradual widening and deepening of European integration.

The Widening of European Integration

As discussed in Chapter 2, the European Community expanded from 6 to 15 full members in three successive enlargements (see Figure 2.4). In the first enlargement, Britain, Denmark, and Ireland joined the EC in 1973; in the second enlargement, Greece joined in 1979 and Spain and Portugal joined in 1986; and in the third enlargement, Austria, Finland, and Sweden joined in 1995. While expanding its membership, the EC was also extending its associate linkages with former colonies and possessions. These associate agreements with LDCs are nonreciprocal: the LDCs do not have to fully reciprocate for the trade preferences they receive from the European Union. This section focuses on the most marked case of "widening" in recent years: the expansion of EU trade linkages with the Central and Eastern European countries.

When the EU was first established, the Soviet Union was extremely hostile to it, and the relationship continued to be strained throughout the 1960s and 1970s. The EU also did not want to give legitimacy to the CMEA (the Soviet-led trade organization for Eastern Europe), and it preferred to negotiate bilateral trade agreements with individual Eastern European countries outside CMEA auspices. Although the Soviet Union insisted that the CMEA be the vehicle for the EC's economic contacts with Eastern Europe, the EC successfully encouraged some Eastern European states to break ranks with the Soviet position. For example, Romania requested and received generalized system of preferences (GSP) treatment from the EC in 1972, and in 1980 Romania and the EC signed a full trade and cooperation agreement.

As economic conditions in Eastern Europe worsened in the 1980s and the Eastern bloc became more dependent on economic linkages with the West, the Soviet Union softened its position. In 1988 (under Soviet Premier Mikhail Gorbachev), an EC-CMEA agreement sanctioned the negotiation of trade agreements between the EC and individual Eastern European countries. From 1988 to 1990, the EC therefore negotiated trade and cooperation agreements with the Soviet Union as well as with most Eastern European countries. These agreements generally involved not only the liberalization of trade but also economic cooperation and economic assistance from the European Union.[44]

A major landmark was the collapse of the Soviet bloc and the Soviet Union itself (in 1991), which led to the dissolution of the CMEA and the development of closer ties between the European Union and the Eastern European states. Thus, the EU concluded "Europe agreements" in 1991 with the former Czech and Slovak Federal Republic, Hungary, and Poland and in 1993 with Bulgaria and Romania. Each of these treaties provides for the establishment of an FTA with the EU with a maximum transition period of 10 years and also recognizes the interest of these countries in eventually attaining full membership in the EU. In December 1992, the Czech and Slovak Republic, Hungary, and Poland also created the Central European Free Trade Agreement (CEFTA), which provides for the eventual establishment of an FTA in manufactured goods and raw materials (other than agriculture). Furthermore, the EU signed free trade agreements with each of the three Baltic states—Estonia, Latvia, and Lithuania—in June 1994.

The European Union has generally viewed these "Europe agreements" as a prelude to full membership, and EU leaders at their December 1995 summit in Madrid concluded that "enlargement is both a political necessity and a historic opportunity."[45] In March 1998, Poland, Hungary, the Czech Republic, Estonia, and Slovenia formally began talks with the EU as a prelude to membership. However, there are several major obstacles to full membership for the Eastern European countries. First, there is substantial resistance in some EU countries to increasing market access in such sectors as agriculture, textiles, and steel. The less developed southern European countries in the EU, such as Spain, Portugal, and Greece, feel especially threatened by the possible expansion of the European Union because they share with Eastern European countries such as Poland and Hungary a comparative advantage in agriculture, traditional manufactures, and resource-intensive products. In contrast, the northern more developed countries in the EU, such as Germany, Britain, and France, have a comparative advantage in higher-technology manufactures and service exports, and they are therefore more open to the EU's expansion to the East. Indeed, Eastern European countries in the EU would provide the more developed states with cheaper workers and more investment opportunities. A consensus on the widening of EU membership is therefore clearly lacking.[46]

Second, and most importantly, the Eastern Europeans' lower level of economic development poses a major obstacle to full membership. Indeed, 10 Central and Eastern European states that have signed Europe agreements with the EU have only one-fourth of the purchasing power of the present EU average, and about 20 percent of their workers have agricultural jobs compared with only 6 percent of EU workers.[47] These countries would greatly add to the pressures on the EU's structural funds directed to poorer EU regions and on funds for agricultural subsidies. The Common

Agricultural Policy (CAP) already absorbs about half the EU budget and structural funds another 30 percent, so countries that contribute more to these funds than they receive (e.g., Germany, France, Britain, and the Netherlands) are extremely concerned. Enlargement could therefore be a long-term process, with the EU requiring transition periods before the Eastern Europeans are eligible for the full range of benefits. Nevertheless, EU rejection of the new democracies could jeopardize their economic and political stability.[48]

In sum, three levels of European integration have developed as a result of trade liberalization: (1) The deepest level of integration exists among the 15 EU member states and extends largely to other Western European countries that have free trade arrangements with the EU. (2) The second level includes countries in Central and Eastern Europe and the Mediterranean area, which have reciprocal trade agreements with the EU. (3) The third level extends to the LDCs that have nonreciprocal associate agreements with the EU.[49]

The Deepening of European Integration

Although the European Community was initially successful in lowering internal trade barriers, the insistence of President Charles de Gaulle on retaining French sovereignty over decision making contributed to a marked slowdown in the development of EC institutions in the 1960s. After 1973, the economic growth rates of EC members also slowed considerably. In addition to external causes such as the OPEC oil crisis, this slowdown was attributed to the persistence of trade distortions in the EC resulting from differential taxation, border inspections, domestic subsidies, and internal impediments to market access. The period from the late 1970s to the 1980s was therefore a period of "Eurosclerosis" marked by a loss of faith in the EC's vitality.[50]

To deal with this stagnation of the integration process, EC members signed the Single European Act in 1986, which was designed to complete the process of freeing the internal market by the end of 1992. This "single-market program" involved ending nontariff barriers to trade in industrial goods, liberalizing trade in services, and facilitating the free movement of labor and capital throughout the EC. A further deepening of economic and political ties occurred with the Treaty on European Union (the *Maastricht Treaty*), which entered into force in November 1993. Whereas the Treaty of Rome had focused mainly on promoting trade expansion, the Maastricht Treaty also included the goals of economic and monetary union, a common foreign and security policy, common citizenship, and cooperation in justice and social affairs. Although the EU is experiencing difficulties in achieving some of its objectives, moves toward institutional and economic reform since 1987 have revitalized the integration process.[51]

The Theoretical Perspectives and the European Union

Realists often focus on European integration as a means of increasing Europe's economic power vis-à-vis other major economic actors. For example, the bipolar system after World War II dominated by the United States and the Soviet Union was certainly a major factor in the decision of Western European states to embark on economic integration to increase their influence. In the late 1960s, Jean-Jacque Servan-Schreiber's book *The American Challenge* focusing on the increased penetration of American capital in Europe also had a major impact on European thinking. Individual European states lacked the resources to develop firms that could rival the U.S. multinational corporations, Servan-Schreiber argued, and only a united Europe could accomplish this task and thereby preserve European autonomy and influence.[52] In the 1980s and 1990s, European concerns about American and Japanese technological leadership were similarly a major factor in the signing of the Single European Act and the Maastricht Treaty.

Liberal economists have been primarily concerned with ensuring that the European Union is an "open" rather than a "closed" integration movement. Their concerns about EU protectionism increased during the moves toward consolidation in "Europe 1992" and the EU struggles with the United States in the GATT Uruguay round. In discussions of the EU's inward orientation, analysts sometimes point to the reorientation of trade from third countries to other EU members following the creation of the Community and the accession of new members. They also focus on specific EU policies, such as the CAP, as examples of extreme protectionism. Liberals often point to the detrimental effects of inward-looking EU policies on member states as well as outsiders. For example, one European specialist has argued that "the use of protection to avoid industrial restructuring has almost certainly contributed to Europe's falling behind the United States and Japan in hi-tech goods."[53]

Despite the concerns of some liberals, there is considerable evidence that the EU is responding to globalization forces with outward-looking policies. Indeed, the largest industrial firms in Europe were a major force behind the single-market program in the late 1980s and the 1990s. These firms are global competitors that would oppose regional protectionism because of fears of retaliation. Furthermore, the EU eventually approved the GATT Uruguay round agreement despite dire predictions that European intransigence over agriculture would lead to the failure of the round. The deepening and widening of integration also promises to add considerably to trade creation among EU members and is furthering the process of integrating the former centrally planned states in the capitalist international economy. Some analysts predict that the EU could eventually expand from its current membership of 15 to more than 25 members, which would account for about 30 percent of world trade and production. Although this has the risk of contributing to trade diversion vis-à-vis outsiders, there would also be a substantial amount of trade creation within such a large regional bloc.[54]

Interventionist liberals have praised the EU for directing more attention to social policy than some other integration agreements, such as NAFTA. For example, the European Community created a European Social Fund as early as the 1960s, with the goal of decreasing the socioeconomic disparities between EC member states. A major reason EC countries agreed to adopt the single-market program in the 1980s was that increased structural funds were pledged to Ireland and the poorer Southern European EC states. Historical structuralists are more inclined to view the European social programs as inadequate solutions to inequality and poverty, and they note that there is division among European states regarding how much funding should be provided for social purposes. Thus, major disparities in wealth continue to exist between Northern and Southern European states and between different regions within European countries.[55]

Interventionist liberals and historical structuralists also differ in their views of the European Union's relations with the associate ACP countries. In the liberal view, associate status has been beneficial to these states. The rich EU countries have been willing to absorb the short-term economic costs of providing aid and trade preferences to the ACP countries in the interests of longer-term economic and political security. Historical structuralists, by contrast, argue that the EU associate agreements are designed to perpetuate the dependence of the weaker ACP countries on their former colonial masters. Indeed, the EU maintains the colonial pattern of trade: EU countries export industrial goods, and the ACP countries depend largely on primary product exports. The EU has also discouraged the manufacture of goods such as textiles in the ACP countries by limiting their access to the EU market. Historical structuralists therefore believe that "prospects for symmetrical EurAfrica relations remain . . . dim despite all the rhetoric to the contrary."[56]

NORTH AMERICA

Although the United States and Canada did not establish a generalized free trade agreement until the 1980s, moves toward free trade between the two countries have a remarkably long history. Indeed, a noted Canadian historian has observed that there is one economic issue in Canada that "comes close to rivalling the linguistic and race question for both longevity and vehemence, and this is, of course, the question of free trade with the United States."[57] The United States also expressed interest in free trade with Canada at various historical junctures, but (unlike the Mexican free trade issue) free trade with Canada has not been a highly emotional issue for most Americans. Although Canada is the United States' largest trading partner, it accounts for only about 20 percent of U.S. exports. The United States, by contrast, accounts for about 80 percent of Canadian exports. Thus, the relationship is marked by asymmetrical interdependence, with Canada far more dependent on the United States.

In 1854, the United States and Canada concluded a Reciprocity Treaty providing for free trade in natural products such as grains, meat, dairy products, and fish. However, the United States abrogated the treaty in 1866, largely in reaction to an unfavorable trade balance with Canada, increased Canadian duties on U.S. manufactures, and the British role in the American Civil War. The two countries tried to renew "reciprocity" in 1911, but this time Canadian manufacturers feared that their tariff protection would be weakened, and they joined with other opponents to defeat the move. In March 1948, the two countries devised yet another plan to remove almost all duties on their bilateral trade, but Canadian Prime Minister Mackenzie King ultimately refused to approve the plan because of domestic political opposition. The first postwar integration agreement in North America that actually came to fruition was the 1965 Canada-U.S. Automotive Agreement providing for free trade in automobiles and parts. The United States obtained a GATT waiver in this case because the automotive agreement did not meet the GATT Article 24 requirement that an FTA should cover "substantially all trade." It was not until 1988 that the United States and Canada established the more generalized CUSTA. In December 1992, the United States and Canada joined Mexico in signing NAFTA, which superseded CUSTA.

The Reasons for Forming CUSTA and NAFTA

The question arises as to why the United States and Canada, and then Mexico, decided to negotiate CUSTA and NAFTA. The United States addressed the free trade issue in the 1974 U.S. Trade Act, which permitted the President to "initiate negotiations for a trade agreement with Canada to establish a free trade area"[58]; and the idea of a "North American accord" or "common market" that would also include Mexico surfaced in the 1980 U.S. presidential campaign. However, the presidential candidates were very unspecific about the form this trilateral accord would take, and the proposals seemed motivated more by U.S. concerns about secure access to Mexican and Canadian energy supplies than by an interest in a broad-ranging free trade agreement.[59]

Despite these early American proposals, it was a Canadian and then a Mexican request for free trade negotiations that resulted in the CUSTA and NAFTA agreements. Protectionist forces were strong in the United States in the mid-1980s because of the massive balance-of-payments deficit that developed during the Reagan administration. Canada was directing over 75 percent of its exports to the United States, so the Canadian government decided that a free trade agreement was essential to gain more assured access to the U.S. market. Of particular concern to Canada were U.S. countervailing duties and U.S. trade unilateralism. Another motivation for free trade with the United States was the perceived need to alter *Canadian* domestic economic policies. Business leaders in Canada (as in many other countries) were critical of the government's central role in the economy in the 1980s, and they felt that the need for reciprocal concessions in an FTA would force Canadians to place more reliance on market forces.

Starting from high levels of protection, Mexico instituted unilateral measures to ease trade restrictions *before* it sought free trade negotiations with the United States. These unilateral moves were impelled by the conditions attached to IMF and World Bank structural adjustment loans to deal with the Mexican debt crisis and by the realization that liberalization was necessary if Mexico was to attract foreign investment. Mexico, like Canada, depends on the United States for more than 70 percent of its exports, and it therefore also shared Canada's concerns about gaining more assured access to the U.S. market. The foreign investment issue, however, was even more important to Mexico than the market access issue as a reason for seeking free trade. Despite Mexico's unilateral liberalization moves, potential foreign investors were skeptical that these changes were permanent because of Mexico's long history of government intervention. A free trade agreement with the United States would give Mexico's liberalization policies more credibility and permanence.[60]

The United States as a major economic power was more concerned about global than regional trade linkages; its decision to conclude the CUSTA and NAFTA agreements was motivated largely by frustration with the slow pace of negotiations in the

GATT Uruguay round. Negotiating regional agreements, in the U.S. view, would induce other large economic powers—especially the EU and Japan—to offer concessions in the multilateral negotiations. Regionalism also has a tendency to breed more regionalism, and the EU's enlargement and consolidation in "Europe 92" provided an additional U.S. incentive to establish a North American free trade area as a counterweight. Because its trade hegemony was declining, the United States was less committed to multilateralism as the sole option and more willing to participate in regional free trade agreements. Regional trade is of course less important to the United States than it is to Canada and Mexico, but it is noteworthy that Canada and Mexico are the United States' largest and third-largest single-country trading partners, respectively (Japan is second). Finally, the United States wanted Canada and Mexico to ease their regulations on foreign direct investment and natural resources, and it was willing to open its market more widely to Canadian and Mexican goods in return.[61]

The IPE Theoretical Perspectives and CUSTA and NAFTA

CUSTA and NAFTA are highly controversial treaties which individuals from different perspectives have often jointly opposed (or supported). While CUSTA was more controversial in Canada than in the United States, NAFTA (and its possible expansion) continues to be a major source of contention for Americans. Individuals and groups opposing NAFTA in the United States stretch across the political spectrum, ranging from interventionist liberals to American nationalists and historical structuralists. Nationalist critics of NAFTA often criticize the terms of the agreement; for example, they maintain that the NAFTA environmental and labor side agreements do not provide genuine protection for U.S. jobs and the environment. Historical structuralists, by contrast, oppose NAFTA in *any* form, arguing that it facilitates the ascendancy of the transnational capitalist class over labor. Because such a wide array of groups oppose (and support) NAFTA, this discussion of the theoretical perspectives is illustrative rather than all-inclusive.

The Orthodox Liberal Perspective

The major concerns of liberal economists included the degree to which CUSTA, and then NAFTA, contributed to trade openness and served as stepping-stones rather than obstacles to multilateral free trade. After addressing these issues from a liberal perspective, we discuss the realist and historical structuralist perspectives of North American free trade.

The Canada-U.S. Free Trade Agreement   Liberal economists generally praised CUSTA for contributing to freer trade and for facilitating trade liberalization in GATT. Average tariff rates on U.S.-Canadian trade were quite low even before CUSTA was formed, so the agreement did not result in a significant increase in trade diversion. CUSTA also demonstrated that the United States might opt for regionalism if the GATT Uruguay round was unsuccessful, and the EU and Japan were therefore more willing to compromise in the Uruguay round negotiations. Furthermore,

CUSTA provisions in some areas such as trade in services and trade-related investment served as important precedents for the Uruguay round negotiations.[62]

Although liberals pointed to the positive aspects of CUSTA, they also referred to its shortcomings. For example, CUSTA resulted in some liberalization of services trade, but important sectors such as transportation, culture, basic telecommunications, and the media were excluded. In response to U.S. pressure, Canada also raised the threshold size for screening U.S. foreign investment, but it could still review large investments, and investment continued to be restricted in such areas as financial services and transportation. In response to Canadian concerns about U.S. contingent trade actions, CUSTA called for the creation of binational panels to assess disputes over each country's countervailing and antidumping duty decisions. Unlike the previous system, in which domestic courts had provided final review of CVD and ADD decisions, the binational panels ensured that both countries' interpretations of trade law would be considered in dispute settlement cases. However, each country retained the right to implement its own contingent trade legislation, and the binational panels could judge only whether a U.S. (or Canadian) CVD or ADD decision was made in accordance with U.S. (or Canadian) law; that is, the panels could not assess the fairness of each country's laws. Liberal economists felt that overall, CUSTA made modest contributions to free trade.

The North American Free Trade Agreement   Liberal economists point positively to NAFTA as the first free trade pact between a developing country and industrial states that does not give special and differential treatment to the LDC member (Mexico). Mexico's commitments under NAFTA should ensure that its moves toward trade liberalization persist in the long term. NAFTA also has had a positive "demonstration effect" on the WTO in services trade, investment, and intellectual property rights, and it goes beyond the WTO in coverage of these areas. For example, NAFTA follows a "negative list" approach to national treatment for trade in services; that is, all services not itemized on a country's list are automatically included. This approach puts the onus on each NAFTA member to identify those services it wants to exclude. The WTO's General Agreement on Trade in Services (GATS), by contrast, takes a "positive list" approach to services trade; that is, national treatment applies only to sectors specifically included in a member's list of commitments. Thus, NAFTA's services trade provisions are more trade-creating than those of GATS.[63]

Liberals also point out, however, that NAFTA has some shortcomings. For example, some other regional agreements go beyond NAFTA in contingency trade legislation. As with the case of CUSTA, these NAFTA panels review disputes among the members over CVDs and ADDs. Nevertheless, dispute settlement panels are to base their decisions on the domestic laws of the importing country, and they cannot make judgments about the fairness of these laws. The NAFTA also places no obligation on the three member states to harmonize their domestic subsidies and contingency trade laws. In contrast, the European Union and the Closer Economic Relations (CER) agreement between Australia and New Zealand have substituted harmonized competition policies for contingency trade measures. Thus, CVDs and ADDs are no longer imposed among members of these agreements.[64] Liberals also criticize NAFTA's complex rules of origin. Indeed, NAFTA's rules of origin are generally more restrictive than those of CUSTA. CUSTA, for example, required 50 percent North American content for automotive products to qualify for preferred treatment. The NAFTA rules of origin, by contrast, require 62.5 percent North American content for passenger automobiles, light trucks, engines, and some transmissions. Finally, orthodox liberals oppose the environmental and labor side agreements in NAFTA because of concerns that they are nontrade issues that can pose obstacles to trade liberalization.

Although U.S. Presidents George Bush and Bill Clinton had talked about extending NAFTA to other countries in a Western Hemisphere free trade agreement, NAFTA provisions are very vague regarding the requirements countries must meet to become members. NAFTA is to make decisions concerning new members by consensus (presumably requiring unanimity); the lack of clear-cut procedures could pose a significant obstacle to enlargement. Indeed, the U.S. Congress has been reluctant to give the President **fast-track authority** in negotiations to extend NAFTA to Chile and other Latin American states. The 1974 U.S. Trade Act introduced fast-track measures to expedite legislative approval of trade agreements negotiated by the U.S. executive. Under the fast track, the President could assure U.S. trading partners that Congress would vote for or against negotiated agreements without amendments within a fixed time period. Such authority was often necessary because U.S. trading partners were unwilling to spend months or years negotiating agreements, only to find that the U.S. Congress would later want to amend them. It was through fast-track authority that the United States negotiated the CUSTA and NAFTA agreements. In 1994, however, the President's fast-track authority expired, and the U.S. Congress had still not agreed to renew this authority as of early 1999. The possibilities and time frame for expanding NAFTA or for concluding a Western Hemisphere free trade agreement are therefore highly uncertain.[65]

Despite the reservations they express about NAFTA, many liberals (especially those inclined toward liberal orthodoxy) conclude approvingly that "on balance . . . the trade created by growth in the NAFTA region should more than offset the trade diverted."[66] Thus, liberal economists tend to view the controversy over fast-track approval as injurious to the U.S. postwar position as the predominant force behind the liberalization of trade.

The Realist and Historical Structuralist Perspectives

Realists and historical structuralists believe that CUSTA and NAFTA have had significant distributional effects, which are determined by major asymmetries in power and/or levels of economic development. Thus, realists strongly reject the liberal view that smaller countries often benefit from free trade agreements even more than larger countries. From the realist perspective, the United States as the larger partner naturally demanded that its benefits from free trade would outweigh those received by Canada and Mexico. For example, Canada sought free trade with the United States to gain more assured access to the U.S. market at a time when U.S. protectionism was increasing. In return for granting free trade, the United States expected a number of side payments, including an easing of Canadian regulations on U.S. foreign investment, greater U.S. access to Canadian energy supplies, and an agreement on trade in services. The United States also agreed to free trade with Mexico, but in return Mexico gave up any claims to receive special and differential treatment as an LDC in NAFTA.[67]

In contrast to realists, historical structuralists focus on transnational capital and on class relationships. From their perspective, NAFTA represents a shift in power in favor of the capitalist class and against the interests of labor groups. For example, NAFTA enables MNCs to avoid more rigorous labor and environmental standards in Canada and the United States by relocating production in Mexico. As capital leaves the United States and Canada, wages and opportunities for employment in these countries decline. Some historical structuralists use the terms *core* and *periphery* to designate social position rather than geographic location, arguing that NAFTA has relegated many impoverished American and Canadian workers to peripheral status.[68]

The losses for American and Canadian workers, according to historical structuralists, do not mean that there are comparable gains for Mexican workers. For example, they argue that NAFTA will destroy the livelihoods of Mexican peasants because U.S. corn, which benefits from a range of government subsidies, will eventually be freely exported to Mexico.[69] Historical structuralists thus argue that NAFTA is increasing poverty and inequality between the rich and poor in all three member countries. Some Gramscian theorists discuss the possibility that more progressive groups opposing NAFTA could form a counterhegemonic bloc based on opposition to the domination of corporate capital in North America. This broad-based coalition would consist of labor, environmental, consumer, and women's groups, among others. A counterhegemonic bloc of this nature would be committed to replacing the current corporate view of liberalization in North America with a more democratic, participatory model.[70]

EAST ASIA

The term *East Asia* is used here to refer to Japan, four newly industrialized countries (Taiwan, South Korea, Singapore, and Hong Kong), four members of the Association of Southeast Asian Nations or ASEAN (Indonesia, Malaysia, the Philippines, and Thailand), and China. This region's impact on trade and other aspects of the global economy has grown markedly in recent years. As Table 9.2 shows, East Asia accounted for only 10.8 percent of world trade in 1970, while North America accounted for almost twice that amount (20.7 percent) and Western Europe accounted for more than four times that amount (48.2 percent). By 1990, East Asia's share of world trade had almost doubled, reaching 19.4 percent, while the shares of North America and Western Europe declined slightly to 18.1 and 46.8 percent, respectively.[71]

East Asia was not involved in the first wave of regional integration among LDCs in the 1960s, and in the current wave of regionalism, free trade agreements involving East Asia are still only in the planning stages. Of the two major groupings in the region, one is subregional (ASEAN), and the other extends beyond East Asia to include countries on both sides of the Pacific (the Asia-Pacific Economic Cooperation or APEC forum). Although formal institutional initiatives to encourage regional integration have been far

TABLE 9.2

REGIONAL SHARES OF WORLD TRADE (PERCENT)

	1970	1990
East Asia	10.8	19.4
North America (US, Canada, Mexico)	20.7	18.1
Western Europe (EU and EFTA)	48.2	46.8
Other countries	20.5	15.7

Source: Derived from Soogil Young, "East Asia as a Regional Force for Globalism," in Kym Anderson and Richard Blackhurst, eds., *Regional Integration and the Global Trading System* (New York: Harvester Wheatsheaf, 1993), p. 130, Table 6.1.

less important in East Asia than in other regions, trade and investment among East Asian countries have demonstrated impressive growth rates. Thus, the East Asian case shows that countries can develop strong regional linkages even without formal institutions.[72] A major reason for the rise in intraregional trade is that dynamic, rapidly growing economies (like those found in East Asia in the 1970s to 1980s) are likely to trade with one another. Indeed, several neighboring provinces of East Asian countries have developed close trade and investment linkages even though the relations among the central governments involved are not particularly friendly. Another stimulus for trade is the wide diversity of Asian economies in terms of size, per capita income, and natural resources, which provides opportunities for specialization.

Besides being informal and market-oriented, East Asian regional linkages are also oriented to increasing the competitiveness of the region's firms in global markets. Thus, the internationalization of the production process in East Asia has contributed to the region's ability to market high-quality goods at competitive prices. While Japan has provided capital and high-technology goods, the East Asian NICs have provided goods and services with increasing levels of sophistication, and low-wage countries such as China, Indonesia, and Vietnam have been involved with labor-intensive assembly operations. East Asian countries are not overly concerned about their lack of regional integration agreements, partly because of the advantages they see in the World Trade Organization: it plays an important role in decreasing trade barriers such as "voluntary" export restraints that have restricted the access of East Asian goods to markets in the developed countries; it provides for special and differential treatment for East Asian LDCs (although the NICs are in the process of "graduating" to more developed country status); and it offers smaller East Asian states some protection from the pressures of major regional powers such as Japan and China.[73]

Despite the declared intentions of ASEAN and APEC to develop FTAs, it is uncertain that East Asian regional relationships will ever become as institutionalized as those of Europe and North America. Slow economic growth provided a major motivation for EC members to develop "Europe 1992" and induced the United States, Canada, and Mexico to establish NAFTA. Until recently, East Asian economic performance, by contrast, has been quite successful, and these countries therefore have felt less need for formal arrangements. Persistent hostility and suspicions among East

Asian states pose an additional obstacle to formal integration, with a number of countries having memories of Japan's military conquest in the 1930s, as well as concerns about dominance by the Peoples' Republic of China. Yet another obstacle is posed by the protectionist and interventionist industrial policies in many Asian countries. Formal regional arrangements would require more policy changes than many of these countries are willing to make. Finally, the United States continues to have considerable military and economic influence in East Asia, and it strongly opposes the establishment of a regional trade arrangement limited to Asian countries. Despite these obstacles to the development of more formal institutions, the East Asian countries are concerned about the protectionist and exclusionary aspects of the EU and NAFTA. If the global trade regime is ever seriously threatened by regional trading blocs, East Asian countries might be more willing to accept formal regional arrangements.[74]

The Association of Southeast Asian Nations

Indonesia, Malaysia, the Philippines, Singapore, and Thailand agreed to establish the Association of Southeast Asian Nations in 1967, with the stated goals of promoting peace, stability, and economic growth in the region. However, ASEAN was largely a political organization for many years, with only a few relatively small programs to promote economic linkages. It was not until 1977 that the ASEAN countries signed an Agreement on Preferential Trading Arrangements (PTA), which provided for preferential treatment in terms of tariffs and nontariff measures on certain exports. The agreement had only limited product coverage, however, and it had little effect on intra-ASEAN trade. In January 1991 the ASEAN countries agreed to establish an ASEAN Free Trade Area (AFTA) by the year 2008 (the target date was subsequently shortened to 2003). However, AFTA will exclude services, unprocessed agricultural products, and natural resources from the free trade rules, and it will do little to address the central issue of nontariff barriers. Regional business elites have been pressuring ASEAN to move more rapidly toward trade liberalization, and this pressure may have some effect in speeding up negotiations.[75]

The Asia-Pacific Economic Cooperation Forum

The largest regional initiative involving East Asia is the Asia-Pacific Economic Cooperation forum, which was first proposed by Australian Prime Minister Bob Hawke in 1989. Initially, foreign and economic ministers attended APEC meetings, but the forum became more prominent in November 1993 when it began to hold annual summit meetings of heads of state. As Table 9.3 shows, APEC emphasizes open regionalism, with its broad range of members from Asia, Australasia, and North and South America. Thus, APEC is "very much a creature of the rise of economic liberalism."[76] The potential importance of APEC stems from the influence of its membership: the 18 members account for about one-half of the world's total annual output and for about 40 percent of the world's merchandise trade. In November 1998, Russia, Peru, and Vietnam joined APEC, further increasing the potential impact of the organization.

TABLE 9.3
MEMBERS OF APEC

Year of Joining	Member
1989	Australia, Brunei, Canada, Indonesia, Japan, Republic of Korea, Malaysia, New Zealand, Philippines, Singapore, Thailand, United States
1991	China, Hong Kong, Taiwan
1993	Mexico, Papua New Guinea
1994	Chile
1998	Peru, Russia, Vietnam

APEC also includes the three largest national economies—the United States, Japan, and China—and each of these countries has a vested interest in the group. Thus, the United States did not want to be excluded from an East Asian trading bloc (East Asia overtook the European Community as North America's largest foreign market region in the early 1980s); Japan wanted to include NAFTA members in APEC to counter any protectionist threats in North America, and it also did not want to alienate its ally the United States; and China, which has not yet been accepted into the World Trade Organization, views APEC as one route to establishing its respectability. Smaller East Asian countries are also supportive of APEC because it prevents dominance by any one of the three largest economies and addresses some of the smaller countries' concerns regarding access to the large U.S. market.[77]

APEC's activities to this point are largely limited to promoting increased linkages through trade liberalization, economic cooperation, and development projects in areas such as monetary relations, tourism, human resources, energy, and infrastructure. However, APEC members are also discussing other issues that would extend integration beyond traditional areas. These include the possibilities of reaching agreements on competition policies, common definitions of product standards, a dispute mediation mechanism, and private investment. The most difficult issue in APEC relates to the idea of forming a free trade agreement. At the November 1994 APEC Summit in Bogor, Indonesia, the member states agreed to the goal of establishing a free and open trade and investment area for developed countries by the year 2010 and for LDCs by 2020. The November 1995 APEC Summit in Osaka, Japan then adopted an "action agenda" to begin implementing this free trade commitment by January 1997.

The agreement is ambiguous, however, on such issues as trade liberalization in services and agriculture and the identification of developed countries and LDCs. China, for example, is reluctant to commit to free trade along with more developed countries by the year 2010, but most APEC members would be unwilling to classify the industrial parts of China along with the LDCs. The 1994 Bogor Summit declaration also does not specify clearly how a free and open investment area is to be established, and it leaves the details for discussion at future meetings. The APEC in this respect "is very Asian with its broad consensus style, and very unlike North American and European regional pacts with their detailed liberalization schedules."[78] Thus, Asian members of APEC dislike the bargaining negotiations that take place in GATT/WTO; they would prefer instead to depend on a process of unilateral liberalization. Under this process, each APEC country would independently develop its own plans for liberalization on a most-favored-nation basis; that is, the liberalization would extend to *all countries,* not only to those in APEC. This type of liberalization would stem from enlightened self-interest and peer pressure rather than from the give-and-take of negotiations.

Implementing such a proposal, however, could prove difficult. Most APEC members other than Canada, Australia, Hong Kong, New Zealand, Singapore, and the United States have tariffs averaging above 10 percent, with levels for some products over 30 percent, and it is highly uncertain that these countries would significantly lower their tariffs on a unilateral basis. Furthermore, the U.S. position could pose obstacles to APEC free trade plans for a number of reasons. First, the United States would be most reluctant to extend its APEC concessions to Europe and other non-APEC areas on a nonreciprocal basis; second, protectionist U.S. groups would argue strongly against having open competition with countries such as Japan and China; third, the United States would be reluctant to give free trade access to China in view of the PRC's human rights record; and fourth, U.S. trade problems with some Asian countries such as Japan and South Korea result not from border measures, such as tariffs, but from domestic policies and societal factors that make it difficult for foreigners to compete. Thus, phasing out tariffs in APEC would not result in reciprocal concessions if domestic policy issues were not also addressed.[79]

The size and diversity of APEC membership could also interfere with plans for an FTA. Malaysia in particular has strongly criticized the size and regional scope of APEC and has argued instead for a regional grouping limited to Asian nations. In December 1990, Malaysian Prime Minister Mahathir Mohamad proposed that an East Asian economic grouping be formed for this purpose. The Malaysian proposal was aimed not only at economic liberalism but also at countering the political power of the United States and Europe. In response to harsh criticism from the United States, an informal East Asian Economic Caucus was formed instead within APEC. If APEC's objectives do not materialize, the idea of a regional grouping limited to Asian countries could reemerge in the future.[80]

The IPE Perspectives and East Asian Regionalism

Liberal economists tend to be highly supportive of APEC as an example of open regionalism that is likely to serve as a stepping stone to global trade liberalization. APEC includes countries in a huge area spanning more than one continent, and liberals sometimes compare it favorably with the European Union, which is more discriminatory. Liberals realize there are obstacles to promoting free trade in a forum as diverse as APEC, but they are hopeful that this brand of open regionalism will succeed in the long term. Indeed, one prominent liberal who was chair of APEC's eminent persons' group from 1992 to 1995 believes that APEC could become "the first big international institutional success of the post–cold war era."[81]

Realists are more inclined to view APEC in political as well as economic terms as an effort by non-Asian countries such as Australia and the United States to prevent the formation of a regional trading bloc limited to Asians (as proposed by the Malaysian prime minister). From this perspective, the United States has used APEC "as a forum to maintain US power, [and] embrace the exclusionary East Asian identity within an inclusionary 'Asia-Pacific' identity."[82] Realists place less emphasis than liberals on the institutional aspects of Asian regionalism, and they point to the central role of Japan in establishing its own brand of regionalism. Indeed, Japanese MNCs, with the support of the government, have greatly increased their foreign direct investment throughout Asia, forging a regional production alliance. Instead of establishing an RIA, "Japan is using its Asian production alliance in part as a platform from which to continuing supplying high-technology products to Western markets."[83] Thus, realists place particular emphasis on the competitive challenge that Japan and the East Asian NICs pose to the West today.

Although APEC to this point has been a forum for discussion rather than an RIA, historical structuralists are concerned that APEC could eventually lead to "the erosion of social programs, downward harmonization of environmental, labour and health standards, and a permanent shift of political and economic power to large corporations."[84] Because some East Asian countries currently have policies that provide minimal protection for the environment, for labor, and for human rights, the freeing of trade and foreign investment in APEC could force other countries to sacrifice their own standards to remain competitive. As in the case of NAFTA, the member countries in APEC would be forced into a "competitive race to the bottom."[85]

Historical structuralists, like realists, also focus on the noninstitutional aspects of East Asian regionalism. In the view of historical structuralists, Japan and its MNCs have acted as the core economic power in the region, supplying the highest-technology products and keeping most of the R&D at home. The East Asian NICs (Hong Kong, South Korea, Singapore, and Taiwan) have acted as a semiperiphery supplying high- to medium-technology inputs, and the Southeast Asian countries and China have performed the role of a periphery, supplying the medium- to low-technology inputs. Since the other Asian countries depend on Japan for its high-technology inputs, they must maintain a trade surplus with the West to compensate for their growing trade deficit with the Japanese. Thus, Japanese capital is playing a dominant role in bringing about a large degree of informal integration in the East Asian region.[86]

CONCLUSION

In the postwar period there were two major waves of regionalism, the first in the 1950s and 1960s and the second since the mid-1980s. There is a fairly wide consensus that the second wave of regionalism is likely to be far more enduring than the first wave. Although there are some contradictions between the global and regional processes, globalization has clearly acted as a stimulus to the second phase of regionalism. Regional institutions are developing to deal with problems of global interdependence that nation-states are unable to deal with individually. States are also joining in regional groups to improve their competitiveness as the intensity and scope of global competition increases. Furthermore, internationalist firms within states that have expanded their exports and imports, multinational operations, and intrafirm trade have pressured for free market exchange at both the regional and global levels.

The revival of regionalism stems not only from globalization pressures but also from changes in North-North and North-South relations. Most significantly, the United States changed from a position of refusing to participate in regional integration agreements to openly supporting them during the 1980s. One of the factors explaining the change in American policy was the decline in U.S. trade hegemony. As long as the United States was undisputed hegemon in the global trade regime, it was firmly committed to the multilateral route to trade liberalization. However, the United States was less willing to provide the public goods to maintain an open multilateral trade regime as its economic leverage declined, and it sought to regain some of its economic influence through joining in RIAs. The less developed countries also turned to regionalism in the 1980s, but they generally supported a far more open regionalism than they had in the 1960s. The 1980s foreign debt crisis had a major effect in inducing LDCs to adopt orthodox liberal reforms, reflected in their new approach to regionalism. For example, Mexico engaged in unilateral liberalization of its trade policies, joined GATT in 1986, and formed NAFTA with the United States and Canada in the early 1990s.

The three IPE perspectives differ in their views of RIAs. Liberals believe that multilateralism is the best possible route to trade liberalization, but they are generally supportive of open RIAs as a second-best option. Most liberals have a positive view of the current phase of regionalism because it seems to be serving as a stepping-stone rather than an obstacle to multilateral free trade. Liberals assume that all member countries will benefit from open RIAs, and they often argue that smaller countries in RIAs will gain even more benefits in terms of economies of scale and expanded market share.

Realists believe that the underlying power relationships between states will be evident in regional agreements and that the more powerful states will gain no less, and probably more, from RIAs than the less powerful. While RIAs give smaller member countries access to larger countries' markets, the larger countries will demand side payments in return. For example, in CUSTA, the United States gained concessions from Canada in energy sharing, foreign investment, and trade in services; and in NAFTA, Mexico gave up any claim to the special and differential treatment often accorded to LDCs in international trade agreements.

Historical structuralists have a far more negative view of regional agreements such as NAFTA. In the historical structuralist view, transnational capital is the main beneficiary of such agreements, and the working class and poorest people within member states are the main losers. Because regional agreements often permit MNCs to locate their production facilities in the states that have the lowest wages and environmental standards, they can have a detrimental effect on environmental, labor, health and safety, public service, and consumer protection standards in all member countries.

Chapters 8 and 9 have focused mainly on international trade issues. There is a close interrelationship between trade and foreign investment. Indeed, the director-general of the World Trade Organization has stated that "businesses now trade to invest and invest to trade—to the point where both activities are increasingly part of a single strategy to deliver products across borders."[87] While the level of international trade has been increasing dramatically, foreign direct investment of MNCs has been increasing at an even faster rate. It is to the issue of MNCs that we now turn.

NOTES

1. World Trade Organization Secretariat, *Regionalism and the World Trading System* (Geneva: WTO, advance copy, April 1995), pp. 25–29.
2. Gerald K. Helleiner, "Considering U.S.-Mexico Free Trade," in Ricardo Grinspun and Maxwell A. Cameron, eds., *The Political Economy of North American Free Trade* (Montreal: McGill-Queen's University Press, 1993), p. 50.
3. Helleiner, "Considering U.S.-Mexico Free Trade," pp. 50–51.
4. Vincent A. Mahler, "The Lomé Convention: Assessing a North-South Institutional Relationship," *Review of International Political Economy* 1-2 (Summer 1994), p. 246.
5. Andrew Hurrell, "Explaining the Resurgence of Regionalism in World Politics," *Review of International Studies* 21 (1995), p. 333. For a detailed study that demonstrates the difficulty in defining a "region" precisely, see Bruce M. Russett, *International Regions and the International System: A Study in Political Ecology* (Chicago: Rand McNally, 1967).
6. Even here there are exceptions. For example, the World Trade Organization categorizes the U.S.-Israel, Canada-Israel, and Canada-Chile free trade agreements as regional integration agreements. The European Union also has special agreements with a large number of ACP (Africa, Caribbean, and Pacific) countries. However, the ACP countries are associate rather than full members of the European Union.
7. Hurrell, "Explaining the Resurgence of Regionalism in World Politics," pp. 345–347; Andrew Wyatt-Walter, "Regionalism, Globalization, and World Economic Order," in Louise Fawcett and Andrew Hurrell, eds., *Regionalism in World Politics: Regional Organization and International Order* (Oxford: Oxford University Press, 1995), p. 77.
8. For a cataloguing of the numerous early attempts to establish RIAs, see Fritz Machlup, *A History of Thought on Economic Integration* (New York: Columbia University Press, 1977), pp. 105–115.
9. See Michael Kaser, *Comecon: Integration Problems of the Planned Economies* (London: Oxford University Press, 1965).
10. The new integration agreement in 1957 was in fact called the European Economic Community, but the name was later changed to European Community. The latter term is used in this book. Britain was the leading force behind the EFTA, which also included Austria, Denmark, Norway, Portugal, Sweden, and Switzerland.
11. Jagdish Bhagwati, "Regionalism and Multilateralism: An Overview," in Jaime de Melo and Arvind Panagariya, eds., *New Dimensions in Regional Integration* (Cambridge: Cambridge University Press, 1993), pp. 28–29.
12. Bhagwati, "Regionalism and Multilateralism: An Overview," pp. 29–31.
13. In 1960, the OEEC was converted into the OECD, which also includes non-European industrial countries as members. On the U.S. role in the formation of the OEEC, see Philip E. Jacob, Alexine L. Atherton, and Arthur M. Wallenstein, *The Dynamics of International Organization* (Homewood, IL: Dorsey Press, revised edition, 1972), pp. 337–347.

14. See Joanne Gowa, "Bipolarity, Multipolarity, and Free Trade," *American Political Science Review* 83-4 (December 1989), pp. 1245–1256; Lawrence Krause, "Trade Policy in the 1990s I: Good-bye Bipolarity, Hello Regions," *The World Today* 46-5 (May 1990), pp. 83–86.

15. Hurrell, "Explaining the Resurgence of Regionalism in World Politics," pp. 341–342.

16. For one view of the troubles confronting GATT in the late 1980s and early 1990s, see Clyde V. Prestowitz, Jr., Alan Tonelson, and Robert W. Jerome, "The Last Gasp of GATTism," *Harvard Business Review* 69-2 (March-April 1991), pp. 130–138.

17. Bernard M. Hoekman and Michel M. Kostecki, *The Political Economy of the World Trading System: From GATT to WTO* (Oxford: Oxford University Press, 1995), pp. 214–216.

18. Marc L. Busch and Helen V. Milner, "The Future of the International Trading System: International Firms, Regionalism, and Domestic Politics," in Richard Stubbs and Geoffrey R. D. Underhill, eds., *Political Economy and the Changing Global Order* (Toronto: McClelland & Stewart, 1994), p. 270.

19. Duncan Cameron, "Introduction," in Duncan Cameron and Mel Watkins, eds., *Canada Under Free Trade* (Toronto: Lorimer, 1993), p. xxi.

20. Quoted in Dean Acheson, *Present at the Creation: My Years in the State Department* (New York: Norton, 1969), p. 30.

21. General Agreement on Tariffs and Trade, *Text of the General Agreement* (Geneva: GATT, July, 1986), Article 24; Richard Gibb and Wieslaw Michalak, eds., *Continental Trading Blocs: The Growth of Regionalism in the World Economy* (Chichester, UK: Wiley, 1994), pp. 7–9.

22. See R. G. Lipsey and Kelvin Lancaster, "The General Theory of Second Best," *The Review of Economic Studies* 24-1 (1956–57), pp. 11–32; and J. E. Meade, *Trade and Welfare* (London: Oxford University Press, 1955).

23. The terms *trade creation* and *trade diversion* were actually coined by Jacob Viner *after* GATT Article 24 was written. However, these terms clearly summarize the intent of Article 24. See Jacob Viner, *The Customs Union Issue* (New York: Carnegie Endowment for International Peace, 1950), pp. 41–55.

24. Hoekman and Kostecki, *The Political Economy of the World Trading System*, pp. 216–226.

25. Robert Z. Lawrence, *Regionalism, Multilateralism, and Deeper Integration* (Washington, DC: Brookings Institution, 1996), pp. 41–42.

26. Gardner Patterson, *Discrimination in International Trade, The Policy Issues: 1945–1965* (Princeton, NJ: Princeton University Press, 1966), pp. 146–147. See also C. Michael Aho, "More Bilateral Trade Agreements Would Be a Blunder: What the New President Should Do," *Cornell International Law Journal* 22-1 (Winter 1989), p. 25.

27. Despite the "substantially all trade" requirement, GATT has occasionally granted waivers for sectoral free trade agreements. Notable examples were waivers for the European Coal and Steel Community in 1952 and for the Canada-U.S. Auto Pact in 1965.

28. Bhagwati, "Regionalism and Multilateralism: An Overview," pp. 25–26.

29. Hoekman and Kostecki, *The Political Economy of the World Trading System*, p. 218; World Trade Organization Secretariat, *Regionalism and the World Trading System*, p. 7.

30. Robert E. Hudec, *The GATT Legal System and World Trade Diplomacy* (New York: Praeger, 1975), pp. 195–196; J. Michael Finger, "GATT's Influence on Regional Arrangements," in Melo and Panagariya, eds., *New Dimensions in Regional Integration*, pp. 136–37.

31. World Trade Organization Secretariat, *Regionalism and the World Trading System*, pp. 12–13.

32. Robert E. Hudec, "Discussion," in Melo and Panagariya, eds., *New Dimensions in Regional Integration*, p. 152.

33. Gary Clyde Hufbauer and Jeffrey J. Schott, *NAFTA: An Assessment* (Washington, DC: Institute for International Economics, revised edition, October 1993), p. 112.

34. The only two active agreements which GATT working parties approved are the Caribbean Community and Common Market (CARICOM) and the Czech and Slovak Republics Customs Union.

35. World Trade Organization Secretariat, *Regionalism and the World Trading System*, pp. 16–17; Jeffrey J. Schott, "More Free Trade Areas?" in Jeffrey J. Schott, ed., *Free Trade Areas and U.S. Trade Policy* (Washington, DC: Institute for International Economics, 1989), pp. 24–25.

36. Enzo R. Grilli, *The European Community and the Developing Countries* (Cambridge: Cambridge University Press, 1993), pp. 7–8.

37. Patterson, *Discrimination in International Trade*, p. 234; Desmond Dinan, *Ever Closer Union? An Introduction to the European Community* (Boulder, CO: Rienner, 1994), p. 457.

38. "European Economic Community—Association Agreements: Report of Working Party adopted on 4 April 1966," in General Agreement on Tariffs and Trade, *Basic Instruments and Selected Documents*, 14th supplement (Geneva: GATT, July 1966), pp. 105–106.

39. "EU, G-5 Consult on Bananas," *Bridges Weekly Trade News Digest*, vol. 2, no. 36, September 21, 1998, pp. 1–2. Marjorie Lister, *The European Community and the Developing World: The Role of the Lomé Convention* (Aldershot, UK: Avebury, 1988), p. 61; L. Alan Winters, "Expanding EC Membership and Association Accords: Recent Experience and Future Prospects," in Kym Anderson and Richard Blackhurst, eds., *Regional Integration and the Global Trading System* (Hertfordshire, UK: Harvester Wheatsheaf, 1993), pp. 117–119; Grilli, *The European Community and the Developing Countries*, pp. 11–14.

40. Hudec, *The GATT Legal System and World Trade Diplomacy*, pp. 205–206; John H. Jackson, *World Trade and the Law of GATT* (Indianapolis, IN: Bobbs-Merrill, 1969), pp. 590–591. Jackson notes that the Havana Charter had a special article for regional agreements among LDCs, which was not incorporated into the GATT.

41. World Trade Organization Secretariat, *Regionalism and the World Trading System*, pp. 18–19; Hoekman and Kostecki, *The Political Economy of the World Trading System*, pp. 219–221.

42. See Gustavo del Castillo V., "NAFTA and the Struggle for Neoliberalism: Mexico's Elusive Quest for First World Status," in Otero, ed., *Neoliberalism Revisited*, pp. 27–42.

43. World Trade Organization Secretariat, *Regionalism and the World Trading System*, pp. 27–29.

44. Grilli, *The European Community and the Developing Countries*, pp. 296–316.

45. Quoted in "Arguments for Enlargement," *The Economist*, August 3, 1996, p. 41.

46. Pier Carlo Padoan, "The Changing European Political Economy," in Stubbs and Underhill, eds., *Political Economy and the Changing Global Order*, pp. 340–342.

47. The 10 countries are Poland, Hungary, the Czech Republic, Slovakia, Bulgaria, Romania, Estonia, Latvia, Lithuania, and Slovenia.

48. Haus, *Globalizing the GATT*, p. 66; "Arguments for Enlargement," pp. 41–42; "Slicing the EU's Shrinking Cake," *The Economist*, March 21, 1998, pp. 57–58.

49. World Trade Organization Secretariat, *Regionalism and the World Trading System*, pp. 31–33.

50. Andrew Moravcsik, "Negotiating the Single European Act," in Robert O. Keohane and Stanley Hoffmann, eds., *The New European Community: Decisionmaking and Institutional Change* (Boulder, CO: Westview Press, 1991), p. 41.

51. Stephen George, "The European Union, 1992 and the Fear of 'Fortress Europe,'" in Andrew Gamble and Anthony Payne, eds., *Regionalism and World Order* (New York: St. Martin's Press, 1996), pp. 26–28; Lawrence, *Regionalism, Multilateralism, and Deeper Integration*, pp. 45–47.

52. See J. J. Servan-Schreiber, *The American Challenge,* translated from the French by Ronald Steel (New York: Atheneum, 1979). The book was first published in 1967.

53. L. Alan Winters, "The European Community: A Case of Successful Integration?" in Melo and Panagariya, eds., *New Dimensions in Regional Integration,* p. 208.

54. J. M. C. Rollo, "The EC, European Integration and the World Trading System," in Vincent Cable and David Henderson, eds., *Trade Blocs? The Future of Regional Integration* (London: Royal Institute of International Affairs, 1994), pp. 57–58.

55. See Stephen R. Sleigh, "The Social Dimensions of Economic Integration," in Jo Marie Griesgraber and Bernhard G. Gunter, eds., *World Trade: Toward Fair and Free Trade in the Twenty-first Century* (London: Pluto Press, 1997), pp. 40–44.

56. Ralph I. Onwuka, "Beyond Lomé III: Prospects for Symmetrical EurAfrican Relations," in Ralph I. Onwuka and Timothy M. Shaw, eds., *Africa in World Politics: Into the 1990s* (London: Macmillan, 1989), pp. 83–84; Mahler, "The Lomé Convention," pp. 244–248.

57. J. L. Granatstein, "Free Trade Between Canada and the United States," in Dennis Stairs and Gilbert R. Winham, eds., *The Politics of Canada's Economic Relationship with the United States,* Royal Commission on the Economic Union and Development Prospect for Canada, (Toronto: University of Toronto Press, 1985) vol. 29, p. 11.

58. "U.S. Trade Act of 1974, as amended (Public Law 93-618)," Title VI, section 612, in *Legislation on Foreign Relations Through 1989* (Washington, DC: U.S. Government Printing Office, 1990), p. 456.

59. For a detailed discussion of the U.S. proposals, see Theodore Cohn, "Canadian and Mexican Trade Policies Towards the United States: A Perspective from Canada," in John Curtis and David Haglund, eds., *Canada and International Trade* (Montreal: Institute for Research on Public Policy, 1985), vol. 1, pp. 7–17. See also U.S. Congress, Senate Committee on Finance, *North American Economic Interdependence: Vols. I and II,* Hearings before the Subcommittee on International Trade of the Committee on Finance, 96th Congress, 1st Session, June 6 and October 1, 1979 (Washington, DC: U.S. Government Printing Office, 1979).

60. See Gilbert R. Winham, "Why Canada Acted," in William Diebold, Jr., ed., *Bilateralism, Multilateralism and Canada in U.S. Trade Policy* (Cambridge, MA: Ballinger, 1988), pp. 41–46; Lawrence, *Regionalism, Multilateralism, and Deeper Integration*, pp. 67–68; and Helleiner, "Considering U.S.-Mexico Free Trade," pp. 47–48.

61. John Whalley, "Regional Trade Arrangements in North America: CUSTA and NAFTA," in Melo and Panagariya, eds., *New Dimensions in Regional Integration,* pp. 352–353.

62. Debra P. Steger, *A Concise Guide to the Canada-United States Free Trade Agreement* (Toronto: Carswell, 1988), p. 74; Lawrence, *Regionalism, Multilateralism, and Deeper Integration*, pp. 62–65.

63. Hoekman and Kostecki, *The Political Economy of the World Trading System,* p. 131; Lawrence, *Regionalism, Multilateralism, and Deeper Integration*, pp. 69–72.

64. Barry Appleton, *Navigating NAFTA* (Scarborough, ONT.: Carswell, 1994), pp. 135–137.
65. See Harold Hongju Koh, "The Fast Track and United States Trade Policy," *Brooklyn Journal of International Law* 18 (1992), pp. 143–180; Gary Clyde Hufbauer and Jeffrey J. Schott, *Western Hemisphere Economic Integration* (Washington, DC: Institute for International Economics, July 1994).
66. Hufbauer and Schott, NAFTA: *An Assessment*, pp. 112–113.
67. Helleiner, "Considering U.S.-Mexico Free Trade," pp. 50–51.
68. Robert W. Cox, *Production, Power, and World Order: Social Forces in the Making of History* (New York: Columbia University Press, 1987), p. 345; Ricardo Grinspun and Robert Kreklewich, "Consolidating Neoliberal Reforms: 'Free Trade' as a Conditioning Framework," *Studies in Political Economy* 43 (Spring 1994), p. 45.
69. Herman E. Daly, "Free Trade: The Perils of Deregulation," in Jerry Mander and Edward Goldsmith, eds., *The Case Against the Global Economy: For a Turn Toward the Local* (San Francisco: Sierra Club, 1996), p. 234.
70. Mark E. Rupert, "(Re) Politicizing the Global Economy: Liberal Common Sense and Ideological Struggle in the US NAFTA Debate," *Review of International Political Economy* 2-4 (Autumn 1995), pp. 679–681.
71. Soogil Young, "East Asia as a Regional Force for Globalism," in Anderson and Blackhurst, eds., *Regional Integration and the Global Trading System*, pp. 127–128.
72. Miles Kahler, *International Institutions and the Political Economy of Integration* (Washington, DC: Brookings Institution, 1995), pp. 107–108.
73. Lawrence, *Regionalism, Multilateralism, and Deeper Integration*, pp. 80–83.
74. Lawrence, *Regionalism, Multilateralism, and Deeper Integration*, pp. 83–86.
75. Young, "East Asia as a Regional Force for Globalism," p. 134; Lawrence, *Regionalism, Multilateralism, and Deeper Integration*, p. 79; Kahler, *International Institutions and the Political Economy of Integration*, p. 112.
76. Richard Higgott and Richard Stubbs, "Competing Conceptions of Economic Regionalism: APEC Versus EAEC in the Asia Pacific," *Review of International Political Economy* 2-3 (Summer 1995), p. 518.
77. Fred Bergsten, "The Case for APEC," *The Economist*, January 6, 1996, p. 62; Shuji Miyazaki, "APEC: The First Seven Years and the Road to Manila," *World Economic Affairs* 1-1 (Summer 1996), p. 20.
78. Gary Hufbauer and Jeffrey J. Schott, "Toward Free Trade and Investment in the Asia-Pacific," in Brad Roberts, ed., *New Forces in the World Economy* (Cambridge, MA: MIT Press, 1996), pp. 217–218.
79. Hufbauer and Schott, "Toward Free Trade and Investment in the Asia-Pacific," pp. 219–220.
80. Higgott and Stubbs, "Competing Conceptions of Economic Regionalism," pp. 522–526; David Arase, "Japan in East Asia," in Tsuneo Akaha and Frank Langdon, eds., *Japan in the Posthegemonic World* (Boulder, CO: Rienner, 1993), pp. 131–132.
81. Bergsten, "The Case for APEC," p. 63.
82. Glenn Hook, "Japan and the Construction of Asia-Pacific," in Gamble and Payne, eds., *Regionalism and World Order*, p. 193.
83. Walter Hatch and Kozo Yamamura, *Asia in Japan's Embrace: Building a Regional Production Alliance* (Cambridge: Cambridge University Press, 1996), p. 36.
84. Grinspun and Kreklewich, "Consolidating Neoliberal Reforms," p. 41.

85. Ralph Nader, "Introduction: Free Trade and the Decline of Democracy," in *The Case Against 'Free Trade': GATT, NAFTA, and the Globalization of Corporate Power* (San Francisco: Earth Island Press, 1993), p. 6.
86. Hatch and Yamamura, Asia in Japan's *Embrace,* chs. 1 and 2; Gary Gereffi, "Mexico's 'Old' and 'New' Maquiladora Industries: Contrasting Approaches to North American Integration," in Gerardo Otero, ed., *Neo-Liberalism Revisited: Economic Restructuring and Mexico's Political Future* (Boulder, CO: Westview Press, 1996), p. 96.
87. Renato Ruggiero, Director General of the World Trade Organization, "Charting the Trade Routes of the Future: Towards a Borderless Economy," address delivered to the International Industrial Conference, San Francisco, September 29, 1997, *World Trade Organization Press Release* (Geneva; Press/77), p. 4.

Multinational Corporations and Global Production

The largest multinational corporations are in many respects the main agents of globalization. The MNCs produce and distribute goods and services across national boundaries; they spread ideas, tastes, and technology throughout the world; and they plan their operations on a global scale. MNCs are most commonly considered to be firms that control productive assets in more than one country. Parent firms in the home countries of MNCs acquire their foreign assets by investing in affiliate or subsidiary firms in host countries. This type of investment involves management rights and control and is referred to as *foreign direct investment (FDI)*. *Portfolio investment,* by contrast, is investment without control; that is, it involves the purchase of foreign stocks, bonds, and money market instruments simply for the purpose of realizing a financial return.

The growing presence of MNCs in the world economy testifies to their role as agents of globalization. By 1988, there were about 19,000 MNCs, which accounted for 25 to 30 percent of the GDP of all market economies and for 80 percent of the trade in managerial and technology skills. Despite variations in different years, FDI has generally increased more rapidly than trade. From 1973 to 1995, annual FDI outflows multiplied more than 12 times (from $25 billion to $315 billion) while the value of merchandise exports multiplied by 8.5 times. Today, about a third of total world trade consists of intrafirm trade within MNCs, another third consists of MNC exports to nonaffiliates, and the remaining third consists of trade among national (that is, non-MNC) firms.[1]

The growing importance of MNCs has caused some analysts to argue that the critical problem in the study of IPE today "is the tension between states and multinationals, not states and markets."[2] Nevertheless, MNCs do not receive as much attention in the IPE literature as one might expect; many international relations theorists continue to place primary emphasis on relations among governments. A major obstacle to the study of multinationals is the limited amount of reliable data. As private enterprises, MNCs are reluctant to provide information about themselves, and they are particularly adept at obscuring their activities. This problem is compounded by the fact that no international organization oversees foreign investment activities the way organizations monitor monetary relations, trade, and development assistance. Furthermore, the study of MNCs is highly controversial, and analysts' views of "the facts" are often colored by their general perspective. Thus, it is not uncommon in public debates on MNCs for "anecdote to replace data" and for "the witty phrase to replace analysis."[3]

Liberals, realists, and historical structuralists have differing views regarding both the power of multinationals and their impact on states and societies. Liberal theorists often maintain that the mobility of MNCs gives them a major advantage over national governments, which are bound to specific territories. In the current age of interdependence, MNCs and private banks have therefore become "the major weavers of the world economy."[4] Historical structuralists also refer to the growing power of MNCs, but unlike liberals they argue that corporate managers constitute a transnational class that maintains and defends the capitalist system. Thus, writers from this perspective often assert that managers of major corporations have a predominant influence over the conduct of U.S. foreign policy.[5] Realists, by contrast, argue that the power of states over multinationals has not decreased and that MNCs retain close ties with their home governments. MNCs would not be able to expand their activities, according to realists, without the support of the most powerful states.[6]

While liberals and historical structuralists agree that the influence of MNCs has increased, they strongly differ over the effects of this change. Many liberals believe that FDI contributes to increased efficiency in the use of the world's resources by stimulating innovation, competition, economic growth, and employment. MNCs also provide countries with numerous benefits, such as capital, technology, managerial skills, and marketing networks. Historical structuralists, by contrast, view MNCs as predatory monopolists that overcharge for their goods and services, limit the flow of technology, and create dependency relationships with host countries in the Third World.[7] MNCs can also have a negative impact on home countries, critics argue, by exporting jobs and imposing downward pressures on labor and on environmental standards.

DEFINITIONS AND TERMINOLOGY

Controversy exists not only over the importance and effects of MNCs but even over definitions and terminology.[8] MNCs are usually defined as firms that control assets in at least two countries, but some writers maintain that MNCs must have more of an international presence. For example, one of the classic studies on multinationals argues that only enterprises with manufacturing subsidiaries in at least six countries are "entitled to" the MNC label.[9] Those who favor more restrictive definitions of this type believe that the most important investment issues relate to the largest firms, which establish a number of foreign affiliates as part of a global strategy. However, restrictive definitions are often problematic because they exclude enterprises on a rather arbitrary basis. This chapter therefore adopts the more expansive definition of MNCs as firms that operate in two or more countries. An enterprise is of course not an MNC simply because it does business in more than one country. To qualify as an MNC, a firm must possess at least one FDI project in which it has management rights or control. FDI is of two types: the creation of new productive assets by foreigners, which is referred to as *greenfield investment;* and the purchase of stocks in an existing firm by foreigners with the purpose of participating in its management.

Although the definition of FDI may appear to be straightforward, there are differences of view over what constitutes "control." Until the 1960s, the U.S. Department of Commerce defined FDI as involving control over at least 25 percent of the equity of a foreign business, but the department subsequently lowered this figure to 10 percent. Japan also defines FDI as involving at least 10 percent equity ownership, but the minimum figures for Britain and Germany are 20 and 25 percent. In reality, the percentage of equity required for control varies in different circumstances. On the one hand, a foreign investor may gain managerial control of an enterprise by owning less than 10 percent of the stock if ownership is widely dispersed. On the other hand, 49 percent ownership may not confer control if a single individual or firm owns the other 51 percent. The important point is that a large shareholder may have considerable control over a company's operations even without holding a majority of shares.[10]

Differences exist not only over definitions but also over the use of the term *multinational corporation* itself. The United Nations and a number of scholars prefer the term *transnational* to multinational corporation because the ownership and control of most of these firms is not really multinational. Instead, a firm normally extends its operations from a single home country across national frontiers.[11] It is true that most multinationals have been *ethnocentric* or home country-oriented, with directives and advice flowing from the headquarters to the affiliates and much of the MNCs' research and development being located in the home country. Nevertheless, a small but growing number of MNCs have become more *geocentric* or *stateless;* that is, they adopt a worldwide approach and are not as closely tied to any single state. Strategic alliances among MNCs from different states further complicate the task of associating an MNC with a specific home government. These alliances can take the form of production-sharing agreements, collaborative research and networking arrangements, and other types of cooperation. Finally, host states in some cases may induce an MNC to engage in activities attuned to the hosts' requirements. For example, MNCs can sometimes gain entry into a foreign country only by agreeing to form *joint ventures* with local firms. Joint ventures involving two or more firms are becoming increasingly common in Eastern European and less developed countries.[12]

The term *transnational* accurately reflects the fact that the home country continues to be significant for most international firms. Nevertheless, the existence of geocentric firms, strategic alliances, and joint ventures demonstrates that corporations differ in the degree to which their nationality has significance. A later section of this chapter discusses the debate over competitiveness; analysts have widely differing views regarding the significance of an MNC's nationality. This text uses the more common term *multinational corporation,* simply to signify that a firm has ongoing managerial and productive activities in more than one country.[13]

WHY DO FIRMS BECOME MULTINATIONALS?

To understand why firms become multinationals, it is important to distinguish between horizontal and vertical integration. A *horizontally integrated MNC* extends its operations abroad by producing the same product or product line in its affiliates in different countries. A *vertically integrated MNC* produces goods and services at different stages of the production process; that is, the outputs of some affiliates serve as inputs to other affiliates of the MNC.

Firms often engage in **horizontal integration** to defend or increase their market shares. Although a firm's exports from the home country may initially meet the demand for products and services in a foreign market, new local suppliers might enter that market and put the firm at a competitive disadvantage. By producing in a foreign market rather than exporting to it, a firm may avoid additional costs such as transportation, and if the firm is producing for the market in a less developed country, producing directly in the LDC may lower the labor costs of production. Firms also become more attuned to the special characteristics of a foreign market by producing in it. If the foreign market is large enough, the firm may find it economically feasible to alter its goods and services to cater to consumer tastes.

Another major reason why firms engage in horizontal integration relates to policies of foreign governments. When governments impose tariff and nontariff measures that interfere with a firm's exports from its home country, the firm may respond by establishing foreign operations to "get behind" the external barriers. For example, Honda had the largest stake of the Japanese automakers in exports to the American market in the early 1980s. When the United States imposed voluntary export restraints on Japanese auto imports from 1981 to 1985, Honda responded by becoming the first Japanese car manufacturer to produce automobiles in the United States. National and subnational governments also provide direct and indirect investment incentives to encourage firms to locate production facilities in their territories. The efforts of subnational governments to attract FDI have been especially notable since the early 1970s. Only 10 U.S. states had committed budgetary resources to attracting foreign investment before 1969, but 47 states had developed active investment programs by 1979.[14]

Firms often engage in **vertical integration** to avoid uncertainty and reduce transaction costs. Instead of depending on uncertain "arm's-length transactions" with different owners at various stages of the production process, vertically integrated MNCs gain control of these transactions by *internalizing* them within the firm. Vertically integrated firms opt for *backward integration* when the raw materials and other inputs they require for production involve high transaction costs or are not readily available. Examples of such backward integration include steel firm investments in iron ore operations, oil company investments in the extraction of crude oil, and rubber manufacturer investments in natural rubber plantations. Backward integration may also enable MNCs to gain control over the quality of inputs. It is no accident that three vertically integrated MNCs accounted for 60 percent of the export trade in bananas in the 1980s; bananas are highly perishable and require specific handling and ripening conditions. When the growers, shippers, and distributors are not vertically integrated, the independent firms at each stage of the production process have more incentive to compromise quality control. The motivations for *forward vertical integration* are similar to those for backward integration: to reduce uncertainty and transaction costs and to ensure the quality of goods and services that reach the consumer.[15]

Another reason why firms engage in vertical integration is to limit competition. When a small number of MNCs control the inputs such as raw materials for a particular industry, they can impose substantial barriers to the entry of new rival firms. As private firms, MNCs also engage in vertical integration to limit the scrutiny of their activities by nation-states. For example, MNCs sometimes manipulate their transfer prices without detection by governments. **Transfer prices** are the prices that affiliates of an MNC charge each other for the internal sales of goods and services. Transfer prices help the MNC to efficiently manage its internal operations and to monitor the performance of its affiliates. However, an MNC can shift its reported profits from high-tax to low-tax countries (and thus avoid paying some taxes) by artificially raising or lowering the prices each affiliate charges. In 1993, for example, the U.S. Internal Revenue Service ruled that Nissan Motor Company had used transfer prices to seriously underreport its income in the United States, and Nissan was required to pay about $150 million to the United States.[16]

Firms that become multinationals must have the ability as well as the incentive to make this transition. Innovations in communications, transportation, and technology have enabled firms to internationalize their production more easily. Firms are also likely to multinationalize successfully if they benefit both from entering the global marketplace and from operating within nation-states, by "thinking globally" and "acting locally."[17] On the one hand, MNCs operate in a world of nation-states in which they must cater to the demands and tastes of local consumers and adhere to national laws. On the other hand, large MNCs have numerous advantages resulting from their worldwide presence, such as economies of scale, access to global financing, special access to raw materials and other inputs, and the reputation of their brand names.

THE HISTORICAL DEVELOPMENT OF FOREIGN DIRECT INVESTMENT

Although the rapid expansion of MNCs is a post–World War II phenomenon, FDI and MNCs have a much longer history.[18] Some scholars trace the origins of the MNC to the transborder business operations of medieval banks such as the Medici bank in fifteenth-century Florence. In the sixteenth through eighteenth centuries, international trading companies such as the English, Dutch, and French East India Companies and the Hudson's Bay Company coordinated large amounts of cross-border business activity. In the nineteenth century, firms that we commonly consider to be MNCs became involved in more sustained, longer-term investments in a wider array of activities and countries. Thousands of these MNCs existed by the time of World War II.

Despite the general growth of MNCs and FDI over time, a number of factors have affected the rapidity of growth—and sometimes the contraction—of MNC activity in different time periods. First, MNC activity has increased more rapidly during periods of major advances in communications, transportation, and technology. These advances have facilitated the establishment and expansion of MNC control over foreign operations. Second, periods of rapid economic growth have often stimulated the expansion of MNCs, while depressed economic conditions have had the opposite effect. Third, MNCs have expanded their operations more rapidly when national governments and the international system have been receptive to such activity. Internationally, for example, the development of rules governing private property encouraged FDI, while major wars had a depressing effect. Fourth, FDI has increased more rapidly during periods of capital liberalization, while capital and exchange controls have discouraged such activity. Finally, it is ironic that FDI has often expanded during periods of trade protectionism because MNCs have shifted production abroad to circumvent the trade barriers.[19] The historical discussion that follows is divided into three broad periods: before World War II, from the mid-1940s to the mid-1980s, and since the mid-1980s.

The Period Before World War II

Most economists traditionally maintained that long-term capital flows in the nineteenth and early twentieth centuries were composed mainly of portfolio investment rather than FDI. However, data on foreign investment flows for this early period were extremely limited, and there was confusion over how investments should be categorized. As economists refined their definitions, they concluded that direct investment accounted for a greater share of total foreign investment than was earlier assumed. Indeed, some studies estimate that FDI accounted for as much as 45 percent of British foreign investment in 1913–14.[20]

As the first country to industrialize and the global hegemon, Britain was the main force behind the dramatic growth of FDI in the nineteenth century. Although there were no government guarantees or international institutions to provide safeguards, investments were fairly secure for several major reasons. First, economic risk was lower under the pre–World War I gold standard because currencies were convertible, dividends could be easily remitted, and exchange rates were reasonably stable. Second, political risk was lower because a large share of European investment was in colonial territories that operated under home country rules. Third, the lack of restrictions on capital flows facilitated the growth of FDI. And fourth, wars during this period were limited in scope. The nineteenth century was also a period of rapid advances in rail and sea transport and communications (for example, the telegraph), which facilitated the task of managing FDI over long distances.[21]

As Table 10.1 shows, British firms were clearly the leading source of FDI before World War II, accounting for 45 percent of the total in 1914 and 40 percent in 1938. Although the United States was an important host country for European FDI in the nineteenth century, it was also beginning to establish its own multinationals. The first major U.S. manufacturing MNC was the Singer Manufacturing Company, which had plants in four countries by the 1880s; and resource-based U.S. firms such as Standard Oil Company also established extensive offshore operations. Thus, Table 10.1 shows that U.S. share of outward FDI increased dramatically from 14 percent in 1914 to 28

TABLE 10.1

SHARE OF OUTWARD STOCK OF FDI
(PERCENTAGES)

	1914	1938
Britain	45	40
United States	14	28
Germany	14	1
France	11	9
Netherlands	5	10
Other Western Europe	5	3
Rest of world	6	9

Source: Geoffrey Jones, *The Evolution of International Business: An Introduction,* pp. 30, 42. Copyright © 1996 by Geoffrey Jones. First published 1996 by Routledge. By permission of International Thomas Publishing Services Ltd.

percent in 1938. Western Europe and the United States accounted for more than 90 percent of outward FDI before World War II.

Table 10.2 shows that in marked contrast to the home countries for FDI, the largest recipients of FDI in 1914 and 1938 were LDCs in Latin America and Asia. Indeed, 63 percent of the world's FDI was directed to Latin America, Asia, and Africa in 1938. Other major recipients were the United States and Canada. While most of the FDI in manufacturing was concentrated in Western Europe and North America, the FDI in less developed countries was mainly in natural resources and services (FDI in natural resources was also directed to Eastern Europe, Canada, and the United States).[22]

The rapid growth of FDI in the nineteenth century continued into the twentieth century and the interwar period. After World War I, however, foreign investment was hindered by the increase in global economic and political instability. For example, a number of host countries began to impose restrictions on inward FDI, the Soviet

TABLE 10.2

SHARE OF INWARD STOCK OF FDI
(PERCENTAGES)

	1914	1938
Latin America	33	31
Asia	21	25
United States	10	7
Eastern Europe	10	2
Western Europe	8	7
Canada	6	10
Africa	6	7
Rest of world	6	11

Source: Geoffrey Jones, *The Evolution of International Business: An Introduction,* pp. 31, 43. Copyright © 1996 by Geoffrey Jones. First published 1996 by Routledge. By permission of International Thomas Publishing Services Ltd.

Union nationalized foreign property, and the gold exchange standard was suspended. As a result of the Great Depression and World War II, there was a severe contraction in MNC activities. Indeed, MNCs accounted for a much smaller share of world economic activity in 1949 than in 1929. It was not until after World War II that the vigorous growth of multinational corporations and FDI would resume.[23]

The Mid-1940s to the Mid-1980s

Britain was the leading source of FDI in the nineteenth and early twentieth centuries, but U.S. multinationals took over the mantle of leadership after World War II. As Table 10.3 shows, U.S. firms accounted for over one-half (53.8%) of outward stocks of FDI in 1967. Under U.S. leadership, FDI entered a period of rapid expansion because of several changes in the postwar period. First, the industrial states experienced a sustained period of economic growth from 1950 to 1973, which was conducive to the expansion of MNC activity. Second, there were major improvements in international transportation and communications: faster jet and ocean transport, telex and satellite communications, and the fax machine all made contributions to the flow of capital. Third, most industrial states relaxed their controls over FDI after the return to convertibility of their currencies. (A notable exception was Japan, which continued to restrict foreign investment flows.)

Although U.S. MNCs accounted for the predominant share of FDI in the postwar period, their share of global investment has declined steadily since the late 1960s. A major reason for the decline in U.S. share was rapid economic growth in Japan, Germany, and other Western European countries as they recovered from the war. Thus, Table 10.3 shows that the U.S. share of total outward stocks of FDI fell from 53.8 percent in 1967 to 36.6 percent in 1985, while Japan's share rose from 1.4 to 6.5 percent and West Germany's share rose from 2.8 to 8.7 percent. Table 10.3 also shows that almost all the outward FDI flows in the postwar period have come from the developed market economies (99 percent in 1960 and 96.9 percent in 1985). Nevertheless, MNCs based in Third World countries increased their share of outward FDI from only 1 percent in 1960 to about 3 percent in 1985. Most of this foreign investment came from OPEC states and from more prosperous LDCs in Asia and Latin America.

Table 10.4 shows that while the U.S. share of outward FDI was declining after the late 1960s, the U.S. share of inward stocks of FDI increased from 11.2 percent in 1975 to 25.1 percent in 1985. Of the industrial states, only Japan maintained an extremely low share of inward FDI, which remained at 0.6 percent in 1985, largely because of governmental, societal, and cultural factors that limited investment flows. Thus, the developed market economies were the largest recipients as well as providers of FDI, accounting for about 75 percent of inward stocks in the 1975–85 period. Although Third World countries had received well over 60 percent of total FDI before World War II, this figure fell to about 30 percent in the postwar period as FDI activities shifted from primary products to manufacturing. From the mid-1970s, the Third World's share of inward FDI declined even further to about 25 percent because of LDC demands for more control over their natural resources, growing LDC external debts, and an increase in technology-related investment in the developed states.

TABLE 10.3
Outward Stocks of FDI, the Group of Seven (billions of U.S. dollars)

	1960 Value	%	1967 Value	%	1975 Value	%	1980 Value	%	1985 Value	%	1990 Value	%	1995[a] Value	%
United States	31.9	47.1	56.6	53.8	124.2	44.0	220.2	42.9	251.0	36.6	435.2	25.8	705.6	25.8
Japan	0.5	0.7	1.5	1.4	15.9	5.7	18.8	3.7	44.3	6.5	204.7	12.2	305.5	11.2
Germany (Federal Republic)	0.8	1.2	3.0	2.8	18.4	6.5	43.1	8.4	59.9	8.7	151.6	9.0	235.0	8.6
Britain	12.4	18.3	17.5	16.6	37.0	13.1	80.4	15.7	100.3	14.6	230.8	13.7	319.0	11.7
France	4.1	6.1	6.0	5.7	10.6	3.8	23.6	4.6	37.1	5.4	110.1	6.5	200.9	7.4
Italy	1.1	1.6	2.1	2.0	3.3	1.2	7.3	1.4	16.3	2.4	56.1	3.3	86.7	3.2
Canada	2.5	3.7	3.7	3.5	10.4	3.7	22.6	4.4	40.9	6.0	78.9	4.7	110.4	4.0
Total G-7[b]	53.3	78.7	90.4	85.8	219.8	77.9	416.0	81.0	549.8	81.0	1267.4	75.3	1963.1	71.9
Total DMEs[c]	67.0	99.0	—	—	275.4	97.7	507.5	98.8	664.2	96.9	1614.6	95.9	2514.3	92.1
Total	67.7	100.0	105.3	100.0	282.0	100.0	513.7	100.0	685.6	100.0	1684.1	100.0	2730.1	100.0

[a]Preliminary figures
[b]G-7 = Group of Seven
[c]DMEs = developed market economies

Source: Centre on Transnational Corporations, *Transnational Corporations in World Development: Trends and Prospects* (New York: United Nations, 1988), Table 1.2, p. 24 (1960 and 1975 figures); UN Economic and Social Council, Commission on International Corporations, *International Corporations in World Development: A Re-Examination*, E/C. 10/38 (New York: United Nations, 1978), Table III-32, p. 236 (1967 figures); United Nations Conference on Trade and Development. *World Investment Report—1996* (New York: United Nations, 1996), Annex Table 4, p. 245–247 (1980–95 figures).

TABLE 10.4
INWARD STOCKS OF FDI (BILLIONS OF U.S. DOLLARS)

	1975		1980		1985		1990		1995[a]	
	Value	%	Value	%	Value	%	Value	%	Value	%
DMEs[b]	185.3	75.1	373.5	77.5	538.0	73.2	1373.3	80.0	1932.7	72.7
Western Europe	100.6	40.8	200.3	41.6	244.8	33.3	758.7	44.2	1087.6	40.9
United States	27.7	11.2	83.0	17.2	184.6	25.1	394.9	23.0	564.6	21.2
Japan	1.5	0.6	3.3	0.7	4.7	0.6	9.9	0.6	17.8	0.7
Other	57.0	23.1	86.9	18.0	103.9	14.1	209.8	12.2	262.7	9.9
LDCs[c]	61.5	24.9	108.3	22.5	196.8	26.8	341.7	19.9	693.3	26.1
Africa	16.5	6.7	20.8	4.3	27.0	3.7	41.6	2.4	59.6	2.2
Asia	13.0	5.3	38.0	7.9	91.8	12.5	175.9	10.2	403.3	15.2
Latin America and Caribbean	29.7	12.0	48.0	10.0	76.3	10.4	121.3	7.1	225.8	8.5
Other	2.3	0.0	1.5	0.3	1.7	0.2	2.9	0.2	4.6	0.2
Central and Eastern Europe	—	—	0.09	0.0	0.2	0.0	1.8	0.1	31.8	1.2
Total	246.8	100.0	481.9	100.0	734.9	100.0	1716.9	100.0	2657.9	100.0

[a]Preliminary figures; [b]DMEs = developed market economies; [c]LDCs = less developed countries.

Source: Centre on Transnational Corporations, *Transnational Corporations in World Development: Trends and Prospects* (New York: United Nations, 1988), Table 1.3, p. 25 (1975 figures); UN Conference on Trade and Development, *World Investment Report 1996* (New York: United Nations, 1996), Annex Table 3, pp. 239–243 (1980–95 figures).

Among the Third World countries, the most prosperous and resource-rich states received by far the most FDI. Thus, Table 10.4 shows that the share of FDI directed to Africa, which contains many of the least developed countries, declined from 6.7 percent in 1975 to only 3.7 percent in 1985. Asian and Latin American LDCs, by contrast, were receiving 12.5 and 10.4 percent of total inward FDI stocks in 1985 (the decline of the Latin American share from 12 percent in 1975 was partly due to the foreign debt crisis). Almost no FDI was directed to the Central and Eastern European socialist states (including the Soviet Union) during the 1975–85 period. By the mid-1980s most FDI was occurring among the developed market economies, and the LDCs had become increasingly marginalized.

The 1980s to the Present

The average annual growth rate of FDI rose in the 1980s to about 14 percent, the fastest growth rate since the late nineteenth century. Thus, Table 10.5 shows that inward and outward FDI as a share of the GDPs of the developed market economies increased dramatically, from 4.8 and 6.5 percent in 1980 to 8.6 and 11.2 percent in 1994. A number of factors account for the rapid growth of FDI since the early 1980s. Most importantly, with the reemergence of orthodox liberalism, many of the restrictions on international business were phased out. An end to restrictions on capital flows, along with deregulation and privatization in many developed and less developed countries, gave MNCs more freedom to expand their activities. Furthermore, the shift of the emerging countries to market-oriented reforms after the breakup of the Soviet bloc opened up large new areas for FDI. Another factor in the expansion of FDI was the problems with international trade. The protracted Uruguay round negotiations, combined with the use of nontariff barriers, caused many MNCs to extend their activities abroad. Finally, further significant advances in information and transportation technologies enabled MNCs to extend their global network.[24]

Several changes in the nature of FDI in the 1980s and 1990s are especially noteworthy. First, the United States lost its dominant position as a source of FDI. As Table 10.3 shows, the U.S. share of outward stocks of FDI fell from 42.9 percent in 1980 to 25.8 percent in 1990. Second, Japan joined the United States and the European Union as a major source of FDI. Until the late 1970s, FDI originated primarily from Western Europe and North America, but starting in the 1980s, a triad (including Japan) accounted for the greatest share of FDI flows. A strong Japanese yen after 1985, combined with rising trade barriers such as voluntary export restraints on Japanese goods, forced Japanese corporations to invest and produce more abroad. Thus, Table 10.3 shows that Japan's share of outward stocks of FDI increased from 6.5 percent in 1985 to 11.2 percent in 1995. Despite the impressive growth of Japanese outward FDI, however, this was largely a catch-up phenomenon. Japan's outward FDI stock accounted for only 6.2 percent of its GDP in 1994, the lowest percentage of any country in the Group of Seven.[25]

A remarkable feature of FDI today is the degree to which the "Big Three"—the United States, the European Union, and Japan—are directing their FDI to each other. U.S. firms have shown a strong preference for investing in Europe, intra-European investment has accelerated, and Japan and Western European countries have invested

TABLE 10.5

SHARE OF INWARD AND OUTWARD FDI STOCK
AS A PERCENTAGE OF GDP

	1980	1985	1990	1995
DMEs[a]				
Inward	4.8	6.0	8.4	8.6
Outward	6.5	7.5	9.8	11.2
United States				
Inward	3.1	4.6	7.2	7.5
Outward	8.1	6.2	7.9	9.1
Japan				
Inward	0.3	0.4	0.3	0.4
Outward	1.8	3.3	7.0	6.2
Germany				
Inward	4.5	6.0	7.4	6.8
Outward	5.3	9.7	10.1	10.9
Britain				
Inward	11.7	14.0	22.3	20.9
Outward	14.9	21.9	23.6	27.5
France				
Inward	3.4	6.4	7.2	10.7
Outward	3.6	7.1	9.2	13.8
Italy				
Inward	2.0	4.5	5.3	5.9
Outward	1.6	3.8	5.1	8.2
Canada				
Inward	20.4	18.5	19.7	19.2
Outward	8.5	11.7	13.7	19.2

[a]DMEs = developed market economies.

Source: World Investment Report 1996, Annex Table 6, pp. 261–262. Copyright © by the United Nations, 1996. The United Nations is the author of the original materials, and material used with permission of the United Nations Publications.

heavily in the United States. Until the late 1970s, Western European integration occurred largely through the expansion of trade, but in the 1980s the growth of intra-European FDI was more significant than the growth of trade. Table 10.6 shows that the nine largest host countries for FDI from 1985 to 1995 were also included among the largest home countries for FDI, and all but one of these nine (China) is an advanced industrial state.[26] The only important home country for FDI that is not also an important host country is Japan. Although Japan has eased some of its formal impediments to inward FDI, a number of informal barriers remain. As shown in Table 10.4, Japan accounted for only 0.7 percent of the total inward stocks of FDI in 1995.

Although the industrial market economies have the highest levels of both outward and inward FDI, a third development in FDI has been that some Third World countries continue to emerge as important actors. Thus, Table 10.6 shows that a small group

TABLE 10.6

LEADING HOST ECONOMIES FOR FDI
(CUMULATIVE INFLOWS, 1985–95[a]

Rank	Country	FDI (billions of dollars)
1	**United States**	477.5
2	**United Kingdom**	199.6
3	**France**	138.0
4	**China**	130.2
5	**Spain**	90.9
6	**Belgium-Luxembourg**	72.4
7	**Netherlands**	68.1
8	**Australia**	62.6
9	**Canada**	60.9
10	Mexico	44.1
11	**Singapore**	40.8
12	**Sweden**	37.7
13	**Italy**	36.3
14	Malaysia	30.7
15	**Germany**	25.9
16	**Switzerland**	25.2
17	Argentina	23.5
18	Brazil	20.3
19	**Hong Kong**	17.9
20	**Denmark**	15.7

[a]Economies in bold are also among the 20 leading home economies for FDI.

Source: World Trade Organization Annual Report 1996, Vol. 1, *Trade and Foreign Direct Investment*, p. 47, Table 4.1. Copyright © World Trade Organization 1996. By permission of the World Trade Organization.

of rapidly growing LDCs, including China, Mexico, Singapore, Malaysia, Argentina, Brazil, and Hong Kong, were included among the 20 leading host economies for FDI between 1985 and 1995. China's position is especially notable: China now accounts for over one-third of all FDI directed to the LDCs.[27] In contrast to the more prosperous LDCs, the LDCs in sub-Saharan Africa are becoming increasingly marginalized. Table 10.4 reveals that Africa accounted for only 2.2 percent of the inward stocks of FDI in 1995, compared with 15.2 percent for Asia and 8.5 percent for Latin America and the Caribbean.

A fourth development is the proliferation of firms engaging in FDI and the new forms of investment activity. Indeed, the number of MNCs headquartered in 15 major developed countries almost quadrupled between 1968 and 1993, from about 7,000 to 27,000. There has also been a marked shift in FDI from manufacturing and petroleum to service industries. Deregulation of the financial and telecommunications sectors in industrial countries and privatization in some LDCs have stimulated this shift to services. New forms of FDI involving nonequity arrangements such as joint ventures, management contracts, technology licensing, and turnkey projects have also become more important. With these nonequity investments, firms provide certain benefits such as management skills or access to technology in return for royalties, fees, or revenue from sales.[28]

Although MNCs are having a growing impact on all states, they obviously have a qualitatively different relationship with home and host states. The sections that follow therefore examine the interactions between home and host states separately. LDCs are normally host rather than home states for multinationals, so considerable discussion of host state–MNC relations is devoted to the LDCs. The discussion of home state–MNC relations is, by contrast, devoted mainly to the developed market economies.

MNCs AND HOST COUNTRY RELATIONS: THEORETICAL APPROACHES

Orthodox liberals had a highly positive view of foreign investment, which stemmed largely from liberal theories of trade. In accordance with the Heckscher-Ohlin theory (see Chapter 8), liberals assumed that countries have different factor endowments and that foreign investment flows to areas where it is most needed or in shortest supply. Thus, inward FDI provides external financing to compensate for inadequate amounts of local savings, export earnings, and foreign aid; tax revenues from MNC profits supplement local taxes; and managerial skills and technology are transferred. Orthodox liberals also viewed MNCs as performing an important role in altering traditional social attitudes and values, a change that was essential for modernization and development. Finally, some orthodox liberals posited the highly questionable assumption that MNCs operate in a perfectly competitive environment.[29]

The first major challenge to these orthodox liberal views came from two economists, Stephen Hymer and Charles Kindleberger. Hymer and Kindleberger argued that FDI cannot simply be equated with the movement of capital from the home to the host country. Instead, MNCs often get financing for FDI from other sources, including the borrowing of funds in the host country. Although FDI supporters espoused the benefits of free markets, Hymer and Kindleberger (and other writers such as Raymond Vernon) also argued that MNCs are oligopolistic by nature. An MNC lacks certain advantages that local firms possess, but it can gain competitiveness by creating an oligopolistic environment. This can be done by raising barriers to the entry of firms through the new technologies it uses, through its economies of scale, and through its privileged access to global finance. Thus, Hymer wrote that "the industries in which there is much foreign investment tend to be concentrated industries, while the industries in which there is little or no foreign investment tend to be unconcentrated."[30]

The strongest critics of the orthodox liberal perspective have been Marxists and dependency theorists. According to dependency theorists, MNCs prevent Third World states from achieving genuine autonomous development: for example, MNCs prevent local firms and entrepreneurs from participating in the most dynamic sectors of the economy; they appropriate local capital rather than bringing in new capital from the outside; they increase income inequalities in the host country; and they use inappropriate capital-intensive technologies that contribute to unemployment. MNCs also undermine the host country's government, culture, and society by co-opting local business and government elites, imposing political and economic pressures on the host country (often with the help of the MNC's home country), and altering consumer tastes and attitudes.[31] Although the newly industrialized countries in Latin America and East Asia have moved along the path to industrialization, dependency theorists believe MNCs ensure that these states do not achieve autonomous development. Thus, one study claims that MNCs in Brazil keep "the innovative side of their businesses as close to home as possible" and ensure that "the industrialization of the periphery will remain partial."[32]

Research over a period of years indicates that the effects of MNCs on host states are neither as positive nor as negative as orthodox liberal and dependency theorists maintain and that host countries often have more options than one would assume from dependency analysis. For example, one factor affecting a host state's options is the amount of competition among investors. If a host state has more investors to choose from, it has more leverage vis-à-vis each investor. Another factor affecting a host state's options is the "obsolescing bargain," which causes host state–MNC relations to change over time.[33] Before an MNC enters a country, the host government is in a weak bargaining position because the MNC can pursue other options and the host state must provide significant incentives to attract the initial investment. Thus, the initial investment agreement strongly favors the MNC. After the investment is made, however, the bargaining leverage shifts toward the host state because the MNC commits itself to immobile resources. The host state can treat these resources as a "hostage," and the host state gains bargaining, technological, and managerial skills through spinoffs from the foreign investment. As a result, the host state is likely to demand a renegotiation of the original bargain with the MNC and thereby gain more favorable terms.

A number of studies indicate that the obsolescing bargain is more applicable in some cases than in others. For example, it is more likely to apply in the case of projects that require large fixed investments. Such projects give foreign investors considerable leverage initially, but the large fixed investments can become hostage to the host government several years later. MNCs with smaller fixed investments, by contrast, can more easily threaten to withdraw from the host state. Another factor to consider is the type of technology an MNC uses for a project. Foreign investors using new technologies that are unavailable to the host state may be less vulnerable to aggressive host state policies at a later date. Yet another factor to consider is the importance of *marketing*, or product differentiation through advertising. When a firm's sales are determined to a large degree by brand identification and consumer loyalty, the firm is in a stronger position vis-à-vis the host authorities.[34]

These three factors—fixed investments, new technologies, and brand identification—have helped us to predict whether a particular industry will be subject to the obsolescing bargain. For example, the obsolescing bargain is less applicable to more sophisticated manufacturing industries, which are less dependent on resources in specific host states, rely on more advanced technologies, and manufacture differentiated products with brand names that are familiar to consumers. In contrast, the obsolescing bargain is more applicable to natural resource industries, which involve large fixed investments and familiar technologies. LDCs can more easily demand a new bargain in these cases, and it is not surprising that LDC nationalizations in the past have been more common in natural resource industries. Studies of natural resource projects confirm that host states have often been successful in their demands for higher taxes, more processing of goods, joint marketing, and the employment of local people in management.[35]

Although an MNC's investment in a host state may be subject to uncertainties resulting from the obsolescing bargain, political unrest in the host state, and other factors, the MNC can follow a variety of strategies to offset these risks. One of the most important strategies open to large MNCs is vertical integration. By placing the various stages of production in different host states and maintaining control over the different stages, the MNC can decrease its vulnerability to the actions of particular host states. Another strategy is selecting local private partners for joint ventures or other types of arrangements. Evidence indicates that MNCs can often avoid strong pressures from a host state by establishing alliances in the local private sector. When an MNC becomes more firmly established in a host state, it can also build a political base of support for itself by creating linkages with local suppliers, distributors, and consumers. One indication that MNCs have been successful in countering the risks of operating in host states is the fact that host country actions are often more circumscribed today than they were in the past. For example, there have been virtually no nationalizations of MNC affiliates in host states since the mid-1980s.

The effects of MNCs on host states are neither as positive as orthodox liberals indicate nor as negative as dependency theorists maintain. Third World host states are normally in a much weaker position vis-à-vis MNCs than advanced industrial host states. Nevertheless, host states in general have some sources of leverage in their dealings with MNCs, and MNCs can pursue a variety of counterstrategies in return.

CHANGES IN HOST COUNTRY POLICIES TOWARD MNCs

Host country policies toward MNCs have varied widely, ranging from nationalization of foreign investment operations on the one hand to efforts to attract MNCs through concessions and incentives on the other. Many governments welcome FDI in some sectors while limiting or blocking it in others (for example, in defense industries). Furthermore, some federal governments follow restrictive policies toward foreign investment at the same time as their subnational governments (for example, states or provinces) compete with each other to attract FDI.[36] Governments also often impose obligations such as performance requirements on MNCs to ensure that the host country benefits are maximized. Because there are extensive differences between LDC and developed country host policies, the following sections discuss these two groups separately.

The Less Developed Countries

Before World War I, there were very few restrictions on MNCs in the Third World. Colonial territories were of course open to foreign investment from the imperial powers, and countries that had gained their independence—for example, in Latin America—generally accepted the liberal view that foreign investment was necessary for their economic modernization and development. In the interwar period, some LDCs shifted to more nationalist policies. An event that had a major impact on Third World attitudes was Russia's nationalization of its oil industry after the Russian Revolution in 1917. (*Nationalization* or *expropriation* means the forced takeover of foreign direct investment, with or without compensation.) Although confrontations with foreign oil companies followed in Iran, Argentina, Venezuela, and Bolivia, very few LDCs actually expropriated foreign assets. Nevertheless, Mexico nationalized most of its foreign oil industry in 1938 and avoided Western retaliation, partly because of the outbreak of World War II.

After World War II, the change to restrictive policies in the Third World was far more notable. In the most extreme instances, the spread of communism to China, North Korea, North Vietnam, and Cuba resulted in the nationalization of Western assets. In other parts of the Third World, many newly independent countries viewed limits on FDI as essential to their establishment of sovereignty. Much FDI bred hostility because it involved foreign control over the LDCs' natural resources and public utilities and was often associated with the former colonial powers. Nevertheless, the ability of LDCs to pressure for a greater share of the benefits from FDI was limited because they lacked experience in dealing with MNCs, they had few alternative sources of external finance, and they were often preoccupied with security concerns. From 1946 to 1959, U.S. MNCs accounted for well over two-thirds of all new foreign-owned subsidiaries in the Third World, and LDCs had few alternative sources of FDI.[37]

In the 1960s and 1970s, several factors contributed to an increase in LDC leverage and activism vis-à-vis MNCs. The development of more non-U.S. multinationals gave the LDCs alternatives in seeking outside finance; LDCs gained more confidence and began to view MNCs as providing both costs and benefits the LDCs could manipulate; and LDCs began to develop more managerial, administrative, and technical capabilities for regulating MNC behavior. Thus, nationalization of foreign firms became widespread in the petroleum and mining industries in the late 1960s and early 1970s.[38] After OPEC succeeded in raising oil prices in 1973, LDCs also posed a major challenge to liberal-economic views of FDI in the United Nations. In the 1950s and 1960s, the liberal regime for FDI had emphasized national treatment, adequate compensation to MNCs, and the right of multinationals to seek support from their home countries. The Third World countries instead pressured for agreements that would restrict the rights of MNCs, permit discrimination between national and multinational corporations, and give host countries' legal institutions the authority to resolve investment disputes.

In the UN General Assembly, Third World views regarding MNCs were embodied in resolutions that the Group of 77 majority passed over the objections of many industrial states. For example, the 1974 Declaration on the Establishment of a New International Economic Order indicated that host states should unilaterally determine what rules to apply to MNCs operating in their territories. Although the G-77 was successful in winning approval for symbolic resolutions of this nature, it was unable to reach authoritative agreements acceptable to the advanced industrial states. For example, the G-77 failed in its efforts to reach an agreement with the industrial countries on a comprehensive code of behavior for MNCs.[39]

By the late 1970s, the LDCs shifted to more conciliatory attitudes toward MNCs, and the number of nationalizations declined for a number of reasons. First, the nationalization of large-scale petroleum and mining industries was largely completed by 1976. Second, the experience of many LDCs with nationalization of their natural resource industries was disappointing. Problems included declining productivity, failure to introduce new technologies, and continued dependence on MNCs for marketing their products. Third, the militancy of LDCs on foreign investment issues in the 1970s caused many MNCs to be reticent about investing in the Third World. Multinationals often preferred to invest in more developed countries with natural resources, such as Australia, Canada, South Africa, and the United States. Finally, the oil price increase of 1979, followed by the world recession and the 1980s foreign debt crisis, led to severe cutbacks in commercial bank lending to LDCs. Third World fears about exploitation by MNCs were therefore largely replaced by concerns that their share of inward FDI was declining.[40]

A number of LDCs significantly liberalized their policies toward MNCs in the 1980s and 1990s. Mexico, for example, unilaterally liberalized its policies toward FDI and participated in drafting the NAFTA provisions to free foreign investment activities. A number of other Latin American states, such as Argentina, Chile, Colombia, and Venezuela, also took unilateral steps to liberalize their investment policies. The most significant turnaround, however, was in the policies of the emerging centrally planned economies, especially China. Although China was largely closed to FDI in the first three decades of its existence, it passed laws in 1979, 1986, and 1988 that were more welcoming to FDI in some sectors, and it even granted foreign investors special treatment not available to domestic firms. MNCs that transfer advanced technology to China or export a substantial share of their output have received especially favorable treatment. Thus, China soon became the largest Third World host country for FDI.[41]

Although LDCs generally shifted to policies of welcoming FDI, some governments have imposed performance requirements on MNCs, such as local content and export requirements, and have also pressured MNCs to enter into joint ventures with local firms. The East Asian NICs, for example, have welcomed investment, but they have also attached a number of conditions to inward FDI. Nevertheless, even the East Asians are liberalizing their foreign investment policies as a result of the Trade-Related Investment Measures (TRIMs) agreement in the GATT Uruguay round and because of concerns that the industrial states may impose trade restrictions on those with performance requirements for foreign investors. Some LDCs are finding it difficult to attract FDI even when they liberalize their investment policies. For example, most African LDCs adopted policies to encourage FDI, partly under pressure from IMF and World Bank structural adjustment programs. Nevertheless, low economic growth rates, civil conflicts, and political crises, and high levels of indebtedness have had a depressing effect on FDI. As shown in Table 10.4, Africa's share of inward stocks of FDI declined from 6.7 percent in 1975 to 2.2 percent in 1995.[42]

The Industrial States

Industrial host states are generally in a different position vis-à-vis MNCs than LDC host states. While MNCs in Third World countries have historically been involved in natural resource extraction and in lower-technology manufacturing, investment in industrial states is usually based on higher-technology production. MNCs also loom larger in LDC economies and create more dependence among LDCs than is the case for most industrial states. Furthermore, industrial states are often major home and well as host countries for FDI, so they are reluctant to restrict incoming foreign investment. Despite these differences, the policies toward incoming FDI have shifted over time in industrial states, as they have for Third World countries.

In the nineteenth century, Western European countries, the United States, and Canada imposed very few controls over foreign-owned firms. This general openness to MNCs resulted from the liberalism of the period, which was largely fostered by British hegemony. After World War I, Western European countries followed more open policies toward inward FDI than the United States, which restricted foreign ownership in a number of sectors, including banking, shipping, and petroleum. However, countries in Western Europe followed a "national champions" strategy in which they promoted the development of local enterprises in key sectors of the economy. At the end of World War II, the United States as the new global hegemon adopted more liberal policies toward FDI than Western Europe. The shift of European countries toward more restrictionist policies toward FDI was especially noticeable in the 1960s. At this time, Europeans were becoming more concerned that U.S. MNCs were contributing to the Americanization of the developed world. A French writer, Jean-Jacques Servan-Schreiber, expressed these concerns forcefully in his book *The American Challenge.*[43]

Servan-Schreiber attributed the American challenge to the dynamism of American society, and he called on Europe to respond by reforming its educational system, industrial policy, and social structure and by establishing its own MNCs. European governments responded partly by upgrading their policies of promoting national champions in key industries through subsidizing research, encouraging mergers, and increasing preferential procurement from national firms. However, European countries also responded to the American challenge by imposing specific requirements on foreign MNCs in such areas as job creation and export promotion. France in particular screened inward FDI carefully, and its rejection rate for FDI proposals in the late 1970s was much higher than elsewhere in Europe. When takeovers were proposed—even from other European Community countries—the French government often tried to find a French buyer instead. Canada also adopted a screening process in the 1970s because about half of its manufacturing output and about 70 percent of its oil production was foreign (that is, largely U.S.) controlled. As Table 10.5 shows, inward FDI accounted for 20.4 percent of Canada's GDP in 1980, a much higher figure than for other G-7 countries. In 1974, the Canadian government established the Foreign Investment Review Agency (FIRA) to determine whether foreign takeovers were of "significant benefit" to the country; and in 1980, Canada developed an interventionist National Energy Program (NEP) that was partly designed to increase Canadian ownership in the oil and gas industry.[44]

Japan, however, had the most interventionist policy of the industrial states, and as Table 10.4 shows, it received far less FDI than other major industrial countries. While this low level of investment resulted partly from the fact that Western MNCs were not prepared to adapt to the cultural and linguistic differences in Japan, there is no doubt that Japanese investment restrictions also played a critical role. Dating back to at least the sixteenth century, Japan's controls on international economic interactions resulted from its fear of foreign intervention and from national pride in its distinct economy, polity, and society. In the 1930s, Japan developed strategies aimed at extracting the benefits of foreign investment, such as access to capital and technology, while avoiding the drawbacks of foreign control. Japan continued to follow restrictive policies on inward FDI in the postwar period with the passage of its 1950 Foreign Investment Law.[45]

Japan, and to a lesser extent other industrial states, restricted and/or imposed conditions on FDI in the 1970s, but most of these countries liberalized their policies and shifted emphasis toward attracting FDI in the mid-to-late 1980s. Several major factors accounted for this change in policy. First, the phasing out of controls on global capital flows and the reemergence of orthodox liberalism under the leadership of U.S. President Ronald Reagan and British Prime Minister Margaret Thatcher caused countries to question the legitimacy of imposing FDI restrictions. Second, the increase in global competitiveness, along with economic problems such as unemployment in the developed world, generated pressures on states to seek rather than restrict incoming FDI. The average unemployment rate in OECD countries rose from 3.3 percent in 1973 to 8.6 percent in 1983; thus, these countries placed considerable value on the jobs that FDI could provide. Developed countries began to view inward FDI as an opportunity to enhance their international competitiveness, and they provided a range of financial incentives and tax concessions to attract MNCs.[46]

A third factor in the shift toward more open FDI policies was the changing position of the Western European states and Japan. As the position of these countries in the global economy became stronger vis-à-vis the United States, they felt pressures to ease their restrictions on incoming FDI. Traditionally, the European Community was unwilling to support international rules on investment, and it was ambivalent about a 1981 U.S. proposal that GATT should compile an inventory of trade-related investment measures in host countries. However, the EC shifted to a position favoring greater discipline over host countries and supported the U.S. position at the TRIMs negotiations in the GATT Uruguay round. This change resulted largely from the fact that European MNCs greatly increased their outward foreign investment in the 1980s. Because much of this investment was directed to the United States, European firms wanted to encourage the United States to retain its liberal policy on incoming FDI.[47]

As the disparity between Japan's growing outward investment and its restrictions on inward investment became increasingly evident, it also felt pressured to ease its inward restrictions on FDI, and Japan had removed most of its legal obstacles to inward FDI by the 1980s. Intangible barriers to entry, however, continue to limit the role of foreign firms in the Japanese economy. Foreign takeovers are less common in Japan because a large percentage of the stock of Japanese firms is held either by shareholders that have close linkages with the firms' management or by members of *keiretsus* (groups with extensive cross-shareholdings). It is also difficult to develop new FDI production projects because of the high cost and complexities of doing business in Japan, the exclusionary business practices of the *keiretsu*, the complex distribution systems, and the bureaucratic practices that discriminate against foreign firms. There is some evidence that the situation is changing, however; the Japanese government is adopting policies to encourage greater openness, and foreign takeovers of Japanese firms are increasing.[48]

A fourth reason for the shift toward more open investment policies related to the pressures imposed on others by the United States. These pressures were felt most strongly in the United States' two neighboring countries, Canada and Mexico. For example, strong U.S. protests and a U.S. challenge in GATT were major factors explaining the Canadian Liberal government's decision to loosen the controls on inward FDI it had instituted through the FIRA and NEP. (Canada was also concerned about a decline in inward foreign investment at the time.) The Progressive Conservative government of Brian Mulroney, which was elected in 1984, then rescinded the NEP and replaced the FIRA with a new institution called Investment Canada. Unlike the FIRA, Investment Canada was far more involved with encouraging inward FDI than with reviewing it. Subsequently, the Canada–U.S. Free Trade Agreement and NAFTA led to a further liberalization of Canadian (and Mexican) foreign investment regulations.[49]

The United States was the main advocate of liberalized foreign investment policies and was highly critical of host government interventionism in the 1970s and the early 1980s. Ironically, it was the only major industrial state that shifted somewhat toward more restrictive policies in the 1980s. This policy shift resulted largely from the declining economic hegemony of the United States and from its increased role as a host as well as a home country for FDI. In 1985, the United States had an unusually small amount of inward FDI, but direct investment into the United States surged after 1986, and U.S. policies began to shift toward greater interventionism. Some congressional leaders were concerned that foreign investors (especially Japanese investors) were acquiring U.S.-owned high-technology firms and that the U.S. military was becoming too dependent on foreign-controlled suppliers.

The more interventionist approach in the U.S. Congress was evident in a number of proposed and actual legislative changes. The most important was the Exon-Florio Amendment to the 1988 Omnibus Trade and Competitiveness Act, sponsored by Senator James Exon (D–Nebraska) and Representative James Florio (D–New Jersey). This amendment enables the President to block foreign mergers or acquisitions of U.S. firms when there is a possible danger to national security. The authority for implementing Exon-Florio rests with an interagency Committee on Foreign Investment in the United States, which undertakes investigations and reports its recommendations to the President. Some more extreme proposed measures were not actually passed in the U.S. Congress, and the Exon-Florio amendment represents a compromise between internationalist interests of the executive branch and the more nationalist pressures in the Congress. U.S. presidents to this point have implemented the Exon-Florio provision with considerable moderation. Nevertheless, an administration wishing to limit inward FDI could do so by liberally interpreting the national security clause in Exon-Florio in the future.[50] Despite the Exon-Florio amendment, the United States continues to strongly support a liberalized foreign investment regime in international forums. For example, the United States was the main force behind the TRIMs negotiations in the GATT Uruguay round, which focused on easing host government policies toward MNCs.

THE RELATIONSHIP BETWEEN HOME COUNTRIES AND THEIR MNCs

The number of major home countries for MNCs has always been surprisingly small. At least 80 percent of FDI before World War I originated in Western Europe, and Britain accounted for by far the largest share. Between World War I and 1980, only three industrial states accounted for 65 to 75 percent of the FDI stock—the United States, Britain, and the Netherlands. Although the sources of FDI became more diverse after 1980, six industrial states accounted for about 75 percent of the total in the early 1990s—the United States, Britain, Germany, France, Japan, and the Netherlands. Some LDCs, such as the East Asian and Latin American NICs, have become more important as sources of FDI, but in 1995 the developed countries still accounted for 92 percent of the outward FDI stock.[51] Thus, this discussion of FDI–home country relations focuses mainly on the advanced industrial states.

The effects of FDI on the home country depend both on the characteristics of the home country and on the characteristics of its MNCs. Realists often focus on the home country's characteristics, differentiating between rising and declining hegemons. When Britain and the United States first emerged as hegemons in the nineteenth and twentieth centuries, FDI was considered to be relatively costless because no powerful domestic groups viewed it as hurting their interests. As a hegemonic state declines, however, some important domestic groups begin to perceive outward FDI as having detrimental effects. In the United States, for example, domestic labor groups experienced rising unemployment in the 1970s, and they began to argue that U.S. FDI was exporting jobs and adversely affecting their interests.[52]

While some theorists focus on the home state, others devote more attention to the MNC as the source of changing MNC–home state relations. Those who focus on the MNC often present evidence that a growing number of multinationals are becoming "denationalized" and are developing interests that increasingly diverge from the interests of their home countries. American oil companies, for example, became less closely identified with the U.S. national interest after the 1973 energy crisis, when they were accused of aiding the Arab oil embargo; and European oil companies refused to give their home markets preferential deliveries during the embargo, despite the requests of the home governments. In more recent years, studies indicate that increasingly mobile capital is limiting the ability of home as well as host states to affect the behavior and activities of MNCs.

Whether policymakers focus primarily on the characteristics of the nation-state or the MNC as a causal factor, the fact remains that questions about the costs as well as benefits of FDI to home countries have increased in recent years. In this section we begin with a discussion of home country policies toward their MNCs. We then examine two contentious questions in regard to home country–MNC relations: (1) What are the costs and benefits of FDI for labor groups in the home country? and (2) What is the relationship between the competitiveness of a home country and the competitiveness of its MNCs?

Home Country Policies Toward Their MNCs

Home country policies toward their MNCs have been generally favorable, but they are also marked by ambivalence. Home countries often give their MNCs favored treatment and protect them from hostile actions of foreigners. The assumptions underlying these actions are that outward FDI is an indication of economic and political strength and that home countries benefit from the competitiveness of their MNCs. However, home governments also sometimes view their MNCs as tools of foreign policy and are willing to coerce the MNCs if necessary to affect their behavior. Finally, home governments sometimes associate outward FDI with a decrease in home country exports, a decline in the country's industrial base, and losses in domestic employment. In such circumstances, home countries may attempt to stem the flow of outward foreign investment.[53]

The Pre–World War II Period   In the nineteenth and early twentieth centuries, home countries adopted policies to support their corporations and protect them from hostile foreign actions. For example, European states sometimes intervened militarily in the colonial period to ensure that their trading and producing companies could develop and prosper. Home governments in Europe also provided subsidies and other types of assistance in the interwar years to support airlines, shipping firms, and oil companies, which they viewed as being closely tied to their strategic interests. The United States was willing to support the interests of its companies in Latin America with military force when necessary in the 1930s. U.S. officials expressed concerns as early as the 1920s that outward FDI could transfer technology and export employment to foreign countries, but no moves were taken to restrict this investment.[54]

The Early Postwar Period   In the postwar period, the United States as hegemonic power followed assertive policies both in protecting its multinationals and in pressuring them when necessary. In 1962, for example, the U.S. Congress responded to corporate lobbying by passing the Hickenlooper Amendment, which threatened to withhold development assistance from LDCs that nationalized affiliates of U.S. industries without providing adequate compensation. The American government also viewed its MNCs as tools of foreign policy vis-à-vis certain Communist countries. For example, the U.S. government used its Trading with the Enemy Act and Foreign Assets Control Legislation in the 1960s and 1970s to limit the trade of U.S. subsidiaries with China, Cuba, North Vietnam, and North Korea. Host governments for U.S. affiliates in Canada, Europe, and Latin America viewed these policies as an infringement on their sovereignty, and they often adopted their own laws to counter the U.S. legislation.[55] The United States also took actions to affect corporate behavior in response to its growing balance-of-payments deficits. In the 1960s, for example, U.S. MNCs were asked to limit the outflow of capital to their foreign affiliates; and in the 1970s, the United States created the Domestic International Sales Corporation (DISC) program, which provided tax incentives to MNCs to encourage them to export from the United States rather than from abroad.

Most European governments recovering from World War II were concerned that outward FDI would adversely affect their balance of payments. However, they did little to either encourage or restrict outward FDI in the 1950s and 1960s. Japan was the only major economy that systematically restricted outward FDI for about two decades after World War II. In its efforts to keep scarce capital at home for postwar reconstruction, the Japanese government scrutinized every possible FDI project and approved only those that would increase exports, provide access to necessary raw materials, and not pose a threat to Japanese producers. Japan did not begin to liberalize its foreign investment controls until the late 1960s, when its balance-of-trade surpluses were rapidly increasing.[56]

The 1980s and 1990s   Although U.S. actions to limit dealings with Communist countries became less frequent with the decline of the Cold War, they sometimes resurfaced in response to international events and domestic political pressures. In 1981–83, for example, the Reagan administration attempted to prevent the construction of a natural gas pipeline from the Soviet Union to Western Europe. Planning was already at an advanced stage; European firms were to provide equipment needed for construction of the pipeline in return for future deliveries of Soviet natural gas. The Reagan administration's opposition to the pipeline stemmed from concerns that Western Europe would become overly dependent on Soviet gas supplies and that the gas exports would provide the Soviet Union with hard currency receipts that would strengthen its economy. Furthermore, the United States was responding to specific events at the time, most importantly the declaration of martial law in Poland.

From a European perspective, the U.S. actions represented a new level of extraterritorial interference. The United States not only prohibited subsidiaries of American MNCs from exporting foreign-produced equipment and technology to the Soviet Union but also ordered non-U.S. companies not to export goods produced with technology acquired under licensing agreements with U.S. companies. Britain, France, West Germany, and Italy reacted harshly by ordering their resident companies to ignore the U.S. restrictions and provide the needed goods and technology to the Soviet Union. A number of companies, such as Dresser-France (a U.S. subsidiary) and licensees of General Electric in Britain, Italy, and West Germany, complied with the European counterorders. The United States then retaliated by imposing penalties against these companies. However, when it became evident that the Europeans would not back down, the Reagan administration eventually removed most of its sanctions, and the European sales proceeded.[57]

Since the breakup of the Soviet Union, U.S. extraterritorial actions of this nature have been aimed mainly at Cuba. The controversial 1996 Helms-Burton Act is a prime example. This legislation penalizes *foreign* companies for doing business in Cuba if they use assets or property of U.S. multinationals (or individuals) that was nationalized after the 1959 Cuban Revolution. Affected foreign governments reacted angrily to this legislation and indicated that their resident companies would not abide by it.[58]

Other home countries have been far less inclined (and less able) than the United States to take such blatant political actions to control the behavior of multinationals. In *economic* areas, however, Japan and the Western European countries have been more willing than the United States to establish close linkages with their MNCs to achieve common purposes. Indeed, the United States has been more inclined than other industrial states to maintain an arm's-length relationship between business and the government (the U.S. defense and oil industries have been exceptions).[59] A number of realists have argued that the United States should develop its own industrial policy to support its corporations and counter the policies of Japan and Europe, especially in high-technology areas. Such a policy would involve the establishment of institutional mechanisms to assess competitive trends in high-technology industries, along with a shift of federal R&D funds from military uses to dual-use and economic areas.[60] The United States has pursued some limited industrial policy initiatives, but certainly not to the same extent as Japan and certain European countries. The adoption of industrial policy measures poses a realist challenge to liberal support for dependence on the market and on firms that are the lowest-cost suppliers, regardless of their nationality.

The Effects of MNCs on Labor in Home Countries

The effects of MNCs on labor groups is one of the most contentious issues in home countries. Liberal supporters of multinational activity often argue that the impact on labor groups is generally positive. Thus, they present evidence to demonstrate that MNCs have a better record than domestic firms with regard to job creation, export performance, and technological innovations in the home country. Liberals can also point to some studies showing that MNCs pay higher wages than domestic firms, although the results of these studies are inconclusive if other factors (such as size of the firm and training of the workers) are controlled.[61] Many labor groups, however, are unconvinced by this evidence, and labor dissatisfaction with outward FDI has taken a variety of forms in different countries. For example, labor groups in the United States have been especially concerned about the employment effects of outward FDI, while British trade unions have focused more on the possible weakening of labor's position in industrial relations.

In the view of many labor groups (and also historical structuralists), the mobility of capital and MNCs puts immobile workers at a distinct disadvantage. While multinationals can increase their flexibility and competitiveness by extending production to many countries, labor unions are largely limited to organizing themselves on a national or even local basis. Labor groups are particularly concerned that the transfer of MNC activities to affiliates in LDCs with lower wages and standards will produce a deterioration of working conditions in the home country. The geographical fragmentation of production by MNCs in different industrial states can also put labor at a disadvantage because of labor's difficulty in organizing on a multicountry basis.[62]

In the 1970s, when the United States was largely a home country for MNCs, organized labor began to strongly oppose outward FDI. U.S. union leaders called for restraints on outward investment, tax incentives to encourage U.S. multinationals to produce at home for export rather than producing abroad, and adjustment assistance for workers.[63] In 1971, for example, the AFL-CIO supported the ill-fated Burke-Hartke Bill, which was designed to end the tax credit MNCs received for foreign income taxes and to give the President authority to block new outward FDI. American labor's opposition to NAFTA is also based largely on concerns that U.S. multinationals will shift their operations to Mexico. Although NAFTA includes side agreements to deal with concerns about the lowering of labor and environmental standards, it is generally conceded that the side agreements provide little enforcement capability. Thus, organized labor in the United States has strongly opposed any moves to extend NAFTA to other countries.[64]

Competitiveness and Home Country–MNC Relations

As a growing number of multinationals have organized their operations on a global level, questions have arisen as to whether MNCs have worldwide interests that differ fundamentally from the interests of their home countries. Robert Reich has suggested that residents of a nation-state today must ask, "Who is *us*?" Does *us* include our multinational corporations?[65] Phrased another way, is the competitiveness of a nation-state today closely linked with the competitiveness of its MNCs? This question has pitted a number of realists against liberals. Realists argue that the nationality of a nation-state's firms and the amount of foreign ownership can have a major impact on the state's competitiveness. From this perspective, "a nation's standard of living in the long term depends on its ability to attain a high and rising level of productivity in the industries in which its firms compete."[66] Thus, some realists argue that a country such as Canada has a good standard of living but can never have the best because of the high degree of foreign ownership in its manufacturing industry. The best jobs, and most of the research and development, are usually located in the home rather than the host country.[67]

Liberals, by contrast, often argue that MNCs now seek profitable opportunities around the world and that "they are becoming disconnected from their home nations."[68] The competitiveness of a nation-state, from this perspective, is no longer closely linked with the competitiveness of its MNCs. Thus, liberals often argue that the economic future of the United States depends more on the education and skills of American workers than it does on American corporate ownership. If Americans have the requisite technical training, foreign as well as U.S.-owned corporations will employ American workers in growing numbers. Some liberals go even further and assert that we are entering a "borderless world" in which the nationality of most corporations will no longer make a difference.[69] The position an analyst takes on either side of this competitiveness debate obviously affects his or her prescriptions for policymaking. Thus, realists argue that governments should pursue active industrial policies to promote their own multinationals in high-technology areas. Interventionist liberals, by contrast, believe that a government's policy should focus more on upgrading the technological skills and sophistication of the working population than on helping its own MNCs. In other words, governments must make their countries attractive so that global firms—regardless of their nationality—will want to do business, invest, and pay taxes there.[70]

Some evidence certainly indicates that large MNCs are becoming more global in their operations and outlook and less closely tied to their home countries. For example, the sales of foreign affiliates of U.S. firms were about four times greater than the total exports of goods from the United States between 1988 and 1990; foreign affiliates of U.S. multinationals accounted for 43 percent of their parent companies' total profits in 1990; and U.S. firms increased their foreign R&D spending by 33 percent from 1986 to 1988, while their R&D spending in the United States increased by only 6 percent. Some companies also are following deliberate policies of internationalization, and no longer see themselves as being based in a single country. One example of such an MNC is Asea Brown Boveri (ABB), formed from a merger of Sweden's ASEA with Switzerland's Brown Boveri. ABB moved its headquarters from Stockholm to Zurich to place itself more centrally vis-à-vis major European markets. The managers of ABB are Swiss, German, and Swedish, the company does its business in English, and it keeps its books in dollars.[71]

Nevertheless, realists are correct when they argue that most MNCs continue to be home-country based and that the competitiveness of an MNC can have an effect on the competitiveness of its home state. A major factor in promoting competitiveness is R&D, and there is evidence that MNCs in industrial countries keep much of their basic R&D activity at home. In 1984, for example, the ratio of R&D to sales for industrial machinery and equipment firms in Canada was only about 40 percent of the ratio in the United States, and much of this difference resulted from the high degree of foreign ownership in the Canadian industry. American multinationals are more willing than Japanese multinationals to invest in R&D abroad, but even U.S. companies spent only 8.6 percent of their R&D funding in foreign countries in 1988.[72] R&D funding is also essential for the development of new technologies, and ownership and control of technologically sophisticated industries can have significance for a country's long-term national security. Another factor in a country's competitiveness is its ability to maintain a favorable trade balance, and there is evidence that U.S. affiliates of Japanese firms have a higher propensity than American firms to import goods and services into the United States.[73]

Although the competitiveness of a state can be tied to the competitiveness of its firms, it is important to note that there are important national differences in the operation of MNCs headquartered in different countries. For example, there is some evidence that U.S. multinationals favor their home country less than Japanese and German multinationals. Studies have shown that U.S. multinationals are more interested in their financial returns on investments while Japanese MNCs place more emphasis on market share; U.S. multinationals are more willing to invest in overseas R&D activities than their Japanese counterparts; and German and Japanese MNCs place more emphasis on exporting from the home country than U.S. multinationals. Robert Reich's questions as to whether "our MNCs" look after "our national interests" may be more relevant in the case of U.S. multinationals than in the case of Japanese and German multinationals.[74]

Some liberal theorists argue that the term *competitiveness* has more meaning when applied to MNCs than to nation-states. A corporation may go out of business if it is not competitive, but countries normally continue to exist. Furthermore, companies such as Coca-Cola and Pepsi Co are rivals involved in a zero-sum game, while the advanced industrial countries are each other's major trading partners even when they are in competition. International trade is not a zero-sum game; a prosperous European economy provides U.S. exporters with larger markets and offers U.S. consumers higher-quality goods at lower prices than a weaker economy would.[75] A number of economists, however, present counterarguments to demonstrate that in an age of globalization, competitiveness is as much of a concern for states as it is for MNCs.[76]

A REGIME FOR FOREIGN DIRECT INVESTMENT: WHAT IS TO BE REGULATED?

Although MNCs have an increasingly important role in the global economy, the principles, norms, and rules regulating MNCs and FDI are far more rudimentary than those guiding many other areas, such as global trade and monetary relations. Furthermore, no international organization has a role in a "foreign direct investment regime" comparable with that of the WTO in the global trade regime. Most government policies related to MNCs are formulated at the national level, but the transnational nature of MNCs makes these policies inadequate. Nevertheless, there has been little consensus regarding what an FDI regime should be regulating—the MNC, the host state, or the home state. The prominent role of private actors (MNCs, multinational banks, etc.) as sources of investment capital also makes international regulation a difficult and contentious issue.

According to orthodox liberals, investment agreements should be mainly concerned with regulating host state behavior so that MNCs can function freely in the global marketplace. Thus, there should be maximum protection for MNCs and FDI against nationalization, performance requirements, and other impediments. Home countries should have the right to intervene on behalf of their MNCs, in the orthodox liberal view, if the purpose is to counter host government actions that inhibit free investment flows. Realists and historical structuralists, by contrast, see some government limitations on multinational activity as legitimate. From a realist perspective, states will understandably want to ensure that MNC activity does not conflict with their national interest or national security. From a historical structuralist perspective, investment agreements should be mainly concerned with regulating MNCs and with protecting host governments. Because investors can easily move their assets across international borders, labor in both host and home countries is at a distinct disadvantage. Third World host countries are also in a particularly dependent position vis-à-vis MNCs, and they require special protection. Thus, international rules are required to limit the power of MNCs and the major home governments that provide them with support.

In the 1950s and 1960s, the United States as global hegemon provided much of the regulatory activity in the foreign investment area. American policy during this period was mainly aimed at protecting FDI flows against hostile actions of host states (such as nationalization) and ensuring that MNC behavior did not conflict with U.S. and Western objectives in the Cold War. European countries also began concluding "bilateral investment treaties" in the 1960s, which provided some regulation of investment on a bilateral basis (see the discussion later in this chapter). In the 1970s, attention shifted to developing an international regulatory framework for FDI, and several economists proposed that "a General Agreement for the International Corporation" be established, similar to GATT.[77] A number of developments in the 1970s contributed to sentiments that the international framework was needed primarily to regulate the behavior of MNCs. For example, MNCs engaged in currency speculation when the Bretton Woods pegged exchange rate regime was faltering; some industrial states such as France and Canada became concerned about the influence of U.S. multinationals and developed mechanisms to screen foreign investment; and LDCs pressured for the international regulation of MNCs as part of their demands for a New International Economic Order.[78] A number of scholars expressed these anti-MNC sentiments in the 1970s, arguing that the multinational corporation is "not accountable to any public authority that matches it in geographical reach" and that "global corporations must be regulated to restore sovereignty to government."[79]

Despite the widespread sentiments in the 1970s to exert some control over MNC behavior, the main initiatives in this direction came from the LDCs. Arguing that the customary rules of international law regarding foreign investment did not take sufficient account of Third World needs and interests, the Group of 77 pressured for resolutions in the United Nations aimed at regulating MNCs rather than host states. As a result of this LDC activism, in 1974 the UN Economic and Social Committee set up a Commission on Transnational Corporations with a mandate to develop a binding Code of Conduct for MNCs. Third World countries also engaged in a series of nationalizations in the 1960s and early 1970s, and the LDCs in OPEC posed a threat to the international oil companies when they moved to gain greater control over oil pricing and production. To counter these developments, the OECD ministers at the urging of the U.S. government decided to develop their own policy on MNCs which sought to achieve a greater balance than the UN in recognizing the responsibilities of host states as well as MNCs.[80] Thus, the OECD adopted a Declaration and Decisions on International Investment and Multinational Enterprises in 1976 that included some guidelines for MNC behavior, but also sought to improve the foreign investment climate in host states.[81]

By the late 1970s, it was evident that the OECD states would not agree to the Third World demands for change in the UN, and the pendulum began to shift back to emphasis on controlling the behavior of host states. Most significantly, the LDC share of inward FDI was declining because of the foreign debt crisis, concerns about LDC political and economic stability, and the emphasis on high-technology investment in developed countries. As the needs of Third World countries for capital inflows increased, LDCs gradually abandoned their interventionist policies toward MNCs. The increased bargaining power of the developed countries enabled them to begin forging a "consensus" in the 1980s that a stronger regime was necessary to facilitate increased flows of FDI and that the behavior of host countries—not MNCs—was in need of regulation. Although bilateral investment agreements had been the predominant source of foreign investment rules, the feeling grew stronger in the 1980s that multilateral rules were required.

BILATERAL INVESTMENT AGREEMENTS

Bilateral agreements to deal with the concerns of foreign investors have a long history. For example, as early as 1788, the United States concluded bilateral "Treaties of Friendship, Commerce and Navigation" to protect its interests in foreign countries. The earlier versions of these treaties were limited to trade and navigation, but with the dramatic increase in U.S. FDI after World War II, the emphasis shifted to protection of investment. In the 1960s, European countries began signing *bilateral investment treaties (BITs)*, which have become a major instrument for regulating the behavior of Third World host countries. The number of BITs has increased significantly in recent years, and by mid-1996 the world's capital-exporting countries (the European countries, the United States, Japan, and Canada) had concluded 1,160 BITs with LDCs and emerging countries.[82] The BITs generally uphold the most favored nation and national treatment principles, under which an MNC is assured of treatment at least as favorable as that granted to domestic firms or to MNCs from third countries. These treaties also often prohibit host country performance requirements that commit MNCs to export goods produced in the host country or to purchase goods and services locally.

Furthermore, the BITs require payment of prompt and adequate compensation in the event of nationalization.

From a Third World perspective, these BITs are very one-sided because they impose "obligations on the host state for the protection of foreign investment, without any corresponding obligations on the part of the home country or the foreign investor."[83] The industrial states also view the BITs as inadequate, but for very different reasons. They are particularly concerned that variation in their terms seriously limits the effectiveness of these bilateral agreements in international law.[84] As a result, there is growing support among industrial states for a multilateral investment agreement. A number of international and regional organizations have provisions dealing with foreign investment issues. The sections that follow focus on four organizations, demonstrating how attitudes toward FDI have changed from the 1970s to the present.

1. The United Nations tried unsuccessfully to develop a Code of Conduct for MNCs; today it has little influence over foreign direct investment issues.
2. GATT/WTO has some provisions dealing with FDI and could play a much greater role in this area in the future.
3. NAFTA has stronger investment provisions than GATT/WTO and could serve as a stepping-stone to a multilateral investment regime.
4. The OECD was negotiating a controversial *multilateral agreement on investment (MAI)*, but the MAI talks are currently suspended.

THE UNITED NATIONS

In the 1960s and 1970s, the Group of 77 adopted a three-pronged approach in its efforts to alter foreign investment relations: the passage of resolutions in the United Nations, the creation of new institutions to deal with MNCs, and the establishment of a Code of Conduct for MNCs. The Third World countries, which had a voting majority in the UN, passed a series of largely symbolic resolutions in the 1970s proclaiming the rights of host states. The UN also established a new institution in 1974, the *UN Commission on Transnational Corporations*. The commission was to provide a forum for exchange of views on multinationals, develop a comprehensive information system on MNC activities, and help to establish a Code of Conduct for MNCs. The commission met only on an annual basis, so a *UN Center on Transnational Corporations* began operating in 1975 as a secretariat to the commission. The center was created to generate data on international business and to provide technical advice to member states in their relations with MNCs.

The development of a comprehensive Code of Conduct for MNCs was a priority objective of the UN commission from the time of its establishment. An intergovernmental working group began preparing a draft text of the Code and submitted its report to the commission in 1982. However, a long period of negotiations on the report followed because of fundamental disagreements among member states. Most LDCs and socialist states supported the draft Code because it focused on MNC behavior and sought to prevent MNC tax evasion, restrictive business practices, and transfer pricing.

However, the industrial states as the leading home countries for multinationals strongly opposed the draft UN Code because they believed that it did not adequately address the issue of host state treatment of MNCs.[85] After years of on-and-off negotiations, the UN finally abandoned its efforts to establish a Code of Conduct for MNCs in 1992, and the UN Center on Transnational Corporations was subsequently dissolved. The UN has served as a venue for LDC demands regarding MNCs, but its influence on the development of rule making in this area has been extremely limited.[86]

GATT/WTO

The World Trade Organization is a natural institution to deal with FDI issues because of the close interaction between foreign investment and trade. A growing percentage of trade is intrafirm trade, and a number of regional as well as multilateral trade agreements today contain investment provisions. FDI has nevertheless been referred to as the *"neglected* twin" of trade; trade rather than investment was the focus of multilateral negotiations and institution building in the postwar period.[87] Indeed, investment was virtually "a forbidden subject in the context of the GATT" for many years because a number of governments were reluctant to accept limits on their rights to control FDI within their territorial boundaries.[88]

Although the United States for years had wanted GATT to regulate host country controls on foreign investment, GATT members did not seriously consider negotiating investment issues until the preparations for the Uruguay round in the 1980s. The decision was eventually made to hold negotiations on trade-related investment measures in the Uruguay round, but Brazil, India, and most other LDCs strongly opposed the TRIMs talks. As a result, TRIMs were very narrowly defined to accommodate governments that opposed any discipline over such issues, and the final TRIMs agreement deals with only the most obvious violations of existing GATT articles.[89] The TRIMs agreement does prohibit host countries from imposing "local content requirements" on FDI—that is, requirements that a certain percentage of an investor's inputs or value added must be of domestic origin. However, the agreement does not address many other issues, such as a host country's export performance requirements (requirements that a certain share of an investor's output be exported from the host country). In addition to TRIMs, the Agreement on Trade-related Intellectual Property Rights (TRIPs) and the General Agreement on Trade in Services (GATS) have provisions related to FDI because intellectual property and services issues involve foreign investment as well as trade. Thus, the provisions on foreign investment are scattered throughout the agreement, and they do not constitute a *comprehensive* body of rules for foreign investment.[90]

The view of most trade analysts is that TRIMs and other investment provisions in GATT/WTO are only "a tentative first step toward a multilateral investment regime."[91] Nevertheless, both the TRIMs and NAFTA agreements created a precedent for the conduct of far more extensive multilateral negotiations on investment in the OECD (see the discussion below).[92]

THE NORTH AMERICAN FREE TRADE AGREEMENT (NAFTA)

While the BITs were concluded between capital-exporting countries on the one hand and LDCs on the other, the European Union and Canada-U.S. Free Trade Agreement included investment accords among advanced industrial states. The treaties creating the EU provide for the free movement of capital and the protection of FDI among the member states on a multilateral basis. However, the institutional structure of the EU is very different from that desired by the NAFTA countries (the United States, Canada, and Mexico), and the EU model has not served as a precedent for CUSTA or NAFTA.[93]

The investment provisions in NAFTA "carry forward on a trilateral basis all of the key provisions of U.S. bilateral investment treaties."[94] For example, NAFTA commits the three member countries to give both MFN treatment and national treatment to foreign investors; to ban all new export performance, local content, and technology transfer requirements of foreign investors; and to phase out most existing performance requirements within 10 years. NAFTA also establishes a precedent that provides for binding arbitration of investment disputes in an international forum rather than in national courts. Indeed, private investors who are not represented by their government may directly submit their complaints against a NAFTA government to a three-member tribunal that has the authority to make final decisions and award damages. In other international agreements such as GATT/WTO, only governments have "standing," and investors must be represented by governments in settling their claims.

Despite the groundbreaking nature of the NAFTA provisions, member states may claim numerous exceptions to the Chapter 11 obligations. For example, the United States has excluded its maritime industry from the investment provisions, while Canada has exempted its cultural industries and Mexico has shielded its energy and rail sectors. The rules of origin in NAFTA also include complex procedures for determining local content, which may disadvantage outside firms wishing to enter North America. Nevertheless, NAFTA establishes major precedents in the area of foreign investment, and in many respects it has served as a model for OECD negotiations on a multilateral investment agreement.[95]

Because the NAFTA provisions go further than those of other regional and multilateral agreements in liberalizing investment flows, they have been a source of considerable controversy. Most liberal economists today believe that "open investment policies should be the norm, with limited . . . exceptions allowed only when justified in the name of national security or some other overriding principle."[96] Liberals therefore generally applaud NAFTA for its significant advances in the liberalization of investment flows. Liberal criticisms of the NAFTA investment provisions stem from the fact that they contain sectoral exceptions and therefore have "not succeeded in completely liberalizing the North American investment regime."[97]

Realists and historical structuralists, by contrast, view the NAFTA investment provisions as a serious threat to national sovereignty and to the ability of labor groups in all three countries to protect their interests. NAFTA severely limits the ability of host countries to use performance requirements, preventing them from gaining positive spinoffs from foreign investment. Canada and Mexico in particular have imposed performance requirements to encourage investment in depressed regions and in certain sectors of the economy, such as manufacturing, and to ensure that foreign investment contributes to local employment and the growth of exports. By preventing these measures, NAFTA makes it difficult for host countries to channel foreign investment so that it promotes their regional and development objectives. The NAFTA investment rules also increase capital mobility and give the capitalist class even greater advantages vis-à-vis labor. Thus, MNCs can now more easily transfer their operations from the United States and Canada to Mexico to benefit from lower labor costs and lower environmental standards, contributing to a competitive "race to the bottom."[98]

THE OECD

In September 1995, the members of the OECD began negotiations to establish what could be the most comprehensive agreement relating to MNCs and foreign investment: a multilateral agreement on investment. The OECD has served as the venue for these negotiations for several reasons. First, the OECD has considerable experience in developing a framework for foreign investment issues. For example, in 1961 the OECD adopted two codes on the liberalization of capital flows, and in 1976 it adopted a Declaration on International Investment and Multinational Enterprises. Second, the OECD countries account for about 85 percent of the outflows and 65 percent of the inflows of FDI. Third, most OECD members are advanced industrial states with similar views in favor of liberalizing foreign investment flows.

The MAI negotiations in the OECD have been highly controversial because "the governments of most OECD countries appear to agree that an MAI should not impose any obligations on firms but that it should be binding on governments."[99] This consensus among OECD members results partly from the negative experiences of industrial states in the 1970s and 1980s with LDC efforts to develop a UN Code of Conduct for MNCs. Even more important, however, has been the revival of orthodox liberalism, which has been most evident in changing attitudes toward the freeing of foreign investment and capital flows. By the beginning of 1997 the OECD members reached a general agreement on basic principles of the MAI, but strong opposition to some of the provisions in a draft MAI agreement eventually led to the scuttling of further negotiations in October 1998. Nevertheless, it is important to discuss some of the provisions of the emerging MAI agreement, because pressures for an MAI are likely to increase again in the future.

The basic purposes of the MAI are to dismantle barriers to foreign investment and to harmonize international investment rules. More specifically, the emerging MAI provisions will focus on three aspects of rule making: protection for foreign investors, liberalization of investment, and dispute settlement procedures. The investment protection provisions will deal with such issues as compensation for expropriation of property, freedom of investors to transfer profits and dividends out of the host country, and fair and equitable treatment for foreign investors. The investment liberalization provisions will impose various obligations on host countries, such as providing MFN treatment and national treatment for foreign investors and limiting performance requirements imposed on investors. The dispute settlement procedures will permit investors as well as states to submit complaints for binding settlement decisions at the international level. A number of these provisions are already included in BITs and in NAFTA; the significance of the MAI is that it will be multilateral in scope and more comprehensive in coverage than previous agreements.

Although the OECD has served as the venue for initial negotiations of an MAI it is unlikely that the OECD could be responsible for the final negotiation and implementation of such an agreement. Unlike GATT/WTO, the OECD lacks dispute settlement and enforcement procedures and normally depends on peer pressure, "gentlemen's agreements," and consensus building rather than rule making in its operations. OECD membership is also limited mainly to the advanced industrial states, and major LDCs would be unlikely to join an agreement sponsored and negotiated only by the OECD. Third World countries now receive about 40 percent of total FDI flows, and it would make no sense to exclude them. Thus, the OECD would have serious shortcomings as the key investment organization.[100]

A number of analysts have viewed GATT/WTO as the best venue for negotiating and implementing a final agreement on FDI. As we have discussed, the WTO already has agreements (TRIMs, TRIPs, and GATS) that deal with some aspects of foreign investment. The WTO would be a good forum for implementing a more comprehensive international investment accord because of its almost universal membership and because of the close linkages between trade and investment issues. The large, diverse membership of the WTO could of course pose some major obstacles to reaching a comprehensive agreement. It is possible that the WTO would begin by negotiating an investment agreement limited to countries willing to participate (as was the case for the nontariff barrier codes negotiated in the GATT Tokyo round), which would gradually include additional countries.

An MAI would have much broader implications than the NAFTA investment provisions because it would be multilateral in scope. It is not surprising, therefore, that the OECD negotiations are highly controversial. Liberal economists praise the proposed MAI, arguing that the "extension of the rules governing the multilateral trading system to include investment-related issues would be a very positive step, and . . . success within the OECD is a necessary step in this direction."[101] According to liberals, an MAI would establish a "level playing field" for foreign investors, with uniform and equitable rules for market access. An MAI would also facilitate the more efficient use of scarce economic resources and would eliminate distortions in investment flows. Realists and historical structuralists, however, strongly oppose an MAI for many of the same reasons that they oppose the NAFTA investment provisions. According to these critics, an MAI would enable MNCs to move operations to countries with lower environmental, labor, and consumer safety standards; ban performance requirements that countries depend on to promote their welfare and development; prevent restrictions on repatriation of profits and the removal of capital from the host country; and generally restrict the ability of host countries to sanction irresponsible corporations.

In view of the competing perspectives on an MAI, it is not surprising that there was considerable controversy over the OECD negotiations. Although the OECD reached a general agreement on the basic principles of an MAI in early 1997, some differences in members' positions on the specific provisions of an agreement soon became evident. For example, the EU and Canada resented the Helms-Burton law which the United States used to sanction foreign companies for investing in Cuba, Iran, and Libya; France and Canada wanted to exempt culture from the agreement to protect their arts and media sectors; and OECD members had differing views regarding the extent to which environmental and labor measures should be included. The differences among OECD members prevented negotiators from reaching an agreement by the original deadline of May 1997, and the prolongation of negotiations gave an opportunity to outside critics such as the LDCs, environmentalists, trade unionists, and consumer advocates to organize opposition to an agreement. LDCs led by India, Egypt, Pakistan, and Malaysia expressed strong hostility to an MAI which was being negotiated in the OECD without their participation. They argued that the financial crisis in East and Southeast Asia in the late 1990s (discussed in Chapter 11) indicated that capital and foreign investment should be regulated rather than given free reign, and that the MAI threatened the autonomous development of LDCs.[102]

The most effective opposition to the MAI was launched by a wide-ranging coalition of nongovernmental organizations. These NGOs argued that the MAI would threaten protection for human rights, labor and environmental standards, and LDCs. A crucial turning point occurred when Ralph Nader and his consumer advocacy group acquired a copy of an OECD draft MAI agreement and put it on the Internet. By the time the OECD decided to suspend their negotiations in October 1998, about 600 groups in 70 countries had expressed their opposition to the draft agreement, mainly through the Internet. Using a variety of Web sites, NGOs mobilized a strong and diverse opposition composed of human rights groups, labor and environmental groups, and consumer advocates. Gramscian theorists would argue that the NGOs representing disaffected groups organized a counter-hegemony which used an electronic information tool—the Internet—"with incredible effectiveness to derail a planned trade pact designed to increase globalization."[103] Although the OECD's negotiations have been suspended, liberal-economic pressures continue for the negotiation of an MAI. One possibility is that the WTO, which already has a committee on global investment, will eventually take over the negotiations.

CONCLUSION

The postwar economy has been marked by increasing global interdependence among states. Initially, the liberalization of trade under GATT was the main factor contributing to globalization. However, since the 1980s, FDI has become even more important than trade as a force behind the growth of interdependence. Technological advances in communications and transportation enabled firms to extend their operations abroad, and MNCs increased their FDI as a means of gaining access to foreign markets, benefiting from economies of scale, and gaining control over all stages of the production process. Fewer than 200 American corporations and a small number of European firms were global in their operations in 1970, but in the 1980s there was a dramatic increase in both the number of global firms and the number of states that served as home countries. Thus, by the early 1990s, at least 1,000 firms could be categorized as global, and the home nations included the United States, most European countries, Japan, East Asian and Latin American NICs, and some other Third World countries.[104]

Despite the extent of globalization of foreign investment, its growth across countries has been very uneven. As Tables 10.3 and 10.4 show, the developed market economies accounted for 92.1 percent of the outward stocks of FDI and 72.1 percent of the inward stocks of FDI in 1995. Thus, a triad including the European Union, North America, and Japan are the main sources of FDI, and these areas also direct most of their FDI to each other. From the 1950s to the early 1970s, the United States as the main source of FDI was highly critical of the restrictions that other industrial states were imposing on inward FDI. Nevertheless, Western Europe and Japan liberalized their inward FDI policies as they became more competitive with the United States and their outward FDI increased. The United States, by contrast, became more sensitive about incoming FDI as its economic hegemony declined. In 1988, for example, the U.S. Congress enacted the Exon-Florio Amendment, which enables the President to block foreign takeovers of U.S. firms that present a possible danger to national security. Despite Exon-Florio, the United States, like other advanced industrial states, is basically committed to an open foreign investment regime. As major home countries for MNCs, the industrial states have a vested interest in removing obstacles to incoming FDI. Thus, it is the OECD countries that have been negotiating a multilateral agreement on investment.

Unlike the industrial states, Third World countries are primarily host countries rather than home countries for foreign investment. MNCs often have a greater impact on Third World countries with their less developed economies; LDCs have therefore been sensitive to the effects of MNCs on their ability to achieve autonomous economic development. In the 1970s, LDCs reacted strongly to the growing impact of MNCs, demanding greater control over their natural resources and the ability to nationalize MNCs as part of their calls for a New International Economic Order. Nevertheless, the oil price increase of 1979, followed by world recession and the 1980s foreign debt crisis, led to severe cutbacks in commercial bank lending to LDCs. Third World fears about exploitation by MNCs were largely replaced by concerns that their share of inward FDI was declining. Today, many LDCs are unilaterally liberalizing their foreign investment policies and competing for incoming investment.

As discussed throughout this chapter, liberals, realists, and historical structuralists have widely divergent views regarding multinational corporations. Liberals view MNCs as positive agents of global change, which contribute to increased efficiency and stimulate innovation, economic growth, and employment. Liberals also tend to downgrade the importance of the nationality of an MNC, and they advise states to upgrade the skills of their populations in order to attract investment, regardless of the source. Realists, by contrast, believe that the nationality of an MNC does make a difference and that the competitiveness of a nation-state and the competitiveness of its multinationals are closely interlinked. Realists also believe that host states should be able to impose performance requirements and other policies on MNCs to promote industrial development and protect their national interest. Thus, unlike liberals, realists have reservations about an MAI that would unduly restrict governmental policymaking abilities. Historical structuralists argue that MNCs as capitalist organizations over-charge for their goods and services, create dependency relationships with Third World host countries, and pose a major threat to labor groups in home as well as host states. Multinationals can extend their operations to many countries, but labor is largely lim-ited to working and organizing itself on a national basis. Thus, MNCs often transfer operations to affiliates in countries with lower wages and environmental standards, producing a deterioration of working conditions and a competitive "race to the bot-tom." In the historical structuralist view, a code of behavior is required not for host states but for MNCs. However, in the present climate of liberal orthodoxy, a multilat-eral agreement on investment would be aimed primarily at limiting the behavior of host states.

NOTES

1. John H. Dunning, *Multinational Enterprises and the Global Economy* (Wokingham, UK: Addison Wesley, 1993), pp. 14–15; World Trade Organization, *Annual Report 1996, Vol. 1, Trade and Foreign Direct Investment* (Geneva: WTO, 1996), p. 44.
2. Lorraine Eden, "Bringing the Firm Back In: Multinationals in International Political Econ-omy," in Lorraine Eden and Evan H. Potter, eds., *Multinationals in the Global Political Economy* (New York: St. Martin's Press, 1993), p. 26.
3. Ethan B. Kapstein, "We Are US: The Myth of the Multinational," *The National Interest* (Winter 1991–92), p. 55.
4. DeAnne Julius, "International Direct Investment: Strengthening the Policy Regime," in Pe-ter B. Kenen, ed., *Managing the World Economy: Fifty Years After Bretton Woods* (Wash-ington, DC: Institute of International Economics, September 1994), p. 269.
5. Robert W. Cox, *Production, Power, and World Order: Social Forces in the Making of History* (New York: Columbia University Press, 1987), pp. 358–359; G. William Domhoff, "Who Made American Foreign Policy 1945–1963?" pp. 25–69, and William Appleman Williams, "The Large Corporation and American Foreign Policy," pp. 71–104, in David Horowitz, ed., *Corporations and the Cold War* (New York: Monthly Review Press, 1969).
6. See Stephen D. Krasner, "Power Politics, Institutions, and Transnational Relations," in Thomas Risse-Kappen, ed., *Bringing Transational Relations Back In: Non-State Actors, Do-mestic Structures and International Institutions* (Cambridge, Cambridge University Press, 1995), p. 279.
7. Stephen Hymer, "The Multinational Corporation and the Law of Uneven Development," in George Modelski, ed., *Transnational Corporations and World Order* (San Francisco: Free-man, 1979), p. 398.
8. See Yair Aharoni, "On the Definition of a Multinational Corporation," *Quarterly Review of Economics and Business* 11-3 (Autumn 1971), pp. 27–37; Grazia Ietto-Gillies, *International Production: Trends, Theories, Effects* (Cambridge, MA: Polity Press, 1992), pp. 17–20.
9. Raymond Vernon, *Sovereignty at Bay: The Multinational Spread of U.S. Enterprises* (New York: Basic Books, 1971), p. 11.
10. Edward M. Graham and Paul R. Krugman, *Foreign Direct Investment in the United States* (Washington, DC: Institute for International Economics, 3rd edition, January 1995), pp.

9–11; Geoffrey Jones, *The Evolution of International Business: An Introduction* (London: Routledge, 1996), pp. 4–6.

11. See, for example, United Nations Centre on Transnational Corporations (UNCTC), *Transnational Corporations in World Development: Third Survey* (New York: United Nations, 1985).

12. Howard V. Perlmutter, "The Tortuous Evolution of the Multinational Corporation," *Columbia Journal of World Business* 4-1 (January–February 1969), p. 11; Wyn Grant, "Perspectives on Globalizational and Economic Coordination," in J. Rogers Hollingsworth and Robert Boyer, eds., *Contemporary Capitalism: The Embeddedness of Institutions* (Cambridge: Cambridge University Press, 1997), pp. 322–325; Susan Strange, "Global Government and Global Opposition, "in Geraint Parry, ed., *Politics in an Interdependent World: Essays Presented to Ghita Ionescu* (Aldershot, UK: Edward Elgar, 1994), pp. 26–27.

13. Although most political scientists and American scholars prefer the term *MNC*, economists, business professors, and British scholars often opt instead for the term *multinational enterprise (MNE)*. MNE is a more accurate term in their view because an "enterprise" includes "a network of corporate and non-corporate entities in different countries joined together by ties of ownership." See United Nations Department of Economic and Social Affairs, *Multinational Corporations in World Development* (New York: United Nations, 1973), p. 4; Eden, "Bringing the Firm Back In," p. 55.

14. Laura D'Andrea Tyson, "They Are Not Us: Why American Ownership Still Matters," *The American Prospect* 4 (Winter 1991), p. 42; John M. Kline, *State Government Influence in U.S. International Economic Policy* (Lexington, MA: Heath, 1983), p. 63.

15. Jean-François Hennart, "The Transaction Cost Theory of the Multinational Enterprise," in Christos N. Pitelis and Roger Sugden, eds., *The Nature of the Transnational Firm* (London: Routledge, 1991), pp. 143–151; Mark Casson, "The Rationale of the Multinational Enterprise," in *Alternatives to the Multinational Enterprise* (London: Macmillan, 1979), p. 45.

16. Graham and Krugman, *Foreign Direct Investment in the United States,* p. 83. For a discussion of transfer pricing, see Lorraine Eden, *Multinational Enterprise and Economic Analysis* (Toronto: University of Toronto Press, 1997); Alan M. Rugman and Lorraine Eden, eds., *Multinationals and Transfer Pricing* (London: Croom Helm, 1985); and Wagdy M. Abdallah, *International Transfer Pricing Policies: Decision-Making Guidelines for Multinational Companies* (New York: Quorum Books, 1989).

17. See Lorraine Eden, "Thinking Globally—Acting Locally: Multinationals in the Global Political Economy," in Lorraine Eden and Evan H. Potter, eds., *Multinationals in the Global Political Economy* (New York: St. Martin's Press, 1993), pp. 1–2; Michael E. Porter, *The Competitive Advantage of Nations* (New York: Free Press, 1990), p. 53.

18. See Charles Wilson, "The Multinational in Historical Perspective," in Keiichiro Nakagawa, ed., *Strategy and Structure of Big Business,* Proceedings of the First Fuji Conference (Tokyo: University of Tokyo Press, 1974), p. 265; Peter Hertner and Geoffrey Jones, "Multinationals: Theory and History," in Peter Hertner and Geoffrey Jones, eds., *Multinationals. Theory and History* (Aldershot, UK: Gower, 1986), p. 1.

19. Jones, *The Evolution of International Business,* pp. 23–25.

20. See Peter Svedberg, "The Portfolio-Direct Composition of Private Foreign Investment in 1914 Revisited," *The Economic Journal* 88 (December 1978), pp. 763–777; and T. A. B. Corley, "Britain's Overseas Investments in 1914 Revisited," *Business History* 36-1 (January 1994), pp. 71–88.

21. Julius, "International Direct Investment," pp. 272–273.

22. Jones, *The Evolution of International Business*, pp. 28–32.

23. Edward M. Graham, *Global Corporations and National Governments* (Washington, DC: Institute for International Economics, May 1996), pp. 25–26, 136–140; John H. Dunning, "Changes in the Level and Structure of International Production: The Last One Hundred Years," in Mark Casson, ed., *The Growth of International Business* (London: Allen and Unwin, 1983), p. 88.

24. Jones, *The Evolution of International Business*, pp. 52–59.

25. Dennis J. Encarnation, *Rivals Beyond Trade: America Versus Japan in Global Competition* (Ithaca, NY: Cornell University Press, 1992), p. 5; Kiyoshi Kojima, *Direct Foreign Investment: A Japanese Model of Multinational Business Operations* (New York: Praeger, 1978), pp. 1–18.

26. Peter J. Buckley and Mark Casson, *The Future of the Multinational Enterprise* (London: Macmillan, 2nd edition, 1991), p. 11. See also United Nations Centre on Transnational Corporations (UNCTC), *World Investment Report—1991: The Triad in Foreign Direct Investment* (New York: United Nations, 1991).

27. World Trade Organization, *Annual Report—1996, Vol. 1*, p. 47.

28. Graham, *Global Corporations and National Governments*, pp. 22–24; Julius, "International Direct Investment," pp. 276–277; Ietto-Gillies, *International Production*, pp. 25–32.

29. Ietto-Gillies, *International Production*, pp. 78–84.

30. Stephen Herbert Hymer, *The International Operations of National Firms: A Study of Direct Foreign Investment* (Cambridge, MA: MIT Press, 1976), p. 100; Ietto-Gillies, *International Production*, pp. 86–90.

31. Theodore H. Moran, "Multinational Corporations and Dependency: A Dialogue for Dependentistas and Non-Dependentistas," *International Organization* 32-1 (Winter 1978), pp. 79–100.

32. Peter Evans, *Dependent Development: The Alliance of Multinational, State, and Local Capital in Brazil* (Princeton, NJ: Princeton University Press, 1979), p. 37.

33. See Vernon, *Sovereignty at Bay*, pp. 46–59; Raymond Vernon, "Sovereignty at Bay Ten Years After," *International Organization* 35-3 (Summer 1981), pp. 521–523.

34. Theodore H. Moran, "Multinational Corporations and the Developing Countries: An Overview," in Theodore H. Moran, ed., *Multinational Corporations: The Political Economy of Foreign Direct Investment* (Lexington, MA: Heath, 1985), pp. 3–24.

35. See Stephen J. Kobrin, "Testing the Bargaining Hypothesis in the Manufacturing Sector in Developing Countries," *International Organization* 41-4 (Autumn 1987), pp. 609–638.

36. On the policies of subnational governments toward FDI, see, for example, Kline, *State Government Influence in U.S. International Economic Policy*; Douglas M. Brown and Earl H. Fry, eds., *States and Provinces in the International Economy* (Berkeley: Institute of Governmental Studies Press, University of California, 1993); and Peter Karl Kresl and Gary Gappert, eds., *North American Cities and the Global Economy: Challenges and Opportunities*, Urban Affairs Annual Review 44 (Thousand Oaks, CA: Sage, 1995).

37. Jones, *The Evolution of International Business*, pp. 288–291.

38. Stephen J. Kobrin, "Expropriation as an Attempt to Control Foreign Firms in LDCs: Trends from 1960 to 1979," *International Studies Quarterly* 28-3 (September 1984), pp. 337–342.

39. Stephen D. Krasner, *Structural Conflict: The Third World Against Global Liberalism* (Berkeley: University of California Press, 1985), pp. 176–195; Horst Heininger, "Transnational Corporations and the Struggle for the Establishment of a New International Eco-

nomic Order," in Teichova, Lévy-Leboyer, and Nussbaum, eds., *Multinational Enterprise in Historical Perspective*, pp. 351–361.

40. Kobrin, "Expropriation as an Attempt to Control Foreign Firms in LDCs," p. 338; Jones, *The Evolution of International Business*, pp. 294–295.

41. Graham, *Global Corporations and National Governments*, pp. 17–20.

42. United Nations Conference on Trade and Development, *World Investment Report 1994* (New York: United Nations, 1994), pp. 91–97; Graham, *Global Corporations and National Governments*, pp. 97–100.

43. J. J. Servan-Schreiber, *The American Challenge*, translated from the French by Ronald Steel (New York: Atheneum, 1979). The book was first published in 1967. See also Jones, *The Evolution of International Business*, pp. 274–277.

44. C. Fred Bergsten, "Coming Investment Wars? Multinational Corporations in World Politics," *Foreign Affairs* 53–1 (October 1974), pp. 136–139; Barbara Jenkins, *The Paradox of Continental Production: National Investment Policies in North America* (Ithaca, NY: Cornell University Press, 1992), pp. 113–117.

45. Mark Mason, *American Multinationals and Japan: The Political Economy of Japanese Capital Controls, 1899–1980* (Cambridge, MA: Council on East Asian Studies, Harvard University, 1992), pp. 243–247.

46. Jones, *The Evolution of International Business*, pp. 280–281.

47. Graham, *Global Corporations and National Governments*, pp. 96–97.

48. See Robert Z. Lawrence, "Japan's Low Levels of Inward Investment: The Role of Inhibitions on Acquisitions," in Kenneth Froot, ed., *Foreign Direct Investment* (Chicago: University of Chicago Press, 1993), pp. 85–107; C. Fred Bergsten and Marcus Noland, *Reconcilable Differences? United States–Japan Economic Conflict* (Washington, DC: Institute for International Economics, 1993), pp. 79–82; and Encarnation, *Rivals Beyond Trade*, pp. 36–41.

49. Jenkins, *The Paradox of Continental Production*, pp. 117–121; Stephen Clarkson, *Canada and the Reagan Challenge: Crisis and Adjustment, 1981–85* (Toronto: Lorimer, new edition, 1985), pp. 83–113.

50. Edward M. Graham and Michael E. Ebert, "Foreign Direct Investment and US National Security: Fixing Exon-Florio," *The World Economy* 14-3 (September 1991), pp. 245–268; Edward M. Graham and Paul R. Krugman, *Foreign Direct Investment in the United States* (Washington, DC: Institute for International Economics, January 1995), pp. 126–132.

51. Jones, *The Evolution of International Business*, pp. 194–195; United Nations Conference on Trade and Development, *World Investment Report—1996: Investment, Trade and International Policy Arrangements* (New York: United Nations, 1996), p. 245.

52. Robert Gilpin, *U.S. Power and the Multinational Corporation: The Political Economy of Foreign Direct Investment* (New York: Basic Books, 1975), p. 62.

53. UNCTC, *Transnational Corporations in World Development—Trends and Prospects* (New York: United Nations, 1988), p. 240.

54. Jones, *The Evolution of International Business*, pp. 219–220.

55. Robert T. Kudrle, "The Several Faces of the Multinational Corporation: Political Reaction and Policy Response," in W. Ladd Hollist and F. LaMond Tullis, eds., *An International Political Economy*, International Political Economy Yearbook (Boulder, CO: Westview Press, 1985), vol. 1, pp. 176–177; Jack N. Behrman and Robert E. Grosse, *International Business and Governments: Issues and Institutions* (Columbia: University of South Carolina Press, 1990), pp. 82–85; Gilpin, *U.S. Power and the Multinational Corporation*, pp. 142–144.

56. Jones, *The Evolution of International Business*, pp. 221–222.
57. Gary Clyde Hufbauer and Jeffrey J. Schott, "The Soviet-European Gas Pipeline: A Case of Failed Sanctions," in Moran, ed. *Multinational Corporations: The Political Economy of Foreign Direct Investment*, pp. 219–245.
58. Paul Lewis, "Cuba Trade Law: Export of U.S. Ire and Politics," *New York Times*, March 15, 1996, pp. C1, C3; "Biter Bitten: The Helms-Burton Law," *The Economist*, June 8, 1996, p. 45.
59. Robert B. Reich, "Who Is Us?" *Harvard Business Review* 90-1 (January–February 1990), pp. 59–60; Vernon, *Sovereignty at Bay*, pp. 214–215.
60. Laura D'Andrea Tyson, *Who's Bashing Whom? Trade Conflict in High-Technology Industries* (Washington, DC: Institute for International Economics, November 1992), pp. 289–295.
61. See Peter Enderwick, *Multinational Business and Labour* (London: Croom Helm, 1985); Richard E. Caves, *Multinational Enterprise and Economic Analysis* (Cambridge: Cambridge University Press, 1962), pp. 131–159; Theodore H. Moran, "Multinational Corporations and the Developed World: An Analytical Overview," in Moran, ed. *Multinational Corporations: The Political Economy of Foreign Direct Investment*, pp. 139–146.
62. Gordon Betcherman, "Globalization, Labour Markets and Public Policy," in Robert Boyer and Daniel Drache, eds., *States Against Markets: The Limits of Globalization* (London: Routledge, 1996), p. 258; Ietto-Gillies, *International Production*, pp. 136–143.
63. See, for example, Sol C. Chaikin, "Trade, Investment, and Deindustrialization: Myth and Reality," in Moran, ed., *Multinational Corporations: The Political Economy of Foreign Direct Investment*, pp. 159–172.
64. Gary Clyde Hufbauer and Jeffrey J. Schott, *NAFTA: An Assessment* (Washington, DC: Institute for International Economics, revised edition, October 1993), p. 159.
65. Reich, "Who Is Us?" pp. 53–64; Robert B. Reich, *The Work of Nations: Preparing Ourselves for 21st-Century Capitalism* (New York: Vintage Books, 1991), ch. 25.
66. Porter, *The Competitive Advantage of Nations*, p. 2; Tyson, "They Are Not Us," pp. 37–49.
67. Lester Thurow, *Head to Head: The Coming Economic Battle Among Japan, Europe, and America* (New York: Morrow, 1992), p. 201.
68. Reich, *The Work of Nations*, p. 8.
69. Kenichi Ohmae, *The Borderless World: Power and Strategy in the Interlinked Economy* (New York: HarperPerennial, 1991), p. 10.
70. Reich, *The Work of Nations*, p. 163; Ohmae, *The Borderless World*, p. 194.
71. Robert B. Reich, "Who Do We Think They Are?" *The American Prospect* 4 (Winter 1991), p. 51; Grant, "Perspectives on Globalizational and Economic Coordination," pp. 323–324.
72. Fred Lazar, "Corporate Strategies: The Costs and Benefits of Going Global," in Boyer and Drache, eds., *States Against Markets*, p. 285; Louis W. Pauly and Simon Reich, "National Structures and Multinational Corporate Behavior: Enduring Differences in the Age of Globalization," *International Organization* 51-1 (Winter 1997), p. 13.
73. See Richard G. Harris and William G. Watson, "Three Visions of Competitiveness: Porter, Reich and Thurow on Economic Growth and Policy," in Thomas J. Courchene and Douglas D. Purvis, eds., *Productivity, Growth and Canada's International Competitiveness*, Proceedings of a Conference at Queen's University (Kingston, ONT: John Deutsch Institute for the Study of Economic Policy, 1993), pp. 254–256; Graham and Krugman, *Foreign Direct Investment in the United States*, p. 84.

74. See Pauly and Reich, "National Structures and Multinational Corporate Behavior," pp. 1–30.

75. Paul Krugman, "Competitiveness: A Dangerous Obsession," *Foreign Affairs* (March/April 1994), pp. 31–33. See also Paul Krugman, "Competitiveness: Does It Matter?" *Fortune* (March 7, 1994), pp. 109–115.

76. Clyde V. Prestowitz, Jr., "The Fight over Competitiveness: A Zero-Sum Debate?" *Foreign Affairs* (July/August 1994), p. 189.

77. Paul M. Goldberg and Charles P. Kindleberger, "Toward a GATT for Investment: A Proposal for Supervision of the International Corporation," *Law and Policy in International Business* 2 (Summer 1970), pp. 295–325.

78. Christopher J. Maule and Andrew Vanderwal, "International Regulation of Foreign Investment," *International Perspectives*, November/December 1985, p. 22.

79. Vernon, *Sovereignty at Bay*, p. 249; Richard J. Barnet and Ronald E. Müller, *Global Reach: The Power of the Multinational Corporations* (New York: Simon & Schuster, 1974), p. 375.

80. Peter Muchlinski, *Multinational Enterprises and the Law* (Oxford: Blackwell, 1995), pp. 578–592; Oswaldo de Rivero B., *New Economic Order and International Development Law* (Oxford: Pergamon Press, 1980), pp. 88–92.

81. See Organisation for Economic Co-operation and Development, *International Investment and Multinational Enterprises: Review of the 1976 Declaration and Decisions* (Paris: OECD, 1979).

82. Paul Bryan Christy III, "Negotiating Investment in the GATT: A Call for Functionalism," *Michigan Journal of International Law* 12-4 (Summer 1991), pp. 754–760; World Trade Organization, *Annual Report 1996*, vol. 1, p. 62; Jon R. Johnson, *The North American Free Trade Agreement—A Comprehensive Guide* (Aurora, ONT: Canada Law Book, 1994), p. 277. Canadian BITs are called foreign investment protection agreements.

83. UNCTC, *Transnational Corporations in World Development: Trends and Prospects,* p. 337.

84. Christy, "Negotiating Investment in the GATT," p. 763. For a discussion of private international legal efforts to regulate MNCs, See A. Claire Cutler, "Public Meets Private: The International Harmonization and Unification of Private International Law," *Global Society* 13–1 (January 1999), pp. 25–48.

85. UNCTC, *The United Nations Code of Conduct on Transnational Corporations* (New York: United Nations, September 1986), pp. 1–6.

86. "Target Practice," *New Internationalist*, August 1993, p. 15; Leslie Sklair, *Sociology of the Global System* (Hertfordshire, UK: Prentice Hall/Harvester Wheatsheaf, 2nd edition, 1995), p. 53.

87. See De Anne Julius, *Foreign Investment: The Neglected Twin of Trade*, Occasional Papers no. 33 (Washington, DC: Group of Thirty, 1991).

88. Christy, "Negotiating Investment in the GATT," p. 746.

89. John Croome, *Reshaping the World Trading System: A History of the Uruguay Round* (Geneva: World Trade Organization, 1995), p. 138.

90. Graham, *Global Corporations and National Governments,* pp. 71–76; Julius, "International Direct Investment," p. 281.

91. Jeffrey J. Schott, with Johanna W. Buurman, *The Uruguay Round: An Assessment* (Washington, DC: Institute for International Economics, November 1994), p. 112.

92. Ernest H. Preeg, *Traders in a Brave New World: The Uruguay Round and the Future of the International Trading System* (Chicago: University of Chicago Press, 1995), pp. 195–196.

93. Johnson, *The North American Free Trade Agreement,* p. 331, footnote 3.

94. Johnson, *The North American Free Trade Agreement,* p. 275.

95. Edward M. Graham and Christopher Wilkie, "Multinationals and the Investment Provisions of the NAFTA," *International Trade Journal* 8-1 (Spring 1994), pp. 9–38; Schott, with Buurman, *The Uruguay Round: An Assessment,* pp. 112–114.

96. Graham, *Global Corporations and National Governments,* p. 47.

97. Alan M. Rugman and Michael Gestrin, "A Conceptual Framework for a Multilateral Agreement on Investment: Learning from the NAFTA," in Sauvé and Schwanen, eds., *Investment Rules for the Global Economy,* p. 170.

98. Fred Lazar, "Investment in the NAFTA: Just Cause for Walking Away," *Journal of World Trade* 27-5 (October 1993), pp. 28–29; Jim Stanford, "Investment," in Duncan Cameron and Mel Watkins, eds., *Canada Under Free Trade* (Toronto: Lorimer, 1993), pp. 164–166.

99. Edward M. Graham and Pierre Sauvé "Toward a Rules-Based Regime for Investment: Issues and Challenges," in Sauvé and Schwanen, eds., *Investment Rules for the Global Economy,* p. 135.

100. Daniel Schwanen, "Investment and the Global Economy: Key Issues in Rulemaking," in Sauvé and Schwanen, eds., *Investment Rules for the Global Economy,* pp. 21–23.

101. Graham and Sauvé, "Toward a Rules-Based Regime for Investment," p. 101.

102. Elizabeth Smythe, "The Multilateral Agreement on Investment: A Charter of Rights for Global Investors or Just Another Agreement?," in Fen Osler Hampson and Maureen Appel Molot, eds., *Canada Among Nations 1998: Leadership and Dialogue* (Toronto: Oxford University Press, 1998), pp. 239–277; "MAI on Six-Month Hold," *Bridges Weekly Trade News Digest* 2-16 (May 4, 1998), pp. 3–4; "MAI in Doubt After France Withdraws from Talks," *Bridges Weekly Trade News Digest* 2-40 (October 19, 1998), pp. 3–5.

103. Peter Morton, "MAI Gets Tangled in Web," *The Financial Post,* October 22, 1998, p. 3.

104. Schwanen, "Investment and the Global Economy," pp. 2–3; Graham, *Global Corporations and National Governments,* p. 27.

CHAPTER 11

International Development

The Bretton Woods system and its institutions have often been credited with contributing "to almost unprecedented global economic growth and change over the past five decades."[1] However, a substantial majority of the world's people living in the less developed countries have received little benefit from this growth. Poverty, hunger, and disease are prevalent in much of the world, and the gap between the rich states of the North and most of the poor states of the South is persistent and growing. As discussed in Chapter 2, Third World countries generally have low levels of economic development, marked by low per capita incomes, inadequate infrastructure facilities (such as communications and transportation), and limited access to modern technology. The economic development problems of LDCs in turn often prevent them from fostering social and political development. Thus, many LDCs have inadequate health and educational facilities, low literacy rates, and high infant mortality rates. Politically, many LDCs have difficulty maintaining stable governments that also allow for some degree of democratic participation.[2]

Although severe economic and social problems confront a substantial majority of people in the South, there are major differences in economic development among the Southern states. As Table 11.1 shows, the newly industrialized countries of East Asia and Latin America and some members of OPEC have relatively high per capita GNPs, reaching $26,730 in Singapore and $17,390 in Kuwait. In stark contrast, the poorest African and Asian LDCs, such as Mozambique, Ethiopia, and Nepal, have per capita GNPs in the $100 to $200 range and even lower. Table 2.2 in Chapter 2 shows that East Asia (excluding China) also ranks higher than other Third World regions in a wide range of human development measures such as infant mortality rates, adult literacy rates, and access to safe water.

The East Asian NICs were also the most rapidly growing Third World economies during the critical periods of the oil and foreign debt crises from 1973 to 1989. Indeed, East Asia managed to increase its average annual economic growth rate to 6.2 percent

TABLE 11.1

PER CAPITA GNP OF LESS DEVELOPED COUNTRIES, 1995

Higher- and Middle-Income LDCs					
East Asian NICs		**OPEC Countries**		**Latin American NICs**	
Singapore	$26,730	Kuwait	$17,390	Argentina	$8,030
Hong Kong[a]	22,990	Saudi Arabia	7,040	Brazil	3,640
South Korea	9,700	Oman	4,820	Mexico	3,320

Low-Income LDCs			
Africa		**Asia**	
Tanzania	$120	Bangladesh	$240
Ethiopia	100	Vietnam	240
Mozambique	80	Nepal	200

[a]Hong Kong is now part of China.

Source: World Bank, World Development Report 1997, Table 1, pp. 214–215. Copyright © 1997 by The International Bank for Reconstruction and Development/The World Bank. By permission of Oxford University Press.

during 1980–89, a period marked by a global recession and the foreign debt crisis. As Table 11.2 shows, sub-Saharan Africa and Latin America, by contrast, had *negative* economic growth rates (of –1.2 and –0.4 percent) during the 1980–89 period. Many scholars therefore refer to the 1980s as a lost decade for much of the Third World, in which the South experienced a serious debt crisis, declining prices for raw material exports, declining foreign investment, and capital flight. In 1991, the World Bank reported that the real income gap between the industrial countries and all LDC regions except East Asia was widening.[3]

In view of their vulnerabilities, LDCs have traditionally been ambivalent about their relations with the industrial states of the North. Although they have looked to the North for trade, foreign investment, development assistance, and technology transfers,

TABLE 11.2

GROWTH OF REAL GDP PER CAPITA
(AVERAGE ANNUAL PERCENTAGE CHANGE)

Group	1965–73	1973–80	1980–89
Industrial countries	3.7	2.3	2.3
Less developed countries			
Sub-Saharan Africa	2.1	0.4	–1.2
East Asia	5.3	4.9	6.2
South Asia	1.2	1.7	3.0
Europe, Middle East, and North Africa	5.8	1.9	0.4
Latin America and the Caribbean	3.8	2.5	–0.4

Source: World Bank, *World Development Report 1991,* Table 1, p. 3. Copyright © 1991 by The International Bank for Reconstruction and Development/The World Bank. By permission of Oxford University Press.

the LDCs have feared that these linkages contribute to their dependence on the North and to Northern threats to their autonomy. Third World countries have also been ambivalent about the keystone international organizations—the International Monetary Fund, the World Bank, and the World Trade Organization. These institutions have helped LDCs gain access to external finance and foreign markets for their exports, but Third World countries resent the fact that the rich Northern states are the dominant actors in the KIEOs. Furthermore, LDC debtor countries often believe that the conditions attached to IMF and World Bank structural adjustment loans inhibit rather than further their development efforts.[4]

Despite the South's ambivalence about its relations with the North, a series of developments have induced Third World countries to increase their Northern linkages, adopt Northern-prescribed liberal-economic policies, and participate more fully in the global economy. First, a major turning point was the 1980s foreign debt crisis, when a number of LDCs were unable to meet their debt repayment obligations. As discussed in Chapter 7, the debtor LDCs were forced to turn to the IMF, the World Bank, and the advanced industrial states for assistance. The failure of inward-looking import-substituting industrialization policies, combined with the conditions of IMF and World Bank structural adjustment loans, induced LDCs to shift to more open economic policies with an emphasis on trade liberalization, deregulation, and privatization.

A second factor inducing Third World countries to open their economies has been the revival of orthodox liberalism in the 1980s. For example, Chapter 8 discussed the growing Northern opposition to special and differential treatment for LDCs in trade and the Northern pressure on Third World countries to liberalize their trade policies. Most LDCs refused to become signatories to the nontariff barrier codes concluded at the Tokyo round of the GATT talks in the late 1970s, but the GATT Uruguay round negotiations were organized as a single undertaking in which the LDCs were expected to be full participants in all the agreements.

A third factor causing the LDCs to participate more fully in the global economy has been the growing fear that most of the Third World is becoming increasingly marginalized. A major reason for this marginalization was the breakup of the Soviet bloc. On the one hand, the downfall of communism and the end of the Cold War deprived the Third World countries of a traditional source of leverage they had in extracting concessions from both the East and the West. On the other hand, the emerging countries in the former Eastern bloc turned to the West for assistance and became competitors with the LDCs for export markets, development finance, and foreign investment. For example, Eastern Europe and the former Soviet Union were foreign aid donors until the end of the 1980s, but in the 1990s they were vying with Third World countries as aid recipients. At the 1991 council meeting of the Organization for Economic Cooperation and Development, the OECD ministers assured the LDCs that "their co-operation with developing countries will not be diminished because of their support for central and eastern Europe";[5] but the statistics on development assistance from the OECD countries indicate otherwise. Thus, official development assistance from the OECD countries to Third World states fell by 16 percent in real terms between 1992 to 1996;[6] and as Table 11.3 shows, in 1995–96 three former centrally planned economics (China, Poland, and Russia) were among the ten largest recipients of bilateral aid from the OECD countries.[7]

TABLE 11.3
TEN LARGEST RECIPIENTS OF BILATERAL DEVELOPMENT ASSISTANCE FROM THE OECD COUNTRIES (1995–96 AVERAGE)

Top Ten Recipients	Amount[a]
1. China	2412
2. Indonesia	2118
3. Poland	2018
4. Egypt	1937
5. India	1708
6. Israel	1484
7. Russia	1228
8. Philippines	1195
9. Thailand	1059
10. Bangladesh	849

[a]Millions of dollars.

Source: "Development Assistance Committee Report," *Development Co-operation Report 1997*, p. 79.   Copyright © OECD 1998. By permission of the Organisation for Economic Co-operation and Development.

This chapter first assesses the various strategies that LDCs have pursued in efforts to promote their economic development, such as import substitution, socialist strategies, and export-led growth. In accordance with the revival of orthodox liberalism, LDCs are now being pressured to follow more open economic policies. Current development policies fall short, however, in meeting the needs of the poorest and most disadvantaged in society (such as Third World women and children) and in looking after the needs of the future as well as the present (for example, in preserving the environment). As background for examining the LDC economic development strategies, it is first necessary to briefly discuss the three major IPE perspectives and to describe the functions of the World Bank, which "enjoys a unique position as a generator of ideas about economic development."[8] In the postwar period, the World Bank and the United States in particular have had considerable influence over the ideological and operational models used to promote Third World development.

THE IPE PERSPECTIVES AND NORTH-SOUTH RELATIONS

This section briefly summarizes some of the main tenets of the three IPE perspectives as they relate to North-South relations. (For a more detailed discussion of these perspectives, see Chapters 3 through 5.)

Realist writers in the advanced industrial states, preoccupied with power and influence, tend to ignore the economic interests of the poorer countries of the South. It is only when Southern states pose a challenge to the economic predominance of the

North that these realists take notice. In the 1970s, for example, realists looked at the increased leverage of OPEC in raising oil prices and at the attempts of Third World countries to gain more power and wealth through their calls for a New International Economic Order. In the 1980s and 1990s, realists became interested in the economic successes of the East Asian NICs. Despite the lack of realist attention to poverty in the Third World, realist ideas have had considerable influence on Third World policies. For example, Alexander Hamilton and Friedrich List emphasized state building and argued that late industrializers require a large degree of government involvement if they are to "catch up" with the leading states. Major Third World strategies such as import substitution and export-oriented industrialization involve a large role for the state in promoting economic development.

Liberals believe that the growth of interdependence has widespread benefits, and they often argue that LDCs gain even more from North-South linkages than the advanced industrial states. The economic problems of LDCs, from the liberal perspective, stem more from inefficient domestic policies than from their dependent position in the global economy. Thus, those LDCs that follow open economic policies and increase their linkages with the industrial states are most likely to achieve successful development. Although all liberals encourage LDCs to follow open, market-oriented policies, interventionist liberals recognize that inequalities between the North and South put the Southern states at a distinct disadvantage. Unlike orthodox liberals, who emphasize equal treatment and reciprocity, interventionist liberals therefore call on Northern states to give more consideration to the special needs of the South. Nevertheless, interventionist liberals believe that the necessary changes can occur within the existing capitalist order, and they share the faith of orthodox liberals in private enterprise and the market.

The historical structuralist views of most interest in this chapter are those of dependency and world-system theorists. (For a discussion of the classical Marxist view of development, see Chapter 5.) Dependency theorists reject both the optimism of liberals and the liberal view that Third World economic problems result primarily from inefficient domestic policies. From the dependency view, structural factors related to the global capitalist economy are responsible for constraining LDC development possibilities. Thus, dependency theorists argue that the advanced capitalist states in the core of the global economy either "underdevelop" Third World countries in the periphery or prevent them from attaining genuine, autonomous development. Dependency theorists are also interested in class linkages, and they maintain that elites in the South collaborate with foreign capitalists in the North to reinforce the pattern of Third World dependency. Because some Third World states such as the East Asian and Latin American NICs were successfully industrializing, world-system theorists modified the classical dependency argument by introducing a third category of countries, the semiperiphery. Countries may move upward (or downward) from the periphery to the semiperiphery and even to the core, but world-system theorists believe that this only rarely occurs. While some historical structuralists call for a redistribution of resources from the core to the periphery, the more extreme theorists believe that the core will never willingly agree to such a transfer of resources. Thus, they call for a domestic social revolution in the Third World and/or a severing of contacts with the advanced industrial states. The solution for disadvantaged groups, according to Gramscian theorists, is the development of a "counterhegemony."

THE WORLD BANK GROUP

The World Bank was one of the three KIEOs formed in the 1940s. Although the bank gives long- and medium-term loans to LDCs, its influence extends far beyond loan giving. It has an influential role in the ongoing debates over economic development; indeed, global "debates on development issues" are often "framed in terms of 'pro or anti' World Bank positions."[9] Several factors account for the bank's influence in generating ideas on development: the World Bank affects the terms under which LDCs gain access to development financing and international capital markets; it has the largest group of development economists and the largest research and policy analysis budget of any development organization; and the global media pay considerable attention to the bank's major studies and reports. In view of the World Bank's influence, it is necessary to describe its organizational characteristics before discussing Third World development strategies.

Located in Washington, D.C., the World Bank is actually a World Bank group composed of four financial institutions (see Figure 2.1 in Chapter 2). The first of these, the International Bank for Reconstruction and Development, was planned at the Bretton Woods conference, along with the International Monetary Fund. When the United States instituted the Marshall Plan in 1948, the World Bank shifted its attention from European reconstruction to providing long-term loans for Third World development. Each member state has a capital subscription (or quota) in the IBRD based on its economic strength, which determines the number of votes the country has in the bank's policymaking bodies. As in the IMF, the Group of Five countries have the largest subscriptions and also the largest number of votes.

Member countries actually pay in only 10 percent of their subscriptions to the bank and hold the remaining 90 percent as callable capital the bank can request if needed to meet its financial obligations. The IBRD receives by far the greatest share of its funds for development loans by borrowing on world capital markets. It has been able to depend on the capital markets for funding because of its good record in LDC repayment of loans and because of its large reserves of members' callable capital. Thus, the principal U.S. bond-rating services have given IBRD bonds a triple-A credit rating. To make its bonds attractive to purchasers, the IBRD must pay market interest rates, and it must in turn therefore charge near-conventional interest rates on loans to LDC borrowers. For example, the interest rate on IBRD loans in 1997 was about 6.8 percent, the grace period was 3 to 5 years, and the maturity period ranged from 15 to 20 years.[10] IBRD loans are directed only to governments, or with a government guarantee. The World Bank largely limited itself to lending for specific development projects for many years, but it responded to the 1980s foreign debt crisis by extending nonproject structural adjustment loans.[11]

To be a World Bank member, a country must also be a member of the IMF. This requirement deterred most Communist countries from joining the bank because members must provide the IMF with detailed information about their economies. The Western industrial states were willing to give the World Bank and its staff considerable discretion in loan giving because of the lack of Communist members, the bank's weighted voting system, and the dominant position of Western countries on the World Bank staff (for example, the World Bank president has always been American). As is the case for the IMF, a country's economic strength determines both its capital sub-scription and its voting power in the World Bank. In 1997, the United States had the most votes in the IBRD with 17.04 percent of the total, followed by Japan with 6.04 percent, Germany with 4.67 percent, and both France and Britain with 4.47 percent.[12]

As in the IMF, the *board of governors* is theoretically the main policymaking body in the World Bank. Although every member state has one governor, the governors have different numbers of votes based on the weighted voting system. The governors meet only once a year to review the bank's operations and policies, admit new mem-bers, and amend the Articles of Agreement; they delegate most of their functions to the *board of executive directors*. The executive board, which also has weighted voting, is responsible for approving all World Bank loan proposals and for developing the gen-eral policies of the bank. While 5 of the executive board's 24 members are always ap-pointed by the countries with the largest number of votes, coalitions of member coun-tries elect the other 19 executive directors every two years, and each elected director casts the votes for the entire coalition group. Directors cannot split their votes and must cast them as a unit.

The United States is the most important single member of the World Bank. There are a number of indicators of its influence. First, the United States has a larger num-ber of votes than any other country. Second, English is the World Bank's only working language, reflecting U.S. influence (and the bank's location in Washington, D.C.). The American view that a single working language contributes to efficiency contrasts with the view of many other countries that cultural and ethnic diversity dictates the need for more than one working language in international organizations.[13] Third, although the executive directors are theoretically responsible for selecting the World Bank pres-ident, the U.S. government's nominee for president is normally accepted. Bank presi-dents have often come from the U.S. financial community and have strongly supported liberal-economic policies. As a result, the policymaking bodies in the bank (that is, the governors and executive directors) have been willing to delegate considerable author-ity to the World Bank president and staff.

Despite the continued influence of the United States, its predominance has clearly declined. In the early years, the IBRD was extremely dependent on the U.S. capital market as a source of funds; markets in other countries were extremely limited. Over time, however, the share of the bank's outstanding securities held in the United States has steadily declined. U.S. voting power in the IBRD has also fallen from about 40 percent of the total to about 17 percent, and this decline is reflected in voting out-comes. While the United States virtually had a blocking veto on loan decisions during the 1940s and 1950s, some World Bank loans have been approved in recent years even when the U.S. executive director has abstained or voted against them. Nevertheless, the bank would not on a regular basis approve loans that the United States strongly op-posed. Thus, under U.S. pressure, the World Bank ended normal lending activity to Chile during the years of Salvadore Allende's leftist-leaning government, even though some Western European governments continued to provide Allende with bilateral aid. When a right-wing military coup replaced Allende in September 1973, the bank promptly resumed lending to Chile. Furthermore, the World Bank president pledged that no further loans would be made to Vietnam when the United States objected to a 1979 bank loan to that country.[14]

The IBRD was the only World Bank institution until 1956, when the International Finance Corporation (IFC) became the second member of the World Bank group. Reflecting the bank group's liberal-economic orientation, the IFC was created to encourage private business and investment in LDCs, and today it is the largest multilateral source of loans and equity financing for private-sector projects in the Third World. To promote private enterprise, the IFC is active in areas where the IBRD cannot operate. Unlike the IBRD, the IFC can make loans to private ventures in LDCs without a government guarantee; indeed, it may not even accept a government guarantee. The IFC also invests in equity shares of corporations and acts as a broker bringing foreign and domestic partners together in joint ventures. Furthermore, the IFC has persuaded commercial banks to lend more to LDCs, partly through joint financing deals with banks as co-lenders. Like the IBRD, the IFC charges near-commercial rates on its loans. In the 1980s, the U.S. Reagan administration's emphasis on the private sector elevated the IFC's importance in the World Bank group, and the IFC reported net profits of $142 million in the 1992–93 fiscal year. These profits, combined with the high interest rate on IFC loans, raise questions among critics as to whether the IFC is primarily a money-making or a philanthropic institution. Nevertheless, the IFC maintains that it promotes development by providing technical, financial, and environmental advice for Third World development projects.[15]

In 1960, the International Development Association (IDA) became the third World Bank group institution. The IDA was formed largely in response to complaints that the poorer LDCs could not pay the high interest rates on the IBRD's hard loans. Even such major LDCs as India and Pakistan were reaching the limits of their borrowing ability on conventional terms in the late 1950s. Third World countries also opposed the World Bank's weighted voting system, and throughout the 1950s they demanded a soft-loan agency in which they would have greater control. When the industrial states finally agreed to create the IDA as a soft-loan agency, they insisted that it be under World Bank auspices, with the bank's weighted voting system. The IDA and IBRD are legally and financially distinct, but they share the same staff and their projects must meet the same criteria.[16]

The IDA provides soft loans or "credits" to Third World governments with no interest rate, 10-year grace periods, and 35- to 40-year maturities, and these loans are reserved for poorer Third World countries. For example, higher-income LDCs such as Argentina, Uruguay, Mexico, Hungary, Malaysia, and the Czech Republic are eligible only for IBRD loans; a middle-range group of LDCs such as Egypt, Armenia, China, Pakistan, India, and Nigeria are eligible for a blend of IBRD and IDA funds; and the least creditworthy LDCs such as Cameroon, Sri Lanka, Albania, Nicaragua, Bangladesh, Tanzania, and Ethiopia receive only IDA credits.[17] Unlike the case with the IBRD and IFC, the interest-free terms of IDA credits give it no basis for borrowing on capital markets. IDA funds therefore come primarily from "negotiated replenishments" from member governments. The negotiations are often protracted and difficult; other donors often wait for the United States to pledge funds before making their own pledges, and the U.S. Congress has regularly delayed its approval of IDA contributions. Thus, orthodox liberal views that LDCs should rely more on private capital and less on World Bank "handouts" pose a serious threat to the IDA's financial viability. In fiscal year 1998, the IBRD's loan disbursements totaled $19,232 million while the IDA's disbursements amounted to only $5,630 million.[18]

The fourth financial institution of the World Bank group—the Multilateral Investment Guarantee Agency (MIGA)—was established in 1988.[19] The MIGA, like the IFC, demonstrates the liberal-economic orientation of the World Bank group. Its main purpose is to encourage the flow of private foreign investment to its LDC member countries. The agency offers guarantees to foreign investors against losses caused by noncommercial risks and also assists LDCs in their efforts to attract foreign investment.

It is important to note that the World Bank has considerable influence over bilateral as well as multilateral aid giving. (In bilateral aid, a donor country provides assistance directly to a recipient.) The bank is a key source of data and analysis on development issues, and its reports, publications, and activities play a central role in debates among development experts and government officials. The World Bank also chairs a large number of aid consortia and **consultative groups.** These groups bring together donor states that provide development assistance to a particular recipient and enable them to coordinate their bilateral aid giving and avoid needless duplication. From the view of Third World countries, however, consultative groups often permit donors to exert undue pressure on a recipient's policies because only one recipient and many donors attend each meeting.[20]

As the most important multilateral development institution, the World Bank has also provided a model for the formation of regional development banks, including the Inter-American Development Bank (established in 1960), the African Development Bank (1964), the Asian Development Bank (1966), and the European Bank for Reconstruction and Development (1991). Like the World Bank, the regional development banks usually raise money on international capital markets and lend this money at near-commercial rates of interest. Because the banks' credit ratings are backed by member countries' subscriptions (most of which are callable rather than paid in), they can borrow and lend money at favorable rates of interest. These banks also have IDA-type soft-loan affiliates, which must raise their funds from government subscriptions. The regional banks perform an important role in supporting smaller development projects at the regional level while the World Bank directs most of its funding to larger projects and programs.[21]

IMPORT-SUBSTITUTING INDUSTRIALIZATION

In the early postwar period, the ideas of several major economists had a significant influence on the development strategies of LDCs. First, Third World development strategies drew on the interventionist liberal ideas of John Maynard Keynes. While Keynes called for a greater role for the government in welfare and job creation in industrial states, his ideas contributed to the view that LDC governments should also have a major role in promoting economic development. Second, Third World development strategies drew on the ideas of Raúl Prebisch and Hans Singer, which contained elements of both realism and historical structuralism. In 1950, Prebisch and Singer separately published studies arguing that there was a growing gap in the incomes of developed and less developed countries because of a long-term decline in the prices of primary products (raw materials and agricultural goods). To close the income gap with the developed countries, LDCs would have to alter the structures of their economies, decreasing their emphasis on the production of primary products and focusing first and foremost on industrialization.[22]

In arguing that LDCs were disadvantaged because of their role as primary product exporters, Prebisch and Singer directly contradicted the views of liberal economists that free trade based on comparative advantage benefits all states. According to the Prebisch-Singer thesis, the demand of individuals for industrial goods such as automobiles and televisions rises as their incomes go up, but the same does not apply to the demand for raw materials and agricultural products. Indeed, the demand for raw materials may even decline in industrial states as technological advances lead to the discovery of substitute products (such as synthetic rubber as a replacement for natural rubber). Thus, Third World countries that depend on the export of primary products suffer from declining terms of trade. When LDCs raise their production of primary goods in attempts to garner more revenue, they are simply faced with lower prices and more abject levels of poverty as surplus stocks accumulate. Prebisch therefore argued that an import-substituting industrialization strategy would permit LDCs to produce manufactured goods at home that they had previously imported.

Realists such as Alexander Hamilton and Friedrich List had supported ISI policies for late industrializers in the eighteenth and nineteenth centuries, and some Third World countries in Latin America and the Middle East had developed ISI policies as a short-term response to the Great Depression in the interwar period. However, it was not until after World War II that the Third World adopted import substitution as a *long-term development strategy*. Central to ISI was the argument that LDCs should protect and support their infant industries through tariff and nontariff barriers to industrial imports and through subsidies and other incentives to promote industrial growth. Only through an emphasis on industrial development (and a de-emphasis on agriculture) would LDCs be able to compete on a more equal footing with the advanced industrial states.

In the 1950s and 1960s, Third World countries in Latin America, South and Southeast Asia, and Africa developed ISI policies, and import subtitution "emerged as the new gospel for Third World industrialization."[23] Although ISI is considered to be a realist development strategy with strong nationalist overtones, it is interesting that the World Bank was generally supportive of Third World ISI policies in the 1950s. The World Bank normally refused to finance government-owned industries, but it was affected by postwar interventionist liberal views that the state had an important role to play in the development process. Thus, the bank provided funding for major infrastructure projects such as transportation and communications facilities, power projects, and port developments, which Third World countries required to promote industrialization.[24]

Initially, ISI policies seemed to provide major gains for Third World countries. For example, Latin America registered healthy industrial growth rates in the 1940s to 1950s, and the Mexican economy grew at annual average rates of 6.5 percent until 1970. India's steel production increased by six times during its first three 5-year plans from 1951 to 1966, and some African countries such as Ghana also registered major industrial gains. International economic conditions were highly favorable to the success of ISI strategies in the 1950s and early 1960s, and the LDCs benefited from a period of prosperity and growth in North America and Western Europe. Furthermore, the Third World output of agricultural products generally did not suffer in the 1960s even though ISI policies downgraded the role of agriculture because the Rockefeller foundation–supported "green revolution" led to the development of new dwarf strains of high-yielding grains. The green revolution exacerbated differences between rich and poor farmers in the Third World because only the rich could afford the large amounts of irrigation, fertilizer, and other inputs required to grow the new high-yielding grains. Nevertheless, increased agricultural output in India and other Asian countries masked the fact that ISI policies were promoting industrialization at the expense of agriculture.[25]

Despite the initial successes of ISI policies, in the late 1960s and the 1970s, both external problems and internal distortions started to become evident in LDCs employing such policies. International economic changes such as the combined food and oil crises of the 1970s were especially important in exposing the weaknesses of the ISI strategy. Inclement weather, Soviet crop shortfalls, and other unexpected events in the early 1970s led to greatly increased demand for food imports, and global food stocks in 1972–73 fell to their lowest levels in twenty years. Many LDCs lacked *effective demand,* or demand backed by purchasing power, so they had less ability than countries such as the Soviet Union and Japan to purchase foodstuffs on global markets at inflated prices. Thus, the global food crisis in the early 1970s had its severest effects on the Third World.[26] When OPEC managed to limit oil supplies and drastically raise prices in 1973, a number of LDC oil importers such as India were doubly hit by the food and energy crises. These new external stresses exposed a number of weaknesses in import substitution as a Third World development strategy.

First, the global food crisis in the early 1970s pointed to the pitfalls for Third World countries in overemphasizing industrialization at the expense of agriculture. The neglect of agriculture under ISI eventually led to poverty in the countryside, the need for foodgrain imports, and the stagnation of agricultural exports. Indeed, the LDC share of world agricultural exports fell from 44 percent in 1955 to 32 percent in 1970. The decline in revenue from agricultural exports simply exacerbated the LDCs' balance-of-payments deficits and lack of funding for investment. Second, despite the emphasis of the ISI strategy on promoting self-sufficiency, ISI ironically increased Third World dependence on the industrial states and their multinational corporations. In view of their shortages of capital and foreign exchange, Third World countries considered foreign direct investment to be "a necessary evil" if they were to succeed in industrializing, and they therefore encouraged inward FDI as part of their import substitution policies. As a result, MNCs were able to set up subsidiaries behind the trade barriers of Third World countries. This fact helps to explain why the American government supported ISI as part of "its vigorous efforts to secure favorable conditions for U.S. foreign direct investment."[27] U.S. policies were less consistently pro–free trade in the postwar period than many hegemonic stability theorists have indicated.

The most serious weakness of the ISI strategy was its inability to accomplish what it was supposed to be best at: promoting industrial competitiveness. Industrialization seemed to proceed well under an "easy" first stage of import substitution, but the second stage of ISI was far more difficult. In the first stage, LDCs replaced imports of nondurable consumer products, such as shoes, household goods, and clothing, with domestic production. LDCs are better able to produce labor-intensive goods that do not require the use of advanced technology, large amounts of capital investment, or a network of component suppliers. There is also a sizable domestic market in LDCs for the purchase of nondurable consumer goods. To maintain high industrial growth rates, however, LDCs had to move on to a second stage of ISI, replacing imports of intermediate goods (e.g., petrochemicals and steel) and producer and consumer durables (e.g., refrigerators and automobiles) with domestic production. More difficult for LDCs to produce, these second-stage products were capital-intensive and depended on economies of scale and higher levels of technology. Because LDC producers had to import much of the technology and inputs required to produce these goods, the cost of the imported inputs often outweighed any savings from producing the goods locally. Finally, the emphasis on increasing capital-intensive production under ISI concentrated development gains in a small percentage of the population in industrial enclaves, and unemployment emerged as a major problem for most of the population. ISI policies therefore simply exacerbated the inequalities of income among individuals within Third World countries.[28]

Those LDCs pursuing the second stage of ISI therefore suffered from a slowdown in the growth of primary product exports, dependence on imports for the production of second-stage goods, and a failure to increase manufactured exports. In response to their balance-of-payments problems, these LDCs sought external loans, aid, and investment and turned increasingly to trade protectionism. By the 1960s, therefore, the World Bank changed its views and began to oppose ISI policies, and a noted liberal economist argued that "an import substitution policy tends to be less and less successful the longer it continues."[29] Even Raúl Prebisch, who had initially encouraged Latin American LDCs to follow ISI policies, began to question these policies, arguing that "the proliferation of industries of every kind in a closed market has deprived the Latin American countries of the advantages of specialization and economies of scale."[30]

Despite the problems with second-stage ISI, many Latin American and South Asian states continued following an ISI strategy because domestic interest groups with vested interests in trade protectionism limited the ability of governments to institute policy change.[31] It was not until the foreign debt crisis of the 1980s that most LDCs finally dispensed with ISI as a development strategy and shifted to a more outward-oriented strategy (see the discussion below). While many LDCs persisted with ISI policies in the 1960s and 1970s, some sought other alternatives. A second group of LDCs adopted a more extreme inward-looking strategy than ISI, turning to socialist central planning based on the Soviet Union model. However, Third World experiments with socialism also encountered a number of problems. A third group of LDCs, the East Asian NICs, changed from ISI to export-led growth strategies at a fairly early stage, and they experienced far more impressive economic growth rates than other LDCs. As a result, the economic development community began to look positively at export-led growth as an alternative strategy to promote economic development.

SOCIALIST DEVELOPMENT STRATEGIES

By the 1960s, there was already growing disillusionment with import substitution policies, which contributed to uncompetitive industries and balance-of-payments problems.[32] Scholars challenged the ISI approach from both the right and the left, and many left-leaning scholars turned to dependency theory (see the discussion of dependency theory in Chapter 4).[33] According to dependency theorists, the ISI strategy did not adequately restructure the peripheral Third World economies or increase their leverage vis-à-vis the core. Third World countries could promote autonomous development, dependency theorists argued, only by turning to socialism and severing their linkages with the North. Some Third World countries, such as China, North Korea, Cuba, Ethiopia, Mozambique, Vietnam, Laos, Cambodia, and Burma, eventually opted for socialist central planning strategies. Many more, however, employed import substitution; China was the only LDC with the size and resources to be able to reap major economic benefits from socialist central planning.

The socialist development strategies were generally patterned after the Soviet model, which involved the abolition of the capitalist market economy and private ownership and the establishment of state control over the economy and its resources. Thus, state central planning largely replaced market signals in economic decisions concerning the allocation of resources and investment and the setting of production targets, wages, and prices. A major problem with the socialist strategy was that Third World economies other than China were simply too small and lacking in resources to engage in central planning on the Soviet/Eastern European model. For example, LDCs lacked both the communications and transportation infrastructure essential for central planning as well as the well-trained technocratic bureaucracy necessary to design and monitor the plans. Third World countries also encountered many of the same problems that plagued the Soviet Union and Eastern Europe. Thus, central planners were more successful in setting production targets and increasing the quantity of output than they were in ensuring the quality of output and the efficient use of resources. Although Third World countries were generally ill equipped to employ socialist central planning, Western aid and investment policies often did not make their task easier. For example, the U.S. Agency for International Development and World Bank officials believed that foreign aid should be designed in part to promote private enterprise. Thus, most LDCs that followed a socialist development model were not major beneficiaries of Western development assistance programs.

Third World countries opting for the socialist route were more concerned than nonsocialist LDCs about the redistributional aspects of economic development. Thus, they often registered more gains than nonsocialist LDCs in reducing economic and social inequities by providing better access to health care and education, improving the status of women, and opening parks and other facilities for use of the public. Despite the advances of some socialist LDCs in social areas such as health and education, these countries encountered a number of economic problems for the reasons outlined above.

A prime example of the problems facing LDCs that pursued a socialist economic development model was the case of Mozambique. Shortly after gaining independence in 1975, a Marxist government in Mozambique sought to loosen its linkages with South Africa's apartheid government and to follow a path of socialist development. To achieve its egalitarian and socialist objectives, however, the state had to intervene massively in the economy, and this was beyond the capacity of a Third World government. In agriculture, for example, Mozambique established communal villages and about 2000 state farms which were intended to be the main source of the country's food supplies. Nevertheless, total agricultural production fell drastically after 1975, because farmers continued to prefer family plots over farming on a communal basis, and the government could devote only limited resources to the state farms and communal villages. Although Mozambique sought to promote cooperative ties with the West as well as socialist countries, a congressional ban on U.S. foreign aid to Mozambique was maintained (often over the objections of the U.S. executive branch) from 1975 to 1984. Partly in response to its support for refugees and liberation movements in southern Africa, Mozambique was also the target of a severe destabilization campaign launched by the South African government. By the end of 1983, Mozambique was facing a severe economic crisis, marked by a lack of foodstuffs for the population, a shortage of foreign exchange, and severe declines in local production. When the government had to default on its debts, it became a major recipient of international aid, and in response to assistance and debt rescheduling negotiations with the IMF, World Bank, and the Paris and London Clubs, Mozambique introduced a series of orthodox liberal reforms.[34]

Mozambique's experiences were repeated with some variations in a number of other LDCs seeking to pursue socialist economic objectives, and when the Soviet bloc collapsed in the late 1980s and early 1990s, the socialist LDCs could no longer look to the Second World for economic and military support. Thus, very few LDCs are persisting with socialist strategies today, and even the few holdouts such as Cuba are seeking to establish closer ties with the capitalist world.[35]

EXPORT-LED GROWTH

The experience of the East Asian NICs—South Korea, Taiwan, Singapore, and Hong Kong—was very different from that of most other Third World countries. The East Asian NICs all adopted export-led growth strategies, and they registered impressive growth rates and improvement in their economic performance. Export-led growth strategies were far more successful than either the socialist or import substitution strategies in the 1970s and 1980s. In examining the effects of export-led growth strategies on economic development, it is more useful to discuss the experience of South Korea and Taiwan because Singapore and Hong Kong have a unique status in the Third World. Both are so small geographically that they are more akin to city-states than countries, and Hong Kong was a British crown colony before it was incorporated into mainland China. Hong Kong was also the only East Asian NIC that never followed import substitution policies.

Taiwan and South Korea adopted ISI policies in the 1950s, and they experienced serious economic problems. Both countries had large balance-of-payments deficits, which were covered mainly by foreign aid, and their exports consisted almost entirely of primary commodities. In the 1960s, Taiwan and South Korea followed the example of Japan and shifted from ISI to a policy that encouraged the growth of manufactured exports. While maintaining a moderate degree of trade protection of the domestic market, these governments encouraged exports with tax incentives, export credits, export targets, and access to duty-free imports for exporters and their suppliers. Taiwan and South Korea also abandoned minimum wage legislation and imposed only minimal taxes on the employment of labor so that employment in export-oriented industries could increase rapidly. In the early 1980s, Southeast Asian economies such as Malaysia, Indonesia, and Thailand followed the path taken by Japan and the East Asian NICs and also switched to export-led growth strategies.

The change from ISI to export-led growth strategies had a dramatic effect on the economic performance of the East Asian NICs. For example, South Korea's GDP grew at an average annual rate of more than 8 percent throughout the 1960s, and its exports rose from about $31 million in 1960 to $882 million in 1970. Of significance was not only the dramatic growth of South Korean and Taiwanese exports but also the change in their composition. In the 1960s and early 1970s, the majority of the rapidly growing exports were industrial products that used relatively little capital and large amounts of unskilled labor. Over time, industrial wages increased, and there was a structural transformation in the two economies as they began to produce more sophisticated industrial goods that required more highly skilled labor. Thus, by the late 1980s Taiwan was the tenth and South Korea was the thirteenth largest exporter of manufactures in the world.[36]

The economic successes of the East Asian NICs from the 1960s to the 1980s were often compared with the less favorable economic fortunes of the Latin American NICs—Argentina, Brazil, Chile, and Mexico.[37] While the Latin American NICs instituted some reforms to provide more incentives for exports in the 1960s, their policies continued to be aimed primarily at ISI. Thus, the first two columns of Table 11.4 show that per capita GDP growth rates were much higher for the East Asian NICs than for the Latin American NICs. For example, while South Korea's GDP per capita of $747 was well *below* the per capita GDPs of all four Latin American NICs in 1963, by 1988 South Korea's per capita GDP of $4,094 was *above* the figures for all the Latin American NICs. The change was even more dramatic for Hong Kong and Singapore: their

TABLE 11.4
GDP*a* PER CAPITA AND EXPORT/GDP RATIOS

	GDP per Capita		Export/GDP Ratios	
	1963	1988	1963	1988
East Asian NICs[b]				
Hong Kong	$2247	$11,952	39.0	51.1
South Korea	747	4094	2.3	35.4
Singapore	1777	11,693	124.5	164.2
Taiwan	980	4607	15.3	51.8
Latin American NICs[b]				
Argentina	$2949	$3474	10.0	10.2
Brazil	1400	3424	6.0	9.5
Chile	3231	3933	11.6	31.9
Mexico	2312	3649	5.1	11.9

*a*GDP = gross domestic product
*b*NICs = newly industrializing countries

Source: Balassa, Policy Choices for the 1990s, pp. 57, 59.

GDPs soared to more than \$11, 000 by 1988. The last two columns of Table 11.4 show that the export-to-GDP ratios were also higher for the East Asian NICs than for the Latin American NICs. South Korea again provides a striking example. While the South Korean export-to-GDP ratio of 2.3 was well below the figures for the Latin American NICs in 1963, its export-led growth policies resulted in an export-to-GDP ratio of 35.4 in 1988, exceeding the ratios of all the Latin American NICs. Finally, there were striking differences in the composition as well as the level of exports. By the late 1980s, Taiwan, South Korea, and Hong Kong were *each* producing more manufactured exports than all of Latin America.[38]

The East Asian NICs had a few years of reduced growth during the debt crisis in the 1980s, but they did not have to seek debt rescheduling, and they soon adjusted their economies and returned to a pattern of rapid growth. Although the East Asian NICs had about the same ratios of debt obligations to GDP as other oil importers, their ratios of debt obligations to exports were much lower. Their relatively healthy export positions, combined with large infusions of foreign investment (especially from Japan), enabled them to garner sufficient revenue to continue their debt payments without depending on World Bank and IMF structural adjustment loans. The Latin American NICs following ISI strategies, by contrast, were more severely affected by the debt crisis and had to seek substantial funding from the IMF and the World Bank.[39]

As we will discuss later, the East Asian NICs, and the Southeast Asian countries that followed in their footsteps, began to encounter some economic problems in the late 1980s. These problems became starkly evident in the late 1990s. Nevertheless, just as ISI had been viewed as the "gospel for Third World industrialization" in the 1950s,[40] so the East Asian export-led growth strategy emerged as the new gospel for many development specialists from the 1970s to the early 1990s. While there was a general consensus that the East Asian export-led growth policies were more successful than the Latin American ISI policies, there was a wide divergence of views as to the reasons for the East Asians' success.

The IPE Perspectives and the East Asian Experience

Liberals, realists, and historical structuralists offered widely differing explanations for the success of the East Asian NICs' export-led growth strategy from the 1960s to the 1980s. According to liberal economists, the East Asian economic "miracle" resulted from the fact that the export-led growth strategy was "outward-oriented," as opposed to the "inward-oriented" import substitution strategy of the Latin American NICs.[41] From this perspective, the East Asians were successful because they did not have "the mistrust of markets and private entrepreneurship that motivates large-scale doctoring in other Asian countries and in African and South American countries."[42] Thus, the East Asian NICs encouraged the growth of free markets, competition, and private entrepreneurship through the liberalization of policies on trade, foreign investment, and exchange rates. In sum, liberals generally attribute the success of the East Asian NICs to their willingness to follow the example of the Western industrial states, which had reaped major benefits from open market policies.

In contrast to the liberals, realists argued that the key to East Asian economic growth (with the possible exception of Hong Kong) was the existence of a strong *developmental state*, which had "a fundamental role in engineering economic growth, development and success in these countries."[43] As early as the eighteenth and nineteenth centuries, Alexander Hamilton and Friedrich List had argued that late industrializers required state intervention if they were to catch up with more advanced nations (see Chapter 3). However, it was not until the early 1980s that Chalmers Johnson first used the phrase *developmental state* in his seminal works on Japan and the East Asian NICs.[44]

According to realists, the developmental states of East Asia have several common characteristics. First, the state provides extensive guidance to the market, strictly controlling investment flows, promoting the development of technology, and protecting selected infant industries. Second, the state identifies development as its top objective, encouraging citizens to increase investment rather than current consumption, and using repression if necessary to enforce its priorities. Third, the state invests heavily in education, to ensure that the population has the skills to meet the standards of global competitiveness. And fourth, the state depends on a highly skilled, technocratic bureaucracy that is committed to instituting economic reforms. Although the ISI and export-led growth models both depend on a large degree of government intervention, realists argue that the policies differ in two critical respects: the East Asian developmental state focuses primarily on developing the country's export industries, while the ISI strategy seeks to build an industrial base mainly to meet domestic demand; and the ISI strategy generally protects all local industries, while the East Asian developmental state supports a small number of key industries that are considered to be "winners."[45]

In marked contrast to the liberals and realists, dependency and world-system theorists argued that the NICs were not in fact achieving genuine economic development. Although the Latin American and East Asian NICs had ascended to a semiperiphery, which was somewhere above the level of the peripheral Third World states, they were simply "more advanced exemplars of dependent development," still dependent on the industrial states in the core.[46] Thus, André Gunder Frank argued that when "the NICs produce end products such as shirts, radios or even cars they are simply increasing their dependent integration into a worldwide division of labor . . . in which they are allocated the least remunerative and technologically obsolete contribution."[47]

In addition to the three main IPE perspectives, a fourth perspective explained the success of the East Asian NICs in terms of domestic social factors, which are often referred to collectively as *political culture*. Political culture can be defined as widely shared social values that affect a state's political economy. Those who emphasized political culture as the key to the East Asians' success argued that the realist focus on the role and strength of the state was insufficient because "the nature of . . . society is important in determining whether or not state policies are effective."[48] The four East Asian NICs (Hong Kong, South Korea, Taiwan, and Singapore) and China and Japan all have political cultures that are strongly influenced by Confucianism.[49] Confucianism is a secular philosophy that emphasizes respect for authority, the role of the government in promoting and protecting the public good, the importance of education, and the value of strong kinship ties in creating incentives for family-based entrepreneurship. Thus, Confucian philosophy is highly supportive of an economic development model based on collective values, hard work and enterprise, and a benevolent state staffed by the most educated individuals. According to some theorists focusing on political culture, Confucianism was a major factor explaining the success of Japan and the East Asian NICs in promoting economic development. (Political culture theorists generally differentiate Southeast from East Asia because the Southeast Asians lack "a unifying cultural force comparable to Confucianism in East Asia.")[50]

Most analysts argued that of the four perspectives, the realist model of the strong developmental state provided the best explanation for the rapid economic growth of the East Asian and Southeast Asian states. However, a financial crisis that beset East and Southeast Asia in the late 1990s raised serious questions about the realist and other models and demonstrated "how rapidly an informed consensus can change."[51]

The Financial Crisis in East and Southeast Asia

Numerous policymakers and academics referred to the "East Asian miracle" from the 1970s to the early 1990s. The emergence of economic problems in this region caused some to question whether the "miracle" was over or even whether it had ever occurred.[52] In July 1997 a financial crisis began in Thailand and then spread to much of Southeast and East Asia. Foreign investors lost confidence in the currencies of these countries, and eventually the crisis spread to Japan. As a result, some countries such as Thailand, Malaysia, Indonesia, and South Korea had to seek large IMF and World Bank loans to bolster their currencies and economies. In view of the financial crisis, it is useful to examine whether analysts had overlooked (or underestimated) some of the shortcomings of the East Asian export-led growth model.

Among theorists, only the historical structuralists had questioned whether the East and Southeast Asian states were achieving genuine, autonomous development, and the financial crisis seemed to add weight to their arguments. It is true that East Asian LDCs grew far more rapidly than LDCs in other regions for most of the 1970s and 1980s, but their development was more fragile and "dependent" in some respects than was earlier assumed. While the existence of strong developmental states did contribute to economic growth in East and Southeast Asia, this growth was also dependent on the policies of the United States and Japan. Countries such as Taiwan and South Korea, with highly strategic positions vis-à-vis the Soviet Union and China, had special linkages with the United States, extending back to the 1950s. Thus, the United States provided South Korea and Taiwan with large sums of military and economic aid and opened its market to their exports while permitting them to follow protectionist policies. East and Southeast Asian economic growth also stemmed from special linkages with Japan. When the Japanese yen increased greatly in value as a result of the Plaza Agreement in 1985, Japanese companies made huge investments in subsidiary plants throughout East and Southeast Asia to take advantage of cheaper costs of production in these countries. These Japanese investments helped the East and Southeast Asians avoid some the worst effects of the debt crisis that ravaged Latin American and African countries in the 1980s.

Beginning in the late 1980s, however, it became evident that the dependence of East and Southeast Asia on the United States and Japan could have major costs as well as benefits. For example, the United States responded to its growing balance-of-payments problems by becoming more protectionist and by charging some East and

Southeast Asian countries with being unfair traders. After the passage of new U.S. trade legislation in 1988, South Korea and Taiwan offered trade concessions they had previously resisted because the United States threatened to retaliate against their "unfair" trade practices. With the breakup of the Soviet Union and the decline of the Cold War, the United States was also less willing to continue supplying large amounts of aid and other support to countries such as South Korea and Taiwan. In sum, changes in the United States' economic and strategic position made it less willing to provide the East Asian NICs with the economic and military support it had given them from the 1950s to the 1970s.[53]

It also became evident in the 1990s that East and Southeast Asian economic development was fragile because of the region's dependent relationship with Japan. These countries were indeed exporting increasing amounts of industrial goods to the West, but often the goods were produced by Japanese subsidiaries; they were designed in Japan, included imported components from Japan, and depended on Japanese technology. For example, South Korea seems to have successfully developed an automobile industry, but the industry is highly dependent on Japanese auto parts and advanced technology. When a large Korean industrial conglomerate (called Samsung) received government approval to enter the auto industry in 1994, it indicated that it would "import all of the advanced technology it needs from Nissan" in Japan.[54] The dependence of East and Southeast Asia on Japan has had negative effects on these countries' balance of trade and payments in recent years. While the East and Southeast Asians generally have large trade surpluses with the West, their trade deficits with Japan have been growing fast.

The problems in East and Southeast Asia are certainly not due only to external factors such as dependence on the United States and Japan. The currency crisis in the late 1990s also revealed that the authoritarian developmental states in the region were not as efficient and immune to political pressures as writers on the East Asian "miracle" often implied. As early as 1968, a prominent U.S. political scientist had argued that authoritarian governments provided needed stability and order in developing societies and that democratic practices were a luxury that should be introduced only later.[55] Third World countries have also often argued that authoritarianism is necessary for the success of the developmental state and that the West should not attempt to impose its concept of democracy on other regions. For a number of years, the authoritarian governments of East and Southeast Asia did oversee some marked improvements in economic growth and prosperity. Although individual freedoms were strictly limited, this policy was justified on both economic and cultural grounds. Such freedoms were not only a luxury that rapidly developing states could ill afford; they also collided with the traditions of political culture in these countries, which emphasized harmony, respect for authority, and collective action.

Some analysts, however, argue that, ironically, these same characteristics "that contributed to [the] economic boom" in East Asia "also provided the necessary conditions for the subsequent bust."[56] For example, the one-party authoritarian states and close government-business linkages in these countries contributed to widespread nepotism; the operation of banks and access to credit depended more on political connections than on market forces. With weak financial regulation, lenders and foreign investors rapidly expanded credit to risky borrowers. Huge sums were spent for questionable building and real estate projects, without regard for their necessity or how they would be financed.[57] These inefficiencies challenge the contention of realists that authoritarian states such as those in East and Southeast Asia facilitate the development process. The forced resignation of President Suharto in May 1998 after 32 years as Indonesia's leader demonstrates that the populace may be less willing to accept one-person rule in Southeast and East Asian countries when economic growth and prosperity falter.

Critics also charge that the liberal-economic measures of economic development, which emphasize composite statistics such as the growth in GNP and per capita GNP, led to an overestimation of East and Southeast Asian development. Thus, environmentalists argue that the East and Southeast Asian recipe for rapid economic growth is not sustainable in the long term. In Indonesia, for example, logging practices are contributing to a deforestation rate of 2.4 million hectares per year; in the Malaysian state of Sarawak, loggers have removed 30 percent of the forest area in 23 years. In Vietnam, resources are being exported with little concern for the social and environmental consequences.[58] Of particular importance in this regard is the concept of *sustainable development,* which was popularized by nongovernmental organizations in the early 1980s and received multilateral approval in the 1987 report of the World Commission on Environment and Development (the Brundtland Report). The Brundtland Report describes sustainable development as a policy that "meets the needs of the present without compromising the ability of future generations to meet their own needs."[59] Sustainable development is a controversial concept because LDCs have argued that they cannot afford to divert resources from their immediate development to pay the costs of following environmentally friendly or sustainable development policies. The LDCs also point out that industrial states did not adopt sustainable policies when they were developing and that the Northern states today produce more global pollutants than the LDCs. Nevertheless, East and Southeast Asia will not be able to sustain their economic growth rates in the long term if they disregard the effects of environmental degradation.

There is no doubt that the export-led growth model has a number of strengths and that the East Asian developmental state outperformed other Third World countries according to most economic indicators in the 1970s and 1980s. However, recent problems in East and Southeast Asia have also demonstrated some serious weaknesses in their export-led growth strategy. Another development strategy was strongly supported by the World Bank, the IMF, and most industrial states in response to the 1980s foreign debt crisis, and more recently in response to the financial crisis in East and Southeast Asia: the orthodox liberal model.

THE REVIVAL OF ORTHODOX LIBERALISM

Development specialists have discussed a number of factors that are likely to prevent other LDCs from adopting the positive aspects of the East Asian developmental state model. For example, two characteristics of the developmental state are critical to its effective functioning: a highly skilled technocratic bureaucracy and close cooperation between major economic groupings such as agriculture, business, and labor. Most

LDCs "still lack the highly professional merit-based bureaucracies and the tradition of cooperation between key economic actors that would permit them to replicate the East Asian model."[60] Successful developmental states have also generally been authoritarian or semiauthoritarian, so they were able to guide the economy and control labor, business, and other private groups. However, current globalization pressures are causing democracy (in a political sense) to spread around the world, and this raises questions as to whether other LDCs could replicate the rapid economic growth rates of the East Asians. The most important constraint on replicating the East Asian developmental state model has been the return of orthodox liberalism and the World Bank/IMF view that "the market rational/market ideological approach is the only correct course for development."[61]

When British Prime Minister Margaret Thatcher and U.S. President Ronald Reagan led a shift to the right with the revival of orthodox liberalism in the late 1970s and early 1980s, the World Bank, IMF, and others launched a strong attack on realist or statist development strategies in the Third World. Liberal scholars often harshly criticized the statist ISI policies in Latin America, comparing them unfavorably with the export-led growth strategies of the East Asian NICs, which they maintained were liberal and market-oriented. (As discussed above, realists strongly disagreed with the liberal interpretation of the East Asian policies.) Orthodox liberal views that the East Asian development successes depended on the operation of liberal market policies played a critical role in the decision by the IMF and World Bank to insist that Third World debtor countries drastically liberalize their policies if they were to receive structural adjustment loans in the 1980s. Thus, IMF and World Bank SALs have been linked with the adoption of policies such as decreased government spending, the privatization of state-owned enterprises, the deregulation of financial and labor markets, and liberal policies toward trade and investment.

Structural Adjustment and Questions About Orthodox Liberalism

In the 1980s, a large number of LDC debtor countries implemented World Bank and IMF-financed structural adjustment programs, and the Third World became "a laboratory for a huge experiment" in promoting economic development through orthodox liberalism.[62] The World Bank/IMF conditions placed on their SALs stemmed from the so-called Washington consensus endorsed in the United States and parts of Europe. An important part of the Washington consensus was the view that the world economy should be as open as possible to the movement of goods, capital, and services.[63] The results of the structural adjustment programs have demonstrated both the strengths and the weaknesses of the liberal perspective on development.

The World Bank's structural adjustment programs were generally most effective in middle-income LDCs that were exporters of manufactures, such as Brazil, Morocco, the Philippines, South Korea, Thailand, Uruguay, and Yugoslavia. These countries had more developed institutions for bringing about policy reforms, and they had better resilience in dealing with the disruptions of adjustment policies. Thus, liberal studies indicate that structural adjustment programs in these countries reduced government budget deficits, increased export earnings, increased financing available for private investment, and enhanced economic efficiency and growth. However, the effect of structural adjustment programs on the poorest and most highly indebted LDCs, and on the poorest groups *within* LDCs, was a far more contentious issue.

In the early 1980s, World Bank officials believed that structural adjustment programs would not hurt the poor. Although these programs were not designed to deal with poverty or promote equity, the bank endorsed liberal-economic views holding that benefits from the efficient allocation of resources under freer markets would naturally filter down to the poor. However, a number of critics argued that the poorest groups were having to bear a disproportionate share of the adjustment burdens. The persistence or exacerbation of poverty in low-income LDCs and in vulnerable groups within LDCs gave credence to these criticisms and eventually forced the World Bank to rethink its approach.[64] The sections that follow examine one Third World region, and one group within Third World states, in which the effects of structural adjustment programs have been most controversial: the sub-Saharan African states and Third World women.

Structural Adjustment and the Sub-Saharan African States

Some of the strongest criticisms of structural adjustment programs have related to their effects on sub-Saharan Africa. The decade of the 1980s, when over two-thirds of sub-Saharan African states were receiving World Bank and IMF structural adjustment loans, is generally considered to be a lost decade for Africa. During this period, economic growth and industrial production stagnated, agricultural output lagged behind population growth, per capita incomes and investment declined, and unemployment increased. Each year the United Nations Development Program ranks countries according to a "human development index," which includes such factors as per capita incomes, adult literacy rates, education, and life expectancy. In 1996, 14 of the 15 lowest-ranked countries in terms of the human development index were African. In 1997, 19 of the 26 poorest countries in the world in terms of per capita GNP were also African.[65] A comprehensive 1988 study by the United Nations Program of Action for African Recovery and Development concluded that although structural adjustment programs had registered a few gains, "for the majority of African states, there has not been even a hint of recovery."[66] (In this section, the term *Africa* refers to sub-Saharan Africa.)

Liberal-economic supporters of structural adjustment argue that these programs are often blamed for problems caused by general economic deterioration. Indeed, the World Bank and IMF were simply reacting to the Third World debt crisis, which had resulted from both inefficient LDC economic policies and a series of unfavorable global economic changes stemming from the 1970s oil crisis. Furthermore, liberals maintain that many problems in Africa, such as political instability, civil wars, and famine, have been unusually resistant to solution and that the economic conditions of Africans would be even worse without World Bank and IMF structural adjustment programs. Liberals maintain that because state-led strategies such as ISI were clearly unsuccessful, the World Bank and IMF market-led prescriptions are the best possible strategies for bringing about adjustment and growth.[67]

Critics, by contrast, argue that World Bank/IMF structural adjustment programs in Africa are defective in several major respects: they place too much emphasis on market-oriented policies, they do not contribute to economic growth, and their costs fall most heavily on the poorest groups and countries. The strongest criticisms relate to World Bank/IMF demands that Third World debtors downgrade the role of the government and emphasize privatization so that market forces can operate. Because the public sector provides a critical source of employment for Africans, a downgrading of the government's role causes unemployment. As the capacity of the government declines, crucial infrastructure such as transportation and communications, and services such as health care and education also suffer. Furthermore, the emphasis on privatization does not take account of the fact that private firms are often unwilling and/or unable to supply essential public goods required for development. Third World countries must therefore rely heavily on their governments to provide the resources for technical and scientific education of the populace and for other aspects of human capital necessary for industrialization and competitiveness.

Critics also oppose the emphasis that World Bank and IMF structural adjustment programs place on trade liberalization. Middle-income Latin American and East and Southeast Asian countries may reap some major benefits from such trade liberalization, but the benefits are far more dubious for lower-income African and Asian LDCs. Because many Latin American and East and Southeast Asian countries have had lengthy periods of sheltering their domestic industries, these industries may now be better able to compete with growing imports. Most African LDCs, by contrast, are only beginning to embark on the path to industrialization, and they require continued protection for their infant industries. Critics charge that World Bank and IMF market-based prescriptions have been ineffective and/or have harmed the economic development process in Africa. This is especially true because most African LDCs are at an early stage in development and continue to require a substantial role for the government.[68]

Structural Adjustment and Third World Women

A major criticism of World Bank and IMF structural adjustment programs is that they have disregarded the issue of gender. Almost all societies (developed as well as less developed) are characterized in varying degrees by gender inequality and the exploitation of women; critics argue that it is therefore not possible for structural adjustment programs to be "gender-neutral." By disregarding the subsidiary role of women, these programs often reinforce male bias and exacerbate the economic and social problems confronting women in LDCs.

The position of Third World women varies widely as a result of diverse cultural values, historical factors, levels of economic development, and types of government in different LDCs. Women in the same society may also occupy vastly different positions depending on such factors as social class and ethnicity. Nevertheless, it is possible to generalize about some characteristics of women's positions in Third World societies:

- In the household, women spend much more time than men, on the average, on unpaid subsistence work involving child care, food production and preparation, health care, and education.

- In work outside the home, women are overrepresented relative to men in the "informal" sector of the economy. Unlike formal-sector employment, work in the informal sector is largely unaffected by government regulations and standards. About three-fourths of those in the informal sector are service providers such as roadside food stall operators, market traders, messengers, and shoe shiners. Informal-sector earnings on average are well below those of the formal sector.
- In the formal sector, women are more concentrated in the lower-skilled, lower-wage occupations, and they also are often paid less than men for doing the same work.
- Compared with men, women are more important in agricultural labor and less important in industry. In Africa, for example, women produce about 90 percent of the food, but they are less important in the production of export crops.
- If one combines women's lower wages in the formal sector with their overrepresentation in agriculture, the informal sector, and work in the household, women's income is normally significantly less than that of men. Thus, female-headed households in which women are the sole breadwinners are among the poorest groups in Third World societies.[69]

The position of women in Third World societies as outlined above should be considered in any structural adjustment programs. However, World Bank policy prescriptions are based on macroeconomic concepts, which view the economy as a whole rather than looking at individual firms or households. Because much of women's time is spent doing unpaid subsistence work in the household, which does not appear in production statistics, the World Bank gives little attention to the effect of its structural adjustment policies on women's work time. For example, structural adjustment programs usually call for cutbacks in government spending, leading to decreases in the provision of public goods in areas such as health, education, and water and sanitation facilities. As a result of these cutbacks, much of the burden of health care and education shifts to the community and household, where women play the most prominent role.

World Bank and IMF policy prescriptions that raise the cost of basic foodstuffs simply add to the problems of Third World women. Structural adjustment programs usually require that LDCs lower government deficits by phasing out food subsidies and provide incentives to farmers by raising the prices they receive for their tradeable goods. Because of the higher food costs, women must use cheaper foods that take longer to prepare, such as coarse grain and root crops rather than wheat products, and they must rely on home baking rather than the purchase of bread. Hospitals, too, may succeed in cutting their costs per patient largely by shifting many of the costs of care to the unpaid economy of the household.[70] The World Bank views cutbacks in government spending and subsidies as an indication of increased efficiency, but in fact costs are simply being shifted from the paid to the unpaid economy, where women do most of the work.

Even if women worked only in the household, the off-loading of government services and subsidies would place unreasonable new burdens on them. The need for income, however, "has forced women into the labour force to protect their families' survival."[71] Thus, women as a proportion of the total labor force rose in Asia from 29 percent in 1950 to 33.8 percent in 1985, and in Latin America they rose from 18 to 24.2 percent. Women have often fared poorly as members of the formal and informal labor force under structural adjustment programs. In sub-Saharan Africa, for example, farmers were paid higher prices to encourage them to produce more crops for the export market. Cash crops, however, tend to be men's crops, while subsistence food crops are more often women's crops. Men also tend to market most of the crops produced by both women and men, and women do not benefit from the increased prices because men often keep a high proportion of the revenue for their own use.[72]

Critics thus argue that structural adjustment programs affect Third World women adversely in their multiple roles as mothers, managers of the household, community leaders, and workers in the formal and informal sectors. Only when the World Bank and IMF dispense with the myth that structural adjustment is gender neutral will they be able to confront the problems that their structural adjustment programs pose for Third World women.

Structural Adjustment and the Theoretical Perspectives

Historical structuralists believe that there is no point in attempting to alter World Bank and IMF structural adjustment programs to take account of the most disadvantaged groups (e.g., women) and states (e.g., in sub-Saharan Africa). From this perspective, structural adjustment programs are not "simply an innocuous remedial package for sustained growth and development." Instead, they are "an almost deliberate scheme for the perpetuation of export dependency . . . and reproduction of existing conditions of global inequality."[73] The World Bank, the IMF, and other Northern-dominated institutions caused the problems of Third World indebtedness in the first place; it is therefore unrealistic to expect that they will ever design structural adjustment programs to alleviate Third World problems.

Interventionist liberals, by contrast, believe that structural adjustment programs are necessary to combat domestic inefficiencies and corruption in Third World economies. However, they are more receptive than orthodox liberals to state interventionism, and they argue that the World Bank and the IMF should be doing more to focus on the human development aspects of adjustment. From this perspective, the World Bank should be more sensitive to the implications of its adjustment policies for the poorest groups and states in the Third World.[74] From a realist perspective, the World Bank and the IMF are not following the correct policies in emphasizing the downsizing of government through privatization, deregulation, and trade liberalization. Realists argue that late industrializers, whether they be the United States and Germany in the nineteenth century, the East Asian NICs from the 1950s to the 1980s, or other LDCs today, *require* a large degree of government interventionism to catch up with the leading powers. A strong state in the realist view is therefore an essential prerequisite for economic development in the Third World.

ANOTHER SHIFT IN DEVELOPMENT STRATEGY?

In the late 1980s and the 1990s, the World Bank became more responsive to criticisms of its structural adjustment policies and began to take a second look at its orthodox liberal approach to development. Two issues are of particular concern here: the bank's approach to the role of the state and its approach to the most vulnerable groups in Third World societies.

The Role of the State in Development

Protracted economic and political problems in the least developed states in Africa and Asia led to a gradual recognition by the World Bank that the state had a significant role to play in economic development. At the same time, however, the bank did not wish to veer too far from orthodox liberal views favoring the unfettered market. The evolution in bank thinking was evident throughout the 1990s. In its 1991 *World Development Report,* the World Bank reiterated its views that "governments need to do less in those areas where markets work, or can be made to work." However, the bank also acknowledged that "governments need to do more in those areas where markets cannot be relied upon" such as health, education, nutrition, family planning, and poverty alleviation.[75] In 1993, the World Bank published a policy research report titled *The East Asian Miracle,* in which it acknowledged that government intervention in some areas may have contributed to economic growth in East Asia.[76] Nevertheless, the bulk of the World Bank's *East Asian Miracle* study attributed the East Asians' success primarily to their liberal "market-friendly" approach.[77]

The World Bank focused its 1997 *World Development Report* specifically on "The State in a Changing World." (Each year's *World Development Report* has a different theme.) In this report, the bank attributed sub-Saharan Africa's severe development problems to a deterioration in the effectiveness and legitimacy of the state. It also indicated that a clear priority for African countries should be "a thorough reform of the state, so that it can deliver quality public services and facilitate private activity."[78] In sum, the World Bank expressed some recognition in the 1990s that the structural adjustment programs of the 1980s had overemphasized downsizing the state without giving sufficient attention to the state's role in promoting economic development. While World Bank supporters generally credit the institution with adopting a more flexible approach, critics argue that the bank's orthodox liberal policies have not really changed. From this perspective, the bank's recognition of the state's role is superficial, and it is still basically committed to "market fundamentalism."[79]

A Focus on Vulnerable Groups

In the 1970s, bilateral aid donors such as the United States, Canada, and the European countries, as well as international organizations such as the World Bank, had placed some emphasis on a basic needs approach in development assistance to the Third World. For example, in 1973, the U.S. Congress made the satisfaction of **basic human**

needs the main declared objective of the Agency for International Development (the main U.S. foreign aid agency). In the same year, the World Bank president, Robert S. McNamara, proposed that a major part of development funding should be used to assist the poorest 40 percent of those living in the Third World. While these declared intentions to focus on basic needs were only partly fulfilled in practice, the World Bank did increase its lending in the 1970s for agricultural and rural development, low-cost urban housing and slum rehabilitation, and primary and nonformal education.[80]

However, the shift toward orthodox liberalism under Prime Minister Margaret Thatcher and President Ronald Reagan, combined with the foreign debt crisis, "led to a complete switch in major international institutions' approach to development."[81] World Bank structural adjustment loans in the 1980s were conditioned upon the implementation of orthodox liberal policies, and the basic needs of vulnerable groups were largely forgotten. Indeed, the discussion above of sub-Saharan Africa and Third World women shows that the poorest and most vulnerable groups in Third World countries often bore a disproportionate share of the burden of World Bank and IMF structural adjustment policies.

Throughout the 1980s, there were growing pressures on the World Bank as the main multilateral development agency to devote some attention to the distributional effects of structural adjustment. For example, in a 1987–88 two-volume study titled *Adjustment with a Human Face*, the United Nations Children's Fund (UNICEF) indicated that it was necessary to include a "poverty alleviation dimension" in adjustment programs.[82] In response to the growing criticism, the World Bank finally shifted its position somewhat in 1989 when it acknowledged that "sub-Saharan Africa has now witnessed almost a decade of falling per capita incomes and accelerating ecological degradation" and that there was a need for "special measures . . . to alleviate poverty and protect the vulnerable."[83] Pursuant to its change in focus, the World Bank devoted the 1990 issue of its *World Development Report* to poverty reduction, and it began to redesign its structural adjustment programs to decrease adverse effects on the poor.[84] The bank also began to give more attention to the education of Third World women and to ensuring that a larger percentage of its loans were directed to human resource development. Furthermore, a larger share of World Bank development loans were directed to poverty reduction, basic education, health conditions, and water supply and sanitation.

A tension nevertheless continues to exist between structural adjustment pressures for orthodox liberal reforms on the one hand and the protection of vulnerable Third World groups on the other. Thus, the World Bank's strategies for poverty reduction continue to have limitations.[85] Furthermore, the pressures of globalization and the end of the Cold War have diminished the concern of the advanced industrial states about poverty and discontent in the Third World. A prime example of the growing marginalization of the poorest Third World countries and peoples is the extent to which foreign aid has become a lower priority for Northern industrial states in recent years. The greatest share of foreign aid is official development assistance (ODA), which consists of grants or loans on concessional terms to LDCs and multilateral institutions provided by official agencies in the industrial states. *Aid grants* do not require repayment. *Concessional loans* have lower interest rates, longer grace periods before repayment begins, and longer repayment periods than commercial loans.

In 1969, a Commission on International Development (the Pearson Commission), which had been formed at the suggestion of the World Bank to study foreign aid, recommended that every advanced industrial state should devote at least 0.7 percent of its GNP to development assistance.[86] Table 11.5 shows that despite this recommendation, the members of the OECD have *decreased* rather than increased the percentage of their GNP devoted to official development assistance to Third World countries in recent years. The OECD countries' ODA as a percentage of GNP amounted to 0.52 percent in 1960, but this figure fell to 0.37 percent in 1980, 0.33 percent in 1990, and 0.25 percent in 1996. Significantly, Table 11.5 shows that the ODA of the two largest bilateral aid donors in 1996, Japan and the United States, amounted to only 0.20 and 0.12 percent of their GNPs, respectively. The decrease in ODA has been especially dramatic in the 1990s, with net ODA falling in real terms by 16 percent between 1992 and 1996.[87]

Although many critics believed that development assistance had not succeeded in its stated objective of promoting economic growth and helping the poorest groups in LDCs, there were also other reasons why ODA declined in the 1980s and 1990s. First, as the pressures of globalization increased, OECD countries began to look to

TABLE 11.5

NET ODA to the Third World Countries as a Percentage of GNP (OECD members)

	1960	1970	1980	1990	1996
Australia	0.38	0.59	0.48	0.34	0.30
Austria	—	0.13	0.23	0.25	0.24
Belgium	0.88	0.48	0.50	0.46	0.34
Canada	0.19	0.43	0.43	0.44	0.32
Denmark	0.09	0.38	0.74	0.94	1.04
Finland	0	0	0.22	0.63	0.34
France	1.38	0.65	0.63	0.60	0.48
Germany	0.31	0.32	0.44	0.42	0.33
Ireland	0	0	0.16	0.16	0.31
Italy	0.22	0.16	0.17	0.31	0.20
Japan	0.24	0.23	0.32	0.31	0.20
Luxembourg	0	0	0	0.21	0.44
Netherlands	0.31	0.63	0.97	0.92	0.81
New Zealand	0	0	0.33	0.23	0.21
Norway	0.11	0.33	0.87	1.17	0.85
Portugal	1.45	0.45	0	0.25	0.21
Spain	0	0	0	0.20	0.22
Sweden	0.05	0.37	0.78	0.91	0.84
Switzerland	0.04	0.14	0.24	0.32	0.34
United Kingdom	0.56	0.37	0.35	0.27	0.27
United States	0.53	0.31	0.27	0.21	0.12
Total	**0.52**	**0.34**	**0.37**	**0.33**	**0.25**

Source: Organisation for Economic Co-operation and Development, *Development Co-operation* (various years).

their aid budgets as a means of cutting spending in an increasingly competitive global environment. Second, with the election of U.S. President Ronald Reagan in 1981, orthodox liberals were "poised for attack on one of [their] . . . long-standing pet peeves: foreign aid."[88] The feeling took hold among conservatives in the United States and other OECD countries that ODA was a form of glorified welfare program that provided only marginal rates of return. A third important factor in the decline of ODA was the breakup of the Soviet bloc. With the end of the Cold War, the Third World lost an important source of leverage in gaining more assistance from the Western industrial states, and it also found that emerging countries such as Poland, Russia, and the Ukraine had become major competitors for development assistance from the OECD countries. Aid from OECD countries to more advanced emerging countries (e.g., Russia, Poland, and the Czech Republic) and also to some more advanced LDCs (e.g., Kuwait and Singapore) is referred to as **official aid (OA)** rather than official development assistance (ODA). When the former Eastern bloc countries became major recipients of OA in the 1990s, the volume of ODA to Third World countries declined.[89]

The World Bank and the advanced industrial states have become more aware of the need to pursue structural adjustment and development programs that recognize the important role of Third World states and are attuned to the needs of the poorest and most vulnerable groups. Nevertheless, in the current environment of global competitiveness and orthodox liberalism, the commitment to these objectives is inevitably limited.

CONCLUSION

The postwar period has generally been marked by prosperity and economic growth for the industrial states of the North, but this has not been the case for many of the poorer countries and peoples in the South. Indeed, other than a small number of newly industrialized countries and the OPEC states, the income gap between the North and the South has been growing. This chapter has examined some of the strategies LDCs have used in attempts to promote their economic development. The discussion of import-substituting industrialization, export-led growth, and socialist and orthodox liberal models provides some basis for drawing preliminary conclusions about the most appropriate development strategies for Third World states.

First, the same development strategy is not necessarily feasible or desirable for all Third World states. Although a number of East and Southeast Asian LDCs achieved impressive economic growth rates through an export-led growth strategy, it is unlikely that many other LDCs could emulate their experience. The East Asian NICs' success resulted from a confluence of favorable external and domestic circumstances, such as U.S. and Japanese support and the presence of highly skilled, technocratic government bureaucracies in East Asia. These characteristics are often lacking in poorer African and Asian LDCs. Indeed, many sub-Saharan African countries with ongoing economic and political crises today would find it impossible to follow the developmental state model of the East Asian NICs. The return to liberal orthodoxy in the 1980s has also precluded many LDCs from following state-led growth policies. Instead, World Bank and IMF structural adjustment programs have pressured LDC debtors to engage in deregulation, privatization, and other measures to downsize the role of the state.[90]

Second, negative experiences with World Bank and IMF structural adjustment programs have pointed to the pitfalls of focusing on the economic aspects of development without looking sufficiently at the human aspects. Thus, the United Nations Development Program began to publish an annual *Human Development Report* in 1990 to emphasize the fact that "there was no automatic link between growth and human development."[91] The human development approach assesses development not only in terms of a country's per capita GNP growth but also in terms of such factors as life expectancy, health and sanitation facilities, education, employment, the income gap between rich and poor, the gender-gap, and the rural-urban gap. In thinking about human development, for example, it is necessary to understand how women's unpaid subsistence work in the household puts them at a disadvantage in markets.[92] Only by taking such human factors into consideration can we understand that the main purpose of economic development should be to improve human well-being.

Third, an economic development strategy should strike a realistic balance "between the state and the market so as to stimulate a positive and dynamic interaction between them."[93] While ISI policies emphasize state intervention and give too little consideration to market signals, orthodox liberal approaches disregard the fact that late industrializers often require an active role for the state. Governments in East and Southeast Asian states were particularly adept at using market interactions to their advantage, and this enabled them to register some striking economic gains, even during the 1980s foreign debt crisis. However, the East and Southeast Asians have also too often substituted "political whim . . . for proper risk assessment for commercial activities," and their failure to provide sufficient banking regulations was a major factor contributing to their 1990s financial crisis.[94] The mixed record of the East Asian governments indicates that it is not government regulation per se that should concern us but finding the amount and type of regulation that will ensure economic stability, confidence, and the proper functioning of market signals.

Finally, an economic development strategy should take account of the difference in wealth and power between the North and the South. Except in a small number of East Asian NICs, the North-South income gap has continued to widen, and the 1980s foreign debt crisis was a reminder of the degree to which the South is still dependent on the North. While Northern linkages in trade, foreign investment, and other economic areas are critical to the South, development strategies should also aim at developing some ability of the South to act independently. One possible route to greater self-sufficiency is through establishing more South-South economic linkages. South-South trade linkages can enable LDCs to foster new comparative advantages. These countries can raise their production and export of industrial goods. Indeed, about 60 percent of the goods traded between Southern countries are manufactures.[95] One example of an important South-South regional integration agreement is Mercosur (the *Mercado Común del Sur*), which was formed by Argentina, Brazil, Paraguay, and Uruguay in the Southern Cone of South America in 1991. The importance of Mercosur stems from the fact that Argentina and Brazil together account for over half of

Latin America's GDP, and that it is the world's fourth largest integrated market after the European Union, NAFTA, and Japan.[96]

All three theoretical perspectives—realism, liberalism, and historical structuralism—have had something important to say regarding the most appropriate strategies for promoting Third World economic development. Scholars who focus on domestic societal factors such as political culture have also improved our understanding of which strategies a Third World state might realistically follow. Furthermore, there seems to be no single "best" development strategy for all Third World states, because of major differences among these states and their positions in the world. A variety of Third World development strategies therefore will be, and should be, pursued in the future, as they have been in the past.

NOTES

1. Bretton Woods Commission, *Bretton Woods: Looking to the Future,* Commission Report, Staff Review, Background Papers (Washington, DC: Bretton Woods Committee, July 1994), p. B3.

2. See Howard Handelman, *The Challenge of Third World Development* (Upper Saddle River, NJ: Prentice Hall, 1996), pp. 3–10.

3. World Bank, *World Development Report 1991* (New York: Oxford University Press, 1991), p. 2.

4. Stephan Haggard, *Developing Nations and the Politics of Global Integration* (Washington: Brookings Institution, 1995), p. 1.

5. Organisation for Economic Co-operation and Development, *Development Co-operation— 1994 Report* (Paris: OECD, 1995), p. 86.

6. Organisation for Economic Co-operation and Development, *Development Co-operation— 1997 Report* (Paris: OECD, 1998), p. 55.

7. *Bilateral aid* is assistance that flows directly from donor to recipient governments. *Multilateral aid* is assistance that flows from donor governments through international organizations (such as the World Bank), whose policies are determined collectively by donors and recipients.

8. Robert Wade, "Japan, the World Bank, and the Art of Paradigm Maintenance: The East Asian Miracle in Political Perspective," *New Left Review* no. 217 (May/June 1996), p. 5.

9. Wade, "Japan, the World Bank, and the Art of Paradigm Maintenance," p. 5. See also Guy Gran, *Development by People: Citizen Construction of a Just World* (New York: Praeger, 1983), p. 28.

10. *The World Bank Annual Report—1997* (Washington: World Bank, 1997), pp. 134–137.

11. Melissa H. Birch and Thomas J. Biersteker, "The World Bank," in Thomas J. Biersteker, ed., *Dealing with Debt: International Financial Negotiations and Adjustment Bargaining* (Boulder, CO: Westview Press, 1993), pp. 40–42.

12. *The World Bank Annual Report—1997*, p. 149.

13. See Theodore Cohn, "Developing Countries in the International Civil Service: The Case of the World Bank Group," *International Review of Administrative Sciences* 41-1 (1975), pp. 47–56.

14. See Stephen D. Krasner, *Structural Conflict: The Third World Against Global Liberalism* (Berkeley: University of California Press, 1985), pp. 146–50; Cheryl Payer, *The World Bank: A Critical Analysis* (New York: Monthly Review Press, 1982), pp. 43–48.

15. *International Financial Corporation Annual Report—1995* (Washington, DC: IFC, 1995), pp. 5–6; "Hey, Big Lender," *The Economist,* April 23, 1994, pp. 81–82.

16. See Ronald T. Libby, "International Development Association: A Legal Fiction Designed to Secure an LDC Constituency," *International Organization* 29-4 (Autumn 1975), pp. 1065–1072.

17. For a full listing of the countries in these three categories, see *The World Bank Annual Report—1997,* pp. 157–158.

18. Paul Lewis, "Clinton Backs Funds for World Bank Agency," *New York Times,* October 12, 1995, p. C4; "Aid for the World's Poorest," *New York Times,* October 18, 1995, p. A18; *The World Bank Annual Report—1998,* p. xii.

19. The idea of establishing a multilateral investment guarantee agency emerged as early as the 1950s (*Convention Establishing the Multilateral Investment Guarantee Agency and Commentary on the Convention* [Washington, DC: IBRD, October 11, 1985], p. 47). For a detailed discussion of the MIGA, see Ibrahim F. I. Shihata, *MIGA and Foreign Investment: Origins, Operations, Policies and Basic Documents of the Multilateral Investment Guarantee Agency* (Dordrecht: Nijhoff, 1988).

20. See Anne O. Krueger, Constantine Michalopoulos, and Vernon W. Ruttan, with Keith Jay, *Aid and Development* (Baltimore: Johns Hopkins University Press, 1989), pp. 106–108; and John White, *Pledged to Development: A Study of International Consortia and the Strategy of Aid* (London: Overseas Development Institute, 1967).

21. See John White, *Regional Development Banks: A Study of Institutional Style* (London: Overseas Development Institute, 1970). The most comprehensive recent studies of the multilateral development banks are contained in a five-volume series published in association with the North-South Institute in Ottawa, Canada: E. Phillip English and Harris M. Mule, *The African Development Bank;* Nihal Kappagoda, *The Asian Development Bank;* Chandra Hardy, *The Caribbean Development Bank;* Diana Tussie, *The Inter-American Development Bank;* and Roy Culpeper, *Titans or Behemoths?* (Boulder, CO: Rienner, 1995–97).

22. See Raúl Prebisch, *The Economic Development of Latin America and Its Principal Problems* (New York: United Nations Economic Commission for Latin America, 1950) 7-1, pp. 1–59; H. W. Singer, "The Distribution of Gains Between Investing and Borrowing Countries," *American Economic Review* 40-2 (May 1950), pp. 473–485.

23. Ozay Mehmet, *Westernizing the Third World: The Eurocentricity of Economic Development Theories* (London: Routledge, 1995), p. 78; John Rapley, *Understanding Development: Theory and Practice* (Boulder, CO: Rienner, 1996), pp. 27–34.

24. Luiz Carlos Bresser Pereira, "Development Economics and the World Bank's Identity Crisis," *Review of International Political Economy* 2-2 (Spring 1995), pp. 215–217; Edward S. Mason and Robert E. Asher, *The World Bank Since Bretton Woods* (Washington: Brookings Institution, 1973), pp. 150–153.

25. See Rapley, *Understanding Development,* pp. 27–36.

26. Theodore Cohn, *Canadian Food Aid: Domestic and Foreign Policy Implications* (Denver, CO: University of Denver, Graduate School in International Studies, 1979), pp. 25–27.

27. Sylvia Maxfield and James N. Nolt, "Protectionism and the Internationalization of Capital: U.S. Sponsorship of Import Substitution Industrialization in the Philippines, Turkey and Argentina," *International Studies Quarterly* 34-1 (March 1990), p. 50.

28. Anne O. Krueger, *Trade Policies and Developing Nations* (Washington: Brookings Institution, 1995), pp. 3–10, 33–44; Rapley, *Understanding Development,* pp. 33–44; Stephan

Haggard, *Pathways from the Periphery: The Politics of Growth in the Newly Industrializing Countries* (Ithaca, NY: Cornell University Press, 1990), pp. 9–14.

29. Anne O. Krueger, "The Effects of Trade Strategies on Growth," *Finance and Development* 20-2 (June 1983), p. 8; Bresser Pereira, "Development Economics and the World Bank's Identity Crisis," p. 216.

30. Raúl Prebisch, *Towards a Dynamic Development Policy for Latin America* (New York: United Nations, 1963), p. 71. See also Raúl Prebisch, "Five Stages in My Thinking on Development," in Gerald M. Meier and Dudley Seers, eds., *Pioneers in Development* (New York: Oxford University Press, 1984), p. 181.

31. See Bela Balassa, "The Process of Industrial Development and Alternative Development Strategies," in Bela Balassa, ed., *The Newly Industrializing Countries in the World Economy* (New York: Pergamon Press, 1981), pp. 5–16.

32. This section draws partly on Rapley, *Understanding Development*, pp. 44–47.

33. Joseph L. Love, "The Origins of Dependency Analysis," *Journal of Latin American Studies* 22 (February 1990), pp. 143–160.

34. James H. Mittelman and Mustapha Kamal Pasha, *Out from Underdevelopment Revisited: Changing Global Structures and the Remaking of the Third World* (London: Macmillan, 2nd edition, 1997), pp. 181–214.

35. David Slater, "The Political Meanings of Development: In Search of New Horizons," in Frans J. Schuurman, *Beyond the Impasse: New Direction in Development Theory* (London: Zed Books, 1993), pp. 101–105.

36. John M. Page, "The East Asian Miracle: An Introduction," *World Development* 22-4 (1994), p. 619; Robert Wade, *Governing the Market: Economic Theory and the Role of Government in East Asian Industrialization* (Princeton, NJ: Princeton University Press, 1990), p. 34.

37. See, for example, Arnold C. Harberger, "Growth, Industrialization and Economic Structure: Latin America and East Asia Compared," in Helen Hughes, ed., *Achieving Industrialization in East Asia* (Cambridge: Cambridge University Press, 1988), pp. 164–194; Haggard, *Pathways from the Periphery*, chs. 3–7; and Bela Balassa, *Policy Choices for the 1990s* (London: Macmillan, 1993), pp. 56–67.

38. Wade, *Governing the Market*, p. 34.

39. Krueger, *Trade Policies and Developing Nations*, pp. 20–23.

40. Mehmet, *Westernizing the Third World*, p. 78.

41. On inward- versus outward-oriented development strategies, see Bela Balassa, *The Newly Industrializing Countries in the World Economy* (New York: Pergamon Press, 1981), pp. 6–24.

42. Staffan Burenstam Linder, *The Pacific Century: Economic and Political Consequences of Asian-Pacific Dynamism* (Stanford, CA: Stanford University Press, 1986), p. 31.

43. Ronen Palan and Jason Abbott, with Phil Deans, *State Strategies in the Global Political Economy* (London: Pinter, 1996), p. 78.

44. See Chalmers Johnson, "Introduction—The Taiwan Model," in James C. Hsiung et al., eds., *Contemporary Republic of China: The Taiwan Experience 1950–1980* (New York: Praeger, 1981), pp. 9–18; and Chalmers Johnson, *MITI and the Japanese Miracle: The Growth of Industrial Policy, 1925–1975* (Stanford, CA: Stanford University Press, 1982).

45. Rapley, *Understanding Development*, pp. 124–127; Adrian Leftwich, "Bringing Politics Back In: Towards a Model of the Developmental State," *Journal of Development Studies* 31-3 (February 1995), pp. 401–403.

46. Peter Evans, *Dependent Development: The Alliance of Multinational, State, and Local Capital in Brazil* (Princeton, NJ: Princeton University Press, 1979), p. 33.
47. Quoted in William Nester, "The Development of Japan, Taiwan and South Korea: Ends and Means, Free Trade, Dependency, or Neomercantilism?" *Journal of Developing Societies* 6 (1990), p. 206.
48. Cal Clark and Steve Chan, "MNCs and Developmentalism: Domestic Structure as an Explanation for East Asian Dynamism," in Thomas Risse-Kappen, ed., *Bringing Transnational Relations Back In: Non-State Actors, Domestic Structures and International Institutions* (Cambridge: Cambridge University Press, 1995), p. 125.
49. For a detailed discussion of Confucian political culture in East Asia, see Lucian W. Pye with Mary W. Pye, *Asian Power and Politics: The Cultural Dimensions of Authority* (Cambridge, MA: Belknap Press of Harvard University Press, 1985), ch. 3.
50. Pye, *Asian Power and Politics*, p. 90; Clark and Chan, "MNCs and Developmentalism," pp. 120–123.
51. Christopher Lingle, "What Ever Happened to the 'Asian Century'?" *World Economic Affairs* 2-2 (Spring 1998), p. 32.
52. See, for example, Seth Mydans, "An 'Asian Miracle' Now Seems Like a Mirage," *New York Times*, October 22, 1997, pp. A1, A8.
53. Walden Bello and Stephanie Rosenfeld, *Dragons in Distress: Asia's Miracle Economies in Crisis* (San Francisco: Institute for Food and Development Policy, 1990), pp. 3–10; I.M. Destler, *American Trade Politics* (Washington, D.C.: Institute for International Economics, 2nd edition, 1992), pp. 131–133.
54. Walter Hatch and Kozo Yamamura, *Asia in Japan's Embrace: Building a Regional Production Alliance* (Cambridge: Cambridge University Press, 1996), p. 37.
55. See Samuel P. Huntington, *Political Order in Changing Societies* (New Haven, CT: Yale University Press, 1968).
56. Lingle, "What Ever Happened to the 'Asian Century'?" p. 33.
57. Edward A. Gargan, "Currency Assault Unnerves Asians," *New York Times*, July 29, 1997, pp. A1, C15; Joseph Stiglitz, "How to Fix Asian Economies," *New York Times*, October 31, 1997, p. A19.
58. Walden Bello, "Overview of Current Economic, Strategic and Political Developments in Southeast and South Asia," *Focus Files* (Bangkok, Thailand), October 1997, p. 3.
59. World Commission on Environment and Development, *Our Common Future* (Oxford: Oxford University Press, 1987), p. 8.
60. Handelman, *The Challenge of Third World Development*, p. 228.
61. Palan and Abbott, *State Strategies in the Global Political Economy*, p. 99.
62. Rapley, *Understanding Development*, p. 76.
63. Wade, "Japan, the World Bank, and the Art of Paradigm Maintenance," p. 5.
64. James H. Weaver, "What Is Structural Adjustment?" in Daniel M. Schydlowsky, ed., *Structural Adjustment: Retrospect and Prospect* (Westport, CT: Praeger, 1995), pp. 12–13; Barend A. de Vries, "The World Bank's Focus on Poverty," in Jo Marie Griesgraber and Berhard G. Gunter, eds., *The World Bank: Lending on a Global Scale* (London: Pluto Press, 1996), pp. 68–69.
65. United Nations Development Program, *Human Development Report 1996* (New York: Oxford University Press, 1996), pp. 136–137; World Bank, *World Development Report 1997* (New York: Oxford University Press, 1997), p. 214.

66. Quoted in Julius O. Ihonvbere, "Economic Crisis, Structural Adjustment and Africa's Future," in Gloria Thomas-Emeagwali, ed., *Women Pay the Price: Structural Adjustment in Africa and the Caribbean* (Trenton, NJ: Africa World Press, 1995), p. 137.

67. For a strong defense of World Bank structural adjustment programs in Africa, see Elliot Berg, "African Adjustment Programs: False Attacks and True Dilemmas," in Schydlowsky, ed., *Structural Adjustment,* pp. 89–107.

68. Rapley, *Understanding Development,* pp. 83–92; J. Barry Riddell, "Things Fall Apart Again: Structural Adjustment Programmes in Sub-Saharan Africa," *Journal of Modern African Studies* 30-1 (1992), pp. 53–68.

69. Frances Stewart, "Can Adjustment Programmes Incorporate the Interests of Women?" in Haleh Afshar and Carolyne Dennis, eds., *Women and Adjustment Policies in the Third World* (New York: St. Martin's Press, 1992), pp. 22–24.

70. Diane Elson, "Male Bias in Macro-Economics: The Case of Structural Adjustment," in Diane Elson, ed., *Male Bias in the Development Process* (Manchester, UK: Manchester University Press, 1991), pp. 175–178.

71. Stewart, "Can Adjustment Programmes Incorporate the Interests of Women?" p. 27.

72. Elson, "Male Bias in Macro-Economics," p. 173; Stewart, "Can Adjustment Programmes Incorporate the Interests of Women?" p. 22.

73. Gloria Thomas-Emeagwali, "Introductory Perspectives: Monetarists, Liberals and Radicals: Contrasting Perspectives on Gender and Structural Adjustment," in Thomas-Emeagwali, ed., *Women Pay the Price,* p. 5.

74. Thomas-Emeagwali, "Introductory Perspectives," pp. 3–4.

75. World Bank, *World Development Report 1991,* p. 9.

76. See World Bank, *The East Asian Miracle: Economic Growth and Public Policy,* Policy Research Report (Oxford: Oxford University Press, 1993).

77. World Bank, *The East Asian Miracle,* p. 26; Wade, "Japan, the World Bank, and the Art of Paradigm Maintenance," pp. 3–36.

78. World Bank, *World Development Report 1997,* p. 162.

79. Alice H. Amsden, "Why Isn't the Whole World Experimenting with the East Asian Model to Develop? Review of the East Asian Miracle," *World Development* 22-4 (1994), pp. 627–633.

80. Robert L. Ayres, *Banking on the Poor: The World Bank and World Poverty* (Cambridge, MA: MIT Press, 1983), pp. 4–6; Anthony Bottrall, "The McNamara Strategy: Putting Precept into Practice," *ODI Review,* 1 (1974), pp. 70–80; Paul Dickson, "A Fresh Look at the World Bank," *Vista* 8-6 (June 1973), pp. 24–49.

81. Giovannia Andrea Cornia, Richard Jolly, and Frances Stewart, eds., *Adjustment with a Human Face, Vol. 1: Protecting the Vulnerable and Promoting Growth* (Oxford, UK: Clarendon Press, 1987), p. 6.

82. Cornia, Jolly, and Stewart, eds., *Adjustment with a Human Face,* vol. 1, p. 7.

83. World Bank, *Sub-Saharan Africa: From Crisis to Sustainable Growth, a Long-Term Perspective Study* (Washington: World Bank, 1989), pp. 17, xi. See also Ihonvbere, "Economic Crisis, Structural Adjustment and Africa's Future," pp. 138–147.

84. See World Bank, *World Development Report 1990, "Poverty"* (New York: Oxford University Press, 1990).

85. de Vries, "The World Bank's Focus on Poverty," pp. 65–73.

86. *Partners in Development,* Report of the Commission on International Development, chaired by Lester B. Pearson (New York: Praeger, 1969), p. 152.

87. Organisation for Economic Co-operation and Development, *Development Co-operation, 1997 Report,* p. 55.
88. Robert L. Ayres, "Breaking the Bank," *Foreign Policy,* 43 (Summer 1981), p. 104.
89. In 1995–96, Poland was the largest recipient of bilateral development assistance from Austria, Canada, the European Community, and Germany; and Russia ranked second as a recipient in the German bilateral aid program, third in U.S. aid, fourth in European Community aid, and seventh in Norwegian aid. See Organisation for Economic Co-operation and Development, *Development Co-operation, 1997 Report,* pp. 79–107, A101.
90. Rapley, *Understanding Development,* pp. 135–154.
91. United Nations Development Program, *Human Development Report 1996,* p. 1.
92. Diane Elson, "Economic Paradigms Old and New: The Case of Human Development," in Roy Culpeper, Albert Berry, and Frances Stewart, eds., *Global Development Fifty Years After Bretton Woods* (New York: St. Martin's Press, 1997), p. 60.
93. Cristóbal Kay, "For a Renewal of Development Studies: Latin American Theories and Neoliberalism in the Era of Structural Adjustment," *Third World Quarterly* 14-4 (1993), p. 695.
94. Lingle, "What Ever Happened to the 'Asian Century'?," p. 33.
95. Rapley, *Understanding Development,* pp. 155–157. See also Elizabeth Parsan, *South-South Trade in Global Development* (Aldershot, UK: Avebury, 1993).
96. "Survey: Mercosur," *The Economist,* October 12, 1996, pp. 3–30.

PART IV

Concluding Comments

The last three decades of the twentieth century have been marked by a series of unexpected and disruptive developments in global politics and economics. Most notable of these developments were the oil crises in the 1970s, the foreign debt crisis in the 1980s, the breakup of the Soviet bloc and Soviet Union in the 1980s–90s, and the financial crisis in East and Southeast Asia in the 1990s. As globalization has increased, events in one part of the world have also had a greater impact on distant areas, and predictions about the future of the global political economy have become more hazardous. Nevertheless, the historical discussion in this book enables us to speculate about current and possible future changes in the twenty-first century. Relying on the major themes of this book, Chapter 12 examines contemporary trends in the global political economy.

Current Trends in the Global Political Economy

This book provides a comprehensive approach to the study of international political economy, introducing the student to the major theoretical perspectives and substantive issue areas. The three perspectives of realism, liberalism, and historical structuralism have evolved and influenced each other over time, and some theoretical approaches such as hegemonic stability theory, regime theory, and the business conflict model draw upon more than one of the major perspectives. Approaches that focus on domestic-international linkages and establish connections between comparative political economy and international political economy are becoming more common, and contributing to further changes in the study of IPE.

To help in linking theory and practice, this book focuses on three themes central to the study of IPE: globalization, North-North relations, and North-South relations. Issues surrounding the emerging states of Eastern Europe and the former Soviet Union are subsumed under these three themes, because the Cold War has virtually ended, and the former centrally planned economies are becoming increasingly integrated in the capitalist global economy. While the more developed former Eastern bloc states such as the Czech Republic and Hungary have levels of development almost comparable with some of the industrial states of the North, the poorer countries of the former Second World face some severe economic problems more comparable with those of less-developed countries in the South. It is useful in this concluding chapter to examine where we are today with these three themes of globalization, North-North relations, and North-South relations and to speculate about the future.

GLOBALIZATION

Globalization is a process that involves both the broadening and deepening of interdependence among societies and states throughout the world. *Broadening* refers to the geographic extension of linkages to encompass virtually all major societies and states, and *deepening* refers to an increase in the frequency and intensity of interactions. This text has *not* adopted an extreme view of globalization which argues that we are entering a "borderless world" where multinational corporations are losing their national identities and nation-states are losing their distinctiveness.[1] In fact, globalization is a process that affects some states and regions more than others; that threatens the state's autonomy in some respects but does not prevent it from making policy choices; and that contributes to fragmentation and conflict as well as unity and cooperation. Although there was a high degree of economic interdependence among states and societies in the nineteenth and early twentieth centuries, globalization is more encompassing today than it was at any time in the past. Advances in technology, communications, and transportation are facilitating the globalization process as never before; the role of the MNC in generating foreign direct investment, trade, and technology is unprecedented; and with the breakup of the Soviet bloc, the capitalist economic system is spreading throughout the globe, and international economic organizations are becoming truly universal in membership.

Realists, liberals, and historical structuralists have widely divergent views of globalization. Realists emphasize the continuing importance of the nation-state and often question whether there is in fact a significant rise in globalization. While realists may acknowledge that global interdependence is increasing in some areas, they believe that this occurs only with the permission or encouragement of the most powerful states and that these states continue to dictate the terms and limits of such transactions. Liberals, by contrast, believe that there is a significant level of globalization that is eroding state control, and they view the growth of global interdependence as a positive development. While realists believe that globalization occurs at the whim of the state, liberals attach far more importance to such factors as technological change and advances in communications and transportation which are beyond state control. Liberals also argue that globalization is increasing as a result of the demands of domestic and transnational societal actors such as internationalist firms.[2]

Historical structuralists, like liberals, believe that globalization is having a significant impact, but unlike liberals, they feel that globalization has extremely negative consequences for the poorer states and classes in the periphery of the global economy. Some Gramscian theorists argue that globalization is leading to the development of a "transnational historic bloc" composed of the largest MNCs, international banks, international economic organizations, and international business groups in the most powerful capitalist states. A crucial element of this transnational historic bloc is the power and mobility of transnational capital, which is putting national groups such as labor unions on the defensive. The only way to counter such a transnational historic bloc, according to Gramscians, is to develop a counterhegemonic bloc composed of the disadvantaged and disaffected such as labor, human rights, environmental, consumer, and women's groups. A counterhegemonic bloc of this nature would be committed to replacing the current corporate view of liberalization with a more democratic, participatory model based on socialism.[3]

Globalization and Triadization

Globalization today is in many respects more akin to "triadization." The integrative processes are most intense among three major regions that contain most of the world's developed market economies: Western Europe, North America, and Japan/East Asia.[4] Countries in these three regions are the main sources of foreign direct investment, and they direct most of their FDI to each other. In 1995, for example, the developed market economies accounted for 92.1 percent of the outward stocks of FDI and for 72.1 percent of the inward stocks of FDI. Western Europe, North America, and Asia also dominate international trade flows, and they trade much more with each other than with other parts of the world. In 1993, North America, Western Europe, and Asia accounted for 84.2 percent of global merchandise exports and for 90.2 percent of world exports of manufactures.[5]

Although some less developed countries have increased their share of inward FDI, the distribution of this investment has been very uneven. On the one hand, 10 LDCs located mainly in East Asia and Latin America (Singapore, Brazil, Mexico, China, Hong Kong, Malaysia, Egypt, Argentina, Thailand, and Colombia) received about three-fourths of total FDI inflows to Third World countries in the 1980s. On the other hand, the least developed countries—most of which are in sub-Saharan Africa—received only 1.5 percent of the FDI inflows to the Third World during 1980–84, and their share fell to 0.7 percent in the 1985–89 period. (The United Nations has designated 48 LDCs as "least developed.")[6] Many of the poorest Third World countries have also received little benefit from the expansion of world trade. Although the Asian countries' share of world trade grew from 4.6 to 12.5 percent between 1970 and 1991, the share for other LDC regions declined. The least developed countries, with about 10 percent of the world's people, accounted for only 0.3 percent of world trade in 1997—which was about half of their share two decades earlier.[7]

Although historical structuralists have warned against Third World dependence on the First World, an even greater problem for most of the poorer Third World countries today is the threat of marginalization. The breakup of the Soviet bloc and the decline of the Cold War decreased the leverage of LDCs in gaining economic concessions from both East and West. This marginalization of the poorer Southern countries is likely to continue because the triad of the European Union, North America, and Japan will be primarily interested in increasing their economic linkages with the more prosperous Third World countries and with the emerging states of Eastern Europe and the former Soviet Union.[8]

Globalization and the Nation-State

Globalization has constrained the ability of industrial states to continue providing the social welfare benefits that citizens came to expect in the 1950s to 1970s; and the

revival of orthodox liberalism has made such social expenditures seem less legitimate. Globalization has also limited the ability of the state to regulate the national
economy. For example, the massive growth of international capital flows has contributed to volatility and misalignment in currency exchange rates. Major fluctuations in exchange rates interfere with the state's ability to promote economic regulation and stability.

Liberal economists generally view the increase in capital flows as a favorable development because financial markets impose necessary discipline on states, and global
savings and resources move to their most productive locations. Historical structuralists, by contrast, view increased capital mobility as a highly negative development because the fear of capital outflows can force governments to adopt policies that adversely affect the poorest and weakest in society. If governments do not adopt
"capital-friendly" policies, MNCs and international banks can readily shift their funds
to more welcoming locations. Thus, MNCs tend to locate their production facilities in
the states with the lowest wages, environmental standards, and taxes. Realists believe
that the increase in global financial flows in recent years has occurred with the permission or even encouragement of the most powerful states and that these states continue
to dictate the terms for such transactions. Although the United States, Britain, and
others adopted policies that contributed to the globalization of finance, this globalization "has had unintended consequences for those who promoted it," and realists overlook the fact that it may be extremely difficult for states to regain control over the
global market forces that they unleashed.[9]

Third World states are especially vulnerable to the freeing of capital flows, as the
financial crisis in the late 1990s demonstrated. East and Southeast Asian countries had
opened their economies to freer capital flows in the years leading up to the crisis, and
a surge of bank lending and portfolio investment contributed to risky and ill-advised
investments in the region. When serious weaknesses in the economies of these countries became evident, there was a "rush of international capital out of the region in
1997–a movement that was more frenzied than its mad rush to get into the area in
earlier years."[10] Although domestic political and economic factors in the Asian
economies contributed to the financial crisis, a major external factor was the volatility
of capital flows or contagion. "Contagion" refers to "the spread of currency and asset
market problems from one market to another."[11] As investor concern spreads from
country to country, even sound financial institutions can be adversely affected. Thus,
one currency after another in East and Southeast Asia was depreciated sharply, countries experienced severe liquidity crises, and the IMF became deeply involved in providing finance.

Even the first deputy managing director of the IMF has acknowledged that the
"factors contributing to contagion suggest it has been excessive—and that a way should
be found to moderate it."[12] There is also a consensus developing that Third World and
emerging countries should not open their capital markets too rapidly, because it may
be difficult for them to make adequate adjustments. In 1993, the Group of Seven released a study that examines possible multilateral approaches to dealing with the negative effects of international capital mobility, but policy coordination among the G-7
countries may be difficult for several reasons. First, states often give priority to their
own national concerns over the need for coordination. Second, it is questionable

whether governments have the will to regain control over capital and foreign invest-ment movements in the present climate of orthodox liberalism. Third, although there is general agreement that LDCs must be more careful in liberalizing capital flows, that is about all the experts agree on. Many analysts blame the IMF for mishandling the fi-nancial crisis in East and Southeast Asia, but there is a notable lack of consensus on proposals for reform.[13] Nevertheless, domestic societal groups are becoming more ac-tivist and demanding that the state reestablish some controls. Chapter 10, for example, discusses the role that disaffected labor and environmental groups, human rights groups, and consumer advocates in industrial states played in organizing opposition to the OECD's negotiation of a multilateral agreement on investment. Societal groups of course do not have the capability to develop regulations over global financial markets, but they may play a role in eventually pressuring the industrial states to cooperate in establishing such global regulatory capabilities.

Globalization and Inequality

Many liberals recognize that globalization may contribute to inequalities among and within states in the short term. However, they believe that the efficiency gains from globalization will reduce these inequalities in the long term. Realists and historical structuralists, by contrast, believe that there will be long-term losers as well as winners from globalization. From the realist perspective, the most powerful states have consid-erable control over the pace and direction of globalization, and they can use the glob-alization process "to reinforce their position and their relative power." For less power-ful states, by contrast, globalization "is a process which is happening to them and to which they must respond."[14] Historical structuralists also believe that globalization benefits the most powerful capitalist states and nonstate actors such as MNCs in the core at the expense of peripheral states and societal groups.

Although the statistics are sometimes conflicting, it does seem that globalization and liberalization in combination have contributed to inequalities. In many industrial states, globalization has resulted in an increase in *overall* income, but also in a rise in unemployment. In 1995, 7.5 percent of the work force or 34 million people in the OECD countries were unemployed; and from 1979 to 1997, unemployment in the European Union more than doubled, to 11 percent. In the United States, the employ-ment picture was healthier in the late 1990s, but there is evidence that the income gap between the rich and poor was widening. Globalization has also contributed to greater inequalities in a number of Third World and former Soviet bloc countries. For exam-ple, the United Nations Development Program reported in 1997 that a falling share of national income was going to the poorest 20 percent of the people in several Latin American countries (Argentina, Chile, the Dominican Republic, Ecuador, Mexico, and Uruguay) and that in 16 of 18 countries in Eastern Europe and the Common-wealth of Independent States (the FSU countries other than Estonia, Latvia, and Lithuania) income distribution had worsened and poverty had increased.[15]

Mexico, a Third World country that has been something of a pacesetter in liberal-izing its economic policies since the mid-1980s, provides a prime example of the fact that there are both winners and losers from globalization. On the one hand, policies such as the privatization of state industries and the 1992 land reform permitting investors to purchase land from smallholders were highly beneficial to owners of capital and to large commercial farms. On the other hand, the share of Mexicans living in absolute poverty rose from 19 percent in 1984 to 24 percent in 1989, and in rural areas the number of poor people increased from 6.7 million to 8.8 million. While large commercial fruit and vegetable producers in Mexico are benefiting from free trade in agriculture with the United States under NAFTA, many Mexican corn and bean subsistence farmers (by far the largest group engaged in agricultural production) could lose what little they have.[16]

It is important to note that there are variations among countries, indicating that the domestic policies of governments (and their positions in the global economy) can make a difference. For example, there is evidence that some Asian LDCs, such as China, India, Bangladesh, and Vietnam, have liberalized their trade and investment policies while also reducing poverty to some extent. Variations among LDCs in the concentration of land ownership, the degree to which production is labor intensive, and other factors can influence the way in which globalization affects the distribution of wealth in society. In the developed world, some Scandinavian countries have liberalized while still maintaining a substantial social safety net. In the short to medium term, then, globalization contributes to inequalities within and among a number of states, but the policies of states can ameliorate these effects. As for the long term, it is difficult to either prove or disprove the orthodox liberal claim that globalization will eventually contribute to a decrease in inequalities.

Globalization and Democracy

Many liberals believe that globalization is helping to promote stable democratic governments throughout the world. Indeed, they can point to the spread of liberal democratic practices in southern Europe in the 1970s, in Africa and Latin America in the 1980s, and in the emerging states of Eastern Europe and the FSU in the late 1980s and 1990s. Historical structuralists, by contrast, argue that globalization is transferring control from democratically accountable governments to MNCs, international banks, and international organizations. For example, the investment chapter of NAFTA prohibits a range of performance requirements that governments have traditionally imposed on foreign investment to ensure that it serves the interests of the national economy. Historical structuralists also argue that income inequalities resulting from globalization contribute to growing disparities in political influence. These inequalities in the economic and political arenas inevitably decrease the opportunities for democratic policymaking.[17]

The liberal and historical structuralist perspectives are in fact both important for understanding the relationship between globalization and democracy. As liberals have noted, globalization has forced a number of governments to open their societies both economically and politically. Thus, liberal democratic practices such as constitutional guarantees, freedom of speech, open elections, and a multiparty system have spread to a number of countries throughout the world. Nevertheless, historical structuralists point out that the poorest individuals in LDCs often lack employment, education, sanitation and health facilities, and even enough food to eat. To these people, the economic right to an adequate standard of living is of far more relevance than Western-oriented political rights such as free speech and democratic elections. Because socio-economic inequalities have increased with globalization, it is difficult to argue that globalization has genuinely contributed to democracy in the Third World. Even in the advanced industrial states, democratically accountable governments have lost some of their authority over social and economic policymaking to MNCs and international bureaucracies. If governments lose too much authority, one must question whether liberal democratic practices such as open elections in fact provide the citizenry with meaningful choices. Real decision-making power under these circumstances may shift away from the majority of the populace "even if political struggles, which give the illusion that genuine power struggles are occurring, persist."[18]

Globalization and Migration

It is quite common for individuals, societal groups, and states to support some aspects of globalization from which they benefit and at the same time to oppose other aspects of globalization that pose a real or presumed threat to them. The cross-border movement of people is one area in which there is often a more generalized negative societal reaction to globalization. While many states and societal groups have supported the freeing of trade and capital flows, they have been far more resistant to the cross-border movement of people. In the area of migration, societies and governments have demonstrated particular resistance to the forces of globalization, and there are growing signs of antiimmigrant sentiment in a number of industrial states. For example, a public opinion survey conducted by the European Union in 1993 found that 52 percent of respondents felt there were too many immigrants; and a 1993 New York Times/CBS national telephone survey reported that 61 percent of Americans favored a decrease in the number of immigrants, compared with 42 percent in a 1977 Gallup poll.[19] Despite these negative societal attitudes, the politics of immigration is complex and there are also countervailing tendencies. For example, the market demand for certain types of foreign workers sometimes makes it difficult for political leaders to limit immigration. Newly naturalized immigrants can also form an important voting constituency, and the Clinton administration adopted a "Citizenship USA" plan in 1996 under which over one million people were sworn in, often in citizenship ceremonies with up to 12,000 to 15,000 individuals. These new citizens provided President Clinton with an important source of votes for his re-election.[20]

The migration issue demonstrates that globalization can produce a highly defensive societal reaction in certain areas. Although citizens and states may wish to regulate people movements because of valid concerns with such issues as illegal immigration, societal groups may also seek to impose limits for more questionable reasons. For example, labor groups are often sensitive about the immigration issue, because there has been a gradual shift in demand away from less-skilled workers in the advanced industrial states. There is no conclusive empirical evidence of a linkage between increased unemployment among semi-skilled and unskilled workers in the industrial states on the one hand, and immigration from Third World countries on the other. Indeed, some analysts argue that migrants often enter low-wage occupations that do not attract the local population, that many migrants are self-employed and create their own jobs, and that migration can stimulate growth and thus in fact reduce unemployment.[21] Nevertheless, concerns about the effects of migration on employment remain. Hostility to immigrants is also often heightened by groups with less legitimate objectives linked with extreme nationalism, racism, and suspicion of those who are different. For example, some extremist groups such as the Federation for American Immigration Reform (FAIR) have called for "a temporary moratorium on all immigration except spouses and minor children of U.S. citizens."[22]

Most IPE scholars who write about globalization focus on such issues as trade, foreign investment, and capital flows. They often do not even discuss migration, because "no other issue remains so much under the thrall of states and so resistant to globalizing effects."[23] Nevertheless, as globalization increases the pressures for migration will grow along with the pressures for other types of international interactions, and it is important that migration becomes a more integral part of the study of international political economy.

NORTH-NORTH RELATIONS

The second theme examined in this book relates to the interactions among the advanced industrial states of the North. The issue of international economic management is primarily a North-North issue because the Northern states in the OECD are the only countries with the wealth and power to look after the management of the global economy. This book has discussed two factors that contribute to international economic management: hegemony and international institutions.

The Current State of U.S. Hegemony

Part III provides a mixed picture of the current state of U.S. economic hegemony. On the one hand, the United States continues to demonstrate a number of strengths as a global hegemon. With the breakup of the Soviet Union, the United States has emerged as the unchallenged military power in the world. As long as the threat of violent conflict persists, a state with hegemony in security matters will also be able to exercise power over economic and other nonsecurity areas.[24] The U.S. dollar continues to serve as the main international currency, and in the weighted-voting Bretton Woods institutions (the IMF and the World Bank), the United States continues to have the most votes. Even more important, the United States has a considerable amount of co-optive power (also referred to as structural or soft power): it is often successful in getting "other countries to *want* what it wants."[25] For example, Part III shows that the United States played a critical role in setting the agenda for the GATT Uruguay round negotiations and in guiding the policy of industrial states on a range of issues extending from liberalized capital flows to the foreign debt crisis and international development.

On the other hand, Part III also provides a number of indications of U.S. hegemonic decline. The U.S. dollar shifted from top-currency to negotiated-currency status in the 1960s; the United States has had chronic balance-of-trade deficits since 1971; the United States has become more dependent on FDI inflows in recent years and has accounted for a declining share of outward FDI; and Japan surpassed the

United States for the first time in 1989 as the largest single-country donor of official development assistance to the Third World.

Despite the conflicting signals about the status of U.S. hegemony, almost all analysts agree that American economic power has declined *in a relative sense* since 1945. Its predominance at the end of the Second World War was so great that the relative position of the United States was bound to decline as a result of economic reconstruction in Europe and Japan. It is therefore useful to examine whether there is a country or group of countries that could replace the United States as global hegemon.

Is There a Candidate to Replace the United States as Global Hegemon?

An extensive body of literature exists on the question of whether Japan could be the next global hegemon.[26] In the late 1980s, some academics and policymakers took a rather positive view of Japan's hegemonic prospects. For example, one scholar wrote that "if any country surpasses the United States as the world's leading economic power, it will be Japan."[27] By the early to mid-1990s, however, most analysts were highly skeptical about Japan's ability and willingness to lead. Arguments against Japan's possible rise to hegemonic status stemmed from the views that Japan lacks both military power and ideological appeal and that it would be unwilling to assume the global responsibility of leadership. In the late 1990s, further questions were raised about Japan's hegemonic potential when a financial crisis hit many countries in East and Southeast Asia. Many hoped that Japan would set an example of reform because it shared some economic problems with other East and Southeast Asian states such as failing banks, questionable bookkeeping methods, and corrupt interlocking corporate relationships.[28] Political indecisiveness and inflexible economic and social practices, however, have prevented Japanese leaders from adopting bold policies to reform the economy. Despite Japan's economic strengths, it is highly unlikely that Japan will replace the United States as a global hegemon.

Some writers speculate that the European Union could become the top power, and one economist has even predicted that "future historians will record that the 21st century belonged to the House of Europe."[29] However, the EU will not have the ability and willingness to lead unless it becomes a more cohesive unit. In early May 1997, the European Union's heads of government agreed that 11 EU members would replace their national currencies with the euro and join in forming an economic and monetary union: Austria, Belgium, Finland, France, Germany, Ireland, Italy, Luxembourg, the Netherlands, Portugal, and Spain. In view of the combined strength of these countries' economies, the euro will be the world's second most important currency and could eventually supplant the U.S. dollar as the key currency in the global monetary regime. Nevertheless, continued divisions among EU countries over a wide range of economic and political issues could prevent the EU from assuming hegemonic responsibilities.

A third possibility is that global leadership is becoming more collective in nature and that the United States is best placed to lead this collectivity because its strength is so multidimensional; that is, it encompasses military, political, economic, scientific, cultural, and ideological power resources.[30] To lead the collectivity, however, the United

States must accept the reality that its ability to act unilaterally is declining. The U.S. capacity for unilateral action is decreasing both because of its relative decline in economic power and because economic management must be collective if it is to deal adequately with capital flows and other economic transactions in this age of globalization.

The most obvious candidates for collective leadership in the core would be the triad: the United States, the European Union, and Japan. However, the possibilities that such a collective leadership will succeed is questionable in view of ongoing disputes among these three actors and the difficulties the EU has in reaching agreements internally among its own member states. Even if the states in the triad reached agreement on major issues, it is uncertain that they could achieve hegemony. A number of newly industrialized countries, along with major powers such as China and India, are gaining economic influence, so it may become less feasible to leave global management to the countries within the triad.[31] A final possibility is that because globalization is upgrading the importance of transnational actors such as MNCs and international banks, no state—or collectivity of states—can become hegemonic. In other words, MNCs and internationally mobile capital may be vying with the nation-state today for global hegemony.[32]

The Role of International Institutions

International institutions—both international regimes and international organizations—are discussed under "North-North relations" because the rich Northern countries have clearly assumed the largest role in setting the principles, norms, and rules for these institutions. Three keystone international economic organizations have performed major functions in overseeing economic management: the IMF, the World Bank, and GATT/WTO. As we have discussed, the three main IPE perspectives present widely differing views of these organizations. While liberals believe that the KIEOs are beneficial organizations that seek to promote economic efficiency and openness, realists view the KIEOs as rather passive creatures of their most powerful member states, and historical structuralists consider the KIEOs to be a mechanism by which the capitalist core countries exploit weaker countries in the periphery. Instead of attempting to decide which of these views of the KIEOs is most accurate (all three perspectives in fact have some validity), this section provides an assessment of the current and possible future influence of these organizations.

The KIEOs have all been quite adaptable in altering their functions to meet changing economic circumstances, and it is likely that they will continue to have important roles in global economic management. As discussed in Chapter 6, the International Monetary Fund lost one of its two main functions—looking after the pegged exchange rate system—when the major economic powers shifted to floating exchange rates in 1973. The IMF also became a less essential source of loans for more creditworthy LDCs in the 1970s when international private banks recycled large sums of petrodollars to the Third World. In the 1980s, however, the IMF regained its stature when it took the lead role (along with the United States) in managing the Third World foreign debt crisis. With the breakup of the Soviet Union, the IMF also became an essential source of funding for Russia and other emerging economies. When a financial crisis affected East and Southeast Asian countries in the late 1990s, the IMF again was given the lead responsibility for dealing with the crisis. Furthermore, the IMF is currently seeking to establish a role for itself in promoting the orderly liberalization of capital movements.[33]

The conditionality the IMF places on its loans has long created resentment in Third World countries, and this resentment increased as the IMF attached more intrusive conditions to its structural adjustment loans to highly indebted countries in the 1980s and 1990s (see discussion of this issue in Chapter 7). Nevertheless, because the IMF retained the confidence of the advanced industrial states, it was able to maintain its important and influential position. The financial crisis of the late 1990s marked somewhat of a turning point, because economists and policymakers in the industrial states began to attack the IMF's stabilization programs in such countries as South Korea, Indonesia, and Russia. For example, critics charged that the IMF imposed the same conditions on loans to South Korea that it had imposed on foreign debtors in the 1980s, even though South Korea had fundamentally different economic problems. South Korea's foreign debt and current account deficit were both low, and its problems were related to a temporary lack of liquidity resulting from short term debts rather than from insolvency. In Indonesia and Russia, serious economic problems persisted despite the IMF's involvement, and the IMF was accused of simply bailing out governments and foreign investors without bringing about longer-term economic solutions. Thus, one noted economist strongly criticized the IMF programs as being "too flawed to be a standard of good or bad performance."[34]

Despite the strong criticisms of the IMF, most analysts in the industrial states believe that abolishing the organization is not the answer, and that emphasis should be placed instead on "refocusing the IMF."[35] The IMF serves an important function for both the industrial states and the Third World countries as a lender of last resort, and if it were dismantled another organization like it would most likely be reinvented. The IMF also performs a useful function in deflecting the anger of Third World countries over the conditionality on loans; without the IMF, this anger would be aimed more directly at the United States, Germany, Japan, and other industrial states. Furthermore, the IMF may seem uncertain about the proper macroeconomic solutions today, but it is certainly not alone in lacking definitive answers. Most analysts who referred to the East and Southeast Asian countries as "miracle economies" did not predict that the fortunes of these countries would change so drastically, and the policy prescriptions of different experts for dealing with the current problems are often contradictory. It is therefore likely that the IMF will continue to play a central role as a lender of last resort, and will adapt its functions to meet changing circumstances as it has in the past.

Of the three KIEOs, the World Bank group is probably in the most uncertain position. The International Bank for Reconstruction and Development or World Bank initially provided long-term loans for European reconstruction and Third World development. When the World Bank lost its reconstruction function, it shifted its attention almost solely to the Third World. The World Bank's importance has stemmed partly from the fact that it is the largest source of multilateral financing for Third World development. In recent years, however, "public support and public resources for official development assistance have declined."[36] The decline in development assistance has resulted from a variety of factors: aid agencies have not succeeded in promoting economic development; the end of the Cold War removed the security rationale for providing aid; and states want to cut spending in an increasingly competitive global environment. "Aid fatigue" in the advanced industrial states has of course had adverse effects on the World Bank's functioning. For example, the United States and other donors have often been reluctant to replenish funding for the World Bank group's soft loan-affiliate, the International Development Association (see Chapter 11).

The foreign debt crisis in the early 1980s gave the World Bank as well as the IMF new functions to perform. However, both the bank and the IMF began to provide structural adjustment loans to Third World debtors, and the IMF rather than the World Bank was given responsibility for coordinating the response to the foreign debt crisis. As IMF and World Bank functions increasingly overlapped, questions were raised about whether or not the bank was "redundant." The World Bank, however, has been highly adaptable, and it will probably continue to function as a separate institution. As discussed in Chapter 11, sub-Saharan Africa is currently facing a development crisis, and the World Bank is the only multilateral organization with the economic resources and technical expertise to deal with the crisis. The World Bank has also managed to carve out for itself "a unique position as a generator of ideas about economic development."[37] Indeed, in its 1997 *Annual Report* the bank indicated that it was placing greater emphasis on "building a sound knowledge base to support nonlending (as well as lending) activities."[38] The bank's influence as a disseminator of ideas depends on the expertise of its operating staff as well as on its important position as a source of development finance. Thus, it seems likely that the World Bank will continue to operate as a KIEO.

Of the three KIEOs, the World Trade Organization is likely to become the most important. Unlike the IMF and the World Bank, which impose conditions only on Third World and emerging country borrowers, the WTO establishes rules for almost all of the world's major trading nations. Even such important countries as China and Russia, which are not yet WTO members, are feeling pressures to alter their trading policies in line with WTO principles, norms, and rules. Both countries have applied to join the organization. The WTO's importance is ironic because its predecessor, the GATT, became a permanent organization only by default when the Havana Charter and proposed International Trade Organization did not receive final approval. Nevertheless, the informal nature of GATT permitted it to be highly adaptable.

Although GATT negotiations were initially designed to lower tariff barriers, the trade organization also began to negotiate reductions in nontariff barriers at the Kennedy round in the 1960s, and it expanded these negotiations on NTBs at the Tokyo round in the 1970s. The GATT Uruguay round in the 1980s and 1990s was by far the most complex and ambitious negotiation. Thus, the new WTO oversees regulations not only for trade in goods but also for trade in services, intellectual property, and trade-related investment measures. It is also possible that the WTO will eventually oversee the implementation of a multilateral agreement on investment. While some analysts warn that the expansion of regional integration is threatening the global trade regime, regional integration agreements today are generally more open than they were in the 1960s. Thus, regional agreements such as the EU, NAFTA, and the

Asia-Pacific Economic Cooperation (APEC) forum are more likely to serve as stepping-stones than as obstacles to global free trade. In sum, the WTO is likely to emerge as the most important of the KIEOs.

NORTH-SOUTH RELATIONS

The population of the Third World accounted for almost 65 percent of the total world population in 1950, and by 1996 the Third World population had climbed to almost 80 percent of the world total. A number of emerging economies that were formerly part of the Second World are now receiving foreign debt and development finance from the advanced industrial states and thus have some characteristics in common with the Third World. Most of the "world" is therefore the Third World. Nevertheless, as this book has shown, Third World countries have had relatively little influence in setting the agenda and making decisions regarding the global political economy.

In addition to the weak economic and political positions of most LDCs, there are major divisions within the Third World which prevent it from taking unified actions. For example, poverty is spread very unevenly among LDC geographic regions. The United Nations has identified 48 LDCs as "least developed" because they have extremely low per capita incomes and literacy rates and are poorly endowed with natural resources. Almost all of these least developed countries are in sub-Saharan Africa and in Asia. Poverty in the Third World also has a differential impact on societal groups in LDCs, with women and children most severely affected. Furthermore, there are indications that globalization is marginalizing the weakest states and societal groups, even as it has contributed to growth in many of the stronger states. For example, the poorest LDCs, which have 20 percent of the world's population, saw their share of world trade fall from about 4 percent in 1960 to less than 1 percent in 1990. Private investment flows to LDCs increased by from $5 billion in 1970 to $173 billion in 1994, but about 75 percent of this investment went to only 10 countries, mainly in East and Southeast Asia and Latin America.[39]

The statistics on the poorest LDCs and societal groups indicate that development strategies over the years have had only limited success—especially if one believes that a certain degree of equity is necessary for development to be considered successful. The sections that follow examine how the concept of "development" is changing and consider whether or not there is a demonstrated best path to development.

Changing Concepts of Development

In the 1950s and 1960s, economic development was usually equated with material economic growth, and the essential indicators of development were a country's GDP and per capita income. In the orthodox liberal view, Western industrial states with high per capita incomes had achieved successful development, and LDCs could acquire similar wealth if they simply followed the same path set by the already developed states. Orthodox liberals were not concerned about redistributing wealth to the poorest groups in LDCs because they believed that the prosperity of Third World countries which followed liberal-economic policies would "eventually trickle down from the top, alleviating the problem of poverty at the bottom."[40]

Although Third World countries experienced unprecedented economic growth in the 1960s, there were indications that unemployment, poverty, and the gap between the rich and the poor were increasing. Thus, a number of development specialists rejected the orthodox liberal view that growth would naturally "trickle down" to the poor, and they proposed that conscious efforts should be made to redistribute income to the poor and meet their basic human needs for health, education, food and clean water, and family planning services. From this perspective, GDP and per capita income are not the only important indicators of economic development, and human development indicators must also be considered. These human development indicators include such measures as life expectancy, health and sanitation, literacy rates, education, employment, malnourishment, the position of women and children, and rural-urban disparities. The human development approach demonstrates that development must be measured "through investment in people and not just in machinery, buildings, and other physical assets."[41]

Another change in the concept of development came from those who are concerned about environmental degradation. Of particular importance in this regard was the concept of sustainable development, which was popularized by some nongovernmental organizations in the early 1980s and received multilateral approval in the 1987 report of the World Commission on Environment and Development (the Brundtland Report). The Brundtland Report describes sustainable development as a policy that "meets the needs of the present without compromising the ability of future generations to meet their own needs."[42] Sustainable development is a controversial concept because LDCs often argue that they cannot afford to divert resources from their immediate development needs to pay the costs of following environmentally friendly policies. The LDCs also point out that industrial states did not adopt sustainable policies when they were developing and that the Northern states today produce more pollutants than LDCs. If the industrial states expect the Third World to follow more environmentally friendly policies, from this perspective, they must be willing to compensate the LDCs with financial resources.[43]

The prevailing concepts of development have a major effect on policymaking, so it is essential that we opt for a broad rather than narrow concept of development, for two reasons. First, recent decades of experience have shown that rapid economic growth does not necessarily enrich people's lives and may even enhance income gaps and poverty under some circumstances. A broader concept of development includes not only economic growth but also human development, the reduction of poverty, and the protection of the environment and sustainability. Second, as global interdependence increases, the form that development takes can have major implications for the entire globe. For example, the World Bank estimates that more than 2 million people in China die each year from the effects of air and water pollution and that the effects of this pollution may extend far beyond the boundaries of China. Aside from the United States, China is now the largest source of greenhouse gases that are linked to global warming, and China and India are the two fastest-growing sources of these gases.[44] In an age of globalization, we can no longer afford to adopt a narrow concept of development that is limited to economic growth. Thus, the industrial states must provide assistance to Third World countries that lack the capacity to transfer scarce resources from economic growth to other critical development objectives such as sustainability and the reduction of poverty.

Is There a "Best" Development Strategy?

Chapter 11 discussed several major development strategies, including import substitution, socialist development models, export-led growth, and orthodox liberalism. Liberals, realists, and historical structuralists disagree as to which strategy is best to follow, and they even sometimes disagree as to the type of strategy a state is actually following. For example, when the East Asian export-led growth model was experiencing its greatest success in the 1970s and 1980s, liberals attributed the success of these countries to their outward, market orientation. Realists, by contrast, attributed the East Asians' success to the existence of a strong developmental state that promoted an effective industrial policy; and historical structuralists argued that the East Asians were following a strategy based on dependency, which was not as successful as the realists and liberals assumed. The experience with different development strategies indicates that *none* of these strategies is necessarily "the best" and that each strategy has both strengths and weaknesses. Furthermore, in view of the diverse nature of the Third World today, a strategy that may be best for one LDC may not be best or even feasible for another. A brief recounting of the strengths and weaknesses of the major LDC development strategies will help to reinforce these points.

As discussed in Chapter 11, import-substituting industrialization was a commonly used development strategy among LDCs in the 1950s and 1960s. The easier first stage of ISI resulted in economic growth and industrialization in a number of LDCs. However, those countries in Latin America and elsewhere that continued on to a second stage of ISI encountered increasing problems with balance-of-payments deficits, the development of uncompetitive industries, and increased dependence on external finance. When problems arose with the ISI strategy, some Third World countries adopted more extreme inward-looking policies and attempted to follow the socialist planning model of the Soviet Union. Central planning contributed to increases in industrial production in some countries, but even larger LDCs such as China were plagued by inefficiencies, low-quality production, and lack of competitiveness. For smaller Third World countries such as North Korea, Cuba, Ethiopia, Mozambique, Vietnam, and Burma, which lacked resources, the attempts at central planning were even more ineffective. Nevertheless, these countries did register some gains in social areas, such as providing better access to health care and education, improving the status of women, and adopting measures to reduce social and economic inequalities.[45]

The East Asian newly industrialized countries, which followed the Japanese model and turned from import substitution to export-led growth policies in the 1960s, were by far the most successful group of LDCs in increasing their economic growth from the 1960s to the 1980s. While liberals and realists often agreed that other Third World states should learn from the example of the East Asian "miracle," they had widely differing interpretations of the reasons for these countries success. The realists in fact were probably more accurate in their interpretations: the East Asian NICs (other than Hong Kong) had strong developmental states that provided extensive guidance to the market, controlled investment flows, promoted the development of technology, and protected selected infant industries.

A financial crisis in the 1990s, however, demonstrated that the developmental state in East and Southeast Asia was not as efficient and immune to political pressures as was earlier assumed. Thus, the crisis stemmed partly from the failure of governments to develop adequate regulations for banking and other financial institutions. It also became evident that the East Asians had benefited from a unique set of circumstances in which the United States and Japan gave them favored treatment in terms of military and economic aid, trade, and foreign investment. The cost of this special treatment was the development of dependent linkages, and when U.S. and Japanese policies changed in the 1990s, the East and Southeast Asian states were highly vulnerable. Environmentalists also raised questions about the sustainability of rapid economic growth in East and Southeast Asia, where little action was being taken to prevent environmental degradation. By the 1990s, few analysts were still claiming that the export-led growth model was the answer to Third World development problems.

In the 1980s, the debt crisis and IMF and World Bank structural adjustment loans ushered in yet another Third World development strategy, based on orthodox liberalism. In marked contrast to import substitution and export-led growth, the orthodox liberal strategy emphasized decreased government spending, privatization, deregulation, and liberal policies toward trade and foreign investment. In middle-income LDCs the structural adjustment programs had some positive effects in reducing government budget deficits, increasing export earnings, and enhancing economic efficiency and growth. However, World Bank and IMF structural adjustment loans also had some negative effects on the poorest LDCs in sub-Saharan Africa and Asia and on vulnerable groups in LDCs, such as women and children. Critics argued that the structural adjustment programs underestimated the need for involving the state in development and for maintaining social, health, and educational programs for vulnerable groups, despite their financial costs. Supporters of orthodox liberalism, however, asserted that Third World countries would benefit most by discarding their traditional policies and following in the path of Western Europe and North America.[46]

In view of the global spread of orthodox liberalism, the question arises whether we have reached the "end of history" for Third World development strategies and whether liberalism has become the only acceptable path to follow.[47] This is not likely to be the case. As we discussed, even the World Bank has now acknowledged that structural adjustment programs will succeed only if they take account of the need for strong, stable Third World governments in promoting development and include some distributional goals vis-à-vis the poorest and most vulnerable groups. The problems with structural adjustment programs also serve as a reminder that development strategies for the future should avoid the "northern ethnocentrism which permeated much of orthodox development thinking" with its "false claim of universality."[48] As realists have noted, strategies that provide an active role for the government, such as import substitution and export-led growth, may be necessary for Third World countries at various stages in their development if they are to catch up with the leading states. Both import substitution and export-led growth strategies have encountered some problems, but this could mean that we need to find the correct regulatory regime rather than simply opting for deregulation and privatization. As for historical structuralists, they have pointed out correctly that we must be concerned with the distributional effects of development strategies and with overdependence on industrial states as a possible hindrance to Third World development.

We have *not* reached the end of history in terms of development strategies. The "best" development strategy is likely to include realist and historical structuralist as well as liberal components, and again, the best strategy for some Third World states may not necessarily be the best strategy for others.

A FINAL WORD ON THEORY AND PRACTICE

This book has tried to join together theory and practice in the study of international political economy. This introduction to IPE has focused on the three major theoretical perspectives: realism, liberalism, and historical structuralism. Significant changes have occurred in recent years, including the breakup of the Soviet Union and the end of the Cold War, the pressures of globalization, and the emergence of common threats to humanity such as environmental degradation. These changes have revealed a need for "new theoretical categorizations."[49] One approach to the shortcomings of the three main IPE perspectives is to develop new theories and models that draw on more than one theoretical perspective. This book has focused on several of these "hybrid" theories, particularly hegemonic stability theory and regime theory. Another approach is to develop new theoretical perspectives in IPE which focus on such issues as environmentalism and feminism that the three traditional perspectives largely ignore.

The globalization phenomenon points to yet another direction theorists should follow: the development of theories that explore domestic-international interactions in the global political economy. With globalization, the sensitivity of national economies to changes in capital, foreign investment, and trade flows has dramatically increased, as the 1990s financial crisis in East and Southeast Asia clearly demonstrates. As states become more interdependent, policies that were traditionally considered to be domestic (e.g., government subsidies) can also have a major impact on outsiders. This text has focused on a number of issues that involve domestic and international interactions, but a more systematic examination of such issues is essential to increasing our understanding of IPE. Although no country today can escape the fact of growing international interdependence, a country's openness to outside influences also depends on domestic factors. A country's policies result from a variety of domestic factors such as the position and influence of socioeconomic groups and the nature of the country's political institutions. As a country becomes more involved in foreign trade and investment, domestic political conflict may increase between societal groups that benefit from greater international openness and groups that depend on protectionism and economic closure. The extent to which the government adopts more open economic policy depends not only the relative influence of these societal groups but also on the country's domestic political institutions. Existing institutions can exert strong pressures on governments to either accede to the forces of globalization or to resist these forces with more protectionist economic policies. The reluctance of the U.S. Congress to give President Clinton fast-track approval to expand the North American Free Trade Agreement and to negotiate other trade liberalization agreements is one example of the important role of domestic institutions. All three of the traditional IPE perspectives have devoted too little attention to domestic variables, and the study of IPE will benefit from the increased attention that is currently being given to domestic-international interactions.[50]

Students have been introduced to a range of theoretical approaches in this book and have seen how these theories are applied to substantive IPE issue areas. As one noted international relations theorist has stated, "to think theoretically one must be constantly ready to be proven wrong,"[51] and this book has shown that all theoretical perspectives have been partially correct and partially incorrect in their assessments of a wide range of IPE issues. It is only through formulating and reformulating our theories that we will be able to understand the issues of international political economy in a broader context.

NOTES

1. The "borderless world" terminology derives from Kenichi Ohmae's *The Borderless World: Power and Strategy in the Interlinked Economy* (New York: HarperPerennial, 1990).

2. See Helen V. Milner, *Resisting Protectionism: Global Industries and the Politics of International Trade* (Princeton, NJ: Princeton University Press, 1988).

3. See Stephen Gill and David Law, "Global Hegemony and the Structural Power of Capital," in Stephen Gill, ed., *Gramsci, Historical Materialism and International Relations* (Cambridge: Cambridge University Press, 1993), pp. 93–124; and Mark E. Rupert, "(Re) Politicizing the Global Economy: Liberal Common Sense and Ideological Struggle in the US NAFTA Debate," *Review of International Political Economy* 2–4 (Autumn 1995), pp. 679–681.

4. Riccardo Petrella, "Globalization and Internationalization: The Dynamics of the Emerging World Order," in Richard Boyer and Daniel Drache, eds., *States, Against Markets: The Limits of Globalization* (London: Routledge, 1996), pp. 77–78.

5. United Nations Conference on Trade and Development, *World Investment Report 1996* (New York: United Nations, 1996), pp. 239–247; General Agreement on Tariffs and Trade, *International Trade: Trends and Statistics 1994* (Geneva: GATT, 1994), pp. 22, 58.

6. For the United Nations list of 48 least developed countries, see United Nations Conference on Trade and Development, *The Least Developed Countries—1997 Report* (New York: United Nations, 1997), p. 152.

7. United Nations Development Programme, *Human Development Report—1997* (New York: Oxford University Press, 1997), pp. 83–84.

8. United Nations Centre on Transnational Corporations, *World Investment Report 1991: The Triad in Foreign Direct Investment* (New York: United Nations, 1991), pp. 9–15.

9. Ethan B. Kapstein, *Governing the Global Economy: International Finance and the State* (Cambridge, MA: Harvard University Press, 1994), p. 6. See also Eric Helleiner, *States and the Reemergence of Global Finance: From Bretton Woods to the 1990s* (Ithaca, NY: Cornell University Press, 1994).

10. Walden Bello, "East Asia: On the Eve of the Great Transformation?" *Review of International Political Economy* 5-3 (Autumn 1998), p. 426.

11. Stephan Haggard and Andrew MacIntyre, "The Political Economy of the Asian Economic Crisis," *Review of International Political Economy* 5-3 (Autumn 1998), p. 383.

12. Stanley Fischer, "Lessons from a Crisis," *The Economist*, October 3, 1998, p. 27.

13. John B. Goodman and Louis W. Pauly, "The Obsolescence of Capital Controls? Economic Management in an Age of Global Markets," *World Politics* 46-1 (October 1993), p. 81; Tony Porter, "Capital Mobility and Currency Markets: Can They Be Tamed?" *International Journal* 51-4 (Autumn 1996), p. 676; "Global Finance: Don't Wait Up," *The Economist*, October 3, 1998, pp. 83–84.

14. Andrew Hurrell and Ngaire Woods, "Globalisation and Inequality," *Millennium* 24-3 (1995), p. 458.

15. United Nations Development Programme, *Human Development Report—1997*, pp. 88–89.

16. United Nations Development Programme, *Human Development Report—1997*, p. 88. For a discussion of the effects of NAFTA on Mexican agriculture, see Theodore H. Cohn, "The Intersection of Domestic and Foreign Policy in the NAFTA Agricultural Negotiations," *Canadian-American Public Policy*, no. 14 (Orono: University of Maine, September 1993), pp. 24–33.

17. Ian Robinson, "Globalization and Democracy," *Dissent* (Summer 1995), pp. 374–377. For a detailed examination of globalization and democracy, see David Held, *Democracy and the Global Order: From the Modern State to Cosmopolitan Governance* (Cambridge: Polity Press, 1995).

18. Marjorie Griffin Cohen, "Democracy and the Future of Nations: Challenges for Disadvantaged Women and Minorities," in Boyer and Drache, eds., *States Against Markets*, p. 407; Stephen Gill, "Globalization, Democratization, and the Politics of Indifference," in James H. Mittleman, ed., *Globalization: Critical Reflections* (Boulder, CO: Rienner, 1996), pp. 213–218.

19. Myron Weiner, *The Global Migration Crisis: Challenge to States and to Human Rights* (New York: HarperCollins, 1996), p. 3.

20. "Immigration: Suspicious Minds," *The Economist,* July 4, 1998, p. 25.

21. Keith Griffin, "Nine Good Reasons to Love Labor Migration," *UC Mexus News*, University of California Institute for Mexico and the United States, p. 2.

22. *http://www.fairus.org*, "What Is the Federation for American Immigration Reform?" p. 1.

23. Malcolm Waters, *Globalization* (London: Routledge, 1995), p. 89.

24. Susan Strange, *States and Markets* (London: Pinter, 2nd edition, 1994), p. 29.

25. Joseph S. Nye, Jr., "Soft Power," *Foreign Policy* 80 (Fall 1990), p. 166. See also Joseph S. Nye, Jr., *Bound to Lead: The Changing Nature of American Power* (New York: Basic Books, 1990); and Susan Strange, "The Persistent Myth of Lost Hegemony," *International Organization* 41-4 (Autumn 1987), pp. 551–574.

26. Good overall surveys of this literature include Alan Rix, "Japan and the Region: Leading from Behind," in R. Higgott, R. Leaver, and J. Ravenhill, eds., *Pacific Economic Relations in the 1990s* (Boulder, CO: Rienner, 1993), pp. 62–82; and Philip J. Meeks, "Japan and Global Economic Hegemony" (pp. 41–67), and Koji Taira, "Japan as Number Two: New Thoughts on the Hegemonic Theory of World Governance" (pp. 251–263) in Tsuneo Akaha and Frank Langdon, eds., *Japan in the Posthegemonic World* (Boulder, CO: Rienner, 1993).

27. See Ronald A. Morse, "Japan's Drive to Pre-Eminence," *Foreign Policy* no. 69 (Winter 1987–88), pp. 3–21.

28. "Dangerous Inertia in Japan," *New York Times,* December 23, 1997, p. A12; "Japan on the Brink," *The Economist,* April 11, 1998, pp. 15–17. See also Ron Bevacqua, "Whither the Japanese Model? The Asian Economic Crisis and the Continuation of Cold War Politics in the Pacific Rim," *Review of International Political Economy* 5-3 (Autumn 1998), pp. 410–423.

29. Lester Thurow, *Head to Head: The Coming Economic Battle Among Japan, Europe, and America* (New York: Morrow, 1992), p. 258.

30. Nye, "Soft Power," pp. 154–155; Samuel Huntington, "The U.S.—Decline or Renewal?" *Foreign Affairs* 67-2 (Winter 1988–89), p. 90.

31. Aaron Segal, "Managing the World Economy," *International Political Science Review* 11-3 (1990), p. 362.

32. Stephen Gill, "Global Finance, Monetary Policy and Cooperation among the Group of Seven, 1944–92," in Philip G. Cerny, ed., *Finance and World Politics: Markets, Regimes and States in the Post-hegemonic Era* (London: Elgar, 1993), p. 105.

33. See Stanley Fischer, "Capital Account Liberalization and the Role of the IMF," paper released by the International Monetary Fund, September, 1997, p. 12.

34. Jeffrey Sachs, "Global Capitalism: Making it Work," *The Economist,* September 12, 1998, p. 25. See also David E. Sanger, "I.M.F.'s Bearer of Bad Tidings," *New York Times,* October 30, 1998, pp. C1 and C3.

35. See Martin Feldstein, "Refocusing the IMF," *Foreign Affairs* 77-2 (March/April 1998), pp. 20–33; Jagdish Bhagwati, "The Capital Myth: The Difference between Trade in Widgets and Dollars," *Foreign Affairs* 77-3 (May/June 1998), p. 11.

36. Organisation for Economic Co-operation and Development, *Development Co-operation: Efforts and Policies of the Members of the Development Assistance Committee—1996* (Paris: OECD, 1997), p. 1.

37. Robert Wade, "Japan, the World Bank, and the Art of Paradigm Maintenance: The East Asian Miracle in Political Perspective," *New Left Review* no. 217 (May/June 1996), p. 5.

38. World Bank, *Annual Report 1997* (Washington, DC: World Bank, 1997), p. 7.

39. World Bank, *World Development Report 1990: Poverty* (New York: Oxford University Press, 1990), pp. 1–2; United Nations Development Programme, *Human Development Report 1996* (New York: Oxford University Press, 1996), pp. 8–9.

40. Mohammed H. Malek, "Towards an Integrated Aid and Development Programme for Europe," in Mohammed H. Malek, ed., *Contemporary Issues in European Development Aid* (Aldershot, UK: Avebury, 1991), p. 142.

41. Wilfred L. David, *The Conversation of Economic Development: Historical Voices, Interpretations, and Reality* (Armonk, NY: Sharpe, 1997), p. 177.

42. World Commission on Environment and Development, *Our Common Future* (Oxford: Oxford University Press, 1987), p. 8.

43. See Maurice F. Strong, "Achieving Sustainable Global Development," in the South Centre, *Facing the Challenge: Responses to the Report of the South Commission* (London: Zed Books, 1993), pp. 305–313.

44. Nicholas D. Kristof, "Across Asia, a Pollution Disaster Hovers," *New York Times,* November 28, 1997, pp. A1, A10.

45. John Rapley, *Understanding Development: Theory and Practice in the Third World* (Boulder, CO: Rienner, 1996), pp. 44–47.

46. See Walter Russell Mead, "Asia Devalued," *New York Times Magazine,* May 31, 1998, pp. 38–39.

47. See Francis Fukuyama, "The End of History?" *The National Interest* 16 (Summer 1989), pp. 3–18.

48. Kay, "For a Renewal of Development Studies," p. 697.

49. Thomas J. Biersteker, "Evolving Perspectives on International Political Economy: Twentieth-Century Contexts and Discontinuities," *International Political Science Review* 14-1 (January 1993), p. 27.

50. See Robert O. Keohane and Helen V. Milner, eds. *Internationalization and Domestic Politics* (Cambridge: Cambridge University Press, 1996); and Helen V. Milner, *Interests, Institutions, and Information: Domestic Politics and International Relations* (Princeton: Princeton University Press, 1997).

51. James N. Rosenau, "Thinking Theory Thoroughly," in James N. Rosenau, *The Scientific Study of Foreign Policy* (London: Pinter, revised edition, 1980), p. 30.

Acronyms and Abbreviations

AASM Associated African States and Madagascar
ACP Africa, Caribbean, and Pacific
ADD antidumping duty
APEC Asia-Pacific Economic Cooperation
ASEAN Association of Southeast Asian Nations
BIS Bank for International Settlements
BIT bilateral investment treaty
CAP Common Agricultural Policy
CARICOM Caribbean Community and Common Market
CEFTA Central European Free Trade Agreement
CMEA Council for Mutual Economic Assistance (also referred to as COMECON)
COCOM Coordinating Committee
CPE centrally planned economy
CU customs union
CUSTA Canada-U.S. Free Trade Agreement
CVD countervailing duty
EC European Community
ECB European central bank
ECLA Economic Commission for Latin America
ECOSOC Economic and Social Council
ECSC European Coal and Steel Community
ECU European currency unit
EFTA European Free Trade Association

EMS European Monetary System
EMU economic and monetary union
ERM exchange rate mechanism
EU European Union
FDI foreign direct investment
FIRA Foreign Investment Review Agency
FSU former Soviet Union
FTA free trade area
GAB General Arrangements to Borrow
GATS General Agreement on Trade in Services
GATT General Agreement on Tariffs and Trade
GDP gross domestic product
GNP gross national product
GSP generalized system of preferences
IBRD International Bank for Reconstruction and Development
IDA International Development Association
IDB Inter-American Development Bank
IFC International Finance Corporation
IMF International Monetary Fund
IPC Integrated Program for Commodities
IPE international political economy
ISI import-substituting industrialization
ITO International Trade Organization
KIEOs keystone international economic organizations
LAFTA Latin American Free Trade Association

LDC less developed country
LIC low-income country
LLDC least developed country
MAI multilateral agreement on investment
MERCOSUR Southern Common Market Treaty
MIC middle-income country
MFA Multi-Fiber Arrangement
MFN most-favored nation
MIGA Multilateral Investment Guarantee Agency
MNC multinational corporation
MTNs multilateral trade negotiations
NAFTA North American Free Trade Agreement
NEM New Economic Mechanism
NIC newly industrializing country
NIEO new international economic order
NTB nontariff barrier
OA official aid
ODA official development assistance

OECD Organization for Economic Cooperation and Development
OEEC Organization for European Economic Cooperation
OPEC Organization of Petroleum Exporting Countries
PRC People's Republic of China
R&D research and development
RIA regional integration agreement
RTAA Reciprocal Trade Agreements Act
SAL structural adjustment loan
SDRs special drawing rights
TRIMs Trade-Related Investment Measures
TRIPs Trade-Related Intellectual Property Rights
UNCTAD United Nations Conference on Trade and Development
UNDP United Nations Development Program
WTO World Trade Organization

absolute advantage A condition in which a country is able to produce a good more efficiently and at a lower cost than another country (or countries). Liberal-economic trade theorists maintain that countries benefit by specializing in the production of goods for which they have an absolute advantage. See also *comparative advantage.*

antidumping duties (ADDs) Duties a country may impose on imported goods if it determines that the goods are being dumped and that this is causing or threatening material injury to its domestic producers. See also *dumping.*

Asia-Pacific Economic Cooperation (APEC) forum An "open" regional initiative that includes the three largest national economies (the United States, Japan, and China) and has members from Asia, Australasia, and North and South America. Initially, foreign and economic ministers attended APEC meetings, but in 1993, the forum began to hold annual summit meetings of heads of state. Although APEC's economic activities to this point have been rather limited, the goal has been established to form a free trade area, and there are possibilities for agreements on competition policies, product standards, dispute settlement, and private investment.

Baker Plan A plan proposed by U.S. Secretary of the Treasury James Baker in 1985, to deal with the LDC foreign debt crisis. The plan emphasized the postponement of some debt payments, the provision of new IMF and World Bank loans as an incentive for continued lending by private banks, and structural changes in debtor country policies.

balance of payments A summary record of all international economic transactions that a country has, normally over a one-year period. The most important components of the balance of payments are the *current account* and the *capital account.*

Bank for International Settlements (BIS) The oldest of the international financial institutions, formed in 1930 to oversee German war reparations. The BIS is located in Basel, Switzerland, and is the main forum for cooperation and consultation among central bankers in the OECD countries. It helps to deal with exchange rate problems and provides credit to central banks that lack liquidity. In response to the 1980s debt crisis, the BIS provided "bridging" finance until IMF and World Bank loans were available and also adopted measures to increase confidence in the international banking system.

basic human needs A foreign aid approach focused on the poorest among and within less developed countries. The basic human needs (or basic needs) approach was prominent in the 1970s and marked a shift from the emphasis on GNP growth in the 1960s. Aid programs, according to this approach, should emphasize basic health, education, family planning, rural development, and services to the poor; the increased involvement of women in development programs; and special attention to the problems of the least developed countries.

bilateral aid A type of foreign assistance that flows directly from a donor to a recipient government. The largest percentage of official development assistance is given bilaterally. See also *foreign aid, multilateral aid, and official development assistance.*

Brady Plan   A plan proposed by U.S. Secretary of the Treasury Nicholas Brady in 1988, after it became evident that the Baker Plan was insufficient to deal with the foreign debt crisis. The Brady Plan introduced the idea that debt relief or reduction was necessary for some LDCs with severe and protracted debt problems, in exchange for structural adjustment of the debtors' economies.

Bretton Woods system   Bretton Woods, New Hampshire, was the location of meetings in July 1994 that culminated in the creation of the postwar economic order. The International Monetary Fund and International Bank for Reconstruction and Development (or World Bank) were established at Bretton Woods, as was the monetary regime of pegged exchange rates. This monetary regime ended in 1973, when major countries shifted to flexible exchange rates.

capital   A factor of production, along with land and labor. Capital consists of physical assets such as equipment, tools, buildings, and other manufactured goods, which are capable of generating income; and it also consists of financial assets such as stocks, which presumably reflect a firm's physical assets. Marxists view capital in social and political as well as economic terms and emphasize capital's exploitation of labor in the capitalist system.

capital account   A major item in the balance of payments, which records the amounts that a country lends to and borrows from nonresidents. Countries often finance their current account deficits with a net inflow of capital, or a surplus in their capital accounts. The transactions in the capital account include *foreign direct investment* and *portfolio investment.*

capital market   A capital market consists of all those institutions in a country (e.g., the stock exchange, banks, and insurance companies) that match supply with demand for long-term capital. Unlike a capital market, a money market deals with shorter-term loanable funding. The World Bank floats bonds on the capital markets of the advanced industrial states to acquire much of its funding for lending purposes.

central bank   The public authority responsible for managing a country's money supply and for regulating and controlling its monetary and financial institutions and markets. All industrial states and most less developed countries rely on a central bank for such regulatory activities.

Committee of Twenty (C-20)   A forum composed of representatives of both developed and less developed countries, which attempted to reform the international monetary regime after the 1971 devaluation of the U.S. dollar. After two years of deliberations, the C-20 proposal failed to receive approval.

common market   The third stage of regional integration, which has the characteristics of a customs union *plus* the free mobility of factors of production (i.e., capital and labor). (See also *customs union, economic union,* and *free trade area.*)

comparative advantage   A country has a comparative advantage in producing good A if it can produce A at a *relatively* lower cost than other goods, even if it does not have an absolute advantage in producing any good. Comparative advantage is a powerful liberal-economic theory justifying specialization and free trade.

competitiveness   A frequently cited definition of competitiveness, developed by the U.S. President's Commission on Industrial Competitiveness, is "the degree to which . . . [a nation] can, under free and fair market conditions, produce goods and services that meet the tests of international markets while simultaneously expanding the real income of its citizens." Wide disagreement exists, however, over the most important factors determining competitiveness and over the relationship between the competitiveness of states and firms.

concessional loans   (or *soft loans*) Loans that have lower interest rates, longer grace periods, and longer repayment periods than *commercial* or *hard loans.*

conditionality   A concept that is most closely associated with the International Monetary Fund but is also associated with World Bank structural adjustment loans. As a condition for receiving IMF loans above a certain level, borrowers must explicitly commit themselves to follow a prescribed set of policies. These policies typically include decreased government spending, increased government revenues, devaluation, deregulation, and privatization.

consultative group   A group that brings together donor states that provide development assistance to a particular recipient. In using consultative groups, donors seek to coordinate their bilateral aid giving and to exert collective pressure on recipient states.

countervailing duties (CVDs)   Duties a country may impose on imported goods if it determines that the goods are benefiting from trade-distorting subsidies in the exporting country and that this is causing or threatening material injury to domestic producers.

current account   A major item in the balance of payments, which records a country's trade in goods and services with foreigners, investment income and payments, and gifts and other transfers paid to and received from foreigners.

customs union (CU)   The second stage of regional integration, in which the member countries eliminate tariffs on all (or substantially all) their trade with each other and develop a common external tariff toward outside countries.

debt service ratio   (or debt-to-export ratio) The ratio of a country's interest and principal payments on its debt to its export income; often used to assess a country's ability to repay its foreign debt. The East Asian NICs had stronger export positions than the Latin American NICs and were better able to service their foreign debts in the 1980s.

dependency theory   A historical structuralist development theory which argues that the world is hierarchically organized, with the leading capitalist states in the core of the global economy dominating and exploiting the poorer states in the periphery.

devaluation   A reduction in the official rate or value at which one currency is exchanged for another. When a country devalues its currency, the prices of its imported goods and services increase, while its exports become less expensive to foreigners. A country can therefore gain certain trade advantages through devaluation of its currency.

dumping   Selling a product in an export market at a lower price than charged in the home market, or below the cost of production.

economic union   The fourth stage of regional integration, which has the characteristics of a common market and also harmonizes the industrial, regional, fiscal, monetary, and other economic policies of member countries. A full economic union also involves the adoption of a common currency by the members.

economism   An overemphasis on the importance of the economic sphere, and a corresponding underemphasis on the autonomy of the political sphere.

Eurocurrencies   National currencies traded and deposited in banks outside the home country, mainly (but not necessarily) in Europe. The most common form of Eurocurrencies are U.S. Eurodollars in European banks. International firms and national governments often prefer to use the Eurocurrency market for deposits and loans because the transactions in this market are free of most government regulations.

European Community (EC)   A regional integration agreement formed in 1957 among six Western European countries for political as well as economic reasons. In economic terms, the EC goals were to establish a customs union and a common market. The EC also established a complex institutional structure, including a Commission, Council of Ministers, European Court of Justice, and European Parliament. Membership in the EC increased to 12 countries by 1986, and in 1993 the EC was superseded by the *European Union.*

European Union (EU)   The European Union became the successor organization to the EC in 1993, largely as a result of the "Europe 92" program. Europe 92 was designed to complete the establishment of a single market by the removal of remaining fiscal, nontariff, technical and other barriers to trade. The EU has moved to both widen and deepen the integration process in Europe. As for widening, EU membership increased from 12 to 15 countries in 1995, and future membership of East European countries was under consideration. As for deepening, 11 members of the EU established an economic and monetary union in 1999 with a common currency (the Euro).

exchange rate   The number of units of one currency that can be exchanged for a unit of another currency. See also *fixed exchange rates* and *floating exchange rates.*

export-led growth An outward-looking economic development strategy that emphasizes the production of industrial goods for export to the advanced industrial states. Export-led growth is commonly associated with the economic success of the newly industrializing countries in East Asia. See also *import-substituting industrialization*.

fast-track authority Measures first introduced in the 1974 U.S. Trade Act to expedite congressional approval of trade agreements negotiated by the U.S. executive. Under the fast track, the President can assure U.S. trading partners that Congress will vote for or against negotiated agreements without amendments within a fixed time period. Such authority is often necessary because other countries are reluctant to negotiate trade agreements with the United States which the U.S. Congress can later seek to amend.

fiscal policy Fiscal policy affects the economy through changes in government spending and/or taxes. When a government uses fiscal policy to deal with a balance-of-payments deficit, it lowers government expenditures and/or raises taxes to withdraw purchasing power from the public. See also *monetary policy*.

fixed exchange rates In a fixed exchange rate system, currencies are given official exchange rates, and governments regularly take actions to keep the market rates of their currencies close to the official rates.

floating exchange rates (or flexible exchange rates) With *free floating exchange rates*, governments do not intervene and the market alone determines currency valuations. With *managed floating*, central banks intervene to deal with disruptive conditions such as excessive fluctuations in exchange rates. While managed floating is considered to be legitimate, the IMF calls on central banks to avoid *dirty floating*, which refers to a government's manipulation of exchange rates to prevent effective balance-of-payments adjustment or to give that country an unfair competitive advantage.

foreign aid The administered transfer of resources to recipient countries for the stated purpose of promoting their welfare and economic development. The greatest share of foreign aid is official development assistance, but aid is also provided by private or nongovernmental organizations. According to the Development Assistance Committee of the OECD, only grants that do not require repayment and concessional loans with a grant element of at least 25 percent should qualify as foreign aid. See also *concessional loans, bilateral aid, multilateral aid, and official development assistance*.

foreign direct investment (FDI) Investment involving the ownership and control of assets in one country by residents of another country. The foreign residents are usually multinational corporations, which have management rights or control in a branch plant or subsidiary. Foreign direct investment may occur through the creation of new productive assets by foreigners (i.e., greenfield investment) or through the purchase of stock in an existing firm. See also *portfolio investment*.

free trade area (FTA) The first stage of regional integration, in which the member countries are to eliminate tariffs on all (or substantially all) trade with one another. However, each member country can continue to levy its own tariffs and follow its own trade policies toward nonmembers.

General Agreement on Tariffs and Trade (GATT) A provisional treaty that became the main global trade organization in 1948 by default when a planned International Trade Organization did not receive final approval. As an organization, GATT provided a written code of behavior, a forum for multilateral negotiations, and a venue for dispute settlement on trade issues. When the more formal World Trade Organization was formed in 1995, GATT reverted back to its original status as a treaty regulating trade in goods.

generalized system of preferences (GSP) In the 1970s, the developed countries agreed to establish a GSP in response to LDC demands. Under the GSP, individual developed countries can waive most-favored-nation treatment and give preferential treatment to imports of specific goods from LDCs. Thus, the import duties for some LDC products are lower than those levied on developed countries' products.

gold standard   A monetary system in which central banks fix the value of their currencies in terms of gold and hold official international reserves in gold. A regime based on the gold standard existed from the 1870s to 1914, and many countries unsuccessfully tried to restore it after World War I. In a *gold exchange standard* (e.g., the Bretton Woods regime), central banks hold their international reserves in two forms—gold and foreign exchange—in any proportion they choose.

gross domestic product (GDP)   The total value of production of goods and services in a country, including those produced by foreigners as well as nationals. See *gross national product*.

gross national product (GNP)   The GNP is similar to the gross domestic product, except that GNP includes the income domestic residents gain from foreign investment and excludes the income foreigners accumulate in the domestic market.

Group of Five (G-5)   The G-5 includes the finance ministers and central bank governors of the largest industrial economies: the United States, Japan, Germany, France, and Britain. It has played a major role at times in coordinating monetary and other economic policies.

Group of Seven (G-7)   The G-5 plus Italy and Canada. The G-7 includes the seven largest industrial democracies, which account for about two-thirds of global output. G-7 members meet regularly in efforts to provide leadership in international economic policy.

Group of Ten (G-10)   The G-10 includes the 10 industrial countries that established the General Arrangements to Borrow with the IMF in 1962. Eleven countries are in fact members of the G-10 today—the G-7 plus the Netherlands, Belgium, Sweden and Switzerland. In addition to providing supplementary finance, the G-10 regularly meets to discuss important matters related to the international monetary regime.

Group of 24 (G-24)   The G-24 was formed by the G-77 in 1972 to represent the interests of less developed countries on international monetary issues. The G-24 is composed of eight finance ministers or central bank governors from each of the three main LDC regions—Africa, Asia, and Latin America.

Group of 77 (G-77)   The principal group representing Third World economic interests in negotiations with the developed countries. The G-77 derives its name from the 77 less developed countries that formed the group in 1964, but well over 100 LDCs are in fact members of the group today.

Heckscher-Ohlin theorem   A theory named after two Swedish economists that postulates that comparative advantage is determined by the relative abundance and scarcity of factors of production (land, labor, and capital). Thus, capital-rich countries (usually the more advanced nations) should specialize in capital-intensive production, while countries with an abundance of cheap labor (many less developed countries) should specialize in labor-intensive production.

hegemonic stability theory   A theory asserting that a relatively open and stable international economic system is most likely to exist when a hegemonic state is willing and able to provide leadership. The hegemonic state may manage the global economic system through coercive tactics and/or the provision of public goods. See also *hegemony* and *public goods*.

hegemony   Leadership, preponderant influence, or dominance in the international system, usually (but not always) associated with a particular nation-state. Gramscian theorists use the term *hegemony* in a cultural sense to connote not only the dominance of a single world power but also the complex of "ideas" that social groups use to legitimize their authority.

horizontal integration   A horizontally integrated multinational corporation extends its operations abroad by producing the same product or product line in plants located in different countries. See also *multinational corporation* and *vertical integration*.

import-substituting industrialization (ISI)   A strategy to promote economic development by replacing industrial imports with domestic production through trade protectionism and government assistance to domestic firms. Import substitution is most commonly associated with the economic problems of a number of Latin American LDCs.

instrumental Marxism   A form of Marxism that perceives formal government institutions as responding in a passive manner to the interests and pressures of the capitalist class. See also *structural Marxism.*

International Monetary Fund (IMF)   An international financial organization formed in 1944 to uphold the Bretton Woods system of pegged exchange rates (until the move to floating rates in 1973) and to provide countries with short-term loans for balance-of-payments problems. The IMF has had a leading role in dealing with the 1980s foreign debt crisis and the 1990s financial crisis.

liquidity   The ease with which an asset can be used at a known price in making payments. Cash is the most liquid form of an asset.

London Club   An informal group of private commercial banks that have provided credit to Third World countries encountering debt repayment problems. The London Club has no formal structure or specific location for its meetings. Meetings often occur in "creditor committees," in which the largest creditor banks coordinate their positions in debt rescheduling negotiations with individual LDC debtor countries. See also *Paris Club.*

macroeconomics   The branch of economics that deals with the behavior of the economy as a whole. For example, macroeconomics is concerned with overall levels of employment, growth, production, and consumption. It examines such issues as monetary and fiscal policy, the banking system, trade, and the balance of payments.

market   An arrangement in which goods, services, and factors of production are bought and sold in response to relative prices, which are determined by the interaction of supply and demand.

market economy   An economy in which the market coordinates individual choices to determine the types of goods and services produced and sold and the methods of production.

mercantilism   A policy of states from the sixteenth to eighteenth centuries to build up their power and wealth relative to other states, largely by maintaining a balance-of-trade surplus. States that rely on government involvement and trade protectionism to increase their power and wealth today are often considered to be *neomercantilist.*

monetary policy   Monetary policy influences the economy through changes in the money supply. When a government uses monetary policy to deal with a balance-of-payments deficit, its central bank limits public access to funds for spending purposes and makes such funds more expensive.

most-favored-nation (MFN) treatment   A principle stipulating that every trade advantage, favor, privilege, or immunity a GATT/WTO member gives to any country must be extended to all other member states. A major exception to MFN treatment is provided for regional integration agreements.

multilateral aid   A type of foreign assistance in which donor governments provide funding through international organizations (such as the World Bank) whose policies are collectively determined. *See also* bilateral aid, foreign aid, and official development assistance.

multinational corporation (MNC)   An enterprise that owns and controls facilities for production, distribution, and marketing in at least two countries. Also referred to as a *transnational corporation* or *multinational enterprise.*

national treatment   A principle stating that all GATT/WTO members should treat foreign products—after they have been imported—as favorably as domestic products with regard to internal taxes and other internal charges and regulations.

New International Economic Order (NIEO)   A set of proposals for extensive international economic reform and concessions from the industrial states of the North, which Third World countries presented in the United Nations in the 1970s. These included LDC demands for control over their economies and natural resources, control over foreign investment, greater assistance for economic development, greater access to markets in developed countries, and increased prices for LDC commodity exports. The Northern states ultimately rejected most of these demands for change.

nontariff barriers (NTBs)   An incredibly large array of measures other than tariffs that restrict imports, assist domestic production, and promote exports. As tariffs declined because of successive rounds of GATT negotiations, nontariff barriers became relatively more important. NTBs are often more restrictive, ill defined, and inequitable than tariffs.

North American Free Trade Agreement (NAFTA)   A free trade agreement joining the United States, Canada, and Mexico, which entered into force in January 1994. The importance of NAFTA stems from the inclusion of the United States, the comprehensive nature of the agreement, and the fact that it is the first reciprocal free trade accord between industrial states and a less developed country. Unlike the World Trade Organization, NAFTA does not give special and differential treatment to the LDC member (Mexico).

official aid (OA)   Flows of foreign aid that meet the same criteria of eligibility as *official development assistance*. The only difference is that recipients of official aid are the more advanced emerging countries (e.g., Russia, Hungary, and Poland) and a small number of advanced Third World countries (e.g., Kuwait and Singapore).

official development assistance (ODA)   Flows of foreign aid to less-developed countries and multilateral institutions from official government agencies. *See also* bilateral aid, foreign aid, and multilateral aid.

Pareto-optimal outcome   A condition of equilibrium in which no one actor can be made better off without making someone else worse off. A Pareto-suboptimal outcome, by contrast, is one in which all actors prefer another outcome to the equilibrium outcome. See *prisoners' dilemma.*

Paris Club   An informal grouping of creditor governments (members of the Organization for Economic Cooperation and Development) that meets with individual LDC debtor governments to negotiate debt rescheduling agreements. The Paris Club normally meets in the French Ministry of Finance, but it has no legal status or written rules, no voting procedure, and no formal organizational structure.

portfolio investment   The purchase of stocks, bonds, and money market instruments by foreigners for the purpose of realizing a financial return, which does not result in foreign management, ownership, or legal control.

prisoners' dilemma   A game used by theorists (often in international relations) to examine situations in which individual rationality induces each state to "cheat" regardless of the actions taken by others. Such individually rational actions, however, can produce a Pareto-suboptimal outcome; hence the "dilemma" in the prisoners' dilemma. See *Pareto-optimal outcome.*

public goods   Also called *collective goods*, these are goods which are *nonexcludable* (i.e., all states have access to them) and *nonrival* (i.e., any state's use of the good will not decrease the amount available for others). Hegemons often provide public goods, according to the liberal interpretation of hegemonic stability theory. A major problem associated with public goods is the existence of *free riders* because even noncontributing states (or individuals) can benefit from the provision of public goods.

Quadrilateral Group of Trade Ministers or **Quad**   An informal grouping composed of the United States, the European Commission, Japan, and Canada, which helps to set the agenda for meetings and negotiations in the global trade regime. It performs some of the same functions in trade that the Group of Seven performs in the monetary and financial regimes.

reciprocity   The GATT/WTO principle that a country benefiting from another country's trade concessions should provide roughly equal benefits in return. *Specific reciprocity*, the more demanding type, requires concessions of equivalent value between two actors within a strict time period. *Diffuse reciprocity* is less demanding, with more flexibility in terms of equivalence of value and the time period for granting reciprocal concessions.

regime   A form of institution dealing with a specific issue area in international relations, in which principles, norms, rules, and decision-making procedures affect actors' expectations and behavior. *International organizations* are more concrete and formal institutions than regimes and are often embedded within regimes. For example, the World Trade Organization is embedded within the global trade regime.

rules of origin   Regulations designed to prevent importers from bringing goods into a free trade area through the lowest-duty member country and then shipping them to partner countries that have higher duties. Rules of origin often provide an excuse for protectionism.

safeguards   Term usually applied to Article 19 of GATT (the general escape clause). This article permits countries to take emergency protection measures to counter unexpected import surges that cause, or are likely to cause, serious injury to domestic industry. Safeguard actions are to be applied on a nondiscriminatory basis, and affected countries can request compensation.

seignorage   The profit and advantages accruing to a "seigneur" or sovereign power from issuing money. The term usually refers to the influence and power a hegemon acquires as a result of its position as the top-currency state.

special drawing rights (SDRs)   Artificial international reserves created and managed by the Group of Ten and used among central banks. SDRs have been issued only three times, and efforts to increase their role as an alternative to the U.S. dollar have been unsuccessful.

strategic trade theory   A realist theory indicating that a state can successfully intervene through industrial targeting to alter its comparative or "competitive" advantage vis-à-vis other states. In deciding on its intervention strategies, a state tends to favor industries with presumed advantages in research and development, technology, economies of scale, and market power.

structural adjustment loans (SALs)   Medium-term balance-of-payments financing provided by the World Bank and IMF to less developed countries. To receive such loans, LDC borrowers must agree to institute structural reforms prescribed by the IMF and/or World Bank.

structural Marxism   Structural Marxists view the state as relatively autonomous of direct political pressure from particular capitalists, but they believe that the state acts in the long-term interests of the capitalist class.

sustainable development   A policy that recognizes the complementarity between economic development and environmental conservation. Sustainable development was popularized by nongovernmental organizations in the early 1980s and received multilateral approval in 1987 by the Brundtland Commission. According to the Brundtland Commission, sustainable development "meets the needs of the present without compromising the ability of future generations to meet their own needs."

tariffs   Taxes levied on products that pass through a customs border. Although tariffs are usually imposed on imports, they may also be applied to exports. Import tariffs are most commonly used as a means of protectionism, but they may also be valued as a source of revenue for the state.

terms of trade   The relationship between the prices of a country's exports and the prices of its imports. In the late 1940s and early 1950s, structuralists such as Raúl Prebisch argued that relations between the core and periphery were marked by unequal exchange, in which there were deteriorating terms of trade for LDCs in the periphery. LDCs were therefore advised to follow *import-substituting industrialization* policies.

transfer prices   Prices used by a business firm for the internal sale of goods and services among its divisions (i.e., for intrafirm trade). A multinational corporation may artificially raise or lower its transfer prices to shift its reported profits from high-tax to low-tax countries.

Triffin dilemma   Named after Robert Triffin, the Triffin dilemma described the position of the United States as the top-currency state. Continued balance-of-payments deficits would create a "confidence" problem in the U.S. dollar; but if the United States moved to reduce its payments deficit, there would be a shortage of U.S. dollars for liquidity purposes. The Triffin dilemma therefore refers to the conflict between the liquidity and confidence functions of a top-currency state.

United Nations Conference on Trade and Development (UNCTAD)   A permanent organ of the United Nations General Assembly, created in 1964 as a result of Third World dissatisfaction with existing international economic organizations such as GATT. UNCTAD is primarily concerned with promoting international trade, economic development, and the interests of less developed countries.

vertical integration   Control and coordination of production of goods and services at different stages of the production process. When such integration occurs across national boundaries, a firm is referred to as a vertically integrated multinational corporation.

voluntary export restraints   A practice by which countries have circumvented the GATT Article 11 ban on import quotas by pressuring other countries to "voluntarily" decrease their exports of specific products.

World Bank group   The largest multilateral group of institutions providing international development financing for Third World countries and emerging centrally planned economies. The group consists of four financial institutions, including the International Bank for Reconstruction and Development (formed at Bretton Woods in the 1940s); the International Finance Corporation (formed in 1956); the International Development Association (created in 1960); and the Multilateral Investment Guarantee Agency (established in 1988).

world-system theory   Like dependency theory, world-system theory rejects the view of modernization theorists that countries in the periphery have problems because they follow traditional practices. World-system theorists argue that problems in the periphery stem from capitalism, a global system for organizing economic activities that has existed since the "long sixteenth century." To explain the fact that some countries in the periphery have experienced some development, world-system theorists introduced the concept of the semiperiphery.

World Trade Organization (WTO)   The main global trade organization, established as the successor to GATT in 1995 by the signatories to the GATT Uruguay round agreement. Under the WTO are various agreements, including the General Agreement on Tariffs and Trade (GATT), the General Agreement on Trade in Services (GATS), and the Agreement on Trade-Related Intellectual Property Rights (TRIPs).

SELECTED BIBLIOGRAPY

TOPICS

I. General Studies— International Political Economy

Ashley, Richard K. "Three Modes of Economism." *International Studies Quarterly* 27-4 (December 1983): 463–496.

Baldwin, David A., ed. *Neorealism and Neoliberalism: The Contemporary Debate.* New York: Columbia University Press, 1993.

Biersteker, Thomas J. "Evolving Perspectives on International Political Economy: Twentieth-Century Contexts and Discontinuities." *International Political Science Review* 14-1 (January 1993): 7–33.

Boyer, Robert, and Daniel Drache, eds. *States Against Markets: The Limits of Globalization.* London: Routledge, 1996.

Caporaso, James A. "Global Political Economy." In *Political Science: The State of the Discipline II,* ed. Ada Finifter, 451–481. Washington, DC: American Political Science Association, 1993.

Cerny, Philip G., ed. *World Politics: Markets, Regimes and States in the Post-Hegemonic Era.* London: Elgar, 1993.

Cox, Robert W. *Production, Power, and World Order: Social Forces in the Making of History.* New York: Columbia University Press, 1987.

Crane, George T., and Abla Amawi, eds. *The Theoretical Evolution of International Political Economy: A Reader.* New York: Oxford University Press, 2nd edition, 1997.

Doyle, Michael W., and G. John Ikenberry. *New Thinking in International Relations Theory.* Boulder, CO: Westview Press, 1997.

Fieleke, Norman S. *The International Economy Under Stress.* Cambridge, MA: Ballinger, 1988.

Frieden, Jeffry A., and David A. Lake, eds. *International Political Economy: Perspectives on Global Power and Wealth.* New York: St. Martin's Press, 3rd edition, 1995.

Gilpin, Robert, with Jean Gilpin. *The Political Economy of International Relations.* Princeton, NJ: Princeton University Press, 1987.

Howlett, Michael, and M. Ramesh. *The Political Economy of Canada: An Introduction.* Toronto: McClelland & Stewart, 1992.

Jones, R. J. Barry. *Perspectives on Political Economy.* London: Pinter, 1983.

Kegley, Jr., Charles W., ed. *Controversies in International Relations Theory: Realism and the Neoliberal Challenge.* New York: St. Martin's Press, 1995.

Kenen, Peter B., ed. *Managing the World Economy: Fifty Years After Bretton Woods.* Washington, DC: Institute for International Economics, September 1994.

Kindleberger, Charles P. *Power and Money: The Economics of International Politics and the Politics of International Economics.* New York: Basic Books, 1970.

Knorr, Klaus. "Economics and International Relations: A Problem in Teaching." *Political Science Quarterly* 62-4 (December 1947): 552–568.

Kresl, Peter Karl, and Gary Gappert, eds. *North American Cities and the Global Economy: Challenges and Opportunities.* Urban Affairs Annual Review 44. Thousand Oaks, CA: Sage, 1995.

Lindblom, Charles E. *Politics and Markets: The World's Political-Economic Systems.* New York: Basic Books, 1977.

McKinlay, R. D., and R. Little. *Global Problems and World Order.* London, UK: Pinter, 1986.

Murphy, Craig N., and Roger Tooze, eds. *The New International Political Economy.* Boulder, CO: Rienner, 1991.

O'Hara, Phillip Anthony, ed. *Encyclopedia of Political Economy,* vols. 1 and 2. London: Routedge, 1999.

Polanyi, Karl. *The Great Transformation.* Boston: Beacon Press, 1965.

Schwartz, Herman M. *States versus Markets: History, Geography, and the Development of the International Political Economy.* New York: St. Martin's Press, 1994.

Staniland, Martin. *What Is Political Economy? A Study of Social Theory and Underdevelopment.* New Haven, CT: Yale University Press, 1985.

Strange, Susan. "International Economics and International Relations: A Case of Mutual Neglect." *International Affairs* 46 (April 1970): 304–315.

———, ed. *Paths to International Political Economy.* London: Allen & Unwin, 1984.

———. *States and Markets.* London: Pinter, 1988.

Strange, Susan, and Roger Tooze, eds. *The International Politics of Surplus Capacity.* London: Allen & Unwin, 1981.

Stubbs, Richard, and Geoffrey R. D. Underhill, eds. *Political Economy and the Changing Global Order.* Toronto: McClelland & Stewart, 1994.

Webb, Michael C. *The Political Economy of Policy Coordination: International Adjustment Since 1945.* Ithaca, NY: Cornell University Press, 1995.

Whitworth, Sandra. *Feminism and International Relations: Towards a Political Economy of Gender in Interstate and Non-Governmental Institutions.* London: Macmillan, 1994.

II. Globalization

Amin, Samir. "The Challenge of Globalization." *Review of International Political Economy* 3-2 (Summer 1996): 216–259.

Burback, Roger, Orlando Núñez, and Boris Kagarlitsky. *Globalization and Its Discontents: The Rise of Postmodern Socialisms*. London: Pluto Press, 1997.

Cerny, Philip G. "Globalization and the Changing Logic of Collective Action." *International Organization* 49-4 (Autumn 1995): 595–625.

Carnoy, Martin, Manuel Castells, Stephen S. Cohen, and Fernando Henrique Cardoso. *The New Global Economy in the Information Age: Reflections on Our Changing World.* University Park: Pennsylvania State University Press, 1993.

"Globalization." Special issue of *International Journal* 51-4 (Autumn 1996).

Held, David. *Democracy and the Global Order: From the Modern State to Cosmopolitan Governance.* Cambridge: Polity Press, 1995.

Hirst, Paul, and Grahame Thompson. *Globalization in Question.* Cambridge: Polity Press, 1996.

Holm, Hans-Henrik, and Georg Sorensen, eds. *Whose World Order? Uneven Globalization and the End of the Cold War.* Boulder, CO: Westview Press, 1995.

Hurrell, Anthony, and Ngaire Woods. "Globalisation and Inequality." *Millennium* 24-3 (1995): 447–470.

Jones, R. J. Barry. *Globalisation and Interdependence in the International Political Economy: Rhetoric and Reality.* London: Pinter, 1995.

Kapstein, Ethan B. *Governing the Global Market: International Finance and the State.* Cambridge, MA: Harvard University Press, 1994.

Mander, Jerry, and Edward Goldsmith, eds. *The Case Against the Global Economy: For a Turn Toward the Local.* San Francisco: Sierra Club, 1996.

McGrew, Anthony G., and Paul Lewis, et al. *Global Politics: Globalization and the Nation-State.* Cambridge: Polity Press, 1992.

Mittelman, James H. *Globalization: Critical Reflections.* Boulder, CO: Rienner, 1996.

Ohmae, Kenichi. *The Borderless World: Power and Strategy in the Interlinked Economy.* New York: Harper Perennial, 1990.

Robertson, Roland. *Globalization: Social Theory and Global Culture.* London: Sage, 1992.

Sklair, Leslie. *Sociology of the Global System.* Hertfordshire, UK: Prentice Hall/Harvester Wheatsheaf, 2nd edition, 1995.

Waters, Malcolm. *Globalization.* London: Routledge, 1995.

III. Institutional Framework for Managing the Postwar World Economy

Acheson, A. L. K., J. F. Chant, and M. F. J. Prochowny, eds. *Bretton Woods Revisited.* Toronto: University of Toronto Press, 1972.

Assetto, Valerie J. *The Soviet Bloc in the IMF and the IBRD.* Boulder, CO: Westview Press, 1988.

Bakker, Age F. P. *International Financial Institutions.* New York: Longman, 1996.

Bergsten, C. Fred, and C. Randall Henning. *Global Economic Leadership and the Group of Seven.* Washington, DC: Institute for International Economics, June 1996.

Bleicher, Samuel A. "UN v. IBRD: A Dilemma of Functionalism." *International Organization* 42-1 (Winter 1970): 31–47.

Brabant, Jozef M. van. *The Planned Economies and International Economic Organizations.* Cambridge: Cambridge University Press, 1991.

Bretton Woods Commission. *Bretton Woods: Looking to the Future.* Commission Report, Staff Review, Background Papers. Washington, DC: Bretton Woods Committee, July 1994.

Camps, Miriam, with C. Gwin. *Collective Management: The Reform of Global Economic Organizations.* New York: McGraw-Hill, 1980.

Cavanagh, John, Daphne Wysham, and Marcos Arruda, eds. *Beyond Bretton Woods: Alternatives to the Global Economic Order.* London: Pluto Press, 1994.

Cutajar, Michael Zammit, ed. *UNCTAD and the North-South Dialogue: The First Twenty Years.* Oxford: Permagon Press, 1985.

Danaher, Kevin, ed. *50 Years Is Enough: The Case Against the World Bank and the International Monetary Fund.* Boston: South End Press, 1994.

Feeney, William. "Chinese Policy in Multilateral Financial Institutions." In *China and the World: Chinese Foreign Policy in the Post-Mao Era,* ed. Samuel S. Kim, pp. 266–292. Boulder, CO: Westview Press, 1984.

Feinberg, Fichard E. "The Changing Relationship Between the World Bank and the International Monetary Fund." *International Organization* 42-3 (Summer 1988): 545–560.

Ferguson, Tyrone. *The Third World and Decision Making in the International Monetary Fund: The Quest for Full and Effective Participation.* London: Pinter, 1988.

Gold, Joseph. "The Relationship Between the International Monetary Fund and the World Bank," *Crerghton Law Review* 15 (1982): 499–521.

Hajnal, Peter I., ed. *The Seven Power Summit: Documents from the Summits of Industrialized Countries 1975–1989.* New York: Kraus International Publications, 1989.

Hart, Jeffrey A. *The New International Economic Order: Conflict and Cooperation in North-South Economic Relations, 1974–77.* London: Macmillan, 1983.

Jacobson, Harold K. *Networks of Interdependence: International Organizations and the Global Political System.* New York: Knopf, 1979.

Jacobson, Harold K., and Michel Oksenberg. *China's Participation in the IMF, the World Bank, and GATT: Toward a Global Economic Order.* Ann Arbor: University of Michigan Press, 1990.

Karns, Margaret P., and Karen A. Mingst. *The United States and Multilateral Institutions: Patterns of Changing Instrumentality and Influence.* Boston: Unwin Hyman, 1990.

Kirshner, Orin, ed. *The Bretton Woods–GATT System: Retrospect and Prospect After Fifty Years.* Armonk, NY: Sharpe, 1996.

Lang, Laszlo. "International Regimes and the Political Economy of East-West Relations." *Occasional Paper Series* no. 13. New York: Institute for East-West Security Studies, 1989, 19–22.

Laszlo, Ervin, et al. *The Obstacles to the New International Economic Order.* New York: Pergamon Press, 1980.

Morgenthau, Henry, Jr. "Bretton Woods and International Cooperation." *Foreign Affairs* 23-2 (January 1945), 182–94.

Polak, Jacques J. *The World Bank and the International Monetary Fund: A Changing Relationship.* Brookings Occasional Papers. Washington, DC: Brookings Institution, 1994.

Prügl, Elisabeth. "Gender in International Organization and Global Governance: A Critical Review of the Literature." *International Studies Notes* 21-1 (Winter 1996): 15–24.

Putnam, Robert D., and Nicholas Bayne. *Hanging Together: Cooperation and Conflict in the Seven-Power Summits.* London: Sage, revised edition, 1987.

Rochester, J. Martin. "The Rise and Fall of International Organization as a Field of Study." *International Organization* 40-4 (Autumn 1986): 777–813.

Ruggie, John Gerard., ed. *Multilateralism Matters: The Theory and Praxis of an Institutional Form.* New York: Columbia University Press, 1993.

Sauvant, Karl P. *The Group of 77: Evolution, Structure, Organization*. New York: Oceana Publications, 1981.

Van Dormael, Armand. *Bretton Woods: Birth of a Monetary System*. London: Macmillan, 1978.

Williams, Marc. *International Economic Organisations and the Third World*. New York: Harvester Wheatsheaf, 1994.

World Commission on Environment and Development. *Our Common Future* (The Brundtland Report). Oxford: Oxford University Press, 1987.

IV. The Realist Perspective

Baldwin, David A. *Economic Statecraft*. Princeton, NJ: Princeton University Press, 1985.

Evans, Peter B., Dietrich Rueschemeyer, and Theda Skocpol, eds. *Bringing the State Back In.* Cambridge: Cambridge University Press, 1985.

Gilpin, Robert. *War and Change in World Politics*. Cambridge: Cambridge University Press, 1981.

———. "The Richness of the Tradition of Political Realism." *International Organization* 38-2 (Spring 1984), pp. 287–304.

Grieco, Joseph. *Cooperation Among Nations: Europe, America, and Non-Tariff Barriers to Trade*. Ithaca, NY: Cornell University Press, 1990.

Hart, Jeffrey A. *The New International Economic Order: Conflict and Cooperation in North-South Economic Relations, 1974–77*. London: Macmillan, 1983.

Heckscher, Eli F. *Mercantilism*. Vol. 2. London: Allen & Unwin, 1934.

Hirschman, Albert O. *National Power and the Structure of Foreign Trade*. Berkeley: University of California Press, expanded edition, 1980.

Johnson, Chalmers. *MITI and the Japanese Miracle: The Growth of Industrial Policy, 1925–1975*. Stanford, CA: Stanford University Press, 1982.

Keohane, Robert O., ed. *Neorealism and Its Critics*. New York: Columbia University Press, 1986.

Krasner, Stephen D. *Defending the National Interest: Raw Materials Investments and U.S. Foreign Policy*. Princeton: Princeton University Press, 1978.

———. *Structural Conflict: The Third World Against Global Liberalism*. Berkeley: University of California Press, 1985.

Lake, David A. "Power and the Third World: Toward a Realist Political Economy of North-South Relations." *International Studies Quarterly* 31-2 (June 1987): 217–234.

List, Friedrich. *The National System of Political Economy*. Translated by Sampson S. Lloyd. London: Longmans, Green, 1916.

Machiavelli, Niccolò. *The Prince and the Discourses*. New York: Modern Library, 1940.

Mastanduno, Michael, David A. Lake, and G. John Ikenberry, "Toward a Realist Theory of State Action." *International Studies Quarterly* 33-4 (December 1989), pp. 457–474.

Morgenthau, Hans. J., rev. by Kenneth W. Thompson. *Politics Among Nations: The Struggle for Power and Peace*. New York: Knopf, 6th edition, 1985.

Rothstein, Robert L. *The Weak in the World of the Strong: The Developing Countries in the International System*. New York: Columbia University Press, 1977.

Syrett, Harold C., ed. *The Papers of Alexander Hamilton*, Vol. 10. New York: Columbia University Press, 1966.

Thucydides. *The History of the Peloponnesian War*. Translated by Richard Crawley. London: Dent, Everyman's Library, 1963.

Viner, Jacob. "Power versus Plenty as Objectives of Foreign Policy in the Seventeenth and Eighteenth Centuries." *World Politics* 1 (October 1948): 1–29.

Waltz, Kenneth N. *Theory of International Politics*. Reading, MA: Addison Wesley, 1979.

V. Hegemonic Stability Theory

Akaha, Tsuneo, and Frank Langdon, eds. *Japan in the Posthegemonic World.* Boulder, CO: Rienner, 1993.

Calleo, David P. *Beyond American Hegemony: The Future of the Western Alliance.* New York: Basic Books, 1987.

Cowhey, Peter F., and Edward Long. "Testing Theories of Regime Change: Hegemonic Decline or Surplus Capacity?" *International Organization* 37-2 (Spring 1983): 157–188.

Gill, Stephen. "American Hegemony: Its Limits and Prospects in the Reagan Era." *Millennium* 15-3 (Winter 1986): 311–336.

Huntington, Samuel P. "Transnational Organizations in World Politics." *World Politics* 25-3 (April 1973): 333–368.

Kennedy, Paul. *The Rise and Fall of the Great Powers: Economic Change and Military Conflict from 1500 to 2000.* New York: Random House, 1987.

Keohane, Robert O. *After Hegemony: Cooperation and Discord in the World Political Economy.* Princeton, NJ: Princeton University Press, 1984.

———. "The Theory of Hegemonic Stability and Changes in International Economic Regimes, 1967–1977." In *Change in the International System,* ed. Ole R. Holsti, Randolph M. Siverson, and Alexander L. George, pp. 131–162. Boulder: Westview Press, 1980.

Kindleberger, Charles P. "Dominance and Leadership in the International Economy: Exploitation, Public Goods, and Free Rides." *International Studies Quarterly* 25-2 (June 1981): 242–254.

———. *The World in Depression, 1929–1939.* Berkeley: University of California Press, 1973.

Mead, Walter Russell. *Mortal Splendor: The American Empire in Transition.* Boston: Houghton Mifflin, 1987.

Morse, Ronald A. "Japan's Drive to Pre-Eminence." *Foreign Policy* 69 (Winter 1987–88): 3–21.

Nau, Henry R. *The Myth of America's Decline: Leading the World Economy into the 1990s.* New York: Oxford University Press, 1990.

Nye, Joseph S., Jr. *Bound to Lead: The Changing Nature of American Power.* New York: Basic Books, 1990.

———. "Soft Power." *Foreign Policy* 80 (Fall 1990): 153–171.

———. "The Changing Nature of World Power." *Political Science Quarterly* 105-2 (Summer 1990): 177–192.

———. "Understating U.S. Strength." *Foreign Policy* 72 (Fall 1988): 105–129.

———. "U.S. Power and Reagan Policy." *Orbis* 26-2 (Summer 1982): 391–411.

Olson, Mancur. *The Logic of Collective Action: Public Goods and the Theory of Groups.* Cambridge, MA: Harvard University Press, 1965.

Russett, Bruce. "The Mysterious Case of Vanishing Hegemony; or, Is Mark Twain Really Dead?" *International Organization* 39-2 (Spring 1985): 207–231.

Snidal, Duncan. "The Limits of Hegemonic Stability Theory." *International Organization* 39-4 (Autumn 1985): 579–614.

Stein, Arthur A. "The Hegemon's Dilemma: Great Britain, the United States and the International Economic Order." *International Organization* 38-2 (Spring 1984).

Strange, Susan. "Finance, Information, and Power." *Review of International Studies* 16-3 (July 1990): 259–274.

———. "The Future of the American Empire." *Journal of International Affairs* 42 (Fall 1988): 1–17.

———. "The Persistent Myth of Lost Hegemony." *International Organization* 41-4 (Autumn 1987): 551–574.

Thurow, Lester. *Head to Head: The Coming Economic Battle Among Japan, Europe, and America.* New York: Morrow, 1992.

Webb, Michael C., and Stephen D. Krasner. "Hegemonic Stability Theory: An Empirical Assessment." *Review of International Studies* 15 (Spring 1989): 183–198.

VI. The Liberal Perspective

Arblaster, Anthony. *The Rise and Decline of Western Liberalism.* New York: Basil Blackwell, 1984.

Balassa, Bela, ed. *The Newly Industrializing Countries in the World Economy.* New York: Pergamon Press, 1981.

Bauer, P. T., and B. S. Yamey. "Against the New Economic Order." *Commentary* 63-4 (April 1977): 25–31.

Black, C. E. *The Dynamics of Modernization: A Study in Comparative History.* New York: Harper & Row, 1966.

Cooper, Richard N. *The Economics of Interdependence: Economic Policy in the Atlantic Community.* New York: McGraw-Hill, 1968.

Cutler, A. Claire. "The 'Grotian Tradition' in International Relations," *Review of International Studies* 17 (1991): 41–65.

Eichner, Alfred S. *A Guide to Post-Keynesian Economics.* White Plains, NY: Sharpe, 1979.

Fox, Annette Baker, Alfred O. Hero, Jr., and Joseph S. Nye, Jr., eds. *Canada and the United States: Transnational and Transgovernmental Relations.* New York: Columbia University Press, 1976.

Friedman, Milton, ed. *Essays in Positive Economics.* Chicago: University of Chicago Press, 1953.

Friedman, Milton, and Rose Friedman. *Free to Choose: A Personal Statement.* New York: Harcourt Brace Jovanovich, 1980.

Fukuyama, Francis. "The End of History?" *The National Interest* 16 (Summer 1989): 3–18.

Hayek, F. A. *New Studies in Philosophy, Politics, Economics and the History of Ideas.* Chicago: University of Chicago Press, 1978.

Jones, R. J. Barry, and Peter Willetts, eds. *Interdependence on Trial: Studies in the Theory and Reality of Contemporary Interdependence.* London: Pinter, 1984.

Keohane, Robert O., and Joseph S. Nye. *Power and Interdependence: World Politics in Transition.* Boston: Little, Brown, 1977.

Keynes, John Maynard. *The General Theory of Employment, Interest, and Money.* New York: Harcourt, Brace and World, 1935.

Krasner, Stephen D., ed. *International Regimes.* Ithaca, NY: Cornell University Press, 1983.

Lerner, Daniel. *The Passing of Traditional Society: Modernizing the Middle East.* New York: Free Press, 1964.

Moravcsik, Andrew. "Taking Preferences Seriously: A Liberal Theory of International Politics." *International Organization* 51-4 (Autumn 1997): 513–553.

Ricardo, David. *The Principles of Political Economy and Taxation.* Homewood, Il: Irwin, 1963.

Rostow, W. W. *The Stages of Economic Growth: A Non-Communist Manifesto.* Cambridge: Cambridge University Press, 1960.

———. *Why the Poor Get Richer and the Rich Slow Down.* Austin: University of Texas Press, 1980.

Schattschneider, E. E. *Politics, Pressures and the Tariff: A Study of Free Enterprise in Pressure Politics, as Shown in the 1929–1939 Revision of the Tariff.* Hamden, CT: Archon Books, 1935. Reprint, 1963.

Smith, Adam. *The Wealth of Nations.* London: Dent & Sons, Everyman's Library, 1910.

von Mises, Ludwig. *Planning For Freedom.* South Holland, IL: Libertarian Press, 1974.

VII. International Institutions and Regime Theory

Cohn, Theodore H. "The Changing Role of the United States in the Global Agricultural Trade Regime." In *World Agriculture and the GATT,* International Political Economy Yearbook, vol. 7, ed. William P. Avery, pp. 17–38. Boulder, CO: Rienner, 1993.

de Senarclens, Pierre. "Regime Theory and the Study of International Organizations." *International Social Science Journal* (November 1993): 45–138.

Haggard, Stephan, and Beth A. Simmons. "Theories of International Regimes." *International Organization* 41-3 (Summer 1987): 491–517.

Hollingsworth, J. Rogers and Robert Boyer, eds. *Contemporary Capitalism: The Embeddedness of Institutions.* Cambridge: Cambridge University Press, 1997.

Jacobson, Harold K. *Networks of Interdependence: International Organizations and the Global Political System.* New York: Knopf, 1979.

Kahler, Miles. *International Institutions and the Political Economy of Integration.* Washington, DC: Brookings Institution, 1995.

Keohane, Robert O. *International Institutions and State Power: Essays in International Relations Theory.* Boulder, CO: Westview Press, 1989.

———. *After Hegemony: Cooperation and Discord in the World Political Economy.* Princeton, NJ: Princeton University Press, 1984.

Krasner, Stephen D., ed. *International Regimes.* Ithaca, NY: Cornell University Press, 1983.

Lang, Laszlo. "International Regimes and the Political Economy of East-West Relations." *Occasional Paper Series* no. 13. New York: Institute for East-West Security Studies, 1989.

Levy, Marc A., Oran R. Young, and Michael Zürn. "The Study of International Regimes." *European Journal of International Relations* 1-3 (1995): 267–330.

Mearsheimer, John J. "The False Promise of International Institutions." *International Security* 19-3 (Winter 1994–95): 5–49.

Rittberger, Volker, ed. *International Regimes in East-West Politics.* London: Pinter, 1990.

Rittberger, Volker, with the assistance of Peter Mayer, eds. *Regime Theory and International Relations.* Oxford: Clarendon Press, 1993.

Rochester, J. Martin. "The Rise and Fall of International Organization as a Field of Study." *International Organization* 40-4 (Autumn 1986): 777–813.

Rosenau, James N., and Ernst-Otto Czempiel, eds. *Governance Without Government: Order and Change in World Politics.* Cambridge: Cambridge University Press, 1992.

Taylor, Phillip. *Nonstate Actors in International Politics: From Transregional to Substate Organizations.* Boulder, CO: Westview Press, 1984.

Zacher, Mark W., with Brent A. Sutton. *Governing Global Networks: International Regimes for Transportation and Communications.* Cambridge: Cambridge University Press, 1996.

VIII. The Historical Structuralist Perspective

Aglietta, Michel. *A Theory of Capitalist Regulation: The US Experience.* Translated by David Fernbach. London: New Left Books, 1979.

Avineri, Shlomo, ed. *Karl Marx on Colonialism and Modernization: His Dispatches and Other Writings on China, India, Mexico, the Middle East and North Africa.* Garden City, NY: Doubleday, 1968.

Baran, Paul A. *The Political Economy of Growth.* New York: Monthly Review Press, 1962.

Blaney, David L. "Reconceptualizing Autonomy: The Difference Dependency Theory Makes." *Review of International Political Economy* 3-3 (Autumn 1996): 459–497.

Brewer, Anthony. *Marxist Theories of Imperialism: A Critical Survey.* London: Routledge, 2nd edition, 1990.

Caporaso, James. "Dependency Theory: Continuities and Discontinuities in Development Studies." *International Organization* 34-4 (Autumn 1980): 605–628.

Cardoso, Fernando Henrique. "The Consumption of Dependency Theory in the United States." *Latin American Research Review* 12-3 (1977): 7–24.

Cardoso, Fernando Henrique, and Enzo Faletto. *Dependency and Development in Latin America.* Translated by Marjory Mattingly Urquidi. Berkeley: University of California Press, 1979.

Chase-Dunn, Christopher. "Comparing World-Systems: Toward a Theory of Semiperipheral Development," *Comparative Civilizations Review* 19 (Fall 1988): 29–66.

———. "International Economic Policy in a Declining Core State." In *America in a Changing World Political Economy,* ed. William P. Avery and David Rapkin, 77–96. London: Longman, 1982.

Clark, Cal, and Donna Bahry. "Dependent Development: A Socialist Variant." *International Studies Quarterly* 27-3 (September 1983): 271–293.

Cox, Robert W. *Production, Power, and World Order: Social Forces in the Making of History.* New York: Columbia University Press, 1987.

De Vroey, Michel. "A Regulation Approach Interpretation of Contemporary Crisis." *Capital & Class* 23 (Summer 1984): 45–66.

dos Santos, Theotonio. "The Structure of Dependence." *American Economic Review* 60-2 (May 1970): 231–236.

Evans, Peter. "After Dependency: Recent Studies of Class, State, and Industrialization." *Latin American Research Review* 20-2 (1985): 149–160.

———. *Dependent Development: The Alliance of Multinational, State, and Local Capital in Brazil.* Princeton, NJ: Princeton University Press, 1979.

Foster-Carter, Aidan. "From Rostow to Gunder Frank: Conflicting Paradigms in the Analysis of Underdevelopment." *World Development* 4-3 (March 1976): 167–180.

Frank, André Gunder, *Capitalism and Underdevelopment in Latin America: Historical Studies of Chile and Brazil.* New York: Monthly Review Press, 1967.

Galtung, Johan. "A Structural Theory of Imperialism." *Journal of Peace Research* 8-2 (1971): 81–117.

Gereffi, Gary. *The Pharmaceutical Industry and Dependency in the Third World.* Princeton, NJ: Princeton University Press, 1983.

Gill, Stephen, ed. *Gramsci, Historical Materialism, and International Relations.* Cambridge: Cambridge University Press, 1993.

Gramsci, Antonio. *Selections from the Prison Notebooks of Antonio Gramsci.* Edited and translated by Quintin Hoare and Geoffrey Nowell Smith. New York: International Publishers, 1971.

Hobson, J. A. *Imperialism: A Study.* Ann Arbor: University of Michigan Press, 1965.

Krader, Lawrence. *The Asiatic Mode of Production: Sources, Development and Critique in the Writings of Karl Marx.* Assen, The Netherlands: Van Grocum, 1975.

Laclau, Ernesto. "Feudalism and Capitalism in Latin America." *New Left Review* 67 (May/June 1971): 19–38.

Lenin, V. I. *Imperialism: The Highest Stage of Capitalism.* Revised translation. New York: International Publishers, 1939.

Lipietz, Alain. *Towards a New Economic Order: Postfordism, Ecology and Democracy.* Translated by Malcolm Slater. New York: Oxford University Press, 1992.

Love, Joseph L. "The Origins of Dependency Analysis." *Journal of Latin American Studies* 22 (February 1990): 143–168.

Marx, Karl, and Frederick Engels. *Selected Works.* New York: International Publishers, 1968.

McGowan, Pat, and Stephen G. Walker. "Radical and Conventional Models of U.S. Foreign Economic Policy Making." *World Politics* 33-3 (April 1981): 347–382.

Miliband, Ralph. *The State in Capitalist Society*. New York: Basic Books, 1969.

O'Leary, Brendan. *The Asiatic Mode of Production: Oriental Despotism, Historical Materialism and Indian History*. Oxford: Basil Blackwell, 1989.

Owen, Roger, and Bob Sutcliffe, eds. *Studies in the Theory of Imperialism*. Burnt Mill, Harlow Essex, UK: Longman, 1981.

Palma, Gabriel. "Dependency: A Formal Theory of Underdevelopment or a Methodology for the Analysis of Concrete Situations of Underdevelopment?" *World Development* 6-7/8 (July/August 1978): 881–924.

Parkin, Frank. *Marxism and Class Theory: A Bourgeois Critique*. London: Tavistock, 1979.

Prebisch, Raúl. *Towards a Dynamic Development Policy for Latin America*. New York: United Nations, 1963.

Sassoon, Anne Showstack, ed. *Approaches to Gramsci*. London: Writers and Readers Publishing Cooperative Society, 1982.

Shannon, Thomas Richard. *An Introduction to the World System Perspective*. Boulder, CO: Westview Press, 2nd edition, 1996.

Skocpol, Theda. "Wallerstein's World Capitalist System: A Theoretical and Historical Critique." *American Journal of Sociology* 82-5 (March 1977): 1075–1090.

Smith, Tony. "The Underdevelopment of Development Literature: The Case of Dependency Theory." *World Politics* 31-2 (January 1979): 247–288.

Valenzuela, J. Samuel, and Arturo Valenzuela. "Modernization and Dependency: Alternative Perspectives in the Study of Latin American Development." *Comparative Politics* 10 (July 1978): 535–557.

Wallerstein, Immanuel. *The Capitalist World-Economy*. New York: Cambridge University Press, 1979.

———. *The Modern World System: Capitalist Agriculture and the Origins of the European World-Economy in the Sixteenth Century*. New York: Academic Press, 1974.

———. *The Politics of the World-Economy: The States, the Movements and the Civilizations*. London: Cambridge University Press, 1984.

Warren, Bill. *Imperialism: Pioneer of Capitalism*. London: New Left Books, 1980.

Williams, Glen. "On Determining Canada's Location Within the International Political Economy." *Studies in Political Economy* 25 (Spring 1988): 107–140.

IX. Domestic-International Interactions

Avery, William P. "American Agricultural and Trade Policymaking: Two-Level Bargaining in the North American Free Trade Agreement." *Policy Sciences* 29 (1996): 113–136.

———. *World Agriculture and the GATT*. Boulder, CO: Rienner, 1993.

Busch, Marc L., and Helen V. Milner. "The Future of the International Trading System: International Firms, Regionalism, and Domestic Politics." In *Political Economy and the Changing Global Order*, eds. Richard Stubbs and Geoffrey R. D. Underhill. Toronto: McClelland & Stewart, 1994.

Cohn, Theodore H. "The Intersection of Domestic and Foreign Policy in the NAFTA Agricultural Negotiations." *Canadian-American Public Policy no. 14*. Orono: University of Maine, September 1993.

Cohn, Theodore H., and Patrick J. Smith. "Subnational Governments as International Actors: Constituent Diplomacy in the Pacific Northwest." *BC Studies* no. 110 (Summer 1996): 25–59.

Coleman, William D., and Grace Skogstad. *Policy Communities and Public Policy in Canada: A Structural Approach*. Mississauga, ONT: Copp Clark Pitman, 1990.

Comisso, Ellen, and Laura D'Andrea Tyson, eds. *Power, Purpose, and Collective Choice: Economic Strategy in Socialist States.* Special issue of *International Organization* 40-2 (Spring 1986).

Cox, Ronald W. *Power and Profits: U.S. Policy in Central America.* Lexington: University Press of Kentucky, 1994.

Eichengreen, Barry. *The Gold Standard and the Great Depression, 1919–1939.* New York: Oxford University Press, 1992.

Evangelista, Matthew. "Domestic Structure and International Change." In *New Thinking in International Relations,* ed. Michael W. Doyle and G. John Ikenberry. Boulder, CO: Westview Press, 1997.

Evans, Peter B., Harold K. Jacobson, and Robert D. Putnam, eds. *Double-Edged Diplomacy: International Bargaining and Domestic Politics.* Berkeley: University of California Press, 1993.

Friman, H. Richard. "Side-Payments versus Security Cards: Domestic Bargaining Tactics in International Economic Negotiations." *International Organization* 47-3 (Summer 1993): 387–410.

Gibbs, David N. *The Political Economy of Third World Intervention: Mines, Money, and U.S. Policy in the Congo Crisis.* Chicago: University of Chicago Press, 1991.

Gourevitch, Peter. *Politics in Hard Times: Comparative Responses to International Economic Crises.* Ithaca, NY: Cornell University Press, 1986.

———. "The Second Image Reversed: The International Sources of Domestic Politics." *International Organization* 32-4 (Autumn 1978): 881–912.

Gourevitch, Peter Alexis. "Squaring the Circle: The Domestic Sources of International Cooperation." *International Organization* 50-2 (Spring 1996): 349–373.

Ikenberry, G. John. "The Irony of State Strength: Comparative Responses to the Oil Shocks in the 1970s." *International Organization* 40-1 (Winter 1986): 105–137.

Ikenberry, G. John, David A. Lake, and Michael Mastanduno, eds. *The State and American Foreign Economic Policy.* Special issue of *International Organization* 42-1 (Winter 1988).

Katzenstein, Peter J., ed. *Between Power and Plenty: Foreign Economic Policies of Advanced Industrial States.* Special issue of *International Organization* 31-4 (Autumn 1977).

Katzenstein, Peter J. "International Relations and Domestic Structures: Foreign Economic Policies of Advanced Industrial States." *International Organization* 30-1 (Winter 1976): 1–45.

Keohane, Robert O., and Helen V. Milner, eds. *Internationalization and Domestic Politics.* Cambridge: Cambridge University Press, 1996.

Kresl, Peter, Karl Kresl, and Gary Gappert. *North American Cities and the Global Economy: Challenges and Opportunities.* Thousand Oaks, CA: Sage, 1995.

Milner, Helen V. *Resisting Protectionism: Global Industries and the Politics of International Trade.* Princeton, NJ: Princeton University Press, 1988.

Milner, Helen. "Resisting the Protectionist Temptation: Industry and the Making of Trade Policy in France and the United States During the 1970s." *International Organization* 41-4 (Autumn 1987): 639–665.

Nowell, Gregory P. *Mercantile States and the World Oil Cartel, 1900–1939.* Ithaca, NY: Cornell University Press, 1994.

Putnam, Robert D. "Diplomacy and Domestic Politics: The Logic of Two-Level Games." *International Organization* 42 (Summer 1988): 427–460.

Risse-Kappen, Thomas, ed. *Bringing Transnational Relations Back In: Non-State Actors, Domestic Structures and International Institutions.* Cambridge: Cambridge University Press, 1995.

Rogowski, Ronald. *Commerce and Coalitions: How Trade Affects Domestic Political Alignments.* Princeton, NJ: Princeton University Press, 1989.

Simmons, Beth A. *Who Adjusts? Domestic Sources of Foreign Economic Policy During the Interwar Years.* Princeton, NJ: Princeton University Press, 1994.

Stolper, Wolfgang F., and Paul A. Samuelson. "Protection and Real Wages." *Review of Economic Studies* 9-1 (November 1941): 58–73.

X. International Monetary and Financial Relations

Bird, Graham. *The International Monetary System and the Less Developed Countries.* London: Macmillan, 2nd edition, 1982.

Britton, Andrew, and David Mayes. *Achieving Monetary Union in Europe.* London: Sage, 1992.

Cerny, Philip G., ed. *Finance and World Politics: Markets, Regimes and States in the Post-hegemonic Era.* London: Elgar, 1993.

Cohen, Benjamin J., ed. *The International Political Economy of Monetary Relations.* Aldershot, UK: Elgar, 1993.

Cohen, Benjamin J. *Organizing the World's Money: The Political Economy of International Monetary Relations.* New York: Basic Books, 1977.

Cooper, Richard N. "Prolegomena to the Choice of an International Monetary System." *International Organization* 29-1 (Winter 1975): 63–97.

Dam, Kenneth W. *The Rules of the Game: Reform and Evolution in the International Monetary System.* Chicago: University of Chicago Press, 1982.

De Grauwe, Paul. *The Economics of Monetary Union.* Oxford: Oxford University Press, 2nd revised edition, 1994.

Dell, Sidney. "On Being Grandmotherly: The Evolution of IMF Conditionality." *Essays in International Finance* no. 144. Princeton, NJ: Princeton University, October 1981.

Eichengreen, Barry, and Jeffry Frieden, eds. *The Political Economy of European Monetary Unification.* Boulder, Westview Press, 1994.

Feldstein, Martin. "Refocusing the IMF." *Foreign Affairs* 77-2 (March/April 1998): 20–33.

Ferguson, Tyrone. *The Third World and Decision Making in the International Monetary Fund: The Quest for Full and Effective Participation.* London: Pinter, 1988.

Frankel, Jeffrey A., and Shang-Jun Wei. "Is a Yen Bloc Emerging?" in Symposium on "Economic Cooperation and Challenges in the Pacific." *Joint U.S.-Korea Academic Studies* 5 (1995): 145–175.

Fratianni, Michele, and Jürgen von Hagen. *The European Monetary System and European Monetary Union.* Boulder, Westview Press, 1992.

Gardner, Richard N. *Sterling-Dollar Diplomacy in Current Perspective: The Origins and Prospects of Our International Economic Order.* New York: Columbia University Press, new expanded edition, 1980.

Gold, Joseph. *Membership and Nonmembership in the International Monetary Fund: A Study in International Law and Organization.* Washington, DC: IMF, 1974.

Gowa, Joanne. *Closing of the Gold Window: Domestic Politics and the End of Bretton Woods.* Ithaca, NY: Cornell University Press, 1983.

Hamouda, Omar F., Robin Rowley, and Bernard M. Wolf, eds. *The Future of the International Monetary System: Change, Coordination or Instability?* Aldershot, UK: Elgar, 1989.

Helleiner, Eric. *States and the Reemergence of Global Finance: From Bretton Woods to the 1990s.* Ithaca, NY: Cornell University Press, 1994.

Horsefield, Keith J. *The International Monetary Fund, 1945–65: Twenty Years of Monetary Cooperation. Vols. I–III.* Washington, DC: IMF, 1969.

James, Harold. *International Monetary Cooperation Since Bretton Woods.* Washington, DC: IMF, 1996.

Kapstein, Ethan B. *Governing the Global Economy: International Finance and the State.* Cambridge, MA: Harvard University Press, 1994.

Lavigne, Marie. "Eastern European Countries and the IMF." In *East-West Economic Relations in the Changing Global Environment,* ed. Béla Csikós-Nagy and David G. Young, pp. 298–311. London: Macmillan, 1986.

McKinnon, Ronald I. "The Rules of the Game: International Money in Historical Perspective." *Journal of Economic Literature* 31-1 (March 1993): 1–44.

Odell, John S. *U.S. International Monetary Policy: Markets, Power, and Ideas as Sources of Change.* Princeton, NJ: Princeton University Press, 1982.

Plumptre, A. F. W. *Three Decades of Decision: Canada and the World Monetary System, 1944–75.* Toronto: McClelland & Stewart, 1977.

Schweitzer, Pierre-Paul. "Political Aspects of Managing the International Monetary System." *International Affairs* 52-2 (April 1976): 208–218.

Solomon, Robert. *The International Monetary System, 1945–1981.* New York: Harper & Row, 2nd edition, 1982.

Strange, Susan. *Casino Capitalism.* Oxford: Basil Blackwell, 1986.

———. *Sterling and British Policy: A Political Study of an International Currency in Decline.* London: Oxford University Press, 1971.

Triffin, Robert. *Gold and the Dollar Crisis: The Future of Convertibility.* New Haven: Yale University Press, revised edition, 1961.

Webb, Michael C. *The Political Economy of Policy Coordination: International Adjustment Since 1945.* Ithaca, NY: Cornell University Press, 1995.

Williamson, John. *The Exchange Rate System.* Washington, DC: Institute for International Economics, revised edition, June 1985.

———. *The Failure of World Monetary Reform, 1971–74.* Sunbury-on-Thames, UK: Nelson, 1977.

XI. Foreign Debt

Biersteker, Thomas J., ed. *Dealing with Debt: International Financial Negotiations and Adjustment Bargaining.* Boulder, CO: Westview Press, 1993.

Bouchet, Michel Henri. *The Political Economy of International Debt.* New York: Quorum Books, 1987.

Busumtwi-Sam, James. "The Role of the IMF and the World Bank in International Development." In *United Nations Reform,* ed. Hanna Newcombe and Eric Fawcett, pp. 248–266. Toronto: Dundurn Press, 1995.

Cline, William R. *International Debt and the Stability of the World Economy.* Policy Analyses in International Economics 4. Washington, DC: Institute for International Economics, 1983.

———. *International Debt Reexamined.* Washington, DC: Institute for International Economics, 1995.

Cohen, Benjamin J. "Balance-of-Payments Financing: Evolution of a Regime." In *International Regimes,* ed. Stephen D. Krasner, pp. 315–336. Ithaca, NY: Cornell University Press, 1983.

Cohn, Theodore H. "The United States and Latin America: Ambivalent Ties." *The Canadian Review of American Studies* 20-2 (Fall 1989): 255–263.

Corbridge, Stuart. *Debt and Development.* Oxford: Blackwell Publishers, 1993.

D'Andrea Tyson, Laura. "The Debt Crisis and Adjustment Responses in Eastern Europe: A Comparative Perspective." *International Organization* 40-2 (Spring 1986): 239–285.

Eichengreen, Barry, and Peter H. Lindert. eds. *The International Debt Crisis in Historical Perspective.* Cambridge, MA: MIT Press, 1989.

Elson, Diane. "From Survival Strategies to Transformation Strategies: Women's Needs and Structural Adjustment." In *Unequal Burden: Crises, Persistent Poverty, and Women's Work,* ed. Lourdes Beneria and Shelley Feldman, pp. 26–48. Boulder, CO: Westview Press, 1992.

————. "How Is Structural Adjustment Affecting Women?" *Development* (1989-1). 67–74.

Feinberg, Richard E., and Ricardo Ffrench-Davis, eds., *Development and External Debt in Latin America: Bases for a New Consensus.* Notre Dame, IN: University of Notre Dame Press, 1988.

Feinberg, Richard E., and Valeriana Kallab, eds. *Adjustment Crisis in the Third World.* New Brunswick, NJ: Transaction Books, 1984.

Fishlow, Albert. "Lessons from the Past: Capital Markets During the Nineteenth Century and the Interwar Period." *International Organization* 39-3 (Summer 1985): 383–439.

Frieden, Jeff. "Third World Indebted Industrialization: International Finance and State Capitalism in Mexico, Brazil, Algeria, and South Korea." *International Organization* 35-3 (Summer 1981): 407–431.

Honeywell, Martin, ed. *The Poverty Brokers: The IMF and Latin America.* London: Latin America Bureau, 1983.

Husain, Ishrat, and Ishac Diwan, eds. *Dealing with the Debt Crisis: A World Bank Symposium.* Washington, DC: World Bank, 1989.

Kahler, Miles. "Politics and International Debt: Explaining the Crisis." *International Organization* 39-3 (Summer 1985): 357–382.

Kahler, Miles, ed. *The Politics of International Debt.* Ithaca, NY: Cornell University Press, 1986.

Körner, Peter, Gero Maass, Thomas Siebold, and Ranier Tetzlaff. *The IMF and the Debt Crisis: A Guide to the Third World's Dilemma.* Translated by Paul Knight. London: Zed Books, 1986.

Krugman, Paul. "LDC Debt Policy." In *American Economic Policy in the 1980s,* ed. Martin Feldstein, pp. 691–739. Chicago: University of Chicago Press, 1994.

Kuhn, Michael G., with Jorge P. Guzman. *Multilateral Official Debt Rescheduling: Recent Experience, World Economic and Financial Surveys.* Washington, DC: IMF, November 1990.

Lipson, Charles. "Bankers' Dilemmas: Private Cooperation in Rescheduling Sovereign Debts." In *Cooperation Under Anarchy,* ed. Kenneth A. Oye, pp. 200–225. Princeton, NJ: Princeton University Press, 1986.

————. "The International Organization of Third World Debt." *International Organization* 35-4 (Autumn 1981): 603–631.

Pastor, Robert A., ed. *Latin America's Debt Crisis: Adjusting to the Past or Planning for the Future?* Boulder, CO: Rienner, 1987.

Payer, Cheryl. *The Debt Trap: The IMF and the Third World.* Middlesex, UK: Penguin, 1974.

————. *Lent and Lost: Foreign Credit and Third World Development.* London: Zed Books, 1991.

Rieffel, Alexis. "The Paris Club, 1978–1983." *Columbia Journal of Transnational Law* 23-1 (1984): 63–110.

————. "The Role of the Paris Club in Managing Debt Problems." No. 161. *Essays in International Finance.* Princeton, NJ: Princeton University, December 1985.

Sachs, Jeffrey D., ed. *Developing Country Debt and Economic Performance.* Vol. 1: *The International Financial System.* Chicago: University of Chicago Press, 1989.

Sachs, Jeffrey. "External Debt and Macroeconomic Performance in Latin America and East Asia." In *Brookings Papers on Economic Activity 2,* ed. William C. Brainard and George L. Perry, pp. 523–574. Washington, DC: Brookings Institution, 1985.

————. "Making the Brady Plan Work." *Foreign Affairs* 68-3 (Summer 1989): 87–104.

Smith, Gordon W., and John T. Cuddington, eds. *International Debt and the Developing Countries: A World Bank Symposium.* Washington, DC: World Bank, 1985.

Stallings, Barbara. *Banker to the Third World: U.S. Portfolio Investment in Latin America, 1900–1986.* Berkeley: University of California Press, 1987.

XII. Global Trade Relations

Aggarwal, V. K. *Liberal Protectionism: The International Politics of Organized Textile Trade.* Berkeley: University of California Press, 1985.

Bhagwati, Jagdish. *The World Trading System at Risk.* New York: Harvester Wheatsheaf, 1991.

Brown, William Adams, Jr. *The United States and the Restoration of World Trade: An Analysis and Appraisal of the ITO Charter and the General Agreement on Tariffs and Trade.* Washington, DC: Brookings Institution, 1950.

Cline, William R., ed. *Trade Policy in the 1980s.* Washington, DC: Institute for International Economics, 1983.

Cohn, Theodore H. *The International Politics of Agricultural Trade: Canadian-American Relations in a Global Agricultural Context.* Vancouver: University of British Columbia Press, 1990.

Conybeare, John A. C. *Trade Wars: The Theory and Practice of International Commercial Rivalry.* New York: Columbia University Press, 1987.

Cortney, Philip. *The Economic Munich: The I.T.O. Charter, Inflation or Liberty, The 1929 Lesson.* New York: Philosophical Library, 1949.

Croome, John. *Reshaping the World Trading System: A History of the Uruguay Round.* Geneva: World Trade Organization, 1995.

Curzon, Gerard. *Multilateral Commercial Diplomacy: The General Agreement on Tariffs and Trade and Its Impact on National Commercial Policies and Techniques.* London: Michael Joseph, 1965.

Dam, Kenneth W. *The GATT: Law and International Economic Organization.* Chicago: University of Chicago Press, 1970.

Destler, I. M. *American Trade Politics.* Washington, D.C.: Institute for International Economics and The Twentieth Century Fund, 2nd edition, June 1992.

Diebold, William, Jr. *The End of the I.T.O. Essays in International Finance.* No. 16. Princeton, NJ: International Finance Section, Department of Economics and Social Institutions, Princeton University, October 1952.

Dunoff, Jeffrey L. "Institutional Misfits: The GATT, the ICJ and Trade-Environment Disputes." *Michigan Journal of International Law* 15-4 (Summer 1994): 1043–1128.

Evans, John W. *The Kennedy Round in American Trade Policy: The Twilight of the GATT?* Cambridge, MA: Harvard University Press, 1971.

Finlayson, Jock A., and Mark W. Zacher. "The GATT and the Regulation of Trade Barriers: Regime Dynamics and Functions." In *International Regimes,* ed. Stephen D. Krasner, pp. 273–314. Ithaca, NY: Cornell University Press, 1983.

Goldman, Patti A. "Resolving the Trade and Environment Debate: In Search of a Neutral Forum and Neutral Principles." *Washington and Lee Law Review* 49-4 (Fall 1992): 1279–1298.

Greenaway, David, Robert C. Hine, Anthony P. O'Brien, and Robert J. Thornton, eds. *Global Protectionism.* London: Macmillan, 1991.

Griesgraber, Jo Marie, and Bernhard G. Gunter, eds. *World Trade: Toward Fair and Free Trade in the Twenty-first Century.* London: Pluto Press, 1997.

Haus, Leah A. *Globalizing the GATT: The Soviet Union's Successor States, Eastern Europe, and the International Trading System.* Washington, DC: Brookings Institution, 1992.

Higgott, Richard A., and Andrew Fenton Cooper. "Middle Power Leadership and Coalition Building: Australia, the Cairns Group, and the Uruguay Round of Trade Negotiations." *International Organization* 44-4 (Autumn 1990): 589–632.

Hirschman, Albert O. *National Power and the Structure of Foreign Trade.* Berkeley: University of California Press, 1945.

Hoekman, Bernard M., and Michel M. Kostecki. *The Political Economy of the World Trading System: From GATT to WTO*. Oxford: Oxford University Press, 1995.

Hudec, Robert E. *Developing Countries in the GATT Legal System*. Thames Essay no. 50. Aldershot, UK: Gower, for the Trade Policy Research Institute, 1987.

———. *Enforcing International Trade Law: The Evolution of the Modern GATT Legal System*. Salem, NH: Butterworth Legal Publishers, 1993.

———. *The GATT Legal System and World Trade Diplomacy*. New York: Praeger, 1975.

Jackson, John H. *The World Trading System: Law and Policy of International Economic Relations*. Cambridge, MA: MIT Press, 1989.

———. *World Trade and the Law of GATT*. Indianapolis: Bobbs-Merrill, 1969.

———. "World Trade Rules and Environmental Policies: Congruence or Conflict?" *Washington and Lee Law Review* 49-4 (Fall 1992): 1227–1278.

Kock, Karin. *International Trade Policy and the GATT, 1947–1967*. Stockholm: Almqvist & Wiksell, 1969.

Kostecki, M. M. *East-West Trade and the GATT System*. London: Macmillan, for the Trade Policy Research Centre, 1979.

Krasner, Stephen D. "State Power and the Structure of International Trade." *World Politics* 28 (April 1976): 317–47.

Krueger, Anne O. *Trade Policies and Developing Nations*. Washington, DC: Brookings Institution, 1995.

Long, Olivier. *Law and Its Limitations in the GATT Multilateral Trade System*. Dordrecht, The Netherlands: Nijhoff, 1985.

Mason, Edward S., and Robert E. Asher. *The World Bank Since Bretton Woods*. Washington, DC: Brookings Institution, 1973.

McGovern, Edmond. *International Trade Regulation: GATT, The United States and the European Community*. Exeter, UK: Globefield Press, 1982.

Odell, John S., and Thomas D. Willett. *International Trade Policies: Gains from Exchange Between Economics and Political Science*. Ann Arbor: University of Michigan Press, 1990.

Organisation for Economic Co-operation and Development. *Integration of Developing Countries into the International Trading System*. Paris: OECD, 1992.

Preeg, Ernest. *Traders and Diplomats: An Analysis of the Kennedy Round of Negotiations Under the General Agreement on Tariffs and Trade*. Washington, DC: Brookings Institution, 1970.

———. *Traders in a Brave New World: The Uruguay Round and the Future of the International Trading System*. Chicago: University of Chicago Press, 1995.

Raghavan, Chakravarthi. *Recolonization: GATT, the Uruguay Round and The Third World*. London: Zed Books, 1990.

Runge, C. Ford, with François Ortalo-Magné and Philip Vande Kamp. *Freer Trade, Protected Environment: Balancing Trade Liberalization and Environmental Interests*. New York: Council on Foreign Relations Press, 1994.

Schattschneider, E. E. *Politics, Pressures and the Tariff: A Study of Free Private Enterprise in Pressure Politics, as Shown in the 1929–1939 Revision of the Tariff*. Hamden, CT: Archon Books, 1963, unaltered from the 1935 edition.

Scherer, F. M., and Richard S. Belous. *Unfinished Tasks: The New International Trade Theory and the Post-Uruguay Round Challenges*. Issues Paper no. 3. Washington, DC: British–North American Committee, May 1994.

Schott, Jeffrey J., assisted by Johanna W. Buurman. *The Uruguay Round: An Assessment*. Washington, DC: Institute for International Economics, November 1994.

Stegemann, Klaus. "Policy Rivalry Among Industrial States: What Can We Learn from Models of Strategic Trade Policy?" *International Organization* 43-1 (Winter 1989): 73–100.

Thomas, Jeffrey S., and Michael A. Meyer. *The New Rules of Global Trade: A Guide to the World Trade Organization.* Toronto: Carswell, 1997.

Tyson, Laura D'Andrea. *Who's Bashing Whom? Trade Conflict in High-Technology Industries.* Washington, DC: Institute for International Economics, November 1992.

Whalley, John, ed. *Developing Countries and the Global Trading System,* vol. 1. Ann Arbor: University of Michigan Press, 1989.

Whalley, John, and Colleen Hamilton. *The Trading System After the Uruguay Round.* Washington, DC: Institute for International Economics, July 1996.

Wilcox, Clair. *A Charter for World Trade.* New York: Macmillan, 1949.

Winham, Gilbert. *International Trade and the Tokyo Round Negotiations.* Princeton, NJ: Princeton University Press, 1986.

———. *The Evolution of International Trade Agreements.* Toronto: University of Toronto Press, 1992.

Wolfe, Robert. *Farm Wars: The Political Economy of Agriculture and the International Trade Regime.* London: Macmillan, 1998.

———. "Global Trade as a Single Undertaking: The Role of Ministers in the WTO." *International Journal* 51-4 (Autumn 1996): 690–709.

XIII. Regionalism and Globalism

Abbey, Michael H., and Nicholas Bromfield. "A Practitioner's Guide to the Maastricht Treaty." *Michigan Journal of International Law* 15-4 (Summer 1994): 1329–1357.

Anderson, Kym, and Richard Blackhurst, eds. *Regional Integration and the Global Trading System.* Hertfordshire, UK: Harvester Wheatsheaf, 1993.

Appleton, Barry. *Navigating NAFTA.* Scarborough, ONT: Carswell, 1994.

Balassa, Bela. *The Theory of Economic Integration.* London: Allen & Unwin, 1962.

Cable, Vincent, and David Henderson, eds. *Trade Blocs? The Future of Regional Integration.* London: Royal Institute of International Affairs, 1994.

Cameron, Duncan, and Mel Watkins, eds. *Canada Under Free Trade.* Toronto: Lorimer, 1993.

Cohn, Theodore H. "Emerging Issues in Canada-U.S. Agricultural Trade Under the GATT and FTA." *Canadian-American Public Policy no. 10.* Orono: University of Maine, Canadian-American Center, June 1992.

———. "NAFTA, GATT and Canadian-U.S. Agricultural Trade Relations." *The North-South Agenda Papers 10.* North-South Center, University of Miami, Coral Gables, FL, November 1994.

Diebold, William, Jr., ed. *Bilateralism, Multilateralism and Canada in U.S. Trade Policy.* Cambridge, MA: Ballinger, 1988.

Dinan, Desmond. *Ever Closer Union? An Introduction to the European Community.* Boulder, CO: Rienner, 1994.

Edwards, Sebastian. "Latin American Economic Integration: A New Perspective on an Old Dream." *The World Economy* 16-3 (May 1993): 317–324.

Fawcett, Louise, and Andrew Hurrell. *Regionalism in World Politics: Regional Organization and International Order.* New York: Oxford University Press, 1995.

Gamble, Andrew, and Anthony Payne, eds. *Regionalism and World Order.* London: Macmillan, 1996.

Gibb, Richard, and Wieslaw Michalak, eds. *Continental Trading Blocs: The Growth of Regionalism in the World Economy.* Chichester, UK: Wiley, 1994.

Globerman, Steven, and Michael Walker, eds. *Assessing NAFTA: A Trinational Assessment.* Vancouver: Fraser Institute, 1993.

Grilli, Enzo R. *The European Community and the Developing Countries.* Cambridge: Cambridge University Press, 1993.

Grinspun, Ricardo, and Maxwell A. Cameron, eds.. *The Political Economy of North American Free Trade.* Montreal: McGill-Queen's University Press, 1993.

Haas, Ernst B. *The Obsolescence of Regional Integration Theory.* Berkeley: University of California, Institute of International Studies, Research Series no. 25, 1975.

Hatch, Walter, and Kozo Yamamura. *Asia in Japan's Embrace: Building a Regional Production Alliance.* Cambridge: Cambridge University Press, 1996.

Higgott, Richard, Richard Leaver, and John Ravenhill, eds., *Pacific Economic Relations in the 1990s: Cooperation or Conflict?* Boulder, CO: Rienner, 1993.

Hufbauer, Gary Clyde, and Jeffrey J. Schott. *NAFTA: An Assessment.* Washington, DC: Institute for International Economics, revised edition, October 1993.

———. *Western Hemisphere Economic Integration.* Washington, DC: Institute for International Economics, July 1994.

Johnson, Jon R. *The North American Free Trade Agreement: A Comprehensive Guide.* Aurora, ONT: Canada Law Book, 1994.

Jovanovic, Miroslav N. *International Economic Integration.* London: Routledge, 1992.

Kahler, Miles. *Regional Futures and Transatlantic Economic Relations.* New York: Council on Foreign Relations, 1995.

Kaser, Michael. *Comecon: Integration Problems of the Planned Economies.* London: Oxford University Press, 1965.

Keohane, Robert O., and Stanley Hoffmann. *The New European Community: Decisionmaking and Institutional Change.* Boulder, CO: Westview Press, 1991.

Kirschner, Heinrich. "The Framework of the European Union Under the Treaty of Maastricht." *Journal of Law and Commerce* 13-2 (Spring 1994): 233–245.

Lawrence, Robert Z. *Regionalism, Multilateralism and Deeper Integration.* Washington, DC: Brookings Institution, 1996.

Lipsey, R. G., and Kelvin Lancaster. "The General Theory of Second Best." *The Review of Economic Studies* 24-1 (1956–7): 11–32.

Lister, Marjorie. *The European Community and the Developing World: The Role of the Lomé Convention.* Aldershot, UK: Avebury, 1988.

Ludlow, Peter. "The Maastricht Treaty and the Future of Europe." *Washington Quarterly* (Autumn 1992): 119–137.

Machlup, F. *A History of Thought on Economic Integration.* London: Macmillan, 1977.

Melo, Jaime de, and Arvind Panagariya, eds. *New Dimensions in Regional Integration.* Cambridge. Cambridge University Press, 1993.

Nader, Ralph. *The Case Against 'Free Trade': GATT, NAFTA, and the Globalization of Corporate Power.* San Francisco: Earth Island Press, 1993.

Patterson, Gardner. *Discrimination in International Trade. The Policy Issues: 1945–1965.* Princeton, NJ: Princeton University Press, 1966.

Robson, Peter. *The Economics of International Integration.* London: Allen & Unwin, 3rd edition, 1987.

Rupert, Mark E. "(Re) Politicizing the Global Economy: Liberal Common Sense and Ideological Struggle in the US NAFTA Debate." *Review of International Political Economy* 2-4 (Autumn 1995): 658–692.

Schott, Jeffrey J, ed. *Free Trade Areas and U.S. Trade Policy.* Washington, DC: Institute for International Economics, 1989.

Smith, Murray G., with C. Michael Aho and Gary N. Horlick. *Bridging the Gap: Trade Laws in the Canadian—U.S. Negotiations.* Toronto: Canadian-American Committee, 1987.

Stairs, Dennis, and Gilbert R. Winham, eds. *The Politics of Canada's Economic Relationship with the United States*, Vol. 29, Royal Commission on the Economic Union and Development Prospect for Canada. Toronto: University of Toronto Press, 1985.

Steger, Debra P. *A Concise Guide to the Canada–United States Free Trade Agreement.* Toronto: Carswell, 1988.

Stone, Frank. *The Canada–United States Free Trade Agreement and the GATT.* Ottawa: Institute for Research for Public Policy, November 1988.

Viner, Jacob. *The Customs Union Issue.* New York: Carnegie Endowment for International Peace, 1950.

Wilcox, Clair. *A Charter for World Trade.* New York: Macmillan, 1949.

Wise, Mark, and Richard Gibb. *Single Market to Social Europe: The European Community in the 1990s.* Essex, UK: Longman, 1993.

World Trade Organization. *Regionalism and the World Trading System.* Geneva: WTO, April, 1995.

XIV. Multinational Corporations and Global Production

Barnet, Richard J., and Ronald E. Müller. *Global Reach: The Power of the Multinational Corporations.* New York,: Simon & Schuster, 1974.

Behrman, Jack N., and Robert E. Grosse. *International Business and Governments: Issues and Institutions.* Columbia: University of South Carolina Press, 1990.

Bergsten, C. Fred, and Marcus Noland. *Reconcilable Differences? United States–Japan Economic Conflict.* Washington, DC: Institute for International Economics, 1993.

Buckley, Peter J., and Mark C. Casson. *The Future of the Multinational Enterprise.* London: Macmillan, 2nd edition, 1991.

Casson, Mark, ed. *The Growth of International Business.* London: Allen and Unwin, 1983.

Caves, Richard E. *Multinational Enterprise and Economic Analysis.* Cambridge: Cambridge University Press, 2nd edition, 1996.

Cutler, A. Claire. "Public Meets Private: The International Harmonization and Unification of Private International Law." *Global Society* 13-1 (January 1999): 25–48.

Dunning, John H. *Multinational Enterprises and the Global Economy.* Wokingham, UK: Addison-Wesley, 1993.

Eden, Lorraine. *Taxing Multinationals.* Toronto: University of Toronto, 1997.

Eden, Lorraine, and Evan H. Potter, eds. *Multinationals in the Global Political Economy.* New York: St. Martin's Press, 1993.

Encarnation, Dennis S. *Rivals Beyond Trade: America versus Japan in Global Competition.* Ithaca, NY: Cornell University Press, 1992.

Enderwick, Peter. *Multinational Business and Labour.* London: Croom Helm, 1985.

Froot, Kenneth, ed. *Foreign Direct Investment.* Chicago: University of Chicago Press, 1993.

Gilpin, Robert. *U.S. Power and the Multinational Corporation: The Political Economy of Foreign Direct Investment.* New York: Basic Books, 1975.

Graham, Edward M. *Global Corporations and National Governments.* Washington, DC: Institute for International Economics, May 1996.

Graham, Edward M., and Paul R. Krugman. *Foreign Direct Investment in the United States.* Washington, DC: Institute for International Economics, 3rd edition, January 1995.

Hennart, Jean-Francois. "The Transaction Cost Theory of the Multinational Enterprise." In *The Nature of the Transnational Firm,* ed. Christos N. Pitelis, and Roger Sugden, pp. 143–151. London: Routledge, 1991.

Hertner, Peter, and Geoffrey Jones. *Multinationals: Theory and History*. Aldershot, UK: Gower, 1986.

Hymer, Stephen Herbert. *The International Operations of National Firms: A Study of Direct Foreign Investment*. Cambridge, MA: MIT Press, 1976.

Ietto-Gillies, Grazia. *International Production: Trends, Theories, Effects*. Cambridge, MA: Polity Press, 1992.

Jenkins, Barbara. *The Paradox of Continental Production: National Investment Policies in North America*. Ithaca, NY: Cornell University Press, 1992.

Jones, Geoffrey. *The Evolution of International Business: An Introduction*. London: Routledge, 1996.

Julius, De Anne. *Foreign Investment: The Neglected Twin of Trade*. Occasional Papers no. 33. Washington, DC: Group of Thirty, 1991.

Kindleberger, Charles P. *American Business Abroad: Six Lectures on Direct Investment*. New Haven, CT: Yale University Press, 1969.

Kindleberger, Charles P., and David B. Audretsch, eds. *The Multinational Corporation in the 1980s*. Cambridge, MA: MIT Press, 1983.

Kojima, Kiyoshi. *Direct Foreign Investment: A Japanese Model of Multinational Business Operations*. London: Croom Helm, 1978.

Krugman, Paul. "Competitiveness: A Dangerous Obsession." *Foreign Affairs* (March/April 1994): 28–44.

———. "Competitiveness: Does It Matter?" *Fortune* (March 7, 1994): 109–115.

Mason, Mark. *American Multinationals and Japan: The Political Economy of Japanese Capital Controls, 1899–1980*. Cambridge, MA: Council on East Asian Studies, Harvard University, 1992.

Mason, Mark, and Dennis Encarnation, eds. *Does Ownership Matter? Japanese Multinationals in Europe*. Oxford: Clarendon Press, 1994.

Modelski, George, Ed. *Transnational Corporations and World Order: Readings in International Political Economy*. San Francisco: Freeman, 1979.

Moran, Theodore H., ed. *Multinational Corporations: The Political Economy of Foreign Direct Investment*. Lexington, MA: Heath, 1985.

Muchlinski, Peter. *Multinational Enterprises and the Law*. Oxford: Blackwell, 1995.

Ohmae, Kenichi. *The Borderless World: Power and Strategy in the Interlinked Economy*. New York: HarperPerennial, 1991.

Pauly, Louis W., and Simon Reich. "National Structures and Multinational Corporate Behavior: Enduring Differences in the Age of Globalization." *International Organization* 51-1 (Winter 1997): 1–30.

Porter, Michael E. *The Competitive Advantage of Nations*. New York: Free Press, 1990.

Reich, Robert B. *The Work of Nations*. New York: Vintage Books, 1992.

———. *The Work of Nations: Preparing Ourselves for Twenty-first Century Capitalism*. New York: Vintage Books, 1991.

Rugman, Alan M., and Lorraine Eden, eds. *Multinationals and Transfer Pricing*. London: Croom Helm, 1985.

Sauvé, Pierre, and Daniel Schwanen. *Investment Rules for the Global Economy: Enhancing Access to Markets*. Policy Study 28. Toronto: Howe Institute, 1996.

Servan-Schreiber, J.J. *The American Challenge*. Translated from the French by Ronald Steel. New York: Atheneum, 1979.

Smythe, Elizabeth. "The Multilateral Agreement on Investment: A Charter of Rights for Global Investors or Just Another Agreement." In *Canada Among Nations—1998: Leadership and Dialogue.*, eds. Fen Osler Hampson and Maureen Appel Molot, pp. 239–277. Toronto: Oxford University Press, 1998.

Stopford, John M., and Susan Strange, with John S. Henley. *Rival States, Rival Firms: Competition for World Market Shares.* Cambridge: Cambridge University Press, 1991.

Teichova, Alica, Maurice Lévy-Leboyer, and Helga Nussbaum. *Multinational Enterprise in Historical Perspective.* Cambridge: Cambridge University Press, 1986.

Trinational Institute on Innovation, Competitiveness and Sustainability. Papers presented at Whistler, B.C., Canada, August 14–21, 1994. Vancouver: Simon Fraser University, Harbour Centre, 1994.

Tyson, Laura D'Andrea. *Who's Bashing Whom? Trade Conflict in High-Technology Industries.* Washington, DC: Institute for International Economics, November 1992.

Vernon, Raymond. *Sovereignty at Bay: The Multinational Spread of U.S. Enterprises.* New York: Basic Books, 1971.

XV. International Development

Afshar, Haleh, and Carolyne Dennis, eds. *Women and Adjustment Policies in the Third World.* New York: St. Martin's Press, 1992.

Amsden, Alice H. "Why Isn't the Whole World Experimenting with the East Asian Model to Develop? Review of the East Asian Miracle." *World Development* 22-4 (1994): 627–633.

Ayres, Robert L. *Banking on the Poor: The World Bank and World Poverty.* Cambridge, MA: MIT Press, 1983.

Balassa, Bela, ed. *The Newly Industrializing Countries in the World Economy.* New York: Pergamon Press.

Baldwin, David A. "The International Bank in Political Perspective." *World Politics* 18-1 (October 1965): 68–81.

Bello, Walden. "East Asia: On the Eve of the Great Transformation?" *Review of International Political Economy* 5-3 (Autumn 1998): 424–444.

Bello, Walden, and Stephanie Rosenfeld. *Dragons in Distress: Asia's Miracle Economies in Crisis.* San Francisco: Institute for Food and Development Policy, 1990.

Benería, Lourdes, and Shelley Feldman. *Unequal Burden: Economic Crises, Persistent Poverty, and Women's Work.* Boulder, CO: Westview Press, 1992.

Cohn, Theodore H. *Canadian Food Aid: Domestic and Foreign Policy Implications.* Denver: Graduate School of International Studies, 1979.

———. "Developing Countries in the International Civil Service: The Case of the World Bank Group." *International Review of Administrative Sciences* 41-1 (1975): 47–56.

———. "Politics in the World Bank Group: The Question of Loans to the Asian Giants." *International Organization* 28-3 (Summer 1974): 561–571.

Cornia, Giovannia Andrea, Richard Jolly, and Frances Stewart, eds. *Adjustment with a Human Face. Vol. 1: Protecting the Vulnerable and Promoting Growth.* Oxford: Clarendon Press, 1987.

Culpeper, Roy. *The Multilateral Development Banks. Vol. 5: Titans or Behemoths?* Boulder, CO: Rienner, 1997.

Culpeper, Roy, Albert Berry, and Frances Stewart, eds. *Global Development Fifty Years After Bretton Woods: Essays in Honour of Gerald K. Helleiner.* New York: St. Martin's Press, 1997.

Dorraj, Manochehr, ed. *The Changing Political Economy of the Third World.* Boulder, CO: Rienner, 1995.

Elson, Diane, ed. *Male Bias in the Development Process.* Manchester, UK: Manchester University Press, 1991.

English, E. Philip, and Harris M. Mule. *The Multilateral Development Banks. Vol. 1: The African Development Bank.* Boulder, CO: Rienner, 1996.

Evans, Peter. *Dependent Development: The Alliance of Multinational, State, and Local Capital in Brazil.* Princeton, NJ: Princeton University Press, 1979.

Griesgraber, Jo Marie, and Bernhard G. Gunter, eds. *The World Bank: Lending on a Global Scale*. London: Pluto Press, 1996.

Haggard, Stephan. *Developing Nations and the Politics of Global Integration*. Washington, DC: Brookings Institution, 1995.

———. *Pathways from the Periphery: The Politics of Growth in the Newly Industrializing Countries*. Ithaca, NY: Cornell University Press, 1990.

Haggard, Stephan, and Andrew MacIntyre. "The Political Economy of the Asian Economic Crisis." *Review of International Political Economy* 5-3 (Autumn 1998): 381–392.

Handelman, Howard. *The Challenge of Third World Development*. Upper Saddle River, NJ: Prentice Hall, 1996.

Hughes, Helen, ed. *Achieving Industrialization in East Asia*. Cambridge: Cambridge University Press, 1988.

Johnson, Chalmers. *MITI and the Japanese Miracle: The Growth of Industrial Policy, 1925–1975*. Stanford, CA: Stanford University Press, 1982.

Kappagoda, Nihal. *The Multilateral Development Banks. Vol. 2: The Asian Development Bank*. Boulder, CO: Rienner, 1995.

Krueger, Anne O. *Trade Policies and Developing Nations*. Washington, DC: Brookings Institution, 1995.

Krueger, Anne O., Constantine Michalopoulos, and Vernon W. Ruttan, with Keith Jay. *Aid and Development*. Baltimore: Johns Hopkins University Press, 1989.

Mason, Edward S., and Robert E. Asher. *The World Bank Since Bretton Woods*. Washington, DC: Brookings Institution, 1973.

Mason, Mike. *Development and Disorder: A History of the Third World Since 1945*. Toronto: Between the Lines, 1997.

Mehmet, Ozay. *Westernizing the Third World: The Eurocentricity of Economic Development Theories*. London: Routledge, 1995.

Mittelman, James H., and Mustapha Kamal Pasha. *Out from Underdevelopment Revisited: Changing Global Structures and the Remaking of the Third World*. London: Macmillan, 2nd edition, 1997.

Otero, Gerardo, ed. *Neoliberalism Revisited: Economic Restructuring and Mexico's Political Future*. Boulder, CO: Westview Press, 1996.

Payer, Cheryl. *The World Bank: A Critical Analysis*. New York: Monthly Review Press, 1982.

Pereira, Luiz Carlos Bresser. "Development Economics and the World Bank's Identity Crisis." *Review of International Political Economy* 2-2 (Spring 1995): 211–247.

Prebisch, Raúl. *The Economic Development of Latin America and Its Principal Problems*. New York: United Nations Economic Commission for Latin America, 1950.

Pye, Lucian W., with Mary W. Pye. *Asian Power and Politics: The Cultural Dimensions of Authority*. Cambridge, MA: Belknap Press, 1985.

Rapley, John. *Understanding Development: Theory and Practice*. Boulder, CO: Rienner, 1996.

Schuurman, Frans J. *Beyond the Impasse: New Direction in Development Theory*. London: Zed Books, 1993.

Schydlowsky, Daniel M., ed. *Structural Adjustment: Retrospect and Prospect*. Westport, CT: Praeger, 1995.

Sen, Gita, and Caren Grown. *Development, Crises, and Alternative Visions: Third World Women's Perspectives*. New York: Monthly Review, 1987.

Shonfield, Andrew. *The Attack on World Poverty*. New York: Random House, 1960.

Singer, H. W. "The Distribution of Gains Between Investing and Borrowing Countries." *American Economic Review* 40-2 (May 1950): 473–485.

Thomas-Eneagwali, Gloria, ed. *Women Pay the Price: Structural Adjustment in Africa and the Caribbean*. Trenton, NJ: Africa World Press, 1995.

Tussie, Diana. *The Multilateral Development Banks. Vol. 4: The Inter-American Development Bank.* Boulder, CO: Rienner, 1995.

Wade, Robert. *Governing the Market: Economic Theory and the Role of Government in East Asian Industrialization.* Princeton, NJ: Princeton University Press, 1990.

———. "Japan, the World Bank, and the Art of Paradigm Maintenance: The East Asian Miracle in Political Perspective." *New Left Review* 217 (May/June 1996): 3–36.

World Bank. *The East Asian Miracle: Economic Growth and Public Policy.* Policy Research Report. Oxford: Oxford University Press, 1993.

———. *Sub-Saharan Africa: From Crisis to Sustainable Growth,* a Long-Term Perspective Study. Washington, DC: World Bank, 1989.

XVI. Documentary Sources

A number of international and regional organizations and national government agencies provide valuable information and data on issues related to international political economy. Below is a selected list of some useful sources from international organizations. (Unless a date is mentioned, most of these sources are serial publications.)

International Finance Corporation (IFC)
  Annual Reports
  Articles of Agreement

International Monetary Fund (IMF)
  Annual Reports
  Articles of Agreement
  Balance of Payments Statistics Yearbook
  Direction of Trade Statistics
  Finance and Development Journal
  Government Finance Statistics Yearbook
  International Financial Statistics
  IMF Survey newsletter
  IMF Working Papers
  IMF Papers on Policy Analysis and Assessment
  Summary Proceedings of the Board of Governors
  World Economic Outlook (a survey of global economic developments)

Multilateral Investment Guarantee Agency (MIGA)
  Annual Reports
  Convention Establishing the MIGA

Organization for Economic Cooperation and Development (OECD)
  Development Co-operation: Efforts and Policies of the Members of the Development Assistance Committee
  Economic Surveys
  Financing and External Debt of Developing Countries (was called External Debt of Developing Countries until 1984)
  International Direct Investment Statistics Yearbook
  Main Economic Indicators: Sources and Methods
  Twenty-five Years of Development Co-operation: A Review—1985 Report

United Nations Centre on Transnational Corporations (no longer exists)
Transnational Corporations
Transnational Corporations in World Development: Trends and Prospects, 1988

United Nations Conference on Trade and Development
Handbook of International Trade and Development Statistics
International Monetary and Financial Issues for the 1990s
Report of the Trade and Development Board
The Least Developed Countries—Annual Report
Trade and Development Report
Transnational Corporations
UNCTAD Bulletin
UNCTAD Review
World Investment Report

United Nations Department for Economic and Social Information and Policy Analysis
International Trade Statistics Yearbook
Monthly Bulletin of Statistics
World Economic and Social Survey (*World Economic Survey* prior to 1995)

United Nations Development Program
Human Development Report

United Nations Industrial Development Organization (UNIDO)
Industry and Development: Global Report

World Bank
Annual Reports
Annual World Bank Conference on Development Economics
Articles of Agreement
Summary Proceedings of the Board of Governors
World Debt Tables
World Development Report

World Trade Organization (WTO) and General Agreement on Tariffs and Trade (GATT)
Basic Instruments and Selected Documents
GATT Activities
GATT Focus newsletter
WTO Focus newsletter
International Trade: Trends and Statistics
Results of the Uruguay Round of Multilateral Trade Negotiations: The Legal Texts
Text of the General Agreement on Tariffs and Trade
Texts of the Tokyo Round Agreements
Trade Policy Reviews
WTO Annual Reports
WTO Press Releases